ALL · IN · ONE

AWS
Certified SysOps
Administrator Associate

EXAM GUIDE

(Exam SOA-C01)

ABOUT THE AUTHOR

Sam R. Alapati works as a data administrator for Solera Holdings in Westlake, Texas, just outside Dallas. Sam has worked as an Oracle DBA for many years and has authored many books for Oracle DBAs, including *Expert Oracle Database 11g Administration* (Apress, 2008), *OCP Upgrade to Oracle Database 12c Exam Guide* (Oracle Press/McGraw-Hill Education, 2014), and *Expert Hadoop Administration* (Addison-Wesley, 2016).

About the Contributor and Technical Editor

Kamesh Ganesan is a seasoned technology and cloud evangelist with more than 21 years of IT experience working with all major technologies including AWS, Azure, GCP, and Alibaba cloud. He holds multiple cloud certifications including five from AWS, three on Microsoft Azure, and three GCP certifications.

ALL·IN·ONE

AWS
Certified SysOps Administrator Associate

EXAM GUIDE

(Exam SOA-C01)

Sam R. Alapati

New York   Chicago   San Francisco
Athens   London   Madrid   Mexico City
Milan   New Delhi   Singapore   Sydney   Toronto

Library of Congress Cataloging-in-Publication Data

Names: Alapati, Sam R. author.
Title: AWS certified SysOps administrator associate all-in-one exam guide
   (Exam SOA-301) / Sam Alapati.
Other titles: Amazon Web Services certified SysOps administrator associate
   all-in-one exam guide (Exam SOA-301)
Description: First edition. | New York : McGraw-Hill, [2019] | Includes index.
Identifiers: LCCN 2019017079 | ISBN 9781260135565 (soft cover : alk. paper)
Subjects: LCSH: Web services—Examinations—Study guides. | Cloud
   computing—Examinations—Study guides. | Amazon Web Services
   (Firm)—Examinations—Study guides.
Classification: LCC TK5105.88813.A447 2019 | DDC 006.7/8—dc23 LC record available at
   https://lccn.loc.gov/2019017079

McGraw-Hill Education books are available at special quantity discounts to use as premiums and sales promotions, or for use in corporate training programs. To contact a representative, please visit the Contact Us pages at www.mhprofessional.com.

AWS Certified SysOps Administrator Associate All-in-One Exam Guide (Exam SOA-C01)

1 2 3 4 5 6 7 8 9   LCR   23 22 21 20 19

ISBN   978-1-260-13556-5
MHID   1-260-13556-X

Sponsoring Editor Lisa McClain	**Technical Editor** Kamesh Ganesan	**Production Supervisor** James Kussow
Editorial Supervisor Patty Mon	**Copy Editor** Lisa Theobald	**Composition** Cenveo® Publisher Services
Project Editor Rachel Fogelberg	**Proofreader** Paul Tyler	**Illustration** Cenveo Publisher Services
Acquisitions Coordinator Claire Yee	**Indexer** Jack Lewis	**Art Director, Cover** Jeff Weeks

This book is dedicated to my good friend,
Eligio (Eddie) S. Colon, to whom I owe
more than he probably remembers.

CONTENTS AT A GLANCE

CONTENTS

ACKNOWLEDGMENTS

First and foremost, I'd like to express my thanks to Lisa McClain, Sponsoring Editor, McGraw-Hill, for accepting my proposal for the book and supporting me through some difficult times early on. I've known Lisa for many years, but this is the first book I have written with her as the editor. Lisa is a consummate professional, and I'm fortunate to have worked with her on the book. I appreciate her patience and the superb guidance she has provided during the writing of this book. Claire Yee, Acquisitions Coordinator, McGraw-Hill, has provided the logistical support, and so much more. With her timely reminders and help with numerous issues during the writing of the book, Claire has helped me stay on track and finish up in time. Thank you, Lisa and Claire, for all your support and kind help for the last year and a half!

The technical editor for this book, Kamesh Ganesan, has helped ensure that I was technically correct in my explanations and has kindly volunteered additional information and insights which helped me enhance the quality of the presentation.

The copy editor, Lisa Theobald, has done a yeoman job of organizing the material and rearranging topics in several chapters to make the book coherent. I appreciate her painstaking work, which helped make this book read much better. The proofreader for the book, Paul Tyler, was simply superb, and I'm grateful for the thoroughness with which he reviewed the pages. Rachel Fogelberg, the project editor, managed the work flow very efficiently, and on more than one occasion accommodated my request for last-minute additions and changes to the manuscript. Thank you, Rachel, for your help!

I am grateful for the kind help provided by my wife, Valerie, and the encouragement and support of my children, Nina and Nick. My family enabled me to devote myself to this book for many months, and I'm forever thankful for their understanding and good cheer.

INTRODUCTION

Amazon Web Services (AWS) is an amazing collection of computing, storage, and networking services that enable you to spin up a complete IT environment very quickly, without a significant upfront investment. The cloud is where almost every organization wants to go, if it isn't there already. Of the major public cloud providers, AWS is the largest by a huge margin. Many organizations seek competent, experienced AWS system administrators. One of the best ways to demonstrate competence in managing an AWS environment and to set yourself apart from others is by certifying as an AWS SysOps Administrator.

This book is designed to help you prepare to take and pass the AWS Certified SysOps Administrator Associate exam offered by AWS. Ideally, you should have a year or so of hands-on experience administering AWS before you sit for the exam. The next best solution would be to sign up for the AWS Quick Labs and read the AWS documentation along with this book.

How to Use This Book
The best way to make use of this book is to go through each of the eleven chapters, starting from the beginning. Read the chapter a couple of times and take the review test at the end of the chapter.

End of Chapter Questions
At the end of each chapter module, you'll find questions that test your mastery of the content discussed in the chapter. The questions closely resemble the actual AWS certification exam questions. It's important that you attempt all the questions at the end of each chapter before proceeding to the next chapter. By reviewing the answers for both the questions that you've gotten right as well as those you've answered incorrectly, you can fill in the gaps in your learning.

Online Practice Exams
Follow the same strategy for the practice exams—take the exam, read the explanations, and look in the book for answers to the questions that you missed.

Preparing for the Real Certification Exam
I recommend the following strategy to pass the AWS certification exam.

Take and Retake the Chapter Review Tests and the Practice Exams
Make sure you look up the relevant material in the text for each question that you miss in a review test. Then take the test again. You should be able to answer *all* the questions correctly in each of the eleven chapters before you attempt the online practice exams. And make sure you can correctly answer *all* the questions in the practice exams before you take the actual exam.

The practice exams that come with this book draw their questions from a test bank of over 250 questions. Each practice exam has 65 questions which are randomly selected from the test bank. So, taking the practice exams multiple times means that eventually you'll encounter all 250 questions. I strongly suggest that you take the practice exams multiple times for another reason too. Many of the answers come with detailed explanations that will help you understand why the answer is correct. Reading these explanations will strengthen your understanding of the key concepts.

Read the Docs
Although the book is comprehensive, it can't go into the details of the many topics that it covers. This book is devoted to helping you pass the AWS certification exam. However, you need to know far more than the contents of this book to become a competent AWS SysOps? Administrator. Review the appropriate AWS documentation for each chapter to learn the topics in depth.

Do the Exercises at the End of the Chapters
Make sure you do every exercise at the end of each chapter. These exercises are designed to provide a hands-on experience with all the AWS services that will be on the exam.

Practice with the AWS CLI
The exercises at the end of each chapter expect you to perform tasks using the AWS console for the relevant service. Try to perform tasks from the command line as well, through the AWS CLI. I have sprinkled examples of AWI CLI usage throughout the book, and you can search online for other examples or find them in the AWS documentation.

Read the FAQS for All the AWS Services
This book reviews many AWS services such as Amazon EC2 and AWS CloudFormation. AWS publishes a very useful FAQ page for each of these services. Do yourself a favor and read the FAQs for each of the services covered in this book. The FAQs serve to help you understand each of the services in more depth and explain the ramifications of using various options with each of the services. You can view all the AWS service FAQs here: https://aws.amazon.com/faqs/. AWS FAQs for various services will help you answer many certification exam questions, so read all the FAQs for each service that is covered in this book, such as Amazon VC and Amazon VPC.

Think Strategically
Most of the exam questions are based on scenarios. Read these scenarios a couple of times and understand exactly what the question is asking. Try not to get lost in the specifics of the scenarios. Try to figure out the AWS services that are involved and how to use them in this scenario. Rule out options that are obviously wrong. From the remaining options, select the most reasonable answer.

Who Should Read This Exam Guide
This book is intended for individuals who have technical expertise in deployment, management, and operations on AWS. It validates an examinee's ability to do the following:

- Deploy, manage, and operate scalable, highly available, and fault-tolerant systems on AWS.
- Implement and control the flow of data to and from AWS.
- Select the appropriate AWS service based on compute, data, or security requirements.
- Identify the appropriate uses of AWS operational best practices.
- Estimate AWS usage costs and identify operational cost control mechanisms.
- Migrate on-premise workloads to AWS.

 NOTE Most of the material in this section is from the AWS Certification site (https://aws.amazon.com/certification/).

Exam Prerequisites

There are no prerequisites for taking the SysOps Administrator Associate examination. AWS recommends, however, that you have the following AWS knowledge before you take the test:

- Minimum of one year of hands-on experience with AWS
- Experience managing operating systems on AWS
- Understanding of the AWS tenets—architecting for the cloud
- Hands-on experience with the AWS CLI and SDKs/API tools
- Understanding of network technologies as they relate to AWS
- Understanding of security concepts, with hands-on experience in implementing security controls and compliance requirements

AWS recommends that you possess the following general IT knowledge:

- One or two years' experience as a systems administrator in a systems operations role
- Understanding of virtualization technology
- Monitoring and auditing systems experience
- Knowledge of networking concepts (such as DNS, TCP/IP, and firewalls)
- Ability to translate architectural requirements

Exam Question Types

There are two types of questions on the examination:

- **Multiple choice** One correct response and three incorrect responses (distractors).
- **Multiple response** Two or more correct responses out of five or more options. Select one or more responses that best complete the statement or answer the question.

Distractors, or incorrect answers, are response options that an examinee with incomplete knowledge or skill may choose. However, they are generally plausible responses that fit in the content area defined by the test objective. Unanswered questions are scored as incorrect; there is no penalty for guessing.

Unscored Content

Your examination may include unscored items that are placed on the test to gather statistical information. These items are not identified on the form and do not affect your score.

Exam Results

The AWS Certified SysOps Administrator Associate (SOA-C01) exam is a pass or fail exam. The examination is scored against a minimum standard established by AWS professionals who are guided by certification industry best practices and guidelines.

Your results for the examination are reported as a score from 100 to 1000, with a minimum passing score of 720. Your score shows how you performed on the examination as a whole and whether or not you passed. Scaled scoring models are used to equate scores across multiple exam forms that may have slightly different difficulty levels.

Your score report contains a table of classifications of your performance at each section level. This information is designed to provide general feedback concerning your examination performance. The examination uses a compensatory scoring model, which means that you do not need to "pass" the individual sections, only the overall examination. Each section of the examination has a specific weighting, so some sections have more questions than others.

The following table lists the main content domains and their approximate weightings.

Domain	Percent of Examination
Domain 1: Monitoring and Reporting	22
Domain 2: High Availability	8
Domain 3: Deployment and Provisioning	14
Domain 4: Storage and Data Management	12
Domain 5: Security and Compliance	18
Domain 6: Networking	14
Domain 7: Automation and Optimization	12
TOTAL	100

Using the Objective Map

The objective map included in Appendix A has been constructed to help you cross-reference the official exam objectives from AWS with the relevant coverage in the book. References have been provided for the exam objectives exactly as AWS has presented them, including the section that covers that objective and the chapter reference.

Online Content

This book includes online content that features the TotalTester exam software that will enable you to generate a complete practice exam or to generate quizzes by chapter module or by exam domain. See Appendix B for more information.

System Operations: An Overview of AWS

In this chapter, you will

- Realize the benefits of running operations in a cloud such as Amazon Web Services
- Learn about the types of cloud services: public, private, and hybrid
- Understand cloud deployment modes: IaaS, PaaS, and SaaS
- Learn about AWS foundational services
- Learn about AWS platform services
- Learn about AWS deployment and management services

Cloud computing is the on-demand delivery of computing capacity, storage, networking, databases, and other IT resources via a cloud services platform that you access over the Internet, paying only for the usage of the various resources and services offered by the cloud provider. Cloud providers also offer private connectivity from on-premise locations to the cloud, in addition to the Internet connectivity.

A cloud provider such as Amazon Web Services (AWS), Microsoft Azure, or Google Cloud Platform (GCP) owns and maintains the hardware and other infrastructure you use to run your applications and services in the cloud. You can provision the services and resources you need for your workloads.

Here's a formal definition of cloud computing, according to the National Institute of Standards and Technology (NIST):

> Cloud computing is a model for enabling convenient on-demand networking access to a shared pool of configurable computing resources (e.g., networks, servers, storage, applications, and services) that can be rapidly provisioned and released with minimal management and effort or service provider interaction.

Cloud computing offers rapid access to IT resources and services at low cost, without requiring you to make large upfront investments, spend time setting up resources, or manage those resources. You can immediately access virtually any amount of computing resources because there is built-in elasticity in provisioning the resources. You also reap the benefits of redundancy, high availability, and higher performance offered by various features of cloud computing, such as more powerful networks and content delivery systems. Finally, cloud environments are more secure overall, because both the organizations who use the cloud to support their operations (cloud consumers) and the cloud provider share the responsibilities for securing the cloud environment.

AWS, a subsidiary of Amazon, is the leading provider of on-demand cloud-based computing infrastructure and services. You can use the products and services that AWS offers to run sophisticated and highly scalable applications, store your corporate data, run your databases, and more. You gain the benefits of speed, elasticity, security, lower costs, efficiency, scale, and performance by moving to cloud computing environments such as AWS.

AWS operates on a pay-for-use subscription model, just as an electric or water utility does. Subscribers have a full-fledged virtual computing environment available at their disposal, although they're charged for actual usage only. In this context, it's important to remember that in addition to the pay-as-you-go on-demand servers (instances), AWS also offers reserved instances and spot instances to lower server costs, and dedicated instances to enhance security.

AWS started out with provisioning virtualized computing environments, and virtual machines (VMs) continue to predominate its infrastructure. However, in recent years, Docker containers have become popular, and AWS fully supports containerized applications. Even more recent is the introduction of *serverless computing* (the AWS Lambda service), where you submit the code you want to execute, and AWS will run it for you on its computing infrastructure, without you ever having to spin up a server at all!

Cloud computing is being used for more than consumers may realize. Practically the entire computing infrastructure of Netflix, for example, runs on the public cloud (AWS). In fact, most of the popular movie, music, streaming video, games, and picture and document storing services use cloud computing to serve their users.

Benefits of Cloud Computing

The immense popularity of cloud computing results from the many benefits it offers, such as the following:

- **Speed of implementation**   Traditional data centers involve ordering and setting up of hardware and provision of power and cooling, all of which take time to accomplish. Often, the projects end up taking multiple years due the budgeting, contracting, and implementation work involved in running on-site data centers. Cloud is extremely fast, and you can spin up virtually unlimited servers and storage in mere minutes.

- **Move the focus to business priorities**   Cloud computing helps organizations focus on their business differentiators, for example, by concentrating on data analysis, and the building of effective applications. The organization's time is better spent on these mission-critical purposes rather than purchasing, deploying, and maintaining servers and storage systems.

- **Pay-for-use billing model**   In a cloud environment, you lease computing resources, paying for them based on a pay-for-use model. You are billed only for your actual usage of the IT resources. Obviously, this has the potential to reduce both your initial infrastructure investment and your operational costs, compared to a data center–based computing model.

- **Cost**   Although you must be smart about how you use cloud computing and use all the "deals" offered by the cloud providers to reduce costs, cloud computing doesn't involve the traditional upfront capital expense of buying hardware and other components required for running a data center. You trade capital expenses for variable operational expenses. You reap the benefits of the massive economies of scale in a cloud-computing environment, where the cloud provider purchases massive amounts of processing and storage capacity.

- **Elasticity**   The ability to ramp up (and down, if needed) computing capacity quickly is a hallmark of cloud computing and serves as a strong separator of a cloud-based computing infrastructure from traditional data center–based computing environments.

In an on-premise computing environment, you need to guess about your capacity requirements, potentially leading to excessive idle resources or running into a capacity barrier. In the cloud, you don't guess: you can acquire as much or as little computing power as your business demands, and you can scale your operations within minutes.

- **Reliability**   Traditional concerns such as disaster recovery and data backups become less worrisome because cloud providers offer built-in resiliency by storing data in multiple zones that are geographically separate from one another.

- **Security**   When you run applications in a public cloud, you follow a shared responsibility model for security, in which you're responsible for mostly application security and the cloud provider worries about securing the computing infrastructure from external threats.

- **Performance**   Because a cloud provider can offer the very latest in computing hardware as well as lower network latency, application performance is usually enhanced in a cloud environment.

Types of Cloud Services: IaaS, PaaS, SaaS

Cloud providers offer various types of services, depending on the depth of the computing stack they offer. Here are the three broad types of cloud delivery models:

- **Infrastructure as a service (IaaS)**   IaaS is the most common type of cloud service, and this is what most people use the cloud for. Under IaaS, the cloud provider will supply just the IT infrastructure, such as servers, storage, and networks, which you'll pay for on a usage basis. The cloud consumer is responsible for installing, configuring, and managing the various services such as databases, web servers, and their applications.

Most of the IT resources offered under the IaaS model aren't preconfigured, meaning that the cloud consumers have a high degree of control over their cloud environment, although they must set up and maintain the bare infrastructure provisioned by the cloud providers.

- **Platform as a service (PaaS)**   PaaS is a computing model in which the cloud provider provisions, configures, and manages all the computing infrastructure, such as servers, networks, and databases, and you do the rest. PaaS offers a ready-to-use computing environment since the resources and services are already deployed and configured.

  PaaS computing services include those that help you develop, test, and deliver custom software applications. Developers can quickly create their applications, with the cloud provider setting up and managing the underlying computing infrastructure. The cloud consumers can replace their entire on-premise computing environment in favor of a PaaS. Or they can use PaaS to scale up their IT environment and/or reduce costs with the cloud environment.

- **Software as a service (SaaS)**   SaaS is how a cloud provider delivers software applications on demand over the Internet. In this mode, the provider manages not only the infrastructure, but also the software applications, with users connecting to the applications over the Internet. The software program is modeled as a shared cloud service and made available to users as a product. Cloud consumers have limited administrative and management control under a SaaS cloud delivery model.

It's important to understand that cloud providers offer all three types of cloud services, and users may subscribe to more than one type of cloud service. AWS provides all three types: IaaS, PaaS, and SaaS. IaaS and PaaS make up most of the AWS cloud products and services.

Types of Cloud Deployments: Public, Private, and Hybrid

Just as there are multiple cloud delivery models, there are multiple ways of deploying a cloud computing infrastructure. You can deploy cloud computing resources in three different ways: public, private, and hybrid.

- **Public cloud**   Also called an "all-in" cloud deployment, a public cloud is run by a third-party cloud provider, such as Microsoft Azure, AWS, or GCP. Users access the cloud publicly over the Internet. All cloud applications are built from scratch on the public cloud or migrated from on-premise computing infrastructure.

- **Private cloud**   Here you maintain the computing infrastructure and services on a private network. Your organization owns the private cloud and helps you employ cloud computing technologies to centralize access to companywide IT resources by users/departments within your organization. An organization can

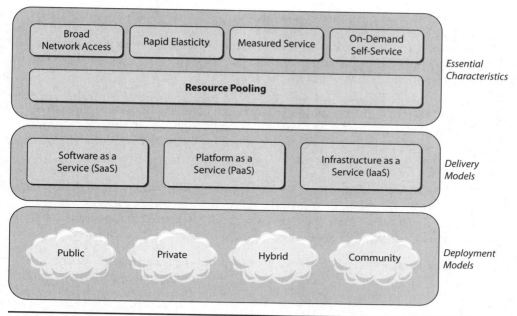

Figure 1-1 The NIST cloud computing taxonomy

run its private cloud in its on-site data center, or it can hire a third-party service provider to host its private cloud.

- **Hybrid cloud** This environment consists of two or more cloud deployment models. Hybrid cloud deployments are common, and they connect the applications and infrastructure in an on-premise environment to the cloud-based infrastructure and applications. Most commonly, the hybrid deployment helps an organization to grow its infrastructure by connecting cloud resources to its internal systems. In a hybrid cloud, your private cloud and the public cloud share data and applications. Data can freely flow between the private and public clouds, or you may use a private cloud for hosting sensitive data and host other cloud services to the public cloud.

Figure 1-1 shows the cloud computing taxonomy according to the National Institute of Standards and Technology (NIST).

The AWS Services

AWS started with a single service, the Simple Storage Service (S3), on March 13, 2006. S3 offered the capability for anyone to store objects such as digital photos, file backups, video recordings, or spreadsheet files and retrieve them. S3 was initially offered in a single region—the United States—although it's now offered throughout the world. Currently, there are 20 AWS regions.

AWS consists of an ever-growing set of services, each of which provides a specific functionality, such as compute, networking, security, monitoring, storage, and so on. There are more than 100 AWS services at the time of this writing. In this chapter, our goal is to learn the function of the most important AWS services. Later chapters will delve into the details of working with each of the key services.

 EXAM TIP The certification exam doesn't give all AWS services the same amount of importance. You're likely to face more questions about the most important or the most commonly used services, such as compute, storage, networking, monitoring, and security.

As an AWS system administrator, you must know how to work with all these services, including the configuration, performance, and security aspects of each AWS service.

Figure 1-2 shows the major AWS cloud services. Users can choose to use any of the services offered by AWS. AWS services can be grouped into three major areas:

- **Infrastructure** These are the data centers and the geographically distributed regions and availability zones. Amazon CloudFront, a content delivery network service, uses a global network of 160 points of presence (149 edge locations and 11 regional edge caches) in 65 cities across 29 countries. These edge locations and edge caches, both of which speed up the distribution of content to users, are also part of the infrastructure layer.

- **Foundational services** There are four main foundational level service areas:

  - **Compute** This refers to the services that provide computational resources such as virtual machines (VMs), Elastic Compute Cloud (EC2), and Elastic Container Service (ECS). Services such as Auto Scaling and Elastic Load Balancing (ELB) help scale and load balance computing services and therefore fall under the this category.

  - **Storage** This refers to multiple types of storage such as object (S3), block (Elastic Block Store, or EBS), and archive storage (S3 Glacier).

  - **Security and access control** Security includes various AWS services such as Identity and Access Management (IAM), AWS Key Management Service (KMS), and AWS Active Directory (AD). A virtual private network (VPN) offers site-to-site (S2S) and point-to-site (P2S) connectivity to AWS from on-premise (S2S) or remote users (P2S).

  - **Networking** This includes the AWS Domain Name System (DNS) called Route 53, a content delivery network (Amazon CloudFront), and the Amazon Virtual Private Cloud (VPC).

- **Platform services** Platform services include the following categories of services:

  - **Database services** These include the managed AWS Relational Database Service (RDS), a NoSQL database named DynamoDB, and a managed caching service based on the Redis or Memcached engines.

- **Analytics** Services that support analytics include Elastic MapReduce (EMR), which offers managed Hadoop clusters in the cloud; and real-time analytical services such as data warehouses (Redshift), AWS Glue, and Amazon QuickSight.

- **App services** These include services that support distributed applications, including queuing (Amazon Simple Queue Service, or SQS), orchestration (AWS CloudFormation), app streaming (Amazon AppStream 2.0), e-mail (Amazon Simple Email Service, or SES), and search (Amazon Elasticsearch Service and Amazon CloudSearch).

- **Deployment and management** Several AWS services are designed to help you deploy and manage your applications, including ECS, which helps deploy and manage containers, and DevOps tools such as AWS CodeBuild, AWS CodeCommit, AWS CodeDeploy, and AWS CodePipeline. AWS CloudFormation is a template-based provisioning service, and you can track API calls with AWS CloudTrail and monitor your AWS resources and the applications running on it with the AWS CloudWatch service.

In the following sections, I describe the key services offered by AWS in each of the three service areas: infrastructure, foundational, and platform. You may be overwhelmed by the wide array of services. I describe each of the services briefly and explain how to work with each in the remaining chapters of this book.

 NOTE It's common to use what's known as a "reference architecture" to understand the various AWS services. A common cloud-based architecture is the three-tier design, which includes the following three layers: a web server (front-end) layer that serves content, an application middle layer, and a backed database layer.

Enterprise Applications	Virtual Desktops			Sharing and Collaboration	
Platform Services	**Databases**	**Analytics**	**App Services**	**Deployment and Management**	**Mobile Services**
	Relational	Hadoop	Queuing	Containers	Identity
		Real-Time	Orchestration	DevOps Tools	
	NoSQL	Data Warehouses	App Streaming	Resources Templates	Syns
			Transcoding		
		Data Workflows	Email	Usage Tracking	Mobile Analytics
	Caching		Search	Monitoring and Logs	Notifications
Foundational Services	Compute (VMs. Auto Scaling and load Balancing)		Storage (Object, Block and Archive)	Security and Access Control	Networking
Infrastructure Services	Regions		Availability Zones	Content Delivery Networks and Points of Presence	

Figure 1-2 The AWS cloud services

AWS: The Global Infrastructure

AWS maintains numerous locations that geographically distribute the data centers around the world. There are two types of locations: regions and availability zones (AZs). A *region* is a specific geographic area, such as Western United States or Eastern Europe. Each region consists of multiple isolated locations called availability zones.

 NOTE AWS currently (January 2019) has 60 AZs within 21 geographic regions. Amazon plans to add 12 more AZs and 4 more regions in Bahrain, Hong Kong SAR, Cape Town, and Milan. AWS has two GovCloud regions (US East and US West).

The way AWS uses its locations provides enhanced availability for the servers and storage you run on the AWS infrastructure. AWS enables you to spread out your infrastructure, such as servers that you use, over multiple geographic regions by locating them in different regions and in different AZs. You can place your resources and data in multiple locations for resiliency. Failure of some servers or storage devices located in a specific AZ won't affect the availability of your applications. AWS itself won't replicate your resources across regions unless you choose to do so.

Regions and Availability Zones

Each AWS region denotes a broad geographical area, such as US East or Asia Pacific, and is independent of, and completely isolated from, the other regions to achieve fault tolerance and stability. AWS consists of 21 regions at the time of this writing:

Code	Name
us-east-1	US East (N. Virginia)
us-east-2	US East (Ohio)
us-west-1	US West (N. California)
us-west-2	US West (Oregon)
ca-central-1	Canada (Central)
eu-central-1	EU (Frankfurt)
eu-west-1	EU (Ireland)
eu-west-2	EU (London)
eu-west-3	EU (Paris)
eu-north-1	EU (Stockholm)
ap-northeast-1	Asia Pacific (Tokyo)
ap-northeast-2	Asia Pacific (Seoul)
ap-northeast-3	Asia Pacific (Osaka-Local)
ap-southeast-1	Asia Pacific (Singapore)
ap-southeast-2	Asia Pacific (Sydney)

Code	Name
ap-south-1	Asia Pacific (Mumbai)
sa-east-1	South America (São Paulo)
cn-north-1	China (Beijing)
cn-northwest-1	China (Ningxia)
us-gov-east-1	AWS GovCloud (US East)
us-gov-west-1	AWS GovCloud (US West)

Although each AZ is isolated from the other AZs in a region, the AZs are connected through fast network links. Figure 1-3 shows the relationship between regions and AZs. Each AZ consists of one or more data centers.

AZs have the following features to enhance resiliency and availability:

- They are in lower-risk flood plains.

- To reduce a single point of failure, the AZs get their power from different grids from independent utilities.

TIP You can protect your applications from a service disruption that impacts a single location by placing your cloud resources in separate AZs. Ideally, an identical copy of an entire application stack should be placed in at least two AZs.

Global, Regional, and Local Resources

Some of the computing resources you use in the AWS cloud can be used in all regions, making them *global* resources. A good example of a global resource is AWS Route 53, AWS's DNS service. Some other resources are specific to a region. A security group (acts as a virtual firewall), for example, is a regional resource because the group is tied to a region and you can assign it only to instances in the same region. Alternatively, the resources could be tied to an AZ, which makes them local resources. For example, an EC2 instance is tied to the AZ in which you launch it. Similarly, Amazon EBS volumes

Figure 1-3
Regions and AZs

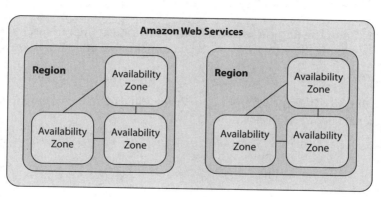

are tied to an AZ and you can attach them to instances in the same AZ. In other words, some resources can be used in all regions (global) and others are specific to a region or AZ in which they reside.

 NOTE Specifying the AZ when creating a resource is important because some resources can be shared across AZs while others can't be shared.

Your resources aren't automatically replicated across regions. There is no data transfer charge between two AWS services within the same region (such as between Amazon EC2 US West and another AWS service in the US West). Data transferred between AWS services in different regions are charged as Internet data transfer on both sides of the transfer.

Regions   By default (except if you have a GovCloud account), various regions are available to you. The multiple regions offer you the chance to launch your EC2 resources in locations that satisfy your requirements. If you have a large number of Asian customers, for example, you can launch instances in the Asia Pacific (ap-south-1) region.

Availability Zones   An AZ is represented by a region code, followed by an identifier—for example, *us-east-1a* or *us-east-1b*. Your AWS account may have a different number of available AZs in a specific region than other accounts.

When you launch an EC2 instance, you launch it in a specific AZ. You can remap an *elastic IP address* from an instance running in one AZ to an instance running in another AZ within the same region to work around problems with your EC2 instance.

Finding Your Regions and AZs   You can describe the regions for your account by running the describe-regions command using the AWS supplied command line tool, AWS CLI (discussed in detail in Chapter 2):

```
$ aws ec2 describe-regions
```

You can describe the AZs for a specific region, such as us-east-2, by running the describe-availability-zones command:

```
$ aws ec2 describe-availability-zones --region us-east-2
```

Specifying the Region with the Command Line   You can specify the region when you run a command, with the -region command line option, as shown here:

```
$ aws ec2 -region us-east-2
```

Setting the Default AZ   You can set the value of an environment variable to a specific regional endpoint, as shown here:

```
$ export AWS_DEFAULT-REGION=https://ec2.us-east-2.amazonaws.com
```

AWS Foundational Services

The AWS foundational services are the common infrastructure services that enable users to run their applications, databases, and other services. Following are the key AWS foundational services:

- **Compute**   Compute services provide the computational foundation for your AWS cloud and include services such as EC2, which provisions the virtual machines on which you run your applications in the AWS cloud; ECS, which provides managed Docker containers; Amazon Batch, which helps you run large batch jobs; and AWS Lambda, which offers serverless computing.

- **Storage**   AWS offers several types of storage, such as object (S3), file (Elastic File System, or EFS), and block storage (EBS and Glacier) services.

- **Security, identity, and access control**   AWS offers a broad range of security features and services to enhance privacy and control network access. IAM, Cloud KMS, cloud hardware security module (CloudHSM), and AWS Directory Service are some of the important AWS security services. The security features include network firewalls built into the Amazon VPC that help you create private networks and control access to your server instances and applications. AWS also provides connectivity options that enable dedicated private connections from your office or on-premise data centers to the AWS cloud.

- **Networking**   AWS networking services such as VPC, VPN, Direct Connect, CloudFront, and Route 53 enable you to isolate your infrastructure in the AWS cloud, scale your capacity to handle user requests, and connect your physical network to your private virtual network.

I'll review the key AWS foundational services in the following sections.

Compute

Whether you're building cloud-based enterprise applications and mobile applications or running massive data science projects on the cloud using huge clusters of computers, compute is the key IT service. AWS offers more than 170 infrastructure services. It also offers a wide variety of computer instance families. All of this helps organizations of all sizes use AWS for their operations.

The following sections summarize the portfolio of computer services offered by AWS to help you develop, deploy, and run your applications and workloads in the cloud.

Amazon Elastic Compute Cloud   Amazon EC2 is the most commonly used and best-known AWS service. EC2 is a web service that provides scalable computing capacity in the form of virtual servers.

The primary components of EC2 are virtual servers (VMs), which are called EC2 instances. AWS enables you to obtain and boot new server instances in minutes, and you can immediately scale capacity up or down to meet your computing requirements. You can create as many instances as you want (subject to service limits), but you're charged only for the computing capacity that you use—that is, only for those instances that are started up and are running.

EC2 makes web-scale cloud computing easy, since you can commission any number of instances virtually instantaneously and pay only for what you use. Common use cases for running EC2 instances are big data (Hadoop, Spark) applications, databases (MySQL, DynamoDB), enterprise applications (Oracle, SAP, SharePoint), and the migration of custom applications from on-premise environments.

You create EC2 instances with Amazon Machine Images (AMI), which are precon-figured templates for creating EC2 instances. You can use either a preconfigured AMI or create your own with the applications, libraries, and configuration settings you want to use.

You have complete control of your EC2 instances and have root access to all your servers. You can stop and restart the instances as you need, using web service APIs or command line tools. You also control the server, OS, and deployment software.

You also have a wide flexibility in the creation of EC2 instances, both from a pric-ing point of view and from the compute and storage capacity viewpoint. On-demand instances are always available and cost the most. Spot instances and reserved instances help you provision your instances at a significant discount. You can choose from multiple EC2 instance types based on various configurations of memory, CPU, and storage. For example, you can choose from GPU compute instances, dense storage instances, and high I/O instances, depending on the type of workload you plan to run on the EC2 instances. With regard to the operating system for the EC2 instances, you can also choose from various Linux distributions as well as the Microsoft Windows Server OS, all of which are available from the AWS Marketplace (https://aws.amazon.com/marketplace/), a digital catalog with numerous software offerings from independent software vendors. This makes it easy for you to obtain, test, purchase, and deploy software that runs on AWS.

AWS Auto Scaling capability enables you to scale your applications and automati-cally adjust your computing capacity based on conditions that you define. For example, you can configure EC2 Auto Scaling to provision a higher number of instances when demand spikes, and when demand slows down, you can automatically lower the number of running instances.

You can build scaling plans using AWS Auto Scaling for resources such as EC2 instances, DynamoDB tables and indexes, and Aurora database replicas.

Amazon Elastic Container Service   Amazon ECS offers *containers*, rather than VMs, as is the case with the EC2 service. Containers are a type of OS virtualization that enables you to run your applications in isolated processes. Using containers, you can package an application's configuration, code, and all its dependencies into an easy-to-deploy format.

You can package your applications and run them as Docker containers. You provision and scale the server capacity and manage the utilization of the containers. AWS manages the fault tolerance of your applications running inside the containers and manages the cluster state and container deployment.

Good use cases for Amazon ECS include web applications, microservices, batch jobs, and Docker workloads.

In addition to ECS, AWS offers two other container-related services or products:

- **Amazon Elastic Container Service for Kubernetes (Amazon EKS)**   This managed service helps you run managed Kubernetes clusters on AWS. Kubernetes is an open-source system for deploying and managing containerized applications.

- **AWS Fargate**   This technology for Amazon ECS and Amazon EKS enables you to run containers without managing servers or clusters.

  You can deploy Amazon ECS and Amazon EKS in two modes: EC2 launch type and Fargate launch type. Under the EC2 launch type, you use ECS and EKS to manage a cluster of servers, and you are responsible for placing the containers on the servers, thus granting you more granular control over the infrastructure that runs your container-based applications. You're also responsible for provisioning patching and scaling the clusters of servers that host the containers.

  With the Fargate launch type, you don't need to provision, configure, and scale clusters of VMs to run your containers. Instead, you focus on designing and building your container applications. Package your applications in containers, specify the CPU/RAM, define networking and security policies, and launch the applications. Amazon ECS and EKS will track the CPU and other resources in your cluster and run the containers on the most appropriate server(s), based on your resource requirements.

Amazon Batch   Amazon Batch is a fully managed service that enables you to run batch computing workloads on the AWS cloud. Batch computing is a mode of computing for engineers and analysts that enables access to large amounts of compute resources.

The Batch service provisions resources in response to jobs submitted to it, ensuring that the jobs don't run into capacity constraints. Batch automatically provisions the computer instances required to complete the batch workload and optimizes the distribution of the batch workload. Based on the volume and resource requirements of the batch jobs you submit, the Batch service provisions the optional quantity and type of compute instances, such as CPU or memory-optimized instances. Batch will plan, schedule, and execute your batch-computing workloads.

AWS Lambda   AWS Lambda is quite different from all the other compute services offered by Amazon. Lambda is at the core of *serverless computing*, which enables you to run applications and services without worrying about servers. AWS Lambda lets you run code for all types of applications or backend services with zero administration. Common use cases for Lambda include web applications, mobile and IoT (Internet of things) backends, and stream- and file-processing workloads. AWS Lambda helps you run your code in response to events.

The deployment unit in AWS Lambda is neither a virtual server nor a container—it's just code! Lambda enables you to run code without provisioning and managing servers. You use AWS Lambda to run applications based on events. Lambda is ideal for running event-initiated, stateless applications that need quick response times.

To use AWS Lambda, just upload your code to it. Lambda takes care of everything that's necessary to run your code, with high availability to boot. Lambda runs your code in its own compute fleet of EC2 instances across multiple AZs. AWS provisions, scales, and manages the utilization of the server capacity it allocates to you to run your code. It also manages the availability and fault tolerance of the applications that you run on the AWS infrastructure.

Most commonly, you create your AWS services resources such as Amazon RDS instances and Amazon Redshift data warehouses inside an Amazon VPC so they can't be accessed over the public Internet. AWS Lambda can run your function code within a VPC by default, but resources that are within a VPC aren't accessible from inside the Lambda function. To enable the function to access resources in your private VPC, you must provide additional VPC-related information such as the VPC subnet IDs. AWS Lambda uses this information to configure elastic network interfaces (ENIs) that enable the Lambda function to connect securely to other AWS resources within your VPC.

AWS Lightsail As its name suggests, Lightsail offers an easy way to launch and manage virtual servers. Common use cases include simple web applications, blogs, web sites; e-commerce web sites; and single-server business software.

 NOTE AWS Lightsail offers less control over server resources and fewer options than EC2 instances.

Lightsail includes everything you need to run simple projects, such as a VM, solid-state drive (SSD) storage, DNS management, and a static IP, for a low price (with plans that start at $5 per month). If you need advanced features, such as a managed database or a content delivery network (CDN), you can connect those AWS services to your Lightsail server.

Storage

Cloud storage is a key component of cloud computing and is used for storing database files, big data analytics, backups, and archive applications. You'll find that cloud storage is more reliable, secure, and easier to scale than on-premise storage systems.

AWS offers a wide variety of cloud storage services to support a whole host of use cases, such as applications and archival compliance requirements. The three main types of AWS storage are block, object, and archive:

- **Block storage** This is persistent local storage, similar to the hard drives you use in an on-premise data center.

- **Object storage** Object storage is a massively scalable, cost-effective means for storing any type of data in its native format. You tag the objects with unique metadata.

- **Archive storage** This affordable, long-term storage option can replace tapes for archiving and regulatory compliance.

Following is a brief description of the main types of cloud storage offered by AWS. (Chapter 3 describes all these storage types in detail.)

Amazon Elastic Block Storage (Amazon EBS) Amazon EBS provides persistent local storage for EC2 instances, relational and NoSQL databases, enterprise applications, big data processing, and backup purposes. AWS automatically replicates each EBS volume within its AZ to protect the data from component failure. AWS also provides ephemeral storage (as opposed to persistent EBS block storage) for EC2 instances (for most instance types) through *instance storage*.

EBS offers low-latency block storage for use with Amazon EC2 instances. EC2 instances use EBS storage for persistent storage, and you can scale your usage up or down in minutes. RDBs such as MySQL or NoSQL databases such as Cassandra and MongoDB, and popular big data analytics engines such as Hadoop use EBS storage.

Amazon Elastic File System (Amazon EFS)   Amazon EFS is a file system interface and file system access mechanism that makes data available to EC2 instances and enterprise applications for content serving, media processing workflows, backups, and big data storage. EFS provides scalable file storage that you can mount on Amazon EC2 instances. When you use EFS, you avoid the burden of deploying and maintaining file systems.

EFS is designed to scale on demand elastically without service interruptions, providing your applications the storage they need at all times. Web services, content management, enterprise applications, as well as media and entertainment processing workflows, database backups, and big data analytics workloads, are good use cases for EFS.

Multiple EC2 instances can simultaneously access an EFS file system, thus enabling EFS to act as a shared file system for workloads and applications running on more than one EC2 instance. EFS offers a simple and secure way to move data from your on-premise or in-cloud file systems. Because EFS provides persistent shared access to files, it's ideal for container storage.

Amazon Simple Storage Service (Amazon S3)   Amazon S3 is a durable object storage platform that lets you access data from an Internet location. You can store any type of data, such as archives, big data (data lakes for analytics), or database backup data in S3. You can access data stored in S3 through an API, from the AWS CLI, and from the Amazon S3 console.

S3 storage is secure, 99.999999999 percent (eleven 9's resiliency) durable, and can scale over tens of trillions of objects. Object storage such as S3 is ideal for backup and recovery, data archiving and compliance, and big data analytics.

You can use Amazon Athena, an Amazon service, with S3 data. Athena offers a unique query-in-place functionality that enables you to run analytics directly on the data that you store in S3 via standard SQL statements. Athena is simple to use, since you just point to the S3 data, define the schema, and query the data with SQL. Athena is a serverless offering, meaning you don't need to set up an infrastructure for it. You just pay for the queries that you execute against data that you've stored in S3.

Athena is fast, often returning query results in seconds, thus making it unnecessary to run typical ETL (extract, transform, and load) jobs to get your data ready for analysis. Athena comes integrated with the AWS Glue Data Catalog, which enables you to create a unified metadata repository across multiple services.

Amazon Glacier   Amazon Glacier is affordable long-term storage that lets you avoid traditional tapes for archiving and for regulatory compliance purposes. Glacier is a durable object storage service for long-term backups and archiving of data. You can use Glacier for data that you access infrequently. It also helps you replace tape for some types of applications. You can also use Glacier to assist with compliance in tightly regulated organizations such as healthcare and financial services.

AWS Storage Gateway   The AWS Storage Gateway is a hybrid storage cloud that supplements your on-premise storage with cloud storage. This software application provides highly optimized connectivity between your local on-premise environment and the AWS cloud storage. The main purpose of the AWS Storage Gateway is to augment your on-premise storage with the AWS cloud storage.

The Storage Gateway is a hybrid storage service that enables your data center–based applications to use the AWS cloud storage. It helps you migrate data to the cloud through common storage interfaces. For example, you can move local files as objects into S3, block storage volumes into EBS, and back up your tapes to S3 as objects, or to Glacier for long-term storage. You can use the Storage Gateway for handling bursts in demand, for maintaining tiered data, for migrating data between environments, and for maintaining multiple tiers of storage.

AWS Cloud Data Migration Services   The AWS cloud data migration services help you move data of all types into and out of the AWS cloud storage. There are several important data migration services:

- **AWS Database Migration Service**   Helps you easily and securely migrate your database to the AWS cloud. The service enables you to migrate databases while they are running, thus minimizing application downtime.

- **AWS Migration Hub**   Provides a single location to track the progress of multiple applications to the cloud. The hub provides visibility into the status of migrations across multiple applications and provides key migration metrics and progress updates for applications.

- **AWS Snowball**   A large-scale (petabytes) data transfer service. Moving large amounts of data into and out of AWS involves high network costs, long transfer times, and security concerns. Snowball enables you to transfer data securely at a fraction of the cost (about one-fifth) of high-speed Internet transfer.

- **AWS Snowball Edge**   A 100-terabyte-scale data transfer service. As with Snowball, you can use Snowball Edge to move data into and out of AWS or to support local workloads in remote or offline locations.

- **AWS Snowmobile**   For moving massive volumes of data, this is probably the best choice. AWS Snowmobile is an exabyte-scale data-transfer service. The service enables you to transfer up to 100 PB of data securely per Snowmobile.

Security, Identity, and Access Control Services

AWS follows a shared security model, which shares security responsibilities with cloud customers. AWS is responsible for managing all the underlying infrastructure, and the organizations that use the AWS cloud must secure anything they deploy and run on AWS. Following are the key AWS security and access control-related services.

Identity and Access Control   AWS offers several services to define, enforce, and manage user access policies regarding access to the various services that are part of the AWS cloud. Following are the main access control mechanisms:

- **Identity and Access Management (IAM)**   IAM helps you control access to your AWS account. It enables you to define individual user accounts with access permissions that control how users access various AWS cloud services and resources. You can create AWS users and groups and allow (or deny) access to these entities for any AWS resource. IAM helps you control various authentication methods such as passwords and access keys.
- **Multi-Factor Authentication (MFA)**   Helps secure accounts by adding an extra layer of protection on top of usernames and passwords. Once you enable MFA, when users log into an AWS web site, their credentials are the first factor, and the authentication response from their AWS MFA device is the second factor. You can use a supported universal 2nd factor (U2F) security key, a hardware device, or a virtual MFA device.
- **Directory Service**   Helps integrate with your corporate directories to reduce the administrative overhead. You can integrate IAM with your existing Active Directory systems with AWS Directory Service.

Inventory and Configuration   AWS offers several tools to ensure that your cloud resources comply with security best practices and your organization's standards, including the following:

- **Amazon Inspector**   This security assessment service automatically assesses applications for security vulnerabilities and security best practice violations.
- **AWS Config**   Along with other inventory and configuration management tools, Config tracks configuration changes to AWS resources over time.
- **AWS CloudFormation**   This template definition and management tool helps create standard, preconfigured environments. CloudFormation is an infrastructure as code (IaC) tool analogous to Chef, Puppet, and Ansible. IaC enables you to code your infrastructure to automate your deployments.

Data Encryption   Data encryption adds an extra layer of security to the data you store in the cloud. All the AWS storage options, such as EBS, S3, and Glacier, and its database services such as Redshift and Relational Database Service (RDS) offer encryption capabilities. There are many types of encryption, such as server-side encryption, client-side encryption, encryption at rest (encrypting data stored on disk), and encryption in transit (encrypting data as it's transmitted through the network).

The AWS KMS helps you choose whether to let AWS manage the encryption keys. You can fully control the encryption keys as an alternative to AWS taking care of the keys by storing them in the KMS. KMS uses a hardware security module (HSM) to secure your encryption keys strongly.

AWS Directory Service   AWS Directory Service for Microsoft Active Directory (AWS Microsoft AD) enables your workloads and AWS resources to use Active Directory in the AWS cloud. AWS Microsoft AD is built on Microsoft Active Directory so you can use normal Active Directory administration tools and features, such as group policy and single sign-on (SSO).

AWS Certificate Manager   You use Secure Sockets Layer/Transport Layer Security (SSL/TLS) certificates to secure network communications and identify web sites in the Internet as well as resources in your private networks. The AWS Certificate Manager service lets you provision, manage, and deploy SSL/TLS certificates for use with AWS services (and your internal connected resources).

AWS Web Application Firewall (AWS WAF)   AWS WAF is a web application firewall that protects a cloud consumer's web applications from known vulnerabilities and web exploits. Using AWS WAF, you can control traffic flowing to your web applications by allowing or blocking them through custom web security rules. For example, WAF makes it easy to create a rule to block SQL injection, a famous hacking technique used to break into web applications.

AWS and Compliance with Security Regulations   AWS global infrastructure is designed and managed according to various security requirements and compliance standards. AWS ensures that users have access to governance-focused service features to ensure that they meet their compliance and audit requirements. The AWS infrastructure follows security best practices and standards and is designed to meet the unique characteristics of cloud security. AWS offers numerous security services, redundant and layered controls, and features to safeguard your data, increase privacy, and control network access. AWS enables you to create private networks to control access to your virtual servers and applications.

AWS complies with many compliance certifications and security standards, such as the following:

- Service Organization Controls (SOC) 1/International Standard on Assurance Engagements (ISAE) 3402, SOC 2, and SOC 3
- Federal Information Security Management Act (FISMA) and Federal Risk and Authorization Management Program (FedRAMP)
- Payment Card Industry Data Security Standard (PCI DSS) Level 1
- International Organization for Standardization (ISO) 9001, ISO 27001, and ISO 27018
- Certifications such as CJIS, DoD SRG Levels 2 AND 4, HIPAA, and FIPS 140-2

AWS helps client organizations meet their regulatory requirements by helping produce reports, certifications, accreditations, and necessary third-party attestations.

Strengthening Security in the Cloud   The Amazon VPC enables you to provision a logically isolated section of the AWS cloud where you can launch AWS resources in your own virtual network. A VPC isolates you from all the other traffic from the many applications that run in a public cloud such as AWS. You fully control your virtual networking environment, such as selecting your own IP address ranges, creating subnets, and configuring network route tables and network gateways.

NOTE   A variety of connectivity options are available for Amazon VPC. You can connect the VPC to the Internet, to other VPCs, or to your data center, based on which AWS resources you want to keep private and which you want to expose to the public.

You can configure custom networks for your Amazon VPC. The VPC will be divided into these subnets, and all the services that you run in the AWS cloud will be assigned to one of these subnets in your VPC. Here's how you control the access to the subnets:

- Use network access control lists (NACLs) to control access between the subnets.
- Control the traffic that flows into and out of the VPC through a gateway that you attach to the VPC. An Internet gateway (IGW) allows traffic to and from external sources (from public IP networks).
- Create public-facing subnets for your web servers that need to access the Internet and place your database and application servers in private-facing subnets that have no Internet access. Public subnets have IGW access. When a subnet doesn't have IGW access, they become strictly private subnets, accessible only to private, and not public, IP networks.
- Use multiple layers of security such as security groups and NACLs to control access to the EC2 instances that run in the subnets you create.
- Create a VPN connection between your on-premise data center and your VPC, thus leveraging the cloud as an extension of your data center.

Regardless of how good your applications are, you're extremely vulnerable in the cloud without an iron-clad security strategy. You start off with a strong security strategy by making sure your system is patched with all available updates, so you're protected against known security vulnerabilities. Tighten access to your AWS account to protect your AWS resources from accidental or intentional damage, and ensure that you control all network traffic to and from your Amazon EC2 instances. Make sure you take advantage of VPC capability to create subnets in your network so that unauthorized outsiders can't break into your systems from the Internet.

Networking Services

AWS networking products help you isolate your cloud infrastructure from the rest of the world. They also let you scale your ability to handle requests and connect your data center physical network to your private virtual network.

Security Groups   A security group acts as a virtual firewall to control inbound and outbound network traffic. Security groups control traffic flowing to all objects in an Amazon VPC, such as all your Amazon EC2 instances. Security groups are stateful, so if you send a request from your instance, the response traffic for that request is allowed to flow in regardless of inbound security group rules. Responses to allowed inbound traffic are allowed to flow out, regardless of outbound rules.

You can create multiple security groups, and you can add two sets of rules to each security group: one to control the inbound traffic to the instances and the other to control all outbound traffic. For example, you can create a security group for the Amazon RDS that accepts traffic only from the Amazon EC2 instances that are in the application tier (middle tier in a three-tier application architecture). In this case, the security group provides a layer of network security around the database component in your three-tier application architecture.

Your VPC comes with a default security group. You usually create your own security groups (firewalls) and specify a default security group when you launch an EC2 instance. If you don't specify a security group, the EC2 instances that you launch in your VPC are by default associated with the default security group (though you can change this later).

 TIP You can also set up NACLs with similar rules as your security groups to add an additional layer of security to your VPCs.

Networking products such as Amazon VPC support the needs of various other AWS services and offer robust networking and security features. AWS system or network administrators should be familiar with the following key AWS networking products:

- Amazon VPC
- Amazon Route 53
- Amazon CloudFront
- Elastic Load Balancing
- AWS Direct Connect

The following sections describe these five key networking products.

Amazon VPC Amazon VPC enables you to create a virtual private cloud that helps isolate your cloud resources from the rest of the world. You launch your AWS resources in the virtual network that you create.

You completely control your virtual networking environment, including the following:

- Selection of your own IP address range
- Creation of subnets
- Configuration of routing tables
- Configuration of network gateways

As mentioned, you can customize the network configuration for your VPC. You can, for example, create a public-facing subnet for web services that should have access to the

Internet, and you can keep your backend database and applications away from Internet access by placing them in a private-facing subnet.

Amazon CloudFront CloudFront is Amazon's global CDN that helps deliver web content to viewers with low latency and high transfer speeds. A CDN helps to minimize the distance between your web servers and your visitors. The CDN does this by storing cached versions of its content in various geographical locations called points of presence (PoPs). The PoPs are responsible for using their caching servers to deliver content to users that are near it. By storing content close to the users, CDNs provide better service to your users. For example, when a user in India accesses your US-based web site, the data can be delivered from a caching server in a local PoP in India.

CloudFront securely delivers data, videos, and applications to viewers. It is closely integrated with AWS via physical locations that connect to the AWS global infrastructure, and via software that works with various AWS services such as Amazon S3, Amazon EC2, and ELB as origins for your applications.

CloudFront can also use Lambda@Edge (programmable CDN) to run custom code close to an application's users. Lambda@Edge helps run code in response to your end users, with a low latency. Amazon CloudFront events such as content requests from origin servers and viewers can trigger your code.

AWS Direct Connect AWS Direct Connect is a dedicated network connection from your on-premise network directly to your Amazon VPC. It provides your own private high-bandwidth connection between your network and your AWS VPC.

Direct Connect helps you establish private connectivity between AWS and your local data center, offices, or other environments. In many cases, Direct Connect reduces your network costs, increases bandwidth throughput, and offers a more consistent network experience when compared with Internet-based connections.

Direct Connect lets you to set up a dedicated network connection between your network and one of AWS's Direct Connect locations. It offers both 1 Gbps and 10 Gbps network connections. Direct Connect maintains network separation between the public and private environments.

Amazon Route 53 Route 53 is a scalable DNS web service. A DNS translates names such as www.example.com into the numeric IP addresses such as 192.0.2.1 that computers use to connect to one another. Route 53 is a highly available and scalable DNS service that connects user requests to your AWS resources. Route 53 offers developers and businesses a highly reliable and cost-effective way to route their end users to Internet applications.

 TIP You can use Amazon Route 53 to connect user requests to AWS infrastructures as well as to infrastructures outside AWS.

Route 53 connects user requests to computing and storage infrastructure running in AWS, such as EC2 instances, ELB load balancers, and Amazon S3 storage buckets. You can also use Route 53 to route users to infrastructures outside of AWS.

Elastic Load Balancing ELB automatically distributes incoming application traffic among targets such as the Amazon EC2 compute instances and the containers that you run in the AWS cloud. Load balancing enables you to achieve a high degree of fault tolerance for your applications, by seamlessly providing the computing capacity to handle high amounts of application traffic. So, in addition to fault tolerance, load balancing ensures scalability, performance, and security. There are three types of AWS load balancers:

- **Application load balancer** Routes HTTP (and HTTPS) layer 7 Internet traffic to compute targets within the Amazon VPC based on the request content. The advanced request routing helps deliver modern application architectures, such as microservices and containers.
- **Network load balancer** This load balancer routes layer 4 TCP traffic to targets within the Amazon VPC and is capable of handling very high volumes (millions of requests per second) of user requests with a low latency.
- **Classic load balancer** This legacy load balancer provides basic load balancing across a set of EC2 instances. It is meant for applications in the older EC2-Classic network.

AWS Platform Services

AWS platform services support a platform as a service (PaaS) model of cloud delivery. These services include database services, analytical services, application services, and deployment and management services.

Databases

AWS offers a broad variety of databases, such as RDBs, data warehouses, NoSQL databases, graph databases, and in-memory database stores for caching data. You can create and manage any type of database on EC2 instances. You can migrate your on-premise databases to the AWS cloud easily with the AWS Database Migration Service. Alternatively, you can subscribe to one of AWS's managed database services, such as Aurora. Following are brief descriptions of the various types of AWS-managed database service offerings.

Amazon Relational Database Service

Amazon RDS is AWS's managed RDS that automates administrative tasks such as creating databases and patching and performing backups. You don't need to provision any infrastructure or install database software. You can access RDS through the command line or via the AWS Management Console.

RDS is available for six familiar database engines:

- Amazon Aurora
- PostgreSQL
- MySQL

- MariaDB
- Oracle
- Microsoft SQL Server

Aurora is a fully managed MySQL- and PostgreSQL-compatible relational database, Aurora is based on open source databases and offers good performance and high availability features. Aurora is up to five times faster than a standard MySQL database.

DynamoDB

DynamoDB is a serverless NoSQL database. DynamoDB is a fast NoSQL database service for applications that need a single-digit millisecond latency at any scale.

DynamoDB is fully managed by AWS and supports both document and key-value store models. Its reliable performance and automatic scaling of throughput capacity makes it ideal for mobile, gaming, web, IoT, and similar applications.

Amazon ElastiCache

ElastiCache is a fully managed caching service that offers the ability to deploy and operate an in-memory data store based on Memcached or Redis. The two Amazon ElastiCache engines are Amazon ElastiCache for Redis and Amazon ElastiCache for Memcached.

ElastiCache serves as an in-memory data store and cache to support demanding applications that require submillisecond response times. You can enhance your application performance by retrieving data from the cache rather than the much slower disk storage.

Amazon Neptune

Amazon Neptune is a fully managed graph database service used to store highly connected datasets. The Neptune database uses a high-performance database engine optimized for storing billions of relationships and querying the graph with very low latency.

Graph database use cases include fraud detection, recommendation engines, drug discovery, and network security, where you need to create relationships among the data and query those relationships. Relational databases have a tough time with these types of data, since they need to use multiple tables with multiple foreign keys to represent the relationships among the data. You'd need to construct complex, nested SQL queries and complex joins to join the tables, making query performance a big problem.

Neptune supports the popular graph models Property Graph and the World Wide Web Consortium (W3C) Resource Description Framework (RDF), and the associated query languages Apache TinkerPop, Gremlin, and SPARQL, which help you query the highly connected datasets stored in Neptune.

NOTE Amazon Database Migration Service helps migrate your on-premise databases and make them Amazon RDS–managed databases.

Amazon Redshift

Redshift is a fully managed petabytes-scale data warehouse that enables you to analyze your business data using standard SQL and business intelligence (BI) tools.

Redshift Spectrum enables you to query data you stored in Amazon S3 using the same syntax SQL and BI tools you use for querying data stored on local disks in Redshift. This enables you to store highly structured, frequently used data on Redshift local disks and keep unstructured data in an Amazon S3 data lake, with the ability to query across both data sources.

Analytics Services

AWS offers several analytics services that help you process, analyze, and visualize data to extract insights and actionable information. AWS analytics services include data warehousing, business intelligence, stream processing, and machine learning. The Amazon Redshift data warehouse service falls under both database and analytics service offerings.

Following is a summary of the key AWS analytics services.

Amazon Athena   Amazon Athena is a serverless interactive query service that helps you analyze data you store in Amazon S3 using standard SQL. Serverless means that you don't have an infrastructure to manage, and you pay just for the queries you run.

Athena is based on the open source database Presto and works with varied data formats such as CSV, JSON, ORC, Avro, and Parquet. Athena enables you to query large datasets in S3, with fast, interactive query performance.

Amazon Elastic MapReduce   EMR is a managed Hadoop framework to process large amounts of data in a cost-effective manner. You can run an open source data processing framework such as Apache Spark, and Apache HBase and Presto on EMR.

EMR is meant for big data use cases such as web indexing, log analysis, data transformations (ETL), machine learning, financial analysis, and bioinformatics.

Amazon Elasticsearch Service   The Amazon Elasticsearch Service makes it easy to deploy and scale Elasticsearch, the popular open source search and analytics engine, in an AWS cloud. Elasticsearch Service is a fully managed service and is designed for use cases such as log analytics, clickstream analytics, and real-time application monitoring.

Amazon Kinesis   Amazon Kinesis is an AWS product that offers an easy way to work with streaming data in the cloud. Web applications, mobile devices, industrial sensors, and similar software applications and services generate large amounts of streaming data, often reaching several TBs per hour. Your streaming data applications that will collect, store, and continuously process this data can use Amazon Kinesis to perform their work.

Amazon QuickSight   Amazon QuickSight is a business analytics service that helps an organization build visualizations, perform ad-hoc analysis, and generate business insights from their data. QuickSight uses an in-memory calculation engine to render rapid visualizations and perform advanced calculations.

AWS Glue   AWS Glue is Amazon's managed ETL service that helps you prepare raw data for analytics and load it to data stores. Glue simplifies and automates the data discovery, conversion, mapping, and other tasks that are part of ETL processes.

AWS Data Pipeline   The AWS Data Pipeline is an orchestration service for data workflows. The pipeline helps you reliably move data between various AWS compute and storage sources, as well as your on-premise data sources. In addition, AWS offers several machine-learning services for developers and analysts, such as Amazon Machine Learning service (for developers who want to use machine-learning technology), and TensorFlow on AWS (an open source machine intelligence library).

Application Services

AWS application services include the Amazon API Gateway that facilitates the creation and maintenance of APIs; the Amazon Simple Workflow (SWF), a workflow service for coordinating applications; AWS Step Functions, which help coordinate the components of distributed applications; message queuing; and message notification services.

 TIP   You can access everything in AWS through APIs.

Amazon API Gateway

Amazon API Gateway is a fully managed service for developers to create, publish, monitor, and secure APIs easily. The APIs act as a "front door" for applications to access the business logic, functionality, and data from your backend services. The API Gateway handles all tasks involved in accepting and processing API calls, such as traffic management, authorization and access control, and monitoring. Users pay for the API calls they receive and the amount of data that is transferred out.

Amazon Simple Workflow

Amazon SWF is a fully managed workflow service for coordinating all the processing steps within an application. SWF helps automate the business processes for complex finance and business applications. It also helps build sophisticated business analytics applications.

In a cloud-based distributed application, coordinating the processing steps in an application across multiple systems is challenging. SWF enables developers to structure an application's processing steps as tasks and coordinates the task execution. SWF manages the task dependencies and scheduling according to the application logic specified by the application developers. SWF provides API calls that can be executed from code written in any language.

Messaging Services

AWS offers two messaging services: the Amazon Simple Queue Service (SQS) is a message queuing service, and the Amazon Simple Notification Service (SNS) is a push-notification service

Amazon Simple Queue Service   Amazon SQS is a hosted queue for storing messages as they travel between computers. Using a messaging service such as SQS, developers move data between applications that perform various tasks, without losing messages. SQS FIFO (first in, first out) queues are designed to guarantee that messages are processed exactly once, in the exact order that they are sent. SQS makes it easy to build automated workflows. It works by exposing Amazon's messaging infrastructure as a web service. Any computer on the Internet can read the messages without needing special software.

Amazon Simple Notification Service   Amazon SNS is a web service designed to send notifications from the cloud. Developers can use SNS to publish messages from an application and immediately deliver them to other applications or subscribers to the message queues.

Instead of periodically checking or polling clients for new information and updates, SNS delivers notifications to clients using a "push" mechanism. You create the notification topics that you want to send to applications or people. Next, you subscribe the clients to these topics, publish the messages, and have SNS deliver the messages over a client's protocol of choice, such as HTTP, e-mail, or SMS.

Deployment and Management Services

AWS offers a large variety of developer tools that facilitate application development and deployment, as well as management services that help you manage your cloud resources.

Developer and Deployment Tools

AWS offers several tools that help developers deploy and manage applications in the AWS cloud. The following sections describe the most important AWS developer tools.

AWS CodeDeploy

AWS CodeDeploy is a service that automates code deployment to computing instances running in the AWS or on-premise. CodeDeploy helps automate your software deployments, eliminating the usual errors of manual deployments. It helps you release new features rapidly and helps avoid downtime during the deployment and updating of applications.

AWS CodePipeline

AWS CodePipeline is a continuous integration/continuous delivery (CI/CD) service. CodePipeline helps you build and test code and automatically deploys your code every time you make code changes based on the release model that you define.

CodePipeline helps you deliver new features and application updates faster and you can integrate it with popular code-hosting services such as a GitHub for building an end-to-end deployment solution.

AWS CodeCommit

AWS CodeCommit is a managed source control service that makes it easy for an organization to host callable private Git repositories to source their code. You can use Code-Commit to store source code, binaries, and other objects, and it works seamlessly with your current Git tools.

AWS Elastic Beanstalk

AWS Elastic Beanstalk is a service for deploying and scaling web applications using web servers such as Apache, Nginx, and Internet Information Services (IIS). To run web applications, you simply upload your code (via the AWS Management Console, a Git repository, or an integrated development environment such as Eclipse) to Elastic Beanstalk, which will take care of everything else. It provisions the capacity, performs load balancing and automatic scaling, as well as monitors the health of the applications that it deploys. You thus start running your applications without having to do any infrastructure provisioning or configuration work.

AWS Management Tools

AWS provides a set of management tools that help you provision, monitor, and automate all components of your AWS cloud. AWS provides four types of management tools that all work together, helping you control the following aspects of your cloud infrastructure:

- **Provisioning** AWS CloudFormation
- **Monitoring and logging** AWS CloudWatch, AWS CloudTrail, AWS Config
- **Operations management** AWS Systems Manager
- **Configuration management** AWS OpsWorks

Provisioning Resources with AWS CloudFormation

The CloudFormation service enables you to describe and provision all your infrastructure resources in AWS. You use a simple JSON/YAML file to model your entire infrastructure and provision the resources across regions and accounts. You can also place a set of approved CloudFormation files in the AWS Service Catalog to ensure that your organization deploys only approved resources compliant with all the regulations and standards.

You "code your infrastructure" with a CloudFormation template (in either JSON or YAML format) using one of the many sample templates. You can then create a stack based on your template code. AWS CloudFormation will provision and configure the stacks and resources you specified in your CloudFormation template. System administrators can build and tear down complex infrastructure systems with a single action using the CloudFormation templates.

With CloudFormation, you treat your infrastructure as just code. You check the code into a version control system and deploy it into production. You can provision resources in a repeatable manner, so you can continue to rebuild and grow your infrastructure and applications without performing manual actions or writing custom scripts. CloudFormation determines the correct sequence of operations when managing your stack, and it automatically rolls back changes when it detects errors.

Monitoring and Logging with AWS CloudWatch

AWS CloudWatch is a monitoring service for the AWS infrastructure and the applications that you run on it. CloudWatch can collect and track metrics, monitor log files, set alarms, and automatically react to changes in the AWS resources.

CloudWatch can monitor your EC2 instances, DynamoDB and RDS database instances, and tables. In addition, you can have it track and react to custom metrics and your application log files. CloudWatch is natively integrated with more than 70 AWS services such as Amazon EC2, Amazon DynamoDB, Amazon S3, Amazon ECS, AWS Lambda, Amazon API Gateway, and more, that automatically publish detailed one-minute metrics and custom metrics with up to one-second granularity.

CloudWatch provides a stream of events that describe your infrastructure and application changes, and you can use the events to configure how AWS should react.

Operations Management

AWS provides the Systems Manager, CloudTrail, and Config tools for systems and operations management to help you control your infrastructure and ensure regulatory compliance.

AWS Systems Manager

The Systems Manager tool enables you to review and monitor resources and automate operational tasks such as patching the OS software. You can remotely manage your servers without having to log in to each server manually. The tool simplifies resource and application management and gives you visibility and offers control of your AWS infrastructure.

Systems Manager provides a unified user interface (UI) to help you view operational data from several AWS services, and it enables you to automate operational tasks. You can group resources such as your EC2 instances, S3 buckets, or RDS database instances by application and act on groups of resources. You can view aggregated operational data by resource group and automate actions across resource groups.

Using the Systems Manager, you can automate maintenance and deployment tasks such as applying server patches and updates and making configuration changes. You can view systems and application configuration, OS patch level, and other environment details through the Systems Manager dashboard.

Systems Manager also helps you maintain your adherence to security and compliance standards by scanning instances against your security and compliance policies. It also provides a centralized store to manage configuration data, so you can keep it separate from code.

AWS CloudTrail

AWS CloudTrail is a tool for logging user activities in your organization. CloudTrail can track both user activity and API usage. The service helps you log, monitor, and retain account activity pertaining to the actions they perform within the AWS infrastructure.

CloudTrail maintains an event history of all your AWS account activity, regardless of how the actions were performed—that is, through the AWS Management Console, AWS SDKs, command line tools, or other AWS services.

CloudTrail records every API call made in the AWS system and tracks information such as the following:

- The API caller's identity
- When the API call was made

- The source IP address of the API caller
- The request parameters
- The response items returned by the web service

The service history maintained by CloudTrail helps in security reviews, resource usage tracking, and troubleshooting. CloudWatch logs help process the API call data captured by CloudTrail. CloudWatch logs mine the text data, looking for patterns that can trigger alerts and automatic actions.

AWS Config

AWS Config helps inventory all resource configurations across your cloud infrastructure. Config helps you continuously assess, audit, and evaluate the configuration of all your AWS resources.

When any configuration change occurs for any AWS resources or any software configuration within EC2 instance, Config records the changes and delivers it to your S3 storage bucket. It also automatically evaluates the stored configurations against your desired configurations. Config displays the evaluations in a dashboard that you can access through the Config APIs, and it can also optionally send the evaluations via Amazon SNS.

 NOTE AWS Config automatically triggers Amazon SNS when any resource configuration changes deviate from your organization's policies and guidelines.

Using Config, you can review configuration changes and analyze the resource configuration histories; this helps you ascertain whether the existing configurations are in accordance with your corporate configuration guidelines. AWS Config also reveals how a resource was configured at any point in time. You can use Config for compliance auditing, security analysis, change management, and troubleshooting operational issues.

AWS Config is well integrated with AWS CloudTrail, which records events related to API calls for your account. Config uses CloudTrail event records to correlate configuration changes to specific events in your account. You can then obtain the details of the event API call (such as who made the request and from which IP address) from the CloudTrail logs.

Configuration Management with OpsWorks

OpsWorks is a fully managed configuration management service that's ideal for existing users of the well-known Chef and Puppet configuration management (CM) tools. OpsWorks hosts the Chef Automate and the Puppet Enterprise servers, eliminating the need for you to install and configure your own configuration management systems. OpsWorks also integrates well with your existing Chef and Puppet tools.

TIP Typically, the services listed under the Other category in the AWS itemized bills account for between 15 to 20 percent of the total spending on AWS services. Though this seems small compared to what companies usually spend on the EC2 service (typically about 60 to 65 percent), these services, which include SQS and SNS, can add up to a sizable amount at the end of the year. You must monitor your usage of the services in the Other category with the same diligence with which you track the EC2 instance usage.

Accessing the AWS Cloud Platform

By now, you've surely learned that the AWS cloud consists of a large number of services. A question you may have at this point is how exactly you access these services. Chapter 2 provides the nuts and bolts of AWS access methods, but following is a summary of the three most common ways you access the AWS cloud services: the AWS Management Console, the AWS command line interface (CLI), and the AWS software development kits (SDKs).

- **AWS Management Console**   This web application helps you manage your AWS cloud services. Each AWS cloud service has its own console, and you can access the individual service console through the main AWS Management Console. Not only do you manage your AWS cloud infrastructure from the Management Console, but you also get your account billing and usage details here.

- **AWS Command Line Interface**   The AWS CLI helps you manage various AWS services from the command line. You'll need to download and configure the tool, as explained in Chapter 2. The AWS CLI helps you automate management tasks by enabling you to include commands inside scripts.

- **AWS Software Development Kits**   SDKs offer an API that interacts with AWS web services. SDKs come in several languages and platforms and provide easy programmatic access for many AWS cloud services.

Chapter Review

In this introductory chapter, I described the benefits of cloud computing and the various types of cloud computing (public, private, and hybrid), as well as the various ways of taking advantage of the cloud—IaaS, PaaS, and SaaS.

One of the goals of this chapter is to introduce you to key AWS concepts such as the shared responsibility security model, virtual private clouds, and automatic scaling.

AWS consists of numerous products, services, and managed services such as RDS. It's bewildering at first, but as you go through the rest of the book, I describe each of the key AWS products in detail and explain how to configure and manage them, so that you can be a successful AWS systems administrator—after you pass the AWS Systems Administrator Certification Exam, of course!

Questions

The following questions will help you measure your understanding of the material presented in this chapter. Read all the choices carefully because there may be more than one correct answer. Choose all the correct answers for each question.

1. Which of the following AWS management tools enables you to retain account activity pertaining to the actions they perform within the AWS infrastructure?

   A. AWS CloudWatch

   B. AWS CloudFront

   C. AWS CloudTrail

   D. AWS Config

2. Which of the following are true when you use the Amazon Elastic File System (EFS)? (Choose two)

   A. Multiple EC2 instances can simultaneously access the same EFS file system.

   B. Multiple EC2 instances can't access the same EFS file system at the same time.

   C. EC2 instances can connect only to EBS storage.

   D. EFS will automatically scale on demand.

3. Which of the following AWS services enables you to view system-wide resource utilization, application performance, and the health of the various AWS system components?

   A. AWS OpsWorks

   B. Amazon CloudWatch

   C. AWS CloudTrail

   D. AWS CloudFront

4. Which of the following tools helps you review configuration changes and analyze the resource configuration histories?

   A. AWS Config

   B. AWS CloudTrail

   C. AWS Systems Manager

   D. AWS CloudWatch

5. Which one of the following AWS services acts as a virtual firewall to control Internet traffic for EC2 instances?

   A. Amazon Virtual Private Cloud

   B. Availability zones

   C. Security groups

   D. Network access control lists

6. You currently run several web servers by hosting them on the Amazon EC2 instances. You learn that you can move the static web sites to which of the following services, instead of using EC2 instances to run them?

   A. Amazon Route 53

   B. Amazon Simple Storage Service (Amazon S3)

   C. Amazon RDS

   D. Amazon CodeDeploy

7. Which of the following location-related concepts provides high availability and fault tolerance for the applications that you run in the AWS cloud?

   A. Availability zones

   B. Content delivery networks

   C. AWS regions

   D. Edge locations

8. Which of the following are true regarding regions and availability zones? (Choose two)

   A. All regions are connected via high-speed links.

   B. Availability zones in all the regions are tightly connected with one another.

   C. All regions are separated from one another.

   D. All availability zones within each region are connected via high-speed links.

9. Which of the following storage types offers "query-in-place" functionality, enabling you to run analytics directly on the data you store (data-at-rest) through Amazon Athena?

   A. Amazon Elastic File Service (Amazon EFS)

   B. Amazon Simple Storage Service (Amazon S3)

   C. Amazon Elastic Container Service (Amazon ECS)

   D. Amazon Glacier

10. Which of the following AWS services helps you connect your on-premise data center to the AWS cloud with a dedicated network connection from your on-premise network directly to your Amazon VPC?

    A. Amazon Virtual Private Cloud (Amazon VPC)

    B. AWS Direct Connect

    C. Amazon Route 53

    D. Availability zone

11. What is the deployment unit in AWS Lambda?

    A. A virtual server

    B. A container

    C. A microservice

    D. Code

12. Which of the following storage types offers a file system interface to storage?

    A. Amazon EFS

    B. Glacier

    C. Amazon EBS

    D. Instance storage

13. Which of the following AWS services helps you treat the AWS infrastructure as code?

    A. Amazon CloudWatch

    B. AWS OpsWorks

    C. Amazon CloudControl

    D. Amazon CloudTrail

14. Which of the following AWS cloud services helps with your IT governance, compliance, and auditing requirements?

    A. Amazon CloudWatch

    B. AWS OpsWorks

    C. Amazon CloudControl

    D. Amazon CloudTrail

15. You periodically run several heavy data processing jobs in the AWS cloud. After you complete the data processing, you'd like to retain the data on the Amazon EC2 file system, although you're going to shut down the Amazon EC2 instance to keep from incurring charges between your jobs. Which of the following AWS cloud services helps you store data in a persistent basis in these types of situations?

    A. Amazon Glacier

    B. Amazon Simple Storage Service (Amazon S3)

    C. Amazon Elastic Block Store (Amazon EBS)

    D. Amazon RDS

16. Which of the following architecture extends your on-premise infrastructure into a cloud such as the AWS cloud so you can connect the cloud resources to your data center?

    A. AWS Direct Connect

    B. Amazon S3

    C. A public cloud architecture

    D. A hybrid cloud architecture

17. You notice huge spurts in your online customer traffic to your e-commerce web site around your heavily promoted quarterly sales events. Which of the following features or services can you use to handle the spurts in customer traffic during the sales events?

A. Auto Scaling

B. Amazon Simple Storage Service (Amazon S3)

C. AWS Lambda

D. AWS Snowball

18. Which of the following architectural layers are part of a three-tier architecture? (Choose three)

A. Storage layer

B. Front-end web server layer

C. Database layer

D. Application layer

19. Which of the following AWS cloud services is a fully managed NoSQL database service?

A. Amazon Relational Database Service (Amazon RDS)

B. Amazon Aurora

C. Amazon ElastiCache

D. Amazon DynamoDB

20. Which of the following AWS cloud services enables you to work in a logically isolated section of the cloud where you can launch your AWS resources into a virtual network you define?

A. Amazon Route 53

B. Amazon Virtual Private Cloud (Amazon VPC)

C. Amazon Security Groups

D. Amazon API Gateway

21. Which of the following AWS cloud services would you use to decouple your user-facing applications from your backend services such as a database?

A. Amazon CloudTrail

B. Amazon Simple Queue Service (Amazon SQS)

C. Amazon Simple Notification Service (Amazon SNS)

D. AWS Lambda

22. Under the shared responsibility security model, which of the following would be the responsibility of the cloud provider? (Choose two)

A. Power supplies to the compute instances

B. Data center physical security

    C. Configuration of the AWS provided security group firewall

    D. Database credentials and roles

23. Which of the following AWS services helps you automate your code deployment?

    A. AWS CodeDeploy

    B. AWS CodePipeline

    C. AWS Systems Manager

    D. AWS CodeCommit

24. You're interested in finding out the origination point for an API call, as well as the times when the call was made. Which of the following tools will help you get the information you're looking for?

    A. AWS CloudWatch

    B. AWS Systems Manager

    C. AWS CodeDeploy

    D. AWS CloudTrail

25. Which of the following information does the AWS CloudTrail service track? (Choose two)

    A. User activity

    B. Resource usage

    C. Application usage

    D. API calls

26. Which of the following is *not* a means of accessing the AWS cloud platform?

    A. AWS SDK

    B. AWS CLI

    C. AWS Management Console

    D. Chef and Puppet

Answers

    1. C. CloudTrail tracks all user activity and records the API usage.

    2. A, D. A is correct because more than one EC2 instance can access the same EFS file system. **D** is correct because EFS automatically scales on demand without your having to provision anything.

    3. B. CloudWatch is a monitoring series that shows resource utilization, application performance, and the AWS system health.

    4. A. AWS Config records configuration changes to all AWS resources.

    5. C. Security groups are like firewalls that control traffic into and out of the EC2 instances.

6. **B.** You can store your static web content in S3 and serve that content directly from S3 instead of launching web servers by hosting them on EC2 instances.

7. **A.** There are multiple availability zones within each AWS region, thus providing a higher availability and resilience for your applications.

8. **C, D.** Regions are geographically separated from one another and all availability zones with in a region are connected via low-latency network connections.

9. **B.** You can directly query data that you store in S3.

10. **B.** AWS Direct Connect enables you to connect your on-premise data centers and offices to the AWS cloud, to enable fast transmission of data.

11. **D.** The deployment unit in AWS Lambda is code because it employs a serverless architecture.

12. **A.** Amazon EFS offers a file system interface to storage in AWS.

13. **B.** AWS OpsWorks is a configuration management service like Chef and Puppet and enables you to treat your infrastructure as code.

14. **D.** CloudTrail tracks user activity and API usage, and this information is useful for auditors who want to examine your governance, compliance, and auditing requirements.

15. **C.** EBS offers persistent storage that will remain intact after you shut down the EC2 instances.

16. **D.** A hybrid cloud architecture is where you use your on-premise and public cloud infrastructures as a single infrastructure.

17. **A.** Auto Scaling is an AWS feature that helps you handle spurts in demand for your applications by automatically scaling your EC2 instances up or down.

18. **B, C, D.** The three-tier architecture consists of the web server, database, and application layers.

19. **D.** Amazon DynamoDB is a fully managed NoSQL database.

20. **B.** Amazon VPC is a logically separated section of the VPC where you can launch your AWS resources into your own private virtual network.

21. **B.** Amazon Simple Queue Service (SQS) is a fully managed message queuing service that helps you decouple and scale microservices, distributed systems, and serverless applications. SQS helps decouple and coordinate components of a cloud application. You can send, store, and receive messages between software components at high volume using SQS as the messaging service.

22. **A, B.** In the shared responsibility security model, the cloud provider (AWS) is responsible for securing the cloud infrastructure. This includes securing the power supplies and physical security of the data center.

23. A. CodeDeploy is a service that automates software deployments to compute services such as EC2, AWS Lambda, and instances running in your on-premise data centers.

24. D. CloudTrail tracks and records all user activity and API usage in the AWS cloud.

25. A, D. CloudTrail tracks and records user activity and API usage in the AWS cloud.

26. D. Chef and Puppet are configuration management tools.

Working with AWS: Signing Up, the AWS Management Console, and Command Line Tools

In this chapter, you will
- Sign up for an AWS account
- Understand AWS security credentials
- Manage AWS through the AWS Management Console
- Work with the AWS Command Line Interface
- Learn about AWS SDKs and Python Boto3

Chapter 1 introduced you to the nature of cloud operations and the large number of services available to you in the AWS platform. In this chapter, our goal is to learn how you manage the services. If you're already an experienced AWS system administrator, you may skip this chapter. If you're new to AWS operations, this chapter will show you how to use and administer your AWS cloud, both via the web-based AWS Management Console and via the powerful AWS Command Line Interface (CLI).

Signing Up for AWS

It's quite possible that you already have an AWS account—either your own, your corporate AWS account, or both. If you are entirely new to AWS, however, before you learn how to administer various AWS services, you must first create your AWS account by signing up for AWS. Here are the steps:

1. Go to https://aws.amazon.com.
2. Select Create an AWS Account.
3. Follow the instructions.

NOTE AWS will require that you enter your credit card information, but you'll start getting charged only when you launch services such as EC2 instances (virtual machines) in the AWS cloud. The *free tier* for Amazon EC2 provides you with 750 hours of usage of Linux (any combination of t1.micro and t2.micro instances), plus 750 hours of usage of Windows (any combination of t1.micro and t2.micro instances).

After you've set up your AWS account and established a set of credentials consisting of your AWS account e-mail address and a password, you are deemed to be the AWS account *root user*. It's a good idea to make a note of two very important things: your AWS account number and the AWS root user credentials. By default, your AWS account is enrolled for all AWS services, whether or not you need them right away. Not to worry, since you're billed just for those services that you use.

Amazon offers a Free Tier (https://aws.amazon.com/free/) to help you get familiar with its AWS cloud platform. You'll also be offered this option when you sign up for your AWS account. The AWS Free Tier offers some services free for 12 months, while some other services are always free. Amazon EC2, for example, is free for up to 750 hours per month for 12 months.

When you sign up for AWS and create your account, you owe nothing to AWS. However, once your Free Tier usage is up, you'll start getting charged by the minute for all services that you use. As you move through this book and its discussions of various AWS services, I'll be sure to specify the cost aspects of using each service.

TIP Be sure to shut down all services you use during your exploration of the AWS platform. If you keep unnecessary services running for days, you'll need to pay for them, whether you use them or not. Avoid unpleasant billing shocks by diligently turning off all services after your work is complete for that day. (I speak from personal experience when I first started using AWS.) You can track your AWS Free Tier usage to help you stay under the limits. AWS automatically provides e-mail alerts through AWS Budgets (discussed in Chapter 11) when you exceed the Free Tier limits or when you are forecasted to go over the limits.

Now that you have an AWS account, you can log in and work with AWS services and resources in the cloud. Before you do that, however, you must understand the various types of AWS security credentials and how to manage them.

Understanding AWS Security Credentials

To work with AWS, you must provide your AWS security credentials, so AWS can verify your identity. The credentials also will enable AWS to ascertain that you have appropriate permissions to access various AWS resources. If you want to access objects you stored in AWS S3, for example, the security credentials you specify will enable AWS to determine whether you are authorized to access those S3 objects.

From a functional point of view, there are two types of security credentials: username/password combinations and access keys. You use a username/password credential for performing tasks such as logging into the AWS Management Console to work with AWS services and resources. Access keys help you make programmatic calls to AWS API operations and run AWS CLI (command line interface) commands.

From an authentication and authorization point of view, there are two types of credentials: root user and Identity and Access Management (IAM) credentials.

AWS Account Root User Credentials

When you create an AWS account, the username (your e-mail address) and the password that you provide are your credentials as an account owner. You use these credentials for signing in to AWS web pages such as the AWS Management Console and the AWS Support Center. These credentials are called *root user credentials* and are all powerful, because they provide you with complete access to all resources in your AWS account.

You must use your AWS account e-mail address and password to sign in to the AWS Management Console as the AWS account root user. To change the root user password, go to the Security Credentials page in the AWS Management Console, which you'll learn about later in this chapter.

Multi-Factor Authentication (MFA) provides an additional layer of security for your AWS account. When you enable MFA, AWS prompts you for your username and password and an authentication code from an MFA device to sign in to the AWS website. MFA isn't enabled by default. AWS recommends that you require MFA on the AWS account root user credentials and privileged IAM users.

You do need root account for some specific tasks, but AWS strongly recommends that you do not use the root user for your everyday tasks, even the administrative ones, because you cannot restrict the permissions for the root user credentials. Instead, adhere to the best practice of using the root user only to create your first IAM user. Then securely lock away the root user credentials and use them to perform only a few account and service management tasks.

Tasks that Require Root User Access

You'll rarely need to use root user access credentials to perform specific administrative tasks. To perform the following tasks, however, you'll need to sign in as the AWS account root user:

- Changing the root user password
- Changing your AWS support plan
- Creating a CloudFront key pair
- Changing or deleting your payment options
- Viewing your account's billing information

TIP You can also enable billing access to an IAM user so that user can view billing information and change or delete your payment options. Costs incurred by an IAM user are billed to the AWS account owner.

IAM User Credentials

As an AWS system administrator, you'll need to perform various administrative tasks. Instead of using root user credentials for performing day-to-day tasks with AWS, you'll create and use AWS IAM user credentials. IAM helps you secure and control access to AWS services and resources.

First, create an IAM user and grant that user full access to AWS. Then use this user's credentials to work with AWS. As an IAM user, you can sign in to the AWS web pages, the AWS Management Console, and the AWS Support Center, just as you can as the AWS root user. You can create multiple IAM users, each with access to specific AWS resources. To further restrict access, you can create as many IAM users as necessary with read-only access to your AWS resources.

 NOTE AWS recommends that you require MFA for both the root credentials and for highly privileged IAM users (such as those for whom you've granted administrative access) to provide an extra layer of security. By default, MFA isn't enabled.

Access Keys and Key Pairs

You use the IAM user credentials for accessing things such as the AWS Management Console and the AWS Support Center, but you must use access keys for programmatic access to AWS services and resources and to use the AWS CLI. Key pairs are entirely different and unrelated to access keys and consist of a public key and a private key. You use key pairs to access Amazon EC2 instances and Amazon CloudFront, the AWS global content delivery network (CDN) service that delivers data and applications to viewers with low latency.

Access Keys

To secure the login information for an instance (such as the Linux instance), AWS uses public-key cryptography. This involves the use of access keys, which consist of two parts:

- An access key ID (such as AGCDDEFGDYYZZEXAMPLE)
- A secret access key (such as kiazrNXjeKUIL/J8KENSE/cPxUkiDOEXAMPLEKEY)

You log into an EC2 instance by using a key pair, which I describe in the following section. You need to specify the access keys when using the AWS CLI, because an EC2 instance doesn't use passwords for Secure Shell (SSH) access. Instead, the commands that you execute from the CLI are signed by your access keys. Similarly, you use access keys when using the AWS SDKs and when you perform AWS API operations. You use access keys for all programmatic access to AWS. As with a username and password combination, you must provide both the access key ID and the secret access key to authenticate your requests.

 CAUTION Never share the access key ID and the secret access key with anyone outside your organization, even if you're led to believe that AWS is requesting the keys. AWS will never ask you for your secret keys!

You create access keys as a set (access key ID and the secret access key). If you lose or forget your access keys, you can create a new set of access keys. An access key that you create has the status of *active*, meaning that you can use the access key for CLI and API calls. You can create access keys from the AWS CLI and from the AWS Management Console. You can have a maximum of two access keys at any time. You can create access keys for both the AWS root user account and for the IAM users. You can create the IAM user access keys from the IAM console.

You can create temporary access keys (which include a security token that must be sent to AWS when using the credentials) for use in less secure environments or when you want to grant users temporary access to resources in your AWS account. For example, you can create temporary access keys for enabling users from a different AWS account to access your AWS resources.

Key Pairs

A *key pair* is a pair of text files: a *public key* and a corresponding *private key*. Each of the keys contains long strings of plain-text characters, such as the following:

```
"KeyMaterial": "-----BEGIN RSA PRIVATE KEY-----\nMIIEogIBAAKCAQEA1gttG+YVcUE7
ZPjoJ2Jk/dhU4pTCaoneJqOcbkZTorvIO2PAqLP4ycFKlt6C\nsUA0iWOhAmKQPDSqWnmLYua6E3i
b0xbzZ2/2dgB40EXsenS/UgOr8/AgQz7a80qI1LS40QM5GybB\
...
/KpoFagaoP7CrKTTCgnMiKNqz+K+YhqqgMXrb37SvM2lHqOu3AtIBR8tim5gO2\n5m0WwXLKbTpQ2
pY7gE8LluXkBIDTa0F1r1GF82fZgZ8wJOCT3EZug8SHyqI5D+kT+5w=\n-----END RSA PRIVATE
KEY-----",
```

The strings inside the private and public key text files are randomly generated numbers and characters, which makes them difficult to guess. The private key helps you create a digital signature. AWS uses the corresponding public key to validate this digital signature.

Only EC2 instances and Amazon CloudFront require key pairs. EC2 uses key pairs to enable access to the instances—for example, when you log into a Linux instance using SSH. CloudFront uses key pairs to create signed URLs for private content—for example, when you distribute restricted content.

You must create your own key pairs. For EC2, you can do this from the EC2 console, the CLI, or via an API. You can create a CloudFront key pair from the Security Credentials page in the AWS Management Console.

As an AWS system administrator, you must know how to manage AWS services and users through the console as well as through the command line. Let's start by looking at how you use the AWS Management Console.

Working with the AWS Management Console

The AWS Management Console (AWS console) is a web application that helps you manage various AWS services by providing a simple and convenient user interface for each service. You can set up users and groups, configure your access credentials, get your billing information, and much more, through the AWS console. It also provides a gateway to the service consoles and dashboards of all AWS services, including compute, storage, networking, databases, and more.

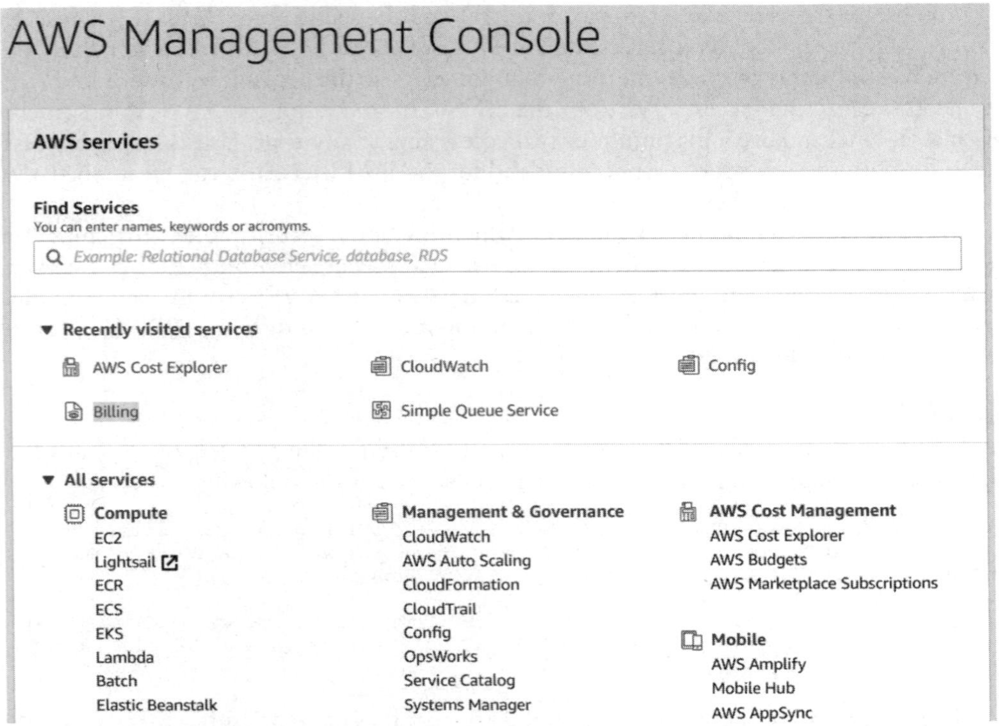

AWS Management Console

AWS services

Find Services
You can enter names, keywords or acronyms.

🔍 *Example: Relational Database Service, database, RDS*

▼ **Recently visited services**

  🏛 AWS Cost Explorer   📑 CloudWatch   📑 Config

  📄 Billing   🔲 Simple Queue Service

▼ **All services**

🖥 **Compute**	📑 **Management & Governance**	🏛 **AWS Cost Management**
EC2	CloudWatch	AWS Cost Explorer
Lightsail ⬈	AWS Auto Scaling	AWS Budgets
ECR	CloudFormation	AWS Marketplace Subscriptions
ECS	CloudTrail	
EKS	Config	📱 **Mobile**
Lambda	OpsWorks	AWS Amplify
Batch	Service Catalog	Mobile Hub
Elastic Beanstalk	Systems Manager	AWS AppSync

Figure 2-1 The AWS Management Console

When you sign in to the console using your credentials, you'll see the console home page, shown in Figure 2-1.

From here, you can manage your entire AWS infrastructure and services. You can also find account information, including billing information, and change your AWS account password. To access a dashboard for a particular AWS service, click the service name from the All Services list. For example, to access the EC2 service dashboard shown in Figure 2-2, you would click EC2 under the Compute heading.

Although you can manage your AWS infrastructure and services from the AWS console, in a production system, where you run numerous AWS services and have many AWS resources, you may want to automate things by scripting your management tasks. That's where the AWS CLI comes in. You can use the AWS CLI to run commands either from an EC2 instance or from any Linux, Windows, or macOS server.

 TIP AWS makes its code for the AWS CLI, AWS SDKs, and other tools available on GitHub. You can incorporate the code behind the tools into your own code. The source code is available at https://github.com/aws/.

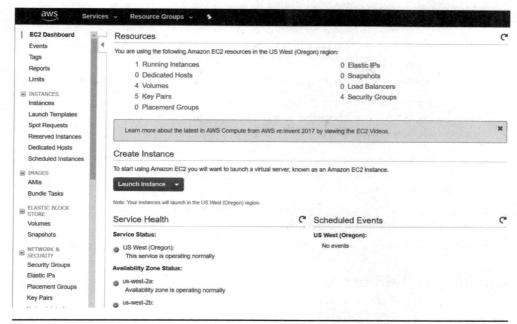

Figure 2-2 The EC2 dashboard

Accessing AWS Services the Right Way

Before you can access an AWS service such as EC2, the service requires that you provide credentials. To access the AWS console, you need a username and a password. To access AWS services through a CLI or an API, you must provide access keys.

Although you can create access keys for your main AWS account and access AWS that way, this is not recommended, because it's not a good idea to grant administrative access to the console to all users in an organization. AWS recommends that you connect as an IAM user rather than connect with your default (and at this point, in our case, the only account) AWS account root user credentials. IAM enables you to control user access to AWS services, as explained in Chapter 5.

You should create an IAM user (instead of a role) in the following cases:

- You created an AWS account and you're the only person who works in that account.

- Other people in your group need to work in your AWS account, and your group is using no other identity mechanism.

- You want to use the CLI to work with AWS.

Create an IAM role (instead of a user) in the following cases:

- You're creating an application that runs on an EC2 instance and the application makes requests to AWS.
- You're creating an app that runs on a mobile phone and makes requests to AWS.
- Users in your company are authenticated in your corporate network and want to be able to use AWS without having to sign in again—that is, you want to allow users to federate into AWS.

To access AWS services, follow these steps:

1. Create an IAM user.
2. Grant the new IAM user administrative permissions (or add the user to an IAM group with administrative permissions).
3. Access AWS using a special URL, which includes the IAM user's credentials.

Creating an IAM User

Follow these steps to create an IAM user from the console:

1. Log into the AWS console using your AWS credentials (AWS account e-mail address and password).
2. In the AWS Management Console page, scroll down to the Security, Identity, & Compliance group of services and click on IAM.
3. On the IAM dashboard page (Welcome to Identity and Access Management), choose Users, and then choose Add User to open the Add User page, shown in Figure 2-3.
4. For User name, enter **administrator** (or any name you want).

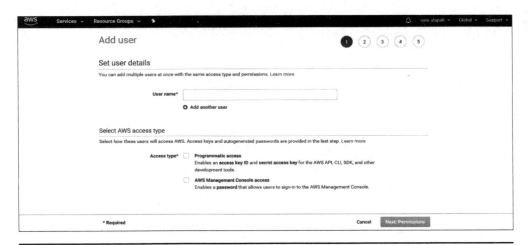

Figure 2-3 The Add User page in the console

5. Under the Select AWS access type section, for Access Type, select how the new IAM user can access AWS: Choose Programmatic Access and AWS Management Console Access. You can limit a user's access to just one access type, but for this example, select both types of access.

6. Under the Select AWS access type, for Console password, select Custom password. Enter the password for the new IAM user. For Require Password Reset, choose No.

7. Click Next: Permissions at the bottom of the page.

8. In the Add user to group page, you can either add the user to an existing group or if you don't have one, you can first create a group by clicking Create group. Select Create Group.

9. In the Create Group page enter **administrators** in the Group name box, and select AdministratorAccess as the policy for this group. Click Create group. You'll be returned to the Add user to group page.

10. In the Add user to group page, your new administrators group will be automatically selected for you. Click Next:Tags.

11. In the Add user page, you have an opportunity to add IAM tags (key-value pairs) to your user. This is optional, and you can skip it for now. Select Next: Review to review your choices.

12. After reviewing your choices, click Create User.

Upon the creation of the IAM user, AWS confirms the user creation:

```
Success
You successfully created the users shown below. You can view and download user
security credentials. You can also email users instructions for signing in to
the AWS Management Console. This is the last time these credentials will be
available to download. However, you can create new credentials at any time.
Users with AWS Management Console access can sign-in at: https://321938860023.
signin.aws.amazon.com/console
```

As indicated by the last line in the message from AWS, 321938860023 is the Account ID. The username I chose was administrator.

Logging In as the New IAM User

To log in as the new IAM user you just created, first log out of the AWS console and then launch the console by entering the following URL (enter you actual *AWS account ID* as indicated):

> https://*AWS account ID*.signin.aws.amazon.com/console

In our example, this would be:

```
https://321938860023.signin.aws.amazon.com/console
```

When you enter this URL in your browser, you'll be taken to the AWS sign-in page. The Account ID will be prepopulated by AWS, and so should be the IAM username that you chose and the password. If not, enter the IAM username and password (we used administrator for the username). Click the **Sign in** bar.

The navigation bar will show "administrator@*AWS account ID*". To avoid showing the AWS account ID on the sign-in page, you can create an account alias from the IAM dashboard. Then your login URL will change to this:

https://your_account_alias.signin.aws.amazon.com/console/

Now you've learned how to create an IAM user and log into the AWS console as that user. For programmatic access to AWS, and for use with the CLI, you'll need to create access keys (consisting of an access key ID and a secret access key), so let's create them now.

Creating an Access Key ID and Secret Access Key (Key Pair) for an IAM User

When we created the IAM user named administrator for administrative access to the AWS cloud in the previous section, "Creating an IAM User," AWS kindly generated the access key ID and a secret access key for the user. The access key ID serves the same function as login name, and the secret access key serves as a password. Rather than have AWS create the keys for you, you can generate an access key ID and secret access key for any IAM users you create.

Here's how to create the access key ID and the secret access key:

1. Open the IAM console.

2. Select Users.

3. Select Security Credentials, and then, select Create Access Key.

4. Download the key ID and the secret access key by choosing Download .CSV File. You can then store the keys for future reference.

 NOTE This is the only time you can download or view the secret access keys. You cannot recover the keys if you lose them. You can, however, create a new set of secret access keys any time.

The CSV file you download will look something like this:

```
Access key ID, Secret access key
AKIAIZO6PO5YKASXZC3A,/qvQ5xXCjXtex20lynAo0dZ62IAGQrrNCk/QUfp1
```

Figure 2-4 shows confirmation from the AWS console, indicating that you've successfully created the access keys.

You can create access keys for a user from the command line with the following command:

```
$ aws iam create-access -key -user-name sam_alapati
```

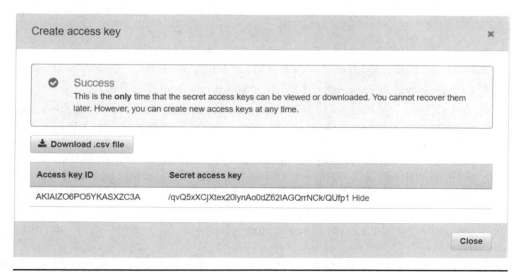

Figure 2-4 Successfully created access keys for an IAM user can be downloaded as a CSV file.

Using a Key Pair to Connect to an EC2 Instance

Remember that you need a key pair for just two things: to connect to an EC2 instance from the command line and to perform certain tasks with Amazon CloudFront. We'll connect to an EC2 instance here, but first we have to create a key pair (there are no default key pairs).

Creating a Key Pair

You can use a key pair for programmatic access and for logging in via SSH. And you can replace this key pair through the AWS console if you happen to lose the original key pair. The presence of a matching set of keys assures openSSH that it's safe to allow the session to start.

When AWS creates a key pair, it embeds the public half of the key pair on the EC2 instance when it starts the instance. You must download the private key and store it on the server from which you plan to connect to an EC2 instance.

NOTE If you want to launch instances in multiple regions, you must create a key pair in each region. A key pair is specific to a region.

Remember that in real life, you must specify a custom security group before you create a key pair. A security group functions as a virtual firewall for EC2 instances and controls inbound and outbound traffic. If you don't explicitly create a security group, AWS will use the default security group.

Follow these steps to create a key pair.

1. Open the Amazon EC2 console: https://console.aws.amazon.com.ec2/.

2. From the navigation bar, select a region for which you want to create the key pair.

3. In the navigation pane, select Key Pairs, and then Create Key Pair.

4. In the *Create Key Pair* dialog box, enter a name for your new key pair. In this case, enter **admin-key-pair-uswest2**. You must provide the name of your key pair when you launch an EC2 instance.

5. Your browser will download the private key file, which has a .pem filename extension. Remember that there is a public and a private component to a key pair; each time you connect to an EC2 instance, you must provide the private key that you've generated in this step.

6. Copy the .pem file to the computer from which you want to connect to an AWS EC2 instance via SSH.

7. Safeguard the contents of your private key file by setting appropriate permissions:

```
$ chmod 400 admin-key-pair-uswest2.pem
```

NOTE You specify the name of the key pair when you create your compute environment and provide the private key when you log in using SSH.

To connect to your EC2 Linux instance from a computer running Mac or Linux, you must specify the .pem file to the SSH client by using the -i option, and you must provide the path to your private key (same as the .pem file). The later section "Connecting to a Running EC2 Instance from the Command Line" shows how to specify the .pem file when connecting to an instance.

Working with the AWS CLI

The AWS CLI is a tool that helps you control multiple AWS services from the command line. The CLI connects to the AWS services through the public APIs of the services. The AWS CLI also helps you automate system administration by enabling you to embed commands in shell scripts. In addition to managing AWS services, you can also manage Amazon S3 objects through file commands.

AWS CLI is built on top of the AWS SDK for Python, also called Boto. You can achieve the same functionality with AWS CLI that you do with the AWS console. You can run AWS CLI commands from the following programs:

- In Linux, macOS, or UNIX, you can run them through shell programs such as Bash and tsch.

- In Microsoft Windows, you can run the commands through the Microsoft Windows PowerShell or the Command Processor.

- You can use remote terminals such as Putty or SSH to run the commands remotely.

NOTE   The primary method for installing AWS CLI on Linux, Windows, and macOS is Python's package manager, pip.

The Structure of AWS CLI Commands

AWS CLI uses low-level, API-equivalent commands to enable you to connect and work with various AWS services. For some services such as Amazon S3, the AWS CLI offers customizations, which are higher-level commands. For example, the AWS S3 commands enable you to manage files in Amazon S3 (Simple Storage Service). Here's an example that shows how to use AWS CLI to upload files to Amazon S3:

```
$ aws s3 cp myvideo.mp4 s3://samalapati/
```

The `aws s3 cp` command in this example is a shell-like copy command that uploads large files to the Amazon S3 storage service.

NOTE   In this book, I explain how to use AWS CLI in the Linux environment, but macOS commands are similar. If you want to use Windows PowerShell, you can do so with the AWS tools for Windows PowerShell. You can find details at https://aws.amazon.com/powershell/.

Installing AWS CLI

AWS CLI is Python-based, and, therefore, you must ensure that your distribution came with Python; if not, you'll need to install Python. Both Mac and Linux require Python for using AWS CLI. For Windows, the installer contains all the necessary dependencies. You can check whether Python is available by running the following command:

```
$ python --version
Python 2.7.12
$
```

NOTE   AWS CLI comes already installed on the Amazon Linux AMI.
An AMI (Amazon Machine Image) is a template for creating an EC2 instance (virtual machine).

Since AWS CLI is Python-based software, you use pip, a Python package manager, to install AWS CLI. You can check to determine whether pip is already installed:

```
$ pip
The program 'pip' is currently not installed.
```

So because pip isn't installed on my server, I can install it by running the following commands on my server. (My server is a Ubuntu Linux server, but commands for other operations systems are similar. Refer to the AWS documentation for details.)

```
$ sudo apt install python-pip
[sudo] password for samalapati:
Reading package lists... Done
...
$
```

Then I can confirm that installation was successful:

```
$ pip -version
pip 8.1.1 from /usr/lib/python2.7/dist-packages (python 2.7)
$
```

Once you confirm that pip is installed, you can install the AWS CLI with the following command:

```
$ pip install awscli --upgrade --user
Collecting awscli
...
$
```

Confirm that you've installed AWS CLI correctly, by running the aws --version command:

```
$ aws --version
aws-cli/1.15.6 Python/2.7.12 Linux/4.10.0-28-generic botocore/1.10.6
$
```

Configuring the AWS CLI

Before you can start using the AWS CLI, you must configure it. To do so, use the aws configure command, which has several options that I will describe. Here's how to run the aws configure command:

```
$ aws configure
AWS Access Key ID [None]: AKIAIZO6PO5YKASXZC3A
AWS Secret Access Key [None]: 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
Default region name [None]: oregon
Default output format [None]: table
$
```

As you can see, AWS CLI prompts you for information:

- **AWS Access Key ID and AWS Secret Access Key**   These represent your AWS account credentials; you've already learned how to generate them.
- **Default region name**   Name of the region you want to work with by default.
- **Default output format**   Specify JSON, text, or table output formats. The default format is JSON.

Changing the values of one or two of the parameters doesn't require you to enter values for all four prompts, because AWS CLI remembers the previous values. So, when you just want to change the default region name from Oregon to us-west-2, and the default output format from table to json, here's how it looks:

```
$ aws configure
AWS Access Key ID [****************ZC3A]:
AWS Secret Access Key [****************Ufp1]:
Default region name [Oregon]: us-west-2
Default output format [None]: json
$
```

This `aws configure` command reconfigures the default region and default output formats.

Run the following command to make sure that you've configured the AWS CLI correctly:

```
$ aws ec2 describe-regions --output table
-----------------------------------------------------------
|                    DescribeRegions                      |
+---------------------------------------------------------+
||                       Regions                        ||
|+-----------------------------------+-------------------+|
||              Endpoint             |    RegionName     ||
|+-----------------------------------+-------------------+|
||  ec2.ap-south-1.amazonaws.com     |  ap-south-1       ||
. . .
||  ec2.us-west-2.amazonaws.com      |  us-west-2        ||
|+-----------------------------------+-------------------+|
$
```

The output tells me that my credentials are correct because I'm able to connect to AWS and retrieve information that I need (regions).

Where AWS CLI Stores the Configuration and Credential Files

AWS CLI stores the credentials you specify with the `aws configure` command in a file named *credentials*, and it stores the file under your home directory, in the .aws subdirectory. For example, my home directory on my Ubuntu Linux server is /home/samalapati. I can view the configuration and credentials files in this manner:

```
$ cd ~
$ pwd
/home/samalapati
$ cd .aws
$ ls
config credentials
```

While the credentials file stores the account credentials, the config file will have the AWS CLI configuration information I had specified when I ran the most recent `aws configure` command.

```
$ cat config
[default]
region = us-west-2
output = json
```

As mentioned earlier, the credentials file stores the secret access keys:

```
$ cat credentials
[default]
aws_access_key_id = AKIAIZO6PO5YKASXZC3A
aws_secret_access_key = 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
$
```

Using Named Profiles

As the previous section explained, when you run the `aws configure` command, AWS CLI stores the credentials (secret keys) in the credentials file and the default values for the region and output in the *config* file, both under the $HOME/.aws directory. Within the *config* file, it stores the values under a *profile* named *default*, as shown here:

```
$ cat ~/.aws/config
[default]
region = us-west-2
output = json
$
```

Instead of all users using the same default profile, you can create custom profiles with different credentials, regions, and output formats. You can create any number of profiles you need. Profiles help you grant separate sets of privileges for different environments, such as development and production environments. You can create a profile and assign it to multiple accounts. Creating and using multiple profiles helps you implement different configurations for different sets of users.

 TIP   AWS also enables you to specify an MFA device to use along with your credentials. You can review the configurations available to you by executing the command `aws help config-vars`.

Creating a Custom Profile Using the Config and Credentials Files   You can create a *custom profile* either by using the config and credentials files or directly from the AWS command line. Here's how to do it by directly adding the custom profile named user2 to the config and credentials files:

```
~/.aws/credentials
[default]
aws_access_key_id=AKIAIOSFODNN7EXAMPLE
aws_secret_access_key=wJalrXUtnFEMI/K7MDENG/bPxRfiCYEXAMPLEKEY

[user2]
aws_access_key_id=AKIAI44QH8DHBEXAMPLE
aws_secret_access_key=je7MtGbClwBF/2Zp9Utk/h3yCo8nvbEXAMPLEKEY
```

As you can see, the user2 profile has different access keys than the default profile.

The following output from the config file shows that the profile user2 can have a different region, as well as a different output format:

```
~/.aws/config
[default]
region=us-west-2
output=json

[profile user2]
region=us-east-1
output=text
```

Now that we've created a test profile, let's see how you can use that profile with the AWS CLI. To use this profile (user2), you must add the `--profile` option to the command

and specify the profile you want to use when running a command. Remember that if you were to use the default profile, as in all our previous examples that showed the AWS CLI in action, you don't need to specify the `profile` parameter.

Here's an example that shows how to specify a named profile (user2) when executing an AWS CLI command:

```
$ aws ec2 describe-instances --profile user2
------------------
|DescribeInstances|
+----------------+
$
```

Note that this command results in no output, because I specified the AWS region as us-east-1 for the new user2 profile. All my EC2 instances happen to be running in the us-east-2 region.

In this section, I showed you how to create a profile by editing the config and credentials files. But you don't have to do it this way; you can create a profile from the command line by specifying the `--profile` option with the `aws configure` command. Here's an example:

```
$ aws configure --profile user2
AWS Access Key ID [None]: AKIAIOSFODNN7EXAMPLE
AWS Secret Access Key [None]: wJalrXUtnFEMI/K7MDENG/bPxRfiCYEXAMPLEKEY

Default region name [None]: us-east-1
Default output format [None]: text
$
```

Configuring the CLI to Use a Role   In the previous section, you learned how to create and use a user profile when accessing the AWS CLI. Instead of using a user profile, you can also create a profile for an IAM role. An IAM role is a way to enable a user to gain permissions to perform actions in a different account. You can configure the CLI to use a role by creating a profile for that role in the ~/.aws/config file. Here's an example:

```
[profile salesadmin]
role_arn = arn:aws:iam:123456780012:role/financeadmin
source_profile = default
```

This configuration enables an IAM user (default profile) to assume the financeadmin role. The named profile here is *source_profile*. Unlike the other profiles I've described in previous sections, you don't configure this named profile with access keys or any other credentials. Instead, you specify two things:

- **The ARN (Amazon Resource Name) of the role**   ARNs help you uniquely identify AWS resources. When you need to specify resources across all of AWS, such as IAM policies, Amazon Relational Database Service (Amazon RDS) tags, and API calls, AWS requires you to use an ARN.

- **The name of the profile that has access to this role profile**   When you specify a command using the role profile, AWS CLI calls the AWS Security Token Service and assumes the role you specify. It uses the source profile's credentials (`role_arn`) to do so.

To use a role profile, you must first do the following:

- Create an IAM role to delegate permissions to a user.
- Allow the IAM user to assume the new role (by modifying what's called the *trust relationship*).
- Grant the IAM user permission to assume the new role.

Once you set up the role profile, role permissions, trust relationship, and the IAM user's permissions, the user can assume the role by specifying the `--profile` option at the command line:

```
$ aws s3 ls --profile financeadmin
```

If you want to use this role for several commands, you can set the AWS_ENVIRONMENT environment variable AWS_PROFILE or your session, as shown here:

```
$ AWS_PROFILE = financeadmin
```

The following section explains how to specify environment variables.

Specifying Environment Variables to Configure AWS CLI

You can specify environment variables at the command line (their values last for the duration of your session), or you can include them in your scripts. In both cases, the values you set through the environment variables will override the values stored in the configuration and credential files (in the ~/.aws directory).

Often, you many need to change some configuration properties temporarily, either when running scripts or when executing commands from the CLI. Environment variables are ideal for these situations.

 NOTE The access and secret key environment variables override credentials stored in the credentials and config files.

You can configure the following environment variables when working with AWS CLI:

- **AWS_ACCESS_KEY_ID**   Specifies the AWS access key.
- **AWS_SECRET_ACCESS_KEY**   Specifies the AWS secret key.
- **AWS_SESSION_TOKEN**   Specifies a session token if you are using temporary security credentials.
- **AWS_DEFAULT_REGION**   Specifies the AWS region. This variable overrides the default region of the in-use profile, if set.
- **AWS_DEFAULT_OUTPUT**   Sets the AWS CLI output format to JSON, text, or table.

- **AWS_PROFILE**   Specifies the name of the CLI profile to use, which can be the name of a profile stored in the credentials or config file, or the default profile.
- **AWS_CA_BUNDLE**   Specifies the path to a certificate bundle to use for HTTPS certificate validation.
- **AWS_SHARED_CREDENTIALS_FILE**   Changes the location of the file that the AWS CLI uses to store access keys.
- **AWS_CONFIG_FILE**   Changes the location of the file that the AWS CLI uses to store configuration profiles.

NOTE   An access key is a combination of an access key ID (such as AGCDDEFGDYYZZEXAMPLE) and a secret access key (such as kiazrNXjeKUIL/J8KENSE/cPxUkiDOEXAMPLEKEY). You use access keys to sign API requests you make to AWS.

Here are some examples that show how to configure environment variables for various properties on a Linux or macOS server, where you use the export command to export the environment variables:

```
$ export AWS_ACCESS_KEY_ID=AKIAIOSFODNN7EXAMPLE
$ export AWS_SECRET_ACCESS_KEY=wJalrXUtnFEMI/K7MDENG/bPxRfiCYEXAMPLEKEY
$ export AWS_DEFAULT_REGION=us-west-2
$ export AWS_PROFILE=user
```

NOTE   In a Windows server, replace export with set.

Configuration Precedence

As you've learned, you can configure AWS CLI settings in multiple ways. You can do so via environment variables, through the credentials and config files, through the config command, and finally, from the command line. If you set different values for a configuration variable such as region, which of the configuration values will the AWS CLI use? In other words, what's the *order of precedence* among the various ways of configuring the AWS CLI?

The AWS CLI looks at credentials and configuration settings in the following order:

- Command line options
- Environment variables
- The AWS credentials file (~/.aws/credentials)
- The CLI config file (~/.aws.config)
- Container credentials (provided by the Amazon Elastic Container Service)
- Instance profile credentials (used on EC2 instances with an assigned instance role)

Now that you've learned how to configure AWS CLI, let's dive into how you use the tool. I describe only a couple of examples in this chapter, but throughout the book, you'll learn many commands in detail.

Using the AWS CLI

To use the AWS CLI, you must know a few things, how to set various command line options, such as those that control the command output, and how to invoke help for the various AWS commands.

Command Line Options

You can set the following command line options, each preceded by two hyphens (--).

- **--profile**   Specify a named profile here; if you don't, AWI CLI will assume you want to use the default profile.

- **--region**   The AWS region where you want to create, or work with, existing AWS resources; you can check your AWS resources in a specific AWS region.

- **--output**   The format in which you want the CLI to display the results of the commands you run. You can configure a different output format when writing AWS administrative scripts, for example.

- **--endpoint-url**   The endpoint to make the call against, such as the address of a proxy or an AWS region's endpoint URL.

AWS CLI Command Structure

Issuing commands from the AWS CLI is no different from executing any other commands. You must first use `aws`, followed by the service name you want to work with, and then a set of options. AWS CLI commands have a multipart structure:

```
$ aws command> <subcommand> [options and parameters]
```

In this generic command structure,

- `aws` issues a base call to AWS.

- `command` shows the top-level command, which is usually the name of an AWS service, such as `ec2` or `s3`.

- `subcommand` specifies the operations you want to perform for that service. Commands issued for each AWS service can include subcommands. For example, `ec2 describe-instances` is a subcommand for the `ec2` top-level command that asks `ec2` to provide information pertaining to EC2 instances.

- `options` enable you to specify exactly what you need the subcommand to do.

- `parameters` have string or numeric values.

In the following example, sam-key-pair is the name of the key pair in the `ec2 create-key-pair` command:

```
$ aws ec2 create-key-pair --key-name sam-key-pair
{
    "KeyMaterial": "-----BEGIN RSA PRIVATE KEY-----\nMIIEogIBAAKCAQEA1gttG+YVcUE7ZP
joJ2Jk/dhU4pTCaoneJqOcbkZTorvIO2PAqLP4ycFKlt6C\nsUA0iWOhAmKQPDSqWnmLYua6E3ib0xbzZ2/
2dgB40EXsenS/UgOr8/
...
 XkBIDTa0Flr1GF82fZgZ8wJOCT3EZug8SHyqI5D+kT+5w=\n-----END RSA PRIVATE KEY-----",
    "KeyName": "sam-key-pair",
    "KeyFingerprint": "a0:a7:7e:36:7b:20:34:76:80:66:fd:40:00:72:81:67:a3:ac:2b:b9"
}
$
```

Earlier, you saw how to generate a key pair from the console. It's good to learn how to do this from the command line as well.

Getting Help Regarding the Commands

To review all the available commands at your disposal, use the `aws help` command:

```
$ aws help
```

The `aws help` command shows all AWS CLI commands, and there are quite a few of them! To view the subcommands available for a specific service such as EC2 (as shown in Figure 2-5), type the following:

```
$ aws ec2 help
```

Figure 2-5 shows the output of the `aws ec2 help` command. You can scroll down the list by pressing ENTER.

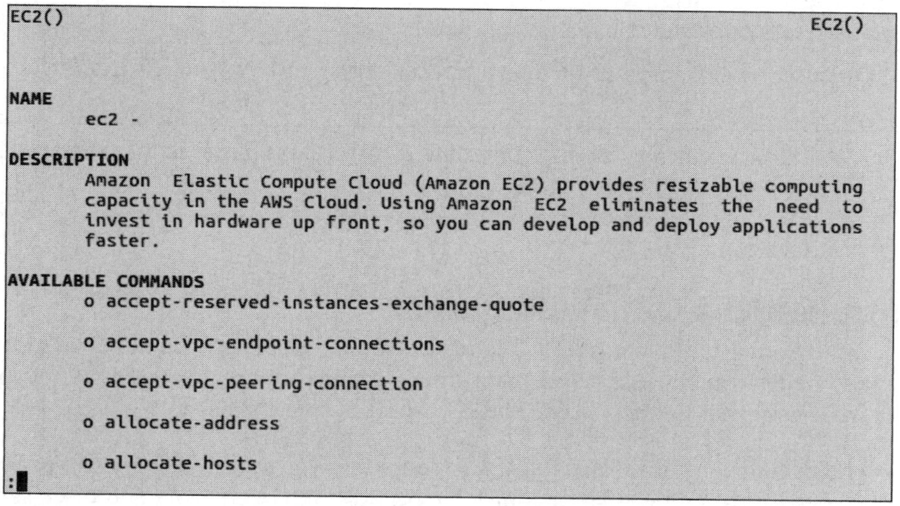

Figure 2-5 Results of the `aws ec2 help` command

There are many subcommands for the top-level command `aws ec2` as well. The `aws ec2 help` command lists all those commands. Let's say you'd like to learn how to use a specific subcommand such as `ec2 describe-instances`. You can learn more about this command by asking the help facility for details:

```
$ aws ec2 describe-instances help
DESCRIBE-INSTANCES()                                    DESCRIBE-INSTANCES()
NAME
       describe-instances -
DESCRIPTION
       Describes one or more of your instances.
       If you specify one or more instance IDs, Amazon EC2 returns information
       for those instances. If you do not specify instance IDs, Amazon EC2
       returns information for  all  relevant  instances.  If you specify an
       instance ID that is not valid, an error is returned. If you specify an
       instance that  you  do  not  own,  it  is not included in the returned
       results.
...
SYNOPSIS
          describe-instances
       [--filters <value>]
       [--instance-ids <value>]
       [--dry-run | --no-dry-run]
...
OPTIONS
       --filters (list)
          One or more filters.
          o availability-zone - The Availability Zone of the instance.
...
$
```

The `aws ec2 describe-instances help` command shows the following:

- **Description** A description of the API operation that the command will invoke.
- **Synopsis** A list of the subcommand and its options—any option in square brackets is optional or has a default value.
- **Options** Lets you filter the output of the command by specifying an AZ.

NOTE You can view the content of all AWS CLI commands' help files online in the AWS CLI Command Reference.

Controlling the Command Output

Unlike many other CLIs, the AWS CLI enables you to select the format of the output a command generates. You can select from three output formats: JSON, text, and table. Here's what you need to know about the AWS CLI output formats:

- The default output format, JSON, is best when you're using a program or jq (a command-line JSON processor). Applications can easily parse and understand JSON data and thus many AWS cloud services such as AWS CloudFormation use the JSON format extensively. You can encode some AWS CLI inputs in JSON format and pass them through by using the `-cli-input-json` parameter.

- The table format is mostly meant for reading by humans, rather than programs. You can read the table output format easily compared to JSON and text.
- The text output format presents output in tab-delimited lines. Text format works best when using text processing tools in scripts, such as sed, grep, and awk.

NOTE The default output format of the AWS CLI is JSON.

You can specify the output format in various ways, discussed next.

Specifying the Output Format by Configuring It   You specify the output format in the config file (or by running the config command) by specifying the value under [default]. This example shows how to set the output format to table:

```
[default]
output=table
```

Specifying the Output Format at the Command Line   The default output format is text, so you'll see the following when you run the aws ec2-describe-instances command:

```
$ aws ec2 describe-instances
{
    "Reservations": [
        {
            "Instances": [
                {
                    "Monitoring": {
                        "State": "disabled"
                    },
                    "PublicDnsName": "ec2-34-209-241-143.us-west-2.compute.amazonaws.com",
                    "State": {
                        "Code": 16,
                        "Name": "running"
                    }
                }
...
$
```

You can specify the --output option on the command line when running a command to control the format of the output. To view the output in a table format instead of text, you'd issue the following command.

```
$ aws ec2 describe-instances --output table
-------------------------------------------------------------------------------------
|                                  DescribeInstances                                 |
+---------------------------------------------------------------------------------+
||                                   Reservations                                  ||
|+---------------------------------------+---------------------------------------+|
||  OwnerId                              |  321938860023                         ||
||  ReservationId                        |  r-0fbdb98d9c6070295                  ||
|+---------------------------------------+---------------------------------------+|
|||                                   Instances                                  |||
||+-------------------------------------+-------------------------------------+||
|||  AmiLaunchIndex                     |  0                                  |||
|||  Architecture                       |  x86_64                             |||
...
$
```

Specify the Output Format via an Environment Variable   You can also set the output format using an environment variable. Here's how to do it:

```
$ export AWS_DEFAULT_OUTPUT="table"
```

 TIP   When you execute a long command with AWS CLI, you can use backslashes (\) after a set of words to indicate that you wish to continue the line after moving to a new line. At the end of the very last line, press the **Enter** key to execute the full command.

Filtering the Output of a Command

Many AWS CLI commands generate a large volume of output, such as the describe-volumes command:

```
$ aws ec2 describe-volumes
{
    "Volumes": [
        {
            "AvailabilityZone": "us-west-2c",
            "Attachments": [],
            "Encrypted": false,
            "VolumeType": "io1",
            "VolumeId": "vol-062eba9ec3e525e94",
            "State": "available",
            "Iops": 100,
            "SnapshotId": "",
            "CreateTime": "2018-04-22T15:16:15.410Z",
            "Size": 100
        },
        {

            "AvailabilityZone": "us-west-2b",
            "Attachments": [
                {
                    "AttachTime": "2018-02-25T21:10:53.000Z",
                    "InstanceId": "i-0fa4707c0e0aac82c",
                    "VolumeId": "vol-0dea915474e305219",
                    "State": "attached",
                    "DeleteOnTermination": true,
                    "Device": "/dev/sda1"
                }
            ],
...
$
```

You may have many volumes attached to an instance, making it difficult for you to go through the entire output when all you want is to find information about a single volume. To avoid getting lost in the voluminous output, you can filter the output by specifying the --query option along with the aws ec2-describe-volumes command. The --query parameter is a powerful tool for simplifying complex cloud deployments.You can display information about only the first volume, for example, by using the --query option, like this:

```
$ aws ec2 describe-volumes --query 'Volumes[0]'
{
    "AvailabilityZone": "us-west-2c",
    "Attachments": [],
```

```
        "Encrypted": false,
        "VolumeType": "io1",
        "VolumeId": "vol-062eba9ec3e525e94",
        "State": "available",
        "Iops": 100,
        "SnapshotId": "",
        "CreateTime": "2018-04-22T15:16:15.410Z",
        "Size": 100
    }
  $
```

The --query option is versatile. You can specify the wildcard notation [*] to go over the entire volume list and print out just the elements that you need. You do this by using the dictionary notation to specify an alias for each key (same as element), which is {Alias1:Key1,Alias2:Key2,Alias3:Key3}. Here's an example:

```
$ aws ec2 describe-volumes --query 'Volumes[*].{ID:VolumeId,AZ:AvailabilityZone,Size:Size}'
[
    {
        "AZ": "us-west-2c",
        "ID": null,
        "Size": 100
    },
    {
        "AZ": "us-west-2b",
        "ID": null,
        "Size": 8
    },
    {
        "AZ": "us-west-2b",
        "ID": null,
        "Size": 100
    }
]
$
```

AWS strongly recommends that you use the text output format along with --query option for consistent behavior. The reason is that the text format orders the output columns alphabetically. AWS may add or remove key-value elements to its resources in the future, which changes the order of the columns. Using the text format ensures that the correct key values will always be shown in the expected column. When you specify the text format, AWS CLI outputs "None" as the value for keys that don't exist.

You can use the Linux grep, awk, and sed commands with text output from a command. In the following example, the first two commands show how to specify the --query option to track the status of all EC2 instances in your AWS account:

```
$ aws ec2 describe-instances --query 'Reservations[*].Instances[*].
[Placement.AvailabilityZone, State.Name, InstanceId]' --output text
us-west-2b      running      i-0fa4707c0e0aac82c
us-west-2b      stopping     i-03ec45c7de2692159
$
$ aws ec2 describe-instances --query 'Reservations[*].Instances[*].
[Placement.AvailabilityZone, State.Name, InstanceId]' --output text
us-west-2b      running      i-0fa4707c0e0aac82c
us-west-2b      stopped      i-03ec45c7de2692159
$
```

Here's how to use the Linux `grep` and `awk` commands to start up all stopped EC2 instances automatically in your account:

```
$ aws ec2 describe-instances --query 'Reservations[*].Instances[*].
[Placement.AvailabilityZone, State.Name, InstanceId]' --output text |
> grep stopped |
> awk '{print $2)' |
> while read line;
> do aws ec2 modify-instance-attribute --instance-id $line --instance-type
'{Value": "m1.medium"}';
> done
$
```

Writing scripts such as this helps you automate your AWS environment as the number of your EC2 instances grows.

Limiting the Command Output with the Pagination Option   If you expect a lot of output from a command, you can modify the default pagination behavior of the AWS CLI to control the output. By default, AWS uses a page size of 1000, meaning that each command will retrieve 1000 items per each call made by CLI to the AWS service. For example, if you issue the `aws s3api list-objects` command, the CLI needs to issue calls to Amazon S3 to retrieve the list of objects.

The default page size of 1000 may be too large when you run a command that retrieves a large list of objects. You can change the default page size to avoid an AWS service from timing out your requests. Here's an example:

```
$ aws s3api list-objects –bucket my-bucket –page-size 100
```

You can also control the output by specifying the `–max-items` option, which will show you the number of items that you specify:

```
$ aws s3api list-objects –bucket my-bucket –max-items 50
```

Reading in Configuration Parameters from a File

In all the examples thus far, I've showed you how to execute commands by typing them at the command line. However, there's an easier way to run a lot of commands at once, without the tedium of typing each command. You can store parameters in a JSON-formatted file and read them in.

To create a file with stored parameters, first generate a *CLI skeleton*, which is an outline (in JSON format) of all the parameters that you can specify for an operation. You can run the `--generate-cli-skeleton` command to view the JSON skeleton for an operation. For example, here's how you'd run the command to view the JSON skeleton for the `run-instances` command:

```
$ aws ec2 run-instances --generate-cli-skeleton
{
    "DryRun": false,
    "ImageId": "",
    "MinCount": 0,
    "MaxCount": 0,
    "KeyName": "",
    "SecurityGroups": [
        ""
```

```
    ],
    "SecurityGroupIds": [
        ""
    ],
    "UserData": "",
    "InstanceType": "",
    "Placement": {
        "AvailabilityZone": "",
        "GroupName": "",
        "Tenancy": ""
    },
...
```

To run commands from a JSON file, do the following:

1. Capture the output of the command to a .json file, to save the skeleton:

   ```
   $ aws ec2 run-instances --generate-cli-skeleton > ec2runinst.json
   ```

2. The ec2runinst.json file captures all the parameters for the run-instances command. Open the file and delete all the parameters you don't need. Modify the parameters that you do need and save the file. In this example, I choose to set the DryRun parameter (the DryRun parameter shows whether your JSON is correctly formed and validates the parameter values) to true:

   ```
   {
       "DryRun": true,
       "ImageId": "ami-dfc39aef",
       "KeyName": "mykey",
       "SecurityGroups": [
           "my-sg"
       ],
       "InstanceType": "t2.micro",
       "Monitoring": {
           "Enabled": true
       }
   }
   ```

Once you make the changes to the parameters you need, pass the JSON configurations to the --cli-input-json command:

```
$ aws ec2 run-instances --cli-input-json file://ec2runinst.json
```

NOTE In addition to AWS CLI, you can use other AWS tools to help you manage AWS resources, such as the AWS tools for PowerShell, and the AWS Software Development Kits (for developers).

Connecting to a Running EC2 Instance from the Command Line

A basic building block of your AWS infrastructure is computing. EC2 is an AWS service that enables you to create virtual servers for your use. Once you have an AWS account, you can start using it, but you must first create an EC2 instance. I'll explain how to create an EC2 instance in Chapter 3. Once you have an instance ready, you can connect to it via the console or from the command line using the AWS CLI.

It's common to use an SSH client such as Putty to connect to an EC2 instance. I'm sure many of you know how to use Putty, but if not, you can download it from https://www.chiark.greenend.org.uk/~sgtatham/putty/latest.html.

Connecting from Another Server

You can log into an EC2 server from another Linux server (or a Cygwin session) by following these steps:

1. Locate your private key file (n2.pem in our case).
2. For SSH to work, your private key must not be publicly viewable. Change the permissions on the private key file (n2.pem) so only you can read it:

   ```
   $ sudo chmod 400 n2.pem
   ```

3. Connect to the EC2 instance by specifying its public DNS (`ec2-34-209-241-143.us-west-2.compute.amazonaws.com` in this example):

   ```
   $ sudo ssh -i "n2.pem" ubuntu@ec2-34-209-241-143.us-west-2.compute.amazonaws.com
   Welcome to Ubuntu 16.04.3 LTS (GNU/Linux 4.4.0-1049-aws x86_64)

    * Documentation:  https://help.ubuntu.com
    * Management:     https://landscape.canonical.com
    * Support:        https://ubuntu.com/advantage
     ...
   *** System restart required ***
   Last login: Sun Feb 25 21:15:02 2018 from 63.89.85.15
   $
   ```

You can get the connection string for an instance from the AWS EC2 console. Click the Connect tab, as shown in Figure 2-6.

Getting the DNS of a Server

You can get the public DNS of an EC2 instance running in your account by going to the EC2 Dashboard console and clicking Instances in the list on the left-hand side. In the page that appears (Instances page), select the Instance ID for which you want to get the public DNS. You'll see the Public DNS (IPv4) of the instance on the bottom right-hand side of the instance page for this instance (for example, ec2-54-91-34-34.compute-1.amazonaws.com).

Alternatively, you can click the Connect button on the Instances page after selecting the instance you want to connect to. AWS will display a Connect To Your Instance page, as shown in Figure 2-7, showing the access details.

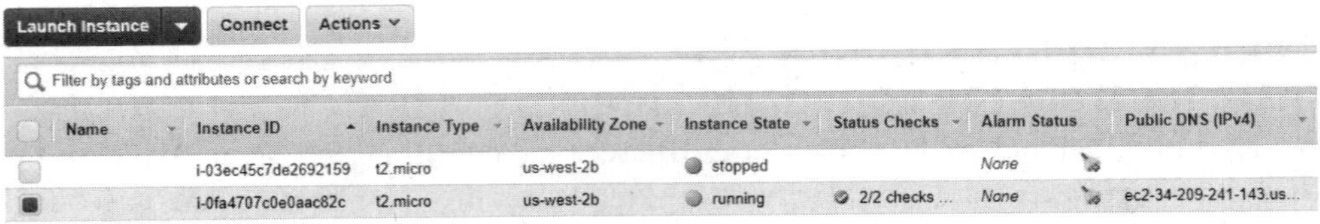
Launch Instance
Connect
Actions
Filter by tags and attributes or search by keyword
Name
Instance ID
Instance Type
Availability Zone
Instance State
Status Checks
Alarm Status
Public DNS (IPv4)
i-03ec45c7de2692159
t2.micro
us-west-2b
stopped
None
i-0fa4707c0e0aac82c
t2.micro
us-west-2b
running
2/2 checks ...
None
ec2-34-209-241-143.us...

Figure 2-6 The Connect tab in the EC2 console

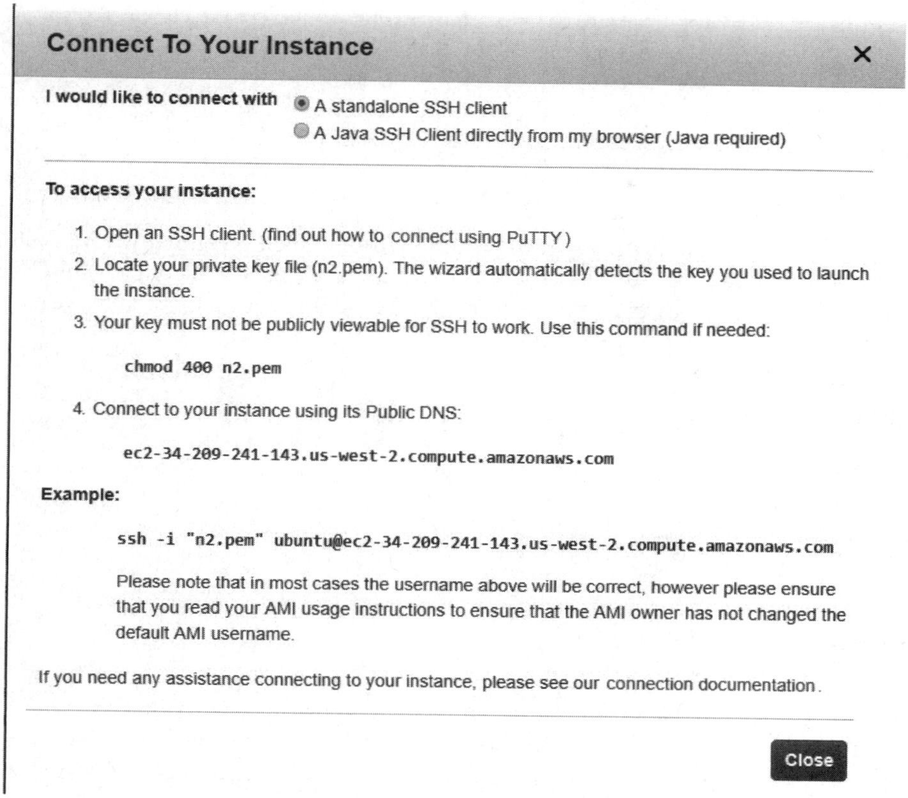

Connect To Your Instance   ✕

I would like to connect with ⦿ A standalone SSH client
                                   ⦾ A Java SSH Client directly from my browser (Java required)

To access your instance:

1. Open an SSH client. (find out how to connect using PuTTY)

2. Locate your private key file (n2.pem). The wizard automatically detects the key you used to launch the instance.

3. Your key must not be publicly viewable for SSH to work. Use this command if needed:

    chmod 400 n2.pem

4. Connect to your instance using its Public DNS:

    ec2-34-209-241-143.us-west-2.compute.amazonaws.com

Example:

    ssh -i "n2.pem" ubuntu@ec2-34-209-241-143.us-west-2.compute.amazonaws.com

    Please note that in most cases the username above will be correct, however please ensure that you read your AMI usage instructions to ensure that the AMI owner has not changed the default AMI username.

If you need any assistance connecting to your instance, please see our connection documentation .

                                                                        Close

Figure 2-7 The Connect to Your Instance page in the AWS console

AWS SDKs and Python Boto3

AWS SDKs enable developers to write code that makes use of AWS services such as EC2 and S3. SDKs make it easy to use AWS services in your applications, with APIs in various languages. AWS SDKs and the APIs that underlie them enable the applications you build in AWS to manage your infrastructure as code (more on infrastructure as code in Chapter 11). As an AWS system administrator, you may not directly use SDKS often, but you'll find it useful to understand them a bit, especially if you're part of a DevOps group, where you perform both administrative and development tasks.

Amazon SDKs are available in the following languages:

- Java
- .NET
- Node.js

- Ruby
- Python
- PHP
- Go
- C++

In this book, I focus on the AWS SDK for Python, which is named Boto3. You can integrate your Python applications or scripts that interact with AWS services using Boto3. Before you can start using Boto3, you must install it and set up credentials.

Installing Boto3

Install Boto3 with pip:

```
$ pip install boto3
Collecting boto3
  Downloading ...
Successfully installed boto3-1.7.6 botocore-1.10.6 docutils-0.14 futures-3.2.0
jmespath-0.9.3 python-dateutil-2.7.2 s3transfer-0.1.13 six-1.11.0
$
```

Setting Up Credentials

Make sure you have the credentials and the default region set up, as shown in the section "Configuring the AWS CLI" earlier in this chapter. You may recall that the credentials and the config files are stored in the ~/.aws/credentials and the ~/.aws/config files, respectively. This is so for both Mac and Linux systems. The credentials are stored in the %UserProfile%\.aws\credentials directory on Windows servers.

Testing the Boto3 Installation

Log into the Python interpreter and run a Boto3 command to get a list of all your Amazon S3 buckets:

```
$ python
Python 2.7.12 (default, Dec  4 2017, 14:50:18)
[GCC 5.4.0 20160609] on linux2
Type "help", "copyright", "credits" or "license" for more information.
>>> import boto3
>>> s3 = boto3.resource('s3')
>>> for bucket in s3.buckets.all():
...     print(bucket.name)
...
sam-alapati-bucket1
>>>
```

Simple as this Boto3 command is, it offers a glimpse of how you can use Boto3 to perform powerful and wide-ranging actions in an AWS cloud environment.

More About Boto3

Here's some more information about Boto3:

- Low-level APIs, also called client APIs, offer one-to-one mapping to the underlying HTTP API operations.

- High-level APIs, also called resource APIs, provide resource objects and collections to perform actions by accessing object attributes.

- Boto3 has several service-specific features, such as automatic multipart transfers for Amazon S3.

- Waiters automatically poll for status changes in the AWS resources. For example, you can use a waiter to track EC2 instances that you've started and have them wait until the instance reaches the "running" state. When you create an instance or an Amazon Redshift cluster, there's a short wait. The waiter allows you to wait for an ordered infrastructure to become available before proceeding further.

Chapter Review

This chapter showed you how to work with AWS basics. You learned how to set up an AWS account. You learned how to work with the AWS Management Console and the AWS CLI. Although you can and will perform many administrative tasks through the AWS Management Console, the AWS CLI is very powerful and is especially helpful when you're creating scripts to perform repetitive or common administrative tasks.

The chapter explained how each AWS command that you can invoke consists of sub-commands, options, and parameters. Understanding how to wield the AWS CLI tool effectively will go a long way toward making you an effective AWS sysops professional.

You learned how to create an IAM user. As an administrator, you must perform all routine administrative tasks through an IAM user account, and not use your initial AWS account root user key to do so. You learned how to create an IAM user, how to create a key pair, and how to access an EC2 server using a key pair.

As a sysops professional, although you may not use the Amazon SDKs and Boto3, it's a good idea to learn what these are so you can help developers who will be often using these tools.

Exercises

The exercises in this chapter show you how to use the AWS CLI and the console to perform various administrative tasks.

Start by creating an AWS account, as explained in this chapter, before attempting the exercises. Use the Free Tier when launching AWS resources.

Exercise 2-1: Create an access key (access ID and secret key) using the AWS Management Console.

In this exercise, you will create a set of access keys from the AWS console.

1. Log into the AWS console with the username and password you provided when creating your AWS account. That is, log in with your AWS account root user credentials.

2. Select **IAM** under the **Security, Identity, & Compliance** group of services.

3. Under IAM Resources, click on Users.

4. Click your username or any username for which you want to create the access keys.

5. Click the **Security Credentials** tab, and then, in the **Access keys** section, select **Create access key**.

You'll see a Create access key page with a message indicating that the access keys were successfully downloaded and informing you that this the only time you can view or download the access keys. Download the .csv file that contains the access key ID and the secret access key by clicking on the the **Download .csv file** link, and store them securely. Click **Close** to exit the **Create access key** page.

Exercise 2-2: Install the AWS CLI on a linux server.

1. Check whether Python is installed on your server.

2. If Python isn't installed, install it using the steps shown in this chapter.

3. Check whether pip is installed.

4. If pip isn't installed on your server, install it using the steps shown in this chapter.

5. Run the following command to install the AWS CLI:

```
$ pip install awscli
```

Exercise 2-3: Configure the AWS CLI.

1. Run the following command to configure AWS CLI:

```
$ aws configure
```

2. AWS CLI will prompt you to fill in values for the access key, secret key, region, and the output format.

3. For the access key and secret keys, use the credentials you obtained in Exercise 1.

4. Enter **us-east-2** as the Region.

5. Choose Table as the Output Format.

6. Run the following command to make sure your configuration is correct:

```
$ aws ec2 describe-availability-zones
```

Exercise 2-4: Change your AWS account password from the AWS Management Console.

1. Log into the AWS Management Console by going to https://aws.amazon.com.

2. Select your account name in the navigation bar at the upper-right-handcorner.

3. Select Security Credentials.

4. Following the console's instructions to change your password.

5. Confirm your new password.

6. Once you complete the password form, select Change Password or Save Changes.

Exercise 2-5: Get billing information from the AWS Management Console.

1. Log into the AWS Management Console by going to https://aws.amazon.com.

2. Select your account name in the navigation bar at the upper right-hand corner.

3. Select My Billing Dashboard.

4. Use the dashboard to find a billing summary and a monthly AWS spending breakdown.

Questions

The following questions will help you measure your understanding of the material presented in this chapter. Read all the choices carefully because there may be more than one correct answer. Choose all the correct answers for each question.

1. Which of the following do you need to do to connect to a Linux EC2 instance using SSH?

    A. Use a certificate.

    B. Use the private and public halves of a key pair.

    C. Use Multi-Factor Authentication.

    D. Specify the private half (.pem) file of a key pair.

2. When you lose your secret access keys, which of the following is true?

   A. You can generate new access keys anytime you need to.

   B. You can go the AWS console and download a CSV file that includes the lost access keys.

   C. You can view the lost access keys by going to the IAM console.

   D. If you lose your access keys, there's no way to generate a new set of keys.

3. Which of the following is the default AWS CLI output format?

   A. Text

   B. Table

   C. HTML

   D. JSON

4. Where are the AWS CLI credentials that you specify with the `aws configure` command stored?

   A. In your home directory, in a subdirectory named .aws, and in a file named credentials

   B. In the AWS root directory, in a file named credentials, and in a directory named .aws

   C. In your home directory, in a file named. aws, and in a directory named .credentials

   D. In your home directory, in a file named credentials in a folder named aws

5. Which of the following shows the correct order of precedence regarding AWS CLI configuration?

   A. environment variables, config files, command line

   B. command line, environment variables, config files

   C. config files, environment variables, command line

   D. command line, config files, environment variables

6. Which of the following AWS CLI options enables you to filter the results of an AWS CLI command?

   A. `--sort`

   B. `--filter`

   C. `--search`

   D. `--query`

7. Which of the following AWS CLI output formats is easiest for viewing by a human?

   A. Table

   B. Text

   C. JSON

   D. Script

8. Which of the following formats must a file be in for an AWS CLI command that accepts formatted files as inputs?

   A. Text

   B. JSON

   C. HTML

   D. Table

9. Which of the following commands do you run to get help on the syntax and options for AWS EC2?

   A. `aws ec2 -help`

   B. `aws ec2 -list-commands`

   C. `aws -help ec2`

   D. `aws ec2 help`

10. Which of the following configuration properties are mandatory when you run the `aws configure` command? (Choose two)

   A. Region name

   B. Output format

   C. Access key ID

   D. Secret key

11. Which of the following tasks does the Python Boto3 waiter do?

   A. It keeps an EC2 instance from being available to users until you approve the access.

   B. It waits for infrastructure that must be provisioned in an orderly fashion to be available before continuing.

   C. It waits for instructions from you before continuing.

   D. It waits for messages from AWS services.

12. Which of the following must be installed before you can run the AWS CLI for Linux and macOS?

   A. Python

   B. Java

   C. JSON

   D. Boto3

13. What is the purpose of using multiple profiles?

    A. Multiple profiles help you implement different configurations for different sets of users.

    B. Multiple profiles enhance security.

    C. Multiple profiles help you implement the same configuration for different sets of users.

    D. If you lose a profile, you can use one of the other profiles.

14. What does AWS recommend that you do with your AWS account root user credentials?

    A. Save the credentials in a safe place, under lock and key.

    B. Lock the credentials.

    C. Encrypt the credentials.

    D. Never obtain the root user credentials.

15. Which of the following enable an AWS-based application to treat infrastructure as code? (Choose two)

    A. SDKs

    B. Python Boto3

    C. Config files

    D. AWS APIs

16. Which AWS CLI output format enables you to use Linux commands such as `grep`, `awk`, and `sed`?

    A. Both text and JSON formats

    B. JSON format

    C. Text format

    D. Table format

17. Which of the following is *not* an AWS CLI command line option:

    A. `--region`

    B. `--endpoint-url`

    C. `--service`

    D. `--profile`

18. Which of the following credentials will enable you to perform administrative tasks when you log into AWS? (Choose two)

    A. IAM user credentials

    B. Root user credentials

    C. Security administrator credentials

    D. AWS resource owner credentials

19. Which of the following type of credentials will enable programmatic access to AWS services and resources?

   A. Access keys

   B. Key pairs

   C. Both access keys and key pairs

   D. Only the secret key

20. Which of the following are you most likely to use when administering an AWS cloud?

   A. Key pairs

   B. Only the secret access key

   C. Access keys (access key ID plus the secret access key)

   D. Account root user credentials

Answers

1. D. You must specify the private half of the key pair when connecting to an EC2 instance via SSH.

2. A. You can create a new access key ID and the secret key anytime you need, either from the console or from the AWS command line.

3. D. JSON is the default AWS CLI command output format.

4. A. The AWS CLI credentials are stored under your home directory, in the subdirectory named .aws, and in a file named credentials.

5. B. The order of precedence goes from the values you specify on the command line when running a command, to the values you specify through an environment variable, and finally to the values stored in the config files, in that order.

6. D. The `--query` option enables you to filter the output of an AWS CLI command.

7. A. The table format is the easiest format for a human to read.

8. B. For an AWS CLI command to accept a file as input, the file must be in the JSON format.

9. C. You must run the command `aws -help ec2` to get information about the syntax and options for AWS EC2.

10. C, D. Both the access key ID and the secret key are mandatory when running AWS CLI commands.

11. B. The Boto3 waiter offers a handler to our code so it can deal with the waits when performing tasks such as launching AWS instances or building a database cluster. The job of the waiter is to wait for infrastructure that must be provisioned in an orderly fashion to be available before continuing.

12. **A.** You must have Python installed before you can use AWS CLI on a server with a Linux or macOS operating system.

13. **A.** The ability to create multiple profiles enables you to create different configurations for different users (or sets of users who share a profile).

14. **B.** AWS strongly recommends that you lock your main AWS account root credentials and use IAM credentials instead.

15. **A, D.** AWS SDKs, which rely on AWS APIs, enable applications to treat infrastructure as code.

16. **C.** Only the text output format enables you to use Linux commands (such as `awk` and `sed`) to search through a command's output.

17. **C.** `service` isn't one of the four command line options, which are `--profile`, `--region`, `--output`, and `--endpoint-url`.

18. **A, B.** You can perform AWS administrative tasks by logging in as the account root user or as an IAM user that has administrative privileges. However, remember that AWS strongly recommends that you secure the root account credentials by locking your account root user credentials after creating an IAM-based user account for performing administrative tasks.

19. **A.** Only access keys (consisting of an access key ID plus a secret key) will enable you to programmatically access AWS services and resources.

20. **C.** You are most likely to use access keys when working with AWS. You use key pairs only for logging into an EC2 instance from the command line, and for working with CloudFront in a few special cases.

AWS Identity and Access Management and AWS Service Security

In this chapter, you will

- Learn about the AWS shared responsibility security model
- Use AWS account security features
- Learn more about AWS Identity and Access Management (IAM)
- Learn how to manage AWS component security
- Learn how to secure your network
- Understand how to secure storage services
- Learn how to secure your databases: Amazon DynamoDB, Amazon RDS, Amazon Redshift, and Amazon ElastiCache Security
- Learn how to secure application services
- Understand how to improve security with AWS monitoring tools and services

AWS security is a very broad topic because of the many ways in which you can secure your AWS resources and the flow of Internet traffic to your cloud-based servers and applications.

The AWS Shared Responsibility Security Model

In an AWS cloud, security and compliance are a shared responsibility between AWS and its customers. AWS manages the infrastructure components, ranging from the host operating system and the virtualization layer, down to the physical security of the facilities that host the services. The customers are responsible for managing the guest OS, including applying all updates and security patches and other application software. This shared responsibility between you and AWS reduces the burden on you to secure your infrastructure in the AWS cloud and provides a stronger security posture.

Figure 3-1 illustrates the AWS shared responsibility security model. This separation of security responsibilities is often referred to as the security "of" the cloud versus security "in" the cloud.

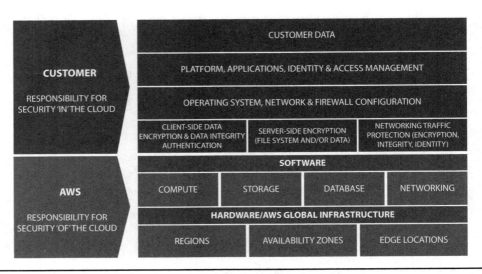

Figure 3-1 The AWS shared responsibility model in the cloud

AWS Responsibility: Security of the Cloud

AWS is responsible for the security of the entire underlying infrastructure on which its customers run the AWS cloud services. Indeed, AWS considers protection of the infrastructure its main priority. The infrastructure consists of all the hardware and software, as well as the networking, storage, and physical facilities that support AWS cloud services. The shared responsibility model means that AWS manages the security for the following assets:

- Physical facilities
- Physical hardware
- Network infrastructure
- Virtualization infrastructure

AWS offers services such as IAM that you can use to manage users and user permissions in AWS services.

 EXAM TIP Remember the distinction between "security of the cloud" and "security in the cloud." This helps you identify which security measures fall under AWS's responsibility. For example, protecting against IP spoofing and packet sniffing falls under the "security *of* the cloud" category, so it falls under AWS's responsibility. Patching EC2 instances and databases belongs to the "security *in* the cloud" and is therefore your responsibility, not AWS's. Similarly, managing the security groups for your EC2 instances and the access key rotation policies for your IAM users also fall under your domain, not AWS's.

Auditing AWS Infrastructure Security

It's not possible for all customers to visit the AWS data centers to ensure that the promised protection is indeed there. However, you can rest assured, because AWS offers several types of third-party auditor reports that verify AWS compliance with several computer security standards and regulations, such as Sarbanes-Oxley and PCI DSS.

NOTE Under the shared responsibility security model, the customer is fully responsible for the security of the guest operating system.

AWS Global Infrastructure Security

AWS locates all its computing resources in a global infrastructure, which includes the physical data centers, network, hardware and host OS software, and virtualization software to support users of these resources.

Physical and Environment Security AWS houses its global data centers in nondescript physical buildings and strictly controls physical access at the perimeter using video surveillance, intrusion detection systems, and other physical security measures. AWS enforces a two-factor authentication for authorized staff to access the data center floors, and all physical access to data centers is logged and audited.

AWS protects its data centers from disasters and failures via the following means:

- **Decommissioning old storage devices** AWS uses a formal decommissioning process that destroys data as part of the decommissioning process. Decommissioned magnetic storage devices are degaussed and physically destroyed.

- **Fire detection and suppression** AWS installs automatic fire detection and suppression equipment in its data centers.

- **Redundant power supplies** Data center electric power systems are fully redundant, using uninterruptible power supplies (UPS) through the use of power generators for provision of backup power in the event of electrical failures.

- **Climate control** Data centers are conditioned to maintain temperatures at the optional levels to prevent overheating and reduce service outages.

Business Continuity Management Business continuity management involves providing high availability for the data centers and fast incident detection and response.

AWS builds its data centers as clusters in multiple geographical regions. If a data center fails, its automatic processes direct customer traffic to the unaffected data centers. Distributing your applications across multiple availability zones (AZs) and regions enhances resiliency against failures caused by natural disasters or system failures. The AZs inside each region are designed as independent failure zones by physically separating the zones and locating them in lower-risk flood plains. Data centers also use power from different grids run by different utilities to reduce the possibility of a single point of failure. The Amazon Incident Management team provides fast incident response by proactively detecting incidents and managing their resolution.

In addition, AWS has implemented various types of internal communications to teach employees about their individual roles and responsibilities, including orientation and training programs, video conferencing, and electronic messages. The customer support teams maintain a Service Health Dashboard to alert customers to issues having major impact. The AWS Security Center offers security and compliance details that pertain to AWS.

The AWS Compliance Program AWS follows strict security best practices and security compliance standards. When you set up your systems on top of the AWS infrastructure, you'll share compliance responsibilities with AWS. AWS ties together governance focus and audit-friendly service features with relevant compliance and audit standards to help you operate in an AWS security–controlled environment.

The AWS infrastructure is designed to align with a variety of IT security standards, including the following:

- Service Organization Controls (SOC 1)/Statement on Standards for Attestation Engagements (SSAE 16)/International Standard on Assurance Engagements (ISAE 3402) (formerly SAS 70)
- SOC 2
- SOC 3
- Federal Information Security Management Act (FISMA), DoD Information Assurance Certification and Accreditation Process (DIACAP), and Federal Risk and Authorization Management Program (FedRAMP)
- DoD CSM Levels 1–5
- PCI DSS Level 1
- ISO 9001/ISO 27001
- International Traffic in Arms Regulations (ITAR)
- Federal Information Processing Standard (FIPS 140-2)
- Multi-Tier Cloud Security Standard (MTCS) Level 3

 EXAM TIP You're likely to see questions relating to compliance and auditing of your AWS systems. Best practices for preparing for audits include gathering evidence of your IT controls; requesting from AWS third-party audited compliance reports and certifications; and requesting approval from AWS to perform network scans and penetration testing of your AWS instances and endpoints.

In addition, the AWS platform complies with other industry-specific security standards such as these:

- Criminal Justice Information Services (CJIS)
- Cloud Security Alliance (CSA) standards
- Family Educational Rights and Privacy Act (FERPA)

- Health Insurance Portability and Accountability Act (HIPAA)
- Motion Picture Association of America (MPAA)

NOTE You can access the AWS security and compliance reports through the AWS Artifact service (https://aws.amazon.com/artifact). AWS Artifact provides compliance-related reports and select online agreements. You can access reports such as AWS Service Organization Control (SOC) reports, Payment Card Industry (PCI) reports, and certifications from accreditation bodies that validate the implementation and effectiveness of AWS security controls. Online agreements include the Business Associate Addendum (BAA) and the nondisclosure agreement (NDA).

Securing its global infrastructure isn't AWS's only responsibility. AWS is fully responsible for securing all its managed services offerings, such as Amazon RDS, Amazon DynamoDB, and Amazon Elastic MapReduce (EMR). When you use any of the managed services, AWS takes care of the overall security configuration, such as patching the guest operating system and databases, firewall configuration, and many other security aspects. Your responsibility would be to take care of the access controls to your servers and databases.

If a third-party auditing services is auditing your organization, and it requires details about your physical network and ritualization infrastructure, you can approach your AWS representative to help the third-party auditors get the information they need. The AWS representative will facilitate the audits by the third-party auditing services. For auditing purposes, you're responsible for the applications that you run on AWS EC2 as well as securing the OS, including managing the system administrators group.

If an external auditor requests a list of your users and their statuses for audit purposes (say, to determine whether you're using Multi-Factor Authentication) you can generate a credentials report by signing into the AWS Management Console, opening the IAM console, and downloading the report. The credentials report shows all your users and their credential statuses, such as passwords, access keys, and MFA devices. You can also generate the credentials report from the command line, IAM APIs, or through AWS SDKs.

TIP If you need to conduct penetration testing for EC2 instances in your AWS account, you can do the testing with prior authorization from AWS.

Customer's Responsibility: Security in the Cloud

While AWS is responsible for the infrastructure and its support, you, as the customer, are responsible for everything you place in the cloud (think data!) or connect to the AWS cloud, in addition to securing the OSs, platforms, and data. AWS customer responsibility varies according to the services that the customer chooses. In the case of services categorized as Infrastructure as a Service (IaaS), for example, such as Amazon EC2, Amazon VPC, and Amazon S3, the customer performs all the security configuration and management tasks.

If you deploy an EC2 instance, you're responsible for managing the guest OS as well as the application software and utilities that you install on the EC2 instance. In addition, you're responsible for configuring the security groups on each of the instances. As you'll recall, a security group acts as a virtual firewall.

The type and extent of security configuration you must perform depends on the specific AWS service and the importance of the data you store in the cloud. With EC2, for example, the customer is responsible for securing the following:

- Amazon Machine Images (AMIs)
- Guest operating systems (including updates and security patching)
- Applications
- Firewalls (security groups)
- Data (stored on disk and in transit)
- Credentials
- Policies and configuration

Regardless of the type of service, you must set up certain security elements such as IAM, Secure Sockets Layer/Transport Layer Security (SSL/TLS) for encrypting data in motion, and a strong logging framework (using AWS CloudTrail) to protect your cloud infrastructure and the data you store in it.

Sharing Security Responsibility for AWS Services

You can categorize security and shared responsibility for the AWS infrastructure and platform services into the following categories, each of which has a slightly different security ownership model:

- **Infrastructure services**   These are the various compute services such as EC2, and associated services such as Amazon Elastic Block Storage (EBS), Auto Scaling, and Amazon VPC. You control the OS and configure and manage the identity management system that enables access to the user layers of the virtualization stack.

- **Container services**   These services typically live in separate EC2 or other infrastructure instances, and for the most part, you don't manage the OS or the platform layer. You are responsible for setting up network controls such as firewall rules and managing the platform-level identity and access management separately from IAM.

- **Abstracted services**   These services include high-level storage, database, and messaging services such as S3, Glacier, DynamoDB, Simple Queue Service (SQS), and Simple Notification Service (SNS). These are services in the platform layer on which you build cloud applications. You use AWS APIs to access the endpoints of these abstracted services. Abstracted services are offered on a multitenant platform that stores your data securely in an isolated fashion.

Responsibility for IT Controls and Compliance

The same shared responsibility model for securing the IT environment also applies to IT control. You follow a distributed control strategy in the AWS cloud for managing, operating, and verifying IT controls. AWS is responsible for managing the controls associated with the physical infrastructure.

There are three types of controls based on how they're managed by AWS, you, and/or both:

- **Inherited controls**   These are controls that you fully inherit from AWS, such as the physical and environment controls managed by AWS.
- **Shared controls**   AWS provides the infrastructure requirements, and you must provide your own control implementation within your use of the AWS services. Here are examples:
  - **Patch management**   AWS is responsible for patching the infrastructure, but you are responsible for patching your guest OS and application software.
  - **Configuration management**   AWS configures its infrastructure devices, but you configure your own guest OS, databases, and applications.
- **Customer-specific controls**   These controls are solely your responsibility, depending on the applications you deploy within AWS services. For example, Zone Security may require you to zone data within specific security environments.

Security for the AWS-Managed Services

Throughout this book, you'll learn about various AWS-managed services, such as the Amazon Relational Database Service (Amazon RDS), where AWS fully manages the relevant service. AWS is responsible for the security configuration of all of its managed services. You need to configure access controls with AWS IAM and account credentials for database user accounts for the managed service, such as a MySQL database service (RDS) and similar services.

Network Security

AWS secures its network infrastructure using several strategies:

- **Secure network architecture**   Network devices such as firewalls and other boundary services use rule sets and access controls lists (ACLs) to control network traffic flow to and from each managed network interface.
- **Secure access points**   Strategically placed cluster customer access points called *API endpoints* enable secure HTTP and (HTTPS) access to your storage and compute instances.
- **Transmission protection**   You can connect to AWS access points using SSL to protect against tampering and message forgery. If you need additional layers of network security, you can use Amazon Virtual Private Cloud (VPC), which provokes a secure subnet within the AWS cloud. VPCs offer the ability to use an IPsec virtual private network (VPN) to provide an encrypted tunnel for transmitting data between your data center and Amazon VPC.

Network Monitoring and Protection

AWS uses several automated monitoring systems to enhance service performance and availability. The monitoring is designed to catch unauthorized activities at incoming and outgoing communication points by monitoring server/network usage, port-scanning activities, application usage, and intrusion attempts.

AWS security monitoring tools help identify the following types of attacks.

Distributed Denial-of-Service (DDoS) Attacks AWS locates API endpoints on world-class infrastructure and uses proprietary DDoS mitigation techniques. It also multihomes its networks across providers to achieve diversified Internet access, which helps in situations such as a DDoS attack.

Man-in-the-Middle (MITM) Attacks AWS encourages its users to use SSL. All the AWS APIs are available via SSL-protected endpoints. EC2 AMIs generate new SSH certificates when you first boot an instance. You can use the AWS Certificate Manager (ACM) to call the console and get the host certificates before logging onto the new instance.

IP Spoofing EC2 instances can't send spoof network traffic. The host-based firewall won't permit an EC2 instance to send traffic with any source IP or MAC address other than its own IP/MAC address.

Port Scanning AWS stops and blocks all unauthorized port scanning. Since, by default, all inbound ports of EC2 instances are closed, port scanning isn't effective with an EC2 instance. By configuring appropriate security groups, you can further minimize the threat of port scans. As a customer of AWS, you can request permission from AWS to conduct vulnerability scans that you need, but you must limit the scans to your own instances and must not violate the AWS Acceptable Use Policy.

Packing Sniffing by Other AWS Tenants EC2 instances that you own and that are located on the same physical hosts cannot listen to one another's traffic. Even if you place a VM into promiscuous mode to receive or "sniff" traffic being sent to other VMs, the hypervisor won't deliver any traffic that isn't addressed to this instance. Well-known security attacks such as Address Resolution Protocol (ARP) cache poisoning aren't possible in EC2 and VPC.

In addition to constant monitoring, AWS also performs regular vulnerability scans on the OS, web applications, and databases.

AWS Account Security Features

You can use various tools and features to protect your AWS account and AWS resources, as summarized in the following sections.

AWS Credentials

AWS uses several types of credentials for authentication to ensure that only authorized users and processes can access your accounts and resources.

AWS recommends that you regularly change your access keys and certificates. You can rotate the access keys of your IAM account as well as your IAM user accounts with the AWS IAM API.

> **TIP** You can download a credentials report for your account from the Security Credentials page. The report shows all your account users and the statuses of their credentials, such as whether they have enabled MFA.

Passwords

AWS requires passwords for accessing the AWS account, as well as the individual IAM user account and the AWS Support Center. You can change the passwords from the Security Credentials page. AWS recommends the creation of strong and hard-to-guess passwords.

You can set a password policy for your IAM user accounts to ensure the use of strong passwords and ensure that they're changed on a regular basis. Several password policy options are available to you, such as preventing password reuse by users.

You can choose to require a password reset by the administrator when user passwords expire or allow some users to manage their passwords. The password expiration requires an administrator reset option in the console and prevents IAM users from choosing a new password when their password expires. If you decide to enable this option, be sure to do one of the following, so you're not locked out of your own AWS account when your password expires:

- Make sure you have the access keys, which will enable you to use the AWS CLI (or the AWS API) to reset your own password, even if you cannot log into the AWS Management Console.

- Alternatively or in addition, ensure that multiple administrators have the necessary administrative permissions to reset IAM user passwords. This way, even if you as the administrator don't have the access keys, other administrators can reset your console password for you.

AWS Multi-Factor Authentication

With Multi-Factor Authentication (MFA), a system checks for more than one authentication factor before granting access. This usually consists of a username/password combination (something you know) and the code from an authentication device (something you have). MFA provides an additional layer of security when users authenticate to the AWS cloud.

When you enable MFA, you need to provide a six-digit single-use code, in addition to a username/password, to gain access to your accounts. The single-use code may be provided by an authentication device you carry with you.

> **NOTE** AWS MFA supports MFA through hardware devices such as Gemalto, virtual MFA devices such as Microsoft Authenticator and Google Authenticator, and Simple Message Service (SMS) messages that run on mobile hardware devices, including smartphones.

You can enable MFA for all the IAM users that you create. You can also add MFA protection for access across IAM accounts. This enables a user in one AWS account to use an IAM role to access AWS resources in a different AWS account. Before the user can assume the role, you can require the user to use MFA.

IAM Access Keys

As you know, access keys consist of two components: an access key ID and a secret access key. A user can have a maximum of two active access keys to enable continued access even while the active key is being rotated. Users can list and rotate their own access keys.

As a best practice, you must regularly rotate all your IAM user's access keys. You can view an access key's usage history to determine whether the key is being used and remove unnecessary active keys from users who don't use them. You can revoke an IAM user's access by disabling their access keys, which makes the keys inactive. You can also delete the access keys of a user.

As described in Chapter 2, the IAM access keys are by default stored in the ~/.aws/ credentials file on a Linux server. AWS recommends that you not use the root access keys and that you lock these keys.

You are required to sign all your API requests with a digital signature to verify your identity. The text of your request and your secret access key serve as inputs to the hash function used to calculate the digital signature. Your applications must calculate the digital signature, but when you use the AWS SDKs, the signature is calculated for you. If a request doesn't reach AWS within 15 minutes of the request's timestamp, AWS turns down the request.

AWS also recommends that you not embed the access keys in your code. Using IAM roles is a safe and easy way to manage access key distribution. IAM roles offer temporary credentials that are automatically loaded to the target instances and are automatically rotated several times daily.

Key Pairs

Instead of passwords, EC2 instances use a public/private key pair to sign in via SSH. The public key is embedded in the EC2 instance. You sign in securely with your private key. You can have AWS generate a key pair for you automatically when you launch an instance, or you can generate your own and load it.

In addition to EC2, Amazon CloudFront also uses key pairs. It does so when creating signed URLs of private content, such as when you distribute restricted content that someone paid for.

X-509 Certificates

X-509 certificates contain a public key and additional metadata such as the certificate expiry date and are associated with a private key. These certificates are used to sign SOAP-based requests. They are also used as SSL/TLS certificates for users who use HTTPS for encrypting their data.

To create a request, you use your private key to create a digital signature and include the signature in the request, along with your X.509 certificate. AWS verifies your identity by decrypting the signature with the public key embedded in your certificate.

As with key pairs, you can let AWS create the certificate and private key for you to download, or you can upload your own certificate. If you're using the X-509 certificates for HTTPS, you can use a tool such as OpenSSL to create a unique private key, which you'll then use to create a Certificate Signing Request (CSR) to submit to a certificate authority (CA) to get the server certificate. Using the AWS CLI, you can upload the certificate, private key, and certificate chain to IAM.

Individual User Accounts

You use AWS IAM to create and manage individual users in your AWS account. A user can be a person, an application, or a system that works with AWS resources programmatically, from the command line, or through the AWS Management Console.

You use IAM to define permission policies that control what your users can do with your AWS resources. Grant users the minimum permissions they need to do their job.

Secure HTTP Access Points

AWS recommends that you use HTTPS (which uses the SSL/TLS protocol that uses public key cryptography to prevent unauthorized use) instead of HTTP for transmitting data. AWS services offer secure customer access points called *API endpoints* to help you establish HTTPS sessions.

Security Logs

AWS CloudTrail tracks and records all requests for AWS resources you own. The logs reveal the services accessed, actions performed, the time when the actions were performed, and the identity of the individual or service.

CloudTrail captures data about all API calls made to all your resources. It delivers its event logs every 5 minutes, and you can configure it so it stores aggregated log files from multiple regions into an Amazon S3 bucket. You can move the logs from S3 to Glacier for long-term auditing and compliance requirements.

You can upload CloudTrail logs from S3 to your own log management solutions to analyze them and detect unusual patterns. The CloudWatch Logs service tracks systems, applications, and more, from EC2 instances and other sources in near real-time, helping you to detect unauthorized login attempts, for example, by monitoring the web server log files.

AWS Trusted Advisor Security Checks

AWS Trusted Advisor offers a set of best-practice checks to help increase your security and performance. The advisor can also inspect your AWS environment and offer security remediation recommendations or close security gaps.

Managing Cryptographic Keys for Encryption

Earlier, you learned how to safeguard your public/private key pairs that help you log into your EC2 instances. You also learned how X-509 certificates help AWS to verify the authenticity of a requester by decrypting their digital signatures (created with a private key) with the public key and X-509 certificates to safeguard interactions with AWS.

You use encryption in various services, such as databases. To protect your cryptographic keys, AWS offers two important services or tools: the AWS Key Management Service (KMS), and the AWS cloud hardware security module (CloudHSM).

The AWS Key Management Service

AWS KMS is a managed service that helps you create and manage the encryption keys that you use to encrypt your data stored in the AWS cloud. KMS helps you create, import, rotate, disable, and define the usage policies for encryption keys that you use.

KMS uses FIPS 140-2 validated hardware security modules to safeguard the keys. KMS is integrated with most AWS services, which makes it easy for you to encrypt data you store in these services with encryption keys that you fully control. It's also well integrated with AWS CloudTrail, thus providing you with a record of all encryption key usage, which helps in meeting many regulatory and compliance needs.

Following are the key features of AWS KMS.

Centralized Key Management   You can create and manage encryption keys from the AWS Management Console or with the AWS CLI and SDK, which offers you centralized control of your encryption keys. You can have KMS create the master keys or import them from somewhere else. These keys are stored in an encrypted format, and you can have KMS rotate the master keys once a year, without having to re-encrypt the previously encrypted data, since KMS keeps older master keys available.

Easy Encryption   You can easily encrypt data through a one-click encryption in the AWS console or use the AWS SDK to incorporate encryption in your application code.

Audit Capabilities   AWS CloudTrail can record all uses of a key that you store in KMS in a log file that it can deliver to an S3 bucket.

Scalability and High Availability   AWS KMS scales automatically as your encryption needs grow over time. KMS stores multiple copies of the encrypted versions of your encryption keys to provide 99.999999999 percent durability. For high availability of the encryption keys, KMS is deployed in multiple AZs inside an AWS region.

Secure Safeguarding of Encryption Keys   Your master keys are stored securely and cannot be exported out of KMS. No one, including AWS employees, can view the KMS service's plain-text keys, which are never written to disk and are pulled into volatile memory during cryptographic operations. KMS uses a FIPS 140-2 validated hardware security module (HSM) to safeguard the keys.

Compliance   AWS KMS has been certified by several compliance standards that include PCI DSS Level 1, IS0 27018, and ISO 9001.

Storing and Managing Encryption Keys

You can use encryption for protecting data in your databases, document signing, transaction processing, and for digital rights management (DRM). Encryption strategies require encryption keys. You can use your own processes for managing encryption keys in the

AWS cloud or rely on server-side encryption with AWS key management and storage capabilities.

If you choose to manage encryption keys yourself, AWS recommends that you store keys in tamper-proof appliance such as an HSM. If you choose to store the keys on premises in an HSM, you can access the AWS keys over secure links such as IPsec VPNs, or AWS Direct Connect.

AWS offers an HSM service, AWS CloudHSM. If you use CloudHSM instead of your own on-premise HSM, you receive a dedicated single-tenant access to CloudHSM appliances, which are resources in your Amazon VPC. The appliance has a private IP and runs in a private subnet. You connect to the appliance from EC2 servers via SSL/TLS, with two-way digital certificate authentication and 256-bit SSL encryption.

If you use CloudHSM, try and choose a CloudHSM service in the same region as your EC2 instance to decrease network latency and thus improve application performance.

CloudHSM appliances can securely store and process cryptographic keys for database encryption, Public Key Infrastructure (PKI), authentication and authorization, transaction processing, and so on. They support strong cryptographic algorithms such as AES and RSA.

Although AWS is responsible for managing, monitoring, and maintaining the health of the CloudHSM appliance, only you control your security keys and the operations performed by CloudHSM. A *cryptographic domain* is a logical and physical security boundary that restricts access to your encryption keys. AWS doesn't have access to the cryptographic domain. You initialize and manage the cryptographic domain of CloudHSM.

When you start working with CloudHSM, you must set up one or more cryptographic partitions on it. A partition is a logical and physical security boundary that restricts access to your cryptographic keys. AWS can't see inside the HSM partitions, although it has admin credentials to the appliance itself in order to monitor the appliance's health and availability. Therefore, AWS can't perform cryptographic operations with your keys.

HSM also offers both physical and logical tamper detection and response capabilities that erase cryptographic key material and log the events when HSM detects tampering.

AWS Identity and Access Management

AWS IAM is a web service that helps you secure access to your AWS resources. IAM helps you centrally manage your users, security credentials (passwords and access keys), and permissions policies that determine which AWS services and resources users can access. More precisely, IAM enables you to do the following:

- Create users and groups in your AWS account.
- Assign unique security credentials for users in your AWS account.
- Share AWS resources among your users.
- Control user access to AWS services and resources.
- Control each user's permissions to perform tasks with AWS resources.

- Allow users in another AWS account to share your AWS resources.
- Create roles and define the users or services that can assume the roles.

IAM enables you to control how AWS products are administered, such as the creation and termination of EC2 instances. IAM controls the administrative tasks that you perform via the console, command line tools, or the AWS SDKs. You can work with IAM through the AWS Management Console, AWS CLI, and AWS SDKs.

It's important to understand that AWS services such as EC2 and Amazon RDS have their own ways of securing access to their resources. These access methods are separate from IAM.

IAM has two main components:

- **Identity**   Who is authenticated legitimately (signed in)
- **Access management**   Who has the authorization (permissions) to use the AWS resources

How IAM Works

IAM provides the infrastructure that manages authentication and authorization for AWS accounts. IAM uses the following elements to perform its tasks:

- Principals
- Requests
- Authentication
- Authorization
- Actions or operations
- Resources

 NOTE   By default, only the AWS account root user has access to all resources in that account. All other users must have permissions granted by a policy.

Principals

A *principal* is any entity that can act on an AWS resource. Originally, when you create your AWS account, you create the administrative IAM user as your first principal. Later, you can allow users and services to assume a role. You can also support applications to programmatically access your AWS account. All users and roles (including federated users and applications) are AWS principals.

Figure 3-2 shows how principals perform actions on resources through authorization granted via IAM policies.

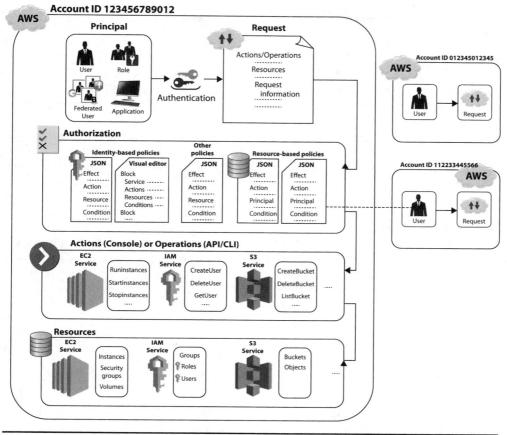

Figure 3-2   How principals perform actions on resources in IAM

Requests

Principals send requests via the AWS console, the AWS CLI, or the AWS API. A request contains information about the following:

- The principal (requestor), including the permissions granted to that principal via IAM policies
- The resources on which the user wants to perform the action, such as the name of a DynamoDB table or a tag associated with an Amazon EC2 instance
- The actions or operations that the principal wants to perform on the resources

AWS takes the request information such as principals, resources, actions, and environmental data (such as the IP address) and forms a request *context*, which it uses to evaluate the request and determine whether it should authorize it.

Authentication vs. Authorization

It's important that you understand the difference between *authentication* and *authorization*. AWS must authenticate and authorize your request before it approves the actions in the request.

Before a principal can access a resource and perform actions on it, AWS must first *authenticate* the user. You authenticate from the console by signing in with your username and password. You authenticate through the API or CLI by providing your access key and secret key.

In authorization, IAM checks the request contexts for matching policies so it can allow or deny the requests. AWS collects all the request information and puts it into a request context, which it uses to evaluate the request and determine whether it should authorize it. Policies specify the permissions that are either allowed or denied for principals or resources.

Actions (Operations)

Once IAM authenticates the user and authorizes the request, AWS will approve the action/operation that you specify in your request. The operations that you can perform are defined by a service, so they can vary. For example, you can perform actions such as the following on a user resource:

- Create user
- Delete user
- Update user

Resources

A resource is an object that exists within a service, such as an EC2 instance or an S3 bucket. I discuss resources in more details in the next section.

Managing the Identity Component of IAM

When you sign up for AWS, the first account that you create is an AWS account, and you use your e-mail address and password as credentials. You can use these credentials to log into the AWS Management Console. You can also create a set of access keys to use when you need to make programmatic calls to AWS via the CLI, the AWS SDKs, or API calls.

IAM enables you to create individual users in your AWS account with their own username/password. The users can log into the console using an account-specific URL. You can also create access keys for users to enable them to make programmatic calls to AWS resources.

 NOTE Remember that as a best practice, AWS recommends that you create an IAM user for yourself (the administrator) and then not use your AWS account credentials for everyday access to AWS services and resources. Instead, use the IAM account.

You must understand two key things in the context of IAM:

- **Principal**   This AWS entity can perform actions in AWS. A principal doesn't have to be a specific human user; it can be the AWS account root user, and IAM user, or a role.

- **Resource**   This object exists within a service, such as an EC2 instance or an S3 bucket. An *Amazon Resource Name* (ARN) uniquely identifies an AWS resource. AWS requires you to use an ARN so that you can unambiguously specify resources across all of AWS, such as when you create an IAM policy or an Amazon RDS tag, for example. Following is the general format of an ARN:

    ```
    arn:partition:service:region:account-id:resource,
    ```

    - *partition*   Where the resource is located. For standard AWS regions, the partition is aws. For resources that live in other partitions, the partition is aws-*partitionname*, as in aws-cn, which is the partition for resources location in the Beijing, China, AWS region.

    - *service*   Identifies the AWS product. For IAM resources, the service is always IAM.

    - *region*   The region the resource lives in. For IAM resources, you leave the region blank.

    - *account-id*   The AWS account ID, such as 123456789012.

    - *resource*   The part of the ARN that identifies a specific resource.

When working with AWS IAM, you must understand both the ARN format as well as IAM identifiers. I explain the two in the following sections.

IAM ARN Formats

An ARN can take slightly different formats, depending on the resource, as shown here:

```
arn:partition:service:region:account-id:resourcetype/resource
arn:partition:service:region:account-id:resourcetype/resource/qualifier
arn:partition:service:region:account-id:resourcetype/resource:qualifier
arn:partition:service:region:account-id:resourcetype:resource
arn:partition:service:region:account-id:resourcetype:resource:qualifier
```

Following are some examples of ARNs for various services.

AWS Batch

```
arn:aws:batch:us-east-1:123456789012:job-definition/my-job-definition:1
```

Amazon DynamoDB

```
arn:aws:dynamodb:us-east-1:123456789012:table/books_table
```

Amazon EC2

```
arn:aws:ec2:us-east-1:123456789012:dedicated-host/h-12345678
```

An AWS account

```
arn:aws:iam:123456789012:root
```

An IAM user in the AWS account

```
arn:aws:iam::123456789012:user/Sam
```

An IAM group

```
arn:aws:iam:123456789012:group/Developers
```

An IAM role

```
arn:aws:iam::123456789012:role/S3Access
```

You can specify all users, groups, or policies in your account by specifying a wildcard for the user, group, or policy portion of the ARN:

```
arn:aws:iam::123456789012:user/*
arn:aws:iam::123456789012:group/*
arn:aws:iam::123456789012:policy/*
```

IAM Identifiers

IAM employs different *identifiers* for users, roles, groups, policies, and server certificates. The three types of identifiers are friendly names and paths, IAM ARNs, and unique IDs.

Friendly Names and Paths   When creating users, groups, or policies, or when you're uploading serer certificates, you can specify a friendly name for the entities, such as Sam, Administrators, ProdApp1, ManageCredentialsPermissions, or ProdServerCert.

When you use the AWS command line to create the IAM entities, you can optionally provide a path for an entity. The path can be a single path or a nested multiple path structure, such as a directory structure.

IAM ARNs   Although many AWS resources have friendly names such as a user named Sam and a group named Administrators, you can't use these in permission policies, which require that you specify the ARN format instead when referring to resources such as users and groups.

Unique IDs   IAM assigns a unique ID to each user, group, role, policy, instance profile, and server certificate that it creates. The unique ID is a string of letters and numbers, such as the following: AIDAJQABLZS4A3QDU576Q.

You use friendly names or IAM ARNs mostly when working with IAM entities such as users and groups, but the unique ID is helpful when you can't use friendly names. All IAM users have a unique ID, even if you assign an IAM user a previously used friendly name. In cases such as this, using unique IDs rather than friendly names helps tighten data access.

You can't get unique IDs for an IAM entity from the IAM console. You can get the IDs via the AWS CLI or an IAM API calls. In AWS CLI, for example, the `get-user`, `get-role`, and `get-group` commands will provide the unique IDs for a user, role, and group, respectively.

Managing the Authentication Component of IAM

AWS IAM enables you to manage secure access to your AWS resources and AWS services. The *identity* portion of AWS IAM deals with the creation and management of AWS users and groups. The *access management* part of IAM deals with how you use permission to allow and deny users access to your AWS resources.

With IAM, you can easily provide users secure access to your AWS resources. You can manage IAM users and their access by creating users in the AWS identity management system and assign those users various types of security credentials, such as access keys, passwords, and MFA devices. In addition to helping you manage IAM users, IAM helps you manage access to federated users in your corporate directory (such as Active Directory), without having to create IAM user accounts for them.

You can access AWS services and resources via different types of identities: the AWS account root user, IAM users, and IAM roles, as explained in the following sections.

AWS Account Root Users

The AWS account root user is the user account (with your e-mail address and password as the credentials) set up when you first create an AWS account. The AWS account root user account has full access to all AWS services and resources in your account. The root user has full, unrestricted access to your entire AWS account. Because you can't restrict the permissions granted to the main AWS account, the best practice is to use the root user to create your first IAM user and lock up the root user credentials. Even if you're the only person who works with your AWS account, it's a best practice to create an IAM user and use that user's identity (and credentials) when working with AWS.

IAM Users

IAM users are unique identities recognized by AWS services and applications. You create IAM users with specific permissions to access services and resources. For example, you can create an IAM user with permissions to create a hosted zone in Amazon DNS, Route 53.

 TIP   You can use the Active Directory Connector (AD Connector) to simplify identity management by sourcing the user identities directly from Active Directory. AD Connector is a directory gateway that redirects directory requests to your on-premises Microsoft Active Directory. Your IAM users can use their existing Active Directory credentials. You can reuse existing Active Directory security policies as well, such as those that control password expiration, and account lockout.

IAM helps you manage access to two broad sets of users: It supports IAM users you create and that are managed in AWS's IAM system. In addition, it enables you to grant access to your AWS resources to *federated users* that are managed outside AWS in your corporate directory.

IAM users can sign in to the AWS Management Console and use the AWS CLI or APIs to make programmatic requests to AWS services. Although you can directly attach permission policies to an IAM user, the recommended way to grant permissions is by making the user part of a group that has the required permission policies.

A user doesn't have to be a person: it can be an individual, system, or an application that requires access to an AWS service. Each user has a unique name and security credentials, such as a password and/or access keys (up to two access keys for use with the CLI or API).

Usernames can be a combination of up to 64 letters, digits, and the characters plus (+), equal (=), comma (,), period (.), at sign (@), and hyphen (-). Names aren't distinguished based on case. So, for example, sam@mycloud is a valid username and so is sammycloud, but not sam#mycloud.

IAM Roles

An IAM role is similar to an IAM user, but unlike a user, a role doesn't have or require credentials and it is temporary, set to expire after a defined time period (the default expiration time is 12 hours). Once a role expires, it can't be reused. An IAM role defines a set of permissions for making AWS service requests. It uses temporary security credentials that enable you to delegate access to users or services that need access to your AWS resources. You can create an IAM role with specific permissions that aren't tied to a specific user or group. Rather, entities such as IAM users, applications, or even AWS services such as EC instances assume the roles. The credentials are automatically loaded, to the target instances, and you don't need to embed them in code, which isn't safe. They are automatically rotated several times daily and stored securely.

NOTE IAM users can request temporary security credentials for their own use by calling the AWS STS GetSessionToken API. The default expiration for these temporary credentials is 12 hours; the minimum is 15 minutes, and the maximum is 36 hours.

You create a role similar to how you create an IAM user: you assign a name and attach an IAM policy to it. IAM roles can be used to solve several security problems. For example, say that you have 1000 employees in your organization for which you need to provide access to your new AWS cloud resources. The best way to do this is to create roles to authorize various users to access the different AWS resources. Creating roles is a best practice for AWS IAM.

An IAM role enables you to delegate access to trusted entities with defined permissions, without your having to share access keys long-term. Roles are helpful when you don't want to create regular IAM users with persistent permissions for accessing resources in your AWS account. With an appropriate IAM role, an IAM user can access not only resources in their own AWS account, but also resources in other AWS accounts.

NOTE You can use the AWS Security Token Service (STS) to provided trusted users with temporary security credentials that allow access to your AWS resources. You can assume an IAM role by calling the AWS STS AssumeRole APIs (`AssumeRole`, `AssumeRoleWithWebIdentity`, and `AssumeRoleWithSAML`). The APIs return a set of temporary security credentials that apps can use to sign their requests to AWS service APIs. There's no limit on the number of IAM roles that you can assume.

Before an IAM user, application, or service can use a role, you must grant the entity permission to switch the role through a permissions policy that you attach to the IAM user or user group. Use the `DurationSeconds` parameter to specify the duration of the role session, with a minimum value of 900 seconds (15 minutes), up to the maximum CLI/API session duration for the role.

IAM roles with temporary credentials are useful in the following cases, where you need to provide limited, controlled access.

Federated (Non-AWS) User Access   You can assign a role to federated users (or applications) that don't have an AWS account when they request access through an identity provider such as Active Directory, Lightweight Directory Access Protocol (LDAP), or Kerberos. The temporary AWS credentials are assigned to the roles provided with the identity federation between AWS and non-AWS users in your organization's identity and access management system. With web identity federation, you don't need to manage identities of your users. Instead, the users of your apps can sign in via an identity provider (IdP) such as Amazon, Facebook, Google, or any other OpenID Connect (OIDC)–compatible IdP and receive an authentication token, which they exchange for temporary credentials in AWS that map to an IAM role with permissions to use resources in your account. The IdP enables you to manage user identities outside of IAM and grant these external users permissions to your AWS resources.

Create Trust Between Organizations   If your company supports Security Assertion Markup Language (SAML) 2.0, you can create trust between your organization (identity provider) and other organizations (service providers).

Allow Externally Authenticated Users to Log In   Roles also enable users to sign in to your applications by logging into Amazon, Facebook, or Google. The users can use information from their successful authentication to assume the roles and, thus, the temporary security credentials for accessing your AWS resources. If you're currently managing identities outside of AWS, you can use IAM IdPs instead of creating IAM users in your account. The best practice here is to use an IAM role that validates the calls to the DynamoDB database with IdPs.

Provide Cross-Account Access   You can use roles to provide users with permissions in an AWS account to access your resources in another AWS account owned by your organization, thus ensuring that only temporary credentials are provided on an as-needed basis to the cross-account users. For details, see the section "Granting IAM Users Permissions to Switch to other Roles" a bit later in this chapter.

Allow Applications to Access AWS Resources   Applications running on EC2 instances require security credentials when they make requests to an AWS resource such as S3 buckets. Roles help you grant AWS services permissions to access your AWS resources. Instead of creating individual IAM accounts for each application and storing access keys on the EC2 instances where applications are running, you can use IAM roles as a way of granting temporary credentials for the applications when they make AWS API requests. This is especially useful when dealing with a large number of EC2 instances that are spawned dynamically, through AWS Auto Scaling.

NOTE When dealing with IAM roles, remember that the permissions policy is attached to the role and not to the IAM user or IAM group member that temporarily assumes that IAM role.

IAM Groups

Use IAM groups to manage permissions that you want to grant to more than one user and to gather users based on their functional roles. Suppose, for example, that there are 50 IAM users in your AWS account. If your company introduces a new policy that changes the access of the IAM users, you don't need to apply the new policy at the individual user level. You can add the new security policy to the group. Remember that there's no default group in your AWS account. You create the groups as needed. An IAM user can be a member of more than one IAM group. When a user joins or leaves your organization, you can add or remove the user from the groups.

 EXAM TIP Be sure you understand the things you can do with groups: You can add or remove users from a group and grant permissions to groups using access control policies. Also, groups can't belong to other groups, but a user can belong to multiple groups.

Know the Difference: IAM Users vs. Groups vs. Roles

A tricky part of IAM is in clearly understanding the differences and the relationships among IAM users, IAM groups, and IAM roles:

- An IAM user has permanent credentials and directly interacts with AWS services.

- An IAM group is a logical entity that you use to grant/modify/revoke permissions for a similar set of IAM users.

- An IAM role is an entity with permissions to make service requests to AWS services such as EC2. A role can't make direct requests to an AWS service; roles are strictly meant to be assumed by entities such as IAM users, applications, and AWS services. Roles help you delegate access within or between various AWS services.

Granting IAM Users Permissions to Switch to Other Roles

You can grant your IAM users permission to switch to other roles in your AWS account. AWS recommends that you adopt this approach to enforce the *principle of least access*— that is, grant users more advanced or more powerful permissions only for times they need them to perform specific tasks, such as terminate an EC2 instance. This reduces your security exposure and minimizes or prevents accidental changes to critical environments. Auditors will also appreciate the fact that you granted role permissions only when you needed to.

A user in an AWS account can switch to another role in the same or a different AWS account. When users switch to a different role, their original permissions are suspended, and they're restricted to just those actions and resources that are permitted by the role they switched to. The user's original permissions are restored when the user exits the new role.

For example, suppose that you have a development and a production environment, and you create separate AWS accounts for the two environments. Your IAM users in the development account may occasionally need to access resources in the production account. Instead of creating separate identities in both environments for the users that need this type of access, you can enable cross-account access to those users. Here's how to do this:

1. In the production account, create a role named ModifyApp and define a trust policy for that role and attach it to the role. This allows an IAM user to assume the role. The trust policy defines the development account as a Principal. This allows authorized users from the development account to use the ModifyApp role. Next, you define a IAM permissions policy for this role that specifies the actions that the IAM user is allowed to perform when the user assumes this IAM role. In this case, the permission policy grants access to the production resources (such as an Amazon S3 bucket in the production environment). The role ARN for an account such as 123456789012 will then look like the following:

   `arn:aws:iam:123456789012:role/ModifyApp`

2. As the AWS SysOps administrator, you must grant the users in the development account permission to switch to the role you've created in step 1 by granting the group—say, the Developers group—permission to call the AWS Security Token Service `AssumeRole` API for the ModifyApp role that you created in step 1. This enables the users in the Development group to switch to the ModifyApp role in the production account.

3. The users in the Development group can now request a switch to the ModifyApp role by choosing **Switch Role** in the AWS console, or they can use the AWS API or AWS CLI to do the same.

4. AWS STS verifies the request with the role's trust policy and returns temporary credentials to the AWS console or to the application.

5. The temporary credentials returned by AWS STS grant the user access to the AWS resources in the production account. The AWS console uses these credentials on behalf of the user for subsequent console actions, such as accessing an S3 bucket in the production account. Similarly, if the user has switched the role through the AWS API or AWS CLI, the application uses the temporary credentials to update the S3 bucket(s) in the production account.

Managing IAM Authorization Policies

So far, you've learned about the identity part of AWS IAM. The second part of IAM, *access management*, also known as *authorization*, enables you to configure what users and other entities can do in their account. Authorization is how you specify permissions that allow or deny users access to AWS resources, as well as specify the actions they can perform in AWS.

You define these permissions with the help of IAM policies. Permissions policies help you control which users can access AWS resources and what actions they can perform on those resources. For example, let's say that you want your IAM users to be able to access the IAM console only from within the organization, and not from outside. You create an IAM policy with a condition that denies access when the IP address range is from outside the organization. The following example shows an IAM policy with a `Deny` condition that prevents access from any IP addresses that are specified as the source IP addresses (`"AWS:SourceIp"`):

```
.{ "Version": "2012-10-17",  "Statement": {    "Effect": "Deny",    "Action":
"*",    "Resource": "*",    "Condition": {"NotIpAddress": {"AWS:SourceIp": [
"192.0.1.0/24",    "202.0.112.0/24"    ]}}  }}
```

All IAM users start with zero permissions. So, by default, a user can't do anything in your AWS account until you explicitly attach a policy to that user or add that user to a group with the relevant permissions.

 EXAM TIP Often an IAM-related question tests your knowledge of the default limits for IAM entities such as users, groups, and roles. Here are some key default limits:

Customer-managed policies in your AWS account: 1500
Groups in your AWS account: 300
Roles in your AWS account: 1000
Managed policies that can be attached to an IAM role or an IAM user: 10

There are two broad types of policies:

- **Permissions policies** A permissions policy is an object that defines an entity's or a resource's permissions. These are mostly stored as JSON documents, which you can attach to an IAM identity or an AWS resource (such as an Amazon S3 bucket) to define their permissions (allow or deny).
- **Permissions boundaries** Permissions boundaries are policies that limit the maximum amount of permissions that a user or entity (principals) can have.

Earlier in the chapter, you learned about a request context. When a principal seeks to perform an action on an AWS resource such as an EC2 instance, IAM looks in the request context for matching permissions policies to determine whether to allow the request.

 EXAM TIP An IAM policy is a document that lists permissions. Understand the different entities an IAM policy can assign permission to. You can use a policy to grant permissions to a user, group, role, or a resource.

Permissions Policies

An IAM policy is a JSON-formatted document with one or more statements. A statement has the following structure and syntax:

```
{
......  "Statement":[{
        "Effect":"effect",
        "Action":"action",
        "Resource":"arn",
        "Condition":{
         "condition":{
          "key":"value"
          }
         }
        }
       ]
}
```

Following are the key elements of a statement:

- `"Effect"` This can take the value `Allow` or `Deny`. By default, users don't have permissions to use resources or perform API actions, so all requests are denied. An explicit deny in the `"Effect"` element overrides any allows, and an explicit allow overrides the default (deny).

- `"Action"` This is the specific API action for which the policy grants or denies permission.

- `"Resource"` This is the resource that's impacted by the action. You specify the resource by using its Amazon Resource Name (ARN).

- `"Condition"` This is an optional attribute that allows you do things such as controlling when your policy is in effect. A condition has one or more key-value pairs, and when there are multiple keys in a condition, AWS evaluates them using a logical AND operation. All conditions must be met before permission is granted. For example, you can have `ec2:AccepterVpc` as the condition key, and `"ec2:AccepterVpc":"vpc-arn"` as the key-value pair. Here, `vpc-arn` is the VPC ARN of the accepter VPC in a VPC-peering connection. You can also set a policy condition that requests must originate from specific IP addresses, or that they use SSL, for example.

EXAM TIP Be sure that you aren't confused as to what the different elements of an IAM policy statement do. The four key elements in an IAM policy statement are *effect, actions, resources*, and *condition*. The effect describes the result of a user request: either allow or deny. Actions refer to the operations that you allow. Any actions that you don't explicitly allow are denied. That means that a user can't access any resources to which you've not granted that user permissions. Each AWS service has its own set of actions, such as the `ListBucket` action in Amazon S3., which returns information about the objects stored in an S3 bucket. Resources are the entities over which you allow the actions. Condition is an optional element.

Following is an example of a permissions policy that permits all requests except those coming from specific IP addresses (NotIpAddress) to terminate EC2 instances using the AWS API or the AWS CLI. Remember that unless a permission is granted explicitly, AWS by default disallows all actions, so the users to whom you attach this policy won't be able to terminate the EC2 instances via the console.

```
{
  "Version": "2012-10-17",
  "Statement": [
    {
      "Effect": "Allow",
      "Action": ["ec2:TerminateInstances"],
      "Resource": ["*"]
    },
    {
      "Effect": "Deny",
      "Action": ["ec2:TerminateInstances"],
      "Condition": {
        "NotIpAddress": {
          "aws:SourceIp": [
            "192.0.2.0/24",
            "203.0.113.0/24"
          ]
        }
      },
      "Resource": ["*"]
    }
  ]
}
```

Here's what you need to remember about how IAM authorizes requests through permissions policies:

- By default, all requests are denied.
- An explicit allow in a permissions policy overrides the default.
- A permissions boundary (an AWS Organizations secure control policy [SCP] or a user or role boundary) or a policy used during AWS Security Token Service (STS) role assumption overrides the allow.
- An explicit deny in a permissions policy overrides any allows.
- If a single policy in a request includes a denied action, IAM denies the entire request.

NOTE Requests that are made using the AWS account root user credentials are always allowed for all resources in that account.

Types of Permissions Policies

There are four broad types of AWS permissions policies:

- **Identity-based policies** Attach managed or inline policies to IAM identities such as users, groups, and roles.

- **Resource-based policies** Attach inline policies to resources, such as an Amazon S3 bucket policy.

- **AWS Organizations SCPs** Apply permissions boundaries to an organizational unit (OU) or an AWS Organizations organization.

- **Access control lists (ACLs)** Specify the principals that can access various resources.

 NOTE You can attach multiple permissions policies to a principal. Each of the policies can contain multiple permissions.

Identity-Based Permissions Policies You can attach permissions policies to IAM identities such as users, groups, and roles. There are two broad types of identity-based policies: *managed policies* and *inline policies.*

Managed policies are permissions policies that you can attach to users, groups, and roles in an AWS account. Managed policies offer various benefits, such as the following:

- **Automatic updates** AWS automatically updates AWS-managed policies when necessary, such as adding permissions for a new AWS service, and applies those changes to the principals.

- **Reusability** You can attach the same managed policy to multiple principals.

- **Central change management** A change to a managed policy applies to all principals to which you attach that policy.

- **Versioning and rollback** IAM stores up to five versions of customer-managed policies. You can revert to an older policy version if you need to.

- **Permissions management delegation** You can allow users to attach and detach permissions policies.

There are two types of managed policies: AWS-managed policies and customer-managed policies.

AWS-managed policies are standalone policies maintained by AWS. A standalone policy has its own ARN:

```
arn:aws:iam::aws:policy/IAMReadOnlyAccess
```

In this ARN, IAMReadOnlyAccess is the name of the AWS policy.

AWS recommends that you start with the AWS-managed policies since you don't have to write the policies yourself. You simply assign the permissions to the user, groups, or roles. You can attach a single AWS-managed policy to principals in different AWS accounts. You typically use these policies for defining permissions for service administrators. You also use them to grant full (AmazonDynamoDBFullAccess) or partial access (AmazonEC2ReadOnlyAccess) to AWS services.

AWS-managed policies are especially useful when you design the policies to match common job functions, such as the PowerUserAccess policy, which grants full access to a user for every AWS service (with limited access to IAM and Organizations).

 EXAM TIP You're very likely to see a question or two about IAM policies, with the question containing a sample IAM policy. You need to focus on the key policy elements *Effect, Allow, Action,* and *Resource* to determine the entitlements that the policy grants to a user or a group.

Here's an example IAM policy for an IAM group that grants full access to all AWS services (similar to a full administrator access) for the IAM users who are members of this group:

```
?{    "Version": "2012-10-17",    "Statement": [        {          "Effect":
"Allow",            "Action": "*",              "Resource": "*"          }    ]}
```

 NOTE You can't change any of the permissions defined in an AWS-managed policy. AWS can update the permissions in a policy, say, when it launches a new AWS service.

Customer-managed policies are policies that you create and manage. These allow a more fine-grained control than AWS-managed policies. Customer-managed policies are also standalone policies that you attach to users, groups, and roles. Customer-managed policies enable you to enforce identical permissions to a group of users by attaching the policy to a group (or groups). You can easily edit a policy to apply policy changes to all members of the group(s).

An easy way to ensure that you've created a policy correctly is by copying an AWS-managed policy and customizing it. You can then assign the policy to one or more principals. As an AWS administrator, you can use IAM policies to control which users can create, update, and delete customer-managed policies in your AWS account. Following is an example policy that allows a user to create, update, and delete customer-managed policies in your AWS account:

```
{
 "Version": "2012-10-17",
 "Statement": {
  "Effect": "Allow",
  "Action": [
   "iam:CreatePolicy",
   "iam:CreatePolicyVersion",
   "iam:DeletePolicy",
   "iam:DeletePolicyVersion",
   "iam:GetPolicy",
   "iam:GetPolicyVersion",
   "iam:ListPolicies",
   "iam:ListPolicyVersions",
   "iam:SetDefaultPolicyVersion"
  ],
  "Resource": "*"
 }
}
```

The second major identity-based permissions policy type, *inline policies*, are policies that you can create and embed directly into a user, group, or role. Unlike managed policies (both AWS-managed and customer-managed), inline policies aren't standalone policies. These policies are *part of a specific principal*, such as a user, group, or rule. So when you delete the principal, the embedded policies in the principal entity are deleted automatically. Inline policies are helpful when you want to establish a strict one-to-one relationship between a permissions policy and a principal. Multiple principals can share the same inline policy that you create.

NOTE Inline policies are ideal when you need to grant access to AWS resources in your account to an external vendor. You create an AWS account for the user and restrict access to your AWS resources for just that user for a brief period, using an inline policy. When you delete the user, the embedded inline policies are deleted automatically, preventing the permissions in the policy from being inadvertently attached to other principals. AWS recommends that you use AWS-managed policies instead of inline policies in most cases.

Resource-Based Permissions Policies   Resource-based policies attach inline policies to AWS resources, rather than to IAM identities. For example, you can attach policies to resources such as Amazon S3 buckets, Amazon SQS queues, and so on. With each resource, you specify which principal can access the resource and the actions they can perform on the resource. All resource-based policies are inline, not managed, policies.

NOTE   Only AWS account root users have permissions to perform any actions on the resources in that account. Even if an IAM user creates a resource, the user doesn't have automatic permissions on that resource.

AWS is composed of collections of resources such as IAM users and Amazon S3 buckets. User requests specify a resource, a principal, a principal account, and the action the user wants to perform on the resource. This information, along with other necessary request information, is part of the *resource context*.

AWS Organization SCPs   AWS Organizations is a service that groups and manages all the AWS accounts that your organization owns. SCPs are JSON policies that apply permissions boundaries that control the maximum services and the actions that entities in an AWS Organizations organization, or an organization unit (OU), can access. The permissions apply to the AWS root user as well.

Access Control Lists   Amazon S3 supports ACLs as a permission mechanism. An ACL is a list of permissions attached to an object, such as a file or an Amazon S3 bucket. The ACL specifies which users or processes can access the objects, as well as what operations they're allowed to perform on the objects.

ACLs are independent of IAM policies and permissions, although you can use both together. ACLs are similar to resource-based permissions policies, but they are the only resource type that doesn't use the JSON policy document structure.

NOTE A resource-based permissions policy is different from resource-level permissions. While you can attach a resource-based policy directly to a resource, a resource-level permission enables you to use ARNs to specify the individual resources within a policy. Only some AWS services support resource-based permissions. If a user with specific resource-based permissions requests a resource with a permissions policy attached to it, AWS evaluates both sets of permissions before it determines whether to grant the user access to that resource.

Permissions Boundaries

Permissions boundaries change the effective permissions for a user or role. While permissions policies (identity, resource-based, ACLs) define permissions for the objects to which you attach them, permissions boundaries help you limit the maximum permissions for an IAM principal or AWS Organizations. Permissions boundaries don't grant any access on their own, but they can *limit* permissions provided by permissions policies.

NOTE You use either an AWS-managed policy or a customer-managed policy to set the maximum permissions for a principal (user or role) using permissions boundaries. Here's an example that shows how to use a policy to set a permissions boundary for an IAM user:

```
{
    "Version": "2012-10-17",
    "Statement": [
        {
            "Effect": "Allow",
            "Action": [
                "s3:*",
                "ec2:*"
            ],
            "Resource": "*"
        }
    ]
}
```

NOTE You can use a permissions boundary only to limit a user's permissions. It doesn't grant any permissions on its own.

This example shows how you can allow the IAM user to perform actions only in Amazon S3 and Amazon EC2. Even if you create a policy allowing the action `iam:CreateUser` and grant the policy to this IAM user, the operation fails, since the permissions boundary doesn't allow operations in IAM.

Creating IAM Policies

You can create policies from the command line or via the console. Here's an example that shows how to create a managed policy with the `CreatePolicy` action

```
https://iam.amazonaws.com/?Action=CreatePolicy
&PolicyDocument={"Version":"2012-10-17","Statement":[{"Effect":"Allow","Action":"s3:ListA
llMyBuckets",
"Resource":"arn:aws:s3:::*"},{"Effect":"Allow","Action":["s3:Get*","s3:List*"],"Resource":
["arn:aws:s3:::EXAMPLE-BUCKET","arn:aws:s3:::EXAMPLE-BUCKET/*"]}]}
&PolicyName=S3-read-only-example-bucket
&Version=2010-05-08
&AUTHPARAMS
```

You can also create an IAM policy in the AWS console. Choose from one of the following methods to create a new IAM policy:

- **Import**   Import and customize either an AWS-managed or a customer-managed policy that you've created.
- **Visual editor**   Create the JSON document for the policy in the visual editor.
- **JSON**   Create a policy using JSON syntax in the JSON tab. You'll do this in Exercise 3-2 later in this chapter.

 NOTE   Remember that you can create both customer-managed and inline policies, but not AWS-managed policies.

IAM Best Practices

AWS recommends the following best practices for securing your AWS resources.

Restrict and Protect the AWS Account Root User Access Key

Your AWS account root user access key (consisting of an access key ID and secret access key) gives access to all your AWS resources, including billing details. Therefore, you should not use your AWS account root user access key. Instead, use your account e-mail address and password to log into the console and create an IAM user that you can use for all administrative work. In addition, you may also want to delete or rotate your AWS account keys and use a strong password to protect the key.

Create Individual IAM Users

Create individual IAM users for working with your AWS account. This enables you to grant a different set of permissions for each IAM user, as needed.

Grant Least Privilege

Granting least privilege means that when you create IAM policies, you must limit the privilege grants to the permissions required to perform a task that each user needs to perform. For example, if a user needs only read-only access to a resource, don't grant the user write permissions. When granting permissions on S3 service, for example, allow only a small set of required users to access Amazon S3 write actions, which enable a user to put objects into an S3 bucket or delete buckets. The Access Advisor tab in the IAM console shows information about the services by user, group, and role. This information helps you identify and remove unnecessary IAM policies.

 EXAM TIP Review the AWS security best practices, along with IAM-specific best practices. Most security best practices include creating IAM users and groups, using roles, configuring users and groups with policies that grant access based on the least privilege principle, securing remote administrative access, and configuring MFA for the root account as well as for all privileged IAM users.

Use Roles and Groups to Delegate and Assign Permissions

Instead of granting permissions directly to individual users, try to create groups based on job functions, and grant permissions for each group. Once you add users to a group, the users inherit all the permissions you assigned to the group. Groups help you easily grant and revoke permissions from users as their assignments in an organization change over time.

 NOTE To pass a role and its permissions to an AWS service, you must have permissions to pass the role to the service. You must grant the IAM user, group, or role the `PassRole` permission to allow the entity to pass a role to an AWS service. You can use the same IAM role on multiple EC2 instances. However, you can associate only one IAM role with an EC2 instance.

Granting credentials to IAM roles rather than users helps secure your AWS services. Applications running on EC2 instance, for example, can use a role's credentials to access AWS resources.

Use AWS-Defined Policies to Assign Permissions

Use the managed policies created by AWS to grant permissions. As you introduce new services, AWS maintains and updates the policies.

Monitor Activity in your AWS Account

Regularly review and monitor all your IAM policies to enhance your security. Ensure that the policies follow the principle of least privilege as the policies evolve over time.

AWS Component Security

Some AWS resources have their own security mechanism that operates beyond IAM, which controls access to management tasks that are performed from the console, command line, or AWS SDKs. The following sections summarize the product-specific security for important AWS services.

Amazon EC2 Security

In EC2, you log into the instances with a key pair (Linux) or use a username/password (Windows). You use security groups to control the traffic to the instance.

AWS offers the following recommendations as security best practices for Amazon EC2:

- Use and identify federation, IAM roles, and IAM users to manage access to all AWS resources and APIs.

- Establish credentials-management policies and procedures for the creation, revocation, and rotation of AWS access.

- Implement the least permissive rules for your security group.

- Perform regular patches and updates of the OS and applications on your EC2 instances.

AWS offers multiple layers of security for EC2 instance, at the host and guest OS levels, and via firewalls and signed API calls. The following sections summarize the OS, network, and security features of EC2 instances.

Managing OS Access to EC2 Instances

In the shared responsibility model, you keep the OS credentials to your EC2 instances. AWS helps you with the initial access to the OS. When you launch an EC2 instance from a standard Amazon Machine Image (AMI), you must authenticate at the OS level to access and configure the instance. You can use secure remote access protocols such as Secure Shell (SSH) or Windows Remote Desktop Protocol (RDP) to access that instance.

Once you authenticate to your new EC2 instance, you can set up standard OS authentication mechanisms, such as local OS accounts, Microsoft Active Directory, and X.509 certificate authentication.

EC2 Key Pairs for Authentication to EC2 Instances

AWS provides asymmetric EC2 key pairs to enable you to authenticate to EC2 instances. You learned about key pairs in Chapter 2. Public key cryptography uses a public key to encrypt something such as a password, and the recipient uses the private key to decrypt the data.

The big difference between the AWS account and IAM user credentials versus the EC2 key pairs is this: you use your account and IAM credentials to manage access to other AWS services, whereas an EC2 key pair controls access to a specific EC2 instance that you launch in your account.

 NOTE You can have multiple EC2 key pairs and launch new instances with different key pairs.

AWS can generate EC2 key pairs for you. When you launch an instance, AWS presents both the private key and the public key that are part of the key pair. You can generate new key pairs through EC2 anytime you want to.

On a Linux server, the public key is stored with the /.ssh/authorized_keys file. You must provide the private key when you connect to the instance. AWS doesn't save the private key, so if you lose it, you must generate a new key pair. Therefore, it's a good idea to secure the private key of the Amazon EC2 key pair.

Instead of having AWS generate a key pair for you, you can use a standard tool such as OpenSSH (with the keygen utility) to generate your own EC2 key pair. You import only the public key of the key pair into AWS and securely store the private key.

Each Linux instance launches with a default Linux system user account such as *ec2-user* (or Amazon Linux and Red Hat), and *ubuntu* for the Ubuntu operating system. Instead of granting access to an account such as *ec2-user* to multiple users, to enhance EC2 security, you must create multiple user accounts. Once you create the users, set up access keys for the users to log into EC2.

NOTE   You mustn't distribute the private key file that you use for the root account to multiple users. If multiple users require access to the same EC2 instance, you should add user accounts (through IAM) to your instance and create a key pair for each user. Then distribute the private key files to your users.

Controlling Access to EC2 Instances

You can access all AWS services with your security credentials. In addition, you have unlimited use of your AWS resources, such as EC2 instances. However, you don't have to share your own security credentials with other users. Instead, use IAM and other EC2 features to control EC2 resource usage by other users, services, and applications. Security groups control access to EC2 instances, and IAM helps you control how users use resources in your AWS account. Following is a summary of how you control access to EC2 instances.

EC2 Security Groups for Linux Instances to Control Network Access   A security group is a virtual firewall that controls traffic into and out of one or more EC2 instances. If you don't specify a custom security group when you launch an instance, the instance uses the default security group. Your AWS account has a default security group (named default) for the default VPC in each AWS region. The default rules for each default security group are as follows:

- Allow all inbound traffic for all the other instances associated with the default security group.
- Allow all outbound traffic from the instance.

NOTE   You can't delete the default security group.

You add rules to a security group to control which traffic you want to accept or deny access to an instance or instances. AWS evaluates all rules from a security group in determining whether to allow traffic to go to an EC2 instance.

Security groups control both inbound and outbound traffic at the instance level. You must set up rules in your security group to enable you to connect to a Linux instance from your IP address, via SSH. Here's how you'd add the rule to the security group using the AWS CLI:

```
$ aws ec2 authorize-security-group-ingress --group-id security_group_id --protocol tcp --port 22 --cidr cidr_ip_range
```

If you create an EC2 instance in a VPC, you must specify a security group created for that VPC. A security group is associated with the network interfaces, and changing the security groups for an instance changes the security groups associated with the primary network interface (eth0).

 NOTE   You can maintain your own firewalls on top of the security groups on any of your EC2 instances.

EC2 Permission Attributes   You can specify which of your AWS accounts can use your AMIs and EBS snapshots. You configure an AMI's `LaunchPermission` attribute to specify the AWS accounts that can access an AMI. The `create VolumePermission` attribute of an EBS snapshot helps you control which AWS accounts can use a snapshot.

IAM and EC2   You can use IAM with EC2 to control which users can perform tasks using specific EC2 API actions, and whether they can work with specific AWS resources.

By default, your IAM users can't create or modify EC2 resources. They also can't perform tasks with the EC2 API, the console, or the CLI. To enable your IAM users to work with EC2 resources and perform tasks, you must first create IAM policies that grant the users permission to use resources and perform API actions. You must then attach these policies to the users for groups that need the permissions.

An EC2 IAM policy contains two things:

- It must grant or deny permission to use one or more EC2 actions.
- It must specify the resources that can be used with the action. Because EC2 only partially supports resource-level permissions, for some EC2 API actions, you can't specify the resources a user is allowed to work with for the action.

You can create an IAM group and attach a policy to that group. For EC2, you can use the following AWS-managed policies:

- PowerUserAccess
- ReadOnlyAccess
- AmazonEC2FullAccess
- AmazonEC2ReadOnlyAccess

Once you create a group with one or more of these AWS-managed policies, you can add users to that group. When you attach the policy to the group or user, it grants or denies permission to perform the tasks that you specify on specific resources in your AWS account.

The following EC2 IAM policy shows how you can control permissions granted to IAM users for EC2 instances. This policy is for requests from the Amazon CLI or an AWS SDK. You can also create policies for working in the Amazon EC2 console. This policy enables a user to describe all EC2 instances (each chunk starting with `"Effect":` is a separate statement), but to start and stop only two specific instances and terminate instances only in a specific region and with a specific resource tag:

```
{
  "Version": "2012-10-17",
  "Statement": [
  {
  "Effect": "Allow",
   "Action": "ec2:DescribeInstances",
   "Resource": "*"
  },
  {
   "Effect": "Allow",
   "Action": [
    "ec2:StopInstances",
    "ec2:StartInstances"
   ],
   "Resource": [
   "arn:aws:ec2:us-east-1:123456789012:instance/i-1234567890abcdef0",
   "arn:aws:ec2:us-east-1:123456789012:instance/i-0598c7d356eba48d7"
   ]
  },
  {
   "Effect": "Allow",
   "Action": "ec2:TerminateInstances",
   "Resource": "arn:aws:ec2:us-east-1:123456789012:instance/*",
   "Condition": {
     "StringEquals": {
      "ec2:ResourceTag/purpose": "test"
     }
   }
  }
  ]
}
```

This policy shows how to control access to EC2 instances. You can also create policies that control access to volumes, snapshots, reserved instances, and those that restrict access to specific AWS regions.

Securing the Operating System and Applications

In the shared responsibility model, you are responsible for both OS- and application-level security. AWS recommends that you standardize the OS and application builds and maintain the security configurations in a secure build repository. Furthermore, you should build preconfigured AMIs that satisfy security hardening standards that address known security vulnerabilities.

Best practices for OS and application security include the following:

- Rotate credentials such as access keys.
- Run regular privilege checks using IAM user's Access Advisor and access key last used.

- Disable password-only access and use MFA to gain access to instances.
- Use *bastion hosts* to enforce control. A bastion host acts as a jump server that lets users hop into your AWS environment to access secure servers running within your private subnets. Ideally, all access to EC2 instances should be through a bastion host.
- Password-protect the .pem file on user servers.
- Restrict access to EC2 instances to a select range of IPs, using security groups (these act as firewalls).
- Use SSH network protocol to secure login to your Linux EC2 instances.
- Disable the root API access keys.
- Disable remote root login.
- Use command-line logging.
- Use sudo for privilege escalation.
- Generate your own key pairs, and don't share them with other customers (or even with AWS).
- Delete unnecessary keys from the authorized keys file on your EC2 instances. An instance's neighbors thus don't have privileged access to the instance compared to any host on the Internet, meaning that you can treat them as belonging to different physical hosts.

 EXAM TIP The SysOps certification exam often includes a question relating to bastion hosts, which are part of a security best practice adopted by many to secure the assets that they run in their private subnets. A bastion host is a server in your network that's specifically designed and configured to withstand security attacks. You generally host a single application such as a proxy server on a bastion host and remove other services to reduce the threat to the server. In AWS, you place a bastion host in a public subnet. Users can log into a bastion host via SSH or RDP and use their session to manage other hosts that live in private subnets.

Securing the Hypervisor
EC2 uses a custom version of the Xen hypervisor, which uses paravirtualization for Linux VMs. Under a paravirtualized system, the guest OS has no privileged access to the CPU, since the guest runs less privileged mode, called a *ring*. This demarcation of the guest and hypervisor means strong security for you.

Instance Isolation
AWS uses the Xen hypervisor to isolate the instances running on a physical machine. All network packets pass through the AWS firewall, which is in the hypervisor layer, helping to control traffic to the VM instance's virtual network interfaces. AWS enforces instance isolation in multiple areas, such as CPU memory.

Your EC2 instances use virtualized disks and have no access to the raw disk devices. The disk virtualization layer resets all used storage blocks, so a customer's data isn't exposed to other users. Memory is returned to the free memory pool for new memory allocation only after the memory is fully scrubbed. The hypervisor scrubs all the memory it reallocates to users.

NOTE For additional security, AWS recommends that you encrypt the file systems that you store on the virtual disks.

Who Secures the Host and Guest Operating Systems? AWS uses specially designed, configured, and hardened servers to serve as administration hosts. It tightly controls access to these servers with MFA and logs and audits the access.

You, the customer, completely control your VM servers. You have root access or administrative control over all accounts and servers and the applications that run on these servers. AWS has no access rights to your VMs.

NOTE AWS has no access rights to your instances and guest operating systems.

API Calls

Amazon EC2 API calls, such as those that terminate instances, must be signed by your Amazon secret access key. This key could be the AWS account secret access key, or an IAM user's secret access key.

TIP AWS recommends that you always encrypt all API calls to EC2 instances with SSL.

Mandatory Firewall

The extent of security provided by a firewall depends on the network ports that you open and the duration for which you leave them open. EC2 comes with a mandatory inbound firewall that by default is in the deny-all mode—that is, no inbound traffic is allowed until you open the necessary ports. You can restrict network traffic by protocol, service, port, and IP address.

You can group instances into various classes, so you can assign different rules for the instances. For example, you can open port 80 (HTTP) and, optionally, port 443 (HTTPS) for all your web servers. Instances functioning as database servers, by running the Oracle database, would have port 1521 open.

You can't control the firewall through your VM's operating system. You need your X.509 certificate and key to authorize all firewall changes, thus offering additional security. AWS recommends that you tighten security by restricting inbound and outbound network traffic with additional host-based firewalls such as iptables (or Windows Firewall) and VPNs.

Managing the Security of Your Custom AMIs

You can create and publish custom AMIs for both internal and external use. You are responsible for the security of the AMI and for ensuring that the private AMIs don't violate AWS's Acceptable Use Policy.

 NOTE AWS reserves the right to remove an AMI from the public catalog if the AMI is in violation of security best practices or if it poses a significant risk to users running that AMI. You can review AWS's Acceptable Use Policy at http://aws.amazon.com/aup/.

Ensure that your published AMIs are patched with the latest security patches, and perform the following cleanup and hardening tasks to minimize your exposure, to protect your credentials, and to conform with good governance practices:

- Disable all nonessential network services on startup.
- Delete all AWS and third-party credentials from disk and configuration files.
- Delete all additional certificates or key material from the servers.
- Check to ensure that installed software doesn't use default internal accounts and passwords.
- Ensure that the server doesn't violate the AWS Acceptable Use Policy, such as using open SMTP relays or proxy servers.

 NOTE Don't leave sensitive credentials on AMIs that you share publicly.

You must also perform additional OS-specific cleanup tasks before publishing the AMIs, such as the following steps for a Linux AMI:

- Configure SSHD to allow only public key authentication.
- Generate a unique SSH host key when you launch an EC instance.
- Remove or disable passwords for all user accounts.
- Delete all user SSH public and private key pairs.
- Delete all shell history and system log files that may contain sensitive data.

Once you initiate the hardened AMI by following the security best practices, you can use bootstrapping applications such as Puppet and Chef to modify and update the security controls. These security software updates include the application of server patches, service packs, and critical updates.

Managing Patches

As with the OS software, you are responsible for all patch management for both AMIs and EC2 instances. AWS recommends that you formalize patch management by keeping an inventory of all software and system components and checking to ensure that the security patches you installed match the latest vendor security patch list. You must also set up processes to track the latest security vulnerabilities, and rank the vulnerabilities, especially the most crucial and highest risk vulnerabilities.

You oversee the updating and patching of your guest operating systems. This includes the application of the latest security updates. AWS regularly updates the Amazon-provided AMIs with the latest patches, enabling you to relaunch the instances with the latest APIs that are updated with the current patches. You can also use Amazon Linux YUM repositories to update the Amazon Linux AMI–based instances.

Elastic Block Store Security

AWS protects data that you store on an EBS volume through redundancy. Since EBS replication is entirely within the same AZ, AWS recommends that you regularly take EBS snapshots and store them in Amazon S3 for durability. The data is stored on multiple physical locations without any extra cost to you. AWS further recommends that you use database-driven backups (for example, Oracle RMAN backups or MySQL database dumps) to protect the database data stored on EBS volumes.

It's a good idea to encrypt EBS volumes and snapshots. The encryption, which is performed in the EC2 instances, protects data as it moves between EC2 instances and EBS storage.

 NOTE   Only EC2's larger and more powerful instance types such as M3, C3, R3, and G2 offer encryption.

Securing the Analytics Services

AWS offers several analytics services, such as EMR and Kinesis, to help you store and analyze large volumes of data. The following sections briefly discuss the security aspects of key AWS analytics services.

Securing Amazon EMR

Amazon EMR is AWS's Hadoop web service that lets you run Hadoop clusters in the AWS cloud. Data for EMR is stored in Amazon S3, and EMR stores its job outputs in S3 as well. Amazon EMR creates two EC2 security groups, one group for each of the master nodes and the other for the worker nodes in the EMR cluster. You can use SSH port access to SSH into the master instances. Worker instances interact only with the master instances. By default, neither security group allows external access.

By default, other IAM users can't view an EMR cluster launched by an IAM user. You can choose to make the cluster viewable and accessible to all IAM users in your AWS account.

You can launch your EMR clusters into an Amazon VPC, so you can control access to the entire private subnet in which the cluster runs. You can enable the EMR cluster to access resources from your local data center using a VPN connection.

If you encrypt data before uploading it to S3, you must also provide a way for the EMR job to decrypt the data when retrieving the encrypted data from S3.

Securing Amazon Kinesis

Amazon Kinesis is an AWS-managed service that performs real-time data streaming. Kinesis helps in real-time data ingestion and processing of data in data sources such as server logs, social media, and web clickstream data.

You control access to Kinesis resources by creating IAM users and configuring IAM policies that specify user permissions. To facilitate running applications, use IAM roles. This helps applications to have the permissions you associate with an IAM role, without using long-term security credentials.

Securing the Network

AWS offers several networking services to help you create a secure, isolated network for your infrastructure, and to establish a private network connection to the AWS cloud.

Amazon Elastic Load Balancing Security

The AWS ELB service automatically distributes application traffic across multiple targets such as EC2 instances, containers, IP addresses, and Lambda functions. ELB offers a predefined cipher set used for TLS negations during the establishing of connections between ELB and clients. ELB offers additional configurations for TLS protocols and ciphers to suit your standards and requirements (such as PCI and SOX).

ELB offers perfect forward secrecy (PFS) for enhanced communication privacy. This strategy uses ephemeral session keys. ELB also enables you to identify the originating IP address of clients, which can be useful when you need more information about visitors while analyzing traffic logs or whitelisting certain IP addresses, for example.

ELB logs all HTTP and TCP requests sent to it, and the logs contain details such as the client IP addresses and ports, the sizes of the requests and responses, the backend IP address of the instance that served the requests, and finally the request line from the client, such as GET http://www.mycompany.com:80/HTTP/1.1.

Securing Amazon Virtual Private Cloud

You use Amazon VPC to create a distinct, isolated portion of the AWS cloud for your use. When you create a VPC, you specify a range of IP addresses for the subnet in the form of a Classless Inter-Domain Routing (CIDR) block. To establish external connectivity, you can create and attach an Internet gateway, a virtual private gateway, or both to the VPC.

You launch EC2 instances inside your VPC and define subnets within the VPC to group sets of EC2 instances together based on IP address ranges. You specify a separate CIDR block for each subnet that you create, and this block is a subset of the VPC's CIDR block. You can use routing and security groups to control traffic flow into and out of your subnets and EC2 instances.

In addition to subnets, Amazon VPC contains several other complementary security features, such as security groups, network ACLs, routing tables, and external gateways.

Subnets and Route Tables

Each EC2 instance in a VPC is connected to one subnet. AWS blocks well-known layer 2 security attacks such as MAC and ARP spoofing.

A subnet is associated with a routing table, which filters all network traffic flowing out of the subnet to determine the traffic's destination. You use a public subnet (the subnet's traffic is routed to an Internet gateway) to run web applications that need to connect to the Internet, and a private subnet (the subnet is not routed to the Internet gateway) to run private applications and databases that don't need to connect to the Internet.

Security Groups (Firewalls)

As with EC2 instances, you can create security groups for an Amazon VPC to filter both incoming and outgoing networking traffic from EC2 instances. Here's what you need to know about the differences between EC2 security groups and VPC security groups:

- You must create VPC security groups explicitly for your Amazon VPC. The EC2 security groups that you may have created won't work within the VPC.
- You can do some things with VPC security groups that you can't with EC2 security groups, such as change the security group after the instance launch or specify multiple protocols instead of being limited to TCP, UDP, and ICMP.

Network Access Control Lists

Network ACLs strengthen VPC security by filtering all inbound and outbound traffic from a subnet within a VPC. The ACL rules can control incoming and outgoing network traffic based on protocol, service, port, and the source or destination IP addresses.

Network ACLs and security groups complement each other, as shown in Figure 3-3.

Virtual Private Gateways and Internet Gateways

Network gateways enable connectivity between networks, including the Internet, and your VPC. A virtual private gateway enables you to connect privately to your VPC and other networks. You can connect securely to your VPC from your data centers by establishing a VPN connection to the virtual private gateway from on-premise gateway devices.

You can also attach an Internet gateway to your VPC to connect to the Internet, as well as to AWS services such as Amazon S3. To be able to connect through an Internet gateway, an EC2 instance must have one of the following:

- An elastic IP address that's associated with the instance
- A NAT instance to route the traffic

Dedicated EC2 Instances

By default, your EC2 instances may share the underlying hardware with other tenants. You can create a VPC with dedicated tenancy, forcing all instances that you launch in that VPC to be physically isolated from other tenants at the hardware level. You may also

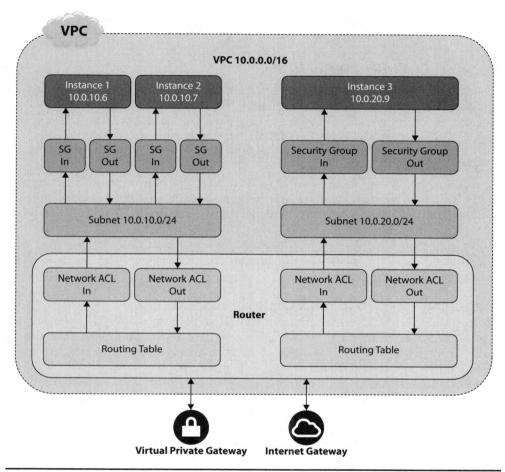

Figure 3-3 How network ACLs and security groups work together to protect instances within your Amazon VPC

specify that specific EC2 instances be created with dedicated tenancy. Be mindful of cost when selecting the dedicated instances.

Elastic Network Interfaces

All EC2 instances have a default network interface with a private IP address in your VPC network. You can add an elastic network interface (ENI) to an instance. ENIs are useful when creating a management network or using network and security appliances in your VPC, or to easily move the instances from one AZ to another.

Amazon Route 53 Security

Amazon Route 53 is Amazon's Domain Name System (DNS) that manages the IP addresses listed for your domain and translates domain names to IP addresses. The Route 53 control API is accessible only through SSL-encrypted endpoints. Route 53 requires all requests made to its control API to be authenticated, and the requests are signed with a signature calculated from the request and the secret access key of the user.

Amazon CloudFront Security

CloudFront is Amazon's content delivery network that delivers web content using a global network of edge locations. User requests for content are routed to the edge location nearest to them, substantially enhancing performance. CloudFront offers several security features to protect your static and dynamic web content.

Limiting Access to APIs

As with Route 53, CloudFront's control APIs are accessible only through SSL-encrypted endpoints. CloudFront also requires all requests made to its control APIs to be authenticated. The requests are signed with a signature calculated from the request and the secret access key of the user.

You can enable CloudFront's *private content feature* to limit who can download content from the service. CloudFront also supports geo restriction, which bases access to content on the viewer's location.

Controlling Access to Original Copies of Content

You can create origin access identities to control access of the original copies of your objects in S3. CloudFront uses the identities to retrieve objects from S3. To prevent the public from viewing the original copies of the object, you can limit access to the origin access identity by using S3 ACLs.

Restrict the Ability to Download Objects from CloudFront Locations

CloudFront uses a stringent system to control who can download objects from the service:

- Although, by default, CloudFront processes access requests in both HTTP and HTTPS, you can call for some objects to be transferred over an encrypted connection (HTTPS) only.
- All users must use a signed URL verification system that uses a public/private key pair.
- You may specify up to five trusted AWS accounts that can sign requests.
- You can create policy documents that specify under what conditions CloudFront serves the content. The document may include items such as the requested object name, the day and time the request was made, and the source IP of the client making the request.

 NOTE By default, all content delivered by CloudFront is publicly readable, unless you enable the optional private content feature.

To reference your objects stored in CloudFront edge locations, you must include the encoded policy document and signature as query string parameters.

Enabling Access Logs   You can enable CloudFront access logs by specifying an Amazon S3 bucket when you're configuring the CloudFront distribution.

Securing AWS Direct Connect

Direct Connect directly links your internal network in an AWS region through a dedicated connection that doesn't involve the public Internet; this lowers your network costs and enhances throughput and consistency. Direct Connect mandates the use of the Border Gateway Protocol (BGP) with an autonomous system number (ASN). You create virtual interfaces directly to the AWS cloud and Amazon VPC. To create the virtual interfaces, you must use either an AWS-generated BGP MD5 cryptographic key or provide your own key.

Securing the Storage Services

AWS offers several types of storage for backup and archiving. You can use Amazon S3 for object storage, for example, and Amazon Glacier for lower-cost archival storage.

Securing Simple Storage Service

Amazon S3 stores your data as objects inside storage buckets, with objects including various types of files, such as a text files or s video files, for example. By adding metadata when you store a file in S3, you can set permissions to control access to the file. S3 permissions can control the following:

- Access to a bucket to indicate who can create or delete objects in that bucket
- Viewing rights to a bucket and its objects access logs
- The choice of the geographical regions where S3 can store a bucket and its objects

Controlling Access to S3 Storage Buckets and Objects

An S3 bucket/object owner is the AWS account owner. The user who creates the bucket/object is *not* the owner of the object or bucket. Only an owner of a bucket or object can access the resources they create.

As the AWS account owner, you can grant or revoke access to S3 buckets and objects in three different ways:

- **IAM policies**   Use IAM policies to control access of IAM users within your own AWS account to S3 buckets and objects. You attach S3 access policies to the IAM users in your AWS account.
- **ACLs**   S3 access control lists (ACLs) help you manage access to S3 buckets and objects. Each bucket and object has an ACL attached to it that defines which AWS accounts or groups have access to the bucket or object. It's important to understand that ACLs allow you to grant access to AWS accounts and groups, but not to individual IAM users.

- **Bucket policies** S3 bucket policies are more broad-ranging that IAM policies and ACLs. Bucket policies enable you to control the access to some or all objects in an S3 bucket. You can attach a bucket policy to users and groups in your own AWS account, as well as other AWS accounts. You can also attach the bucket policies to S3 buckets.

EXAM TIP Carefully review the various types of Amazon S3 access policy options. Broadly speaking, you configure two types of S3 access policies: resource-based policies and user policies. You attach resource-based policies to your S3 resources, such as buckets and objects. Both bucket policies and ACLs are resource-based policies. You attach user policies to your IAM users. You can use user policies, resource policies, or a combination of the two to manage Amazon A3-related access permissions.

Granting Conditional Access to S3 Resources

You can use action-specific *policy keys* available in S3 to grant conditional access to specific S3 resources. You can use conditions such as request time, whether the request used SSL, the requester's IP address, or the requester's client application.

Query String Authentication

You can time-limit access to S3 objects through the use of *query string authentication*. This enables you to share your S3 objects through URLs that are valid for a specific length of time.

Protecting Data at Rest

You can manage your own encryption of S3 data by encryption data with the Amazon S3 encryption client (a client encryption library) before storing it in S3. You can also use Amazon S3 server-side encryption (SSE) to have Amazon S3 manage the encryption for you. You encrypt data with either an AWS-generated key or a key that you supply. Decryption is automatic upon retrieval of data.

TIP S3 metadata isn't encrypted; therefore, AWS suggests that you not put sensitive data in metadata.

S3 Access Logs

You can enable logging for an S3 bucket. Logging captures the access to the bucket and its objects, such as the requested resource, the request type (PUT, DELETE for example), the requestor's IP, and the time of the request.

Cross-Origin Resource Sharing (CORS)

Many web browsers use a same-origin policy that blocks JavaScript and HTML5 from allowing cross-origin requests from other sites or domains. You can enable CORS so that external web pages, style sheets, and HTML5 applications can safely access assets such as images stored in an S3 bucket.

Securing Glacier

Amazon Glacier is an archival service for infrequently used data. Archives are data such as photos, videos, and documents and can contain one or more files. Glacier stores the files as archives, inside vaults.

Security of Data Loads

You must compute and supply a tree hash to AWS when moving data to Glacier. A tree hash is a combination of hashes for each megabyte-sized data you send to Glacier, organized in a treelike fashion, to allow addition of new segments of that data. Glacier checks your tree hash to ensure that your data wasn't tampered with. Similarly, when you retrieve data from your Glacier archives, you can use the supplied checksums to ensure the file integrity.

Encryption

Glacier automatically encrypts all your data and offers an average annual durability of 99.999999999 percent for your archives. It protects your data by storing it in multiple data centers on multiple devices. It also performs regular data integrity checks and includes automatic self-healing features.

Securing the AWS Storage Gateway

The AWS Storage Gateway helps your local data center–based storage devices to connect with the Amazon S3 storage service. Using the Storage Gateway, you can securely upload data to S3 for backup and disaster recovery purposes.

The Storage Gateway moves offsite data to S3 storage via Amazon EBS snapshots, which are replicated over multiple AWS data centers and multiple storage devices. AWS stores the data in the region that you specify.

The Storage Gateway transfers data asynchronously from your data center–based storage devices to AWS via SSL. AWS then stores the data in S3, using the symmetric key advanced encryption standard Advanced Encryption Standard (AES) 256.

Securing AWS Import/Export

AWS Import/Export is a way to use portable storage devices to transfer large amounts of data to S3, EBS, or Glacier storage. You prepare the storage devices and ship them to a secure AWS facility and AWS transfers the data off the storage devices. You can similarly export data from AWS to a portable storage device.

To identify and authenticate your storage devices, you obtain a unique identifier for a job from AWS and a digital signature for authenticating the storage devices. AWS uses the signature file for authentication. When using S3, you place the signature file on your storage device's root directory, and for EBS, you affix the signature barcode to the device itself.

You can encrypt your storage devise in different ways, depending on whether you're importing or exporting and which AWS service (S3, EBS, or Glacier) you're using:

- **Importing to S3** Encrypt your storage device using a PIN-code device and/or TrueCrypt before shipping it. AWS decrypts the data and imports it into S3.

- **Exporting from S3** Provide a PIN code and/or a password so that AWS can encrypt your data on your storage device. You use a PIN-code device and/or TrueCrypt to decrypt the files.
- **Importing to Glacier or to EBS** Encrypt the data with your favorite encryption method before shipping the storage device. AWS doesn't decrypt your storage device.

Securing Databases

All AWS database services, including DynamoDB, RDS, Redshift, and ElastiCache, offer strong security features, as the following sections explain.

Securing DynamoDB

You can control who can access your DynamoDB resources and API by using IAM permissions policies. IAM policies help you control access at the resource level and the database level. Database-level permissions enable you to set up fine-grained access controls at the item (rows) and attribute (column) levels.

Instead of creating IAM users that can access DynamoDB, you can use web identity federation to grant access to users who authenticate by logging into Amazon, Facebook, or Google. IAM users log into an identity provider to obtain temporary security credentials from the AWS Security Token Service (STS). These temporary AWS credentials enable the applications to access specific DynamoDB tables.

All requests to the DynamoDB services must contain a HMAC-SHA256 signature. AWS SDKs automatically sign all your requests, but you must provide the signature when writing your own HTTP POST requests. To calculate the signature, you request temporary security credentials from AWS STS.

Securing RDS

You can secure access to your Amazon RDS DB instances and your RDS resources. You can use one or more of the following to control access to RDS.

Using a VPC to Control Network Access to RDS

For maximum network access control, run your DB instances in a VPC. Locating your RDS DB instances within a VPC enables you to run the instance in your own secure, private subnet. A common scenario for creating an RDS instance in a VPC is when you want the instance to share data with an application server running an EC2 instance within the same VPC.

To access a DB instance that lives in a different VPC from the one an EC2 instance lives in, you can use *VPC peering*. A VPC peering connection between two VPCs enables you to route traffic between the two VPCs using a private IP address, enabling instances to communicate as if they're within the same network. You can create VPC peering connections between your own VPCs or with a VPC in a different AWS account. The VPCs in a peering connection must all be in the same region, use security groups to control access, and must not have overlapping IP ranges. Chapter 6 discusses VPC peering.

Using IAM Policies to Control Access to Database Resources

Create IAM policies to grant permissions that control which users can manage RDS resources. You can, for example, create IAM policies to specify which of your users can create and delete DB instances.

Using DB Security Groups to Control Database Access

Use DB security groups to control which IP addresses can connect to your DB instances. A DB security group helps you secure DB instances running within your Amazon VPC by acting as a firewall to control network access to the DB instances. By default, when you create a database, the DB security group (firewall) disallows any database access unless you specify access through an existing EC2 security group rule. You must associate this security group with the DB instance.

 NOTE A DB security group allows access to the database server port (such as 1521 for the Oracle database) and blocks all other ports.

Since the DB security group by default denies all access to the database, you must explicitly authorize network access by doing one of the following:

- Authorizing a network IP range
- Authorizing an existing EC2 security group

Using SSL Connections

An SSL connection encrypts the connections between your applications and your DB instances. Most of RDS's DB engines enable you to configure SSL connections to the DB instances, which enables the connections to be encrypted.

Encrypting Data

For an additional layer of data protection, you can use RDS encryption to encrypt data-at-rest in DB instances, automated backups, Read Replicas, and snapshots. RDS uses the standard AES-256 encryption algorithm to encrypt data. RDS handles the data decryption transparently, with little overhead.

For Oracle or SQL Server DB instances, you can also use Transparent Data Encryption (TDE) along with encryption-at-rest. For Oracle databases, you can use Oracle Native Network Encryption (NNE), which enables you to encrypt data as it moves via the network to and from an Oracle instance.

You use AWS Key Management Service (KMS) to create the encryption keys and define the policies for key usage. Remember that you must protect the use of the encryption keys by setting up appropriate access control policies. Encryption keys stored by KMS in a region can't be used in other regions, because key usage is limited to a specific region.

Using Built-in Database Security Features

All databases come with a host of built-in security features, such as password verification features. Use all the built-in security capabilities of your databases to protect your data.

When you create a DB instance in RDS, you'll create a master user account to manage the instance. The master user account is all powerful. After you create the database instance, you log into the database with the master user credentials and create additional user accounts, with limited capabilities.

Securing Redshift

Amazon Redshift, Amazon's petabyte-scale SQL data warehouse service, typically is run as a multinode cluster, with a leader node and two or more compute nodes. The leader node manages the connections and manages the query execution that the compute nodes perform. The compute nodes store data and perform the queries under the supervision of the leader node.

AWS runs the all-important compute node on a separate, isolated network, and you never directly access this node.

You can secure Amazon Redshift by controlling access to the database at four levels:

- Cluster management through IAM policies
- Cluster connectivity
- Database access
- Temporary database credentials and single sign-on (SSO)

Authentication and Access Control for Amazon Redshift

Any user who needs to access a Redshift database requires credentials that have permissions to access a Redshift cluster. You can control the ability of a user account to create, configure, and delete clusters by granting permissions to the users or accounts via IAM policies. Use IAM policies to control user access to a Redshift database and authenticate the user actions in the database.

The primary resource in Redshift is a cluster. There are also subresources, such as snapshots, parameter groups, and event subscriptions. Redshift provides a set of operations to use with the Redshift resources. A principal entity such as the root account, an IAM user, or an IAM role can create a resource such as a cluster. The resource owner is always the AWS account owner of the principal entity.

Earlier, you learned about IAM permissions policies such as identity-based permission policies, and policies that you attach to a resource, called resource-based policies. Redshift supports only identity-based IAM policies. You can attach these policies to IAM identities such as a user, group, or role. Customer-managed IAM policies can allow or deny access to RedShift actions and resources.

AWS provides several standalone IAM policies that it creates and administers. These AWS-managed policies provide permissions for common use cases. Here are the AWS-managed Redshift-specific policies that you can attach to your users:

- **AmazonRedshiftReadOnlyAccess** Grants read-only access to all Redshift resources in your AWS account
- **AmazonRedshiftFullAccess** Grants full access to all Redshift resources

- **AmazonRedshiftQueryEditor**   Grants full access to the Query Editor in the Redshift console

Following is an example policy that allows an IAM user to create, delete, and modify a Redshift cluster.

```
[
  "Version": "2012-10-17",
  "Statement": [
    {
      "Sid":"AllowManageClusters",
      "Effect":"Allow",
      "Action": [
        "redshift:CreateCluster",
        "redshift:DeleteCluster",
        "redshift:ModifyCluster",
      ],
      "Resource":"*"
    }
  ]
```

When creating a policy, you can specify a condition such as one that specifies that a policy be applied only after a specific date. You can also use two condition keys to restrict access to resources based on their tags. The `redshift:Request` tag condition key applies to Redshift API actions that create a resource. The `redshift:Resource` tag restricts user access to resources based on tag keys and values.

Redshift uses IAM *service-linked roles*. A service-linked role is a predefined Redshift IAM role that includes the permissions the service requires to call AWS services on behalf of a Redshift cluster. When you create a cluster, Redshift creates a service-linked role in your account.

 NOTE   A service-linked role links to an AWS service, which is also called a *linked service* in this context. Only the linked service can assume the role, which means that you can't assume the role. You use a service-linked role to delegate permission to AWS services to manage AWS resources on your behalf.

The service-linked role named `AWSServiceRoleforRedshift` allows Redshift to call AWS services on your behalf. The role has predefined permissions that allow Redshift to do things such as describe VPCs and subnets.

Redshift Cluster Connectivity

By default, nobody has access to a Redshift cluster that you provision. To grant users access to the cluster, you must associate the cluster with a security group. The security group consists of rules that control cluster access, such as a range of IP addresses from which users can access Redshift. You can either use an existing VPC security group or define a new one and associate it with the cluster. You can associate multiple security groups with a cluster and also multiple clusters with a single security group.

Managing Redshift Database Security

Like all databases, Redshift offers built-in security features. Redshift logs all connection and use activity information for security purposes, a process called *database auditing*. It stores the logs in S3 buckets. The information in the logs is also stored in internal database system tables, but log files are easier to view than the log data stored in tables, since they don't require database permissions to query the data.

In addition to Redshift database audit logging, you can use AWS CloudTrail to view actions taken by a user, role, or AWS service in Redshift. You can find out the IP address from which a request was made to Redshift, as well as the time of the request and the identity of the requestor.

Database User Credentials

The common way to log into a Redshift database is by providing a database username and password. Instead of maintaining credentials in the Redshift database itself, you can allow users to create credentials to log into the database based on their IAM credentials. You can use IAM authentication to generate database user credentials. In other words, you can generate temporary database credentials based on permissions you grant through an IAM permissions policy.

The SQL client needs to call the `GetclusterCredentials` action on your behalf, and you must provide this authorization by creating an IAM user or role and attach a permissions policy that grants the permission to call the `redshift:getClusterCredentials`.

Redshift enables you to grant database permissions on a per-cluster level, and not on a per-table basis. The creator of an object is its owner, and only the owner can modify or delete the object. You can grant necessary permission to users or groups to use an object.

Backups

To protect the data, Redshift mirrors data on each of its nodes to disks on another node. In addition, it also backs up all its data to Amazon S3 through snapshots. You can have S3 store the backups from a period of 1 to 35 days.

Encrypting Redshift Databases

You can enable encryption for a Redshift cluster to protect data-at-rest. Although encryption is optional, AWS recommends that you use it for clusters with sensitive data, or when regulations such as the PPCI DSS and SOX require it.

There are two ways to handle the top-level encryption keys when you decide to encrypt Redshift databases. You can use the AWS Key Management Service (KMS) or an encryption hardware security module (HSM) to store the encryption keys.

Encryption with AWS KMS There is a four-tier hierarchy of encryption keys in AWS KMS:

- **Data encryption keys** These keys encrypt the data blocks in the Redshift cluster, using the database encryption key.
- **Database encryption key (DEK)** A randomly generated AES-256 key stored on disk separately from the Redshift database and encrypted by a master key.

- **Cluster encryption key (CEK)** Encrypts the database encryption key. You can use either AWS or a third-party HSM to store the CEK. HSMs enable you to manage keys separately from the application and the database.

- **Master key** Used for encrypting the cluster key, if you use AWS to store it (and not an HSM). If the cluster key is stored in an HSM, the master key encrypts the CEK-encrypted DEK.

NOTE *Key policies* are the main way to control access to the customer master keys (CMKs) in AWS KMS. You use key policies to configure who can access the keys in the KMS service.

Redshift randomly generates an AES-256 key that it uses as the DEK. It uses the decrypted DEK to encrypt and decrypt the keys for the data blocks in the Redshift database.

By default, Redshift uses the default key that's created for your AWS account (for use in Redshift) as the master encryption key. For more flexibility in creating, rotating, managing the access, and auditing the encryption keys that you use, you can create your own custom master key separately in AWS KMS.

After you choose a master key, Redshift requests AWS KMS to generate a CEK and encrypt it with the master key. AWS KMS stores the customer master key and sends the encrypted CEK to Redshift, which stores it on a separate network from the cluster.

Encryption Using an HSM Instead of using AWS KMS, you can use an HSM to manage encryption keys. As explained earlier in the section, "Storing and Managing Encryption Keys," an HSM is a device for generating and managing encryption keys. Because key management is separated from the database layer, an HSM offers more security.

Rotating the Encryption Keys You can rotate the encryption keys for an encrypted Redshift cluster. Redshift rotates the CEK for the cluster and its snapshots. It also rotates the DEK for the cluster, but it can't do so for the snapshots while they are stored in Amazon S3.

The frequency of key rotation depends on your regulatory compliance and industry standard requirements. A cluster is temporarily unavailable during the key rotation process because it's put in the `ROTATING_KEYS` state during this time. So be careful about frequently rotating the encryption keys!

Securing ElastiCache

Amazon ElastiCache is a web service that helps you set up and manage a distributed in-memory cache environment in the AWS cloud. ElastiCache helps web applications serve information faster by enabling them to retrieve information from a fast in-memory caching site, instead of slow disks.

ElastiCache lets you create cache clusters, which are collections of one or more cache nodes, each running an instance of the Memcached (or Redis) service. The cache nodes are chunks of network-attached RAM, and each cache node runs a Memcached (or Redis) service instance, with its own DNS name and port.

TIP All clients of an ElastiCache cache cluster must be a part of the EC2 network and authorized through ingress rules in cache security groups.

You can control access to an ElastiCache cluster by setting up cache security groups, which are like firewalls that control network access to the cache cluster. By default, network access is denied for all your cache clusters, and you must configure a cache security group and associate it with your cache clusters. By setting up ingress rules, you must explicitly enable access from hosts in the EC2 security group so your applications can access your cache cluster.

After you create a cache security group, you can execute the `authorize cache security group ingress` API or CLI command to authorize the EC2 security group. This determines which EC2 instances, and therefore which applications running on those instances, can access the cache cluster.

Data Security

ElastiCache offers encryption features for data on clusters running in Redis and Memcached. There are two types of encryption in ElastiCache: in-transit encryption and at-rest encryption.

In-Transit Data Encryption In-transit data encryption is designed to protect data moving between two places, such as the cluster and its applications, or between a primary node and a read replica node within a replication group.

In-transit encryption does the following:

- Encrypts connections
- Encrypts replicated data moving between primary and replica nodes
- Enables clients to authenticate that they're connecting to the right server
- Authenticates clients using a security feature such as Redis AUTH

NOTE The Redis AUTH command enhances security by requiring users to enter a password before they're allowed to execute Redis commands on a Redis server.

At-Rest Encryption At-rest encryption protects data stored on disk, including during backup operations. It's designed to enhance data security by encrypting data during sync, backup, and snapshot operations. Because of the processing involved in encryption/decryption, the overhead may impact performance.

Securing Network Access

ElastiCache is fully integrated with Amazon VPC, meaning that your cluster is automatically deployed into a VPC. If you don't define an ElastiCache security group for your VPC, ElastiCache uses the default security group. When creating an ElastiCache cluster in a VPC, you must specify a subnet group. ElastiCache will then choose the subnet and IP address to associate with your nodes. If you don't specify a subnet when launching the cluster, it's launched into your default VPC.

Application Services Security

AWS offers services to support applications, such as the Amazon Simple Queue Service (SQS) and the Amazon Simple Notification Service (SNS). Let's review how you secure the application services.

Securing Amazon SQS

Amazon SQS is a message queueing service that enables asynchronous messaging between a distributed application's components, such as EC2 instances and web servers. As with all other AWS services, SQS access requires credentials that have permissions to access resources such as SQS queues and messages. SQS has a resource-based permission system that's written in the same language as IAM policies. So you can achieve similar things with IAM and SQS policies. In most cases, the end results are the same with the SQS policy system or the IAM policy system.

The only SQS resource is the *queue*. SQL offers a set of actions that work with the queue resource.

Configuring Access with SQS Policies

Although you can use SQS policies to specify the AWS accounts that can work with it through IAM policies, SQS has a separate policy infrastructure. You can create SQS policies for a queue to control AWS account access to that queue. You can specify access conditions such as those that grant permissions to send or receive messages if the request is made before a certain date.

SQS doesn't support resource-based permissions policies; it supports only identity-based (IAM) policies. Here's an example policy:

```
{
  "Version": "2012-10-17",
  "Statement": [{
   "Effect": "Allow",
   "Action": "sqs:*",
   "Resource": "arn:aws:sqs:*:123456789012:sam_queue_*"
  }]
}
```

The SQS service defines a set of actions for each resource. SQS defines the set of actions you can specify in a policy to grant permissions for the actions. You can create SQS policies to allow users to create queues, to allow developers to write messages to shared queues, to allow a partner to send messages to a queue, and so on.

To grant permissions, you can specify conditions for when a policy should take effect by using the SQS Access Policy Language.

Protecting Data with Server-Side Encryption and AWS KMS

AWS doesn't encrypt data stored in Amazon SQS, but you can encrypt data before it is uploaded to Amazon SQS. SSE helps you transmit sensitive data in encrypted queues. It uses keys that are managed by AWS KMS to protect message contents in SQS queues. It's important to remember that all requests that are made to queues for which you've enabled SSE must use HTTPS Signature Version 4, which is a process that adds authentication information to AWS requests. When you use KMS, the data keys that encrypt the messages are encrypted as well as stored together with the data. SSE encrypts the message body in an SQS queue without affecting the normal functioning of SQS. To be able to use SSE for Amazon SQS, you must configure KMS key policies to allow the encryption techniques as well as messages that are stored in the queues. You can do this with either IAM policies or AWS SMS key policies.

You can choose to have SQS encrypt messages stored in both standard and first in, first out (FIFO) queues using an encryption key provided by AWS KMS. You can do this when you create your queue or later.

NOTE SSE encrypts the body of the message, but not the queue and message metadata or the per-queue metrics. Adding encryption to an existing queue doesn't encrypt the backlogged messages. Removing encryption doesn't affect any encrypted messages in the queue.

Securing Amazon SNS

Amazon SNS is a web service that enables users and applications to send and receive notifications from the AWS cloud. SNS coordinates and manages the delivery of messages to endpoints or clients. The two types of clients in SNS are called *publishers* and *subscribers* (or producers and consumers). Publishers send messages asynchronously to a *topic*, which is a communication channel, and subscribers such as web servers and AWS Lambda functions consume the messages by subscribing to the topic.

You control access to a topic by defining policies that specify which publishers and subscribers can use the topic. You allow an account to publish to a topic using the Amazon SNS API action `AddPermission`.

NOTE An SQS policy controls access to a queue, and an SNS policy controls access to a topic.

The key resource in SNS is a *topic*, and you must decide whether you want to grant AWS accounts the ability to perform specific topic actions, such as publishing messages to a specific topic. The SNS access control mechanism enables you to secure topics and messages against access by unauthorized users. A topic owner can set access policies for the topic to control who can subscribe or publish to it. The topic owner can also specify that all message delivery mechanisms must use HTTPS.

By default, access to a topic is limited to the AWS account that created the topic. You can allow other IAM users access to SNS through an SNS-generated policy or a policy that you configure.

AWS Monitoring Tools and Services that Help with Security

AWS provides several useful monitoring tools that help you secure your AWS infrastructure and AWS resources through event notifications and other means. Following are the key monitoring services that help with security:

- Amazon CloudWatch
- AWS Trusted Advisor
- Amazon Inspector
- AWS Config
- Amazon CloudTrail
- AWS Web Application Firewall (WAF)
- AWS Certificate Manager

Amazon CloudWatch

Amazon CloudWatch is a monitoring tool that helps you track your AWS resources and the applications that you run in AWS. CloudWatch collects and processes raw data into useful, near real-time, easily readable and understood performance and security metrics.

CloudWatch is a metrics repository. AWS services such as EC2 store operational metrics in this repository, and you retrieve standard summary statistics based on the metrics. You can also place custom metrics into this repository. You can present the summary metric data in the CloudWatch console in a graphical format. CloudWatch logs enable the monitoring of OS and other service logs. CloudWatch logs can also monitor Cloud-Trail logs in real time.

In Chapter 6, you'll learn about Amazon VPC Flow Logs, which capture information pertaining to the IP traffic flowing into and out of the network interfaces in your VPC. The CloudWatch Logs service stores the VPC Flow Logs data.

You can configure CloudWatch with alarm actions that stop, start, or terminate EC2 instances when certain criteria are met. An alarm can automatically initiate actions on your behalf.

AWS Trusted Advisor Tool

Some Premium Support plans include access to the AWS Trusted Advisor tool, which offers a snapshot of your AWS infrastructure and helps you identify potential security misconfigurations.

Trusted Advisor checks for compliance with the following security configurations:

- Configuration of IAM to ensure that AWS access controls are in place
- Enablement of MFA to provide two-factor authentication for your root AWS account
- Limited access to common administrative ports, such as the ports 22 (SSH), 23 (Telnet), 3389 (RDP), and 5500 (VNC)
- Limited access to common database ports, including ports 1433 (SQL Server), 3306 (MySQL), and Oracle (1521)

Amazon Inspector

Amazon Inspector is a security vulnerability service that helps you secure your AWS resources and comply with various security regulations. Amazon Inspector detects deviations from security best practices and security vulnerabilities in AW services and resources, and it produces a comprehensive list of findings ordered by severity level.

As with other security vulnerability tools, Amazon Inspector relies on a knowledge base of security rules that map to known security vulnerabilities and common security standard definitions. AWS security researchers maintain the security knowledge base and keep it up-to-date.

You can monitor Inspector with CloudWatch, which enables you to access historical information and understand how Inspector is performing. By default, Inspector sends data to CloudWatch every 5 minutes.

Following are the key features of Amazon Inspector:

- **Automation**   You can fully automate Inspector via an API, including executing security checks and reporting their results.
- **Configuration scanning and activity monitoring engine**   Inspector provides an engine that analyzes configuration of resources and monitors activity. This offers a comprehensive picture of the assessment targets and their security and compliance postures.
- **Built-in content library**   Inspector contains a built-in library of rules that checks against best practices, common security standards, and known security vulnerabilities. It also provides detailed recommendations for resolving the security loopholes.

Service-Linked Roles for Amazon Inspector

Inspector is easy to set up because you don't need to add permissions manually. Inspector uses an IAM service-linked role, which is a unique type of IAM rule that links directly to Amazon Inspector. A service-linked role is predefined and includes all the permissions the service requires to all other AWS services on your behalf. Inspector defines the permissions of its service-linked roles, including the trust policy and the permissions policy.

AWS Config

AWS Config is a tool that offers a detailed view of your AWS resources, such as their configuration, their interrelationships, and how both have changed over time. You use AWS Config for troubleshooting, resource discovery, change management, audit compliance, and security analysis.

AWS Config helps you do the following:

- Get a snapshot of the current resource configurations.
- Retrieve the history of the configuration of the resources.
- Receive a notification when a resource is created, deleted, or altered.
- View interrelationships among resources—for example, finding all resources that share a security group.

AWS Config continually tracks resources as you create, delete, or modify them. When AWS Config detects that a resource isn't compliant with your security or other rules, it marks that resource as noncompliant and notifies you. For continuous configuration assessment, you can use AWS Config rules, both the set of prebuilt rules as well as custom rules of your own, to check the configuration changes that AWS Config captures.

AWS Config helps spot potential security weaknesses by providing detailed history information about key resource configuration, such as the IAM permissions that you've granted to users or the EC2 security groups you've configured to control access to AWS resources.

You can configure AWS Config to trigger automatic evaluation of rules when resource configurations change (say, a security group's rules are changed). You can also configure periodic evaluation of rules, such as every 24 hours or every 7 days.

AWS Config enables you to view the IAM policies assigned to users, groups, or roles. This helps you ascertain whether a user or role had permissions to perform certain actions at a specific time. By tracking the configuration of the EC2 security groups, you determine things such as whether specific port rules were open or whether incoming TCP traffic on that port was blocked at a certain time.

AWS CloudTrail

AWS CloudTrail is an AWS service that helps perform governance, compliance, and operations and risk auditing of an AWS account. All activity that occurs in an AWS account is recorded in a CloudTrail event. The activity could be an action that you, a rule, or an AWS service performs via the AWS Management Console, the AWS CLI, and AWS SDKs and APIs. Using CloudTrail, you can get a history of AWS API calls for your account.

CloudTrail helps you identify the users and accounts that called AWS APIs. It captures information about the API calls made to an AWS resource, such as the IP address the calls were made from and the time of the API calls. If the API call resulted in an error, CloudTrail shows the details of the error, including authorization failure messages if any. CloudTrail also captures all AWS console sign-in events and records when an AWS account user, federated user, or an IAM user signed into the console.

NOTE When you turn on CloudTrail logging, CloudWatch writes log files to the Amazon S3 bucket that you listed when configuring CloudWatch.

CloudTrail delivers event logs every 5 minutes to an Amazon S3 bucket that you specify. You can review recent events in the CloudTrail console by visiting Event History, where you can view and download the past 90 days of activity.

You can integrate CloudTrail into applications and automate trail creation for your organization. You can create a CloudTrail *trail* to archive changes to your AWS resources. A trail enables delivery of events to an Amazon S3 bucket you specify. In addition, you can deliver events to the CloudWatch Logs and CloudWatch Events services, and analyze the events there.

CloudTrail log files are stored indefinitely by default. The files are automatically encrypted using Amazon's S3 SSE. You can set up S3 lifecycle configuration rules to delete old logs automatically or move them to Amazon Glacier if you need long-term log storage.

CloudTrail Events

A CloudTrail *event*, which is in the JSON format, is a record of an activity in your AWS account performed by a user, role, or service. CloudTrail events offer a history of both API and non-API account activities. These actions could be from the AWS Management Console, AWS SDKs, CLI, or other AWS services. A trail enables the delivery of Cloud-Trail events to an S3 bucket, CloudWatch logs, or CloudWatch events. You can encrypt the event log files and set up SNS notifications for log file delivery. There are two types of trail events: *management events* and *data events*.

Management Events

Management events track management operations (also called control plane operations) you perform on AWS resources. For example, a management event can relate to configuration of security through an IAM `AttachRolePolicy` API operation or a network routing data configuration rule event (EC2 `CreateSubnet` API operation). Management events also can be non-API events such as when a user signs in to your AWS account, which is logged as the `ConsoleLogin` event.

Data Events

Data events, also called data plane operations, track the operations performed on your AWS resources. For example, a data event can be a `DeleteObject` API operation in Amazon S3. A data event can also be the Invoke API for executing AWS Lambda functions.

AWS Web Application Firewall

AWS WAF protects the applications from common web security exploits such as SQL injection and cross-site scripting. Using WAF, you determine which traffic is allowed or blocked with custom web security rules. WAF pricing is based on the number of rules you deploy and the number of web requests the applications receive.

NOTE   You may deploy AWS WAF on CloudFront, the Application Load Balancer that fronts your web servers, or ElastiCache origin servers running on EC2.

Instead of creating your own set of security rules, you can use the managed rules for AWS WAF, a set of rules provided and managed by the AWS marketplace. These managed rules help secure your web applications and APIs against commons threats such as the OWASP (Open Web Application Security Project) Top 10 security risks and vulnerabilities listed in Common Vulnerabilities and Exposures (CVE).

AWS Certificate Manager

ACM is a service that helps you provision and manage public and private SSL/TLS certificates for using with various AWS services and your AWS resources. The SSL/TLS certificates help secure network communications and establish web site identity over the Internet.

You can request certificates and deploy them on AWS resources such as Elastic Load Balancing and CloudFront distributions and APIs on the API Gateway. ACM also helps create private certificates for your internal use and takes care of the certificate renewals.

Both public and private certificates that you provision through ACM for use with AWS services are free. If you use the ACM Private Certificate Authority, you pay a monthly charge for operating the private CA for the certificates that you issue.

Chapter Review

This chapter provided a thorough review of AWS security topics. You learned about the AWS shared responsibility security model, which explains how AWS and you share the security responsibilities for your AWS resources and AWS services running in the AWS cloud.

AWS Identity and Access Management helps you handle the two key security functions—authentication and authorization—through the creation of IAM principals such as users, groups, and roles, and granting these entities permissions to perform actions on AWS services.

AWS offers several ways to secure your network and storage services. Each of the database services offered by AWS, such as RDS, DynamoDB, and Redshift, provides built-in security measures that you should use.

AWS provides several monitoring tools and services to help you monitor AWS security and resource configuration, such as Amazon Inspector, AWS Config, and AWS CloudTrail.

Exercises

These exercises are designed to teach you how to perform important AWS security-related administrative tasks through the console. If you make a mistake, retrace your steps and ensure that you've correctly performed the steps. You'll know that you've correctly completed the exercise if you achieve the goal set for you in each exercise, such as creating an IAM user.

Exercise 3-1: Create an IAM user from the AWS Management Console.

1. Sign in to the AWS Management Console and open the IAM console at https://console.aws.amazon.com/iam/.

2. Choose Users in the navigation pane, and then choose Add User.

3. Enter the username for the new IAM user (names aren't distinguished by case, and they must be truly unique).

4. Select the type of access you want to grant to the new IAM user. You can select one of the following, or both:

   - **Programmatic Access**   If the user requires access to the API, AWS CLI, or the tools for Windows PowerShell

   - **AWS Management Console**   If the user requires access to the console (this creates the password for the new user)

5. For the Console password type, choose Autogenerated Password or Custom Password. AWS recommends that you choose Require Password Reset to force users to change their password when they sign in the first time.

6. Choose Next:Permissions.

7. On the Set Permissions page, choose how you want to assign permissions to the new user. You must select from one of the following three options:

   - **Add User To Group**   Add the new user to an existing group or choose Create Group to create a group.

   - **Copy Permissions From Existing User**   Copy the group memberships, attached managed policies, embedded inline policies, and any existing permissions boundaries from a current IAM user to the new IAM user.

   - **Attach Existing Policies To User Directly**   Attach an AWS-managed or custom-managed policy to the new user. Or choose Create Policy to create a new policy. AWS recommends, as a best practice, to attach policies to a group and make users members of the appropriate group.
     Optionally, you can set a permissions boundary by opening the Set Permissions Boundary section and choosing Use A Permissions Boundary to set the maximum user permissions.

8. Choose Next:Review to review your choices, and if you're satisfied, choose Create User.

9. Save the new user's access keys (access key ID and secret access key) by choosing Download .csv and saving the file. The new IAM user needs the secret keys to use the AWS API.

Exercise 3-2: Create a new IAM permissions policy from the AWS Management Console.

1. Sign in to the AWS Management Console and open the IAM console at https://console.aws.amazon.com/iam/.

2. Choose Policies in the navigation pane.

3. In the Welcome To Managed policies page, choose Get Started.

4. Choose Create Policy.

5. Choose one of the following options and follow the steps in that option to create the policy:

   - Import Existing Managed Policies
   - Create Policy With The Visual Editor
   - Create Policies In The JSON Tab

After you create the policy, you can attach it to IAM users, groups, or roles.

Exercise 3-3: Create an Administrator IAM user and an Administrators Group from the console (create the group, assign the user to the group).

1. Log into the IAM console as the AWS account root user, using your AWS account e-mail address/password: https://console.aws.amazon.com/iam.

2. Select Users | Add User in the Navigation pane.

3. Type **Administrator** for the User Name.

4. Check the box next to AWS Management Console Access. Select Custom Password and enter a password in the text box.

5. Select Next:Permissions

6. In the Set Permissions page, select Add User To Group.

7. Select Create Group.

8. In the Create Group dialog box, type **Administrators** for Group Name.

9. For Filter Policies, select the check box for AWS Managed – Job Function.

10. In the policy list, select the check box for AdministratorAccess. Then select Create Group.

11. In the list of groups, select the new group (you may have to select Refresh before you see your new group appears in the list).

12. Select Next:Review to see the group memberships AWS IAM grants to the Administrator user. Select Create User.

Exercise 3-4: Create an IAM role.

1. Log into the IAM console as the AWS account root user, using your AWS account e-mail address/password: https://console.aws.amazon.com/iam/.

2. Select Role | Create Role.

3. For Role Type, select Another AWS Account.

4. Under Account ID, enter the AWS account ID for which you want to grant access.

5. Select Next:Permissions.

6. Select an existing AWS-managed or customer-managed policy in your account. Or select Create Policy to create a new policy, as in Exercise 3-2.

7. Select Next:Tagging.

8. Select Next:Review.

9. Under Role Name, type a name for the role (for example: devrole).

10. Review the role and select Create Role.

Exercise 3-5: Disable an IAM user's access keys via the console.

1. Log into the IAM console as the AWS account root user, using your AWS account e-mail address/password: https://console.aws.amazon.com/iam/.

2. Select Users.

3. Select the name of the user and choose the Security Credentials tab.

4. In the Access Keys section, select Make Inactive to disable the active access key.

Questions

The following questions will help you measure your understanding of the material presented in this chapter. Read all the choices carefully because there may be more than one correct answer. Choose all the correct answers for each question.

1. Which of the following AWS services can you use to track and visualize changes made to the resources in your AWS account?

   A. AWS Config

   B. Amazon Inspector

   C. AWS CloudFormation

   D. Amazon CloudTrail

2. When you are in the AWS cloud, which aspects of security is AWS responsible for? (Choose three)

   A. Redundant power supplies

   B. Fire detection and protection

   C. Climate control in the AWS data centers

   D. Database security

3. Which of the following credentials must an IAM user have to be able to log into the AWS Management Console and the AWS Command Line Interface (CLI)? (Choose two)

   A. E-mail address/password combination

   B. Username/password combination

   C. A key pair

   D. Access keys

4. Which of the following does AWS CloudTrail provide?

   A. Information about the incoming IP traffic

   B. Utilization information regarding the AWS resources in your account

   C. A trail of configuration changes made to AWS resources in your account

   D. Logs of the API requests for AWS resources in your account

5. Which of the following IAM permissions policies are standalone policies? (Choose two)

   A. Inline policy

   B. AWS-managed policy

   C. Customer-managed policy

   D. AWS built-in permissions policy

6. Which of the following statements are true regarding a CloudHSM? (Choose two)

   A. You and AWS share the responsibility for managing, monitoring, and maintaining the health of the CloudHSM appliance.

   B. AWS administrators manage, monitor, and maintain the health of a CloudHSM appliance.

   C. AWS initializes and manages the cryptographic domain of the CloudHSM.

   D. You initiate and manage the cryptographic domain of the CloudHSM.

7. Which of the following are AWS account security features? (Choose several)

   A. Key pairs

   B. X-509 certificates

   C. Access keys

   D. AWS Multi-Factor Authentication (MFA)

8. Which of the following aspects of security are your responsibility? (Choose two)

   A. Providing a whitelist of users that can enter an AWS data center

   B. Updating the hypervisors your EC2 instances run on

   C. Configuring security groups to restrict access to EC2 instances

   D. Configuring network ACLs to restrict access to and from the subnets in your Amazon VPC

9. Which of the following statements is/are true in securing Amazon SQS and Amazon SNS?

   A. Both Amazon SQS and Amazon SNS encrypt data-at-rest.

   B. Neither Amazon SQS nor Amazon SNS encrypts data-at-rest.

   C. Amazon SQS encrypts data-at-rest, but Amazon SNS doesn't.

   D. Amazon SNS encrypts data-at-rest, but Amazon SQS doesn't.

10. Which of the following AWS services handles centralized management of authentication and authorization of AWS users?

    A. AWS Security Config

    B. AWS Identity and Access Management service

    C. Amazon Cloud Directory

    D. AWS Key Management Service

11. Which of the following Amazon VPC security features can you implement to protect an RDS instance you're running inside an Amazon VPC? (Choose two)

    A. Security groups

    B. Network ACLs

    C. Key pairs

    D. Encryption with a hardware security module (CloudHSM)

12. Which of the following do you need to use to work with an AWS service from the AWS Command Line Interface (CLI)?

    A. An access key ID and a secret access key

    B. Your e-mail address for the AWS account and a password

    C. Your private key and AWS's public key

    D. Secret access ID and secret access key

13. Which of the following can you do to protect data-at-rest inside an Amazon DynamoDB database?

    A. AWS-provided Server-Side Encryption (SSE)

    B. Secure Socket Layer (SSL) connections

    C. Appropriate AWS IAM permissions policies

    D. Client-side encryption that you perform

14. Which of the following will enable you to send traffic security from your local data center network to your AWS resources within your Amazon VPC (in other words, what type of gateway can you use on the VPC)?

    A. Virtual private gateway

    B. Internet gateway

    C. Gateway VPC endpoints

    D. NAT gateway

15. Which of the following are AWS security best practices for securing AWS accounts? (Choose three)

    A. Creating individual IAM users and not using the root AWS account for routine work

    B. Requiring Multi-Factor Authentication (MFA) for root access

    C. Sharing AWS credentials to ensure secure cross-account access

    D. Disabling remote login for the root user

16. Which of the following does Amazon CloudTrail track and record?

    A. Flow of IP traffic passing through all the network interfaces in your VPC

    B. Configuration changes to AWS resources owned by you

    C. Resource utilization patterns for AWS resources owned by you

    D. All API request activity, such as who made the call, the time of the call, and the change made by the call

17. Which of the following is true when using AWS Identity and Access Management?

    A. All IAM members belong to a default user group if you don't place them in a custom group.

    B. An IAM user can be a member of a single group only.

    C. IAM roles can be members of a group.

    D. You can grant roles to a group or a member of a group.

18. Which feature of an Amazon VPC can you use to control network traffic flowing to an Amazon EC2 instance that lives in an Amazon VPC, based on the source IP address and port number?

    A. Main route table

    B. Security groups

    C. Subnets

    D. Network access controls lists (ACLs)

19. Which of the following statements are true regarding network access control lists and security groups? (Choose two)

    A. Subnets use network access control lists to control the network traffic flowing into and out of the subnet.

    B. EC2 instances use network access control lists to control the traffic flowing into and out of an EC2 instance.

    C. Subnets use security groups to control the network traffic flowing into and out of the subnets.

    D. EC2 instances use security groups to control the network traffic flowing into and out of the EC2 instances.

20. Which of the following logs does Amazon CloudWatch store? (Choose three)

    A. EC2 operating system logs

    B. AWS CloudTrail logs

    C. Amazon VPC logs

    D. Amazon RDS login activity logs

21. Which AWS monitoring and security tool performs automated security assessments to enhance the security and compliance of applications and operating systems that you deploy on Amazon EC2 instances?

    A. AWS Trusted Advisor

    B. Amazon Inspector

    C. Amazon Config

    D. Amazon Secure

22. Which of the following types of Multi-Factor Authentication (MFA) devices can you use for the AWS IAM service? (Choose three)

    A. Amazon Simple Message Service (SMS) via mobile devices such as smartphones

    B. Hardware devices such as Gemalto

    C. Virtual MFA applications such as Microsoft Authenticator or Google Authenticator

    D. Amazon Simple Queue Service (SQS)

23. Which of the following does Amazon CloudFront require as query string parameters in a request for content from the service?

    A. Valid policy documents only

    B. Matching signatures only

    C. Valid policy documents and matching signatures

    D. Valid policy documents, matching signatures, and an origin access identity

24. Which of the following are ways to control access to Amazon S3 buckets and objects? (Choose three)

   A. Identity and Access Management (IAM) policies

   B. Access control lists (ACLs)

   C. Security groups

   D. Bucket policies

25. Which of the following does the AWS Security Token Service (STS) help you do? (Choose two)

   A. Users who sign in with an identity provider can obtain temporary security credentials from AWS STS.

   B. You can use AWS STS to request temporary credentials when calculating the signature for your requests to the DynamoDB service.

   C. STS enables you to grant temporary security credentials for the new IAM users that you create.

   D. STS enables you to create fine-grained access controls for Amazon DynamoDB.

Answers

   1. A. AWS Config enables you to track and visualize changes in resources.

   2. A, B, C. AWS is responsible for the security of its cloud infrastructure. This includes the provision of redundant power supplies to ensure uninterrupted power, fire detection and protection, as well as climate control at the AWS data centers.

   3. B, D. IAM users need an IAM username and password to log into the AWS Management Console. IAM users also require access keys to work with AWS services through the AWS CLI.

   4. D. AWS CloudTrail logs all API requests made to all the AWS resources in your AWS account.

   5. B, C. Both AWS-managed and customer-managed policies are standalone policies.

   6. B, D. B is correct because the AWS administrators are responsible for managing and monitoring and maintaining the health of a CloudHSM appliance. **D** is correct because you initiate and manage the cryptographic domain of the CloudHSM.

   7. A, B, C, D. All four of the choices are AWS account security features.

   8. C, D. You are fully responsible for creating both security groups for controlling access to your EC2 instances, and configuring network ACLs for controlling traffic flowing into and out of the subnets in your Amazon VPC. AWS doesn't secure your VPC, subnets, EC2 instances, and services such as databases that you install and run on those instances.

   9. C. You can configure SQS to encrypt messages stored in the SQS queues, but SQS does not encrypt data-at-rest.

10. **B.** AWS Identity and Access Management (IAM) service helps you manage authentication and authorization of AWS users through the provision of identities (principals) and permissions policies that control the actions the identities can perform on your AWS resources.

11. **A, B. A** is correct because you can configure rules in a security group to control traffic to the EC2 instances that host the RDS database instances. **B** is correct because network ACLs help you control the traffic flow to and from the subnet in which the EC2 instances are running.

12. **A.** You need an access key ID and a secret access key to work with AWS services from the AWS CLI.

13. **D.** You must perform client-side encryption of the data-at-rest in an Amazon DynamoDB database to protect sensitive data. DynamoDB doesn't support SSE.

14. **A.** To transmit data securely from your local data center network to your resources inside an Amazon VPC, you must use a virtual private gateway. All other gateways mentioned here aren't designed for safe and protected transmission of data.

15. **A, B, D.** Not using the root AWS account for performing routine tasks, requiring Multi-Factor Authentication for the root user, and disabling remote login capability for the root user are all part of AWS-recommended best practices for securing your AWS account.

16. **D.** Amazon CloudTrail records all API calls made to all AWS resources in your account. The information includes the identity of the user that made the API call, the day and time when the API call was made, and the specific changes made by the API call.

17. **D.** You can grant roles to an IAM group or to individual members of a group.

18. **D.** Network access controls lists (ACLs) enable you to control network traffic based on IP address and port number.

19. **A, D. A** is correct because you configure a network ACL to control network traffic flowing into and out of a subnet in your VPC. **D** is correct because you configure a security group to control the network traffic going into and out an EC2 instance.

20. **A, B, C.** Amazon CloudWatch stores the EC2 OS logs, AWS CloudTrail logs, and the Amazon VPC logs. It doesn't store any database login activity related logs.

21. **B.** Amazon Inspector uses a vulnerability database to check for known security vulnerabilities by performing automatic security assessment of the applications and operating systems that you deploy on Amazon EC2 instances.

22. **A, B, C.** You can use the Amazon SMS, a hardware device, or a virtual MFA application such as the Microsoft Authenticator to provide MFA.

23. **C.** A request for content from Amazon CloudFront must have valid policy documents and matching signatures as two of the query parameters for the service to honor the request.

24. A, B, D. IAM policies, ACLs (permissions policies), and bucket policies are all valid ways to control access to buckets and objects in Amazon S3.

25. A, B. A is correct because AWS STS returns temporary AWS credentials to applications that sign in to an identity provider. **B** is correct because AWS STS also grants you temporary security credentials to calculate the signature that you must provide to sign your requests to Amazon DynamoDB.

Computing in the Cloud: AWS Compute Services and Amazon EC2

In this chapter, you will

- Learn what Amazon Elastic Compute Cloud (EC2) can do
- Understand how to use an Amazon Machine Image (AMI), a template you use to create and run (launch) an EC2 instance
- Learn how to choose and purchase the best AMI instance types
- Learn about the four different types of storage that you can use with EC2 instances
- Learn about the importance of the root device volume
- Be exposed to EC2 features
- Learn how to monitor your EC2 instances
- Learn how to tag your EC2 resources
- Understand EC2 configuration options

Amazon Elastic Compute Cloud (EC2) is a highly reliable web service that enables you to build fault-resistant applications, fully control your computing resources, and provision new server instances in minutes, to scale your infrastructure both up and down. AWS EC2 offers a service level agreement commitment with 99.99 percent availability for each EC2 region. You pay only for the capacity that you use.

Because AWS offers a variety of compute services, I've devoted two chapters to discussing the key offerings. This chapter focuses on EC2, while the next chapter explains the following key AWS compute services:

- **AWS ECS**   Containers
- **AWS Lambda**   Run code without provisioning or managing servers
- **Amazon Lightsail**   Virtual private server instance
- **AWS Batch**   Run batch computing jobs on AWS
- **AWS Elastic Beanstalk**   Deploy and scale web applications and services

Let's start off our discussion of AWS compute services with Amazon EC2.

What Is Amazon Elastic Compute Cloud?

Amazon EC2 is a web service that offers resizable computing capacity in the form of EC2 *instances*, which are the equivalent of virtual servers. With EC2, you can obtain and boot new server instances in minutes and easily scale capacity up and down as your computing needs change over time. AWS enables you to increase or decrease the number of running instances seamlessly.

Because of Amazon's mammoth scale, you reap the benefits of low costs for your servers. You can use EC2 for running databases, web servers, and enterprise applications, as well as for migrating your computing from your on-premise environments to the cloud. In EC2, you control the server, OS, and the deployment software. So, if you need to apply an operating system patch, you, and not AWS, is responsible for it. AWS will maintain the infrastructure that hosts your EC2 instances.

You can commission large numbers of instances, paying only for what you use. AWS provides a wide range of EC2 instance types that cater to various use cases and offer multiple ways of payment. For example, AWS offers lower prices for instances that you reserve ahead of time and for *spot instances*, in which you specify a bid price for instances and areas assigned the instances.

Amazon Machine Images

Because Amazon Machine Images (AMIs) are the source of the EC2 instances that you create, it's important that you first understand AMIs. An AMI is a template that you use to create and run (launch) an EC2 instance. Once you launch the EC2 instance, you can connect to it and work with it just as you would on any other Linux server. You can do the following with an AMI:

- Launch multiple instances from a single AMI.
- Copy an AMI to a different availability zone (AZ) or multiple AZs within the same AWS region or to a different AWS region.
- Use AMI in EC2 Auto Scaling.
- Share the AMI with different AWS accounts.
- Sell an AMI in the AWS Marketplace.

An AMI includes the following three key components:

- A template for the root volume of the instance, such as the one that hosts an OS or an application server, or some other application.
- Permissions that control which AWS accounts can launch instances with an AMI.
- A block device mapping scheme that specifies which storage volumes will be attached to an instance when you launch it.

You hear about AMIs usually in the context of creating and running EC2 instances. However, it's important to understand that an AMI may contain more than just an OS.

It may contain an application server, for example, on top of the OS. It all depends on the AMI you choose to launch the EC2 instance from.

There's a one-to-many relationship between an AMI and an instance that you generate from that AMI. This means that you can launch any number of instances from the same AMI. The AMI contains the definition and configuration of each instance (which is a virtual server) that you launch, connect to, and work with in the cloud.

Obtaining an AMI

There are multiple ways to obtain an AMI.

- AWS publishes AMIs with common software configurations.
- You can purchase AMIs from third parties. For example, Red Hat Linux offers AMIs that also come with service contracts if you need them.
- You can buy a custom AMI from another EC2 user.

The AWS developer community publishes custom AMIs, or *shared AMIs*, since developers create them with various components and make them available to other developers. You can further customize a shared AMI to suit your needs. You can also share any AMIs that you create. Developers can sell their AMIs by placing them on the AWS Marketplace, an online store that offers software for AWS. An AMI that you can purchase from a developer is called a *paid AMI*.

 CAUTION   Shared AMIs don't come with an AWS assurance of integrity or security, so you use them at your own risk.

You can create your own AMIs that contain custom software and configurations. For example, you can launch an instance from an existing Amazon Linux AMI, install a PostgreSQL database on a 64-bit Amazon Linux instance, and save the updated configuration as a custom AMI. You can make the AMI shareable within a set of AWS accounts that you specify. Alternatively, you can make the AMI public, so the entire community can use it.

 NOTE   You can easily tell an AWS AMI, since they have the name *Amazon* in the account field as an aliased owner. Only AWS can alias an AMI.

Selecting an AMI

You can select an AMI based on several characteristics, as summarized here:

- **Provider**   Select an AMI offered by AWS, Oracle, IBM, Microsoft, or the community.
- **Region**   Select any AWS region that's available to you; you can launch the instance here.

- **Operating system**   Select Linux or Windows.
- **Architecture**   Select a 32-bit (i386) or 64-bit (x86-64) architecture.
- **Launch permissions**   The owner of an AMI specifies the launch permissions, which determine its availability. Launch permissions can be public, implicit, or explicit.
  - A *public* launch permission means any AWS account can launch those AMIs.
  - An *explicit* launch permission grants permission to specific AWS accounts.
  - An *implicit* launch permission means that only the owner can launch EC2 instances from that AMI.
- **Storage for the root device**   An AMI can be Amazon Elastic Block Storage (EBS)-backed, or instance store–backed. (Because this is an important aspect of choosing an AMI, I discuss this characteristic in a separate section.)

Not all instance compute families are available for all AMIs. The CPU family availability is determined by the AMI that you choose.

On the EC2 console, you can search for an AMI on the images page or from the Quick Start tab. When launching an instance, you can choose the instance from the Choose An Amazon Machine Image (AMI) page during the launch process. When launching an instance from the command line, you can first find the image you want to use by running a command such as the following:

```
$ aws ec2 describe-images –owners self amazon
```

The attribute `self` will show the AMIs owned by you, and the attribute `amazon` shows the AMIs owned by Amazon. As mentioned, all Amazon public images have the aliased owner named amazon.

 NOTE   An AMI is tied to the region where its files are located within Amazon S3—that is, AMI IDs are unique to each region. However, you can copy an AMI from one region to another. You can use the `CopyImage` API to do this (make sure you remove the launch permissions and user-defined tags).

The following `aws ec2` command will list all public AMIs:

```
$ aws ec2 describe-images –executable-users all
```

You can save the AMI ID you want to use and specify it when launching an instance from the command line with the `launch-instance` command.

Using a Custom AMI to Launch Instances

To use a custom AMI to create instances, do the following:

1. Create the AMI.
2. Register the AMI.
3. Launch the instance from the AMI.

4. Deregister the AMI. Once you deregister an AMI, you can't create anymore instances with it. However, all instances that you've you launched with this AMI will continue running unaffected.

NOTE The Amazon Linux AMI is a Linux image offered by AWS at no additional cost to the EC2 user. It offers repository access to multiple versions of MySQL, Python, Tomcat, and other applications and software. This AMI contains the AWS CLI, the Amazon EC2 API, and other AWS tools that help you work with AWS services.

Backing the AMI: EBS or Instance Store

An AMI can be backed either by Amazon Elastic Block Store (EBS) or by an instance store. Amazon EBS provides persistent block storage volumes in the AWS cloud. When you launch an instance with an AMI, the instance's root device will be based on the AMI's root device type. The Amazon EBS-backed root device for an instance that you launch from an EBS-backed instance is an Amazon EBS volume created from an Amazon EBS snapshot. The root device for an instance you launch from an instance store–backed AMI will be an instance store volume created from a template stored in Amazon S3.

AWS recommends that you use EBS-backed AMIs, since they launch faster and use persistent storage. Data on any instance store volume will persist only during the life of the instance. If the instance fails or terminates, all data on an instance store volume is deleted.

TIP You can stop and restart EBS-backed EC2 instances. You can't stop or restart instance store–backed instance. These instances are either running or terminated.

An instance that you launch with an EBS-backed AMI will launch faster than an instance launched with an instance store–backed AMI. With an EBS-backed AMI, only the boot-related components are retrieved from the snapshot when launching an instance. Since the state of the instance is stored in an EBS volume, restarts are faster as well.

NOTE Because AWS replicates each Amazon EBS volume automatically within its AZ, you're protected against component failures and gain high availability and durability for your storage. EBS volumes also offer consistent low-latency performance.

Finding the Root Device Type of an AMI

You can find the type of an AMI from the console, as explained in Exercise 4-1, or from the command line with the `aws ec2 describe-images` command:

```
$ aws ec2 describe-images --image-ids ami-e251209a
    {
        "ImageId": "ami-e251209a",
        "Name": "amzn-ami-hvm-2018.03.0.20180508-x86_64-gp2",
        "Description": "Amazon Linux AMI 2018.03.0.20180508 x86_64 HVM GP2",
    ...
```

```
        "RootDeviceType": "ebs",
    ...
        "VirtualizationType": "hvm"
}
$
```

The output reveals, among other things, that this AMI is the EBS-backed type:

```
("RootDeviceType": "ebs")
```

NOTE   When you use an instance store–based AMI, AWS charges you for the AMI storage. When you an EBS-backed AMI, you're charged for the AMI as well as for volume storage. AWS charges you for volume storage even after you stop the instance.

Linux AMI Virtualization Types

You use an AMI to launch a virtual instance. There are two types of AMI virtualization, depending on the boot mechanism and special hardware extensions that offer enhanced performance:

- **Hardware virtual machine (HVM)**   Enables you to run an OS directly on the VM, just as you would run it on bare-metal hardware. The host server emulates the hardware it presents to the guest server (VM). HVM virtualization makes use of hardware extensions that enhance performance, such as the CPU virtualization extension. All instance types (described later in the chapter) support HVM virtualization.

- **Paravirtual (PV)**   Enables instances (guests) to run on hardware that doesn't formally support virtualization. The drawback, however, is that the guests can't use special hardware extensions such as GPU processing. Only some instance types such as the C3 current generation type support PV AMIs.

TIP   As an AWS best practice, you should use an HVM AMI instead of a PV AMI.

Creating a Linux AMI from the Command Line

As mentioned, you can create an EBS-backed or an instance store–backed AMI. In this section, I first explain how to create an EBS-backed AMI.

Creating an EBS-Backed Linux AMI

You can create an EBS-backed Linux AMI in one of two ways:

- Create it from an EC2 instance that you've launched from another Amazon EBS-backed Linux AMI.

- Create an AMI from a snapshot of the root device volume of an instance.

You can create the AMI using both techniques either from the EC2 console or from the command line.

Creating an EBS-Backed AMI from an EC2 Instance   The first step in creating an EBS-backed AMI is to launch an instance off an AMI that's similar to the AMI that you want to create. You can customize the instance, and then AWS automatically registers the Amazon EBS-backed AMI that you create. You can then use this AMI to launch new instances that contain your customizations.

To make sure that the instance is consistent, you must stop the instance before creating the AMI from it. If you don't, EC2 powers down the instance before creating the AMI. You can choose to specify that EC2 not reboot the instance, especially if you're using a file system such as XFS, which lets you safely create an image off a running instance.

EC2 makes snapshots of the instance's root volume and other EBS volumes that are attached to the instance. Since these snapshots could sometimes take a long time (from a few minutes up to 24 hours) to complete, it's a good idea to create the snapshots of your EBS volumes before creating the AMI. When you do this, EC2 needs to make just incremental snapshots of the volumes before creating the AMI.

You'll have the new AMI and a snapshot of the root volume at the end of the AMI creation process. When you launch an instance with this new AMI, AWS creates an EBS volume for the new instance's root volume, using the snapshot.

It's a good practice to initialize both the root volume and any additional EBS volumes when you launch an instance for the first time from an EBS-backed AMI. Although a new EBS volume offers maximum performance from the time it's available to the instance, you must initialize the EBS volumes that you restore from a snapshot to avoid a performance hit. Volume performance may drop below 50 percent of the expected level and may result in the volume showing a warning state in the I/O performance status check. The performance hit is in the form of an increase in the I/O latency the first time you access data blocks on a block.

On a Linux system, you can use the dd (available by default) or fio (you must install it, but it's much faster than dd) utility to read all the blocks on the device, as shown here:

```
$ sudo dd if=/dev/xvdf of=/dev/null bs=1M
$ sudo fio --filename=/dev/xvdf --rw=read --bs=128k --iodepth=32
--ioengine=libaio --direct=1 --name=volume-initialize
```

You initialize the volume by pulling down the data from S3 and writing it to the volume. You do this by reading all the blocks on the volume before using the volume.

 EXAM TIP   Know when you must initialize an EBS volume. You need to initialize an EBS volume only if you've restored it from a snapshot. New EBS volumes don't require initialization.

If there are instance-store volumes or EBS volumes that you've attached to the instance (in addition to the root device volume), the block device mapping for the new AMI and the block device mappings for the instance that you launch from the new AMI will contain information about those volumes. The instance-store volumes for the new instances are new, but the data on the EBS volumes will persist.

Exercise 4-3 asks you to create a Linux AMI from an instance using the EC2 console. From the command line, execute the `ec2 create-image` command to create an AMI from a running or stopped EBS-backed instance, as shown here:

```
$ aws ec2 create-image --instance-id i-1234567890abcdef0 --name "My server"
--description "An AMI for my server" —no-reboot
```

The `no-reboot` option keeps the instance from being rebooted before the image is created.

The `ec2 create-image` command generates output similar to the following:

```
{
    "ImageId": "ami-98234e"
}
```

Use this AMI ID to launch your instance.

You can copy an AMI within or across an AWS region. Copying an AMI will create an identical AMI, but with a different AMI ID.

Creating a Linux AMI from a Snapshot   You can also create an AMI from a snapshot of the root device volume of an instance from the AWS Management Console or the command line. From the console, in the EC2 Dashboard, choose Elastic Block Store | Snapshots | Actions | Create Image, and enter the relevant values in the Create Image from EBS Snapshot page. Then click Create to create the AMI.

You can also run the `register-image` command from the AWS CLI to create an AMI from a snapshot. You specify the snapshot by specifying values for the `-block-device-mapping` attribute in the `register-image` command.

Creating an Instance Store–Backed Linux AMI

You create an instance store–backed Linux AMI after launching an instance and bundling the volume and registering a new AMI. The bundling process results in an image manifest (image.manifest.xml) and a set of files (image.part.*xx*) that contain a template for the root volume.

Once you create the bundle, you must upload it to an S3 bucket. When you launch an instance with the new AMI that you've created, EC2 creates the root volume for the instance using this bundle. The block device mappings for the new AMI that you've created, and the instances that you launch from that AMI, contain information about any additional instance store volumes that exist along with the root device volume.

Copying an AMI

You can copy an AMI within or across an AWS region. Copying an AMI across regions that are geographically distant from each other helps both scalability and high availability and facilitates consistent deployment across the globe. If you have an EC2 instance running in the us-east-1a region, for example, and you want to provide disaster recovery support by creating a similar instance in Europe, you can do so by creating an AMI of the US-based instance, copying the AMI to the EU region, and launching the instance from the EU AMI.

EXAM TIP You should understand how copying an AMI helps you run similar EC2 instances within or across AWS regions. You can also change the AZ in which an instance runs by creating an AMI of the running instance and launching the instance in a different AZ. You can't simply stop an instance and change its AZ, because by default, any AMIs that you create aren't available across all regions and all AZs.

Note the following about copying AMIs:

- You can copy both EBS-backed and instance store–backed AMIs.
- You can copy encrypted AMIs.
- You can copy AMIs with encrypted snapshots.
- You can copy an unencrypted source AMI to an encrypted target AMI, an unencrypted source AMI to an encrypted target AMI, and an unencrypted source AMI to an unencrypted target AMI. However, you can't copy an encrypted source AMI to an unencrypted target AMI.

EXAM TIP Understand the nature of permissions when using an AMI. Because the copy process doesn't copy the launch permissions, any tags that you may have defined, or the Amazon S3 bucket permissions, you must apply these permissions and tags to the new AMI. Thus, if User A shares an AMI created in the us-east region from that user's account with User B, when User A copies the AMI to the us-west region, User B can't automatically access the copied AMI in User A's account. Because copying an AMI doesn't automatically copy the permissions on the AMI, you must do this manually.

You can also share an AMI with another AWS account by copying an AMI. This is called a *cross-account AMI copy*. The original owner of the AMI continues to remain the owner of a shared AMI and is charged for storing the target AMI in the destination region.

EXAM TIP The certification exam asks several questions about AWS pricing. One of them may concern the charges for data transfers between EC2 instances running in different regions. AWS charges such data transfers at Internet data transfer rates.

With this background of AMIs, let's turn to managing EC2 instances, which are at the heart of the AWS compute services.

Launching an EC2 Instance

Launching an instance lets you create an EC2 instance from an AMI and start it up. You can launch an instance from the command line or from the EC2 console or by using AWS CloudFormation. CloudFormation enables you to create your infrastructure *stacks* through templates, similar to how you do so with a configuration management tool such as Puppet or Chef. In production settings, where you may need to launch and manage multiple virtual servers, the command line is better, since it enables you to script the commands.

EXAM TIP The exam will almost certainly quiz you on your understanding of the difference between using a local instance store and the Amazon EBS for storing the root device of an EC2 instance. You can store the root device data on EBS or a local instance store. If you choose EBS, data on the root device will persist independent from the instance's lifecycle. You can therefore start and stop the instance. The local instance store persists only during the instance's life. When would you do this? You choose a local instance store when you aren't storing any data to the root device. A local instance store offers a cheaper way to launch instances since you don't have to pay for any EBS devices to store the root device data. If you're running large web sites where each instance is a clone, the local instance store is a smart way to go.

If you're starting out with AWS, you can take advantage of the *AWS Free Tier*, which enables you to launch and use a micro instance (such as T2) for 12 months. This instance will have a small amount of RAM (1 GB), CPU (one virtual CPU), and disk storage (20Gb). The t2.micro instance is the lowest cost (currently, $0.0058 per hour) Amazon EC2 instance option and is ideal for many applications such as microservices, development, small databases, and code repositories. This instance is sufficient for you to learn everything you need about EC2 instances. If you decide to launch a non-free tier instance, you'll be charge standard usage fees for the instance.

You can launch an instance in multiple ways:

- Use an AMI via the Launch Instance Wizard or from the command line.
- Create a *launch template* with the configuration information to launch an instance, so you don't have to specify the launch parameters for every instance launch. A launch template will contain the AMI ID and instance and network settings for launching an instance.
- Launch an instance from an existing EC2 instance. Click the Launch More Like This button in the EC2 console to use the instance as the basis for a new instance. This option replicates some configuration data from the source instance but doesn't clone the instance. If you need an exact copy of a current instance, create an AMI first, and then launch instances from that AMI.
- Launch an instance from the backup you make of an EC2 instance. Create a backup of the root device volume of an EBS-backed Linux instance by creating a snapshot. This, however, only enables you to launch a new instance using the same image as the AMI that launched the original instance. The snapshot doesn't copy the data and software from the source database.

Exercise 4-4 shows the steps for launching an instance based on an AMI via the EC2 console. Alternatively, you can use the `ec2 run-instances` command to launch a new instance from the command line:

```
$ aws ec2 run-instances –image-id ami-31394949 –instance-type t2.micro –
security-group-id my_sg_group
{
    "Instances": [
        {
            "RootDeviceName": "/dev/xvda",
            "State": {
                "Name": "pending",
...
"PrivateIpAddresses": [
                {
                    "PrivateIpAddress": "172.31.44.100",
                    "PrivateDnsName": "ip-172-31-44-100.us-west-2.
compute.internal",

                    ...
                    "InstanceId": "i-0e31e181430530f03",
}
$
```

This command will launch an EC2 instance based on the AMI ID that I provided (ami-31394949), within the security group my_sg_group. Note the instance ID (`Instance-Id": "i-0e31e181430530f03`), which you'll need for managing the instance, such as stopping and restarting it from the command line.

 NOTE   An instance is tied to the AZ where you launch it.

The `ec2 run-instances` command comes with numerous options and parameters. Here I show how to run the command with just a few of the options and parameters to illustrate how to use the command. As soon as you execute this command, AWS swings into action, initializing and starting the new instance.

When you launch an instance, it is given a public DNS name by AWS. You can use this public IP address to connect to the instance from the Internet, via PuTTY or another Secure Shell (SSH) client. In addition to the pubic IP address, AWS also gives each instance a private DNS name. Instances within an Amazon Virtual Private Cloud (VPC) can connect to other instances via this private DNS name. Chapter 2 explains how to connect to a Linux instance via SSH.

 EXAM TIP   The certification test often includes one or more questions that test your knowledge of the EC2 instance lifecycle. Know the difference between running, stopped, and terminated instances. AWS bills you for EC2 instance usage only when the instances are in the running state. Stopped or terminated instances don't cost you anything while they're in that state.

Troubleshooting EC2 Instances

You may run into various types of problems with EC2 instances. I review several typical problems in this section.

Instance Launch Issues

You may receive the following types of errors when launching an instance (a new or a restarted instance):

- **InstanceLimitExceeded**   This error means that you've reached the limit on the number of EV2 instances that you can launch in a region. AWS sets default limits on the instances that you can run in a region.

- **InsufficientInstanceCapacity**   You receive this error when AWS EC2 doesn't have sufficient On-Demand instances to fulfill your request in an AZ. You can resolve this error by waiting for a few minutes and resubmitting your request, submitting a request with a reduced number of instances, or purchasing *reserved instances* (a way to reserve capacity long-term).

- **Instance moves from the PENDING to the TERMINATED state**   If an instance is terminating soon after you start it, you may have reached your EBS volume limit, you may have a corrupt EBS snapshot, or you may not have the permission to access the Key Management Service (KMS) key to decrypt an encrypted root volume. If it's an instance store–backed AMI that you're launching your instance with, the AMI may be missing an image.part.*xx* file.

 NOTE   Security groups are *stateful*. This means that if you send out a request from an instance, the responses to that request are allowed to flow into the instance, regardless of your inbound security group rules. Similarly, responses to allowed inbound traffic are allowed to flow out, irrespective of the outbound security group rules.

Connection Issues

Following are some typical connection-related issues and error messages that you're likely to encounter.

Network Error: Connection Timed Out or Error Connecting To   These types of instance connection errors result from improperly configured security group rules and route tables. You can do the following to handle these errors:

- Check your security group rules to ensure that they include a rule that allows inbound traffic from your public IPv4 address on the correct port.

- Check that a rule allows traffic from your computer to port 22 (SSH) for Linux servers.

- Check that the route table for the subnet has a route that sends all traffic destined to go to hosts outside your VPC to the Internet gateway for your VPC.

- Check the network access control list (NACL) for the subnet in which the instance is running. The NACL must permit inbound and outbound traffic from your local IP address on the proper port. (I explain NACL in Chapter 6.)

- Check to ensure that your internal firewall allows inbound/outbound traffic from your server on port 22 for Linux servers and port 3389 for Windows servers.

- Ensure that the instance has a public IPv4 address, or associate an elastic IP (EIP) address with the instance.

- Check the CPU load on the EC2 instance to ensure it isn't overloaded.

User Key Not Recognized by Server Error   When you try to connect to an instance with a key that the server doesn't recognize, you see the following at the end of the error message:

```
Permission denied (publickey)
```

You must verify that your private key (.pem) has been converted to the correct format (.ppk), if you're using PuTTY to connect to the instance. Also, verify that you're using the correct username for the AMI. For example, for Amazon Linux AMI, the username is ec2-user, and for an Ubuntu AMI, the username is ubuntu. You can also receive the following error messages when connecting with the wrong username for your AMI:

```
Server refused our key
No supported authentication methods available
```

Username-Related Errors   If you get errors such as the following, you need to verify that you are attempting the connection with the correct username for the AMI, and that you're specifying the correct private key (.pem) file for the instance. Common errors when you don't use the right username and the correct private key file include the following:

```
Host key not found
Permission denied (publickey)
Authentication failed
Permission denied
```

 EXAM TIP   Review the various types of error messages in this section, as the certification exam may ask you about the reasons why you would receive a specific error message (such as an "Unprotected Private Key File" error message) when trying to connect to an EC2 instance. Questions may also quiz you about your knowledge of the fixes for the various types of errors.

Unprotected Private Key File Error   You must protect your private key file so other users can't read or write to it. If you use open file permissions such as 0777 (which allows anyone to read/write to the file), SSH ignores your key files because of its insecure permission level. You should set the file permissions to 044 so that you can SSH to your instances using a private key file.

Ping Failures   You may experience two types of ping failures: you may be unable to ping your EC2 instance or to issue a `ping` command from the instance. Since the `ping` command is a type of ICMP traffic, you must ensure that for the first type of failure, you configure the inbound security group rules to allow ICMP traffic for the `Echo request` message either from all sources or from a specific instance. Similarly, you must configure the outbound security group rules to allow ICMP traffic for the `Echo Request` message to the instance you are trying to ping.

Another situation in which you may not be able to ping an instance successfully is when you patch the OS of an instance and issue a `reboot` command from the OS. You may find that you aren't able to ping the instance's public IP address successfully following this, even after several minutes. This could be due to the OS patching causing a problem with the instance's network interface card (NIC) driver.

Instance Stopping and Termination Issues

If your instance takes a long time to come out of the stopping state after you stop the instance, you can force the instance to stop from the console or from the AWS CLI with this command:

```
aws ec2 stop-instance –instance-ids <instance-id> –force
```

You can create a replacement instance from the AMI of a stuck instance and launch another instance from the AMI that you create. You can do this from the EC2 console by going to Instances | Actions | Image | Create Image | No Reboot. You can also do this from the command line with the following pair of commands:

```
$ aws ec2 create-image --instance-id i-0123ab456c789d01e --name "AMI"
--description "AMI for replacement instance" --no-reboot
$ aws ec2 run-instances --image-id ami-1a2b3c4d --count 1 --instance-type
c3.large --key-name MyKeyPair --security-groups MySecurityGroup
```

Once the new instance is running, you can terminate the stuck instance with the `terminate-instance` AWS CLI command.

If the instance stays a long time in the shutting-down state, it could be due to the shutdown scripts being still run by the instance. It could also result from issues with the server on which the instance (VM) is running. If the instance remains in this state for several hours, EC2 considers the instance stuck and terminates it.

Instance Recovery Failures

An automatic instance recovery can fail due to the following reasons:

- The instance has reached the maximum of three recovery attempts per day.
- An ongoing Service Health dashboard event may prevent the recovery process from running.
- There may be a temporary lack of replacement hardware.

Instances with Failed Status Checks

An instance may show a failed status check for numerous reasons. Instance checks monitor the software and the hardware of an EC2 instance. Thus, a loss of network connectivity, system power, or software issues on the physical host of the instance won't mark the instance's state as *failed*. An incompatible kernel, however, can mark the instance state as failed. You can investigate these failures from the EC2 console or retrieve the system logs and look for errors.

You can create a CloudWatch recovery alarm that automatically recovers failed instances. If the instance is using an EBS-backed AMI, you can try restarting the instance; if it's using an instance store–backed AMI, you can terminate the instance and launch a new instance. If your instance is part of an Auto Scaling group, the EC2 Auto Scaling service automatically launches an instance to replace the failed instance.

When AWS detects an irreparable failure in the hardware that hosts an instance, it schedules the instance for retirement by a scheduled retirement date, on which the instance is stopped or terminated by AWS. If the root device of the retired instance is an EBS volume, you can restart it any time, at which point the instance moves to new hardware. If the instance's root device is an instance store volume, you cannot restart that instance after retirement. Here's a typical notification from AWS about a pending retirement of an instance:

```
EC2 has detected degradation of the underlying hardware hosting your Amazon
EC2 instance (instance-ID: i-011739f6fff4f1a69) associated with your AWS
account (AWS Account ID: 321938868864) in the us-west-2 region. Due to this
degradation your instance could already be unreachable. We will stop your
instance after 2019-03-14 14:00 UTC.
```

Listing Your Instances from the CLI

AWS CLI's ec2 describe-instances command shows details about one or more of your instances. If you issue the command ec2 describe-instances without specifying any instance IDs, EC2 will show you details about all your instances. Obviously, if you have more than just a couple of instances, this could prove to be too much information. Therefore, it's a good idea to specify one or more instance IDs.

Here's an example using the ec2 describe-instances command:

```
$ aws ec2 describe-instances --instance-ids i-1234567890abcdef0
```

Remember several important things about the describe-instances command:

- The results of the command may show instances that were terminated in the last hour.
- The command will fail if you attempt to describe instances for an AZ that's undergoing service disruption.

The EC2 Instance Lifecycle

Once you launch an instance from an AMI through the EC2 console, the CLI, or via CloudFormation, the instance transitions sequentially through the following states:

1. Pending
2. Running
3. Shutting-down
4. Terminated
5. Stopping
6. Stopped

The state of the instance determines whether you can restart the instance and whether you get to keep the storage volumes you assigned to the instance. Let's review the lifecycle of an instance, starting with its launch.

EXAM TIP Know how your workload and the features that you select for an instance determine the scaling of the number of instances. If your workload is variable and you configure Auto Scaling and Elastic Load Balancing, you can automatically scale your EC2 instances (up or down). On the other hand, if your workload is growing gradually, you can consider moving to a larger instance type to handle the workload.

The Pending and Running States

When you launch an instance, it starts in the pending state. After a couple of minutes, the instance moves into the running state, at which point you can connect to the instance. AWS starts billing you for an instance once the instance enters the running state. From here on, until you either stop or terminate the instance, you're billed for every second the instance remains in the running state. This is true even if you aren't connected to the instance.

TIP Once an instance is in the running state, billing starts and won't stop until you terminate or stop the instance. Billing won't stop simply because you log out of the instance. Therefore, be sure to stop (or terminate) instances you aren't using to prevent unnecessary billing.

Stopping, Rebooting, and Terminating an Instance

After you have launched an instance, it's running and will continue to do so until you do one of two things: stop it or terminate it. There are major differences between stopping and terminating an EC2 instance. As the following sections explain, the key differences lie in your ability to restart the instance, retain the storage attached to the instance, and so on.

Stopping an instance is also different from rebooting an instance. It's important to know the differences among the three types of actions: stopping, rebooting, and terminating an instance, all of which involve changing the state of a running instance.

Stopping an Instance

Stopping an instance brings the instance to a stopped state, and you can restart it later. You can stop an instance only if the root device is on an EBS volume (that is, if an instance is EBS-backed). The EBS storage volumes for the instance remain attached to the instance after stopping the instance.

NOTE If an instance device type for its root volume is instance store (instance store–backed instance), you can't stop the instance—you can only terminate it.

You can stop an instance from the console or through the CLI. Using the console, select the instance you want to stop, and then choose Actions | Instance State | Stop. If the root device is an instance store volume, the Stop button is disabled in the console.

EXAM TIP The exam is likely to test your knowledge of what happens to the data on the root volume when you terminate an EC2 instance. Regardless of whether the instance is backed by S3-based AMI (EBS volume) or an instance store–based root volume, the root volume is always deleted. You can create EBS snapshots regularly for backing up data on EBS volumes. Unlike managed services such as AWS RDS, AWS ELB, and AWS DynamoDB, where AWS takes care of high availability through backups and other features such as Multi-AZ (for RDS), system administrators must manage high availability for EC2 instances through scripts, such as those that make backups.

Run the `ec2 stop-instances` command to stop an instance from the command line:

```
$ aws ec2 stop-instances --instance-ids  i-00c387b3389ac07f0
{
    "StoppingInstances": [
        {
            "CurrentState": {
                "Name": "stopping",
                "Code": 64
            },
            "PreviousState": {
                "Name": "running",
                "Code": 16
            },
            "InstanceId": "i-00c387b3389ac07f0"
        }
    ]
}
$
```

NOTE You can *hibernate* an Amazon Linux instance, which makes AWS save the contents of the instance's RAM to the EBS root volume. When you restart the instance, EC2 restores the EBS root volume to its original state, reloads the RAM's contents, and resumes all previously running instances. You can utilize hibernation as a strategy to "pre-warm" an instance by launching the instance, bringing it to a state that you want, and then hibernating it. When you are ready, you can resume the instance by restarting it with the state it had when you hibernated it. AWS doesn't charge you for a hibernated instance when it's in the stopped state.

You can also bring an instance to the stopped state by using the `shutdown`, `halt`, or `poweroff` command. Each of these commands will stop the instance by default (and not terminate it).

Here's what happens when you stop an instance:

- The instance enters the *stopping* state, from which it transitions to the *stopped* state.
- The instance is shut down.
- AWS stops charging you for the instance.
- If the instance belongs to an Auto Scaling group, AWS may mark the stopped instance as unhealthy and terminate the instance. It may also replace the instance.

Some things remain the same between instance restarts:

- The instance retains its instance ID.
- The instance retains all the EIP addresses associated with it.
- All EBS volumes stay attached to the instance (with their data intact).
- AWS will continue to charge you for the EBS volume usage.

Between reboots, an EC2 instance keeps its public IP address. If you shut down the instance, the public IP address is removed. When the instance is turned back on, AWS assigns a new public IP address to the instance because, in the background, AWS starts your machine on a different physical machine within the same AZ.

How Many EC2 Instances Can You Run?

You can run a maximum of 20 EC2 instances at any time. AWS sets this soft limit in order to save your AWS account from getting a huge bill, and also to protect you against misuse of your account by hackers (and bitcoin miners). Regardless of how you provision the EC2 instances, the number cannot exceed 20 instances. In addition, certain instances types are limited per region. You can increase a soft limit by submitting a request to AWS, but a hard limit cannot be changed.

The 20 EC2 instances can be provisioned in multiple ways:

- 20 On-Demand instances across the instance family. On top of this, certain instance types are also limited on a per-region basis.
- 20 Reserved instances
- Request Spot instances per your dynamic Spot instance limit per region (default account limit is 20 Spot instances per region).

You can request AWS to increase the number of instances you can run by creating a case requesting a change in your basic Support Plan. This is a formal request to the AWS Accounts and Billing Support, asking for a Service Limit increase. You need to describe your use case when you request an increase. You can request an increase in the soft limit of not only the number of EC2 instances that you can run, but all other AWS services such as Auto Scaling, AWS Batch, AMIs, EIP addresses, key pairs, dedicated hosts, placement groups, CloudFormation deployment stacks, Amazon EBS volumes, databases, and more.

Restarting an Instance

You can restart an instance from the console by choosing Actions | Instance State | Start. You can restart an instance from the command line with the `ec2 start-instance` command:

```
$ aws ec2 start-instance –instance-ids i-1234567890abcdef0
```

NOTE The instance performs a normal shutdown when you shut down or terminate an instance.

You can perform the following actions while an instance is in the stopped state (and *only* when an instance is in the stopped state):

- Detach and attach the EBS volumes (and make changes to the EBS volume before reattaching).
- Change the kernel and RAM.
- Change the instance type.
- Change the user data.

NOTE You can stop and terminate an EBS-backed instance but can only terminate an instance store–backed instance.

When you restart a stopped instance, it enters the pending state and then transitions to the running state. Usually, AWS moves the instances to a new host computer following a restart.

Once you stop an instance, no more charges will accrue for instance usage. You'll continue to be billed for the usage of the EBS volumes for the instance, even when the instance is in the stopped state.

Rebooting an Instance

An instance reboot is the same as rebooting the operating system and takes only a few minutes. You can reboot the instance from the console or from the CLI. To reboot from the console, choose Instances | Actions | Instance State | Reboot. To reboot from the command line, issue the ec2 reboot-instances command:

```
$ aws ec2 reboot-instances –instance-ids i-123456789abcdef5
```

 NOTE An instance reboot is the equivalent of an operating system reboot and is usually a fast operation.

If an instance doesn't reboot within four minutes after you issue the reboot command from the console (Amazon EC2), EC2 will perform a *hard reboot*. EC2 might also schedule a reboot for any necessary maintenance (during a scheduled EC2 determined maintenance window), such as when EC2 needs to apply some types of updates that require a reboot.

When you reboot an instance (or when EC2 does it) the following applies:

- The public DNS name (IPv4) won't change after the reboot.
- The instance stays on the same physical host.
- The instance retains all the data on its instance store volumes.

 TIP AWS recommends that you use Amazon EC2 console, a CLI, or the EC2 API instead of the OS reboot command to reboot an instance. This will help EC2 perform a hard reboot if your reboot command continues to hang for a while (that is, if the instance doesn't shut down within four minutes).

Terminating an Instance

When you terminate an instance, the instance is deleted. Hence, you can't restart the instance. You terminate an instance when you decide that you don't need it any longer.

When you terminate an instance, the following happens:

- The instance transitions from the running state to the shutting-down state, and then to the terminated state.
- Data on all instance store volumes associated with the instance is deleted.

- All EBS root device volumes are automatically deleted. This occurs because EC2 determines whether it should preserve or delete an EBS volume based on each volume's `DeleteOnTermination` attribute. For a root device, this attribute is set to true. You can change the value to false, which will persist the root device volume after you terminate an instance.

By default, all EBS volumes that you've attached to an instance (at launch time or later on) when you launched the instance persist after you terminate the instance. This occurs because for all EBS volumes except the root device volume, the `DeleteOnTermination` attribute is set to `false`.

NOTE A terminated instance will continue to show up in the EC2 console for about an hour after you terminate the instance.

Managing Instance Termination You can terminate an instance from the console or from the CLI. To terminate from the console, in the navigation pane, choose Instances | Actions | Instance State | Terminate.

Alternatively, you can terminate an instance with the AWS CLI command `ec2 terminate-instances`. Here's an example:

```
$ aws ec2 terminate-instances --instance-ids  i-00c387b3389ac07f0
{
    "TerminatingInstances": [
        {
            "PreviousState": {
                "Name": "stopped",
                "Code": 80
            },
            "InstanceId": "i-00c387b3389ac07f0",
            "CurrentState": {
                "Name": "terminated",
                "Code": 48
            }
        }
    ]
}
$
```

In this example, I terminated an instance that I had stopped earlier. You can also terminate running instances, in which case the instance first transitions into the stopped state and then moves to the terminated state.

NOTE You can find the reason for an instance termination by going to the EC2 console and looking up "Instance description" under the State Transition Reason label.

Obviously, instance termination is a big deal, since the instance will disappear when you terminate it. You also need to deal with the potential impact on storage. You can control the default behavior of EC2 that impacts the termination of instances, the deletion of the root device, and the deletion of the EBS volumes, as explained in the following sections.

Preventing Accidental Termination of Instances   By default, AWS allows the termination of instances from the console, the CLI, and through APIs by any user or role with proper access. That is, by default, there's *no termination protection* for instances. You can prevent an accidental termination of an instance by setting the `DisableApiTermination` attribute to `true` (the default value is `false`). You do this, for example, when you want to prevent administrators in a production team from accidentally terminating critical instances.

NOTE   You cannot enable termination protection for Spot instances, since they're automatically terminated when the Spot price crosses your bid price.

You can set the `DisableApiTermination` attribute from the console or the CLI. To configure this when you launch an instance, go the EC2 console, and in the dashboard, on the Configure Instance Details page, select the Enable Termination Protection check box. Choose Actions | Instance Settings | Change Termination Protection.

TIP   You can enable termination protection for a running or a stopped instance.

To configure termination protection from the command line, run the following command:

```
$ aws ec2 modify-instance-attribute –instance-id 1234567890abcdef0
-DisableApiTermination true
```

Even after setting the `DisableApiTermination` attribute to `true`, you can still terminate an instance by shutting down the instance itself, using an operating system command such as shutdown, halt, or poweroff. By default, any of these commands will stop an instance, not terminate it. You can, however, set the `InstanceInitiatedShutdownBehavior` attribute for an instance so the instance will terminate instead.

You can set the `InstanceInitiatedShutdownBehavior` attribute from the EC2 console or the command line. To change the value for this attribute from the console, in the navigation pane, select the instance, and then choose Actions | Instance Settings | Change Shutdown Behavior. The default value is Stop, as shown in Figure 4-1. Select the Terminate option, and then click Apply.

Alternatively, run the `ec2 modify-instance-attribute` command from the AWS CLI to change the shutdown behavior:

```
$ aws ec2 modify-instance-attribute –instance-id 1234567890abcdef0
-InstanceInitiatedShutdownBehavior terminate
```

Figure 4-1
Changing the
shutdown
behavior of
an instance

Instance Termination and EBS Volumes

Instance Termination and EBS Volumes   By default, EC2 deletes the root volume of an instance when you terminate an instance. You can change this behavior. When launching an instance, you can do this through the console during the instance launch process, in the Add Storage page. Here, you can deselect the Delete on Termination check box for the root volume and then click Launch to start the instance.

If the instance is running, you can't change the `DeleteOnTermination` property from the console. You must use the command line to configure this property to persist the root volume, by running the `ec2 modify-instance-attribute` command in the following way:

```
$ aws ec2 modify-instance-attribute --instance-id i-1234567890abcdef0
--block-device-mappings file://mapping.json
```

The mapping.json file should look like the following:

```
[
  {
    "DeviceName": "/dev/sda1",
    "Ebs": {
      "DeleteOnTermination": false
    }
  }
]
```

NOTE   If you use an EBS volume as a root partition, you must set the `DeleteOnTermination` attribute to `false` if you want the EBS volume to persist outside the life of the instance. By default, the `DeleteOnTermination` attribute for the root volume of an instance is `true`. Hence, the default behavior is to terminate the root volume when the instance terminates.

The `DeleteOnTermination` attribute also apples to the EBS volumes (non-root) that you attach to an instance. By default, this property is set to `false`, which means the EBS volumes are retained along with their data. Following the termination of an instance, you can attach the instance's EBS volumes to another EC2 instance if you want.

Recovering EC2 Instances

You can have AWS automatically recover an instance that's unusable due to a hardware or software issue on the underlying physical host, a loss of power or network connectivity, or any problem that requires an AWS fix. You can do this by setting up an Amazon Cloud-Watch alarm to monitor your AWS instances and recover them.

 NOTE For more on setting up an Amazon CloudWatch alarm, see Chapter 10.

A recovered instance is identical in all respects, such as the instance ID, EIP address, and instance metadata to the original instance it's replacing. You can set up the recover action only for EBS volume-backed instances. Furthermore, your instance must belong to one of the C3, C4, C5, M3, M4, M5, R3, R4, T2, or X1 instance types. Remember that the numbers following the letter denoting the instance family represent the generation of that family. Thus, C represents the instance family and 4 denotes the generation of the C class family instance.

Scheduled Events for Instances

AWS may occasionally perform a *scheduled event* for your EC2. There are four types of scheduled events for an EC2 instance: stopping an instance, retiring an instance, rebooting an instance (or the server that hosts the instance), and system maintenance (network, power, and so on).

You don't need to worry about AWS arbitrarily scheduling instance events, however. The maintenance work will affect you very rarely, and when it does, AWS sends you an e-mail with details about the scheduled event and the start and end dates for the work, so you can plan around the event.

You can proactively check for scheduled events from the console or from the command line. From the console, there are two ways to do this: Click Events in the navigation pane. Alternatively, in the same navigation pane, choose EC2 dashboard and view the resources with an associated pending event displayed under Scheduled Events.

To view the scheduled events for any of your EC2 instances from the command line, issue the following AWS CLI command:

```
$ aws ec2 describe-instance-status –instance-id i-1234567890abcdef0
```

Selecting the EC2 Instance Type

AWS offers a huge amount of choices for creating (launching) an EC2 instance. The *instance type* that you choose determines the hardware of the host computer that supports your instances (virtual servers). As you know by now, EC2 instances are virtual servers that run on a host physical computer, and each of which may have a different combination of CPU, RAM, and other resources. When you launch an instance (create an instance and run it), you must choose the instance type, which tells AWS on which type of server the virtual instance will run.

NOTE You pay for your EC2 Linux instance usage on a per-second basis. Instances that you launch in On-Demand, Reserved, and Spot forms (as well as your EBS volumes) are billed in 1-second increments, with a minimum of 60 seconds.

EC2 runs multiple instances on the host computer. A specific instance is allocated some of the resources of the host computer, such as CPU, RAM, and storage capacity. EC2 will share other resources of the host computer (such as the network and storage) among other instances.

There are many instance types, based on the instance's processing power, memory, network capacity, and storage capacity, and each instance type is optimized for a different use case. For example, EC2 allocates a larger amount of the shared resources to an instance type with a high I/O performance to ensure stable I/O performance.

TIP It's a best practice to separate EBS volumes for the OS and your data. You must also configure the EBS volumes to be retained after an instance termination so you don't lose data. You can delete the EBS volumes that you don't need any longer to avoid orphan volumes and to reduce costs.

Choices for an Instance Type

AWS offers a set of instance types that fall under the *current generation instances*, and an overlapping set of instance types that it calls *previous generation instances*.

TIP AWS recommends that you choose from the current generation of instances because they offer the best performance.

As mentioned, each instance type comes with a combination of CPU, memory, storage capacity, and networking capability. AWS groups its available instance types into *instance families*, based on the capabilities of the servers. The currently available current generation instance types are grouped into the following instance families:

- Burstable performance instances
- General purpose instances
- Compute optimized instances
- Memory optimized instances
- Storage optimized instances
- Linux accelerated computing instances

You can view all the available instance types when you launch a new instance, as shown in Figure 4-2.

t1.micro	m5.2xlarge	m3.medium	c5.2xlarge	c3.xlarge	g3.8xlarge	r4.large	r3.8xlarge	m2.2xlarge	i2.8xlarge
t2.nano	m5.4xlarge	m3.large	c5.4xlarge	c3.2xlarge	g3.16xlarge	r4.xlarge	x1.16xlarge	m2.4xlarge	h1.2xlarge
t2.micro	m5.12xlarge	m3.xlarge	c5.9xlarge	c3.4xlarge	g2.2xlarge	r4.2xlarge	x1e.xlarge	cr1.8xlarge	h1.4xlarge
t2.small	m5.24xlarge	m3.2xlarge	c5.18xlarge	c3.8xlarge	g2.8xlarge	r4.4xlarge	x1e.2xlarge	d2.xlarge	h1.8xlarge
t2.medium	m4.large	m1.small	c4.large	c1.medium	p2.xlarge	r4.8xlarge	x1e.4xlarge	d2.2xlarge	h1.16xlarge
t2.large	m4.xlarge	m1.medium	c4.xlarge	c1.xlarge	p2.8xlarge	r4.16xlarge	x1e.8xlarge	d2.4xlarge	i3.large
t2.xlarge	m4.2xlarge	m1.large	c4.2xlarge	cc2.8xlarge	p2.16xlarge	r3.large	x1e.16xlarge	d2.8xlarge	i3.xlarge
t2.2xlarge	m4.4xlarge	m1.xlarge	c4.4xlarge	f1.2xlarge	p3.2xlarge	r3.xlarge	x1e.32xlarge	i2.xlarge	i3.2xlarge
m5.large	m4.10xlarge	c5.large	c4.8xlarge	f1.16xlarge	p3.8xlarge	r3.2xlarge	x1.32xlarge	i2.2xlarge	i3.4xlarge
m5.xlarge	m4.16xlarge	c5.xlarge	c3.large	g3.4xlarge	p3.16xlarge	r3.4xlarge	m2.xlarge	i2.4xlarge	i3.8xlarge

Figure 4-2 Available EC2 instance types

 NOTE Previous generation instances contain five instance families. These instance families are the same as in the current generation instances, except that they contain the micro instances family instead of the accelerated computing family.

Burstable Performance Instances

Burstable performance instances (T2 and T3) offer a baseline level of CPU performance but can burst to a higher level when your workloads require it. Burstable performance instances are ideal for a wide variety of applications such as microservices and low-latency interactive applications. This is the only instance type that uses CPU usage credits. The smallest burstable performance instance type (t2.nano) comes with a single default virtual CPU (vCPU) and a memory of 0.5GB. The largest instance type (t3.2xlarge) comes with eight vCPUs and a memory of 32GB.

General Purpose Instances

You can use general purpose instances for a variety of workloads, since they offer a balance of compute, memory, and networking resources. There are three types of general purpose instance families: T2 instances, and M4 and M5 instances.

T2 instances provide a baseline level of CPU performance but can burst to a higher level when needed. T2 instances are best suited for applications such as web sites, code repositories, developing and testing environments, and microservices. The smallest T2 instance (t2.nano) has 1 vCPU and 0.5GB RAM. The largest T2 instance (t2.2xlarge) comes with four vCPUs and 32GB RAM.

The M4 and M5 instances are EBS-optimized, which helps you get consistently high performance for your EBS volumes, by eliminating contention between regular network traffic generated by your instance and the EBS I/O. In other words, these instances provide additional dedicated capacity for EBS I/O. M5 instances are the latest generation in the general purpose instance family. M5, M5a, and M5b instances are best suited for running small and medium-size databases, gaming servers, and backend servers for enterprise applications such as SAP. The smallest M5 instance type (m5.large) has 2 vCPUs and 0.5GB RAM. The largest M5 instance type (m5.24xlarge) comes with 96 vCPUs and 384GB RAM.

Compute Optimized Instances

Compute optimize instances are designed for compute-heavy applications that require high-performance processors. Applications such as batch processing workloads, high-performance computing (including high-performance web servers), scientific modeling, and machine learning benefit from using this instance type.

There are two general purpose instance families, C4 and C5, which come in various sizes. The smallest C4 instance type (c4.large) has 2 vCPUs and 3.75GB RAM. The largest C5 instance type (c5d.18xlarge) comes with 72 vCPUs and 144GB RAM.

Memory Optimized Instances

Memory optimized instances have high amounts of memory and use techniques such as Scalable Memory Buffers that provide a very high (300GB) sustainable memory-read bandwidth and high (140 Gbps) sustainable memory-write bandwidth.

The high amounts of memory and the speed-up technologies used by several instance types in the memory optimized instance family are ideal for applications such as high performance relational and NoSQL databases, in-memory databases such as SAP HANA, and applications that analyze high amounts of unstructured data in real time, caching servers such as Memcached that are used as a cache by multiple applications, and Apache Hadoop/Apache Spark clusters.

There are three classes of memory optimized instance families: R4, X1, and X1e. The smallest R4 instance type (r4.large) has 2 vCPUs and 15.25GB RAM. The largest X1e instance type (x1e.32xlarge) comes with 128 vCPUs and 3904GB RAM.

Storage Optimized Instances

Storage optimized instances are ideal for workloads that perform high amounts of sequential read and write accesses to very large data sets. They make this possible by delivering tens of thousands of fast, random operations per second (IOPS). Storage optimized instances are well-suited for applications such as massively parallel processing (MPP) data warehouses, log or data processing workloads, and high volume online transaction processing (OLTP) systems.

There are three classes of memory optimized instance families: D2, H1, and I3. The smallest D2 instance type (d2.xlarge) has 4 vCPUs and 30.5GB RAM. The largest I3 instance type (i3.metal) comes with 72 vCPUs and 512GB RAM.

Linux Accelerated Computing Instances

Accelerated computing instances offer more parallelism, which enhances throughput for compute-intensive workloads. To provide the higher throughput, the instances have access to hardware-based computing accelerators such as graphics processing units (GPUs) or field programmable gate arrays (FPGAs). GPU-based instances provide access to NVIDIA GPUs, which contain thousands of cores. FPGA-based instances offer access to large FPGAs that contain millions of parallel system logic cells.

There are four types of memory optimized instance families: P2, P3, G3, and F1. The smallest P2 instance type (p2.xlarge) has 4 vCPUs and 61GB RAM. The largest F1 instance type (f1.16xlarge) comes with 64 vCPUs and 976GB RAM.

TIP AWS offers *enhanced networking* capabilities for supported instance types. Enhanced networking offers significantly faster performance, with lower network jitter and latency. The enhanced performance is achieved by taking advantage of single root I/O virtualization (SR-IOV). If your EC2 instances are required to support a low inter-instance latency, high bandwidth and high packet-per-second (PPS) performance, you should consider the EC2 enhanced networking feature (for supported instance types).

Optimizing the CPU Options

Multiple threads, each represented as a vCPU, can run in a single Intel Xeon CPU core, which supports an EC2 instance. Depending on its type, each instance has a default number of CPU cores. For example, the m5.xlarge instance type has two CPU cores, and by default two threads can run per core. Thus, the m5.xlarge instance has four vCPUs by default.

You can customize an instance for your specific needs by specifying the following CPU options during instance launch:

- **Number of CPU cores** You can set the number of CPU cores for the instance within a permissible range.
- **Threads per core** For certain high-performance computing workloads, you can specify just a single thread per CPU core rather than multiple cores.

Changing the Instance Type

After running an EC2 instance for a while, you may realize that the instance size is either too big or too small. You can easily change the size of your instance any time. For example, you can change the instance type from m3.medium to t2.micro, and vice versa.

For an EC2 instance that uses an EBS volume for its root device, you can change the instance type in an operation called *resizing*. If your instance's root device is an instance store volume, you must perform a *migrate* operation to move to a new instance with the instance type you need.

To resize an instance, the new instance and the current instance type must have compatible virtualization types (IPV or HVM) and platform (32-bit versus 64-bit AMIs). Additionally, if you are resizing a current instance to an instance type such as M5, which exposes EBS volumes as NVMe (non-volatile memory express) block devices, you must install the NVMe drivers on the current instance before the resize operation.

TIP Resizing an instance (changing the instance type) requires a restart of the instance.

You must be aware of the following when resizing an EBS-backed instance:

- The instance is moved to a new host computer but will retain its instance ID.
- The instance retains its private IPv4 addresses, EIP addresses, and any IPv6 addresses.

- If the instance is running in a VPC with a public IPv4 address, it gets a new public IPv4 address and you can attach an EIP to avoid changing the public IP every time you stop and start the instance.

- During the resizing operation, you must stop the instance and change its instance type. So, there is a service interruption when you resize an instance. It's a good idea to suspend scaling processes for the Auto Scaling group, if the current instance belongs to one. This will keep the Auto Scaling service from marking the stopped instance as unhealthy and launching a replacement instance.

 NOTE Exercise 4-6 shows the procedures for resizing an EBS-backed instance from the AWS Management Console.

While this discussion of the various instance types offered by AWS helps you choose the best instance types for your needs, you must also be aware that a given instance offered by AWS doesn't always have a fixed price. You can optimize your costs by selecting from various instance purchase options.

Instance Purchase Options

You can lower your spending on EC2 compute resources by taking advantage of the various purchase and payment options offered by AWS. Amazon EC2 offers you several options regarding the way you purchase computing resources such as EC2 instances. For example, you can lower your costs substantially by using Reserved instances; you commit to buy the instances for a period of one to three years. Another way to lower costs is to consider purchasing Spot instances, which are allocated to you from Amazon's unused server capacity, and hence are much cheaper than instances you purchase by just launching them (On-Demand instances).

Following are the available instance purchasing options:

- **On-Demand instances**   Pay for an instance by the second.

- **Reserved instances**   Purchase instances for a term from one to three years, at a significant discount (up to a 75 percent discount compared to the price of On-Demand instances).

- **Scheduled instances**   Purchase, for a one-year term, instances that are available during a specific schedule that you specify.

- **Spot instances**   Purchase unused, surplus EC2 computing capacity at significantly lower cost, by placing a bid on the instance (up to 90 percent discount compared to the price of On-Demand instances).

- **Dedicated hosts**   Use a physical host that's exclusively dedicated to running your virtual instances.

- **Dedicated instances**   Pay an hourly price for instances that run on hardware without any other AWS tenants sharing the hardware with you.

NOTE The default mode for EC2 is shared tenancy.

Purchasing Options and the Instance Lifecycle

The length of an instance's lifecycle depends on the purchase option you choose for that instance. For an On-Demand instance, the lifecycle starts when you launch the instance and ends when you terminate the instance. For a Spot instance, the lifecycle lasts as long as two things are true: there is sufficient capacity available and the maximum price offered by you is more than the Spot price of the instance.

You can find the instance lifecycle from the console by going to Instances | Description and viewing the instance lifecycle information at the lower-right of the page. Figure 4-3 shows the lifecycle data for an instance.

To do the same from the command line, run the `ec2 describe-instances` command:

```
$ aws ec2 describe-instances –instance-ids i-12345678901bcdef0
...
"Placement": {
                    "GroupName": "",
                    "AvailabilityZone": "us-west-2b",
                    "Tenancy": "default"
...
$
```

As the output shows, the default value for the `Tenancy` attribute for an On-Demand instance is `default`. If this were an instance running on a dedicated host, the `Tenancy` attribute's value would be `host`. For a Spot instance and a Scheduled instance, the output would show the following, respectively:

```
"InstanceLifecycle": "spot"
"InstanceLifecycle": "scheduled"
```

A Reserved instance won't have the `InstanceLifecycle` element in its output.

Instance: i-01fda470bea59e90b Public DNS: ec2-54-91-34-34.compute-1.amazonaws.com			▬ ▬ ▭
Description Status Checks Monitoring Tags			
Instance ID	i-01fda470bea59e90b	Public DNS (IPv4)	ec2-54-91-34-34.compute-1.amazonaws.com
Instance state	running	IPv4 Public IP	54.91.34.34
Instance type	t2.micro	IPv6 IPs	-
Elastic IPs		Private DNS	ip-172-31-35-240.ec2.internal
Availability zone	us-east-1b	Private IPs	172.31.35.240
Security groups	launch-wizard-1 . view inbound rules . view outbound rules	Secondary private IPs	
Scheduled events	No scheduled events	VPC ID	vpc-882c97f2
AMI ID	amzn2-ami-hvm-2.0.20190228-x86_64-gp2 (ami-02da3a138888ced85)	Subnet ID	subnet-1o6f0440
Platform	-	Network interfaces	eth0
IAM role	-	Source/dest. check	True
Key pair name	administrator1	T2/T3 Unlimited	Disabled
Owner	321938860023	EBS-optimized	False
Launch time	March 2, 2019 at 12:39:32 PM UTC-6 (154 hours)	Root device type	ebs

Figure 4-3 Viewing the lifecycle data for an instance from the console

EXAM TIP Be sure to understand the relationship between an instance type, an instance family, and an instance size. An instance type is composed of the instance family and the instance size. Thus, m4.large is an instance type that comprises the m4 instance family and the large instance size.

In the following sections, I explain the intricacies of the various purchase options for EC2 instances.

On-Demand Instances

The default purchase option for an EC2 instance, On-Demand instances, is where you pay per hour or per second, depending on the instances that you run. You'll use this purchase option if you launch an instance by following the steps described in Exercise 4-3.

Here's what you need to remember about provisioning On-Demand instances:

- You don't need to make any commitments for the long term.
- You don't need to pay anything up front.
- Depending on which instances you run, you pay either per hour or per second.
- You can increase or decrease the number of instances based on your workload, paying the hourly rates for the instances that you're running. (AWS doesn't bill you for stopped or terminated instances.)

NOTE On-Demand instances aren't interrupted by EC2.

On-Demand instances are ideal for new applications that you're testing on EC2, and applications that involve workload spikes, or workloads that are unpredictable, and can't be interrupted.

AWS charges per instance-hour consumed for each instance, from the time you launch an instance until you terminate or stop the instance. AWS bills each partial instance-hour that the instance is running for, on a per-second basis for Linux instances and on a full-hour basis for all other instance types.

Reserved Instances

Reserved instances are especially useful in lowering your computing costs, so I discuss these in detail. You pay by the second for each On-Demand instance, the rate depending on the instance type. Reserved instances offer a huge discount compared to the price of an On-Demand instance, with the discount reaching up to 70 percent compared to On-Demand instance pricing.

In addition to Reserved instances offering a significant discount compared to On-Demand instances, by purchasing Reserved instances for a specific AZ (called a *zonal* Reserved instance), you can make these instances provide a *capacity reservation*, bolstering your confidence in your ability to launch the instance when your workloads need them. When you purchase a Reserved instance for a region (called a *regional* Reserved instance), the instance doesn't provide a capacity reservation.

Reserved instances offer significant savings for applications that have a steady workload or a predictable usage pattern. Let's say you have an application that runs for an hour or so and must be available at all times. A Reserved instance is a good option here since it minimizes the instance cost while enhancing the availability of the instance. You can commit to using EC2 for a one- to three-year term to reduce your computing costs.

NOTE It's important to understand that a Reserved instance is not a physical (or virtual) instance—it's a *billing discount* applied to the On-Demand instances you own. In this sense, it's somewhat like a purchase contract and doesn't refer to a server.

Figure 4-4 shows how you purchase and use Reserved instances.

By purchasing a Reserved instance with the same attributes as an On-Demand instance, you get a discount on the running instance. If you don't have a running instance that matches the Reserved instance, the discount will apply as soon as you launch an On-Demand instance with the attributes of the Reserved instance that you've purchased. In Figure 4-4, a Reserved instance is bought for an T2 instance and is immediately applied, since a T2 instance is running. The Reserved instance for a C4 instance was bought before that instance is launched. The C4 instance gets a discounted rate when you launch the C4 instance.

TIP Reserved instances don't renew automatically. When the Reserved instance expires, you go back to paying the regular On-Demand price for the instance, unless you purchase a new Reserved instance.

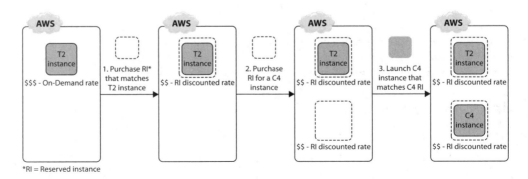

Figure 4-4 Purchasing and running Reserved instances

Standard and Convertible Offering Classes

There are two *offering classes* for Reserved instances:

- **Standard Reserved instance**   Allows you to modify just some attributes of the instance, such as instance size, and you can't *exchange* the instances (when EC2 allows you to trade one Reserved instance for a different instance, and several rules apply).

- **Convertible Reserved instance**   Allows you to exchange the instance during its term for another Convertible Reserved instance with different attributes. Convertible Reserved instances offer more flexibility by allowing you to exchange an instance for a different one with alternative attributes such as instance family, instance type, platform, and tenancy to apply discount credits.

  A Convertible Reserved instance is a good option when your applications will be running daily throughout the year, you're looking for the most cost-effective pricing option for the instances, and you also expect that you may have to upgrade the instances to handle the increasing workloads that you're expecting.

 NOTE   You can *sell* a Standard Reserved instance in the Reserved Instance Marketplace, but you cannot sell a Convertible Reserved instance.

Terms and Payment Options for Reserved Instances

You purchase Reserved instances for a specific term: either a one-year or a three-year term. As mentioned, when the term expires, you'll go back to being charged the higher On-Demand prices for a running instance. You can lower your costs by using various *payment options* for Reserved instances. There are three payment options:

- **All Upfront**   You pay everything when you start the purchase term, and there are no additional costs, regardless of the number of hours you use the instance.

- **Partial Upfront**   You pay part of the cost up front and the rest at a discounted hourly rate, whether you use the instance or not.

- **No Upfront**   You don't pay anything when you start the term and are billed a discounted hourly rate per hour of usage; you pay whether you use the instance or not.

As you can tell, regardless of the payment option you select, you pay for an entire term irrespective of the actual usage of the instance. In general, as in the case of purchasing a house or a car, the more you pay up front, the more you'll save on your total instance costs.

Maximum Number of Reserved Instances

There's a soft limit on how many Reserved instances you can purchase. You can purchase a maximum of 20 Reserved instances per AZ in your region, per month. In addition, you can also purchase 20 Regional Reserved instances. Once you purchase a Reserved instance, you can't cancel the purchase. However, you can modify, exchange, or sell the instance to others. You can sell the Reserved instance on the Reserved Instance Marketplace.

Suppose your instance type requirements change, or your project ends earlier than you planned. You can give up your capacity reservation by listing Reserved instances that you don't need on the Marketplace. Similarly, you can purchase Reserved instances offered by third parties on the Marketplace. You can often purchase Reserved instances at a lower price or for a lower term from the third-party sellers.

Purchasing Reserved Instances

You can purchase Reserved instances from the EC2 console or from the command line. To purchase from the console, in the navigation pane, choose Reserved Instance | Purchase Reserved Instance, and specify the options you want, such as offering class and term.

You can purchase Reserved instances from the command line by running two separate commands, the first (`describe-reserved-instances-offerings`) to find the available instances, and the second (`purchase-reserved-instances-offering`), to purchase the Reserved instances. Here are the commands:

```
$ aws ec2 describe-reserved-instances-offerings --instance-type
t2.large --offering-class standard --product-description "Linux/UNIX"
--instance-tenancy default --filters Name=duration,Values=31536000
Name=scope,Values=Region
```

This command helps you find the available Reserved instances. You can then purchase the Reserved instances with the following command:

```
$ aws ec2 purchase-reserved-instances-offering --reserved-instances-offering-
id ec06327e-dd07-46ee-9398-75b5fexample --instance-count
```

You can view the Reserved instances you've purchased with the following command:

```
$ aws ec2 describe-reserved-instances
```

Scheduled Reserved Instances

At times, you may need some computing capacity to meet recurring needs. You may not need these resources all the time, but you need them on a recurring basis, with set times and for a specific duration. For certain instance types (C3, C4, C5, M4, and R3), you can purchase *Scheduled instances,* also called Scheduled Reserved instances. Scheduled instances enable you to reserve computing capacity for specific times during which you'll need the additional capacity. For example, you can employ a Scheduled instance to run nightly batch processing workloads at 3 A.M.

You can purchase capacity reservations via Scheduled Reserved instances on a recurring daily, weekly, or monthly basis. You must specify a start time and duration.

NOTE You pay for Scheduled Reserved instances even if you don't use them.

You can purchase a Scheduled instance up to three months in advance, and there's a required term of one year and minimum utilization of 1200 hours per year. Scheduled instances are limited to the C3, C4, C5, M4, and R3 instance types.

TIP If you need to reserve instances not on a schedule but continuously, go for *Reserved instances*, which cost less.

You can launch a Scheduled instance only during the instance's scheduled period. As with a Reserved instance, the instance launch configuration must match the following attributes of the schedule you've purchased:

- Availability zone or region
- Network
- Platform
- Instance type

You cannot stop or reboot a Scheduled instance; you can only terminate the instance and relaunch it before the scheduled period for that instance expires.

Execute the `describe-scheduled-instance-availability` command to list available schedules that suit you. Run the `purchase-scheduled-instances` command to purchase the scheduled instance and launch the instance with the `run-scheduled-instances` command.

Spot Instances

You can significantly lower your spending on EC2 instances by purchasing *Spot instances*, which help you make use of unused EC2 instances. Unlike in the case of On-Demand instances, whose price stays fixed, the hourly price of the Spot instance varies based on the supply and demand for the instance.

Spot instances take advantage of spare capacity in the AWS cloud and offer a steep discount over the price of On-Demand instances. You can save up to 90 percent of the cost of On-Demand instances by selecting Spot instances.

Spot instances are ideal for applications that have flexible start and end times, as well as for applications that are cost-efficient only at very low prices for the compute instances. They are also a good choice when you have an urgent need to provision a large amount of additional compute capacity. If you have a batch application that can be interrupted and resumed without any issues, for example, you can choose Spot instances to minimize your compute costs for the application.

NOTE   A Spot instance will run until you terminate it, until capacity becomes unavailable, or until the current Spot price becomes greater than your maximum Spot price bid.

Once you create a Spot request and the request is active, there's no guarantee that you can immediately launch the instance. The Spot instances will launch only if capacity is available. If no capacity is available, the Spot request will keep trying to make the launch request until capacity becomes available.

EXAM TIP   The exam will test your knowledge of Spot instance pricing. The price you pay for a Spot instance (the Spot price) is the Spot price in effect at the beginning of each instance hour of a running instance. If the Spot price changes after you launch the instance, AWS charges you the prevailing new price for your instance usage in each subsequent hour.

There's one catch, though, which may make Spot instances unsuitable for you. Any time EC2 needs additional compute capacity, it can interrupt your instance with just two minutes of notice. If your applications are flexible and can handle this interruption, Spot instances are a great way to reduce your EC2 spending. Financial modeling, image and media encoding, testing, big data, geospatial analysis, web crawling, and analytical and machine learning applications are ideal use cases for choosing Spot instances.

NOTE   AWS's Spot Fleet can help you manage capacity automatically.

Amazon EC2 sets the Spot price for the Spot instance. The Spot price isn't fixed—it varies continuously (updated every five minutes), based on current demand and supply for Spot instances. You must specify a maximum price (per hour) and you'll be allocated the instances if the price you specify exceeds the Spot price set by Amazon EC2.

So, when do you buy Spot instances? Spot instances are ideal for applications such as those that use batch jobs and non-mission-critical jobs such as big data analytics for research, where you can withstand potential interruptions. If you want to have your cake and eat it too, you may do so by launching Spot instances called *spot blocks*, which will run for a required duration without interruptions, regardless of the changes in the Spot price for the instance.

TIP   You must be prepared for interruptions when you use Spot instances, since Amazon EC2 can interrupt the instances whenever the Spot price for an instance exceeds your maximum price.

Spot Instance Terminology

Following are the key terms you must understand to work with Spot instances:

- **Spot price**   The current EC2 hourly price for a Spot instance that's set by Amazon EC2. The Spot price represents the *asking price* for the instance. The default maximum price for spot instance is the On-Demand price.

- **Spot instance request**   The maximum hourly price that you're willing to pay for a Spot instance. This is your *bid price* for the instance. You can set a maximum Spot price of up to 10 times the On-Demand price.

- **Spot instance pool**   The set of available Spot instances (identical instance type and AZ).

- **Spot Fleet**   A set of Spot instances you can launch based on your own criteria. You can use automatic scaling to increase or decrease the target capacity of a Spot fleet, based on policies that you specify.

The Mechanics of Spot Instances

You create a Spot instance request or a Spot Fleet request to use Spot instances. The Spot instance request includes the number of instances, an optional On-Demand portion, the instance type, the AZ, and the maximum price that you're willing to pay for the Spot instances.

As I mentioned earlier, EC2 can interrupt your Spot instance. The interruption can occur under any of the following conditions:

- **Price**   The Spot price exceeds the maximum price you've specified.

- **Capacity**   The demand for Spot instances rises and there aren't enough unused EC2 instances to meet the demand, or when the supply of Spot instances decreases.

- **Constraints**   Spot instances can be terminated as a group when EC2 can't meet a constraint that requires it to launch instances in a launch group or in an AZ group.

EC2 will provide a two-minute notice before it interrupts a Spot instance, and by default, EC2 will terminate Spot instances when it interrupts the instances. You can modify this default behavior (for specific instance types such as C3, C4, R3, and R4) by specifying that it should instead hibernate or stop the Spot instances by choosing the appropriate interruption behavior in the console or using the `InstanceInterruptionBehavior` property in the instance launch configuration.

Unlike an On-Demand Spot instance, you can't start a Spot instance. EC2's Spot service starts and stops all Spot instances. You may, however, reboot or terminate the Spot instances. If you shut the instance down from the command line, it terminates the Spot instance.

As mentioned, you can use a Spot block to keep EC2 from terminating a Spot instance when the Spot price changes. A Spot block is a Spot instance with a specific duration of one to six hours. When your request is fulfilled, the price of the Spot instance is fixed and will remain the same until the instance is terminated. The Spot instance terminates when you terminate it or when the duration ends.

Automatic Scaling for Spot Fleet

AWS offers an *automatic scaling* feature that will increase or decrease the target capacity of the Spot fleet based on demand. The Spot fleet will launch more instances or terminate them, within a range that you specify, based on the scaling policies you create.

Requesting a Spot Instance

You can request a Spot instance by choosing Spot Requests in the EC2 console. Alternatively, you can run the ec2 request-spot-instances command:

```
$ aws ec2 request-spot-instances --instance-count 5 --type "one-time"
--launch-specification file://specification.json
```

You use a specification.json file to provide the launch configuration to use with the command and create a Spot instance request. A typical specification.json file looks like the following:

```
{
"ImageId": "ami-1a2b3c4d",
"KeyName": "my-key-pair",
"SecurityGroupIds": [ "sg-1a2b3c4d" ],
InstanceType": "m3.medium",
"IamInstanceProfile": {
  "Arn": "arn:aws:iam::123456789012:instance-profile/my-iam-role"
}
}
```

Choosing Among On-Demand, Reserved, and Spot Instances

You can mix On-Demand, Reserved, and Spot instances when you're planning the provisioning of EC2 instances for your workloads and applications. You base your choice among the three types of instances on criteria, such as the minimum number of instances that you must have running at all times, the number of instances you may need to add during specific times of the day, and any potential spikes in workloads that may require a large number of instances occasionally during the year.

Let's say, for example, that you're running a web application where you place the web servers in an Auto Scaling group. Based on your workload patterns for the past year, you realize that you need 10 web servers to handle the minimum workload. During the day, when there's more traffic, you need 20 web servers. There are about ten days during the year when you may need up to 30 web servers.

To minimize your compute spending, here's how you may want to plan your instance purchases:

- 10 Reserved instances, which ensures that you can handle the minimum workload at all times.

- 10 On-Demand instances to meet the daytime requirement of up to 20 servers.

- Spot instances to cover anything above 20 instances (you expect that you'll need approximately a total of 30 servers during the peak days in the year). Since you need to go beyond 20 servers for only 10 days during the year, you can use Spot instances to get these additional instances at the lowest cost.

Dedicated Hosts and Dedicated Instances

An EC2 *dedicated host* is a physical server whose capacity for EC2 instances is dedicated just for your use. You can use your existing server-bound (per-socket, per-core, and per-VM) software licenses (such as those for SUSE Linux Enterprise Server, SQL Server, and Windows Server) in EC2. Unlike in the case of a shared computer, a dedicated host is an isolated physical server whose configurations you can control; thus, it has the additional benefit of helping you satisfy your compliance requirements. A dedicated host enables you to use your current server-based software licenses, so it helps you satisfy your corporate compliance and regulatory mandate.

A dedicated host can support a single instance type, and the number of instances you can launch from that host depends in the instance type the host supports. For example, a c3.xlarge dedicated host allows you to launch a maximum of eight c3.xlarge instances on it.

You can purchase dedicated hosts On-Demand (hourly), or as a reservation, for up to 70 percent of the On-Demand price.

TIP EC2 bills you per-instance for your dedicated instances. It uses per-host billing for dedicated hosts.

A *dedicated instance* runs in a VPC, on hardware dedicated to you. This is also called *single-tenant hardware*, unlike the default of *shared hardware*. However, unlike in the case of a dedicated host, you don't have visibility and control over how your instances are placed on the host server. You also don't have visibility into the number of sockets and physical cores of the host server, which is possible with a dedicated host. In addition, you can't deploy your dedicated instances to the same physical server over time.

NOTE The On-Demand, Spot, Scheduled, and Reserved instances run on shared host computers.

A dedicated instance runs in a VPC on hardware that's dedicated to a single customer. All dedicated instances that belong to your account are physically isolated at the hardware level. However, a dedicated instance may share hardware from non-dedicated instances from your AWS account.

EXAM TIP It's easy to trip over the differences between a dedicated host and a dedicated instance. A key difference between a dedicated host and a dedicated instance is that a dedicated host offers you visibility and control over how your instances are placed on the underlying physical server. Let's say your software licensing model specifies that you must limit the number of CPU cores on the underlying hardware. A dedicated host enables you to do this by specifying the number of CPU cores on the physical server. You can also deploy your instances consistently to the same physical server over time.

There are two ways to create a dedicated instance:

- *Create a VPC with its instance* `tenancy` *attribute configured to* `dedicated`. Following this, all the instances that you launch into this VPC are dedicated instances. By default, all instances that you launch into your VPC run on shared hardware.
- *Create the VPC with its instance* `tenancy` *attribute set to* `default`. Specify a `tenancy` attribute of `dedicated` for instances that you launch into this VPC.

 TIP AWS use per-host billing for dedicated hosts and per-instance billing for a dedicated instance.

To use a dedicated host, you must first allocate the hosts in your account. You can then launch an instance on one of these hosts by specifying the attribute `host` for the `tenancy` attribute for the instance. You can launch the instance on a specific host or let EC2 launch the instance on any host that matches the instance type and for which you have enabled *auto-placement*. When you restart the instance, the host affinity setting that you've configured determines whether the instance starts on the same host.

You can't change the tenancy once you launch an instance. Thus, if you launch an instance with the default tenancy and you decide that you need to move the instance to dedicated hardware, you can't simply change the setting for the `tenancy` attribute for this instance to the value `host` (dedicated host). To move the instance to a dedicated host, you must stop the instance and create an AMI first. Following this, launch the new instance with `tenancy=dedicated`, and terminate the old instance.

 NOTE While both dedicated hosts and dedicated instances enable you to launch instances on host physical servers that are dedicated to you, there are some key differences. Dedicated hosts offer visibility of the sockets, cores, and host ID, and allow you to deploy your instances to the same physical server each time, besides offering you control over how the instances are placed on the physical server.

Storage for EC2 Instances

When you launch EC2 instances, you must provision enough storage for running your applications and services. AWS offers four different types of storage that you can use with EC2 instances, each serving a different purpose. You don't necessarily need to use all four storage types:

- **Amazon EC2 instance store**   Non-durable data storage
- **Amazon Elastic Block store (EBS)**   Durable storage
- **Amazon Elastic File System (Amazon EFS)**   Durable storage
- **Amazon Simple Storage Service (Amazon S3)**   Durable storage

In Chapter 7, I discuss the Amazon S3 storage, Amazon Elastic File System, and Amazon Glacier, which is a storage option for cheaper, long-term storage of infrequently used data. Here, my focus is on explaining how to use EBS and the EC2 instance store for running an EC2 instance. I also show how you can use S3 storage for storing the backups and snapshots that you create for an EC2 instance.

Amazon EC2 Instance Store

An EC2 instance store, also referred to as instance storage, is a set of disks attached to the host computer on which an EC2 instance runs. This set of temporary block-level storage volumes are meant for data that changes often, such as caches and buffers. The size of the instance store varies according to the instance type.

Each EC2 instance store uses a specific instance store and not multiple stores. However, an instance store can serve as temporary storage for multiple instances. Figure 4-5 shows how instance stores support instances. Each host server has a single instance store that contains one or more storage volumes. In this example, there are four volumes in the instance store in each host computer, but Server 1 supports two instances and Server 2 just one instance.

 NOTE Instance store data is stored only during the lifetime of the instance.

In Figure 4-5, there are four volumes in the instance store on each of the two host computers. The devices are named ephemeral0, ephemeral1, ephemeral2, and ephemeral3, which is the naming convention for instance store volumes.

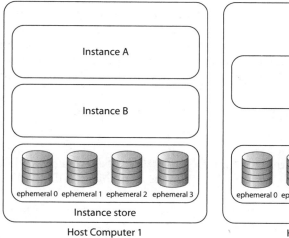
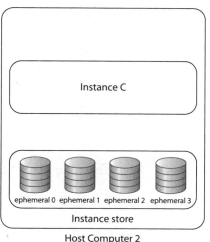

Figure 4-5 Relationship between an instance store and an instance.

Instance Store: Key Facts

Here are key things to remember about an instance store:

- You must specify the instance store volumes when you launch an instance. You can't add instance store volumes after the instance starts running.
- The data on an instance store volume persists only while the instance to which the volume is attached is running.
- When you stop or terminate the instance, the instance store data is lost, because AWS resets all the storage blocks in the store. If you reboot the instance, however, the instance store data remains intact.
- Not all EC2 instance types support instance storage.
- EC2 instances that use instance storage take longer to boot than instances that use EBS storage.
- If the disk drive supporting the instance store fails, the data is lost.
- You specify the instance store volumes for an instance with a block device mapping file (the file's entries include the device and the volumes it maps to).
- You can use an instance store as swap space.
- The cost of the instance storage volumes is included in the pricing of the EC2 instance.

 TIP For optimal instance store volume performance, initialize the disk drives by writing once to each drive location, with the Linux dd command.

Size of the Instance Store

The size of the instance store depends on the instance type that you choose and the hardware type used to create the instance store's volumes. For example, the ds.xlarge instance type comes with 3X2000 GB (6TB) instance store volumes, and the m1.small instance type with a single 160GB volume. AWS doesn't charge you extra for the instance store volumes—as mentioned earlier, it includes the volumes in the instance's usage cost.

 TIP Some instance types don't support an instance store.

Each instance type comes with one of the following disk types for the instance store: HDD, SSD, or NVMe. The SSD and NVMe disk types offer high random I/O performance and are suitable for use cases where you need low latency.

You specify the instance volumes at the instance launch time. Once the instance starts running, it depends on the instance type whether the instances are already mounted. If the volumes aren't mounted, you must mount them. Most volumes are formatted with the ext3 file system. If the volumes are unformatted in a Linux system, you can format them with the `mkfs` command, and then mount the drives with the `mount` command.

Amazon Elastic Block Store

Amazon EBS consists of storage volumes that persist across the lifecycle of instances. If you need to persist your data, EBS is the way to go. EBS also offers fast access, making it an ideal storage format for use by databases and other applications that frequently update data and require persistence.

When you run a database such as Oracle or Apache Cassandra, you store the data on the EBS volumes. EBS volumes are suitable for both database-style applications that require random reads/writes as well as applications that require heavy throughput and perform long, continuous reads/writes.

EBS is, in many ways, the most important storage type for an EC2 instance, and it's something that administrators will deal with often.

EBS volumes are like raw, unformatted disk drives, and you can create a file system on these drives, just as you can on any other block device such as a hard drive. EBS encrypts data using AWS Key Management Service (KMS), which means you don't need to worry about managing your own key management infrastructure.

Both EBS disk volumes and any snapshots you make of them are encrypted. Since the encryption is done on the server that hosts the EC2 instance, data is encrypted when it's in transit between the instance and EBS storage.

Here are key things to remember about EBS:

- You create EBS volumes in a specific AZ.
- You can mount multiple volumes on a single instance.
- You can attach EBS volumes to a running EC2 instance.
- When you shut down the instance, the EBS storage volumes aren't affected; their existence is independent of the instance lifecycle.
- You can attach an EBS volume only to one instance at any time.
- You can detach the EBS volume from one instance and reattach it to another running instance in the same AZ.
- You can take backups of the EBS volumes, called *snapshots*, which are stored in Amazon S3.
- You can create new EBS volumes from a snapshot.
- Since EBS is a separate service, it's priced separately from the EC2 instance to which you attach the EBS volumes.

Restoring an EBS-Backed EC2 Instance

If you find that you are unable to restore a session for an EBS-backed instance, you can use snapshots of the EBS volume to create a new AMI and launch a new instance from this AMI. Exercise 4-5 includes the steps you need to perform to restore the instance.

There are several types of EBS volumes you can choose from, as the next section explains.

 NOTE An Amazon EBS volume is tied to its AZ, and you can attach a volume only to instances in the same AZ.

EBS Volume Types

There are four EBS volume types you can choose from, with the main difference among the different types being their price/performance ratio:

- General purpose SSD
- Provisioned IOPS SSD
- Throughput-optimized HDD
- Cold HDD

Chapter 7, which is dedicated to AWS storage options, explains the four EBS volume types, as well as the key EBS administration topics.

Creating an EBS Volume

You can create an EBS volume either when launching an instance or later, while the instance is running.

 TIP You can attach an encrypted EBS volume only to select instance types.

You can create an EBS volume either through the EC2 console or through the command line. Chapter 5 shows how to create an EBS volume through the console.

Run the EC2 CLI command `create-volume` to create an EBS volume. This command creates the volume and attaches it to an instance in the same AZ as the instance. Always tag your EBS volumes so you can track them. Here's an example that shows how to create a volume and apply two tags to it, named `purpose` (`Value=production`) and `department` (`Value=accounting`):

```
$ aws ec2 create-volume --availability-zone us-east-1a --volume-type gp2
--size 80 --tag-specifications 'ResourceType=volume,Tags=[{Key=purpose,Value=
production},{Key=department,Value=cc123}]'
```

The `ec2 create-volume` command shown here creates an EBS volume of type gp2 (General Purpose SSD), sized 80GB. If you were to create a volume of the Provisioned IOPS SSD type, you need to specify the maximum number of IOPS that the volume should support.

Specifying a Block Device Mapping

Every EC2 instance that you launch will have a root device volume (EBS or instance store volume). Use *block device mapping* to specify extra volumes to attach to the instance when you launch it.

A block device is a storage device that supports random access and uses buffered I/O, such as hard disks and flash drives. Block devices can be attached to the computer physically or accessed remotely.

Although you can attach additional EBS volumes to a running instance, the only way to attach instance store volumes is to attach them at instance launch by specifying block device mapping.

Availability of EBS Volumes

An EBS volume is available right away for full use after you create it. You don't need to pre-warm or initialize the volume. If you were to create a volume by restoring it from a snapshot, however, EC2 must first initialize it by retrieving the snapshot from Amazon S3 storage and writing it to the EBS volume. Therefore, the first time an I/O operation accesses the volume, there's a slight delay. However, once the initial data is accessed, the maximum performance of the EBS volume is fully available.

Amazon Elastic File System

Amazon offers scalable file storage you can use with EC2 instances. You create a single EFS file system and mount it and make the file system available for multiple instances. EFS is a separate service and you must pay a separate cost for using it. You can use EFS only for Linux-based EC2 instances. Chapter 7 discusses EFS.

The Root Device Volume

Each EC2 instance has a *root device volume* that contains the AMI that you used to launch the instance. Although you can choose between an AMI backed by an instance store (for the instances that allow you to use an instance store—you can't do this for the T2 instance type, for example) or one that's backed by Amazon EBS, Amazon recommends that you use EBS-backed AMIs because of their faster speed and the fact that they offer persistent rather than ephemeral storage.

 TIP AWS recommends that if you use an instance store–backed instance to distribute the data on the instance store volumes across AZs. You should also frequently back up the instance store volumes to persistent storage.

If you use an instance store for the root device, when you launch the instance, the AMI that you use to boot the instance is copied to the root volume. You can't stop an instance store–backed instance, however; you can only terminate it. If you terminate the instance or the instance fails, you'll be unable to restore the instance. If you instead use an EBS volume for your instances, you can stop and start the instance without losing the data on the attached EBS volume.

 NOTE AWS strongly recommends that you use an encrypted EBS volume for your root volume, so that data is encrypted both at rest and when the data is moving between the instance and the volume.

Choosing the Root Device Type

You know by now that you launch an instance with the help of an AMI. The AMI you choose determines the root device type; some AMIs are EBS-backed and others are instance store–backed. When you choose the AMI in the EC2 console, specify either EBS Images or Instance store for the Root Device Type option.

Finding the Root Device Type

You can find the root device type an instance is using from the EC2 console or the command line. In the console, in the navigation pane, choose Instances; then, after selecting the instance you want to check, view the root device type by clicking the Description tab. For example, if you're using an EBS-backed instance, you'll see something like the following:

```
device type
ebs
Root device
/dev/sd1
```

From the command line, the ec2 describe-instances command's root-device-name and root-device-type attributes show you details about the root device being used by the instance.

Additional EC2 Features

In the following sections, I briefly describe additional EC2 features.

Instance Placement Groups

A *placement group* is a logical grouping of EC2 instances. It determines how an instance (VM) is placed on the hardware. You can create a placement group and launch instances into that placement group. All instances in a placement group must belong to the same AZ and region.

If your applications can benefit from low network latency and/or high network throughput, you should think about configuring placement groups. For best results, choose an EC2 instance type that supports *enhanced networking*. There's no extra charge for using the enhanced networking EC2 feature.

There are two ways in which you can create a placement group:

- **Use a cluster strategy**   To launch instances in a single AZ to reduce latency. The placement groups are called *cluster placement groups*.

- **Use a spread strategy**   To spread instances across the hardware. The placement groups are called *spread placement groups*.

TIP   To take full advantage of a placement group that you configure and attain a high packet-per-second network performance for the group, choose an EC2 instance type that supports enhanced networking.

Auto Scaling

Amazon EC2 Auto Scaling helps you dynamically scale your EC2 capacity up or down, according to the conditions you specify. If there is a sudden increase in demand, the Auto Scaling capability will automatically increase the number of EC2 instances to meet the additional demand. Chapter 11 discusses EC2 Auto Scaling.

Amazon EBS-Optimized Instances

An *EBS-optimized instance* is a special type of instance that's optimally configured and provides extra, dedicated capacity for supporting EBS I/O. EBS-optimized instances enhance the performance of an EBS volume by reducing contention between EBS I/O and other instance traffic. Not all instance types support EBS optimization. Chapter 7 discusses EBS-optimized instances.

You can enable EBS optimization either at instance launch time or enable/disable optimization for a running instance.

If you are running performance-sensitive workloads that require high performance minimal variability, such as production databases or business-critical applications, AWS recommends that you use EBS-optimized instances. Alternatively, or in conjunction with the EBS-optimized instances, you can choose an instance type that offers a 10Gb network connectivity capability.

Backing Up Instances and Volumes with EC2Rescue for Linux

You can back up an instance or one or more volumes with EC2Rescue for Linux. Here's how you run the backup commands.

You can back up an instance:

```
$ ./ec2rl run -backup-ami
```

You can back up all volumes attached to an instance:

```
$ ./ec2rl run -backupallvolumes
```

Monitoring EC2 Instances

Amazon CloudWatch and Amazon CloudTrail are both useful for monitoring much more than just EC2 instances (and are discussed in detail in Chapter 10). Both are essential tools for monitoring EC2 instances, however.

Amazon CloudWatch Monitoring

Amazon CloudWatch monitors EC2 instances metrics such as CPU utilization, disk reads/writes, and instance/system status checks. By default, CloudWatch is enabled for all your EC2 instances, with basic monitoring (collects metrics at five-minute intervals) enabled by default.

You can use CloudWatch to trigger alarms that can stop, reboot, terminate, or recover instances. You can create a CloudWatch alarm that monitors instances and automatically recovers them when they become impaired.

You must assign an IAM role to the EC2 instance at launch time, with permissions to write to CloudWatch, so that custom EC2 CloudWatch metrics scripts can send the metrics data to CloudWatch.

NOTE   You must always use an IAM role when providing permissions to any AWS service (such as AWS CloudWatch) from an EC2 instance. Roles allow you to control the ability to execute AWS APIs.

Amazon CloudTrail Logging

CloudTrail stores the history of all AWS API calls and other events for your AWS account. It also logs all EC2 actions, such as who made API calls to EC2. This enables you to find out if the requests that were generated to EC2 were made with root or IAM user credentials or by other AWS cloud services.

Tagging EC2 Resources

As you ramp up with EC2, you'll find yourself creating and owning many EC2 resources. *Tags* are metadata that you can assign to an EC2 resource. Tags are optional, but tagging is a best practice because it helps you categorize and track your resources. For example, if you want a specific group of IAM users to be able to access only your test instances and not the production servers, you can define tags on the test and production servers and add a condition to the IAM policy that permits access to specific tags, such as development or production tags. You can tag resources to create categories of AWS resources, based on the owner, purpose, or environment. This helps you easily identify sets of instances of the same type. For example, you can assign Category as the key name and Testing and Production as the values for a tag.

You can use tags to provide better oversight of your resource usage, by organizing your AWS bills and setting up a cost allocation report with tags. Cost allocation tags help you determine which resources are contributing the most to your AWS spending.

Most EC2 resources, such as AMIs, EC2 instances, EBS volumes, and snapshots, enable you to place tags on them. You can even attach a tag to a Spot instance request. All taggable resources enable you to attach a tag specification when you create the resource. In addition, you can also tag most EC2 resources that already exist.

Creating Tags

You can create a tag for an instance or an EBS volume when you launch an instance or when you create a volume. Both the Instance Creation Wizard and the volume creation process offer you a chance to tag the instance or the volume.

There are a few basic restrictions when you apply a tag, such as staying within a maximum number of tags per resource (50) and ensuring that tag keys and values are case-sensitive. The maximum length of the tag key is 127 Unicode characters in UTF-8. The maximum length of the tag value is 255 characters. The commonly allowed tag values (across AWS services) are letters, spaces, and numbers representable in UTF-8, and the special characters +, −, =, ., _, :, /, and @.

An easy way to create and manage tags centrally is through the Tag Editor in the AWS Management Console. In the console, choose Resource Groups in the navigation bar and then choose Tag Editor. If you need to tag a bunch of resources, the Tag Editor is the way to go. The editor makes it easy for you to find all resources in your account and create tags by adding keys for the resources. You can then choose either to add individual tag values or to use the bulk add feature to add the same values to many resources.

As with most other things, you can run an EC2 CLI command to attach tags to a resource. The following example shows you how:

```
$ aws ec2 run-instances --image-id ami-abc12345 --count 1 --instance-
type t2.micro --key-name MyKeyPair --subnet-id subnet-6e7f829e --tag-
specifications 'ResourceType=instance,Tags=[{Key=cost-center,Value=cc123}]'
'ResourceType=volume,Tags=[{Key=cost-center,Value=cc123}]'
```

As this example shows, you can attach tags to more than one resource at a time. The run-instances command attaches the same tag both to the instance it's launching and to the EBS volume that it's attaching to the instance.

Resource Groups and Tags

A *resource group* is a collection of resources that share at least one tag. By setting up resource groups, you can view metrics, alarms, and the configurations for a set of resources in a single view. To do this, you must specify the tag (or tags) when searching for the resources.

Viewing Tags

You can view the tags for a specific resource, such as an EC2 instance, by going to the EC2 instance resource page and viewing the tags in the Tags tab in the details pane. To view the tags you've created for all resources, select Tags in the EC2 console navigation pane.

You can run the `ec2 describe-instances` command and filter the instances using tags. Here's an example that shows how to list all instances with a specific tag (`Stack=production`).

```
$ aws ec2 describe-instances –filters Name=tag:Stack, Values=production
```

This example shows how to describe all instances with the value `Production`. The key is unspecified because we are interested in all instances that have `Production` as the value for the key.

Creating EBS Snapshots

A *snapshot* helps you take a point-in-time backup of an EBS volume. A snapshot creates an incremental backup of an EC2 volume that EC2 stores in S3. You can create a new EC2 volume using data stored in a snapshot by specifying the snapshot's ID. AWS stores all snapshots in Amazon S3.

 NOTE An EBS snapshot is tied to its region, and you can use a snapshot to create volumes in the same region.

When you delete a snapshot, only the data unique to that snapshot is deleted. An active snapshot contains all the data you need to restore an EBS volume by creating a new EBS volume from the snapshot. Creating a snapshot could take some time, depending on the size of the source EBS volume. You can create up to five snapshots concurrently. Chapter 7 shows you how to create EBS snapshots.

Configuring EC2 Instances

An EC2 instance that you launch will contain software and utilities for running basic server operations. The Amazon Linux instances have a preconfigured ec2-user account, and Ubuntu Linux has a preconfigured ubuntu account. You can add other user accounts, just as you do in a regular Linux server. Similarly, after launching the instances, you can change the instance's hostname.

The important thing to know in the instance configuration area is that you can pass configuration data, called *user data*, at runtime. The instance uses the data that you supply to perform configuration tasks at instance start time. You can pass two types of user data: *shell scripts* and `cloud-init` directives.

Passing User Data with Shell Scripts

The easiest way to send instructions to an instance at launch time is through a shell script. Here's what you need to know about passing user data at launch time:

- You can specify user data when you launch an instance. You can also stop an instance and update its user data (if the root volume is an EBS volume).

- The scripts that you use to specify user data are run as the root user.
- Adding user-defined tasks at boot time makes the bootup process longer, since the user tasks that you specify in the script must complete before the instance is available.
- You can add user data when launching an instance from an AMI. You do this by copying your shell script in the User Data field during the instance creation process.

The following example shows how to pass user data in a file called my_script.txt. The file my_script.txt has the following user data:

```
#!/bin/bash
yum update -y
yum install -y httpd24 php56 mysql55-server ph6-mysqlnd
service httpd start
chkconfig httpd on
groupadd www
usermod -a -G www ec2-user
chown -R root:www /var/www
chmod 2775 /var/www
find /var/www -type d -exec chmod 2775 {} +
find /var/www -type f -exec chmod 0664 {} +
echo "<?php phpinfo(); ?>" > /var/www/html/phpinfo.php
```

You can then execute the ec2 run-instances command and point to the file my_script.txt with the –user-data attribute to launch an instance. The instance will boot up after executing the commands in your shell script (my_script.txt).

```
$ aws ec2 run-instances --image-id ami-abc1234 --count 1 --instance-type
m4.large --key-name keypair --user-data file://my_script.txt --subnet-id
subnet-abcd1234 --security-group-ids sg-abcd1234
```

You can also specify user data to build an AMI that is modified by the configuration data supplied at launch time. For example, you can specify user data that modifies an AWS Linux AMI into a web server.

Passing User Data with Cloud-Init Directives

You can pass cloud-init user directives at instance launch time. As with the running of commands by including them in a shell script, adding tasks at boot time through the cloud-init directives makes an instance take more time during its bootup, since it must ensure that the directives have completed their tasks.

Here's a cloud-init equivalent for the shell script that I showed earlier:

```
cloud-config
repo_update: true
repo_upgrade: all

packages:
 - httpd24
 - php56
 - mysql55-server
 - php56-mysqlnd
```

```
runcmd:
 - service httpd start
 - chkconfig httpd on
 - groupadd www
 - [ sh, -c, "usermod -a -G www ec2-user" ]
 - [ sh, -c, "chown -R root:www /var/www" ]
 - chmod 2775 /var/www
 - [ find, /var/www, -type, d, -exec, chmod, 2775, {}, + ]
 - [ find, /var/www, -type, f, -exec, chmod, 0664, {}, + ]
 - [ sh, -c, 'echo "<?php phpinfo(); ?>" > /var/www/html/phpinfo.php' ]
```

As with commands inside a shell script, you can provide `cloud-init` directive commands through the EC2 console or from the command line.

 TIP User data is limited to 16KB in the raw form. However, you can link user data to a location such as an Amazon S3 bucket to load a larger file at instance launch time.

Run the `ec2 describe-instance-attribute` command to view the user data for an instance:

```
$ aws ec2 describe-instance-attribute --instance-id i-1234567890abcdef0
--attribute userData
```

If you stop an instance, change its user data, and restart the instance, it won't update the user data that was executed when you originally started the instance.

Instance Metadata

Instance metadata is the data about an instance that you can use to configure or manage a running instance. For example, you can determine the public and private IP addresses of an instance by querying the instance metadata. There are several categories of instance metadata, such as block device mapping, hostname, and instance-type.

 TIP You can access instance metadata and user data only from the instance. However, since that data isn't safeguarded with cryptographic methods, you shouldn't store passwords and other sensitive data as user data.

You don't have to run a command with the AWS CLI or go the EC2 console to retrieve instance metadata. Instead, you can view all the instance metadata directly from the running instance itself. The following URI lets you view all categories of instance metadata from a running instance: http://169.254.169.254/latest/meta-data/.

 NOTE AWS doesn't charge you for the HTTP requests that retrieve instance metadata and user data.

You can view top-level metadata items like this, with the `curl` tool:

```
[ec2-user ~]$ curl http://168.252.168.252/latest/meta-data/
ami-id
ami-launch-index
ami-manifest-path
block-device-mapping/
hostname
iam/
instance-action
instance-id
instance-type
...
```

The following `curl` command gets you the public hostname:

```
$ curl http://168.252.168.252/latest/meta-data/public-hostname
ec2-203-0-113-25.compute-1.amazonaws.com
```

Alternatively, you can download and install the Instance Metadata Query tool (https://aws.amazon.com/code/ec2-instance-metadata-query-tool/) to query the instance metadata.

An EC2 instance can also use dynamic data such as an instance identity document, which is generated during instance launch. The instance identity document is a JSON file that describes various instance attributes such as its private IP address and the instance ID. The document is exposed to the EC2 instance through instance metadata and helps validate instance attributes such as the instance type, subscribed software, OS, and the AMI.

You can use the user data you supplied during the launch of an instance to create a generic AMI that can be modified by configuration files that you supply at instance launch time. For example, you can run multiple web servers for different organizational units in your organization, all using the same AMI, and retrieving content from an S3 bucket that you specify in the user data at launch time.

EC2 Network and Security

EC2 employs several network and security features to safeguard access to your EC2 instances.

Protecting Access from the Command Line (or API)

Linux instances have no password. You use an access key ID and a secret access key (a key pair) when accessing EC2 using a command line tool such as AWS CLI or an API. (Chapter 2 explained how to do this.) Security is enhanced because you use your private key instead of a password. In a Windows instance, you obtain the admin password with a key pair and log in via Remote Desktop Protocol (RDP).

AWS's Trusted Advisor is part of AWS Support and can be useful in checking open ports on security groups and levels of access to the EC2 instance. The tool also recommends improvements in infrastructure security.

What to Do if You Lose Your Private Key

If you lose your private key, you won't be able to log into the instance via SSH. You need to do the following to regain access to the instance:

1. Stop the instance.
2. Detach the root device volume and attach it to another instance as a non-root (data) volume.
3. Modify the authrorized_keys file.
4. Move the volume back to the original instance as the root device volume.
5. Start the instance.
6. You can now log into the instance again.

Configuring Security Groups to Control Network Traffic

Security groups act as virtual firewalls to control network traffic into and out of an EC2 instance. You add rules to a security group to specify which traffic is allowed into and out of an instance. Following this, you associate an instance at launch time with one or more security groups.

 TIP Security groups control access to instances, and IAM policies control how users use your EC2 resources.

You can configure a security group to allow access via ports, protocols, and sources. Sources can be IP addresses or a different security group.

Here are the key things to know about security groups in relation to EC2 instances:

- You must attach a security group with either SSH (for Linux instances) or RDP (for Windows instances) to log into the guest OS.
- You can't set up a security group with a deny rule.
- By default, security groups allow all outbound access.
- It's recommended that you use security groups mainly for controlling inbound access (though you can control outbound access as well).

Controlling Access to EC2 Resources

Use AWS IAM *policies* and *roles* to control how users, services, and applications use your EC2 resources. IAM enables you to create roles in your AWS account and specify users or services that can assume those roles. It also helps you control user permissions to perform tasks using AWS resources by creating IAM policies and attaching them to the users or groups that need those permissions.

Here's an IAM policy that grants users permission to perform API actions listed under the `Action` element of the policy, such as describing instances and starting, stopping, or terminating the instances:

```
{
    "Version": "2012-10-17",
    "Statement": [{
        "Effect": "Allow",
        "Action": [
            "ec2:DescribeInstances", "ec2:DescribeImages",
            "ec2:DescribeKeyPairs", "ec2:DescribeSecurityGroups",
            "ec2:DescribeAvailabilityZones",
            "ec2:RunInstances", "ec2:TerminateInstances",
            "ec2:StopInstances", "ec2:StartInstances"
        ],
        "Resource": "*"
    }
}
```

IAM roles help applications make secure API requests from your EC2 instances. Instead of distributing your AWS credentials to each instance, you delegate permission to make API requests using IAM roles. For example, you can create an IAM role that grants permissions to applications running on your EC2 instances to use specific Amazon S3 buckets. You can create IAM policies to specify permissions for IAM roles. These policies are like policies you create for IAM users.

Amazon Virtual Private Cloud

Amazon Virtual Private Cloud (VPC) enables you to define your own virtual network within the AWS cloud and launch instances and other resources into the VPC. An Amazon VPC works much like a network in your own data center: you can configure it, select your own IP address ranges, create subnets, and configure routing and security settings. For additional protection, you can create security groups and network access control lists (NACLs) for each subnet in your VPC.

You can connect a VPC to your own data center, thus helping you extend your data center into the AWS cloud. Chapter 6 discusses Amazon VPC.

Elastic, Private, and Public IP Addresses

There are three types of IP addresses you must be aware of, in the context of EC instances: private, elastic, and public.

Private IP Addresses

When you launch an EC2 instance, AWS assigns a private IP address to the network interface of that instance. The exact IP address depends on the VPC and the subnet in which you launch the instance. The private IP address is assigned from that subnet block's list of addresses.

The private IP address is attached to the instance's network interface, and when you stop and restart the instance, it remains attached to the interface. Once you delete the instance, the address is released.

Elastic IP Addresses

Your AWS account is also associated with an elastic IP (EIP) address, which is reachable from the Internet. When an EC2 instance experiences failure and doesn't have a public IPv4 address, you can associate an EIP address with that instance to mask the failure of the instance. When you associate an EIP address with an instance, that instance's public IPv4 address is released back into Amazon's pool of public addresses. You can't reuse the address. The public DNS hostname of the instance will also change to match the new EIP address.

When you delete an EC2 instance with an EIP address, that address isn't returned to AWS's pool of available IP addresses. Your account retains that IP address and the IP address will be later reassigned to other instances in your own account.

Here are some key facts about an EIP address:

- An EIP is associated with your AWS account.
- You can ensure that the IP address for an instance doesn't change after it stops and restarts by launching the instance with an EIP. If, for example, you're mapping an instance's IP address to a custom domain in AWS Route 53, you should associate an EIP with the instance.
- An EIP is a static IPv4 address that helps in dynamic cloud computing scenarios.
- EIPs help you mask instance or software failures by quickly remapping the IP address of the failed instance to a different EC2 instance in your account.
- There's a charge for using EIP addresses. AWS charges you for any unassigned EIPs, to discourage you from hoarding the addresses.

Public IP Addresses

Like an EIP address, a public IP address is also assigned to an interface. However, when you delete an instance with a public IP address, that IP address is returned to AWS's IP address pool and will be reassigned to another instance (most probably to instances that belong to other AWS accounts).

Amazon Systems Manager

Amazon Systems Manager is an unified interface that helps you centralize operational data and automate tasks throughout AWS. It provides you visibility into your AWS infrastructure and gives you control over that infrastructure. With the help of Systems Manager, you can group resources such as EC2 instances and RDS instances by application and view the operational data for troubleshooting problems and taking action on the groups of resources that you configure. The tool helps you automatically collect inventory information, apply patches, create system images, and configure operating systems.

By automating things, Amazon Systems Manager helps you easily track system configuration and maintain software compliance. You can use the tool both for EC2 instances (Windows and Linux) running in your AWS infrastructure and for on-premise servers in your own data center.

NOTE Amazon Systems Manager was previously called Amazon EC2 Systems Manager.

Following are the essentials of the Systems Manager:

- **Resource groups** A resource group is a collection of resources within a single AWS region. You can create resource groups to simplify management tasks on a set of resources through various tools in Systems Manager.

- **Insights** Insights show details about a single resource group at a time, such as CloudTrail logs and Trusted Advisor reports. The Inventory Manager and the Configuration Compliance tools gather system and OS configuration metadata and scan managed instances for patch compliance and configuration consistency.

- **Actions** Systems Manager offers tools to automate deployment and maintenance tasks (the Automation tool), run commands to update applications (the Run Command tool), manage your EC2 instances through a browser-based shell or through the AWS CLI (the Session Manager tool), manage patching of instances (the Patch Manager tool), and set up recurring schedules for performing administrative tasks in the managed instances (the Maintenance Windows tool).

  - The Systems Manager Session Manager capability makes it easy for you to comply with corporate security policies that require you to control instance access.

  - If your organization has mandated that all your EC2 instances be patched with the most up-to-date security patches, AWS Systems Manager Patch Manager is an ideal tool in ensuring that this mandate is fulfilled. Patch Manager automates the process of patching instances with security updates. (for Linux instances, it can also install patches for non-security updates.) Remember that AWS doesn't test patches for Windows or Linux servers before making them available in the Patch Manager action.

- **Shared resources** Systems Manager uses shared resources such as managed instances, Systems Manager documents (defines actions that the Systems Manager performs on your managed instances), and the Parameter Store (securely stores configuration data and secrets such as passwords) to manage and configure AWS resources.

You can access Systems Manager through the Systems Manager console, AWS CLI, and AWS SDKs.

Chapter Review

Amazon EC2 is a vast topic, and this chapter reviewed all the key aspects of working with EC2 instances. You learned about various aspects of working with EC2 instances, such as the various instance types and how to choose from among them. The chapter explained the lifecycle of an EC2 instance and showed you how to perform common tasks such as starting and stopping the instances.

I explained the various types of storage, such as instance storage and EBS volumes, in this chapter. Chapter 8, which is all about AWS storage, will delve into the details of EBS and other storage types.

A key aspect of your job as an AWS SysOps administrator is to save on the costs of running your AWS infrastructure. Knowing how and when to use Spot instances and Reserved instances are key to minimizing your EC2 instance costs.

Exercises

The exercises are designed to teach you how to perform critical EC2-related administrative tasks through the EC2 console. To perform the tasks, follow the steps and refer to the guidance provided by the EC2 console. There are no answers to any of the exercises; if you make a mistake, retrace your steps and ensure that you've correctly performing the steps. You'll know that you've correctly completed the exercise if you achieve the goal set for you in each exercise, such as creating an instance from a snapshot.

Exercise 4-1: Find the root device type of an AMI using the console.

1. Open the EC2 Console.

2. In the navigation pane, select AMIs.

3. Select an AMI.

4. In the Details tab, find the Root Device Type. If the device type is ebs, then the AMI is EBS-backed. If the device type is instance store, it's an instance store–backed AMI.

Exercise 4-2: Launch an EC2 Linux instance from the EC2 console (with the Instance Launch Wizard).

1. Go to the Amazon EC2 console at https://console.aws.amazon.com/ec2/.

2. At the upper-right, click the region name that's showing and select a region that meets your needs, such a US East (Ohio).

3. From the EC2 console dashboard, select Launch Instance.

4. On the Step 1: Choose An Amazon Machine Image (AMI) page, choose an AMI. For this example, under Quick Start, select Free Tier Only to select an AMI that's eligible for the free tier.

5. On the Step 2: Choose an Instance Type page, select the t2.micro instance type to remain eligible for the free tier. Then click Next: Configure Instance Details at the bottom of the page.

6. On the Step 3: Configure Instance Details page, for Number Of Instances enter the value **2**. This will launch two EC2 instances. Click Next: Add Storage.

7. On the Step 4: Add Storage page, do the following:

   a. Click Add New Volume to specify an additional volume to attach to the two instances (by default, the instance will have one or more storage volumes, including the root device volume).

   b. By default, the additional volume is an unencrypted EBS volume. Under Size, specify 20GB as the value to stay within the free tier, which allows you a maximum of 30GB storage.

   c. For Volume Type, select General Purpose SSD (the default volume type).

   d. Click Next: Add Tags.

8. On the Step 5: Add Tags page, click Add Tag. Under Key, enter **Test**, and under Value, enter **Webserver**. Click Next: Configure Security Group.

9. On the Step 6: Configure Security Group page, create a new security group by selecting Create A New Security Group (the wizard creates an inbound rule that enables you to use SSH to connect to your new instances). Click Review And Launch.

10. On the Step 7: Review Instance Launch page, make any final changes via the appropriate Edit links. Select Launch to launch the two EC2 instances you've configured.

11. In the Select An Existing Key Pair Or Create A New Key Pair dialog box, select Create A New Key Pair. Enter **TestKeyPair** as the key pair name.

12. Click Download Key Pair to download the private key file (TestKeyPair.pem) and store the file from where you can retrieve it later. You'll need this file when connecting to the instances via SSH from the command line.

13. Click Launch Instance. You'll see a launch Status page in a few seconds, informing you that the two instances launches were initiated.

14. Click View Instance at the bottom of this page. You can now go to the EC2 home page and click the 2 Running Instances link to view your new instances.

Exercise 4-3: Restore a failed (or old) EC2 instance by creating a new AMI with a snapshot.

1. Create a snapshot of the root volume.

2. Register a new AMI using the snapshot from step 1.

3. Launch an EC2 instance with the new AMI.

4. Detach all the non-root EBS volumes from the failed (or old) instance.

5. Attach the EBS volumes from the original instance to the new EC2 instance.

Exercise 4-4: Create an AMI from an instance using the console.

1. Go to the Amazon EC2 console at https://console.aws.amazon.com/ec2/.

2. In the console's navigation pane, choose Instances, and select your instance. Then choose Actions | Image | Create Image.

3. In the Create Image page, provide values for the Image Name and Image Description attributes, and select No Reboot to avoid an instance restart. Click Create Image.

4. You'll see a notification from EC2 stating Create Image Request received, along with the image ID. Click View pending image ami-0bbee3a8dfa3ecf15.

5. In the EC2 console, you can watch the status of the AMI creation. The initial status will show up as "pending" and changes to "available" once the AMI is created.

6. You can launch an instance from the new AMI using the procedure explained in Exercise 4-2.

Exercise 4-5: Associate an Elastic IP address with an EC2 instance.

1. Go to the Amazon EC2 console: https://console.aws.amazon.com/ec2/.

2. In the EC2 dashboard, under the Network and Security heading (on the left side), select Elastic IPs.

3. Click Allocate A New Address.

4. Associate the address with a running EC2 instance by clicking Allocate.

5. Make sure that AWS responds with the "New address request succeeded" message.

Exercise 4-6: Resize an Amazon EBS-backed instance.

1. Go to the Amazon EC2 console: https://console.aws.amazon.com/ec2/.

2. Choose Instances and select the instance whose instance type you want to modify.

3. Stop the instance by selecting Actions | Instance State | Stop.

4. Confirm that you want to stop the instance by selecting Yes, Stop. Wait for the instance to stop.

5. Once the instance state shows "Stopped," select Actions | Instance Settings | Change Instance Type.

6. The Change Instance Type dialog box then shows the instance types that are compatible with the current instance. Select the instance type you want from Instance Type.

7. Click Apply.

8. Restart the instance by selecting the instance and choosing Action | Instance State | Start.

9. Confirm that you want to restart the instance by selecting Yes, Start. Wait for the instance to indicate that it has entered the running state.

Exercise 4-7: Create a security group using the Amazon EC2 console.

1. Go to the Amazon EC2 console: https://console.aws.amazon.com/ec2/.

2. Select Security Groups.

3. Select Create Security Group.

4. Provide a name and description for your security group.

5. Choose a VPC ID to create a security group for the VPC.

6. Optionally, add rules now or click Create to create the security group and add the rules later.

Questions

The following questions will help you measure your understanding of the material presented in this chapter. Read all the choices carefully because there may be more than one correct answer. Choose all the correct answers for each question.

1. You've purchased some Reserved instances. Currently, you have no running instances in your environment. When can you start using your Reserved instances?

   A. You start using the Reserved instances as soon as you purchase them.

   B. The Reserved instances are unused until you launch an instance that matches the specifications of the Reserved instances you've purchased.

   C. Reserved instances are automatically applied to all On-Demand instances that are running.

   D. Reserved instances are automatically applied to running instances that match the specifications of the Reserved instances.

2. You're flexible about the times when your applications run, and the applications can handle interruptions. Which of the following instance purchase type will best meet your needs and also save on costs?

   A. Spot instance

   B. Reserved instance

   C. Scheduled instance

   D. On-Demand instance

3. Which of the following are true about Amazon Elastic Block Storage? (Choose two)

   A. When you stop an instance, the attached EBS volume is lost.

   B. AWS automatically replicates data you store on EBS volumes within an availability zone.

   C. You can encrypt EBS volumes in a manner that's transparent to the workload you're running on the instance the EBS volume is attached to.

   D. AWS automatically backs EBS data to a tape.

4. Which of the following EC2 features ensure(s) that your EC2 instances don't share a physical host with instances run by other AWS customers?

   A. Placement groups

   B. Security groups

   C. Amazon Virtual Private Cloud (VPC)

   D. Dedicated instances

5. When you take a snapshot of an EBS volume, when will the volume be available?

   A. The volume is available immediately.

   B. The availability is directly related to the size of the EBS volume: the larger the volume, the longer it takes for the volume to become available.

   C. If the volume is EBS-optimized, it will be available immediately; otherwise, it will take a few minutes before the volume is available.

   D. Availability of the volume depends on how much data is stored on the EBS volume.

6. A workload normally requires 1TB of durable block storage at 1500 IOPS. Every night you run a more intensive task that requires 3000 IOPS for 30 minutes. Which of the following volume types would be appropriate for this type of workload?

   A. A magnetic volume

   B. A general-purpose SSD volume

   C. A Provisioned IOPS SSD volume at 3000 IOPS

   D. An instance store volume

7. Which of the following will provide very low latency and a high bandwidth between the EC2 instances in an EC2 cluster you plan on creating?

   A. Enhanced networking on the instances

   B. Placement of the instances in a placement group

   C. Using an elastic IP address

   D. Using an instance type with 10 Gbps network performance

8. You have been tasked with identifying an appropriate storage solution for a NoSQL database that requires random I/O reads of greater than 100,000 4KB IOPS. Which EC2 option will meet this requirement?

   A. EBS Provisioned IOPS

   B. SSD instance store

   C. EBS optimized instances

   D. High storage instance configured in RAID 10

9. When an EC2 instance that is backed by an S3-based AMI is terminated, by default, what happens to the data on the root volume?

   A. Data is automatically saved as an EBS volume.

   B. Data is automatically saved as an EBS snapshot.

   C. Data is automatically deleted.

   D. Data is unavailable until the instance is restarted.

10. Growing business volumes require you to enlarge your EC2 instance size. Which of the following is the best way to increase the instance size?

    A. Stop the running EC2 instance and start it back up after raising the size of the instance.

    B. Create an AMI from the running instance. Use this AMI to create a new EC2 instance with the instance type you need.

    C. Take a snapshot of the running EC2 instance. Use this snapshot to create a larger EC2 instance.

    D. You can increase the size of a running EC2 instance by going to the EC2 console and clicking Resize Instance.

11. Which of the following would be *not* be the reason for your inability to access an Amazon EC2 instance through SSH?

    A. You have the wrong role.

    B. You have an incorrect private key.

    C. There's no public IP address attached to this EC2 instance.

    D. You're using an incorrect username or password.

12. Which of the following would be true of a dedicated EC2 instance? (Choose two)

    A. A dedicated instance is dedicated to a set of AWS customers.

    B. A dedicated instance is dedicated to a single AWS customer.

    C. A dedicated instance is the same as a dedicated host.

    D. A dedicated instance may share hardware from other instances in your account that aren't dedicated instances.

13. Which of the following instance properties is determined by the instance type you choose?

    A. The operating system

    B. The CPU family availability

    C. The instance's virtual IP address

    D. The location of the instance (region)

14. Which of the following options will offer the fastest boot time for an Amazon EC2 instance?

    A. An EBS-backed AMI with user data

    B. An EBS-backed AMI with no user data

    C. An instance store–backed AMI with user data

    D. An instance store–backed AMI with no user data

15. Which of the following strategies would enable the most secure way for an EC2 instance to access an object in an Amazon S3 bucket?

    A. Create an IAM role with the necessary permissions to access the S3 bucket and grant the role to the user who logged into the EC2 instance.

    B. Grant the EC2 instance appropriate permissions directly to access the XS3 bucket.

    C. Create a virtual private network.

    D. Create an IAM role with the necessary permissions to access the S3 bucket and attach the role to the EC2 instance.

16. Which of the following can you *not* do with an instance store–backed EC2 instance? (Choose two)

    A. Stop it.

    B. Delete it.

    C. Start it.

    D. Restart it.

17. What is a placement group?

    A. A collection of Auto Scaling groups in the same region

    B. A feature that enables EC2 instances to interact with each other via high bandwidth, low latency connections

    C. A collection of Elastic Load Balancers in the same region or availability zone

    D. A collection of CloudFront edge locations for a distribution

18. You want to ensure that a long-running AWS Batch job completes within a reasonable amount of time. Which of the following options will ensure that the job completes?

   A. Configure Spot pricing, and make sure your bid is much higher than the On-Demand price for the EC2 instances.

   B. Configure the number of instances to one more than what you need.

   C. Configure Spot pricing, making sure that your bid price is the same as the On-Demand price for the EC2 instances.

   D. Configure On-Demand pricing.

19. When can EC2 Spot service interrupt a Spot instance that you're running? (Choose two)

   A. When the Spot price falls below the maximum price that you've offered

   B. When the Spot prices goes beyond the maximum price that you've offered

   C. When there's no more capacity

   D. When the Spot price and your bid price become equal

20. What is Spot block in the context of Spot instances?

   A. It helps you block a set of Spot instances ahead of time.

   B. It helps you block other tenants of AWS from taking your Spot instances.

   C. You use a Spot block to keep EC2 from terminating a Spot instance when the Spot price changes.

   D. You use a Spot block to keep a Spot instance's price the same, regardless of demand for instances.

21. The instance type you specify when launching an EC2 instance determines which of the following?

   A. The hardware of the host computer for your instance

   B. The software of the host computer for your instance

   C. The hardware and software of the host computer for your instance

   D. The software you will be able to install and run on the instance

22. When AWS determines an irreparable failure of the hardware hosting an instance running with an EBS-backed root device, which of the following actions will AWS take?

   A. It immediately stops the instance.

   B. It immediately retires the instance.

   C. It reboots the instance when the instance reaches its retirement date.

   D. It stops or terminates the instance when the instance reaches its retirement date.

23. Which of the following actions can you perform when an instance is in the Stopped state? (Choose all that apply)

    A. Detach and attach the EBS volumes (and make changes to the EBS volume before reattaching).

    B. Change the kernel and RAM.

    C. Change the instance type.

    D. Change the instance name.

24. Which of the following are valid ways of launching an EC2 instance? (Choose all that apply)

    A. Launch an instance using an AMI, using the Launch Instance Wizard.

    B. Launch an instance using a launch template.

    C. Launch an instance from an existing EC2 instance.

    D. Launch a Linux instance from a backup.

25. Which of the following techniques can you use to clone a current instance?

    A. Select the Launch More Like This option in the EC2 console.

    B. First create an AMI from the current instance and launch an instance from that AMI.

    C. You can't clone an EC2 instance; you must always start from scratch to launch an instance with the same configuration.

    D. Back up the root device of an EBS-backed Linux instance by creating a snapshot. Launch a new instance from the snapshot.

Answers

1. B. Reserved instances aren't instances that you can use right away. Instead, they represent your right to launch EC2 instances that match the Reserve instances specifications. So, the Reserved instances aren't really used until you launch an instance that matches the specifications of the Reserved instances you've purchased.

2. A. If you are flexible about the scheduling of the instance and interruption of the instance availability isn't a problem, then a Spot instance is your best bet. Spot instances cost a lot less than the other instances but you aren't assured of their availability at a specific time. Also, if the Spot price exceeds your bid price for the Spot instances, AWS may terminate the Spot instances (with a two-minute notice).

3. B, C. AWS automatically replicates EBS volume data within an availability zone. You can also transparently encrypt EBS volumes.

4. D. Dedicated instances don't share physical hardware with instances (dedicated or not) from other AWS accounts.

5. A. When you take a snapshot of an EBS volume, the volume is available immediately.

6. C. A Provisioned IOPS SSD volume at 3000 IOPS would address this type of workload.

7. B. Placement groups are designed for applications that benefit from low network latency and/or high network throughput.

8. A. EBS Provisioned IOPS is the right solution for this use case.

9. C. Data is automatically deleted by default, but you can change this behavior by setting the `DeleteOnTermination` attribute for an EBS volume. For an EBS-based root device, this attribute is set to `true`. You can change the value to `false`, which will persist the root device volume after you terminate an instance.

10. A. It's easy to resize an EC2 instance. You must stop the instance first, choose a larger size for the instance, and start the instance back up.

11. A. IAM roles play no role in logging into an EC2 instance via SSH. Roles come into play when you execute an API.

12. B, D. A dedicated instance runs in a VPC on hardware dedicated to a single customer. A customer's dedicated instances are physically isolated at the host hardware level from other instances that belong to other accounts, but they may share hardware with non-dedicated instances from your own account.

13. B. Your choice of the AMI determines the CPU family availability, since some AMIs offer only some of the CPU families.

14. B. EBS-backed EC2 instances will boot faster than instance store–backed instances. And not having user data leads to faster book times, since user data slows down the boot process.

15. D. To enable the most secure way for an EC2 instance to access an object in an Amazon S3 bucket, create an IAM role with the necessary permissions to access the S3 bucket and attach the role to the EC2 instance.

16. A, D. You can't stop or restart an instance store–backed EC2 instance—you can only start it or delete it.

17. B. Placement groups enable EC2 instances to interact with each other via high bandwidth, low latency connections.

18. D. On-Demand pricing (the default for EC2 instances) is the best strategy here. Spot pricing depends on the presence of excess capacity, and if there's no excess capacity, the instances won't launch.

19. B, C. EC2 Spot service may interrupt a Spot instance when the Spot price goes beyond the maximum price you offered, or if there's no more available capacity.

20. C. You use a Spot block to keep EC2 from terminating a Spot instance when the Spot price changes. *Spot blocks* ensure that the instance will run for a required duration without interruptions, regardless of the changes in the Spot price for the instance.

21. **A.** The instance type you specify at instance launch time determines the hardware of the computer that hosts the instance.

22. **D.** When AWS detects an irreparable failure of the hardware that hosts an instance, it schedules the instance for retirement. It then stops or terminates the instance when the instance reaches its retirement date.

23. **A, B, C, D.** You can perform all four of the actions when you stop an instance.

24. **A, B, C, D.** You can launch instances through all four methods.

25. **B.** You can clone an instance, with its configuration, application software, and all data, by creating an AMI from the instance and using this AMI to create an instance, which will be an exact copy of the source instance. Selecting the Launch More Like This option only replicates some of the configuration details and backing up the root device with a snapshot and launching an instance from the snapshot doesn't copy the data and software from the source instance.

Computing in the Cloud: ECS, Batch, Lambda, and Other Compute Services

In this chapter, you will
- Learn how to manage containers with Amazon Elastic Container Service
- Learn how to manage and optimize workloads with AWS Batch
- Understand serverless computing using AWS Lambda
- Understand virtual private servers using AWS Lightsail
- Learn to quickly deploy and manage applications with Amazon Elastic Beanstalk

In Chapter 4, you learned about the well-known Elastic Compute Cloud (EC2) compute service. There are several other important AWS Compute services as well, and I discuss these in this chapter.

Docker and the Amazon Elastic Container Service

Docker is a software platform that uses *containers*, lightweight standardized units (based on Linux container technology) that enable you to build and deploy applications faster than you can with traditional full-fledged servers. Containers are created from templates called *images*. You normally build an image from a Dockerfile, a plain-text file wherein you specify the components of the container. Images are stored in a container registry from which you download and run the image on your cluster.

Docker packages everything that an application needs to run, such as the code, libraries, and runtime, into the containers. This helps you deploy the application into any environment you want without having to worry about the differences among the environments. Docker offers portability and speed. Your applications run the same regardless of the environments, and you can easily move applications from a development environment to a production deployment. Because you don't need to worry about the usual software dependency–related headaches, Docker helps you ship your applications much faster than you can with traditional means of development and deployment.

Although containers are excellent for building microservice applications and running ETL (extract, transform, and load) workloads, for example, managing them is not a trivial task. To schedule large numbers of containers across your cluster, you need to use a scheduling tool such as Kubernetes.

Amazon Elastic Container Service (ECS) is a container management service that helps you run Docker containers in the cloud, enabling you to run applications in a managed cluster of Amazon EC2 instances without the need for a specialized tool such as Kubernetes, a popular container orchestration framework. Amazon ECS helps you configure and manage your containers. You launch and place containers across your ECS cluster using API calls. Containers are highly available because they run across multiple availability zones (AZs) within an AWS region.

Amazon ECS makes it easy for you to create and manage Docker containers on a set of EC2 instances, together called a cluster. In addition to helping you manage container clusters, ECS helps greatly in scheduling the running of containers. You can have ECS schedule the placement of the containers based on your availability requirements and resource needs, thereby avoiding having to use a specialized cluster management system.

Container Launch Types

You can run a cluster of containers in one of two launch types, depending on whether ECS manages the container infrastructure or you do it manually:

- **AWS Fargate launch type**   Helps you run your containers in a serverless infrastructure managed by ECS. Everything runs in the AWS infrastructure, and you don't need to worry about managing the infrastructure components. You package your application in containers, specify the CPU/RAM, define the networking and security (Identity and Access Management [IAM]) policies, and launch the application.
- **Amazon ECS launch type**   Enables you to host your containers on a cluster of Amazon EC2 instances. You are responsible for overseeing the EC2 infrastructure because AWS doesn't manage it for you.

Currently the AWS Fargate launch type supports container images hosted in Amazon Elastic Container Registry (ECR) or on the public Docker Hub registry. Only the EC2 launch type supports private Docker repositories (self-hosted registries).

 NOTE   Use the Docker command line utility to manage a Docker instance as well as the containers that run in that instance.

Installing Docker

If you're going to use Amazon ECS, it's good to know something about Docker. Docker is easy to install, configure, and use. Use the following steps to install Docker on an Amazon EC2 instance, so you can get started with Docker operations:

1. Launch and connect to an Amazon Linux EC2 instance.
2. Update the installed packages and the package cache:

```
$ sudo yum update -y
```

3. Docker comes in both an Enterprise Edition (paid) and the Docker Community Edition 4 (free). Install the latest Docker Community Edition package:

```
$ sudo yum install -y docker
```

4. Use the Docker utility to manage Docker from the command line. Start the Docker service with the following command:

```
$ sudo service docker start
```

5. To avoid having to use sudo with every Docker command, execute the following usermod command to add the *ec2-user* to the docker group:

```
$ sudo usermod -a -G docker ec2-user
```

Once you install Docker, you are equipped to create containers and architect your applications to run in those containers.

The next section shows you how to create Docker containers and images, which are something like a blueprint for creating containers.

Creating Docker Containers and Images

Amazon ECS abstracts several things for you to make it easy for you to create, configure, and manage a cluster of Docker containers. To optimize your use of ECS, you need to understand the basics of creating and managing Docker containers directly with Docker commands, without using ECS. Once you get the hang of running Docker containers in an AWS cloud, you can use AWS EC2 commands to create and manage real-life Docker-based applications.

You create a Docker container from a template called an *image*. You create the image in turn from a Dockerfile. A Dockerfile is a manifest that tells Docker the base image (for example Linux 16:04) and the software and applications that you want the container to have. Once you create the image, you store it in a *registry* from where Docker will download the image and run it to create a new container. All of this is much easier than it sounds, as I show soon!

Before you create an image and a container from that image, it's good to know where you can access a Docker image. You've three main sources from where you can obtain the images for creating your Docker containers, as explained in the following section.

Hosting the Images

You access images from a container image repository. Following are the three types of container image repositories:

- **Amazon ECR**   You can use ECR registries to host your images and manage them. Amazon maintains ECR, and AWS provides each AWS account with a default Amazon ECR registry. The URL for the default registry is https://aws_account_id.dkr.ecr.region.amazonaws.com.

- **Docker Hub**   This cloud-based registry server enables you to build and test Docker images and obtain public images.

- **Private registry**   You maintain this registry in your own environment.

Creating a Docker Image

When you start the Docker service, you just have the Docker instance running, but because there's no container yet, you must use a Docker image to create a container. The following example shows how to create a simple Docker image.

In this example, the Docker image we're about to create includes the following components:

- An Ubuntu 16:04 server
- The Apache 2 web server
- A simple web page that prints "Hola ElMundo!" when you run the containerized application

Here's how you create a Docker image:

1. Open a new file named Dockerfile.

```
$ vi Dockerfile
```

2. Add the following lines to the new Dockerfile:

```
FROM ubuntu:12.04

# Install dependencies
RUN apt-get update -y
RUN apt-get install -y apache2

# Install apache and write hello world message
RUN echo "Hola ElMundo!" > /var/www/index.html

# Configure apache
RUN a2enmod rewrite
RUN chown -R www-data:www-data /var/www
ENV APACHE_RUN_USER www-data
ENV APACHE_RUN_GROUP www-data
ENV APACHE_LOG_DIR /var/log/apache2

EXPOSE 80

CMD ["/usr/sbin/apache2", "-D", "FOREGROUND"]
```

3. Now that you have your Dockerfile ready, you can create a Docker image from it by running the docker build command:

```
$ docker build  test_image .
```

4. Confirm that the image was built by running the docker images command:

```
$ docker images
```

Creating a Docker Container

Once you have your Docker image ready, it's easy to creating a container based on the image. Follow these steps to create a container and test it:

1. Execute the docker run command to run the Docker image you just built, test_image:

```
$ docker run -p 80:80 test_image
```

2. Open a browser and point to the EC2 server that's running the new containers. Since I'm using an EC2 instance, I see the Public DNS of this server.

3. Open the Apache web server's index page from your browser by going to http://localhost:80/. You should see the following statement on the web page that opens in your browser: "Hola ElMundo!"

Amazon ECS Architecture

Amazon ECS consists of a handful of key components: clusters, the container agent, containers and images, and task definitions that define the tasks you run on the container clusters. These components are described here:

- **Clusters**   A logical grouping of tasks or services. A cluster can contain tasks with the Fargate and EC2 launch types. If you're running the tasks or services with the EC2 launch type, a cluster is also a set of container instances in which you can place tasks. A cluster is region-specific and can contain multiple instance types.

- **Container agent**   Runs on each infrastructure resource in an ECS cluster, sends information about tasks to ECS, and starts and stops ECS tasks when ECS requests it to do so.

- **Containers and images**   Containers are created from templates called images.

- **Task definitions and tasks**   A task definition contains the parameters for a container-based application, such as the containers to use and the ports to be opened for them. A task is a task definition put into action.

You deploy containers by performing the following three steps:

1. Define a task.

2. Define the service.

3. Create the ECS cluster.

Amazon ECS Clusters

When you run Docker containers in an AWS cloud, you don't run them as a bunch of containers, each running unrelated tasks. ECS expects you to create clusters of containers instead. A cluster is a logical set of tasks or services. ECS creates a default cluster for you, and you can create other clusters to separate your applications and the resources they require.

An *ECS container instance* is an EC2 instance that runs an ECS container agent and is registered into a cluster. When you run a task with ECS using the EC2 launch type, the task runs on the ECS container instances. In Chapter 4, you learned about EC2 instance types, each with a different CPU, storage, memory and networking capacity. The type of EC2 instances you select for an ECS container instance determines the amount of resources available in an ECS cluster.

ECS requires a basic ECS container instance to have version 3.10 of the Linux kernel, the ECS container agent, and a Docker daemon running at least version 1.9.0, along with all Docker runtime dependencies. The ECS-optimized AMI from Amazon is pre-configured with these requirements, and AWS recommends that you use this AMI for your container instances.

Here's what you need to know about clusters:

- Each cluster is specific to an AWS region.
- You can include both Fargate and EC2 launch types in a cluster.
- If you're using the EC2 launch type, your cluster can contain multiple instance types for the containers.

Creating an ECS Cluster　　You create an ECS cluster either through the familiar AWS Management Console or through the ECS CLI (ecs-cli). To create a cluster through the console, you must choose between the Fargate and the EC2 launch types. In the following example, you'll learn how to create a cluster from the command line, with tasks that use the EC2 launch type.

You can create a cluster from the command line by running the command ecs-cli up. By default, when you run this command, ECS will create a cluster whose tasks will use the EC2 launch type. This command will bring up the number of EC2 instances that will host the Docker containers that you'll be running. This example shows how to create a cluster that consists of six c4.large instances:

```
$ ecs-cli up -keypair <keypair_name> --capability-iam -size 6 -instance-type
c4.large -cluster test1
```

NOTE　When you execute the ecs-cli up command, you can monitor the command's progress in the AWS Management Console.

This command will create an ECS cluster named test1. As you can tell, the size parameter specifies the number of EC2 instances (applicable only for tasks with the EC2 launch type), and the instance_type tells ECS the type of EC2 instances that will serve as hosts for the containers that you'll be launching into this cluster later. The ecs-cli up command creates a new VPC with two subnets. The capability_iam parameter indicates that this command may create IAM resources (use this option only for tasks with the EC2 launch type).

Since the default for the launch type is ECS, I didn't have to specify a launch type option in the previous command. If you need to create a cluster with tasks that will use the Fargate launch type, you must specify the -launch-type parameter, as shown here:

```
$ ecs-cli up -launch-type FARGATE -capability-iam -cluster test1
```

In both cases, the ecs-cli up command will create a AWS CloudFormation stack named test1.

Grouping Cluster Instances Together   When you're working with many cluster instances, it's a good idea to group together instances based on attributes such as the instance type or AZ. Grouping instances facilitates the specification of where ECS places tasks in your cluster.

Use the *cluster query language* to group the cluster instances. The cluster query language uses an expression syntax that enables you to specify attributes for container instances. The language makes liberal use of comparison operators such as == (equal), != (not equal), in, and !in (not in) to keep together or separate cluster instances based on the value of the instance attributes you specify. For example, the following expression groups together cluster instances in the us-east-1a or us-east-1b AZs:

```
attribute:ecs.availability-zone in [us-east-1a, us-east-1b]
```

Cluster query language permits compound expressions. The following example groups all G2 instances running in your cluster, except for those instances running in the us-east-1d AZ:

```
attribute:ecs.instance-type =~ g2.* and attribute:ecs.availability-zone != us-east-1d
```

You can also use the task affinity or the anti-affinity attribute as a criterion to group instances together. By specifying task affinity, you tell ECS to select instances that are hosting tasks in a specific group, such as the `service:production` group. The anti-affinity attribute directs ECS to select instances that are not hosting tasks in a group. The following example uses an expression to select instances that aren't hosting tasks in the database group:

```
not(task:group == database)
```

The Container Agent

The container agent performs tasks on behalf of ECS. It runs on all the infrastructure resources within an ECS cluster. The agent allows container instances to connect to the cluster. Its key tasks are the following:

- Start and stop tasks when ECS requests it to do so.
- Monitor and report on the status of running tasks and resource allocation to ECS.

If you use the Fargate launch type, you don't need to do much to configure the agent, because it is already installed in the AWS-managed infrastructure that this launch type uses for running tasks. For the EC2 launch type, you must install the container agent on all EC2 instances in the cluster.

Task Definitions

Once you create an ECS cluster, you are ready to launch your containers into the new cluster. How does ECS know the number of containers it must create and run on the cluster? You provide the container definitions to ECS through a *task definition*, which you specify in a JSON format text file. You can use a task definition to define properties for up to ten containers that are part of your application.

ECS uses the Docker images that you specify in a task definition to launch containers on EC2 instances in your cluster. A task definition specifies various attributes or parameters for the containers ECS will create for you. You can specify several task definitions (the available parameters vary with the launch type you choose), such as the following:

- The type of container—that is, the specific image you want the container instance to be based on
- Linux parameters
- The resources (CPU/RAM) per each container
- The launch type—the default is EC2, but you can specify Fargate instead
- Ports that should be open on the container instance
- Data volumes to be used with the containers

Here's an example of a simple task definition:

```
{
    "family": "webserver",
    "containerDefinitions": [
        {
            "name": "web",
            "image": "nginx",
            "memory": "100",
            "cpu": "99"
        },
    ],
    "requiresCompatibilities": [
        "FARGATE"
    ],
    "networkMode": "awsvpc",
    "memory": "512",
    "cpu": "256",
}
```

This task definition contains a single container of the Fargate launch type. The container runs a NGINX web server.

Specifying the Number of Tasks   When you create a task definition, you've just provided ECS a description of the containers it must launch. This doesn't automatically launch the containers in your cluster. To launch the containers, you must specify the number of tasks that EC2 must run in the cluster. The instantiation of a task definition is called a *task*.

Scheduling the tasks is how ECS creates tasks in the cluster. ECS takes your task definitions and schedules the tasks by placing tasks on various containers in the ECS cluster. This brings us to the next component in the ECS architecture: the scheduling of ECS tasks.

Scheduling ECS Tasks

When you launch tasks into a cluster, ECS needs to know which instances may have the resources, such as the required RAM/CPU, and open ports to support the task definition. Similarly, when you scale down the tasks, ECS needs to find the correct tasks it should terminate.

ECS makes use of two techniques to optimize where (on which container instances in the cluster) it places tasks and where it terminates them:

- **Task placement strategies**   These are algorithms that guide ECS in the selection of the right instance where it should place tasks or terminate tasks.

- **Task placement constraints**   These are absolute rules that EC2 evaluates before placing tasks. You specify attributes for your container instances and then create a constraint that determines the placement of tasks based on the attribute values.

It's important to understand that a constraint is absolute, in the sense that it can prevent the placement of a task that violates a constraint; a task placement strategy isn't absolute. EC2 tries its best to place tasks in an optimal fashion, but when it can't do so, it chooses the next best option and goes ahead and places the tasks anyway. Placement strategies and the placement constraints aren't mutually exclusive: you can use both together to optimize the distribution of tasks.

Amazon ECS uses the task placement strategies and constraints that you specify in a specific order. It first finds the instances that satisfy the placement constraints and then narrows down the instances that satisfy the placement strategies you configure. Based on its analysis of the strategies and constraints, it determines where it should place tasks.

The Container Deployment Process

You've learned about task definitions, tasks, ECS instances, and clusters. Here's a simple outline of how to deploy a container:

1. *Create a cluster.* Provide a cluster name and specify the number of instances to run.

2. *Register a task definition.* Before you can run a task on the ECS cluster, you must register task definitions, which are lists of containers grouped together. You assign the task name, provide the image name, and specify the amount of memory and CPU that you need. Here's an example task definition that creates a web application written in PHP:

```
{
    "family": "sample-fargate",
    "networkMode": "awsvpc",
    "containerDefinitions": [
        {
            "name": "fargate-app",
            "image": "httpd:2.4",
            "portMappings": [
                {
                    "containerPort": 80,
                    "hostPort": 80,
                    "protocol": "tcp"
                }
            ],
```

```
                              "essential": true,
                              "entryPoint": [
                                  "sh",
                       "-c"
                          ],
                              "command": [
                                  "/bin/sh -c \"echo '<html> <head> <title>Amazon ECS
        Sample App</title> <style>body {margin-top: 40px; background-color:
        #333;} </style> </head><body> <div style=color:white;text-align:center>
        <h1>Amazon ECS Sample App</h1> <h2>Congratulations!</h2> <p>Your appli-
        cation is now running on a container in Amazon ECS.</p> </div></body></
        html>' >  /usr/local/apache2/htdocs/index.html && httpd-foreground\""
                              ]
                          }
                  ],
                  "requiresCompatibilities": [
                      "FARGATE"
                  ],
                  "cpu": "256",
                  "memory": "512"
          }
```

3. *Define the service.* You create a service for the registered task in your cluster. You can specify the number of instances of the task that you want to run in the cluster.

 NOTE Exercise 5-2 walks you through the steps to create an ECS cluster with a Fargate task.

Using the Amazon ECS CLI

Use the Amazon ECS CLI to create, manage, and monitor clusters and tasks from local development environments. In addition to the cluster creation and management commands, ECS CLI also supports Docker Compose, a command line tool that helps you create, configure, and run applications that use multiple Docker containers.

Here are some of the most common `ecs-cli` commands, along with brief descriptions:

- **ecs-cli configure**   Lets you configure the AWS region, the ECS cluster name, and a prefix for resource creation.
- **ecs-cli up**   Creates an ECS cluster and the resources necessary for the cluster to operate.
- **esc-cli down**   Removes the CloudFormation stack for a cluster, as well as all associated resources. You must use the `-force` option with this command.
- **ecs-cli ps**   Lists all running containers in a ECS cluster.
- **ecs-cli scale**   Modifies the desired and maximum instance count in the Auto Scaling group for a cluster.
- **ecs-cli push**   Pushes an image to an Amazon ECR repository.
- **ecs-cli pull**   Pulls an image from an Amazon ECR repository.

- **ecs-cli images**   Lists the images in an Amazon ECR repository.
- **ecs-cli-compose**   Helps you run Docker Compose–style commands to manage ECS tasks.

You can create an ECS cluster with either AWS CLI or ECS CLI. You can use ECS CLI to manage only those tasks, services, and container instances that you create with the tool. To manage entities *not* created with ECS CLI, you must use the familiar AWS CLI (`aws cli`) or the AWS Management Console.

The ECS CLI Compose Command and Docker Compose

The `ecs-cli compose` command helps you manage Amazon ECS tasks with `docker-compose` type commands in an ECS cluster. The `ecs-cli compose` command is based on the Docker Compose tool, which helps you define and run Docker applications that involve multiple containers. You use a YAML file to configure your applications and create and start all the services with a single `docker-compose` command.

Using Docker Compose involves the following three steps:

1. Define the application environment with a Dockerfile.
2. Define the services that the application comprises in a docker-compose.yml file. This helps run the services together in an isolated environment.
3. Run the `docker-compose` command to start and run the entire application.

The `ecs-cli compose` command helps you manage Amazon ECS tasks within an ECS cluster. You use a Docker compose file to create your task definitions and manage the tasks. The `ecs-cli compose` command by default looks for the compose file named docker-compose.yml in the current directory (you can use a different filename and path if you want).

Monitoring Amazon ECS

ECS metric data is sent to Amazon CloudWatch in one-minute intervals. Use CloudWatch to monitor your ECS resources. The statistics are stored for a period of two weeks, so you can access historical data about the clusters. Once you enable CloudWatch metrics for ECS, you can view the metrics from both the ECS and the CloudWatch consoles.

It's a best practice to establish a baseline for ECS performance by monitoring at least the CPU and memory and reservation utilization metrics for ECS clusters and services. You can use the following automated monitoring tools to monitor ECS:

- **CloudWatch alarms**   These help monitor a single metric over time and perform actions based on the values of the metric relative to a threshold value. CloudWatch alarms can scale the number of container instances up or down based on metrics such as memory and CPU reservation (the percentage of memory and CPU reserved by running tasks in the cluster compared to the total CPU and memory registered for each running container instance in the cluster).

- **CloudWatch Logs** Logs help you store and access log files from the containers in ECS tasks.
- **CloudWatch Events** You can match events and route them to functions or streams to make changes or take corrective action.
- **CloudTrail log monitoring** You can monitor CloudTrail log files in real-time by sending them to CloudWatch logs.

NOTE AWS doesn't charge extra for using ECS. Your only charges are for the EC2 instances on which the containers run.

Because CloudWatch alarms don't cover everything, you can use the CloudWatch home page, Trusted Advisor, and other AWS console dashboards to view container clusters and service information. Finally, the log files on the container instances and the containers in your tasks provide valuable information.

ECS IAM Policies, Roles, and Permissions

By default, an IAM user can't create or modify EC2 resources or run tasks using the ECS API. As the AWS system administrator, you must create IAM policies that grant an IAM user permission to create or modify resources and perform tasks and to enable an IAM user to create task definitions and/or deploy clusters.

EC2 container instances execute work in ECS and call EC2 APIs on your behalf, and thus will need to authenticate with your credentials. You must create an IAM role for your container instances and associate it with your container instance while launching the instance.

AWS Batch

Batch computing refers to the use of large amounts of computing resources to run jobs with large workloads, where the jobs can run for several hours or even days. AWS Batch is a fully managed service that automatically provisions, configures, and manages batch computing resources for you and optimizes the workload distribution based on the size of the workloads.

There are several default limits for AWS Batch for a single AWS account:

- Number of compute environments: 10
- Number of job queues: 5
- Number of compute environments per job queue: 3
- Number of job dependencies: 20

You can change the first three limits but not the last one, which is the maximum number of dependencies for a job.

Batch-Related Concepts

Understanding four key concepts—compute environment, jobs, job definitions, and job queues—is critical to working with AWS Batch.

Compute Environment

The *compute environment* is the set of compute resources that Batch uses to run batch jobs. Compute resources in this context refer to the EC2 instances where AWS Batch will run the Docker containers that process the containerized batch jobs. A compute environment is linked to one or more job queues, which determine the order in which jobs are executed. The scheduler will attempt to run the job in the compute environment that has sufficient resources to handle the job.

You can deal with the compute environment in two ways: Set up your own *unmanaged compute environment*, where you handle the instance configuration yourself, with AWS Batch creating the instances in an Amazon ECS cluster. Or let AWS Batch launch and manage the EC2 instances as needed, with you maintaining some control by specifying things such as the instance types (for example, c4.2xlarge). You can specify the minimum, desired, and maximum number of vCPUs and also a percentage value for bids on the Spot market (so that you can use less expensive Spot instances, as opposed to On-Demand instances), and a set of VPC subnets in which to launch the containers. AWS Batch launches and terminates the instances as necessary.

AWS Batch uses Docker container images to run your batch jobs. AWS Batch pulls the container images from container registries, both in your AWS infrastructure and from external registries. The Docker Hub registry is available by default.

Jobs

A job refers to a unit of work such as a shell script or a Linux executable that you submit to AWS Batch. Each job runs as a container application on an EC2 instance. You specify the job parameters in the job definition. When you define a job, you choose the Docker image to use for the job.

 TIP Only Docker container–type jobs are supported in AWS Batch.

You implement a Batch job by following these steps:

1. Define the job.
2. Configure the compute environment.
3. Configure the job queue.
4. Submit the job.

When you submit a job, it either succeeds or fails, and you can configure the number of job attempts for a failed job. A job failure could be due a non-zero exit code from the job or an EC2 instance failure, termination, or other errors and outages in an AWS service.

NOTE You can configure an automatic retry of a failed Batch job, up to a maximum of 10 tries.

Job Definitions

A *job definition* is a blueprint for the job resources that dictates how AWS Batch should run the job. You can specify a name for the job definition, the type of job, container properties, environment variables, and the storage mount points in the job definition.

You typically use the job definition to specify attributes such as the following:

- The Docker image you want to use with the job container
- The CPU/RAM for the container
- The environmental variables that should be passed to a container, and the command that the container must run when it starts
- The job retry strategy

You can create job definitions through the AWS Batch console. You can also use an empty job definition template to create your job definitions and save it to a file. Use the `register-job-definition` command to generate a task definition template:

```
$ aws batch register-job-definition –generate-cli-skeleton
```

Job Queues

A *job queue* is a queue to which you submit your batch jobs; it specifies the priority for job execution. Jobs stay in a queue until the AWS Batch scheduler schedules the job to run on an EC2 instance (in your compute environment).

You can set up multiple job queues. You link a job queue to a specific computing environment, and you can create high and low priority queues to which you submit the appropriate jobs. For example, you can use EC2 On-Demand instances for higher priority jobs and another queue that uses Spot instances for lower priority tasks. The Batch scheduler will run the jobs in the high priority queue first, providing that all the job's dependencies on other jobs have been met. To set up AWS Batch jobs, you must create a job definition and a job queue in the AWS Batch console.

You can specify other jobs as dependencies for a job, to make sure that a job runs only after all its dependencies have been successfully completed first. Once the dependencies are all satisfied, the job status moves through the PENDING, RUNNABLE, STARTING, and then RUNNING states. If any of the dependency jobs fails, the job status goes from PENDING to FAILED.

AWS Lambda

AWS Lambda is the core of *serverless computing*, which enables you to run applications and services without worrying about servers. Lambda runs the code you upload in response to *events*, both those that emanate from within the AWS infrastructure and those that emanate from external sources.

NOTE Unlike with EC2, where you install, configure, and run your applications, you don't provision or manage the servers with Lambda.

Lambda helps you run your code without your having to set up any server infrastructure. Simply upload your code to AWS Lambda in the form of a *Lambda function*, and Lambda automatically provisions the necessary number of servers, manages those servers, and runs your code (applications or backend services). You pay just for the compute time you use, and there's no charge when your code isn't running. You can run code for applications or backend services, with no administrative responsibilities on your part.

Once you upload the code in one of the languages that Lambda supports (as of this writing, Python, Go, Node.js, Java, PowerShell, Ruby, and C#), AWS takes care of the rest, such as setting up the servers and maintaining the OS, capacity provisioning, and automatic scaling. You can set your code to be triggered automatically from an AWS service, or call it directly from a web or mobile app. Lambda offers the following benefits:

- No need to manage servers
- Flexible scaling
- Automated high availability

NOTE Lambda@Edge enables you to run Lambda functions at AWS Edge locations by responding to Amazon CloudFront events.

As you can imagine, Lambda offers a tradeoff: Because AWS manages the compute services for you, leaving you just the responsibility for the code, you can't log into the instances or customize the OS. AWS is fully in charge of performing all operational and administrative activities for the computing infrastructure.

AWS Lambda has several limitations that you should be aware of:

- It's not efficient for running long-lived applications.
- Lambda function deployment package size is limited to 50MB (compressed).
- The non-persistent scratch area available for Lambda is 500MB.
- The well-known *AWS Lambda Cold Start* happens when you execute inactive functions. The delay is due to AWS needing some time (greater than 5 seconds) to provision your runtime container and then run the Lambda function. It also takes some time for the Lambda function to handle a first request.

Implementing Lambda

Follow these steps to implement Lambda:

1. Create a Lambda function.
2. Create a deployment package.

3. Upload the deployment package.

4. Create an invocation type.

Developers can create Lambda-based applications using various tools, such the Lambda Console, AWS CLI, and the SAM CLI, which enables you to iteratively develop and test serverless applications (Lambda function code) before you upload to the Lambda runtime. You can install SAM CLI using pip:

```
$ pip install aws-sam-cli
```

You can use a Docker image called docker-lambda to locally invoke Lambda functions, to run the apps in a simulated environment, without deploying them to AWS Lambda runtime. For example, the following AWS CLI command lists your Lambda functions:

```
$ aws lambda list-functions –profile adminuser
```

Where You Can Use Lambda

Lambda is designed primarily for running your code in response to events such as changes to data in your DynamoDB tables or in response to HTTP requests. You can build data-processing triggers for services such as Amazon S3 and Amazon DynamoDB.

Lambda also helps you build serverless applications that consist of functions that events can trigger and automatically deploy the functions using AWS CodePipeline and AWS CodeBuild.

NOTE Although you are an AWS system administrator and not a developer, Lambda is not only part of the certification exam objectives, but it also falls under your domain, since you need to understand the basics of how to create and manage Lambda-based applications.

Lambda-Based Application Concepts

An AWS Lambda application consists of Lambda functions, event sources, and other resources that work as a single unit to perform a specific task, or tasks. You can use configuration management tools such as AWS CloudFormation to gather together a Lambda application's components into a package that you can deploy and manage as a single AWS resource. Following are brief explanations of the key building blocks of a Lambda-based application.

When a Lambda function is invoked, AWS launches containers, with their configuration depending on the configuration specifications of your Lambda function.

Lambda Functions

Functions are the foundation of Lambda. They contain your code and any dependent libraries, plus memory, maximum execution time, IAM role, and a handler name. The code, a Lambda function, contains other elements such as memory, the maximum execution time (*timeout*), an IAM role (*execution role*), and the *handler* (*entry point* that executes the Lambda function) name. The IAM role controls the access levels for the

Lambda function when it needs to access AWS resources. The handler is the method inside your code where Lambda starts its execution.

 NOTE   A key recommendation for writing Lambda code is to make the code *stateless*, which avoids referencing the infrastructure that executes the code.

Event Source

The event source is an AWS service like a DynamoDB table that triggers the execution of the Lambda functions.

Downstream Resources

Upon triggering by an event, the Lambda function calls the downstream AWS resource (for example an Amazon S3 bucket).

AWS SAM

The AWS Serverless Application Model (SAM) defines serverless applications through simplified syntax for expressing serverless resources. AWS SAM is an extension of the AWS CloudFormation template language that helps you define serverless applications at a higher level. AWS CloudFormation supports AWS SAM, plus you can gain additional functionality through AWS CLI and the AWS SAM CLI.

 NOTE   The AWS Serverless Application Repository is a collection of AWS Lambda applications that you can easily deploy to your AWS account.

Invoking a Lambda Function

Lambda applications have two core components: functions and event sources. The Lambda function is the code that processes the events. An event source is an AWS service or a custom application that publishes the events.

For example, Amazon S3 can publish events such as PUT, COPY, and DELETE objects events on an S3 bucket. You can use this bucket notification capability to direct S3 to invoke a Lambda function when a specified type of event such as PUT, COPY, or DELETE occurs. Suppose a user creates an object in an S3 bucket. S3 detects the new object creation event and invokes your Lambda function.

Lambda supports *synchronous* and *asynchronous* invocation of functions. The invocation type depends on whether a supported AWS service or a custom application is the event source. When you write a custom application that invokes a function or when you invoke a function manually to test it, you can specify either synchronous or asynchronous as the invocation type. However, when an AWS service is the event source, the event type determines the invocation type. For instance, S3 always invokes functions asynchronously.

To get a flavor of Lambda, let's create a Lambda function and invoke it.

Lambda in Action

Near the end of the chapter, Exercise 5-4 shows how to create a Lambda function via the Lambda console. Once you create the Lambda function, you can come back here to learn how to invoke the function using some event data.

In Exercise 5-4, you'll create a Lambda function named TestLambda. Here's how to invoke this Lambda function using the same event data in the Lambda console:

1. In the TestLambda page, select Test in the Configure Test Event page.

2. Select Create New Test Event.

3. For the Event Template option, leave the default Hello World value as is.

4. For Event Name, enter **TestEvent**.

5. The Lambda function will execute, and you'll see the results in the Lambda console. Click Details to see results of the function execution and the logs. Figure 5-1 shows the Execution Result page.

6. After running the simple Lambda function a few times, select the Monitoring tab to view the CloudWatch metrics from the TestLambda function.

Although you don't manage the infrastructure for running the Lambda code, you do pay for the resources used to run the code. To prevent a Lambda function from accidentally running indefinitely, you can choose a timeout, ranging from 1 to 300 seconds (5 minutes). Once the execution crosses the timeout period, AWS terminates the Lambda function.

 NOTE If a Lambda function execution fails, Lambda makes two additional attempts to run the code.

Figure 5-1 Lambda function execution results

Securing Lambda

Since Lambda is serverless, you can't log into the instances that run the code or customize the OS. Lambda functions have a role attached to them, which determines the AWS resources the function can access. You use Lambda *function policies* to have a source event invoke a Lambda function.

 NOTE CloudWatch provides Lambda metrics such as invocation counts and duration, number of requests, request latency, and execution duration.

AWS Lightsail

While virtual machines are the deployment unit for EC2, Lightsail offers *virtual private servers* (VPSs) that enable you to run simple applications and web sites for a low price (you pay a flat monthly rate for your plan, starting at $5, and varying according to the CPU/RAM/SSD you need). You have fewer options and less control when compared to EC2 instances, but you also don't need to worry about things such as security groups. Lightsail contains a virtual machine, SSD-based storage, DNS management, and a static IP. Lightsail is designed for developers or personal hobbyists, who can use Lightsail instances to jumpstart their projects without wasting time installing software or frameworks. Lightsail also helps users learn cloud services, such as VMs and networking. You can use Amazon Linux or Ubuntu as your operating system, but not a Windows system.

Development environments where you want to quickly spin up an instance for performing some basic code configuration and running websites that don't need to highly available are both good use cases for Lightsail.

Lightsail enables you to do the following:

- **Quickly spin up instances** You can quickly spin up instances with preconfigured OS and applications and add advanced features such as managed databases on the Lightsail server later.

- **Add storage and peer your VPC** Although the instances are lightweight to begin with, you can add block storage disks as well as peer your VPC so the instances can work with your other AWS resources.

- **Run other apps** Using Lightsail, you can run an application such as WordPress or a LAMP (Linux, Apache, MySQL, and PHP/Python) in a few seconds. You can even employ a Lightsail load balancer to create highly available applications with Lightsail instances.

- **Use images and stacks** Lightsail offers both images with just a base OS and development stacks like LAMP, plus applications like WordPress and Drupal.

Exercise 5-3 shows you how to create a Linux-based Lightsail instance (the instance starts running automatically once you create it) and connect to it. When you connect to a LAMP instance, for example, you will land in the Linux terminal. Once the Lightsail instance starts running, you can also connect to it via SSH.

TIP You can't change the number of vCPUs, RAM, or the SSD disk size of a Lightsail instance. To change the instance size, you must first take a snapshot of the instance and launch a new instance with the size you want.

AWS Elastic Beanstalk

AWS Elastic Beanstalk helps you quickly deploy and manage applications without having to worry about the infrastructure these applications need. Simply upload your applications, and Beanstalk will handle the provisioning of the servers, scaling, load balancing, and even the management and the monitoring of the application health. A good use case for Elastic Beanstalk is when you want to quickly set up a website for your internal users (you can set up both internal facing and external facing infrastructures), something that doesn't have to be highly available and you don't need to scale for a large user base.

Elastic Beanstalk supports applications you develop in the Java, PHP, .NET, Node .js, Python, and Ruby languages. Elastic Beanstalk automatically deploys the computing environment for running the applications you upload, such as the VPC, EC2 instances, security groups, S3 buckets, CloudWatch alarms, and so on. However, you can make any changes to the environment that you need.

Elastic Beanstalk also supports deploying applications from Docker containers. You can deploy a single Docker container for each application with AWS Elastic Beanstalk. So, both ECS and Elastic Beanstalk enable you to deploy Docker containers, and you can also deploy Docker containers on EC2 instances. The environment variables that you define in the Elastic Beanstalk console are passed to the Docker containers. If one of the Docker containers running in an Elastic Beanstalk environment crashes, Elastic Beanstalk automatically restarts the container.

Building Blocks of Elastic Beanstalk

Elastic Beanstalk uses the following key concepts and terminology.

Environment

Elastic Beanstalk manages all application resources as an *environment*, which is the heart of an application. An environment runs a single application version at a time—it's an application version that's deployed in AWS. When you create an environment, Elastic Beanstalk sets up all the resources required for that application version to run.

Environment Tier

Elastic Beanstalk offers several *environment tiers*, such as a web server environment and worker environment. Each tier will help you create a different type of application environment. For example, an application that serves HTTP requests must run in the web server environment. Similarly, the worker environment supports applications that pull tasks from an Amazon Simple Queue Service (SQS).

Environment Configuration

An *environment configuration* is a set of parameters and configurations that determine how an environment and the resources in that environment will work.

Configuration Templates

A *configuration template* helps you create a set of environment configurations. You can create a configuration template through the Elastic Beanstalk CLI (eb) or APIs.

Application

An application is a collection of all the components such as environment and version that pertain to an application. An application is like a folder. You deploy an application by uploading a source code bundle, in the form of a ZIP or WAR (web application archive) file.

Application Version

An *application version* is a labeled version of web application code. The application version points to an S3 object that connects the code in the form of a binary file, such as a Java WAR file.

 NOTE Elastic Beanstalk is highly available by default. It creates multiple instances in two availability zones.

Creating and Deploying Applications

You can create and deploy applications from the Elastic Beanstalk console or from the command line. An exercise at the end of the chapter walks you through the process of creating an application from the console, and I show how to create the application from the command line here.

You can create and manage your Elastic Beanstalk applications and create and monitor environments from a local repository using the Elastic Beanstalk CLI. It's simpler to use the EB CLI for your development and testing work rather than using the AWS Management Console.

The following shows how to create an application:

1. Create a directory for the application and move to that directory:

```
$ mkdir HelloWorld
$ cd HelloWorld
```

2. Use the `eb init` command to create a local repository for the application:

```
$ eb init -p PHP
```

3. Use the `echo` command to create the index.html page:

```
$ echo "Hello World" > index.html
```

4. Use the `eb create` command to create an environment, which I named dev-env in this example:

```
$ eb create dev-env
$ eb open
```

You can deploy updates to this application by running the `eb-deploy` command.

NOTE You must create two IAM roles when creating an Elastic Beanstalk environment: a *service role*, which Elastic Beanstalk uses to access other AWS cloud services; and an *instance profile*, which Elastic Beanstalk applies to the EC2 instances to enable them to perform tasks such as uploading logs to S3.

Monitoring the Elastic Beanstalk Environment

You can use basic health reporting or enhanced health reporting to monitor the Elastic Beanstalk environment. While basic reporting provides the overall environment status, it doesn't publish metrics to CloudWatch. Enhanced reporting helps you find the severity of the problem as well as its root cause.

Chapter Review

This chapter covered several important AWS compute services, other than EC2, which was discussed in Chapter 4. I explained how to use the AWS Elastic Container Service (ECS). In addition, you learned how to use AWS Batch to run thousands of batch computing jobs on AWS. AWS Lambda enables you to run hundreds of thousands of batch jobs on AWS, and it takes care of provisioning the right amount and type of the computing resources based in the batch job requirements.

Amazon Lightsail lets smaller organizations take advantage of the reliability and security of Amazon Web Services by providing everything they need to jumpstart projects on AWS, such as the compute, storage, and networking resources.

Amazon Elastic Beanstalk helps you deploy and scale web applications and services developed with Java, .NET, PHP, Node.js, Python, Ruby, and Go on servers such as Apache, Nginx, and IIS. Users simply upload their code and Elastic Beanstalk automatically handles all aspects of the deployment, such as provisioning the capacity, auto scaling, and load balancing for the applications.

Exercises

The exercises are designed to teach you critical AWS administrative tasks through the EC2 console. To perform the tasks, follow the steps and refer to the guidance provided by the EC2 console. There are no answers to any of the exercises; if you make a mistake, retrace your steps and ensure that you're correctly performing the steps. You'll know that you've correctly completed the exercise if you achieve the goal set for you in each exercise.

Exercise 5-1: Set up Amazon ECS to prepare for launching an ECS cluster.

You must complete Exercises 4-1 through 4-5 in Chapter 4 before you continue.

Exercise 5-2: Create and launch an ECS cluster with a Fargate task.

You must complete Exercise 5-1 before starting this exercise. Although your account receives a default cluster when you launch your first ECS cluster instance, it's a good idea to create a cluster with a unique name:

```
$ aws ecs create-cluster –cluster-name fargate-cluster
```

In this case, you'll be using the Fargate launch type, so you don't need to worry about creating the EC2 instances to run the containers in your cluster.

1. Register a task definition:

```
$ aws ecs register-task-definition –cli-input-json file://$HOME/tasks/
fargate-task.json
```

Make sure the fargate-task.json file contains a simple task definition, such as the one I showed earlier in this chapter in the section "Task Definitions."

2. Create a service for the registered task in your cluster. The following `aws ecs create-service` command will create a service with at least two instances of the sample-fargate:1 task that will be kept running in the cluster:

```
$ aws ecs create-service --cluster fargate-cluster --service-name
fargate-service --task-definition sample-fargate:1 --desired-count 2
--launch-type "FARGATE" --network-configuration "awsvpcConfiguration={su
bnets=[subnet-abcd1234],securityGroups=[sg-abcd1234]}"
```

3. List the services for the new cluster to view the services you've created in the previous steps:

```
$ aws ecs list-services –cluster fargate-cluster
```

4. Describe the service, using the service name you retrieved in step 3:

```
$ aws ecs describe-services –cluster fargate-cluster –services fargate-
service
```

Exercise 5-3: Create a Linux-based Lightsail instance and connect to it.

1. In the main AWS page (Service), select Lightsail under the Compute list of services.

2. Click on the Create Instance button.

3. In the Create an Instance page, under Instance Location, accept the region shown or choose a different region.

4. On the same page, under Pick Your Instance, select the Linux/Unix platform.

5. On the same page, under Select A Blueprint, select Apps + OS. Also select Lamp Stack or WordPress (or any of the alternatives you want).

6. Under Choose Your Plan, select an option. The most inexpensive option costs $5 and is free for a month (up to 750 hours).

7. Under Select A Name, you can either keep the default name for your Lightsail instance or change it.

8. Click Create at the bottom of the page.

9. In the Lightsail home page displayed next, you can review the CPU/RAM/SSD settings. The page shows that your Lightsail instance is running.

10. On the Lightsail home page, select the menu shown to the right of the instance name, where you'll see five options: Connect, Manage, Stop, Restart, and Delete. Select Connect. You'll be presented with the Linux command line for your Lightsail instance's Linux terminal.

Exercise 5-4: Create a Lambda function.

1. From the AWS console, open the AWS Lambda console by clicking Lambda under the Compute Service list.

2. In the Get Started section, click Create A Function.

3. In the Create Function page, select Author From Scratch (it's preselected for you).

4. In the Author From Scratch section, enter the following information:
   - Name: Enter **TestLambda**.
   - Runtime: Select Python 3.6.
   - Role: Select Create New Role From Template(s). Lambda will then automatically create a role from a policy template.
   - Role name: Enter **testRole.**

5. Click Create Function.

6. In the TestLambda page, you'll see two sections. You'll be in the Configuration page by default, where you can configure various things such as triggers, function code, environment variables, tags, network, and concurrency. This is a simple precoded Lambda application, so you can leave all these alone.

7. Review the code for your Lambda function, which is in a file named lambda_ function.py.

Exercise 5-5: Create and deploy an application with AWS Elastic Beanstalk.

In this example, you use a sample application provided by AWS to create and deploy your application.

1. Open the Elastic Beanstalk console by clicking on this link: https://console.aws.amazon.com/elasticbeanstalk/home#/gettingStarted?applicati onName=getting-started-app.

2. In the Create A Web App page, shown next, the application name is already filled in (getting-started). Choose a platform and select Sample Application for Application Code. You can later upload your own code, but in this example, you can use AWS code to run your first app.

3. Click Create Application. The next illustration shows the application creation process.

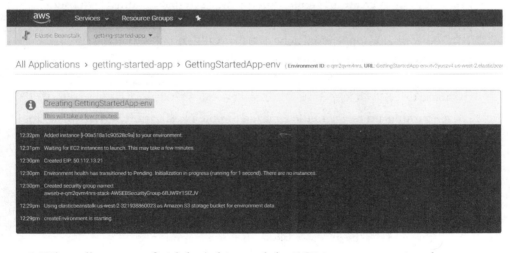

4. When all resources finish launching and the EC2 instances running the new app pass their health checks, the web site is ready to use. To view the environment in the environment dashboard, open the Elastic Beanstalk console.

5. Click the Elastic Beanstalk link to view the application dashboard. From here, you can modify your application code and perform other application deployment–related tasks.

Questions

1. What is a good reason for deploying a web application in multiple availability zones under AWS Elastic Beanstalk?

    A. You can add more compute instances if you use multiple availability zones.

    B. Multiple availability zones ensure high availability for your applications.

    C. Multiple availability zones improve the response time of your applications.

    D. Multiple availability zones improve the throughput of heavy read/write applications.

2. Which of the following can you specify when configuring an instance in AWS Batch?

    A. Only the minimum number of vCPUs

    B. Only the maximum number of vCPUs

    C. Only the desired number of vCPUs

    D. The minimum, maximum, and the desired number of vCPUs

3. Which of the following would be good reasons for creating and using an AWS Elastic Beanstalk application? (Choose two)

    A. You want to create an application for your internal business users without worrying about setting up the infrastructure for running the app.

    B. You want to create an application for your external customers without worrying about setting up the infrastructure for running the app.

    C. You want the application to be automatically run in response to events.

    D. You want to test your applications without deploying them to the Internet.

4. Which of the following events will trigger an AWS Lambda function? (Choose three)

    A. Publishing a message to the Amazon Simple Notification Service (SNS) topic

    B. Retrieving an object from an Amazon Simple Storage Service (S3) bucket

    C. Adding a new message in an Amazon Simple Queue Service (SQS) queue

    D. Adding a row to an Amazon DynamoDB table

5. You want to deploy a highly available application that runs for an hour, while minimizing the cost. Which of the following would be an appropriate strategy?

    A. Create and deploy an AWS Elastic Beanstalk application.

    B. Create an AWS Lambda function that will be triggered by an Amazon SNS notification.

    C. Deploy the application on a dedicated host.

    D. Create an Amazon EC2 Reserved Instance for running the application.

6. Which of the following are possible with Amazon Lightsail? (Choose three)

    A. Create a quick web site that doesn't require high availability.

    B. Bring up an EC2 instance quickly for testing basic code configuration.

    C. Achieve a high degree of control over the instance cost.

    D. Quickly spin up an Amazon Linux, Ubuntu, or a Windows instance.

7. Which of the following are true regarding ECS task constraints and task placement strategies? (Choose two)

    A. A task constraint can prevent the placement of a task that violates a constraint.

    B. A task placement strategy can prevent the placement of a task that violates the strategy.

    C. Placement strategies and placement constraints are mutually exclusive.

    D. You can use both placement strategies and constraints together.

8. Which of the following is a valid way to monitor your Elastic Beanstalk environment?

    A. Use enhanced health reporting and monitoring to publish metrics to CloudWatch as custom metrics.

    B. Use basic health reporting to publish metrics to CloudWatch.

    C. Use CloudTrail.

    D. Use BeanstalkWatch to monitor Beanstalk.

9. Which of the following can a task definition specify in an ECS cluster? (Choose several)

    A. Which containers to use

    B. Which launch type to use

    C. Which ports to be opened for your application

    D. Which data volume to use

10. Which of the following is not a part of the key AWS Batch terminology?

    A. Job definition

    B. Task definition

    C. Job queue

    D. Scheduler

11. Which of the following can you do to configure a Lambda function? (Choose two)

    A. Specify the number of VCPUs (virtual CPUs).

    B. Set a maximum execution time.

    C. Assign an IAM role.

    D. Specify a dedicated instance for the Lambda function to run.

12. Which of the following is ideal for web developers who plan to launch highly scalable, available web applications in a short time?

   A. AWS Batch

   B. AWS Lightsail

   C. AWS Elastic Container Service

   D. AWS Elastic Beanstalk

13. Which of the following configurations options can you configure when using Elastic Beanstalk?

   A. You can add a developer stack such as LAMP or an application stack such as WordPress.

   B. You can select the Linux or Windows OS versions.

   C. You can Auto Scale EC2 instances.

   D. You can deploy Amazon S3 buckets.

14. Once an AWS Lambda function reaches its timeout limit, what does AWS do?

   A. It terminates the Lambda function.

   B. It re-executes the Lambda function.

   C. It starts billing you for invoking the Lambda function.

   D. It invalidates the Lambda function.

15. Which of the following components of a Lightsail instance can you resize after launching the instance?

   A. CPU

   B. RAM

   C. SSD storage

   D. You can't resize a Lightsail instance after launching it.

Answers

1. **B.** Multiple availability zones ensure high availability for your applications.

2. **D.** You can specify the minimum, maximum, and the desired number of virtual CPUS (vCPUs).

3. **A, B.** You use AWS Elastic Beanstalk to create applications without having to worry about setting up the infrastructure for running the apps. The apps can be internal facing or external facing.

4. **A, B, D.** Publishing new messages to SNS topics, performing a GET operation to retrieve objects from an S3 bucket, and adding rows to a DynamoDB database table are all valid events that will trigger a Lambda function.

5. **D.** If you want an application to be highly available, but for only an hour, while costing the least, the best strategy would be to create an Amazon EC2 Reserved Instance for running the application.

6. **A, B, C.** Lightsail is ideal for creating quick, simple web-sites; testing basic instance configuration; and tightly controlling your instance costs.

7. **A, D.** Violating a task constraint can prevent the placement of a task. Task constraints and placement strategies aren't mutually exclusive; you can use them together to complement each other.

8. **A.** You must configure enhanced health reporting and monitoring (basic health reporting doesn't publish metrics to CloudWatch) to publish Elastic Beanstalk metrics to CloudWatch as custom metrics.

9. **A, B, C, D.** A task definition can specify the containers, the launch type, the ports to be opened, and the data volumes to be used with the containers in the task.

10. **B.** Task definitions are analogous to job definitions and belong to Amazon ECS, not Amazon Batch.

11. **B, C.** You can set a maximum execution time for a Lambda function, after which it will be terminated. You can also assign an IAM role to an AWS Lambda function if the function requires access to AWS resources.

12. **B.** AWS Lightsail is designed for developers who want to quickly launch highly scalable and available web applications without worrying about the setting up of the infrastructure.

13. **A.** When using Elastic Beanstalk, you can add a developer stack such as LAMP or an application stack such as WordPress.

14. **A.** AWS terminates a Lambda function whose execution reaches the timeout you specify.

15. **D.** You can't resize a Lightsail instance after launching the instance. You must take a snapshot of the instance and spin up a new instance to change the instance size.

Networking in the AWS Cloud

In this chapter, you will

- Learn about basic AWS networking concepts
- Learn about virtual networking with Amazon Virtual Private Cloud (VPC)
- Learn how AWS Direct Connect lets you bypass the public Internet to access your resources in the AWS cloud
- Learn how Elastic Load Balancing (ELB) helps you balance your workloads among multiple EC2 instances in an AWS region
- Understand how to use Amazon Route 53 to manage your network domains and connect to AWS
- Learn how Amazon CloudFront helps deliver web content faster to your users

AWS networking is a crucial component of AWS, as networking underlies everything you do in AWS. You're likely to be quite familiar with several of the networking features that I'll be discussing in this chapter, while some are specific to AWS, such as virtual private clouds and Amazon's Route 53, its Domain Name System (DNS) service.

The certification exam expects you to know the basics of networking, such as IP addresses, subnets, and so on. I introduce the basics first, and following that, explain the key AWS networking features.

Basic AWS Networking Concepts

Before we jump into AWS networking concepts such as Amazon VPC, you need to understand the definitions of several common networking terms and concepts.

Virtual Private Cloud

A VPC is an isolated virtual network dedicated to your account. This logically isolated network is inside the AWS cloud, where you can launch your AWS resources such as EC2 instances within your VPC and run AWS services safely. You manage the VPC entirely.

You must specify a range of IPv4 addresses when you create the VPC in a Classless Inter-Domain Routing (CIDR) block (such as 10.0.0.0/16). The first block you create will be the primary CIDR block, and you can associate secondary CIDR blocks later to the VPC if required.

Subnets

A subnet is a range of IP addresses in your Amazon VPC. After you launch services such as EC2 into specific subnets in your VPC, you place them into a *public subnet* if you want those services to be connected to the Internet. Otherwise, you use a *private subnet* to launch the services.

A VPC is divided into public subnets and private subnets, and further segmented into availability zones (AZs), as shown in Table 6-1. Remember that when you create a subnet, it's mapped to an AZ, and you can attach only a single AZ to a subnet.

 NOTE If your VPC supports only IPv4, you can configure IPv6 support for the VPC and the resources in your subnets. The default VPC and EC2 IP addressing system is IPv4, and you can't disable it. However, you can enable your VPC and the subnets in it to use IPv5 by configuring the VPC to operate in a dual stack mode.

Subnets of a PC must be in the same address space as the VPC. Thus, if you create a VPC with the CIDR of 10.0.0.0/16, you can create a pair of subnets (one public, the other private) such as 10.0.1.0/24 and 10.0.2.0/24, but not a pair such as 10.1.0.0/24 and 10.2.0.0/24.

VPC	10.0.0.0/16
Private subnets	10.0.0.0/17
Private-Subnet-01-in-AZ1	10.0.0.0/19
Private-Subnet-02-in-AZ2	10.0.32.0/19
Private-Subnet-03-in-AZ3	10.0.64.0/19
Private-Subnet-04-in-AZ4	10.0.96.0/19
Public subnets	10.0.128.0/18
Public-Subnet-01-in-AZ1	10.0.128.0/20
Public-Subnet-02-in-AZ2	10.0.144.0/20
Public-Subnet-03-in-AZ3	10.0.160.0/20
Public-Subnet-04-in-AZ4	10.0.176.0/20

Table 6-1   VPC Divisions

Route Tables

A *route table* is associated with each subnet and specifies the permissible routes for outbound traffic from that subnet. A route table includes a set of rules, or *routes*, that you configure, which are used to determine where network traffic is directed. Every subnet in a VPC must be associated with a route table. Your VPC has a *main route table*, and by default, every subnet you create is associated with your VPC's main route table.

Security Groups

A *security group* controls inbound and outbound traffic for your EC2 instances. It is a virtual firewall that controls traffic to an instance. If you don't specify a security group when you create an instance, AWS uses the *default security group*. Here are the default rules for a default security group:

- Allow all inbound traffic from all other instances associated with the default security group
- Allow all outbound IPV4 traffic from the instance

A *custom security group* enables you to control the type of role an instance plays, such as a web server or a database server. Here are the default rules for a custom security group:

- Allow no inbound (ingress) traffic
- Allow all outbound (egress) traffic

 NOTE AWS security groups are stateful—that is, you do not need the same rules for both outbound traffic and inbound.

You can add rules in a security group that control traffic flow to or from the instances you associate with that security group. By default, a security group allows all outbound traffic. AWS evaluates all the rules from all the security groups you associate with an instance before determining whether it should allow traffic to reach the instance. You can also assign multiple security groups to an instance. AWS aggregates the rules in all the security groups you assign to an instance to determine whether it should grant access.

Network Access Control Lists

Network access control lists (NACLs) control both inbound and outbound traffic for your subnets. Each subnet that you create in your VPC must be associated with an NACL, and by default, all subnets are associated with your VPC's default NACL.

Security groups and ACLs offer additional layers of security for AWS resources in each subnet in a VPC. Unlike a security group, an NACL is stateless. That means that any changes applied to an incoming rule will *not* be applied to the outgoing rule. So, for example, if you allow an incoming request on port 80, you would also need to apply the rule for port 80 for outgoing traffic. Network ACLs are tied to the subnet, so the rule applies to all instances within the subnet group.

Domain Name System

DNS uses a distributed directory that resolves human-readable hostnames, such as example .com, into machine-readable IP addresses, such as 192.161.1.132.

Amazon Virtual Private Cloud

An Amazon VPC is *a virtual network* dedicated to your AWS account. A VPC is isolated from other networks in the AWS cloud. Amazon VPC enables you to launch your AWS resources such as EC2 instances into your own virtual private network (VPN), and it thus acts as the network layer for EC2. The virtual network, as its name says, is private to you and is quite similar to traditional networks that you work with in your data centers, which means that it includes entities such as routing, ACLs, and firewalls.

 NOTE A private subnet doesn't have a route to the Internet gateway.

You can specify an IP address type (IPv4 and/or IPv6) and range for the VPC that you create and add subnets to the VPC. You can also associate security groups with the VPC as well as configure route tables.

 NOTE You can use multiple VPCs; your AWS account entitles you to five VPCs, which is a soft limit that you can have raised by contacting AWS. Because a VPC can't span AWS regions, if you're running AWS services in multiple regions, you must create multiple VPCs—at least one per region.

IP Address Types and IP Ranges

You can use either or both IPv4 and IPv6 address types for a VPC; the IPv4 type is the default and mandatory, and IPv6 is optional. It's important to understand that all IPv6 address types are reachable from the Internet. By default, your VPC and subnets must have IPv4 CIDR blocks, but you can optionally associate an IPv6 CIDR block with the VPC. You must specify a range of IP addresses (CIDR block) for your VPC when you create the VPC. If you're creating multiple VPCs, each one must have a separate address range.

NOTE   Make sure the CIDR block IP ranges are not in conflict with your on-premise IP ranges if you want to connect both networks.

The size of the CIDR block for your VPC depends on the address range that you choose, and it can range from a /16 (65,536 IP addresses) to a /28 (16 IP addresses) netmask. You can associate one or more secondary CIDR blocks, with a maximum of four secondary IPv4 blocks, with the VPC after you create it, enabling you to increase the size of the VPC.

Here are some key factors about CIDR blocks and a VPC:

- You can't change the size of a VPC's CIDR block after creating it—that is, you can't increase or decrease the size of an existing CIDR block.
- A subnet's CIDR block is a subset of the VPC's CIDR block if you create multiple subnets.
- CIDR blocks of different subnets can't overlap.
- If you have a single subnet in your VPC, the CIDR block of the subnet and the VPC can be identical.

Each subnet in a VPC must have its own distinct CIDR block. Let's say, for example, that you create a VPC with the CIDR block 10.0.0.0/24. You want to create two subnets within this VPC. The /24 netmask allows 256 IP addresses, meaning that each of your subnets can have a maximum of 128 IP addresses (if you decide to assign each subnet the same number of IP addresses). One of the subnets uses the CIDR block 10.0.0.0/25, with the IP address range 10.0.0.0–10.0.0.127. The other subnet uses the remaining portion of the VPC's CIDR block, which will be 10.0.0.0/25, with the IP address range 10.0.0.128–10.0.0.0.255.

AWS recommends that you specify a CIDR block of /16 or smaller and dedicate that network to your VPCs to allow for future needs. AWS further recommends that you specify the CIDR block (/16 or smaller) from the following set of private IPv4 address ranges:

- 10.0.0.0–10.255.255.255 (10/8 prefix)
- 172.16.0.0–172.31.255.255 (172.16/12 prefix)
- 192.168.0.0–192.168.255.255 (192.168/16 prefix)

 NOTE   AWS refers to *private IP addresses* as the IPv4 addresses that are within the CIDR range of a customer's VPC.

One you create a VPC with a CIDR block such as 20.0.0.0/24, you can create both public and private subnets in the VPC. In this case, you can create, for example, two subnets: one public subnet with the CIDR block 20.0.0.0/25 (128 IP addresses, in the range 20.0.0.00–20.0.0.127) and a private subnet with the CIDR block 20.0.0.0/25 (128 IP addresses, with the IP range 20.0.0.128–20.0.0.0-255).

AWS reserves certain IP addresses in the network for its own use, as shown in the following list. If, for example, you create a subnet with the CIDR block 10.0.0.0/24, AWS reserves the first four IP addresses, as well as the last address.

- **10.0.0.0** The network address.

- **10.0.0.1** Reserved for the Amazon VPC router.

- **10.0.0.2** Reserved for the IP address of the DNS server, which is always the base of the VPC network range, plus two. However, AWS also reserves the base of each *subnet's* range plus two. If you have multiple CIDR blocks, the DNS server's IP address is located in the primary CIDR.

- **10.0.0.3** Reserved for future use by AWS.

- **10.0.0.255** Reserved as the network broadcast address, because AWS doesn't support broadcast in a VPC.

 TIP If you happen to create a subnet with the CIDR 20.0.0.0/16 and the VPC has the same CIDR, you can't create another subnet in this VPC with another CIDR such as 20.0.0.0/24, because you can't have overlapping CIDRs. You can't modify a subnet, however, so you must therefore delete and re-create the first subnet with a different CIDR block (that's smaller than the VPC's CIDR block), before creating the second subnet.

The reservation of these IP addresses means that you can't assign any of them to an instance running in either a private or a public subnet inside your VPC. So, in the earlier example of a VPC with the CIDR 20.0.0.0/24 (256 IP addresses), you can assign any of the following IP addresses (private IP address) for an EC2 instance, but not 20.0.0.0/255, since it's the network broadcast addresses reserved for AWS use:

- 20.0.0.132
- 20.0.0.55
- 20.0.0.122

Accessing the Internet from a VPC

Each default subnet in a VPC is a public subnet. The EC2 instances you launch into the default VPC have both private and public IPv4 addresses. You communicate with the Internet from your VPC through an *Internet gateway*, which helps your EC2 instances connect to the Internet via the EC2 network edge. You need the Internet gateway to

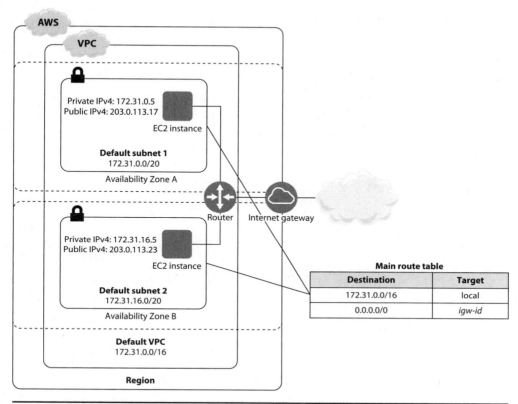

Figure 6-1 Accessing the Internet from inside a VPC

connect to services that are outside your VPC. Some AWS services such as Amazon S3 have *endpoints* that eliminate the need for an Internet gateway, but not every service has such an endpoint. A default VPC comes with an Internet gateway, and for a non-default VPC, you must create a gateway to communicate with the Internet.

Figure 6-1 shows how EC2 instances in a VPC communicate through an Internet gateway.

Amazon Virtual Private Cloud Components

To work with a VPC, you must understand various networking components that play a key role, such as subnets and route tables. I've been using several of these terms out of necessity, but I'll provide clear definitions and explanations for all the VPC network-related terms and concepts here.

Figure 6-2 shows a VPC with a CIDR block of IP addresses and a main route table.

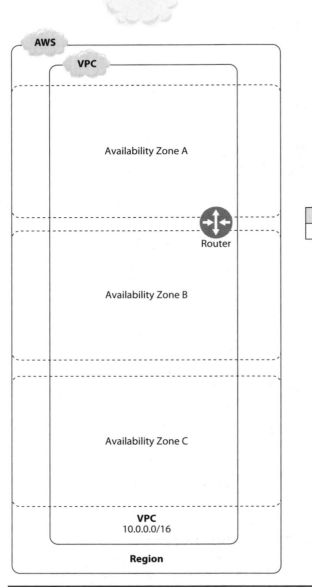

Figure 6-2 A simple VPC

A VPC comes with several components that work together to enable networking. Figure 6-3 shows the VPC dashboard, listing all the VPC resources you can use in your VPC.

In the following sections, I explain each of the key VPC resources.

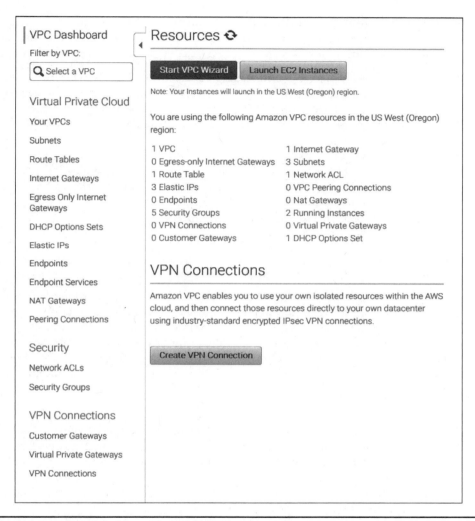

Figure 6-3 The VPC dashboard lists all the VPC components.

Subnets and a VPC

When you create a VPC, you can launch AWS resources such as instances into that VPC. As part of the VPC creation process, you must specify a range of IP addresses (IPv4) for the VPC. The VPC further subdivides that into one or more ranges of IP addresses, called a *subnet*. You specify the IP addresses in the form of a CIDR block, such as 10.0.0.0/16, which is the primary CIDR block for the VPC.

NOTE Exercise 6-4 walks you through the steps for creating a subnet in your VPC.

Subnet Types   There are two main types of subnets: private and public. A *private subnet* is used for resources such as databases that don't need to connect to the Internet. A *public subnet* is used for resources such as web servers that must connect to the Internet.

Default and Nondefault Subnets and Access to the Internet   When you create a VPC, you create a *default subnet* as well, which is a public subnet. The EC2 instances you launch into these subnets have private IPv4 addresses as well as public IPv4 addresses. These instances can communicate among themselves and are able to access the Internet through an Internet gateway.

When you launch an EC2 instance into a nondefault subnet, the instance has only a private IPv5 address. Thus, these instances can communicate only among themselves, with no Internet access. You can, however, assign a public IPv4 address at instance launch time or modify the subnet's public IP address attribute.

You can enable Internet access for the EC2 instances that you launch into a custom nondefault subnet in one of the following ways:

- Attach an Internet gateway to the VPC (if it isn't a default VPC) and associate an elastic IP (EIP) address with the instance.

- For IPV4 traffic, to enable EC2 instances in a VPC to initiate outbound connections to the Internet but disallow random, unsolicited connections from the Internet, you can use a *network address translation* (NAT) device, or a NAT gateway. The NAT device uses an EIP and communicates with the Internet via an Internet gateway. You can connect EC2 instances in a private subnet to the Internet through the NAT device, which routes traffic from the EC2 instance to the Internet gateway and routes the responses to the EC2 instance.

 EXAM TIP   Look out for questions that probe your understanding of how a NAT instance works. Remember that you can make your EC2 instances very secure by placing them in a private subnet with no EIP and routing all traffic through a NAT instance that lives in a public subnet. Amazon offers Linux-based Amazon Machine Images (AMIs) that are configured to run as NAT instances. You launch these instances into your public subnet.

When you create subnets, they inherit the VPC's route table, security groups, and network ACLs. You must therefore modify the route table, security groups, and network ACLs to change the routing of Internet traffic to the subnet you created.

AWS recommends that you create a public subnet and private subnet for every AZ. The public subnet (used for the web layer) includes a route to the Internet. It has either a public IP or an EIP assigned to it. The private subnet (used for the database and application layer) has no route to the Internet and is assigned only a private IP address for internal communications inside the VPC.

If you want to set up the private subnet to send and receive Internet traffic, you must configure it to do so. If you want the private subnet to *send* network packets to the Internet, you must create a route in the subnet's route table, specifying that the IP packets must be routed through either a NAT gateway or a NAT instance. For the private subnet to *receive* traffic from the Internet, the network packets must go through a load balancer of some type, such as the Classic Load Balancer or the Application Load Balancer (both described later in the section "Elastic Load Balancing"). A private subnet with a NAT gateway attached has a route table with the NAT gateway specified in a route, as shown here:

```
Destination      Target              Status      Propagated
10.0.0.0/16      local               Active      No
0.0.0.0/0        nat-gateway-id      Active      No
```

Accessing Your Corporate Network from Your VPC

You can connect your corporate data center with your Amazon VPC through an AWS-managed VPN connection. This in effect makes the AWS cloud an extension of your corporate data center. A VPN connection uses two gateways: a *virtual private gateway* on the AWS side and a *customer gateway* in your data center. The virtual private gateway is attached to your VPC and the customer gateway is a physical device or software appliance located in your data center.

 NOTE   If your AWS VPC doesn't have an Internet gateway attached to any of its subnets, the only way to SSH into your EC2 instances is by creating a VPN connection.

Accessing AWS Services Through AWS PrivateLink   AWS PrivateLink helps you privately connect your Amazon VPC to supported AWS services and to services that are hosted by other AWS account (*VPC endpoint services*). The traffic between your VPC and these services remains within the Amazon network. You don't need an Internet gateway, a NAT device, an AWS Direct Connect connection, or a VPN connection to communicate with the services. When you create a VPC endpoint for a service in your VPC, you create an elastic network interface with a private IP address that the traffic sent to the service uses as an entry point.

Launching an EC2 Instance Inside Your VPC   Follow these steps, in this order, to launch EC2 instances in a VPC:

1. Create an empty VPC, either with the AWS CLI command `create_vpc` or from the Amazon VPC console. (See Exercise 6-2 to create a VPC.)

2. Next, you can create subnets. To add a new subnet to a VPC, you need to specify an IPv4 CIDR block for the subnet from the IP range of a VPC. You can create a subnet with the `create-subnet` command or from the Amazon VPC console, as shown in Exercise 6-3.

3. After you create a subnet, you must configure routing. By default, a subnet you create is a private subnet. To make the subnet a public subnet, you must attach an Internet gateway to your VPC. So, you need to do the following:

   - Create and attach an Internet gateway to the VPC.

   - Create a custom route table and add a route to the Internet gateway.

4. Also, you can do the following to enhance the instance's security in your VPC.

- Create a security group.
- Create network ACLs.

5. After you've created your subnet, configured routing, and secured the VPC, you can launch an EC2 instance into your subnet (from the EC2 console or via the command line with the `create-instance` command).

For the EC2 instance to communicate with services outside your VPC, you must associate a public IP address with the instance by assigning one when you create the instance. Alternatively, NAT can assign the IP address with the NAT service being provided by a NAT gateway.

 NOTE The exercises at the end of this chapter help you perform each of the steps listed here to launch an EC2 instance in a VPC that you create after creating a subnet and configuring routing, followed by a configuration of a security group and network ACLs.

The Default VPC

Your account comes with a *default VPC* with a *default subnet* in each AZ. If you don't create your own VPC, your EC2 instances will launch in the default VPC. The VPC you create is called a *nondefault VPC*. Subnets that you create in this VPC are called *nondefault subnets*.

The default VPC has the following components:

- A default subnet in each AZ
- A size /16 CIDR block (172.31.0.0/16), which provides up to 65,536 private IP addresses
- A default subnet /20, which provides up to 4096 addresses
- An Internet gateway
- A main route table, which routes all IPv4 traffic destined for the Internet to the Internet gateway
- A default security group and a default ACL that allow all traffic
- A default DHCP option set

Elastic Network Interfaces

An *elastic network interface* (ENI) is a virtual network interface that includes attributes such as these:

- A primary and one or more secondary private IPv4 addresses
- An EIP for each private IPv4 address
- A public IPv4 address that can be assigned to the eth0 network interface
- One or more IPv6 addresses

- One or more security groups
- A MAC address
- A description

Every instance in a VPC has a default network interface, which is the *primary network interface* (eth0). This interface has a private IPv4 address. Though you can't detach an instance's primary network interface, you can configure and attach multiple network interfaces to instances in your VPC. Among other things, multiple network interfaces offer an inexpensive high availability solution for instances in your VPC.

Let's say, for example, that you have an application inside your VPC with hard-coded IP addresses. You can enable the application to fail over to new instances without having to reconfigure the application by assigning a secondary private IP address to the primary ENI that can be moved to a failover instance. You can also achieve the failover capability by creating a secondary ENI that can be moved to a failover instance. You can do both of these when launching an instance (*cold attach*), when you are allowed to specify up to two network interfaces. You can also add network interfaces to a running instance (*hot attach*) or when the instance is stopped (*warm attach*). If you specify more than one network interface for an instance, you can't auto-assign a public IPv4 address to that instance.

The maximum number of network interfaces depends on the instance type. For example, the c4.8xlarge instance type can have a maximum of eight network interfaces and up to thirty IPv4 addresses per interface.

An elastic network interface is a static public IPv4 address associated with your account. The interfaces are associated with your AWS account, not to the instances. You can thus associate an ENI with any instance or network interface in your VPC. When you turn off an instance, the ENI that you've associated with that instance remains. If you delete the instance, the ENI continues to be associated with your account, because you created it.

When you create a network interface, it inherits the public IPV4 address from the subnet. After you create a network interface (same as an ENI in our context), you can attach it to an instance, detach it from that instance, and attach it to another instance. The network interface carries over the attributes that you've defined, and network traffic is sent to the new instance to which you attached the network interface. If you want, you can modify the network interface's attributes—say, by changing its security groups and managing its IP addresses.

 NOTE The network interface determines the public IPv4 addressing attribute of an instance when you launch an instance and specify an existing network interface as its primary network interface (eth0).

You can monitor IP traffic going to and from a network interface by enabling a *VPC flow log* on the network interface. Once you create the flow log, you can view its data in CloudWatch Logs.

Attaching Multiple Network Interfaces to an Instance
You can attach multiple network interfaces to an instance in the following use cases.

Create a Low Budget High Availability Solution   You can keep a hot-standby instance running and preconfigure it for the same role as the primary network interface. When the primary instance fails, you attach the primary network interface to the hot-standby instance. When you attach the network interface to the secondary instance, the interface maintains its private IP addresses, EIPs, and MAC address, which helps network traffic to start going to the standby instance.

Create a Management Network   Multiple network interfaces help support a management network. You set up the primary network interface (eth0) to handle public traffic and a secondary network interface (eth1) to take care of management traffic.

You configure different access controls for the primary network (public traffic) and the secondary network (management traffic) interfaces. Typically, the access to the public network is less restrictive, and the security group that you associate with this interface permits access to the server from the Internet.

The security group associated with the secondary network interface doesn't face the Internet. It's a private-facing interface for management purposes. The security group associated with the secondary interface allows SSH access for a small set of IP addresses (in the Internet or in your own VPC, or a virtual private gateway).

Create Dual-Home Instances   Multiple network interfaces help you manage workloads (and roles) on separate subnets. Suppose you have two web servers that connect to a middle tier where an application server runs. In this scenario, you can also configure the application server as dual-homed to a backend network (subnet) such as the database server's network. Each of the dual-homed instances can receive requests on the front end and send their requests to the servers running in the backend network.

NOTE   Several network and security appliances such as load balancers, proxy servers, and NAT servers require that you configure them with multiple network interfaces.

Creating, Attaching, and Detaching a Network Interface

You can create a network interface from the command line with the ec2 create-network-interface AWS CLI command or create it from the Amazon EC2 console. You can create a network interface in a subnet, but you can't move it to a different subnet.

You can attach a network interface to an instance while the instance is running or while it is stopped. You can also attach the network interface (both primary and secondary) when you're launching an instance. And you can attach the interface to instances running in the same AZ.

You can't detach the primary interface (eth0). However, you can detach a secondary (ethN) network interface while the instance is running or is stopped.

NOTE   Exercise 6-4 shows how to create a network interface using the Amazon EC2 console.

Elastic IP Addresses

An EIP is a static public IPv4 address reachable from the Internet that you can associate with an instance or network interface in a VPC. An EIP is associated with an account while a public IP is assigned to a specific instance. If you reboot an instance, neither a public IP nor an EIP that is associated with the instance is removed. If you stop an instance, while a public IP is removed from the instance, the EIP stays with the instance. If an instance fails, the IP address can be quickly remapped to another EC2 instance in your VPC.

Here's what you need to remember about an EIP:

- You can associate an EIP address to an EC2 instance or a network interface.

- You can move an EIP from one EC2 instance to another.

- If you associate the EIP with a network interface, you can move all the attributes for the interface from one EC2 instance to another.

- When you associate an EIP with an instance that has a public IPv4 address, the public DNS name of the instance changes and becomes the same as that for the EIP.

- An EIP is a regional entity.

- An EIP is accessed through a VPC's Internet gateway.

- You must first allocate an EIP for use in your VPC, before you can associate it with an instance or a network interface. (Exercise 6-1 shows how to perform both tasks.)

- If you associate an EIP to an instance or its primary network interface, the instance's public IP address, if you've assigned one, goes back to Amazon's pool of public IPv4 addresses.

- You can assign an EIP only to one instance at a time.

- You associate an EIP with an EC2 instance by configuring the network interface that you've attached to that interface.

- When you move an EIP from an instance, the new instance can be in the same or in a different VPC.

- You can disassociate an EIP from an instance or network interface and re-associate it to a different instance or interface. An EIP you've disassociated from a resource remains allocated to you until you release it.

- You can have a maximum of five EIP addresses, which is a soft limit that can be increased by submitting a request to AWS. Use a NAT device to conserve your limited EIPs. AWS won't charge you for one EIP associated with a running instance but will charge you for any additional EIPs you've associated with that instance.

Route Tables

A VPC that you create will have one or more subnets. Each of those subnets must be associated with a *route table*, which contains a set of rules (routes) that determine where network traffic is directed in a subnet.

NOTE A subnet can have only one route table at a given time. However, multiple subnets can use the same route table.

Main and Custom Route Tables

Each VPC comes with a *default route table* called the *main route table*. If you don't associate a subnet explicitly with any custom route table of your own, the subnet is implicitly associated with the main route table.

The default route table for a VPC with the CIDR range of 10.3.0.0/16 looks like the following, with a *single route*:

```
Destination        Target      Status       Propagated
10.3.0.0/16        local       Active       No
```

This route table specifies that all IP packets with the destination address in the 10.3.0.0/16 network (addresses between 10.3.0.0 and 10.3.255.255) are delivered within this VPC. Suppose you create a private subnet with CIDR range 10.3.55.0/24 in this VPC. The default route table for this subnet will be 10.3.0.0/16, since a subnet inherits its default route table from the VPC.

By default, the main route table doesn't contain a route to an Internet gateway. You can modify the main route table, and add other addresses, as shown here with *two routes*, the second one added by you:

```
Destination        Target                Status       Propagated
10.0.0.0/16        local                 Active       No
0.0.0.0/0          Internet-gateway-id   Active       No
```

As with the first example, the first route delivers all network traffic bound for the 10.155.0.0/16 network within this VPC. The second route ensures that all other network traffic bound for this network is routed to the Internet gateway.

You can make a private subnet a public one by adding a route to an Internet gateway. You must first create an Internet gateway and then add a route with a destination of 0.0.0.0/0 for IPv4 traffic or ::/0 for IPv6 traffic, along with a target of the Internet gateway ID (*igw-xxxxxxxxx*).

You may explicitly associate a subnet with the main route table, although it's not common. You do this temporarily when replacing the main route table. Custom route tables that you create help you explicitly control how a subnet routes outbound traffic.

Creating a Route Table

You can create a route table with the `aws ec2 create-route-table` command. You must specify the VPC. Here's an example:

```
$ aws ec2 create-route-table --vpc-id vpc-66e02103
{
    "RouteTable": {
        "Associations": [],
        "VpcId": "vpc-66e02103",
        "PropagatingVgws": [],
        "RouteTableId": "rtb-bf1e01c7",
```

```
        "Routes": [
            {
                "Origin": "CreateRouteTable",
                "GatewayId": "local",
                "DestinationCidrBlock": "172.31.0.0/16",
                "State": "active"
            }
        ],
        "Tags": []
    }
}
$
```

Connecting to the Internet or Other External Networks from a VPC

You can create a VPC that has no connectivity to the Internet or to your other AWS services or networks, but that wouldn't be of much use to you. Instead, you can set up external connectivity from a VPC through various means:

- **Internet gateway**   This VPC component enables communications between the EC2 instances in a VPC and the Internet. It is a redundant and highly available component that provides a target in the route tables for traffic to or from the Internet, and it performs NAT for instances with public IPv4 addresses.

- **NAT gateway**   This gateway enables EC2 instances in a private subnet to connect to the Internet and to other AWS services. The big difference between the NAT and Internet gateways is that the NAT gateway prevents the Internet from initiating connections to your EC2 instances.

- **VPN gateway**   This gateway enables VPN connections through the Internet to your on-premise data centers.

- **VPC endpoints**   VPC endpoints enable a VPC to connect to services such as Amazon Simple Storage Service (S3) that don't live inside your VPC (remember that EC2 instances live inside the VPC).

- **VPC peering connections**   These enables connectivity between a VPC and another VPC, both owned by you as well as those outside your AWS account.

   NOTE   AWS doesn't charge you for using a VPC, and you continue to pay the standard rates for instances and other EC2 features. You must pay a charge for using the AWS-managed VPN connection and for using a NAT gateway.

Enabling Internet Access for an EC2 Instance Inside a Subnet

For an instance inside a VPC subnet to access the Internet, you must first attach an Internet gateway to the VPC. Then you must ensure that the subnet's route table points to the Internet gateway. The scope of the route can be all destinations not explicitly known to the route table, such as 0.0.0.0/0 for IPv4 addresses or ::/0 for IPv6 IP addresses. You can also narrow the route to a specific range of IP addresses, such as the EIP of EC2 instances outside the VPC.

Each instance in the subnet must have a globally unique IP address, such as a public IPv4 address, an EIP that's associated with a private IPv4 address on the instance, or an IPv6 address. The Internet gateway provides the NAT on behalf of the instance. The reply address field of the traffic going to the Internet is thus set to the public IPv4 instead of the private IP address of the instance. Similarly, the destination address of traffic sent to the public IPv4 or the EIP of the instance is translated by NAT to the instance's private IPv4 address to deliver the inbound Internet traffic to the VPC.

NOTE The network ACLs and security groups rules must allow the Internet traffic to flow to and from the instances.

Creating a VPC

Although AWS does offer you a default VPC, it's a good practice to create your own VPC. You can create a VPC through the VPC Wizard in the Amazon VPC console. When you use the VPC Wizard to create your VPC (follow the steps in Exercise 6-3), the wizard does the following for you:

- It creates a VPC with a /16 IPv4 CIDR block.
- It associates a /56 IPv6 CIDR block with the VPC.
- It attaches an Internet gateway to the VPC.
- It creates a subnet with a /24 IPv4 CIDR block and a /64 IPv6 CIDR block in your VPC.
- It creates a route table and associates it with the subnet it creates, to facilitate network traffic between that subnet and the Internet gateway.

EXAM TIP The exam probes deeply into your understanding of a VPC, including things such as private and public subnets. Remember that a subnet that you associate with a route table that has a route to an Internet gateway is a *public subnet*. Also, a VPC's default settings will only assign a private UP address for the instances in a subnet (the Auto-assign Public IP property is by default set to no). You must also configure any EIPs and the Internet gateway, since these aren't configured by default when you create a subnet.

From the AWS CLI, you can execute the `create-vpc` command to create a VPC:

```
$ aws ec2 create-vpc –cidr-block 10.0.0.0/16
```

To create a VPC manually with a single public subnet that supports Internet access through an Internet gateway, follow these steps:

1. Create the subnet. (Exercise 6-3 shows how to do this.)
2. Create and attach an Internet gateway (or a NAT gateway) to the VPC. (Exercise 6-7 shows how to create a NAT gateway.)

3. Create a custom route table and associate that with the subnet, since, by default, the main route table doesn't contain a route to an Internet gateway. (Exercise 6-8 shows how to create a route for a NAT gateway.)

4. Update the security group rules.

Common VPC Scenarios

I described the generic process for creating a VPC, but you can create a VPC under various scenarios, with different configurations for your subnets, route table, and other VPC components. Let's run through two basic VPC configuration scenarios.

A Simple Single Public Subnet Scenario

This simple VPC has a single public subnet and an Internet gateway that allows Internet communications. AWS recommends this type of configuration for a simple public-facing web applications, such as a small web site or a blog.

In this simple scenario, the VPC's configuration can have the following components:

- A VPC with a size /16 IPv4 CIDR block (remember, this is the maximum size you choose for a VPC's CIDR block and supports 65,536 private IPv4 addresses).

- A single subnet, which can be as large as /16, but is usually something like size /24 IPv4 CIDR block (for example, 10.0.0.0/24), providing 256 private IPv4 addresses.

- An Internet gateway to connect this VPC to the Internet as well as other AWS services. An Internet gateway isn't automatically attached to a VPC by default; you must attach the gateway to your VPC and ensure that the subnet's route table points to the gateway.

- Assigned instances running in this subnet private IPv4 addresses in the subnet's range, which is 10.0.0.0–10.0.0.255. You can assign an instance the private IP address of 10.0.0.8, enabling the instance to communicate with other instances in this VPC. You also assign an EIP such as 198.51.100.4, which is a public IPv4 address that enables these instances to be reached from the Internet.

- The custom route table associated with the subnet, which enables instances in this subnet to communicate with other instances running in your VPC, and to communicate directly over the Internet.

 EXAM TIP　The certification exam quizzes you on your knowledge of an Internet gateway. Remember that an Internet gateway does two things: it provides a target in the route tables for Internet routable traffic, and it performs network address translation (NAT) for instances to which you've assigned public IPv4 addresses. You must explicitly create the gateway and attach an EIP to an instance so you can connect to the Internet from the instance.

A VPC with a Public and a Private Subnet

Another common scenario is a VPC with *both* public and private subnets. AWS recommends this configuration when you want to run public-facing web applications while also running backend servers (such as those that host database servers) without any public access.

In this scenario, instances that run in the public subnet can directly send outbound traffic to the Internet, and instances in the private subnet can access the Internet only via a NAT gateway. The NAT gateway is located in the public subnet.

Although the database servers can access the Internet (for things such as software and security updates) via the NAT gateway, the Internet won't be able to initiate inbound connections to the database servers.

A typical configuration of two subnets, one private and the other public, includes the following entities:

- A VPC with a size /16 IPv4 CIDR block such as 10.0.0.0/16
- A public subnet, such as 10.0.0.24, associated with a route table with a route to an Internet gateway
- A private subnet, such as 10.0.1.24
- An Internet gateway to connect the VPC to the Internet as well as to other AWS services
- Instances in this VPC may have difference connectivity capabilities:
  - **Instances with private IPv4 addresses** in the subnet range, such as 10.0.04 and 10.0.1.5, are allowed to communicate with each other within the VPC.
  - **Instances in the public subnets** can have an EIP address, such as 198.51.100.1, that enables them to be reached from the Internet. You can also assign a public IP address for these instances when you launch them, instead of assigning them an EIP.
  - **Instances in the private subnet that run in the backend** won't have any public IP addresses since they don't need to accept traffic from the Internet. However, these instances can send requests to the Internet via the NAT gateway (located in the public subnet).
- A NAT gateway in the public subnet with an EIP, which allows instances in the private subnet to send requests to the Internet.

The public subnet has a *custom route table* associated with it. This route table contains two entries: The first entry enables instances in this subnet to communicate with other instances in the VPC. The second entry enables the instances to communicate directly with the Internet (over IPv4). The route table looks like this:

```
Destination     Target
10.0.0.0/16     local      (within the PC)
0.0.0.0/0       igw-id     (the Internet gateway's ID, for example, igw-1a2b3d4d)
```

EXAM TIP   Be sure to understand the difference between the main route table and a custom route table. In a VPC, the main route table is associated with the private subnet and the custom route table with the public subnet.

The private subnet has the *main route table* associated with it. This route table also contains two entries. The first entry enables instances in this subnet to communicate with the other instances in the VPC, and the second entry enables the instances to communicate with the Internet via the NAT gateway.

```
Destination    Target
10.0.0.0/16    local            (within the PC)
0.0.0.0/0      nat-gateway-id   (the NAT gateway's ID, for example, nat-124567890123456701234567)
```

If a subnet doesn't have a route to the Internet gateway, but instead has its traffic routed to a virtual private gateway (this is called a *site-to-site, or S2S, connection*), the subnet is a *VPN-only subnet*. Only IPv4 traffic is currently supported over a S2S VPN connection.

 NOTE   If you have a running NAT instance in your VPC, you can't delete the VPC. If you have other EC2 instances in a subnet, you also can't delete that subnet.

Securing Your VPC

Let's say, for example, that one of the instances in a subnet is running a database and another instance in another subnet is running a web application that needs to talk to the database. To ensure that the database and the web application can talk to each other, you must ensure that you configure the VPC's security groups so that they allow the application host to talk to the database on the correct protocol. You must also configure a NACL that allows communication between the two subnets.

Amazon VPC offers three main features or capabilities to secure your VPC: security groups, NACLs, and VPC flow logs, which monitor network traffic going to and coming from VPC, rather than a full-fledged security feature. Both security groups and network ACLs can enhance your VPC's security.

Security Groups

A security group serves as a virtual firewall to control the traffic for one or more EC2 instances. You can specify one or more security groups when you launch an instance or use the default security group of the VPC.

Security groups provide strong security for the instances, but NACLs (discussed next) offer an additional layer of security at the subnet level. The EC2 instances in your VPC don't have to belong to the same security group; they can each belong to a separate security group.

Security Group Rules   You add rules to each of your security groups to control traffic into the instances. One set of rules controls inbound traffic, and another set controls outbound traffic from the instances:

- **Inbound rule**   Consists of the traffic source and the source port (or port range). The source may be another security group, a single IP address, or an IPv4 or IPv6 CIDR block.
- **Outbound rule**   Contains the traffic destination and the destination port (or port range). The destination may be another security group, a single IP address, or an IPv4 or IPv6 CIDR block.

NOTE   Security groups are stateful, which means that the return traffic is automatically allowed, regardless of any rules that you may configure.

A security group rule contains the following entities:

- Any protocol with a standard protocol number
- An optional description of the rule

NOTE   Security groups let you filter only on destination ports, not source ports.

You can specify *allow rules* that allow traffic, and *deny rules* that keep traffic from flowing into or out of an entity. You can specify allow rules only for a security group, not deny rules. The type of security group rules that you add depend on the role that the EC2 instance plays. A database server would need a security rule that allows inbound MySQL access, for example.

A rule for a security group for a web server looks different from that of a database server. A web server usually needs to receive HTTP/HTTPS traffic from all IPv4/IPv6 addresses. So its inbound rules would be something like that shown in Table 6-2.

NOTE   Remember that if you want anyone to be able to access an application running in one of your instances, the source IP range must be 0.0.0.0/0. If, on the other hand, you want to, say, SSH into an instance from a specific IP address, then the source IP is that of the address from which you want to allow the SSH connectivity.

Source	Protocol	Port Range	Comments
0.0.0.0/0	TCP	80	Allow inbound HTTP access from all IPv4 addresses
::/0	TCP	80	Allow inbound HTTP access from all IPv6 addresses
0.0.0.0/0	TCP	443	Allow inbound HTTPS access from all IPv4 addresses
::/0	TCP	443	Allow inbound HTTPS access from all IPv6 addresses
Your network's public IPv4 address range	TCP	22	Allow inbound SSH access to Linux instances from IPv4 IP addresses in your network
Your network's public IPv4 address range	TCP	3389	Allow inbound RDP access to Windows instances from IPv4 addresses in your network

Table 6-2   A Security Group's Inbound Rules

The same set of web servers also needs to send Microsoft SQL Server and MySQL traffic to a database server, so the outbound rules for the security group could look like this:

Source	Protocol	Port Range	Comments
Database server security group's ID	TCP	1433	Allow outbound Microsoft SQL Server access to instances in this security group
Database server security group's ID	TCP	3306	Allow outbound MySQL access to instances in this security group

Default Security Group Behavior   The default security group has an initial set of rules that enables all instances associated with the security group to communicate with each other. However, instances from other security groups by default can't communicate with each other, unless you add security rules explicitly allowing those instances to communicate.

Here are a few summary points about a default security group:

- A security group has an outbound rule, and the rule allows all outbound traffic. You can remove the outbound rule entirely or add outbound rules that allow only specific outbound traffic.

- There are no inbound rules by default. Therefore, all traffic from other hosts is denied, until you add appropriate inbound rules to the security group.

- All traffic between instances in a default security group is allowed.

- You can't delete a default security group, but you may change its rules, just as you can with any other security group.

Security Group Statefulness   A security group is *stateful*. In other words, all responses to requests that an instance sends out are allowed in, irrespective of the inbound security group rules. Similarly, responses to all permitted inbound requests are also allowed to flow out, irrespective of the security group's outbound rules.

Creating Security Groups   Every VPC comes with a default security group, but you need to create your own custom security groups to control the traffic into and out the various instances that you run in your VPC. You can create a security group from the AWS CLI by executing the `create-security-group` command:

```
$ aws ec2 create-security-group --group-name MySecurityGroup --description
"My security group" --vpc-id vpc-1a2b3c4d
```

Run the `describe-security-groups` command to describe one or more security groups, as shown in this example:

```
$ aws ec2 describe-security-groups --group-ids sg-123008a4
```

This command displays information about the security group with the ID sg-123008a4.

 NOTE   Exercise 6-5 shows how to create a security group from Amazon VPC console.

Network Access Control Lists

NACLs help you control inbound and outbound traffic to a subnet. While a security group controls traffic going to and from an instance, ACLs offer an additional layer of protection at the subnet level. Each subnet must be associated with a NACL, and the rules that you configure for the ACL apply to the *entire subnet*. Every VPC comes with a *default* NACL that allows all inbound traffic. Each subnet must be associated with a NCL, and if you don't associate a subnet with a network ACL, the subnet is associated with the default NACL. You can add or remove rules from the default network ACL and associate a subnet with a different custom ACL that you create. You can also change the default ACL if you want. A custom network ACL that you create and associate with a subnet by default denies all inbound and outbound traffic. You can associate a network ACL with multiple subnets, but the opposite isn't true. In other words, you can associate a subnet with only one network ACL.

You can divide your VPC into logical areas by configuring a NACL that restricts which subnets in your VPC can talk to each other—for example, if you don't want development team members working in a development subnet to impact production instances that you're running in a separate production subnet.

Security groups and NACLs work in tandem. If an instance running Subnet A can't ping another instance running in Subnet B, there are two possible reasons:

- The NACL in Subnet B doesn't allow outbound ICMP traffic (ping uses ICMP).
- The security group that you attached to Subnet B doesn't allow inbound ICMP traffic.

NACL Rules   As with security group rules, NACLs have separate inbound and out-bound rules that can either allow or deny traffic:

- **Inbound rule**   Consists of the traffic source and the destination port (or port range). The source may be another security group, a single IP address, or an IPv4 or IPv6 CIDR block.

- **Outbound rule**   Contains the traffic destination and the destination port (or port range). The destination may be another security group, a single IP address, or an IPv4 or IPv6 CIDR block.

Unlike security groups, NACLs are *stateless*, meaning that responses to any allowed inbound external traffic depend on the NACL rules for outbound traffic. The same principle applies to requests sent via outbound traffic.

A NACL rule has the following components:

- **Rule number**   Each rule has a number, and the rules are evaluated starting with the lowest numbered rule. As soon as a numbered rule matches the traffic (network packet), the rule is applied.

- **Protocol**   Any protocol with a standard protocol number can be used.

- **A choice of ALLOW or DENY for the specified traffic**   Suppose you configure an ACL for Subnet A that specifies two rules: Rule #100 explicitly denies TCP traffic on port 21 from 0.0.0.0/0 and Rule #110 explicitly allows TCP traffic on the same port from 0.0.0.0/0. Since rules are evaluated starting from the lowest numbered rule, Rule #100 is evaluated first. Rule #110 is ignored, since there's already a match with a lower numbered rule (#100). The explicit deny in Rule #100 overrides the explicit allow in Rule #110, and traffic is disallowed.

If you need to block access for specific IP addresses to your VPC, you can modify the NACLs associated with the public subnets in the VPC to prevent requests from the IP addresses to access your VPC. You must create an inbound rule for the NACL that denies traffic coming from one or more IP addresses so that the inbound request is stopped at the subnet level. So, if you suspect that a web server is under a phishing or a Denial of Service (DoS) attack and you identify a specific IP address or a set of IP addresses as the source of the attack, you can configure an ACL rule to block all traffic coming from this IP address. You place a DENY rule in the NAL to deny access to the IP addresses.

   NOTE   Both the default NACL and all custom NACLs include a rule whose number is an asterisk (*). This rule's purpose is to ensure that all packets that don't match any of the numbered rules are denied. You cannot remove or alter this rule.

Security Groups vs. NACLs

Following are the key differences between security groups and NACLs.

- **Level of operation**   A security group operates at the instance level, while a NACL works at the subnet level.

- **Type of rules supported**   Security groups support allow rules only, whereas network ACLs support both allow and deny rules.

- **How rules are processed**   Security groups evaluate all rules before determining whether the traffic should be allowed. NACLs process rules in number order (priority), one by one, when deciding whether to allow traffic.

- **Statefulness**   Security groups are stateful and automatically allow all return (response) traffic, regardless of rules. NACLs are stateless and allow return traffic only if the rules allow it.

- **Application**   A NACL applies automatically to all instances in the subnets that you associate with the ACL. A security group applies to an instance only if you specify the security group when launching the instance or associate the security group with the instance later.

VPC Flow Logs

VPC Flow Logs enable you to capture information about the IP traffic passing to and from your VPC's network interfaces. You can choose to publish the flow log data to Amazon S3 and CloudWatch Logs, from where you can view the flow log data.

VPC Flow Logs help you secure your instances by monitoring your network traffic. They also help in troubleshooting certain issues, such as when network traffic fails to reach an instance because of security group rules with overly restrictive filtering rules.

 NOTE   When you use flow logs, CloudWatch charges apply, regardless of whether you configure the storage of the flow logs in CloudWatch Logs or Amazon S3.

You can create a flow log for a VPC, a subnet, or a network interface. AWS monitors all network interfaces in a VPC or subnet when you create a flow log at the subnet or VPC level. Each network interface traced by flow logs has a separate log stream, which consists of log records that store the log events pertaining to the network traffic for a specific network interface.

When you create a flow log, you specify the following key entities:

- **Resource**   VPC, subnet, or network interface
- **Traffic type**   Accepted, rejected, or all traffic
- **Destination at which to publish the records**   Amazon S3 or to the CloudWatch Logs service.

Although you can create flow logs for network interfaces created by AWS services such as Amazon RDS, Elastic Load Balancing (ELB), and Amazon ElastiCache, you cannot do so from the consoles or APIs that belong to these services. You must create the flow logs for these network interfaces from the Amazon EC2 console or the Amazon EC2 API. In addition, you cannot create the log streams from the CloudWatch Logs console or API.

The *capture window* for a flow log record is the duration of time for which the flow logs service aggregates data before it publishes the flow log records via S3 or CloudWatch Logs. The capture window is around 10 minutes but can be extended to 15 minutes. This means that you can't expect flow logs to capture the real-time log events for the network interfaces.

You cannot enable flow logs for VPCs that are peers of your VPC unless the other VPCs are also in your AWS account. Flow logs don't capture all IP traffic. For example, they don't log DHCP traffic and traffic generated by EC2 instances when they contact the Amazon DNS service.

Amazon VPC Optional Components

Amazon VPC offers several optional components that you can use for various purposes:

- **NAT gateways**   NAT gateways enable instances in private subnets to connect to the Internet and other services but prevent the Internet from initiating connections with the instances in the subnet.

- **DHCP options sets**   The Dynamic Host Configuration Protocol is a standard for passing configuration parameters to hosts on a TCP/IP network. The parameters include the domain name, domain name server, and the netbios-node-type.

- **VPN connections**   These are private connections you establish between the Amazon VPC and remote networks or an on-premise network.

- **VPC peering**   VPC peering is a networking connection between two VPCs that helps you transmit traffic between the VPCs with private IPv4 or IPv6 addresses. The two VPCs communicate as if they were in the same network.

We'll review these optional VPC components in the following sections.

NAT Instances and NAT Gateways

You use a NAT device when you want to let instances in a private subnet connect to the Internet or to other AWS services, but block the Internet from initiating connections to those instances. You also use the NAT device to forward traffic from instances that live in a private subnet. NAT forwards the traffic from the instances to the Internet and returns the response back to the instances. When the NAT device forwards the traffic from the instances to the Internet, it replaces the instance's IP address with the NAT device's address. Similarly, when the NAT device sends response traffic to these instances, it translates the address back to the instance's private IP address.

NOTE Because NAT devices aren't supported for IPv6 traffic, you must use an egress-only Internet gateway for IPv6. AWS offers two types of NAT devices: NAT gateways and NAT instances. Though you must manage a NAT instance yourself from a NAT AMI, AWS manages the NAT gateway service. NAT instances are meant for use in special cases where you want more control. There is a charge for creating and using a NAT gateway.

How a NAT Gateway Works You must specify a public subnet and an EIP to create a NAT gateway. The NAT gateway lives in this public subnet. You can associate only one EIP to a NAT gateway. After you create the NAT gateway, you must update the route table of the private subnet (could be multiple) to direct all Internet-bound traffic to the NAT gateway, allowing the instances in that private subnet to talk to the Internet.

For availability purposes, AWS creates a NAT gateway in an AZ and implements redundancy in that zone. If the AZ goes down, the resources from other AZs that use this gateway lose their Internet access. To keep your operations running despite an AZ failure, you must create a NAT gateway in each AZ.

Any ACLs that you create in a subnet in which you locate the NAT gateway apply to the NAT gateway's traffic. You can thus use network ACLs to control traffic to and from this subnet.

Let's say you're running a set of EC2 instances in a private subnet such as 10.0.1.0/24. You've also set up a NAT instance in your public subnet. The EC2 instances running in the private subnet need to download their updates from the Internet via HTTPS. You must add an incoming rule to the security group for the NAT instance that allows incoming requests from Source 10.0.1.0/24 on port 443.

VPC Endpoints, VPC Peering, VPN, AWS Direct Connect, and NAT Gateways You won't able to use a NAT gateway to send traffic over VPC endpoints, VPN, Direct Connect, or a VPC peering connection. The instances in the private subnet must use the subnet's route table to route traffic directly to these devices. Similarly, resources on the other side of the VPC peering connection, a VPN connection, or Direct Connect can't route traffic to a NAT gateway.

Here's an example of a private's subnet's route table's routes:

- Internet-bound traffic (0.0.0.0) is routed to a NAT gateway.
- The traffic for 10.25.0.0/16, which is more specific than 0.0.0.0/0, is routed to a VPC peering connection.
- The instance's Amazon S3-bound traffic uses (*pl-xxxxxxxx*), a specific IP address range for Amazon S3, and is routed to a VPC endpoint.

Creating a NAT Gateway You can use the Amazon VPC console to create a NAT gateway. To create the gateway, you must specify a public subnet and an EIP.

NOTE Exercise 6-7 walks you through the steps for creating a NAT gateway.

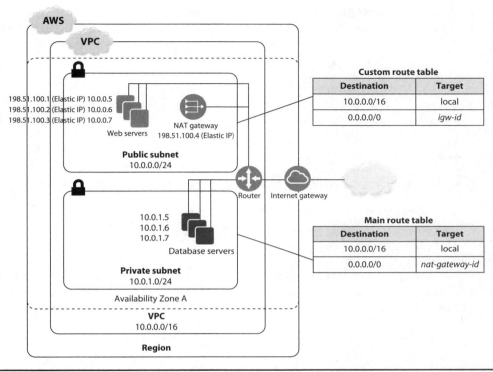

Figure 6-4   Architecture of a VPC with a NAT gateway

After you create the NAT gateway, you must update the route table of the private subnet (or subnets) so it can direct Internet traffic to the NAT gateway. Figure 6-4 shows the architecture of a VPC with a NAT gateway.

DHCP Option Sets

DHCP is a standard for passing configuration information to hosts running on a TCP/IP network. You can configure what are known as *DHCP options sets* for a VPC. When you launch an EC2 instance into your VPC (custom, not the default VPC), by default, the instance has only a private IP address, and not a public IPv4 address. You can change this default behavior by specifying a public IP for the instance when you launch it, or by modifying the subnet's public IPv4 address attribute.

AWS assigns all instances in a non-default VPC that you create an unresolvable host-name, such as *ip-10-0-0-204*. AWS automatically creates a set of DHCP options for a VPC when you create the VPC. The default DHCP options set contains two DHCP options:

- **domain-name-servers**   The AmazonProvidedDNS points to an Amazon DNS server that provides DNS for EC2 instances that want to connect to the Internet over the VPC's Internet gateway.

- **domain-name**   Domain name for your region.

AWS provides an EC2 instance that you launch into a nondefault VPC with a private DNS hostname. It might also provide a public DNS hostname, if your instance has a public IPv4 address *and* you've also configured the required DNS attributes for your VPC. The two VPC attributes that you must set are

- **enableDnsHostnames**   If you set this attribute to true, the instances in your VPC get public DNS hostnames, but only if you've also set the enableDnsSupport attribute to true.

- **enableDnsSupport**   If you set this attribute to true, DNS resolution is supported for your VPC.

When you set both attributes to true, this is what happens:

- The instances in this VPC receive public hostnames.
- The Amazon-provided DNS server resolves Amazon-provided private DNS hostnames.

If you haven't set both attributes to true, your instance gets a custom private DNS hostname, if you've specified a custom domain name in your DHCP options set.
The default public DNS hostnames for the instances have the following form:

- ec2-public-ipv4-address.compute-1.amazonaws.com (for the us-east-1 region)
- ec2-public-ipv4-address.region.compute.amazonaws.com (for all other regions)

The private hostnames take the following forms:

- ip-private-ipv4-address.ec2.internal (for the us-east-1 region)
- ip-private-ipv4-address.region.compute.internal (for all other regions)

You can configure the supported options for a DHCP options set for use with your VPC, to do things like assigning your own domain name to your instances. Here are the five DHCP options you can set:

- **domain-name-servers**   You can provide the IP addresses of up to four domain name servers if you don't want to use the default Amazon DNS server, AmazonProvidedDNS. Suppose, for example, your corporate policies dictate that the DNS name for your internal applications must be resolved internally and not publicly over the Internet. You can create a DHCP option set that includes both options for the domain name servers—AmazonProvidedDNS and your internal DNS server name.

- **domain-name**   If you're using AmazonProvidedDNS in the us-east-1 region, specify ec2.itnernal land region.compute.internal for all other regions. If you're not using AmazonProvidedDNS, you must specify a domain name such as mycompany.com.

- **ntp-servers**   You can specify up to four Network Transfer Protocol (NTP) servers by providing their IP addresses.

- **netbios-name-servers** You can specify up to four NetBios name servers by suppling their IP addresses.

- **netbios-node-type** You can specify a NetBios node type, such as point-to-point, broadcast, and multicast. AWS recommends specifying node type 2 (point-to-point, or P-node). The broadcast and multicast types aren't supported at this time.

VPN Connections

A VPN connection is a connection between your AWS VPC and your own network. You can also connect your VPC to a remote network through a Virtual Private network (VPN) connection. You can choose to use AWS Managed VPN (hardware VPN) to set up the connection to your remote networks. Alternatively, you can do the same thing by configuring an EC2 instance in your VPC that runs a third-party software VPN appliance that is provided by the AWS Partner Network and the open source community. A software VPN offers you more control, but you also become responsible for managing it and ensuring that the software is working as designed. AWS doesn't provide support or maintain a third-party VPN appliance.

When using an AWS Managed VPN, you can enable connectivity between your VPC and your own remote networks by attaching a virtual private gateway to the VPC and creating an AWS-managed VPN connection.

A VPN connection contains several components, such as a virtual private gateway and a customer gateway. You must ensure that a customer gateway is in place, attach a virtual private gateway to your VPC, and create the VPN connection.

 NOTE Most organizations use either, or both, AWS Direct Connect and VPN connections to connect their WANs (wide area networks) to AWS.

VPN Gateway A VPN gateway (also called a *Virtual Private Gateway* or *VGW*) works on the Amazon side of the VPN connection. You create the VPN and attach it to your VPC from where you want to create the VPN connection to your remote network. You can use a VPN gateway to provide either a VPN connection through the Internet to your on-premise location or an AWS Direct Connect connection to your location. Remember the following:

- If you're setting the VPN gateway to provide a VPN connection, two connections are configured for availability purposes, and the gateway supports both static routing and Border Gateway Protocol (BGP).

- When you set up a VPN gateway for an AWS Direct Connect connection, it supports only BGP.

By enabling *route propagation*, you allow a virtual private gateway to automatically propagate routes to the route tables, removing the need for you to manually enter the VPN routes to the route tables. So, if don't see any network traffic on the AWS side of your VPN connection to your VPC, ensure that route propagation is turned on in your VPC's main route table, after you attach the virtual private gateway to your VPC.

Customer Gateway   The customer gateway is a physical device (or virtual software application) that you configure on your remote network. You create the customer gateway resource in AWS to provide information about the device, such as the IP address of its external interface and the type of routing (static/dynamic) used. After creating the resource in AWS, you must configure the device (or software application) in the remote network to enable the VPN connection. You must set up routing so that any traffic from your VPC to your remote external network is routed to the Virtual Private Gateway.

Route Tables   You must add a route to your remote network in your route table, with the virtual private gateway as the target. This ensures that the VPC's traffic going to your remote network passes through the Virtual Private Gateway and over a VPN tunnel.

Configuring VPN Tunnels and High Availability   When traffic is generated from the remote network side of the VPN connection, the customer gateway initiates VPN tunnels. A VPN gateway comes with two publicly reachable IP addresses routed through a pair of IPsec tunnels, each using a separate Virtual Private Gateway public IP address. Both tunnels must be working for redundancy purposes. Figure 6-5 shows the two tunnels of a VPN connection.

To protect against the unavailability of one customer gateway, it's a good idea to configure a second customer gateway to set up a redundant, secondary VPN connection to your VPC and Virtual Private Gateway. The two public IP addresses that you need to provision for the tunnels can be on a single customer gateway or on two customer gateways in the same or a different location. More than one customer gateway can connect to a VPN gateway.

A software VPN supports two tunnels. To make a hardware VPN redundant, download the router configuration from the AWS Management Console and configure two customer gateways, each with endpoints for the hardware VPN's virtual private gateway.

If you are deploying Direct Connect to replace your VPN connection to your VPC, failover to the new Direct Connect connection is automatic, using the BGP. Once established, the Direct Connect connection path will always be the preferred path.

AWS VPN CloudHub   If you have several VPN connections, you can enable the multiple remote sites to communicate with one another and not just with the VPC, by setting up the AWS VPN CloudHub. VPN CloudHub uses a VPN gateway and a hub-and-spoke architecture to connect multiple customer gateways. VPN CloudHub uses BGP, with each customer location assigned a different autonomous system number (ASN).

To configure the AWS VPN CloudHub, you must first create multiple customer gateways. Then you create a VPN connection between each of the customer gateways to the same virtual private gateway.

Using VPN as a Backup for AWS Direct Connect   You can use a VPN connection as a backup to AWS Direct Connect. Let's assume, for example, that you've configured both a VPN connection and AWS Direct Connect. Should the Direct Connect connection fail for any reason, your VPN can act as a backup for transmitting your data. This is provided

Figure 6-5
Configuring
both tunnels for
redundancy of a
VPN connection

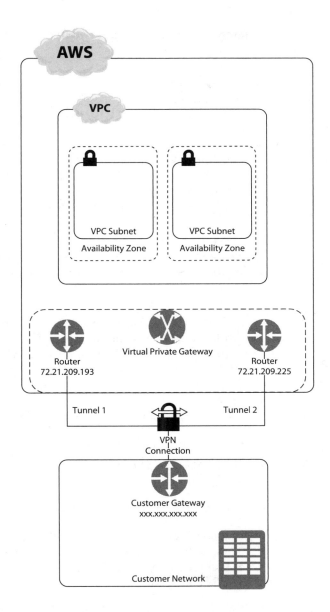

Figure 6-5 Configuring both tunnels for redundancy of a VPN connection

by the AWS *route preference* algorithm, when it has multiple routes to choose from. The route preference is in the following order:

- A VPC's local routes
- Longest prefix first from the route tables
- Static routes
- AWS Direct Connect BGP

- VPN static routes that you've configured in your VPN connection
- VPN BGP

You can use a Direct Connect connection as your main means of connectivity to your VPC, but configure a VPN backup as a lower-cost backup connection.

VPC Peering

A VPC *peering connection* enables two VPCs to communicate as though they are part of the same network. These connections enable a VPC to access resources in one of your other VPCs. You can create a peering connection between VPCs in your own AWS account, VPCs in a different AWS customer's account, or VPCs in a different AWS region. Creating a peering connection provides the other VPC(s) an entry in the VPC's route table.

NOTE A VPC peering connection is different from a VPN connection or a gateway because there's no physical hardware involved.

A VPC peering connection makes it easy to transfer data between multiple AWS accounts you own by creating a file sharing network to transfer the data easily.

You can set up VPC peering connections that provide access (routes) to parts of a CIDR block, an entire CIDR block, or a specific instance within the peer VPC. The CIDR blocks of the VPCs that you want to set up a peering connection for can't match or overlap with each other.

Your VPC peering configurations can include the following:

- Two VPC peered to two subnets in one VPC
- Two VPCs peered to a specific CIDR block in one VPC
- One VPC peered to specific subnets in two VPCs
- Instances in one VPC peered to instances in two VPCs

The VPCs in a peering connection must belong to the same region and should not have overlapping IP ranges. The VPCs must use security groups to control access, and they should not have overlapping IP ranges. If you need to connect VPCs in different regions, you must use a VPN connections between all the VPCs.

Setting Up VPC Peering   Here are the steps to create a VPC peering connection:

1. The owner of the VPC that requests the peering connection (requester VPC) sends a request to the owner of the target VPC (accepter VPC) to create the connection.

2. The owner of the accepting VPC accepts the connection request.

3. The owners of both VPCs in the peering connection add a route to at least one of their VPC route tables that point to the IP address range of the other VPC—the peer VPC in this context.

4. The owners of the two VPCs may also need to update the security group rules to ensure that traffic from the peer VPC is allowed.

You must enable DNS hostname resolution for the VPC connection. Then, when instances in the VPC peering connection address each other using a public DNS hostname, that hostname resolves to the private and not the public IP address of the instance.

After you configure VPC peering, you must ensure that you update all the route tables in each VPC with the appropriate peering configuration. Let's say, for example, that you have set up a VPC peering connection between VPC A (10.0.0.0/16) and VPC B (20.0.0.0/16). The peering connection ID is pcx-1a2b1a2b. Following this, you need to add the following route entries to the route tables of the two VPCs so that traffic can flow between them:

- For VPC A: Destination 20.0.0.0/16 and Target pcx-1a2b1a2b
- For VPC B: Destination 10.0.0.0/16 and Target pcx-1a2b1a2b

Multiple VPC Peering Connections You can create more than one peering connection for one of your VPCs. However, you must create a unique VPC peering connection between different VPCs, because AWS doesn't support a *transitive peering relationship*, even if the VPCs belong to the same AWS account.

For example, if you have set up a peering connection between VPC A and VPC B and also between VPC A and VPV C, there's no automatic transitive peering relationship between VPC B and VPC C. You must explicitly set up a peering relationship between any pair of VPCs. In this case, you must set up a peering relationship between VPC B and VPC C as well, if you want those VPCs to have a peering relationship.

NOTE A VPC peering relationship is always a 1:1 relationship between two VPCs.

VPC Endpoints

A VPC endpoint is a virtual device that enables communications between VPC-based EC2 instances and AWS services, without affecting your network traffic bandwidth. A VPC endpoint helps you privately connect your VPC to supported AWS services and VPC endpoint services powered by AWS PrivateLink. For example, to connect to a service outside a VPC, such as Amazon S3, you can use a VPC endpoint, which makes an Amazon S3 bucket an entry in the VPC's route table.

VPC endpoints enable connections without the use of an Internet gateway, an NAT device, or a VPN/AWS Direct Connect connection. The VPC instances don't need public IP addresses to communicate with AWS resources.

NOTE IAM users don't have permission to work with endpoints until you create user policies that grant the users the permissions to create, modify, describe, and delete endpoints.

The following example shows a route table with a VPC endpoint.

```
Destination        Target             Status          Propagated
10.0.0.0/16        local              Active          No
0.0.0.0/0          nat-gateway-id     Active          No
Pl-xxxxxxxx        vpce-xxxxxxxx      Active          No
```

There are two VPC endpoint types: interface endpoints and gateway endpoints.

Interface Endpoints

An *interface endpoint* is an elastic network interface with a private IP address. It acts as the entry point for traffic sent to supported AWS services such as AWS CloudFormation, AWS CloudWatch, AWS Config, Amazon Simple Notification Service (SNS), *endpoint services* hosted by other AWS customers and partners in their own VPCs, and supported AWS marketplace partner services.

A service provider is the owner of the service, and you, as the service consumer, are the principal that creates the interface endpoints and provides the name of the AWS service or endpoint services to which you want to connect. After you create an interface endpoint, it's available for use only after it's accepted by the service provider, which must configure either automatic or manual acceptance of requests by the service.

An endpoint retunes responses to traffic sent to resources in your VPC. Services won't be able to initiate requests to your resources inside your VPC through the endpoint.

Gateway Endpoints

A *gateway endpoint* serves as a target for a specified route in your route table, for traffic going to a supported AWS service. As of this writing, the supported services are Amazon S3 and DynamoDB.

You specify one or more route tables to control the routing of the traffic between your VPC and the other services. Subnets using the route tables can access the endpoints. You must change the route table for a private subnet to route traffic through an endpoint. Traffic from instances within the subnets to other services is sent through the endpoint.

Troubleshooting AWS Network Connectivity Problems

You might occasionally run into an issue related to AWS networks. Troubleshooting network connectivity issues in the cloud is similar to how you do so on premises. There are several network tools that you can use to troubleshoot connectivity issues. You may also need to check your security group rules to ensure that they allow the connectivity you're looking for.

The `ping`, `nslookup`, and `traceroute` Utilities

A quick tool for testing AWS network connectivity is the `ping` utility, which sends an ICMP package from a server to another server. Here's an example:

```
$ ping www.amazon.com

Pinging d3ag4hukkh62yn.cloudfront.net [52.84.60.162] with 32 bytes of data:
Reply from 52.84.60.162: bytes=32 time=48ms TTL=241
Reply from 52.84.60.162: bytes=32 time=47ms TTL=241
Reply from 52.84.60.162: bytes=32 time=49ms TTL=241

$
```

If ping doesn't respond with an IP address, the server name may be incorrect. A ping test may fail when an AWS target is offline or inaccessible. You can view the AWS Service Health Dashboard (https://status.aws.amazon.com/), which reports up-to-the-minute information on AWS service availability, to see if the service you're trying to connect to, such as EC2 in a specific region, is unavailable.

If you are unable to ping your instance, ensure that the security group's inbound rules allow ICMP traffic for the Echo Request message for all sources or from the server where you're issuing the ping command. If you are unable to issue the ping command from an instance, check the security group's outbound rules and make sure they allow ICMP traffic for the Echo Request message to all destinations or to the destination you are trying to ping.

You can use the nslookup command on a Linux system to resolve the target hostname from the IP address. If there's an error when you run this command or if the name that's returned isn't associated with the right node or server, there may be either a DNS failure or a configuration error. Here's an example:

```
$  nslookup apps.system-prod.chdc20-cf.example.com
Non-authoritative answer:
Server:   axnadc02.na.example.com
Address:   10.66.74.141

Name:     apps.system-prod.chdc20-cf.example.com
Address:   10.35.31.252
$
```

The Linux traceroute command (or the Windows tracert command) helps trace the path and checks delays between a data center and the AWS-based instances. The utility shows details about each router hop and helps find potential network bottlenecks across the public Internet. Pay attention to hops with persistenly high packet losses or packet losses that accumulate to a sizable number over multiple hops.

Errors Connecting to an Instance

You may receive error messages such as Network error: Connection timed out, or Error connecting to [instance], reason: -> Connection timed out: connect. When you see these types of errors when connecting to an instance with an IPv4 address, follow these steps:

- Check the security group's inbound rules to ensure it has a rule that allows inbound traffic from your public IP address on the correct port. For SSH connectivity errors from a Linux server, ensure that there is a rule that allows traffic from your server to port 22. For the same errors from a Windows server, the port is 3389 (RDP).
- Check the route table for the subnet to ensure that there's a route that sends all traffic destined outside your VPC to the VPC's Internet gateway.
- Ensure that there's an Internet gateway attached to your VPC. If there is not, create the gateway and attach it to the VPC.
- Ensure that the route table has a route with 0.0.0.0/0 as the destination and the Internet gateway for your VPC as the target.

- Check the NACL for the subnet and ensure that it allows inbound and outbound traffic to and from your local IP address on the proper port. The default NACL allows all inbound and outbound traffic.

- If your server is on a corporate network, make sure that the internal firewall allows inbound and outbound traffic from your server on port 22 for Linux servers and port 3389 for Windows servers. If you have a firewall on your computer make sure it allows the same traffic as the internal corporate firewall.

- Check your instance's CPU load to make sure it is not overloaded. You can do this with CloudWatch metrics and by checking the instance status in the EC2 console. If your workloads are variable, try using Auto Scaling and ELB to manage the workload. If your workload is growing steadily over time, move to a larger EC2 instance type.

AWS Direct Connect

In some use cases, you won't want to use the Internet to access your AWS resources. That's where AWS Direct Connect comes in; it enables you to bypass the public Internet to access your resources in the AWS cloud. Direct Connect links the internal networks in your data centers to an AWS Direct Connect location. This helps you create direct virtual interfaces to public AWS services such as Amazon S3, bypassing Internet service providers. So, in a scenario where you are performing a daily backup of, say, 10GB of data from your on-premise data center to Amazon S3, you can drastically reduce the time it takes to move this data by moving it via Direct Connect between your data center and your AWS VPC. (As you'll learn in Chapter 7, doing a multipart upload to S3 can also speed up the upload process.)

A Direct Connect connection provides access to AWS in the region in which the direct connection is associated. You can use this connection to access public AWS services in any public region. Figure 6-6 shows the AWS Direct Connect architecture and how it works with your internal networks.

 NOTE You connect to Direct Connect via a virtual private gateway attached to the VPC. Therefore, you must configure and associate the virtual private gateway with your VPC.

Direct Connect offers several benefits for transferring data between your own network and your VPC:

- **Lowers your network bandwidth costs** Because AWS charges reduced rates for data transfers via your dedicated connection, compared to Internet data transfer rates, you end up lowering your bandwidth costs. Costs can be further reduced by reducing your bandwidth commitment to your Internet service provider.

- **Provides consistent network performance** Because you can choose how data is routed through Direct Connect, you gain more consistent network performance, without the variable and inconsistent network latency that's common in public Internet–based network connections.

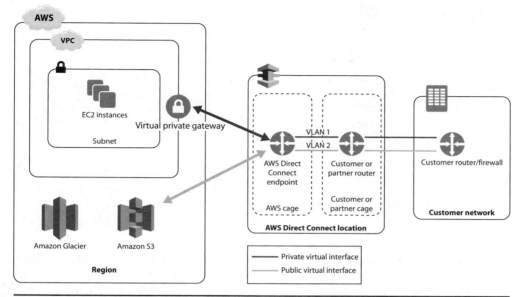

Figure 6-6 How AWS Direct Connect interfaces with your internal networks

- **Facilitates large data transfers** A VPN connection requires specialized VPN hardware and has problems handling large data transfers (over 4 Gbps). With Direct Connect, you can select a 10 Gbps Direct Connect connection and set up multiple connections to enhance your data transfer capacity.
- **Provides a private connection to AWS** Direct Connect helps you set up a private, secure, and fast network connection between your own network and your VPC.

Setting Up Direct Connect

You don't necessarily have to set up your Direct Connect connection at an AWS Direct connection location offered by AWS. You can also set up the connectivity through a network carrier or a member of the AWS Partner Network (APN). Instead of setting up your own Direct Connect connection, you can opt for a hosted connection that's provided by an APN member.

Direct Connect Components

The two key components of Direct Connect are *connections* and *virtual interfaces*. Because Direct Connect supports only the BGP routing protocol, you need a router that supports BGP. To use Direct Connect, your network must be collocated with an existing AWS Direct Connect location, or you must work with an independent service provider to connect to Direct Connect.

Connections

To create a dedicated connection between your network and a Direct Connect location, you must work with a partner in the APN. This enables you to set up a network circuit between your data center (or colocation environment) and an AWS Direct Connect location. When you request a connection, AWS authorizes the connection via a Letter of Authorization and Connecting Facility Assignment (LOA-CFA). Your network provider or the colocation provider requires this to order a *cross-connect* (a cross-network connection) for you. AWS recommends that you request two dedicated connections to AWS to provide failover of the Direct Connect connection.

TIP You can aggregate multiple connections as a single Direct Connect endpoint via a link aggregation group (LAG). This logical interface enables you to treat the multiple connections as a single connection.

Virtual Interfaces

After you create a connection, you must create a *virtual interface* (VIF) to use a Direct Connect connection. For each Direct Connect connection that you configure, you can configure multiple virtual interfaces. There are two types of virtual interfaces:

- **A private virtual interface** A private VIF is a logical interface that enables you to connect to an EC2 instance within your VPC. Each VPC needs a separate private VIF to connect to Direct Connect (or you can use a Direct Connect gateway). The private virtual interface handles traffic originating from your onsite network, destined for resources in your VPC that may not have either a public IP address or an EIP.
- **A public virtual interface** This connects to AWS services that don't live in your VPC, such as Amazon S3 or Glacier. The public interface is meant for handling traffic to other AWS services or to the Internet.

If your traffic is coming both from your onsite network and from other AWS services and the Internet, you need both a private and public virtual interface. After creating a virtual interface, you download the router configuration for the Direct Connect connection. To implement Direct Connect, you also need a public Autonomous System Number for the public VIF and a private Autonomous System Number for the private VIF.

NOTE Remember that a virtual interface supports only the BGP network routing protocol.

For high availability, you must create multiple Direct Connect connections, and the best practice is to create these in different regions. When you set up a redundant Direct Connect connection, in case of a failure, traffic fails over to the second link automatically.

The best practice is to enable Bidirectional Forwarding Detection (BFD) to enable fast failure detection and failover.

Direct Connect Gateways

A *Direct Connect gateway* connects your Direct Connect connection to VPCs in your account over a private virtual interface. You can link this gateway to the virtual private gateway for a VPC. Following this, you create a private virtual interface for the Direct Connect connection to the Direct Connection gateway. You can attach a single or multiple public virtual interfaces to a Direct Connect gateway.

You can use a Direct Connect gateway that you create in a public region in all other public regions. Figure 6-7 shows you how a Direct Connect gateway enables you to use a Direct Connect connection in one region to access VPCs in two regions.

Direct Connect Costs

Direct Connect costs much less than it costs to transfer data via the Internet, and it includes the following components:

- Port costs (billed on hourly basis)
- Data transfer costs
- Direct Connect partner circuit charges
- Cross-connect charges, if you're in a colocation facility

NOTE   You must pay Direct Connect transfer charges for the virtual interfaces. You must also pay the cross-connect or network circuit charges.

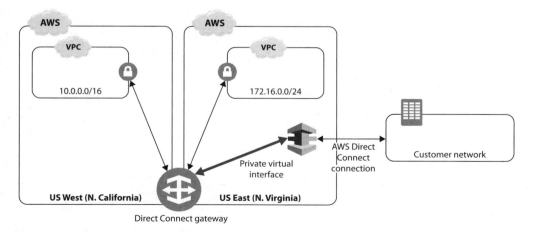

Figure 6-7   A Direct Connect gateway that enables Direct Connect connection to access VPCs in multiple regions

Elastic Load Balancing

AWS offers the *Elastic Load Balancing* (ELB) capability to distribute your applications and their network traffic automatically across multiple targets. For example, if the incoming traffic's target is a web server, ELB can spread the traffic among multiple web servers.

In addition to ELB, which is an Internet-facing load balancer, you can also configure an internal load balancer to distribute your internal traffic. An architecture with both types of load balancers enables you to register your web servers with ELB and your backend database servers with the internal load balancer. The instances in an internet-facing load balancer have public IP addresses. Hence, the DNS name of an internet-facing load balancer is publicly resolvable to the public IP addresses of the instances, and the load balancer can route requests over the Internet. Because the nodes of an internal load balancer have private IP addresses, the DNS name of this load balancer is publicly resolvable to the private IP addresses of the nodes. Hence, the load balancer can only route internal requests.

ELB supports three types of load balancers:

- Application Load Balancers
- Network Load Balancers
- Classic Load Balancers

A Network Load Balancer can handle all your volatile workloads and scale to millions of requests per second.

 NOTE AWS classifies both Application Load Balancers and Network Load Balancers as ELB – Version 2. It places classic load balancing under ELB – Version 1.

ELB can scale itself as traffic to your application changes over time. Besides helping share the workload among multiple compute resources such as EC2 instances, a load balancer enhances the availability of your applications and makes them more robust when they encounter error conditions.

How Load Balancing Works

Clients send their connection requests to the load balancer. The load balancer, in turn, distributes the requests among targets such as EC2 instances that live in one or more AZs.

How Client Requests Are Routed

A client first receives the load balancer's domain name from the DNS server. The Amazon DNS servers return one or more IP addresses to the client. These IP addresses point to the load balancer nodes of the load balancer that you've set up. The client then chooses one of the IP addresses to send requests to the load balancer. The load balancer picks a healthy target and sends the request to the target.

By default, when you use TCP for both front-end and back-end connections, the load balancer forwards requests without any changes to the request headers. If you look in the web server's access logs, you'll find the load balancer's IP address instead of the IP address of the client that originated the request. If you enable Proxy Protocol, a header with the connection information (source and destination IP addresses and port numbers) is added to the request header and the header is sent to the web server as part of the request. The X-Forwarded-For request header reveals the IP address of a client when you use an HTTP or HTTPS load balancer.

Routing Algorithms

The Application Load Balancer uses *listener rules* to select a target from the target group, using the round-robin routing algorithm. Listener rules forward requests to target groups that you specify. A Network Load Balancer selects targets from the target group using a *flow hash algorithm*. It uses the source IP address, protocol, port destination IP address/ port, and TCP sequence number to route to different targets. It may use one of two different routing algorithms: the round-robin algorithm for TCP listeners and the least outstanding requests algorithm for HTTP/HTTPS listeners.

In *connection multiplexing*, the requests from multiple clients can be routed to a target through a single backend connection. This helps lower latency and reduce application load. Both the Classic and Application Load Balancers support connection multiplexing.

Availability Zones and ELB

You must enable one or more AZs for the load balancer when you create it; you cannot do so later. Enabling multiple AZs, which AWS recommends, offers fault tolerance for your applications. ELB can route traffic to healthy targets in a different AZ if one AZ becomes unavailable or if there are no healthy targets in the AZ.

NOTE An Application Load Balancer *requires* you to enable multiple AZs (at least two). This is recommended for the other two types of load balancers.

When you create a load balancer, you must specify one public subnet from at least two AZs. You specify the subnet from the AZ when you enable the zone. ELB creates a load balancer node in that zone and a network interface for the subnet. The load balancer node(s) in the zone use this network interface to get static IP addresses. If you create an Internet-facing load balancer, you can associate an EIP per node.

If you want a web application to accept traffic only from specific IP addresses, you can do so by configuring the following:

- Configure ELB security groups to allow traffic only from the IP address that you want.

- Configure the web servers to filter their traffic based on the ELB's X-Forwarded-For header.

Cross-Zone Load Balancing

A load balancer node distributes traffic evenly among the registered targets in the AZ where you created the load balancer. This is the default behavior. By enabling *cross-zone load balancing*, you can make the load balancer node distribute traffic among registered targets in *all* enabled AZs.

 NOTE Cross-zone load balancing is always enabled for an Application Load Balancer.

Cross-zone load balancing is enabled by default for Application Load Balancers and disabled for Network Load Balancers. If you create a Classic Load Balancer with the API or CLI, cross-zone load balancing is disabled by default, and it is enabled if you create the load balancer from the AWS Management Console.

 EXAM TIP You may see questions about the Classic Load Balancer on the certification exam. Make sure you understand how connecting draining and stick sessions work, and be familiar with the Server Order Preference option.

Here are key things that you need to know about the Classic Load Balancer:

- You can set up *connection draining* to allow inflight requests to proceed while an instance is being deregistered via Auto Scaling. By default, ELB allows inflight request traffic to continue for 300 seconds, and the maximum time limit is 3600 seconds. You can disable connection draining.

- You can ensure that user requests always go the instance where the user created the session by enabling *sticky sessions*. The sticky session ELB algorithm uses cookies to track sessions and inserts a cookie in the response, whether it finds the cookie in the request or not. Sticky sessions help an application manage user sessions.

- The Server Order Preference option in the ELB's security policy specifies which ciphers and protocols are supported during SSL negotiations between the client and ELB. You can choose a Predefined Security Policy or a custom policy. This option helps match the ciphers (encryption algorithms that use encryption keys to create a coded message) on the client side in the order (which indicates the order of preference) they are specified in the ELB cipher list (or table), when the client requests ELB DNS over an SSL connection. If you don't enable this option, ELB uses the ciphers in the order the client presents them. If you haven't configured a specific security policy, ELB chooses the latest version of the policy.

Creating a Load Balancer

You can create a Network Load Balancer, an Application Load Balancer, and a Classic Load Balancer in a similar fashion, with appropriate differences.

To configure load balancers after you create them, you must create a *target group*. You register your targets, such as EC2 instances, with the target groups that you create. A best practice is to ensure that each AZ has at least one registered target.

A Network Load Balancer requires that you create a *listener*, which listens for connection request at a port (such as 80 that accepts HTTP requests, and 443 that accepts HTTPS requests) and a protocol (such as TCP) that you specify. You define rules for the listener that dictate how the load balancer sends requests to multiple targets in a target group.

The following example shows how to create a Network Load Balancer from the command line:

1. Execute the `create-load-balancer` command to create the load balancer:

```
$ aws elbv2 create-load-balancer --name my-load-balancer --type network
--subnets subnet-12345678
```

2. Specify a public subnet for each AZ in which you've launched EC2 instances.

3. Create a target group by executing the `create-target-group` command:

```
$ aws elbv2 create-target-group --name my-targets --protocol TCP --port
80 --vpc-id vpc-12345678
```

4. Register your instances with the target group you created in the previous step by running the `register-targets` command:

```
$ aws elbv2 register-targets --target-group-arn targetgroup-arn
--targets Id=i-12345678 Id=i-23456789
```

5. Specify an EIP for your load balancer:

```
$ aws elbv2 create-load-balancer --name my-load-balancer --type network \
--subnet-mappings SubnetId=subnet-12345678,AllocationId=eipalloc-12345678
```

You can specify one EIP per subnet via subnet mapping.

 EXAM TIP   Review the different types of ELB-related errors captured by CloudWatch metrics. For example, the HTTPCode_Backend_5XX error is caused by issues with the backend servers. The HTTPCode_Backend_4XX error is due to a client error response (such as "A malformed or canceled request from the client") from the registered instances. The HTTPCode_3XX error indicates a redirect response from the instances. Finally, a HTTPCode_Backend_2XX error message indicates a normal, successful response from the instances. Other possible errors are HTTP 502: Bad Gateway, HTTP 503: Service Unavailable, and HTTP 504: Gateway Timeout. You can bypass the load balancer temporarily and send requests directly to an instance to view the responses in the access logs or the error logs of the instances.

You can enable ELB *access logging* to trace requests sent to the ELB. The logs contain information about the time of the request, the server responses, latency, and the client's IPA address. Once you enable access logging, ELB captures the logs and stores them in an Amazon S3 bucket.

NOTE If you happen to accidentally delete an ELB, instances registered with it continue running.

Amazon Route 53

Amazon Route 53 is AWS's DNS web service. It helps route users to web sites by translating domain names such as www.example.com into numeric IP addresses that computers can use to connect to each other. You use Route 53 to do the following:

- Register domain names (such as example.com).
- Route Internet traffic to your web sites or web applications.
- Check the health of your resources, such as web servers.

You don't have to use Route 53 for all three functions listed here, although you can. When you use Route 53 to perform all three of these functions, you register your domain name with Route 53, configure Route 53 to route your Internet traffic to your domain, and finally use the service for checking the health of your AWS services such as the web servers that you run in the AWS cloud. Alternatively, you may decide to use a separate domain registrar to register your domains and use Route 53 to route your traffic and check the health of the AWS services.

Implementing Route 53 involves two main steps:

1. Create a *hosted zone* or zones.
2. Create your resource record sets.

You configure the routing for traffic to your domain and subdomains via a hosted zone. Route 53 assigns a set of unique nameservers for each hosted zone that you create. Because Route 53 can manage both public and private hosted zones, you can use it for distributing traffic both within an AWS region as well as between AWS regions.

If you choose Route 53 as the domain registrar, Route 53 automatically creates a hosted zone for you. If you're using a different organization as the domain registrar, you must create the hosted zone. Route 53 also automatically creates a hosted zone for you when you transfer an existing domain over to Route 53.

The next step after you create the hosted zones for your domain (for example, mycompany.com) is to create *resource record sets*. A resource record set consists of a record type and routing policy. Routing polices tell Route 53 how to respond to queries directed to your domain. You configure different routing polices for each of the record types.

Because Route 53 is a DNS, it's important to learn the basics of DNS.

Basics of the Domain Name System

Every host (server) has at least one numerical *IP address*, a number assigned to devices such as laptops or web servers that enables the devices to communicate with other devices on the Internet—just as every home in a city has a unique address to enable folks to find the house. However, since it's cumbersome for us to use a numerical IP address, we use the friendlier concept of *hostnames* to refer to the host. For example, it's much easier to search for www.google.com rather than 74.125.224.147, which happens to be the main Google numerical IP address.

When a client talks to your web site, the DNS is the very first contact point. Clients reaching out to your web services or web sites must first find your server's IP address before they can connect to it. DNS maps hostnames to IP addresses and vice versa (*reverse DNS*). It translates simple names such as example.com into IP addresses. The DNS is a distributed database that contains a hierarchy of DNS servers.

 NOTE In practice, a DNS server and a name server are interchangeable terms.

DNS Domains

The structure of the DNS is like that of an inverted tree, with the roots and the branches known as *domains*. At the very top is the aptly named *root* domain. The root domain consists of a blank area, and it is expressed by a period, or dot (.). In browsers today, it's not necessary to enter this dot, since the browser will add it itself. There are 13 geographically separated root servers. Root servers really don't hold much information, although they sit on top of the inverted root tree—they simply point to a set of domains called *top-level domains*, which are named .com, and .net, for example.

A fully qualified domain name (FQDN) for a site includes the following: [*hostname*]. [*domain*].[*tld*]. In practice, it looks like this: *www.mydomain.com*. The FQDN contains information about all the domains that are part of the hostname. Even though we don't write it out, there's an implicit dot (.) after every FQDN for a site: so *www.mydomain .com* is *www.mydomain.com.* (note that the dot at the end is not a period here but represents the root domain).

After the root domain is the *top-level domain* (TLD). The TLD names are well known to us: they include the generic domains (.org, .com, .net), country-code domains (.us, .uk, .nz), and branded domains (.linux, .microsoft).

A *second-level domain* name is the domain name that's typically allocated to an organization or even an individual. So in our example, *mydomain.com* is the second-level domain.

The *third-level domain names* are not mandatory unless the user has a specific requirement. A third-level domain can add clarity to a domain name, however. For example, third-level domains can show the hostnames within an organization or can be assigned to subdomains within that organization. So, for example, if *mydomain.com* has a file transfer protocol (FTP) server to let users download files, its third-level domain name would be *ftp* and the full domain name would be *ftp.mydomain.com*. A domain name like *support. mydomain.com* or *membership.mydomain.com* indicates that the company has a support department or a membership department, respectively, and each of these subdomains would get its own zone

Types of Name Servers

A *name server* in the DNS helps translate domain names into IP addresses. DNS employs a distributed architecture with a large number of name servers located throughout the world, so it can scale. There are three *classes* of name servers: root DNS servers, top-level domain (TLD) DNS servers, and authoritative DNS servers—that are organized in a hierarchy, with the root DNS server at the very top of the inverted root structure. The root name servers are special, and there are only 24 of them, managed by various providers. Root name server names look something like this: a.root-server.net, b.root-server.net, c.root-server.net, and so on.

Root DNS servers really don't do much; basically, they publish a *root zone file* to other DNS servers. The root zone file tells requesters where the authoritative servers for the top-level domains such as .com and .org are to be found.

There are three main types of name servers:

- **Authoritative servers** These are the primary DNS servers and are aware of all the hosts and subdomains under them. They also store the domain's configuration files. Any updates to the domain's DNS tables are performed on the authoritative servers. The authoritative name server has definite information about a part of the DNS and responds to requests from DNS resolvers.

- **Secondary servers** Like the primary servers, secondary servers store the configuration files for domains. Because secondary servers need to download the latest information from the authoritative servers, they are occasionally behind the primary servers, but they are mostly trustworthy. Secondary servers act as both backups for the primary servers and also help to lessen the load on those servers.

- **Recursive servers or DNS resolvers** Also referred to as caching servers, these servers don't carry any configuration files at all. In general, they answer name resolution requests in a non-authoritative fashion.

When you enter a domain name in a browser, the DNS query goes to a *DNS resolver* first. If the IP addresses aren't present in their local cache, the servers ask the DNS name server for the names and cache that information. A DNS resolver is often called a *recursive name server* because it requests a sequence of authoritative DNS name servers for the IP addresses, which it then returns to the request's service, such as a web browser that runs on your laptop.

How a DNS Request Works

Let's say, for example, that you open your browser and type a domain name in the address bar—say *www.google.com*. Your browser then submits a DNS query to obtain the IP address associated with the web server. The DNS query first contacts one of the root servers, which returns the IP addresses for the TLD servers for the top-level domain named *.com*. The request then hops to one of the TLD servers, which returns the IP address of an authoritative server, for *google.com*. Finally, the DNS request contacts the authoritative server, which returns the IP address for *www.google.com*.

Working with Records

Each name server stores resource records (RRs), including those that provide the host-name-to-IP mappings. A DNS record defines how Route 53 (DNS) will route traffic for a domain. You select the type of DNS record based on how you want Route 53 to respond to DNS queries. For example, you may create a record specifying that for your domain, traffic should be routed to the web server running on the server with the IP address 192.0.3.234.

Each DNS reply sent by a DNS server carries one or more DNS records. A DNS record has the following fields (name and value fields depend on the type of resource records in use):

- **Name** The name of the domain, or a subdomain.
- **Value** Depends on the record type.
- **Type** The record type, such as MX for routing e-mail. Each record type has a unique set of information. For example, an MX type record contains the hostname of the mail server and a priority for each mail server.
- **TTL** The time to live, which specifies how long a resource record is stored in the DNS cache.

DNS Record Types Following are the main DNS resource record types:

- **SOA (start of authority)** These records start the description of the site's DNS entries. An SOA record contains information about a domain and its hosted zone. Here's an example:

  ```
  ns-2048.awsdns-64.net hostmaster.awsdns.com 1 1 1 1 60
  ```

- **NS (name server)** These records specify which name server stores the records for a hosted zone. Thus, if Type=NS, the Value field shows the authoritative DNS server that knows how to obtain the IP addresses for all hosts in a domain (or zone). In other words, the NS record's value is the domain name of the domain server. Here's an example:

  ```
  ns-1.example.com
  ```

- **A (address record)** This resource record provides the standard hostname-to-IP mapping. The A record maps the hostnames to the IP addresses. Here's an example for the Route 53 console:

  ```
  192.0.2.2351 (IPv4 address format)
  ```

- **PTR (pointer record)** This is the opposite of the A record—it performs reverse name resolution and is in the same format as a domain name, as shown here:

  ```
  hostname.example.com
  ```

- **MX (mail exchanger)** This record tells a host where the site's mail server is. The values in an MX record show the domain name and the priority of the mail server (if you have multiple mail servers). The priority indicates the order or priority—that is, which mail server is sent e-mails first, second, third, and so on.

The mail server with the lowest priority value has precedence. Here's an example MX record, showing the priority and the domain name to specify a mail server:

```
10 mailserver.example.com
```

- **CNAME (canonical name)** This element has the same format as a domain name. The canonical name doesn't provide an IP address; it points to another hostname. CNAME records enable you to create *aliases* for hostnames. Route 53 uses alias records, which belong to a non-standard DNS record type, to route traffic to AWS resources such as CloudFront distributions, an Application Load Balancer, an Elastic Beanstalk environment, and an S3 bucket that you've configured as a static website (see Chapter 7). Instead of pointing to an IP address or a domain name like an A record does, an alias record type points to the AWS resources. You can also configure alias records to route traffic from one record to another in a hosted zone, since an alias record enables you to point to another Route 53 record set
  You can't create a CNAME record for the zone apex, which is the top node of the DNS namespace. So if your domain name in DNS is example.com, the zone apex is example.com, and you can't create a CNAME for example.com (but you *can* create a CNAME for sales.example.com).

- **Alias** A virtual record type that provides CNAME-like behavior on apex domains. Aliases are similar to CNAME record types, but unlike CNAME records, you can create an alias for the zone apex. That is, you can create an alias record that is named the same as the hosted zone which is the zone apex. Suppose your domain is mycompany.com and you want to point it to a name such as myapp.herokuapp.com. You can use an alias record, which will automatically resolve your domain to one or more A records, and the name resolvers see your domain just as if it had A records.

Routing Policies

A DNS query is a request to the DNS for a resource that's associated with a domain name. DNS uses a *routing policy* to determine how it should respond to a DNS query. There are several types of routing policies, as explained in the following sections.

Simple Routing Policy The simple routing policy routes traffic to a single resource that performs a specific function for a domain, such as a web server for one of your domains. You can only configure standard DNS records, with no special routing such as weighted or latency routing. Route 53 responds to DNS queries based on the values you specify in the resource record set, such as the IP address in an A record.

You can't create multiple records with the same name and type. However, you can specify multiple values (say, IP addresses) within the same record.

Failover Routing Policy The failover routing policy helps you configure active-passive failover by designating primary and secondary resources. You can route traffic to the primary resource (such as a web server) so long as it's healthy (as determined by a health of the resource's record set), and when the resource's health status turns to unhealthy, traffic can be automatically routed to an alternate resource, such as a different web server. Route 53 returns the primary record set when both primary and secondary resources' record sets are healthy.

You can use failover routing polices to send users to a primary ELB load balancer within a region if the load balancer is healthy, or to a secondary load balancer when the primary load balancer is unhealthy or unavailable due to maintenance or another reason.

Geolocation Routing Policy   The geolocation routing policy, which maps IP addresses to locations, enables you to route traffic based on the location of your users—that is, where the DNS requests originate from. You can use geolocation routing policies to route all users for a country to a single endpoint. For example, you can configure all DNS queries from Asia to be routed to a load balancer (ELB) in Tokyo. If some IP addresses aren't mapped to specific locations, you can create a default record to handle the queries from those IP addresses that aren't mapped to locations to avoid a "no answer" response from Route 53.

Geoproximity Routing Policy   Geoproximity routing policies consider the geographic location of your resources as well as your users. To use this policy, you must use Route 53 Traffic Flow, described later in the section "Using Traffic Flow to Route DNS Traffic."

You can specify a value, called a *bias*, that grows or shrinks a geographic region's size to route more or less traffic, respectively, to a resource. You can configure a negative bias with a range between −1 and −99, and a positive bias in the range of 1 and 99. With a positive bias setting, Route 53 treats the DNS query's source as being closer to a resource (such as an EC2 instance) than the reality. If the geoproximity record for a web server has a positive bias value of 50, Route 53 acts as if the distance (*biased distance*) between the source of the query and the web server is half of the actual distance.

Not every IP address is mapped to a geographic location, and thus, Route 53 can receive DNS queries from geographic locations that it can't identify. You create a default resource record set to handle these types of queries, to avoid Route 53 having to send a "no answer" response to these queries.

Latency-based Routing Policy   You use latency-based routing policies to route traffic to the resource in a location that offers the lowest latency. You can, for example, use latency routing policies to route users to AWS regions based on the latency between those users and the AWS regions. Route 53 uses the latency record that you create to determine the region with the lowest latency and selects the latency record for that region to route a request. Route 53 sends the DNS query the IP address of a web server, or a similar value, from the latency record that it selects.

 TIP   Remember that AWS determines latency on the basis of the AWS region.

Latency routing policy is helpful when you run AWS services such as web servers in multiple EC2 data centers, and you want Route 53 always to pick the web servers in the data center with the best latency at that time.

Here's a good scenario for creating a latency-based routing record: Suppose you have ten EC2 instances in five AWS regions, with two instances in each region. To enhance availability in case one of the regions loses its network connectivity, you can do the following:

- Create a latency-based routing record set that resolves to an ELB in each of the five regions,
- Set the corresponding Route 53 health check for each ELB.

Latency between Internet hosts can change over time, and, therefore, the same request may be routed to different regions at different times.

Multivalue Answer Routing Policy A multivalue answer routing policy enables Route 53 to return multiple values for a resource (such as web server IP addresses). Although it's not meant for load balancing per se, this routing policy enhances availability and offers load balancing of resources such as web servers.

If you associate health checks with each record, Route 53 responds to DNS queries with all the healthy records (up to eight healthy records), providing different answers to different DNS resolvers. If you don't associate a health check with a multivalued answer routing record, Route 53 considers the record healthy.

Weighted Routing Policy The weighted routing policy routes traffic to multiple resources (within the same domain, such as example.com) in a weighted fashion, based on weights that you specify. Since you can configure how much traffic goes to each resource, such as to each web server, you can use this policy for load balancing of web requests to your domain. It's also a helpful policy when rolling out software changes, since you can limit the traffic that uses the new releases, thereby limiting potential adverse effects of the changes.

Under the weighted routing policy, you assign each record a weight to select the percentage of traffic you want to send to that resource. Thus, if you want to send just 10 percent of your Internet traffic to a web server, and 90 percent to a second web server, you can do so by assigning the two web servers weights of 10 and 90, respectively. If you set a resource record's weight to 0, it means that no traffic is to be routed to that resource. You would create two resource records in this case.

Creating Resource Records

You can create resource records through the Amazon Route 53 console or by importing a *zone file*. Exercise 6-9 at the end of this chapter shows how to create a resource record through the Route 53 console.

For complex routing configuration, you may want to check out the Traffic Flow Visual Editor. You can associate the traffic policies that you create with this editor to a domain name in any hosted zone.

To create a bunch of records for a Route 53–hosted zone, you can import a zone file. This is useful if you're migrating from another DNS service provider to Route 53; simply export your current DNS settings as a zone file and import that file into a Route

53–hosted zone. Zone files use a standard format called BIND to represent resource records in a text format. It's simple to import a zone file:

1. In the Route 53 Management Console, under Hosted Zones, click Import Zone File.

2. Paste the contents of the zone file you want to import in the text box.

3. Click Import.

Configuring Amazon Route 53 to Route Traffic for a Domain

Using Amazon Route 53 as your DNS is optional, and you can choose to use any DNS you like. However, Route 53 offers several built-in advantages and works well with AWS resources. When you use Route 53 as your DNS, a key function it can perform is to route Internet traffic to your domain. To configure this routing, you must do three things:

- Register your domain.
- Use the public hosted zone that Route 53 automatically creates.
- Create resource record sets in your hosted zone, specifying how you want traffic to be routed for your domain.

Registering a Domain　To register a new domain via the Route 53 console, you choose a name for the new domain, provide the requested contact details, and register your domain by paying the annual charge for the domain registration.

Once you register your domain, Route 53 returns the domain name status code (also called an EPP status code) and the Route 53 name servers that will handle the DNS queries for your new domain. You can add, change, or delete the name servers.

Using Hosted Zones　A hosted zone is a container for records that specify how you want to route Internet traffic for a specific domain and its subdomains. It's a set of DNS records that make up a single domain's configuration. You must create a hosted zone for each domain that you configure in Route 53. A hosted zone has the same name as its corresponding domain, such as example.com. There are two types of hosted zones:

- Records in a *public hosted zone* specify how to route traffic for your domain on the Internet.
- Records in a *private hosted zone* specify how to route traffic in an Amazon VPC.

When you register with Route 53, it automatically creates a public hosted zone for the domain, for which there's a small monthly fee. If you create records in a hosted zone other than the one Route 53 creates for you, you must update the name servers for the domain by selecting name servers for the new hosted zone.

The other way to get a public hosted zone is by creating it when you transfer DNS service for a domain to Route 53. Regardless of how you get the public hosted zone, your next step is to create records in it to specify how you want to route traffic for the domain. For example, you might create a record that specifies that Internet traffic be routed to a web server in your own data center.

You create private hosted zones yourself and specify the Amazon VPCs you'd like to associate with the zone. Services such as databases and web servers that run on an EC2 instance in one of the VPCs that you associate with a private hosted zone can submit DNS queries for the domain to Route 53. If you want to ensure that the instances in your VPC only respond to the DNS queries via your domain, you can do by setting up a private hosted zone.

Creating Resource Record Sets Following your registration of a domain name, Route 53 automatically creates a public hosted zone for you. To route traffic to your AWS resources such as RDS databases and web servers, you create records (also called resource record sets, or just record sets) in your hosted zone. You add records such as the CNAME record to Route 53 as record sets.

For example, you can create records that specify how Internet traffic for your domain (such as example.com) is routed to the IP address of a web server in your data center. There are no charges for the records you add to a hosted zone.

A resource record contains details about how you want to direct traffic to your domain, such as the following:

- **Name of the record** The record name is the same as the domain name (example.com) or the subdomain name (retail.exmple.com) to which you want to route traffic.
- **Record type** This refers to the *type* of resource to which you want to route traffic. For an e-mail server, the record type is MX, and for a web server (IPv4 IP address), it is the record type A.
- **Value** The value is dependent on the record type. For example, for a web server it could be something like 192.0.2.136.

 NOTE A record includes the domain (or subdomain name), the record type, and information applicable to that record type.

An *alias record* is a special Route 53 record that routes Internet traffic to AWS resources such as S3 buckets that you've configured as a static web site, CloudFront distributions, Elastic Beanstalk environments, Application Load Balancers, and another Route 53 resource record set in the same hosted zone.

Using Traffic Flow to Route DNS Traffic

It's difficult to manage numerous resource records that use multiple Route 53 routing policies (failover, weighted, geolocation, and so on). You're likely to have problems keeping track of the relationships among the many resource records that you create.

Route 53 Traffic Flow offers a visual editor to make it easy for you to create and manage complex DNS configurations. You create and save the configuration as traffic policies. You can then associate the traffic policies with a domain (mycompany.com) or a subdomain (www.mycompany.com) name.

NOTE Traffic Flow lets you route traffic to both AWS and non-AWS resources.

You can use Traffic Flow only for configurations for public hosted zones. You can associate a traffic policy in the same or in multiple public hosted zones. Traffic Flow makes it easy to apply updates to DNS names or to roll back updates if the configuration doesn't show good performance.

In a nutshell, this is how Traffic Flow works:

1. You create a traffic policy via the visual editor. The traffic policy contains the routing configuration you want to create, such as the resources (IP address of EC2 instances or the domain name of an ELB load balancer) you want to send DNS traffic to, and the routing policies that you want to use. You have the option of ensuring that Route 53 sends traffic only to healthy endpoints by associating health checks with the endpoints.

2. Create a policy record, where you specify the hosted zone in which you want to create the configuration laid out in the traffic policy you created in step 1. You also specify the DNS name (such as www.mycompany.com) that you want to associate the configuration with. You can use the same traffic policy to create multiple policy records, in the same or a different hosted zone. Route 53 creates a tree of records when you create a policy record, with the root record having the DNS name that you specified.

3. When users go to the DNS name you've specified (www.mycompany.com in our example), Route 53 routes the request based on the traffic policy you used as the basis for the policy record that you created in step 2.

Handling Service Failovers (Enhancing Resiliency) with Health Checks

Route 53 helps greatly in making your systems resilient. Using Route 53, you can survive Elastic Load Balancing and application outages.

Route 53 monitors the health and performance of web applications, web servers, and other resources by performing periodic health checks (for example, by requesting web pages from various URLs that you specify). Therefore, it's important that you understand Route 53 health checks, so that you can understand how Route 53 manages service failovers to healthy resources.

Route 53 Health Checks

If you're running multiple resources such as web servers or mail servers, Route 53 can monitor the health of the resources and ensure that the DNS queries are always sent to the currently healthy resources. You can monitor the status of the health checks on the Route 53 console. You can also set CloudWatch alarms from the console to get automatic notifications when a resource's health status changes. When you update the port for a health check (such as for an Application Load Balancer), you won't see the health check in the Amazon CloudWatch console unless you also update the security group rules to allow traffic into and out of the new port.

A Route 53 health check monitors the health and performance of various resources such as web servers. For all failed health checks, except calculated health checks, you can see the reasons for failure in the Route 53 console. A specific health check can monitor one of the following: health of a resource, status of a health check, and status of a CloudWatch alarm.

Health of a Specific AWS Resource   These health checks monitor an endpoint for a resource, such as an IP address or a domain name. Once you create a health check that monitors an endpoint, the health checks send requests to the endpoint to determine its health. For example, for an HTTP and HTTPS health check, the individual health checker must be able to establish a TCP connection within four seconds.

You specify the interval between the health checks, which could be 10 or 30 seconds. The endpoint health checkers determine the endpoint health based on response time and the *failure threshold*, which is the number of consecutive health checks the endpoint must respond to. You specify the failure threshold.

Route 53 will gather data from its health checks, and if more than 18 percent of health checks report that an endpoint is healthy, Route 53 deems it to be in a healthy state of operation, and unhealthy otherwise. The 18 percent value ensures that health checkers in multiple regions consider the endpoint healthy, and may change in the future, based on the number of AWS regions.

Status of a Health Check   Some health checks monitor other health checks; these are called *calculated health checks*. For example, a health check can monitor the status of web server health checks, and it can notify you when the number of available web servers drops below a threshold you specify. The monitoring health check is called the *parent health check*, and the monitored health checks are called *child health checks*. A parent health check can monitor up to 255 child health checks

Status of a CloudWatch Alarm   A CloudWatch alarm monitors the status of various metrics, such as the number of throttled read events for a DynamoDB database. You can create health checks to monitor the same metric stream that CloudWatch monitors for an alarm to get advanced notice of adverse conditions. In a healthy metric, the alarm's data stream indicates that the state of the alarm is "OK"; the state changes to "Alarm" if the check is deemed unhealthy. Even before the state of a CloudWatch alarm changes to "Alarm," the status of a Route 53 health check can become unhealthy.

Configuring DNS Failover

When you have multiple AWS resources that can perform the same function, such as multiple web servers in a domain, you can ask Route 53 to check the resources' health and direct DNS queries to the healthy resources, thus enhancing availability. This feature is called *DNS failover*, since Route 53 transparently directs (or fails over) the requests from an unhealthy web server to a healthy server. You can configure Route 53 to perform health checks through both simple and complex configurations.

In a *simple configuration*, you create a set of resource records that are all the same record type and name, such as a set of weighted records of record type A. You create a record and a health check for a resource such as a web server and associate the health checks with the resource. The health checks will keep periodically probing the resource's health, and Route 53 directs traffic to the healthy resources. You can't use alias records, however, because the alias records can route traffic directly to a resource such as an ELB; they can't direct traffic to another Route 53 record.

Complex configurations require you to create a tree of resource records to route traffic based on multiple criteria instead of a single criterion, as is the case in a simple configuration. For example, you can combine latency- and weight-based records to route traffic to EC2 instances. Complex configurations can include a combination of alias and non-alias records in a multilevel tree. Once you create the records for complex routing configurations, you must associate the records with health checks. When you configure health checking for a set of records with the same type (for example, A) and the same routing policy (such as weighted), Route 53 chooses a healthy record and returns the values in that record as its response to a DNS query. Route 53 selects from a set of health records based on the routing policy you've configured; for example, if you've specified the weighted routing policy, it selects a record based on the weights you've configured for each record.

Configuring Active-Active and Active-Passive Failover

You can configure two types of DNS failover: *active-active* and *active-passive*. In both cases, you use Route 53 health checking.

Configure active-active failover if you want all the resources such as web servers to be available most of the time. In this configuration, all records with the same name, type, and routing policy are active, so long as the underlying resources are deemed healthy by Route 53. Route 53 will respond to DNS queries by routing traffic to any healthy resource. You can configure active-active failover with any routing policy or policies other than the failover routing policy. So, if you want to ensure that a website loads pages in the shortest time and is also always available, you can place the web site in two regions and use latency-based routing together with DNS failover.

In active-passive failover, you distinguish between primary and secondary resources (or groups of resources). You configure this when you want the primary resource to be available most of the time, and you want a secondary resource to be on standby for the times when the primary resource is unavailable. When the primary resources are all unhealthy, Route 53 starts routing traffic to healthy secondary resources. You must use the failover routing policy to configure an active-passive failover.

Monitoring Route 53

The Amazon Route 53 dashboard is your best friend for monitoring Route 53. The dashboard shows new domain registrations and domains that are nearing expiration.

You use health checks along with CloudWatch and CloudTrail to monitor Route 53. CloudWatch tracks the number of health checks with a healthy status and related metrics, such as the time it took for a health check to receive the first byte. CloudTrail records all Route 53–related API requests.

CloudFront: Amazon's Content Delivery Network

CloudFront is AWS's content delivery network (CDN) service. CloudFront lets you speed up the delivery of both static and dynamic web content, such as HTML, CSS, image, and media files, as well as streaming media, to users. CloudFront serves content faster via a network of data centers called *edge locations*. *Edge servers* are located in an edge location. CloudFront routes user requests through the AWS network to the edge location that can assure the fastest delivery of content to users. Typically, this is the edge location that's closest to the user who makes a request for content.

 NOTE Latency is the time it takes to load the first byte of a file. The lower the latency, the higher the data transfer rate.

When clients request content, such as an image file, if the files are already in an edge location with the lowest latency, CloudFront delivers it from that location. Otherwise, CloudFront retrieves the images from an origin that you specify, such as an Amazon S3 bucket or a HTTP server.

The key thing here is that the users aren't aware of what CloudFront does behind the scenes—routing requests from among networks to obtain the resource that was requested.

CloudFront Use Cases

You can use CloudFront wherever faster delivery content is critical. Here are some common use cases:

- **Faster static web content delivery** CloudFront can help you deliver static content such as images and JavaScript faster to your users spread across the globe.

- **On-demand or live streaming video** CloudFront can stream data in common formats such as MPEG DASH to any device. For live streaming, you can cache media fragments on the edge servers to reduce the origin server's load.

- **Encrypt specific fields** By setting up *field-level encryption* through the addition of a public key to CloudFront, you can protect specific data, so that only specific applications at your origin can view the data.

- **Customize the edge server** You can use the edge servers to customize the web content and web experience for your users, such as returning custom instead of generic HTTP error messages. You can also use Lambda@Edge with CloudFront to customize the CloudFront content by creating and deploying functions with CloudFront.

Configuring CloudFront to Deliver Content

When you want CloudFront to distribute web content, you store the objects in an *origin server* (S3 buckets, or *custom origins* such as an HTTP server or a directory in the specified domain) and expose a CloudFront link to the files to your users. Origin servers are locations where you store your web content's original versions. When it receives a request for files, CloudFront gets the files from the origin and distributes them at the edge locations. You can use both S3 buckets and HTTP servers as your origin servers.

Configuring CloudFront to deliver web content faster to users involves the following steps:

1. Specify the source of the web content that CloudFront distributes from edge locations. Content sources, or origin servers, can be an AWS resource—such as an S3 bucket (mybucket.s3.amazonaws.com) or a custom origin server completely outside of AWS. An origin server can also be another AWS resource, such as EC2, or the ELB service. When serving content over HTTP, the origin server is either an S3 bucket or an HTTP (web) server. The web servers can be run on EC2 instances or your own servers. Web servers that you maintain on your own servers are called *custom origins*. An Amazon S3 bucket is always the origin for distributing media files on demand.

2. You can specify the directory path as the origin name, which means that when configuring the origin server, you specify the directory path as well as the domain name. This enables you to deliver multiple types of content through CloudFront, without making major changes to the origin infrastructure.

3. Upload the web content, or *objects*, such as web pages, images, and media files, to the origin servers. If the content is originating from Amazon S3, you must make the objects in the S3 bucket publicly readable.

4. Create a CloudFront distribution—a set of origin servers where CloudFront can get your files to satisfy requests for those files made by users through your applications or web sites. You can create distributions to serve content such as static and dynamic content (.html, .js, and image files), video on demand, and live streaming.

5. Your users can then access the objects that you stored in Amazon S3 buckets either directly from S3 or have CloudFront get the objects from S3 and distribute them to the users. If the users access your S3 objects frequently, it's smarter to use CloudFront, since the data transfer costs for CloudFront are lower than those from transferring data from S3. Since CloudFront restores the objects in edge servers that are nearer to the users, the data is sent faster to the users as well.

6. You can optionally configure the origin server to add headers to the content files. The headers help control the length of time the files can remain in the cache on CloudFront edge locations.

   CloudFront assigns a domain name to the distribution you created in step 4. You can choose to specify a custom domain name to use for URLs for your objects. For example, CloudFront may assign an URL such as the following to an object named image.jpg that you have stored in your Amazon S3 bucket.: http://d111111abcdef8.cloudfront.net/image.jpg. Alternatively, you can configure your CloudFront distribution to use your domain name, in which case, the URL for the object image.jpg will be:

   http://www.example.com/image.jpg

   You can do this by creating or updating a CNAME record in Route 53 (or another DNS) to route requests for www.example.com to d111111abcdef8cloudfront.net.

7. CloudFront transmits the distribution's configuration to all its edge locations, which are located all over the globe. CloudFront caches copies of the objects at the edge locations.

How CloudFront Delivers Content

CloudFront stores the data that it retrieves from origin servers in edge server caches and regional edge caches. Here's how CloudFront delivers content to your users:

1. A user requests an object, such as an image file or an HTTP file, by accessing a web application or one of your web sites.

2. Route 53 (or another DNS) routes the user request to the CloudFront edge location nearest to the user, in terms of latency.

3. If the requested files are in the CloudFront cache at this edge location, the files are returned to the user.

4. Or, if the requested files aren't in the cache at this edge location, CloudFront forwards the request to an origin server, such as an S3 bucket (for image files) or an HTTP server (for HTML files).

5. The origin server sends the requested files to the CloudFront edge location. For faster content delivery, CloudFront maintains persistent connections with the origin servers.

6. CloudFront starts forwarding the files to the user as soon as the first byte arrives from the origin server.

7. CloudFront stores the files to its cache at the edge location and serves all subsequent requests for this content directly from this cache.

Restricting Access to Amazon S3 Content via Origin Access Identities

When you set up an S3 bucket as the origin for a CloudFront distribution, you can restrict access to the bucket by using CloudFront signed URLs or signed cookies. You can restrict access to the content by ending the access after a specific date and time, and also control which IP addresses can be used to access the content. However, you also might want to prevent your users from accessing the S3 files by directly using the S3 URLs, bypassing the control provided by the CloudFront signed URLs or signed cookies.

To ensure that your users access the S3 files only via CloudFront URLs (signed or not), you must do the following:

- Create an *origin access identity* (a special CloudFront user) and associate it with your distribution.

- Change the permissions on the S3 bucket or the objects in the bucket (files) so that only the origin access identity has read permissions (you can also grant the download permission). The origin access identity will get the S3 files on behalf of the users when they access the files, but if the users request the files directly, the requests are denied.

Regional Edge Caches

A *regional edge cache* helps with faster delivery of popular content such as user-generated videos and photos, e-commerce objects such as product photos and videos, and new and event-related content. As objects become less popular, individual edge locations may remove those objects to make room for more popular content.

Regional edge caches are located closer to the viewers of content and are situated in between your origin servers and the global edge locations. Their caches are larger than the caches of individual edge locations, thus enabling these locations to retain objects longer in their cache.

Edge servers contact the nearest regional edge cache to retrieve objects, instead of going to the origin server. When CloudFront requests objects from origin servers (when it can't find the object in its cache), it adds the files to the caches in both the regional edge cache location and the edge location. All edge locations within an AWS region share a local cache.

There are some similarities and differences between regional edge caches and edge locations:

- A cache invalidation removes objects from both edge caches and regional edge caches.
- Proxy methods such as PUT/POST/DELETE don't proxy through regional edge caches; instead, they go directly to the origin servers from the edge locations.
- Amazon S3 origins don't use regional edge caches.
- Dynamic content doesn't go through regional edge caches; instead, it goes straight to the origin.

Configuring an Amazon CloudFront Distribution

As explained earlier, the CloudFront distribution instructs CloudFront about the origin servers from which it should retrieve the content, following a user request for the content made through a web application or a web site.

Configuring a CloudFront distribution involves setting the following values:

- Delivery method
- Origin settings
- Cache behavior
- Custom error pages and error caching

You can specify these values during the creation of or while updating a distribution. The following section describes each of these confirmation elements.

 TIP You can use the optional *private content* feature to limit who can access your CloudFront-distributed content. You do this by requiring users to use either a signed URL or have a signed HTTP cookie when requesting content from your web site or through an application.

Configuring the Delivery Method

The two types of delivery methods are Web or RTMP. If you're using Adobe Flash media Server, the delivery method is Real Time Messaging Protocol (RMTP). For everything else, choose Web. You can specify the delivery method when creating or updating a distribution through the CloudFront console or programmatically. In the console, you choose Create Distribution=>Get started, and then configure values for the distribution, including delivery method, origin settings, and so on.

Origin Setting Values

There are three basic origin values you can configure: origin domain name, origin path, and origin ID:

- **Origin domain name** This is the DNS domain name of the Amazon S3 bucket or the HTTP server from where CloudFront gets the objects for this origin. Here are some examples:
  - Amazon S3 bucket: myawsbucket.s3.amazon.com (this is theS3 bucket name)
  - An Amazon S3 bucket configured as a web site: http://bucket-name.s3-website-us-west-2.amazonaws.com (this is the S3 static web site hosting endpoint for your S3 bucket)
  - An Amazon EC2 instance: ec2-1111-0-222-33.compute-1.amazonaws.com
  - Your local web server: http://mycompany.com
- **Origin path** Specify a directory path to make CloudFront request content from a directory in your custom origin or an AWS resource.
- **Origin ID** Set the origin ID to help uniquely identify the origin or origin group in a CloudFront distribution.

You can configure several other origin-related parameters, such as `origin keep-alive timeout`, which specifies how long CloudFront tries to maintain a connection to a custom origin after it receives the last packet of a response.

Configuring Cache Behavior

You can also configure *cache behaviors*, which are sets of rules for a specific URL pattern for files on your web site, based on file extension (such as *.jpg*), filename, and any part of a URL path on your side. You can configure one or more cache behaviors for a web distribution. CloudFront matches user requests with the URL pattern that you provide and enforces the cache behavior that you've configured for the URL pattern.

A cache behavior lets you configure settings for the following types of CloudFront functionality:

- The path pattern
- The origin from which you want CloudFront to forward requests (if you've configured multiple origins)
- Whether to forward query strings to the origin

- Whether to force users to use HTTPS to access files on the origin (you can also configure the redirecting of HTTP requests to HTTPS protocols)
- The minimum and maximum lengths of time files can stay in the CloudFront cache (overriding the value of any cache-control headers that the origin adds to the files).

 TIP   Each origin requires a different cache behavior. If you have four origins, for example, you must configure four cache behaviors (including the default cache behavior).

Following are some of the many cache behavior parameters you can configure.

Configuring the Viewer Protocol Policy   By default, when using an Amazon S3 origin, CloudFront accepts requests using HTTP or HTTPS. It also forwards the requests to the S3 bucket, using the same protocol that was used by the requests. CloudFront handles HTTP and HTTPS requests differently for a custom origin. You can specify whether CloudFront accesses the origin using only HTTP or HTTPS, or both HTTP and HTTPS.

Caching Content Based on Request Headers   By default, CloudFront ignores headers when caching objects in edge locations. Even if the origin returns two objects, if the request headers are the only difference between the two objects, CloudFront caches only one version of the object.

For most web distributions, you can configure CloudFront to forward headers (none, all, or a whitelisted set of request headers) to the origin and to cache multiple versions of an object based on the header values in the requests. This makes it possible for you to serve custom content based on a viewer's location, device, language, or other criteria.

Let's say, for example, that a user request for *logo.jpg* has *Amazon* or *Walmart* as the value for a custom Company header. If you configure CloudFront to cache objects based on the value of the Company header, it includes the Company header and the two possible values (*Amazon* and *Walmart*) when it forwards requests from logo.jpg to the origin. CloudFront also caches logo.jpg twice: once for requests with the value *Walmart* for the Company header, and the other for requests with the value *Amazon* for the Company header.

You can configure cache behavior based on request headers in one of the following ways:

- *Forward all headers to your region.* When you configure this, CloudFront sends every request to the origin, and doesn't cache the objects that match this cache behavior.
- *Forward a whitelist of headers that you specify.* CloudFront caches objects based on the values in all the headers that you specify.
- *Forward only default headers.* CloudFront won't cache objects based on the request header values.

Caching Duration and Minimum TTL   This behavior is the same for both S3 origins and custom origins. You set the Caching Duration and Minimum TTL to control how long web objects remain in the CloudFront cache before CloudFront forwards new requests on to your origin. You can set the caching duration and Minimum TTL by doing one of the following:

- Adding a Cache-Control or an Expires header to each object.
- Specify a value for a Minimum TTL in CloudFront cache behaviors.
- Use the default value, which is 24 hours.

By default, all objects are cached in an edge location for 24 hours, after which the object expires. You can configure the duration of caching, with there being no maximum expiration time limit.

NOTE   Not all content is good to cache! By setting Cache-Control header directives such as a private and no-store, you can direct CloudFront not to cache that content.

Using Query String Parameters to Determine Caching Content   Some web applications send information to the origin via *query strings*. A query string is the portion of a web request that comes after a ? character and can contain one or more parameters. The following example shows two parameters: `color=red` and `size=large`:

`http://d111111abcdef8.cloudfront.net/images/image.jpg?color=red&size=large`

Query strings help customize web content that's generated by a script that runs on the origin server. By default, CloudFront doesn't forward query string parameters to the origin, and it also ignores the query string portion of the URL, thus treating multiple objects with different query parameters as not being unique.

Because query strings enable the customization of user web pages, you can configure CloudFront not to forward the query strings to the origin. You can alternatively configure it to forward query strings to the origin and cache the content based on all or some of the parameters in the query string.

Handling Cookies   HTTP cookies help deliver a customized or personal dynamic content. By default, CloudFront doesn't consider cookies when caching objects in edge locations. You can configure CloudFront to forward cookies to an origin, which makes CloudFront cache the objects, using the forwarded cookie values to identify the unique objects in its cache.

You can configure a cache behavior in a web distribution to do one of the following:

- *Don't forward cookies to your origin.* CloudFront won't cache objects on cookie values. It also removes the Cookie header from requests that it forwards to the origin and removes the Set-Cookie header from responses it sends back to the users.

- *Forward all cookies to your origin.* CloudFront includes all cookies in the user request that it forwards to the origin.

- *Forward a whitelist of cookies that you specify.* CloudFront forwards requests to the origin after stripping out the cookies that aren't on the whitelist of cookies that you specify.

Cross-Origin Resource Sharing (CORS)   Client web applications loaded on one domain interact with resources in another domain *via Cross-Origin Resource Sharing* (CORS). For both S3 origins and your custom origin servers, you can configure Cloud-Front to forward the request Origin header to your origin, thus ensuring that Cloud-Front adheres to the CORS settings.

Serving Compressed Files   CloudFront can compress certain file types and serve them to your users. For compression to occur, the user request must include Accept-Encoding: gzip in the request header. In addition, you must ensure that you've specified automatic CloudFront file compression in your cache behavior settings.

Downloading compressed content is faster, because the files are much smaller after compression. Faster downloads mean quicker rendering of web pages to you users. On top of this, it cuts your CloudFront costs to transfer data since it's cheaper to serve the smaller compressed file.

Because CloudFront doesn't compress all file types, you can configure your origin (custom or S3 origin) to compress those file types. You can set this up with or without CloudFront's automatic compression. CloudFront knows when it receives a compressed file from the origin and doesn't compress the file further.

Adding, Updating, and Removing Content that CloudFront Distributes

You, as an administrator, must know the basics of how to add, update, and delete content from the origins.

Adding Content

To add content that you want CloudFront to distribute, add the content (objects in the form of files) to an origin that you've listed in your CloudFront distribution. In addition, expose a CloudFront link that enables access to the files. The CloudFront edge location retrieves the files you've added to the origin when it receives a new user request for that content.

If you're using a custom origin, you must add the file you want CloudFront to distribute to a directory in the domain you've specified. If Amazon S3 is the origin, ensure that you add the files to an Amazon S3 bucket that you've specified in the distribution.

 TIP   Make sure that *path pattern* in the cache behavior that applies to the content sends the requests to the appropriate origin. If the only applicable cache behavior for the content is .html, CloudFront forwards only .html files, and nothing else.

Updating Content

You can update existing content that you've configured CloudFront to distribute by updating the files using the same name, or by updating them using a version identifier in the filename. AWS recommends that you use a version identifier in your file or directory names to control your content better. You can use identifiers such as sequential numbers or a date-time stamp. So, for example, instead of updating the file image_1.jpg with the same name, you could call the updated file named image_2.jpg, and update the web application's or web site's links to point to this new version of the file.

If you choose to update an existing file in an origin with a new version of the same name, you must be aware that the edge location can't immediately access the new file version. Indeed, the new version may not be served for up to 23 hours. When the new version is sent to the edge location of the origin, both of the following must be true:

- The previous file version in the cache must expire. By default, CloudFront caches the files in edge locations for 24 hours.
- A user must request the file at that specific edge location.

 TIP Since you can't control how CloudFront starts serving new files, it's preferable to use different filenames when updating content.

Removing Content

If you want to remove content from a CloudFront distribution, you can remove the files from the origin. However, CloudFront will continue retrieving and sending the content to your users by serving it from edge location's cache until the files *expire*. This is not good, of course, so you can remove the files immediately either by invalidating them or by using file versioning.

Invalidating Files   You can invalidate the files in an edge cache to override the expiration period you've configured for that object on the origin server. When there's a subsequent request for this content, CloudFront is forced to contact the origin server to retrieve the latest file version.

 NOTE   You'll use file invalidation only in unusual circumstances, such as to invalidate changes made in error to a web site's CSS file.

You can invalidate a CSS file, for example, to ensure that your changes propagate almost immediately. Suppose you update your application's UI, and its CSS file takes 16 hours to propagate into the cache, whereas the layout changes take only 4 hours. You have a situation where it'll take 12 hours for the new layout that you pushed out to be styled properly. Invalidating objects in CloudFront's cache helps in situations like this. You can invalidate only files that are associated with a web distribution. You can invalidate an entire S3 bucket.

You can remove a large number of objects in a single move by sending a list of up to 3000 invalidation paths in an XML document. You can also request up to 15 invalidation paths with a wildcard (*) character. You can specify either an individual file's path or a path with the * wildcard to invalidate files, as shown here:

- /images/image1.jpg
- /images/image*
- /images/

When you invalidate a file, it removes *all* copies of an object—that is, it removes the object from all CloudFront edge locations.

NOTE   AWS doesn't charge you for a specific number of invalidation paths per month. If you go over the specified number of paths, you pay a fee for each additional invalidation path.

File Versioning   File versioning is another option to update your cached files living on the CloudFront edge locations. By creating a unique name for each version of a file and specifying the most recent filename in your web applications and web pages, you ensure that CloudFront caches the latest version of the object. Then CloudFront doesn't have to wait for the older object to expire in the cache before it can serve the newer version of the object.

If you frequently update your files, AWS recommends that you use file versioning for the following reasons:

- You can serve different file versions to different sets of users.
- Versioning makes it easy to roll back file revisions.
- Versioning has no charges, except the cost to transfer the new file version to edge locations; invalidation incurs costs above a specific threshold of files.
- If you invalidate files instead of using file versioning, some users may still see old versions of a file since they have cached it locally or behind a corporate caching proxy. Thus, file versioning helps you more tightly control when your changes go into effect.

How CloudFront Handles HTTP Status Codes from an Origin

When CloudFront requests objects from an origin (S3 bucket or custom origin server), the origin sometimes doesn't return the object, instead returning an HTTP 3xx , 4xx, or 5xx status code, indicating the error that prevented the origin from returning the object.

NOTE   Some of the caching strategies for requests and responses are similar to both Amazon S3 origins and to custom origins, while others are different.

HTTP 3xx Status Codes

HTTP 3xx codes include the following:

- 301, URL has changed (Moved Permanently)
- 307, URL has changed (Temporary Redirect)
- 304, Not Modified: Object hasn't change the last time CloudFront requested it.

 NOTE CloudFront doesn't follow the redirect to the new location if the origin returns a 301 or 307 status code.

CloudFront caches all 3xx response for the duration you've specified in your Cloud-Front distribution, and the header files that the origin returns with an object.

HTTP 4xx and 5xx Status Codes

HTTP 4xx and 5xx codes indicate errors. CloudFront caches the following HTTP 4xx and 5xx status codes returned by an origin:

- 400: Bad Request
- 403: Forbidden
- 404: Not Found
- 405: Method Not Allowed
- 414: Request-URI Too Large
- 500: Internal Server Error
- 501: Not Implemented
- 502: Bad Gateway
- 503: Service Unavailable
- 504: Gateway Time-out

When an origin returns the HTTP 4xx or 5xx status code, CloudFront can behave in different ways, depending on whether you've configured custom error pages, the duration you want CloudFront to cache the origin's error responses, and whether the requested object is present in the CloudFront edge cache.

Error Processing When You've Configured Custom Error Pages The CloudFront behavior depends on whether the requested object is in the edge cache. CloudFront continues to try to get the requested object from your origin when all of the following are true:

- A viewer requests an object.
- The object isn't in the edge cache.
- Your origin returns an HTTP 4xx or 5xx status code instead of returning a 304 status code (Not Modified) or an updated version of the object.

CloudFront then does the following:

1. In the CloudFront edge cache that received the viewer request, CloudFront checks your distribution configuration and gets the path of the custom error page that corresponds with the status code that your origin returned.

2. CloudFront finds the first cache behavior in your distribution that has a path pattern that matches the path of the custom error page.

3. The CloudFront edge location sends a request for the custom error page to the origin that is specified in the cache behavior.

4. The origin returns the custom error page to the edge location.

5. CloudFront returns the custom error page to the viewer that made the request and caches the custom error page for the amount of time specified by the error caching minimum TTL (five minutes by default).

6. After the error caching minimum TTL has elapsed, CloudFront tries again to get the requested object by forwarding another request to your origin. CloudFront continues to retry at intervals specified by the error caching minimum TTL.

Error Processing When You Haven't Configured Custom Error Pages   CloudFront behavior depends on whether the requested object is in the edge cache. CloudFront continues to try to get the requested object from your origin when all of the following are true:

- A viewer requests an object.
- The object isn't in the edge cache.
- Your origin returns an HTTP 4xx or 5xx status code instead of returning a 304 status code (Not Modified) or an updated version of the object.

CloudFront then returns the 4xx or 5xx status code to the viewer. It also caches the status code in the edge cache that received the request. For the duration of the error caching minimum TTL, CloudFront responds to subsequent viewer requests for the same object with the cached 4xx or 5xx status code. After the error caching minimum TTL has elapsed, CloudFront tries again to get the requested object by forwarding another request to your origin.

Chapter Review

AWS networking is a vast topic, and in this chapter, I've reviewed the essentials of all the major networking capabilities offered by AWS. You learned how Amazon VPC enables you to set your own logically separate and secure network in the AWS cloud. You learned about key VPC components such as subnets and routes, and how to secure your AWS resources with security groups and network ACLs.

The chapter also reviewed ways to establish secure direct connections to Amazon VPC, such as Amazon Direct Connect. You learned about several optional VPC features, such as VPC peering, VPN connections, and configuring DHCP option sets.

Networking also includes understanding how to configure and work with various load options offered by Elastic Load Balancing.

Amazon's Route 53 service is a DNS service you can use. You learned the basics of DNS, as well as how to work with Route 53 to register domains, route traffic to your domains, and perform health checks.

Finally, the chapter described AWS's content delivery service, Amazon CloudFront, and how to secure it.

Exercises

The exercises are designed to teach you how to network. There are no answers to any of the exercises; if you make a mistake, retrace your steps and ensure that you've correctly performed the steps. You'll know that you've correctly completed the exercise if you achieve the goal set for you in each exercise, such as creating an Amazon VPC.

Exercise 6-1: Create an Elastic IP (EIP) address.

To create an EIP, you must first allocate an EIP, and then associate it with an EC2 instance. Here are the steps:

1. Open the VPC console: https://consile.aws.amazon.com/vpc/.

2. In the navigation pane, select Elastic IPs.

3. Select Allocate New Address.

4. Select Allocate.

5. Select the EIP that you've allocated for use with a VPC in the previous step and choose Actions | Associate Address.

6. Select Instance or Network interface. Then, depending on your choice, select the instance or network interface ID.

7. Select the private IP address you want to associate the EIP with. Then click Associate.

Exercise 6-2: Create an Amazon Virtual Private Cloud (VPC).

1. Go to the Amazon VPC console at https://console.aws.amazon.com/vpc.

2. In the navigation pane, select Your VPCs, VPC, and then Click Create VPC. Create VPC.

3. Specify the VPC name tag, CIDR Block, and Tenancy:

- **Name Tag:** This is an optional VPC name.
- **IPv4 CIDR Block:** Choose a CIDR block for the VPC. AWS recommends that you specify a CIDR block from the non-publicly routable, private IP address CIDR blocks such as 10.0.0.0/16, or 192.168.0.0/16, and no preference for the Availability Zone.
- **Tenancy:** Select a tenancy option, such as Dedicated Tenancy.

4. Click Create VPC.

Exercise 6-3: Create a subnet in a VPC.

Before you can create a subnet, you must have a VPC, so make sure you complete Exercise 6-2 before starting Exercise 6-3.

1. Open the Amazon VPC console: https://console.aws.amazon.com/vpc/.

2. In the navigation pane, choose Subnets | Create Subnet.

3. Specify the subnet details that you need and click Create Subnet.

4. Of the five subnet properties, the Name Tag, Availability Zone, and IPv4 CIDR Block are optional. You must, however, choose the VPC and also specify the IPv4 CIDR block for your subnet, such as 10.1.1.0/24.

Exercise 6-4: Create a network interface.

1. Open the Amazon EC2 console: https://console.aws.com/ec2/.

2. In the navigation pane, select Network Interfaces.

3. Select Create Network Interface.

4. Under Description, enter a name for the new interface.

5. Select the subnet for Subnet.

6. For Private IP (or IPv4 Private IP), enter the primary private IPv4 address. Otherwise, AWS selects a private IPv4 address from the subnet you chose earlier.

7. Select one or more security groups for Security Groups.

8. Click Yes, Create.

Exercise 6-5: Create a security group.

1. Open the Amazon VPC console: https://console.aws.amazon.com/vpc/;

2. In the navigation pane, select Security Groups.

3. Select Create Security Group.

4. Enter a name for the security group (my-sg, for example) and a description.

5. From the VPC menu, select your VPC's ID and then click Yes, Create.

Exercise 6-6: Launch an EC2 instance in a subnet.

1. Open the Amazon EC2 console: https://console.aws.amazon.com/ec2/.

2. From the dashboard, choose Launch Instance.

3. Select an AMI and instance type and click Next: Configure Instance Details.

4. On the Configure Instance Details page, select the VPC, and then select the subnet in which you want to launch the instance.

5. Select Next: Add Storage.

6. On the next page, configure the storage settings for the instance. Choose Next: Configure Security Group.

7. On the Configure Security Group page, choose an existing security group or create a new security group.

8. Select Review And Launch.

9. Review the instance settings and select Launch.

10. Select a key pair you own, or create a new one. Then select Launch Instances.

Exercise 6-7: Create a NAT gateway.

1. Open the Amazon VPC console: https://console.aws.amazon.com/vpc/.

2. In the navigation pane, select NAT Gateways | Create NAT Gateway.

3. Specify the subnet in which you want to create the NAT gateway.

4. Select the allocation ID of the EIP you want to associate with the NAT gateway.

5. Choose Create A NAT Gateway.

6. Once the status of the new NAT gateway changes to Available, you can start using it.

Exercise 6-8: Create a route for a NAT gateway.

1. Open the Amazon VPC console: https://console.aws.amazon.com/vpc/.
2. In the navigation pane, select Route Tables.
3. Select the route table associated with your private subnet and choose Routes | Edit.
4. Select Add Another Route.
5. For Destination, type the value **0.0.0.00**.
6. For Target, select the ID of the NAT gateway you created in Exercise 6-7.
7. Open a command prompt from one of the EC2 instances in your private subnet, and ping amazon.com to verify that the Internet connectivity is set up.

Exercise 6-9: Configure Amazon Route 53 to route traffic to an Amazon EC2 instance.

There are some prerequisites for performing this task. You must first do the following:

1. Register your domain name.
2. Choose Route 53 as the DNS service for the domain.
3. AWS recommends that you also create an EIP and associate that with your EC2 instance.

Perform the following steps to configure Route 53 to route traffic to an EC2 instance:

1. Get the IP address for the EC2 instance by going to the EC2 console and looking up the value of the Elastic IP on the Description tab. If you didn't associate an Elastic IP with this instance, get the value of the IPv4 Public IP.
2. Open the Route 53 console: https://consoile.aws.amazon.com/route53/.
3. In the navigation pane, select Hosted Zones. Select the hosted zone with the same name as the domain for which you're routing the traffic.
4. Select Create Record Set. Specify the following values:
   - **Name:** the domain name (default value is the hosted zone's name). For example, if the hosted zone has the name example.com, and you want to use test.example.com to route traffic to this instance, enter **test**.
   - **Type:** A-IPv4 Address
   - **Alias:** Accept the default value.

- **TTL (seconds):** Accept the default value of 300 seconds.
- **Value:** Enter the IP address you retrieved in step 1.
- **Routing Policy:** Accept Simple, the default value.

5. Select Create.

Within 60 seconds, the changes propagate to all Route 53 servers. Following the propagation, you can route traffic to the EC2 instance by using the name of the record that you created in this exercise.

Exercise 6-10: Create and update a Route 53 health check.

1. Sign in to the AWS Management Console and open the Route 53 console: https://console.aws.amazon.com/route53/.

2. Choose Health Checks in the navigation pane.

3. Choose Create Health Check to create a health check. Choose Edit Health Check to update a health check.

4. In the Configure Health Check page, enter the applicable values for each setting for the health check.

5. Create an alarm by choosing Create Alarm so that CloudWatch can send you an SNS notification when the status of a health check changes to unhealthy

6. Click Create Health Check. You should see a confirmation such as the following:

   Health check with id c912740b-d9e3-4646-94b3-fdbcefe6985f has been created successfully

7. Associate the new health check with at least one Route 53 record.

Exercise 6-11: Create a CloudFront distribution.

Before you start this exercise, you must ensure that you've finished the prerequisites:

1. Create at least one Amazon S3 bucket or configure HTTP server as your origin servers.

2. Upload your content to the origin servers, such as Amazon S3, and grant object permissions. You must grant public read permissions to the buckets if you want the objects to be publicly readable and ensure that users can access the objects in your S3 buckets through CloudFront URLs. You will learn how to grant S3 object permissions in Exercise 8-4.

Once you've performed the prerequisite tasks, you are ready to create your CloudFront distribution. Follow these steps to create the distribution:

1. Open the CloudFront console at https://console.aws.amazon.com/cloudront/.

2. Select Create Distribution.

3. In the Select A Delivery Method For Your Content page, click Get Started.

4. On the Create Distribution page, enter the S3 bucket name, path, and other details under Origin Settings, by accepting the default values for most of the settings.

5. Under the Default Cache Behavior settings, accept the default values.

6. Under Distribution Settings, select the values for the distribution, such as the Price Class (maximum price prices you want to pay for the CloudFront service).

7. Once the status of the new distribution changes to Deployed, you can test the links to your objects. For example, to test the link to an object named image.jpg, copy the following HTML to a file:

```
<html>
<head>My CloudFront Test</head>
<body>
<p>My text content goes here.</p>
<p><img src="http://domain name/object name" alt="my test image"/>
</body>
</html>
```

If your object is image.jpg and your domain name is d111111abcdef8.cloudfront, your URL for the link to the object is http://d111111abcdef8.cloudfront.net/image.jpg.

8. Open your web page in a browser and it should return the page with the embedder image file from the edge location where CloudFront has saved the object.

Questions

The following questions will help you measure your understanding of the material presented in this chapter. Read all the choices carefully because there may be more than one correct answer. Choose all the correct answers for each question.

1. What's the best way to set up a highly available connection between your Amazon VPC and your on-premise data center?

   A. Launch EC2 instances across multiple availability zones and set up route tables so that a different EC2 instance automatically takes over when an EC2 instance fails.

   B. Create an AWS Direct Connect setup between your Amazon VPC and your data center.

   C. Create a virtual private gateway with a route to your data center.

   D. Create a virtual private gateway and ensure that you configure two customer gateways.

2. What is the reason for launching EC2 instances in a private subnet?

A. To enable users to connect to the EC2 instances faster

B. Because AWS requires you to place EC2 instances in private subnets

C. Because a public subnet has no way to reach the Internet

D. To provide an additional layer of security for the EC2 instances

3. Which of the following is *not* a benefit you gain from Amazon Direct Connect?

A. Lower data transfer costs

B. Higher latency

C. Connect to VPCs in different regions

D. Direct connectivity between your VPC and your onsite data center network

4. Which of the following does a default VPC have?

A. An Internet gateway and a virtual private network gateway

B. A route table that directs all IPv4 traffic destined for the Internet to the Internet gateway

C. A NAT instance

D. A physical firewall

5. Which of the following statements is true about Amazon CloudFront?

A. It delivers the latest version of a file to the users.

B. It will wait until the entire file downloads, so it can perform error checking before sending the file over to the user.

C. It forwards a file to the user as soon as it receives the first bytes of the file.

D. It waits for the user to request the file.

6. You are tracking your web page users with a tracking image that loads on each web page. You are now serving this image from us-east, but your research shows that it takes too long to load the image for users on us-west. What are the ways in which you can speed the image serving? (Choose two)

A. Use CloudFront to serve the image.

B. Serve the image directly from an Amazon S3 bucket.

C. Use Route 53 as your DNS service, and choose its latency-based routing to serve the image out of both us-east-1 and us-west-2.

D. Use cookies rather than loading the images with each web page load.

7. Which purposes does an Internet gateway server serve? (Choose two)

A. It facilitates private internal communications between the EC2 instances within a VPC.

B. It enables a public, but not a private, subnet to communicate with the Internet.

    C. It provides a target in your VPC route tables for Internet-routable traffic.

    D. It performs network address translation (NAT) for instances that have been assigned IPv4 addresses.

8. Which of the following are true with regard to securing your VPC with security groups and network ACLs? (Choose two)

    A. Security groups control inbound and outbound traffic for your EC2 instances.

    B. Security groups control inbound and outbound traffic for your subnets.

    C. Network ACLs control inbound and outbound traffic for your EC2 instances.

    D. Network ACLs control inbound and outbound traffic for your subnets.

9. Which of the following features can you use to investigate a suspected brute-force hacking attempt into one of your EC2 instances? (Choose three)

    A. Check the access logs.

    B. Enable VPC flow logs and examine the logs.

    C. Check GuardDuty's findings.

    D. Explore the EC2 instance's operating system logs.

10. How would you collect information regarding the IP address of the client making requests on a Classic Load Balancer that you've implemented?

    A. Use access logs to gather the information.

    B. Enable CloudWatch and monitor the HostConnect metric.

    C. Monitor the eventSource API in AWS CloudTrail.

    D. Use flow logs.

11. Which of the following are true? (Choose two)

    A. You can modify the main route table.

    B. You can't modify the main route table.

    C. By default, the main route table doesn't contain a route to an Internet gateway.

    D. By default, the main route table always has a route to an Internet gateway.

    E. By default, the main route table contains a route to an Internet gateway.

12. When you configure CloudFront to speed up the delivery of content to your web users, which of the following is true?

    A. CloudFront starts forwarding the files to the user as soon as the first byte arrives from the edge server.

    B. CloudFront starts forwarding the files to the user as soon as the last byte arrives from the edge server.

    C. CloudFront starts forwarding the files to the user as soon as the last byte arrives from the origin server.

    D. CloudFront starts forwarding the files to the user as soon as the first byte arrives from the origin server.

13. Which of the following is an origin server in Amazon CloudFront? (Choose two)

   A. An HTTP server or an Amazon S3 bucket for distributing static content

   B. An Amazon S3 bucket for distributing media files on demand

   C. A HTTP web server that you run on-premises for distributing media files on demand

   D. An Amazon S3 bucket for static content only

14. If you don't see a heath check for an Application Load Balancer in the CloudWatch console after updating the health check's port, what could be the reason?

   A. You must look for the health checks in the Application Load Balancer's console.

   B. You failed to restart the Application Load Balancer after making the port change.

   C. You haven't enabled your security group's rules to ensure that they allow traffic to the new port.

   D. You can't change a health check's port.

15. Which of the following would be good reasons to set up an AWS Direct Connect connection? (Choose three)

   A. Lower network latency

   B. Lower network data transfer costs

   C. Private connectivity to AWS

   D. Faster network data transmission through Internet-based connections

16. Which of the following statements are correct regarding inbound and outbound rules when adding security rules to a security group? (Choose two)

   A. An inbound rule consists of the traffic source and the destination port (or port range). The source may be another security group, a single IP address, or an IPv4 or IPv6 CIDR block.

   B. An outbound rule contains the traffic destination and the destination port (or port range). The destination may be another security group, a single IP address, or an IPv4 or IPv6 CIDR block.

   C. An inbound rule consists of the traffic destination and the destination port (or port range). The source may be another security group, a single IP address, or an IPv4 or IPv6 CIDR block.

   D. An outbound rule contains the traffic source and the destination port (or port range). The destination may be another security group, a single IP address, or an IPv4 or IPv6 CIDR block.

17. You can create VPC flow logs for which of the following entities?

    A. VPC only

    B. VPC or subnet only

    C. Network interface only

    D. VPC, subnet, or network interface

18. Which of the following statements are true regarding the statefulness of security groups and network ACLs? (Choose two)

    A. Security groups are stateful and allow responses to allowed traffic, even if the security group's rules don't permit it.

    B. Security groups are stateful and allow responses to allowed traffic, only if the security group's rules permit it.

    C. Network ACLs are stateless and allow responses to allowed traffic, subject to network ACL rules.

    D. Network ACLs are stateless and allow responses to allowed traffic, regardless of the network ACL rules.

19. You can control traffic routing within a VPC and into and out of a VPC by using which of the following?

    A. Route tables only

    B. Network ACLs and security groups only

    C. Route tables, network ACLs, and security groups

    D. DHCP

20. An alias record type can point to which of the following? (Choose three)

    A. An Application Load Balancer

    B. An Amazon S3 bucket that you've configured as a static web site

    C. Another Route 53 resource set in the same hosted zone

    D. An IP address or a domain name

21. Which of the following are true of object versioning and cache invalidation when using Amazon CloudFront? (Choose two)

    A. Calling the invalidation API to remove an object removes only the copy of the object on a single CloudFront edge location.

    B. Calling the invalidation API to remove an object removes all copies of an object from all CloudFront edge locations.

    C. If you frequently update your web files, you should use object versioning.

    D. If you frequently update your web files, you must use cache invalidation by calling the invalidation API.

22. Which of the following statements are true? (Choose two)

    A. A security group automatically applies to all instances that you launch.

    B. A security group applies to an instance only if you specify the security group at the instance launch time or associate the security group with the instance later.

    C. A network ACL automatically applies to all instances in the subnets you associate the ACL with.

    D. A network ACL applies to an instance only if you specify a security group for the instance.

23. You're running a web application in your data center located in New York and in the London AWS region. If you're using Route 53, how would you minimize your web application's load times?

    A. Configure a latency-based routing policy.

    B. Configure a weighted routing policy, with the weights heavily oriented toward New York, where the application's data center is located.

    C. Implement a simple routing policy to route all US-based traffic to New York with the least delay.

    D. Run the application in a London data center.

24. Which of the following are good ways to restrict access to your web content stored on CloudFront edge locations? (Choose two)

    A. Signed cookies

    B. Signed URLs

    C. Georestrictive polices

    D. Origin access identity

25. When you terminate an EC2 instance after having assigned it an Elastic IP, what happens to the Elastic IP that you've assigned?

    A. The Elastic IP remains associated with your AWS account, and you'll continue to be charged for it.

    B. The Elastic IP is disassociated from your AWS account.

    C. The Elastic IP remains associated with your AWS account, but you won't be charged for it.

    D. The Elastic IP goes back to the pool of AWS's available IP addresses.

26. You are using AWS Direct Connect to connect to your Amazon VPC. How do you configure your networking so you can use Direct Connect while keeping your Amazon VPC without connectivity to the Internet?

    A. Configure only a VPN gateway for your VPC.

    B. Configure a Direct Connect gateway for your VPC.

    C. Configure an Internet gateway and a VPN gateway for your VPC.

    D. Configure just a local Internet gateway.

27. Which of the following is true regarding the differences between a private subnet and a public subnet in an Amazon VPC?

    A. The public subnet's route table has a route to the Internet gateway, and the private subnet's route table doesn't have one.

    B. The public subnet's route table has a route to network address translation (NAT), and the public subnet's route table doesn't have one.

    C. A private subnet has a security group, and a public subnet doesn't have one.

    D. A private subnet has a network ACL associated with it, and a public subnet doesn't.

Answers

  1. D. To establish a highly available connection, you must set up a virtual private gateway and configure two customer gateways, so you can avoid a single point of failure.

  2. D. An instance inside a private subnet can't be accessed directly by anyone from the Internet. Rather, they'd have to access it from within a VPC, thus providing an additional layer of security.

  3. B. Lower, not higher, latency is a benefit of Direct Connect, since it is on a managed network. All the other alternatives point to benefits offered by Direct Connect.

  4. B. A default VPC comes with a route table that reflects the Internet gateway, which is part of the default VPC.

  5. C. CloudFront doesn't wait until the entire file completes downloading and doesn't perform any error checking. It forwards the file to the users as soon as it gets the first bytes of the file.

  6. A, C. CloudFront can speed up the delivery of content by avoiding a new trip to the origin server each time a user needs to view a file. In addition, latency-based routing of DNS requests will route the user requests to the faster of the two locations.

  7. C, D. An Internet gateway provides a target in your VPC for Internet-routable traffic. In addition, an Internet gateway performs NAT for instances with assigned IPv4 addresses.

  8. A, D. Security groups control inbound and outbound traffic for your EC2 instances. Network ACLs control inbound and outbound traffic for your subnets.

  9. B, C, D. VPC flow log output will show traffic from a single source to a specific port. Amazon GuardDuty (discussed in Chapter 11) reports on suspicious EC2 network activity. Finally, operating system logs will show evidence of any brute-force attacks.

 10. A. Access logs offer the most comprehensive information, such as details about the IP addresses from which the client requests are coming. The information is more detailed than that offered by Amazon CloudWatch.

11. **A, C.** You can modify the main route table any time, and the main table doesn't contain a route to the Internet gateway by default.

12. **D.** CloudFront doesn't wait for the file download to complete. It starts forwarding the files to the user as soon as the first byte arrives from the origin server.

13. **A, B.** A is correct because, for static content, the origin server can be an S3 bucket or an HTTP server (run on an EC2 instance or on-premises). B is correct because for distributing media files on demand, the origin server must be an S3 bucket.

14. **C.** You must ensure that the security group has a rule that allows traffic to and from the new port for the health check.

15. **A, B, C.** Direct Connect offers consistently lower network latency, lowers your network data transfer costs, and lets you establish a private virtual interface from your on-premise network directly to your VPC.

16. **A, B.** Security groups let you filter only on destination ports, and not source ports. An inbound rule consists of the traffic source and the destination port (or port range). An outbound rule contains the traffic destination and the destination port (or port range).

17. **D.** You can create a flow log for a VPC, subnet, or network interface.

18. **A, C.** Security groups are stateful and allow all responses to traffic it has allowed to go out of the network, even if the security group's rules don't permit it. Network ACLs are stricter in a sense, because they are stateless but allow responses to allowed traffic only if the network ACL rules permit it.

19. **C.** You can use route tables, network ACLs, and security groups to control routing both within a VPC and into and out of a VPC.

20. **A, B, C.** An alias record type can point to a CloudFront distribution, an Elastic Beanstalk environment, an Amazon S3 bucket that you've configured as a static web site, an Application Load Balancer, or another Route 53 resource record set in the same hosted zone.

21. **B, C.** When you call the invalidation API to remove an object, it removes all copies of the object from all CloudFront edge locations. AWS recommends that you use object versioning instead of calling the invalidation API because of the many benefits offered by object versioning, including lower costs.

22. **B, C.** A security group applies to an instance only after you specify the security group when launching an instance or if you associate a security group with the instance later. A network ACL automatically applies to all instances in the subnets the network ACL is associated with.

23. **A.** AWS creates latency record sets in an AWS region, and not on a customer's location. Your web application's latency measurement isn't based on its data center location (New York). Rather, the latency is based on the AWS region with which you've associated this record. Instead of associating the resource record with the London region, associate it with the us-east-1 region, located in the eastern U.S.

24. A, B. Signed cookies and signed URLs are the most effective ways to control access to content stored in the edge locations.

25. A. Elastic IPs are associated with your AWS account and not to EC2 instances to which you may assign them. When you delete the EC2 instance, the Elastic IP remains associated with your account, and you'll be charged for it, to keep you from accumulating too many unused Elastic IPs.

26. A. By configuring just a VPN gateway and not an Internet gateway as well, you can use AWS Direct Connect without opening up your EC2 instances to the public Internet.

27. A. The route table in a public subnet has a route to the Internet gateway, whereas the route table in a private subnet doesn't have one.

Storage and Archiving in the AWS Cloud

In this chapter, you will

- Learn how Amazon Elastic Block Storage (EBS) provides block-level storage volumes for use with your EC2 instances
- See how Amazon Simple Storage Service (S3) provides object storage in the AWS cloud
- Understand Amazon S3 Glacier, a storage service optimized for infrequently accessed data that's ideal for data archiving and backup storage
- Learn how Amazon Elastic File System (EFS) provides scalable file storage for your EC2 instances
- Learn about Amazon Snowball, a service that helps you transport large quantities of data to and from AWS with the help of an AWS-provided storage appliance
- Learn about the Amazon Storage Gateway, a service that connects your on-premise software appliances with AWS S3 storage

This chapter discusses the various storage options offered by AWS. These storage options are wide ranging—from object storage in the cloud, to an elastic file system that lets you access an AWS-based file system as a local file system.

Overview of AWS Storage Options

AWS offers a broad range of storage options that offer plenty of flexibility. You can move between various storage tiers and storage types at any time. Your goal is to choose the AWS storage option that suits your organization's needs, including cost, availability, durability, and performance considerations. Before you consider the various storage alternatives offered by AWS, you must identify your storage requirements.

Identifying Your Storage Requirements

There's no one AWS storage type that suits all workloads. Different storage types are geared toward different purposes, such as durability, speed of access, cost efficiency, and security. You must therefore understand the performance profiles of your workloads and choose a specific storage type that matches each type of workload that you manage.

Following are the key factors that determine the type of storage required for a workload:

- **Performance**   You can measure performance in terms of throughput, or IOPS (I/O per second). Throughput (measured in megabytes per second) is the amount of data transferred in a set time period; IOPS relates to the latency or speed of data access. Some workloads require a high throughput, while others require a high IOPS. AWS offers storage types that are optimized for either, so you can pick the right storage for your needs.

- **Availability**   This criterion measures the ability of the storage volumes to return data when it's requested.

- **Frequency of data access**   AWS offers storage types designed for frequent, less frequent, or infrequent access to data.

- **Data durability**   If your data is critical and must be stored indefinitely, you must choose the storage type that meets these requirements. Transient data such as clickstream and Twitter data, for example, doesn't require high durability, because it's not critical data.

- **Data sensitivity**   Some types of data are critical from a business point of view, and others are critical from a security or regulatory point of view.

- **Cost of storage**   Probably one of the most important criteria in choosing the storage type is the cost of storing data. Your storage budget, the importance of the data that you store, and the speed with which you must retrieve the data are pertinent factors in evaluating the storage cost factor.

Choosing the right AWS storage service means that you evaluate these key storage-related factors, keeping in mind your budget, compliance and regulatory requirements, and your application requirements for availability, durability, and performance of the data storage.

AWS Storage Categories

AWS offers three basic storage service categories: *object*, *block*, and *file*. Each of these storage services satisfies a different set of storage requirements, thus providing you a way to choose the storage service, or services, that work best for you.

Object Storage

Amazon S3 is an all-purpose object storage option that offers the highest level of data durability and availability in the AWS cloud. Object storage means that the files that you store in this type of storage are saved as *single objects*, and not as data blocks. If you store a file sized 40MB, it's saved as a single, 40MB-sized object in S3.

As you'll learn in the next section, block storage is provided as mountable storage volumes that you can format and use. Object storage is completely different from block storage in this regard: With block storage, you don't have direct access to the object storage volumes in S3; instead, you use APIs to make calls to the S3 service to read, write, update, or delete data that you store in S3 buckets. (I describe buckets and the objects that you store in them in the sections "Buckets" and "Objects," later in the chapter.)

As with most AWS object storage types, S3 is a *regional service*. The data that you store in S3 is automatically replicated across several data centers in different availability zones (AZs). This is a true advantage of S3 storage, because if you had to provide the same level of data durability on your own, you'd need to store your data in multiple data centers.

A key difference in the way you work with S3 and EBS (block storage) is that with S3, there's no need for you to provision the storage. Use whatever storage you need, and AWS bills you for that storage volume. This is much simpler than provisioning several EBS volumes ahead of time and having to pay for all those volumes, regardless of your usage of those volumes.

S3 comes in three *storage tiers* for hot, warm, and cold data. To optimize your storage costs, you can move data between the three storage tiers based on how your data changes over time. *Hot data* is data that your applications and services request quite frequently. *Cold data* is data that you access infrequently or rarely (such as archived data and backup data). *Warm data* falls in between the hot and cold data types, in terms of cost and the speed of access. The hotter data costs the most to store but is much faster to access. The reverse is true of the coldest data—it's the cheapest to store but slowest in access time.

S3 is ideal for storing unstructured data such as media content. Here's how the three S3 storage tiers differ:

- **Amazon S3 Standard** Delivers low latency and high throughput and is ideal for storing frequently accessed data, such as cloud applications, gaming, dynamic web sites, and data analytics.

- **Amazon S3 Standard – Infrequent Access (Amazon S3 Standard – IA)** Ideal for less frequently accessed data, such as backup data. It's cheaper than S3 Standard, but it also costs more to retrieve or transfer data.

- **Amazon Glacier** Ideal for storing data long-term—for example, storing data for meeting compliance and regulatory requirements. There are various methods to retrieve data from Glacier that differ in their speed and cost of access. You can't retrieve data that you store on Glacier immediately; retrieval can take a few minutes to several hours. So use Glacier when you don't need to retrieve the data often and you can afford to wait a long time to view it. In addition, content can't be searched or served directly from Glacier storage, unlike other S3 storage types.

Here's the pricing structure for S3 storage as of February 2019, based on the US East (N. Virginia) prices (costs may vary across AWS regions):

S3 Storage Tier	Monthly Charge per GB Storage
Amazon S3 Standard	0.023 (first 50TB per month)
Amazon S3 Standard – IA	$0.0125 (plus an additional retrieval charge of $0.01 per GB)
Amazon Glacier	$0.004

As you can tell, there's an inverse relationship between the speed of access and its cost. AWS charges you only for usage of S3 storage, so it doesn't bill you on the basis of your provisioned S3 storage. Take advantage of this by using S3 wherever possible.

Block Storage

Amazon EBS is block-level storage that you can use with EC2 instances. Files are stored in block storage volumes (similar to hard drives), and data is divided into chunks, or blocks, of a certain size, such as 512-byte blocks. A file of 20KB in size could be chunked into 40 blocks, for example. The OS tracks each of the data blocks independently of the other blocks.

The block storage that your provision with EBS is in the form of disk drives that are mountable to EC2 instances. The drives come unformatted, and you can format them and specify their block sizes. Although the Amazon Machine Image (AMI) you may use determines things such as the block size, you can make changes to a drive by specifying attributes such as the format and the file size of the disk drives.

An EBS volume can be a boot volume or a data volume. You can make the same EBS volume serve as both a boot and a data volume, but this means that you'll need to shut down the instance when resizing the volume. Many EC2 servers are stateless, so there's no need to maintain separate boot and data volumes for those instances.

Although a boot volume (root device volume) is automatically destroyed when you terminate an instance, additional EBS volumes that you've attached to an instance (data volumes) are independent of the instance lifecycle, and thus stay intact after instance termination if the Delete on Termination option is not selected. Once you attach the block storage to an instance, you can copy, share, resize, restore, and detach the drives as you'd do with any other disk drive.

 NOTE AWS is aware of an EBS volume's properties such as encryption, IOPS, and size, but it can't see what's on the blocks of the block storage volumes.

EBS storage is meant for storing data that requires both long-term persistence and quick access. There are two types of block stage: *solid-state drive* (SSD) and *hard disk drive* (HDD). Here are the differences between the two EBS block storage types:

- SSD storage is best for transactional workloads, where you need high performance with a high IOPS. You can choose from the following SSD types:
  - **SSD Provisioned IOPS SSD (io1)** If your workloads are latency sensitive and require a minimum guaranteed IOPS, the io1 SSD volumes are right for you. These storage volumes require you to pay separately for the Provisioned IOPS you ask for.
  - **EBS General Purpose SSD (gp2)** The gp2 SSD volumes offer a cost and performance balance and are meant for general use where you don't need high levels of Provisioned IOPS. The gp2 volumes cost less than the io1 volumes.

- HDD storage disks are designed for throughput-heavy workloads such as data warehouses. As with Provisioned IOPS SDD, you have two choices:

  - **Throughput Optimized HDD (st1)**   The st1 volumes are optimized for frequently accessed workloads.

  - **Cold HDD (sc1)**   The sc1 volumes are designed for infrequently accessed workloads.

TIP   AWS charges for all the EBS volumes that you provision, regardless of your usage of those volumes. For S3 and EFS, however, AWS charges you only for what you use, and not for what you provision.

Here's the pricing structure for EBS storage as of February 2019, based on the US East (N. Virginia) prices:

EBS Storage Type	Monthly Charge per GB Storage
General Purpose SSD (gp2)	$0.10 per GB-month of provisioned storage
Provisioned IOPS SSD (io1)	$0.125 per GB-month of provisioned storage plus $0.065 per Provisioned IOPS-month
Throughput Optimized HDD (st1)	$0.0.45 per GB-month of provisioned storage
Cold HDD (sc1)	$0.025 per GB-month of provisioned storage

Not only is EBS Provisioned IOPS storage more expensive, but you pay for the EBS volumes that you provision, *regardless of the extent of your usage*. Therefore, you must consider using these volumes only if your applications strongly demand the Provisioned IOPS.

File Storage

Amazon EFS provides scalable file storage for your EC2 instances without your having to provision storage. Big data, content management, and web serving applications can benefit from EFS file storage. Its fast file synchronization capability enables you to synchronize your on-premise files to EFS at speeds that are up to five times faster than normal Linux copy mechanisms.

In the same N. Virginia region as in the previous two cases (S3 and EBS), EFS storage costs you $0.30 per GB-month. EFS is, therefore, generally more expensive than EBS and S3, but you don't need to provision storage; instead, you can simply use EFS for scalable file storage.

In Chapter 3, I discussed the instance store as a storage option. The instance store is also a block storage type but is often referred to as *ephemeral storage* because it's best for temporary work, not for persistent storage such as EBS. Instance storage, unlike EBS storage volumes, isn't separate from the instance. It's located on the same hardware as an instance and its cost is included in that of the instance per hour. This means that when you stop the instance, the instance volume isn't available and all data on it is lost. You can run a root volume on the instance store instead of an EBS volume, but if you do, you can't really stop the instance, as a stop terminates the instance.

Unlike EBS volumes, which you can attach to all EC2 instance types, some instance types don't support instance stores; they support only EBS volumes. Also, unlike EBS volumes, you can choose an instance store–based storage volume only when creating an instance, but not later. Finally, any encryption that you want to perform for the data on instance store volumes is at the OS level, and you're fully responsible for it.

Now that you have a basic idea of the various AWS storage options, it's time to dive into the details of each of the key storage choices.

 TIP   As a best practice, tag all your EC2 resources such as EBS volumes. Tagging helps you easily keep track of your resource inventory.

Amazon Elastic Block Storage

Amazon Elastic Block Storage (EBS) provides block storage volumes that you can attach to your EC2 instances. You can use the volumes like any other physical hard drives. The EC2 instance can format the EBS volume with a file system such as ext3 or ext4 and use the volume as it would any local physical drive. Once you attach the EBS volumes to an EC2 instance, they persist independently from the instance, meaning that they'll remain intact after you terminate the instance, unlike instance store volumes, which are ephemeral.

AWS recommends that you use EBS volumes when you require quick access and want to store data for long periods. Thus, EBS volumes work well for storing file systems and databases, and they are the best choice when you need raw, unformatted block-level storage. EBS volumes are appropriate for applications that perform random reads and writes and for throughput-heavy applications that perform massive continuous reads or writes.

An EBS volume and the EC2 instance to which you attach the volume must belong to the same AZ. You can attach multiple EBS volumes of varying sizes to an EC2 instance, but you can attach an EBS volume only to one EC2 instance at any time.

Benefits of Amazon EBS Storage

EBS storage volumes offer several benefits:

- **Persistent storage**   EBS volumes live independently of the EC2 instance to which you attach the volumes. However, you continue to pay for the volumes even if you terminate the instance. Data on an EBS volume stays intact through instance starts and terminations. The data remains persistently on the volumes until you delete the data. When you delete an EBS volume, AWS will zero-out (wipe out all data from the disk) the volume before assigning it to other AWS accounts. By default, the volumes are detached from an instance upon instance termination, and you can reattach them to another EC2 instance, if you want.

- **Dynamic changes** If you use a current generation EBS volume by attaching it to a current generation EC2 instance type, you can increase the instance size, the Provisioned IOPS capacity, and the instance type while the volume continues to be attached to the EC2 instance.

- **Snapshots for backups** You can create backups of EBS volumes in the form of snapshots and store the snapshots in Amazon S3 in multiple AZs. You pay for the S3 storage charges based on the EBS volume size. EBS backups are *incremental backups*, which means that for newer snapshots, you pay only for the data that's beyond the volume's original size.

- **Replication** AWS automatically replicates an EBS volume in the AZ in which you create the volume.

- **Encryption** You can encrypt your EBS volumes to satisfy various data-at-rest encryption requirements or regulations. The snapshots that you make of an encrypted EBS volume are automatically encrypted. To protect your sensitive data, it's a best practice to encrypt data or use EBS-encrypted volumes.

Enhancing EBS Performance and Best Practices

For best performance, AWS recommends that you use an EBS-optimized instance. EBS optimization offers the best performance for EBS volumes by minimizing the network contention between EBS I/O and the other traffic flowing to and from an EC2 instance. Depending on the EC2 instance type, an EBS-optimized instance provides a dedicated bandwidth that's between 425 Mbps and 14,000 Mbps.

You can choose from various EBS volume types, each of which offers a performance delivery that's guaranteed to be very near to its baseline and burst (when workload is heavy) performance if you attach it to an EBS-optimized instance. For instance, General Purpose (gp2) EBS volumes will deliver performance that's within 10 percent of their baseline and burst performance, 99 percent of the time, throughout a year. So if you want guaranteed disk performance to meet the needs of your critical applications, use EBS-optimized EC2 instances.

In addition to configuring EBS-optimized instances, you may want to consider following these best practices for getting the most of your EBS storage volumes:

- Instead of attaching just a single EBS volume to an instance, consider stringing together multiple EBS volumes in a RAID 0 configuration to take advantage of the maximum bandwidth for the instance.

- For the st1 and sc1 EBS volume types (described in the following section), consider increasing the read-ahead setting to 1MB to achieve the maximum throughput for your read-heavy workloads. This setting is ideal for workloads with large sequential I/Os (but detrimental to workloads that consist of many small, or random, I/Os).

- If you create an EBS snapshot from an EBS backup, it pays to initialize the volume ahead of time by accessing all the blocks in the volume before making the volume accessible to users and applications. This strategy avoids a significant latency hit when an application first accesses a data block on the restored EBS volume.

EBS Volume Types

Amazon EBS offers the following EBS volume types:

- General Purpose SSD (gp2)
- Provisioned IOPS SSD (io1)
- Throughput Optimized HDD (st1)
- Cold HDD (sc1)
- Magnetic (standard, a previous-generation type)

I discuss the first four volume types in this chapter. These four EBS volume types differ in performance and price, and you should choose the volume that best fits your performance and cost requirements. The main difference among the instance types is their price/performance ratio.

Throughput and I/O per second (IOPS) are the key performance attributes of a disk. *Throughput* is the rate at which data is processed. For the two HDD volume types, which are throughput oriented, the dominant performance attribute is *mebibyte per second* (MiBps). *IOPS* are a unit of measure (the operations are measured in *kibibytes*, or KiB) representing input/output operations per second. For the two SSD volume types, the dominant performance attribute is IOPS.

The four volume types fall under two broad categories:

- **SSD-backed volumes**   For workloads that involve heavy read/write operations of small I/O size and whose primary performance attribute is IOPS. They can offer a maximum of 64,000 IOPS, whereas the HDD storage type can offer 500 IOPS at best.

- **HDD-backed volumes**   For large workloads where high throughput (MiBps) is more important than IOPS.

Before we delve into the performance details of the four types of EBS volumes, you need to understand two key concepts that play a role here: the *bucket and credit model*, which involves burst performance, and *throughput and I/O credits*.

Bucket and Credit Model: I/O and Throughput Credits and Burst Performance

When evaluating the four volume types, you should consider two important interrelated concepts: *burst performance* and *I/O and throughput credits*, which together are referred to as the *bucket and credit model*. Of the four volume types, three instance types—gp2 (General Purpose SSD), st1 (Throughput Optimized HDD), and sc1 (Cold HDD)—use the bucket and credit model for performance.

The performance of a volume depends directly on the size of the volume. The larger the volume, the higher the baseline performance level in terms of IOPS or throughput, depending on the type of disk. Often, a disk volume is expected to support a sustained increase in IOPS or throughput required by the workload. For example, a database may require a high throughput when you're performing a scheduled backup. You obviously don't want to pay the cost of a more powerful volume type just because your workload may spike at times. Ideally, your volumes should be able to support the higher throughput or IOPS for short periods of time by being able to burst through their provisioned performance levels when the workload demands it.

AWS provides I/O and throughput credits to enable a volume to burst occasionally through its baseline performance. I/O and throughput credits represent the ability of a volume to acquire additional capability to burst beyond its baseline performance to reach the higher performance level that you require for a short period. There is a maximum on the number of IOPS or throughput for the burst performance. Each volume receives an *initial I/O credit balance* and the volumes add to their I/O at a certain rate per second, based on the volume size.

 NOTE The baseline IOPS or throughput performance level is the rate at which a volume earns I/O or throughput credits.

For a volume type with IOPS as the dominant performance attribute (such as gp2), burst performance provides the ability to go above their minimum IOPS for an extended period. Once the volume uses up its credit balance, the maximum IOPS performance stays at the baseline IOPS performance level. At this point, the volume starts acquiring (earning) I/O credits. The IOPS performance of the volume can again exceed the baseline performance if its I/O demands fall below the baseline level, and as a result, more credits are added to its I/O credit balance. Larger drives accumulate I/O credits faster since their baseline performance is higher.

For a volume type with throughput (MiBps) as its dominant performance attribute (such as st1), burst performance means the volume can support higher throughput than the baseline throughput of the volume. Once a volume uses up all its I/O or throughput credit balance (the maximum IOPS or throughput), the volume reverts to its base IOPS or throughput performance.

Now that you've learned the key concepts of throughput credits and burst performance, you're ready to learn the details of the four types of EBS storage volumes. It's easy to analyze the performance characteristics of the various volume types by focusing on the SSD and HDD drives separately. As I go through the various volume types, I describe the bucket and credit model in greater detail where it's relevant.

Hard Disk Drives

HDD-backed volumes are throughput optimized and are ideal for large workloads where you are focusing on throughput rather than IOPS. There are two types of HDD: Throughput Optimized HDD (st1) and Cold HDD (sc1).

Throughput Optimized HDD (st1)   Throughput Optimized HDD storage provides low-cost HDD volumes (magnetic storage) designed for frequently accessed, throughput-heavy sequential workloads such as those you encounter when working with data warehouses or big data environments such as a Hadoop cluster. You measure performance for a st1 volume in terms of throughput, and not IOPS. Throughput Optimized HDD volume sizes range from 500GiB to 16TiB.

As with the gp2 volume type (discussed in the following sections), st1 volumes rely on the burst bucket performance model, with the volume size determining both the baseline throughput, the rate at which throughput credits accrue, and the burst throughput of the volume. Remember that an HDD volume (such as st1) bases its bursting on throughput (measured in MiBps), and not on IOPS, as an SSD volume (such as gp2), which uses IOPS as the criterion for bursting.

You can calculate the available throughput of an st1 volume with the following formula:

$$\text{Throughput} = (\text{size of the volume}) \times (\text{credit accrual rate per TiB})$$

Let's take, for example, a small st1 volume, sized 1TiB. Its base throughput is 40 MiBps, meaning that it can fill its credit bucket with I/O credits at the rate of 40 MiBps. The maximum size of its credit bucket is 1TiB worth of credits. You can calculate the baseline throughput of a 5TB-sized volume thus:

$$\text{Throughput} = 5 \times 40 \text{ MiBps} / 1\text{TiB} = 200 \text{ MiBps}$$

The *baseline*, or *base throughput*, ranges from 20 MiBps to 500 MiBps for volumes ranging from 0.5 to 16TiB. The maximum of 500 MiBps is reached by a volume sized 12.5TiB:

$$12.5\text{TiB} \times 40 \text{ MiBps} / 1\text{TiB} = 500 \text{ MiBps}$$

Burst throughput starts at 250 MiBps per tebibyte (TiB) and is capped at 500 MiBps. You will hit the cap at a volume size of 2TiB:

$$\text{TiB} \times 250 \text{ MiBps} / 1\text{TiB} = 500 \text{ MiBps}$$

Figure 7-1 shows the relationship between st1 volume size and throughput. You can see that both burst throughput and base throughput max out at 500 MiBps.

Cold HDD (sc1)   Cold HDD (sc1) offers the lowest-cost HDD volumes; it's designed for workloads that you access infrequently. These volumes are ideal where cost, rather than the access speed, is your main objective.

The sc1 type volume ranges in size from 0.5TiB to 16TiB. The sc1 volume type uses a burst-bucket performance model and works like the st1 model discussed earlier. For a small 1TiB sc1 volume, the credit bucket fills at the rate of 12 MiBps, with a maximum of 1TiB of credits. Its burst throughput is capped at 80 MiBps.

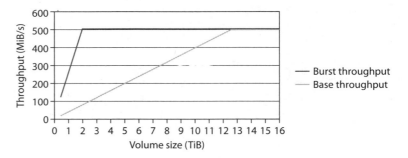

Figure 7-1
Relationship between an st1 volume's size and its throughput

You use the same formula as for the st1 volume type to calculate the baseline throughput for sc1. To figure out the baseline throughput for the largest-sized sc1 type volume:

16 TiB × 12 MiBps / 1TiB = 192 MiBps

The maximum burst throughput is capped at 250 MiBps, and you reach this level with a 3.125TiB volume as shown here:

TiB × 80 MiBps / 1TiB = 250 MiBps

NOTE The four EBS volume types I discussed here all fall under the Current Generation volume type. To cut your storage costs, you can also use a magnetic or standard volume for storing data that you rarely access. The magnetic volumes range in size from 1GiB (gibibyte) to 1TiB and support roughly 1000 IOPS.

Choosing Between the st1 and sc1 HDD Volume Types   The scan time for reading data is a critical performance indicator for both HDD types (st1 and sc1). *Scan time* is the time it takes to complete a full volume scan and is a function of the volume size and throughput of the volume:

scan time = volume size / throughput

Regardless of the volume size, the scan times for the sc1 HDD type are much longer (almost twice as long) than the scan times for the st1 HDD type. If you often need to support workloads that involve many full volume scans, it's a good idea to go for st1. The sc1 volume type is suitable for workloads that you access infrequently, and where scan performance isn't important.

Finally, for both HDD types st1 and sc1, the throughput is the smaller of the volume throughput and the instance throughput.

TIP   High performance storage requires sufficient network bandwidth. If you're planning on using a Provisioned IOPS SSD (io1) volume type, or either of the HDD volume types (st1 and sc1), it's a good idea to attach the EBS volume either to an EBS-optimized instance or to an EC2 instance with 10Gb network connectivity.

Solid-State Drives

Solid-state drives (SSDs) are designed for high performance. There are two types of SSD-backed volumes: General Purpose SSD (gp2) and Provisioned IOPS SSD (io1).

General Purpose SSD (gp2)   General Purpose SSD (gp2) volumes offer a balance between price and performance and are suitable for many workloads, such as interactive applications that require low latency, as well as large development and test databases.

The gp2 volumes offer very fast performance, with single-digit millisecond latencies. A gp2 volume can range in size from 1GiB to 16TiB. The volumes have a baseline performance that scales linearly at 3 IOPS/GiB and can burst to a maximum of

3000 IOPS for extended period of time. A 100GiB gp2 volume, then, has a baseline of 300 IOPS (3×100), and a 1TiB volume has a 3000 IOPS baseline performance. The minimum performance is 100 IOPS (at 33.33GiB and smaller sized volumes) and the maximum IOPS is 16,000, offered by large gp2 volumes sized at 5334GiB and higher, up to a maximum size of 16TiB. A gp2 volume delivers 90 percent of its provisioned performance 99 percent of the time.

A key point that you must understand here is that when you attach multiple EBS volumes to an EC2 instance, the maximum amount of performance for that instance is calculated as the combined performance of all the EBS volumes that you've attached to the instance. As Table 7-1 shows, the maximum IOPS for gp2 volumes is 16,000 IOPS. You can attain this performance with a single, large gp2 volume sized 16GiB (the maximum size for a gp2 volume), or you can cobble together a set of four 4TiB-sized gp2 volumes and stripe them as a single RAID 0 device, giving you a logical gp2 volume sized 16TiB, with a combined performance of 64,000 IOPS.

Each gp2 volume comes with an initial I/O credit balance of 5.4 million I/O credits. For smaller (under 1TiB) gp2 volumes, these I/O credits can sustain a maximum burst performance of 3000 IOPS for 30 minutes. The volumes earn I/O credits at the baseline performance rate of 3 IOPS per GiB of volume size. A 500GiB-sized volume will thus have a baseline performance of 1500 IOPS.

When a gp2 volume requires more IOPS than its baseline performance level, it draws down the I/O credits it has accumulated in its credit balance. A volume can use its I/O credits to burst to a maximum of 3000 IOPS. For example, a volume sized 500GiB has a baseline performance of 1500 IOPS and offers a maximum burst duration of 1 hour at 3000 IOPS.

Figure 7-2 shows how both baseline performance and burst IOPS are based on the size of a gp2 volume.

 NOTE For a gp2 volume type, EBS will deliver the performance you provision 99 percent of the time.

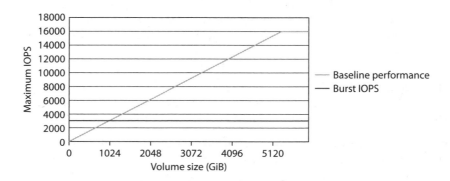

Figure 7-2 Volume size and maximum IOPS for a gp2 EBS volume

A volume's ability to burst beyond its baseline performance is based on the I/O credits that the volume accumulates at a rate of 3 credits per GiB of provisioned storage per second. Once the burst performance window opens, the volume consumes the credits at the rate of 3 credits per IOPS. A volume can accumulate a maximum of 54 million credits, which means that it can burst for a maximum of 3000 IOPS for 30 minutes. After the volume exhausts all its credits, its performance falls back to its baseline performance.

Burst performance and I/O credits are applicable only to volumes under 1000GiB. For these volumes, burst performance is allowed to exceed their baseline performance. A 16TiB-sized volume (the largest-sized volume in the gp2 volume type) has a baseline performance of 16,000 IOPS, which is greater than the maximum burst performance, and, therefore, it always has a positive I/O credit balance. This maximum 16,000 IOPS baseline performance is for volumes sized 5334GiB and higher. For all volumes sized 5334GiB to 16,384MiB (the 16TiB maximum volume size for a gp2 volume), the baseline performance remains at the maximum level of 16,000 IOPS.

 NOTE A gp2 volume larger than 1000GiB has a baseline performance that's equal to or greater than the maximum burst performance, which is 3000 IOPS. Their I/O credit balance never depletes as well.

You can use the following formula to calculate the burst duration of a volume, which is directly related to volume size:

$$\text{burst duration} = \text{credit balance} / \text{burst IOPS} - 3 \ (\text{volume size})$$

Provisioned IOPS SSD (io1) Provisioned IOPS SSD (io1) volumes are the most expensive as well as the highest-performance storage volumes and are ideal for missional-critical business applications such as online transaction processing databases that rely on low latency operations, as well as high throughput–demanding large NoSQL databases such as Cassandra and MongoDB.

 TIP Because of Provisioned IOPS storage's much higher cost, you shouldn't choose it when a cheaper gp2 volume can provide the same baseline IOPS.

Minimum and Maximum IOPS It's a good idea to mention the minimum and maximum IOPS you can specify for a Provisioned IOPS volume. AWS recommends that you specify a minimum of 2 IOPS for each GiB of a Provisioned IOPS volume. This is to ensure adequate performance and minimize latency. So, if you're provisioning a gp2 volume sized 6000GiB, you assure that the volume has a performance of at least 12,000 IOPS.

There's also a maximum amount of IOPS that you can provision for a Provisioned IOPS volume. You can specify a maximum of 50 IOPS per GiB unto a maximum of 20,000 IOPS per volume. So, you can provision a 200GiB-sized gp2 volume for 10,000 IOPS. You can provision a gpc2 volume sized 400GiB or higher for the maximum amount of IOPS.

EC2 Instance Maximum IOPS and Throughput There's a practical limit to the number of IOPS and throughput that you can provision for a single EC2 instance. The maximum IOPS a single EC2 instance can handle is set at 65,000 IOPS. If you need more IOPS than this for your applications, you must provision multiple instances.

As with IOPS, there's also a practical limit on the throughput a single EC2 instance can handle. If you turn on EBS optimization for a volume, the instance can achieve a 12 GiBps maximum throughput.

You can specify from 100 to 64,000 IOPS per a single Provisioned IOPS SSD volume. The maximum ratio of Provisioned IOPS to volume size is 50. This means that a 200GiB io1 volume can be provisioned with a maximum of 10,000 IOPS. As mentioned earlier, the maximum IOPS you can provision is 64,000 IOPS per volume, Thus, for a volume that's 1280GiB or larger, you can provision up to the 64,000 IOPS maximum, since 1280GiB × 50 IOPS = 64,000 IOPS.

 NOTE EBS delivers the IOPS performance that's within 10 percent of the rate you specify, 99.99 percent of the time during a year.

Provisioned IOPS SSD volumes range in size from 4GiB to 16TiB, with the 16TiB-sized volume offering a maximum of 32,000 IOPS. This volume type doesn't use the bucket and credit performance model like the gp2 volumes. Instead, it lets you specify the IOPS you require, and EBS will deliver that performance. If you're using a gp2 volume and find that your workloads require IOPS of greater than 16,000 IOPS (maximum offered by a gp2 volume type) for long periods, you may consider the Provisioned IOPS volume type.

Comparing the EBS Volume Types

Table 7-1 shows the performance storage characteristics of each of the four EBS volume types.

Volume Type	Solid-State Drives (SSD)		Hard Disk Drives (HDD)	
	General Purpose SSD (gp2)	Provisioned IOPS SSD (io1)	Throughput Optimized HDD (st1)	Cold HDD (sc1)
Volume Size	1GiB–16TiB	4GiB–16TiB	500GiB–16TiB	500GiB–16TiB
Max. IOPS/Volume	16,000	64,000	500	250
Max. Throughput/Volume	250 MiBps	1000 MiBps	500 MiBps	250 MiBps
Max. IOPS/Instance	80,000	80,000	80,000	80,000
Max. Throughput/Instance	1750 MiBps	1750 MiBps	1750 MiBps	1750 MiBps
Dominant Performance Attribute	IOPS	IOPS	MiBps	MiBps

Table 7-1 EBS Volume Types and Their Performance and Storage Characteristics

NOTE Although Table 7-1 indicates that the maximum throughput per instance (for all volumes types) is 1750 MiBps, not all instance types support this high a throughput. You must launch an r4.8xlarge or an x1.32xlarge to get this throughput.

Now that you know a bit about IOPS and throughput performance, and IOPS and throughput–related bursting behaviors of the various EBS volume types, let's compare several aspects of the EBS volume types. We'll look at cost, maximum throughput, and maximum IOPS.

Pricing and Cost A Provisioned IOPS volume is the most expensive storage volume type, since it not only costs more per GB-month of storage, but you also must pay an additional $0.05 per Provisioned IOPS per month (at current prices). So if you use a 10,000 IOPS volume, it's going to cost you $650 a month on top of the storage cost per month.

If you focus just on the cost per GB-month, the Cold HDD (sc1) volume type may look like the best choice. However, there's a minimum size of 500GiB for a sc1 volume. If you're storing only 20GiB of data, then you'll be paying for a lot more storage than you need.

Maximum Throughput You can compute throughput as a product of the IOPS offered by a volume type and the packet size. Both Throughput Optimized HDD (st1) and Cold HDD (sc1) have very small maximum IOPS (500 for st1 and 250 for sc1), and thus have a small maximum throughput, especially for small random writes. A General Purpose SSD (gp2) volume, on the other hand, offers the highest throughput for such small random writes, at 16,000 IOPS. With a maximum IOPS of 64,000 a Provisioned IOPS SSD volume (io1) offers four times more maximum throughput that a gp2 volume (1000MiB versus 250MiB).

Maximum IOPS Table 7-1 showed the maximum IOPS for all the volume types. EBS specifies the IOPS ratings based on 16KB-sized packets for the SSD volumes and 1MB packets for the HDD volumes. You can go to a maximum packet size of 256KB for SSD volumes and 1MB for HDD volumes.

The difference in the sizing of the packets for the SSD and HDD volumes helps SSD volumes efficiently process a large number of small packets, while HDD handles fewer large packets more efficiently.

Packet size has a huge bearing on the IOPS for a volume and could lead to a lower IOPS than the rated IOPS for the volume. For example, a 100GiB-sized gp2 volume is rated at 300 IOPS if the packet size is 16KB. The 300 random read/write operations are sustained only if the packet size remains at or under 16KB. Should the packet size increase, say to an average of 64KB, the 100GiB volume can support read/write operations at the rate of only 75 IOPS.

Managing Amazon EBS

To use an EBS volume to store your data persistently, you must create the volume and attach it to an EC2 instance. In this section, I'll show you how to perform common EBS-related administrative tasks such as the following:

- Create an EBS volume
- Attach an EBS volume to an EC2 instance
- Make an EBS volume available for use
- Detach an EBS volume
- Delete an EBS volume

Creating an EBS Volume

You can create and attach an EBS volume when launching an EC2 instance or create the volume and attach it to an existing instance. To keep latency low, however, EBS doesn't permit attaching volumes to an instance across AZs. This means that both the instance and the volume that you'd like to attach to it must be located in the same AZ. Here are the key things to know regarding the creation of EBS volumes:

- You can create encrypted EBS volumes as long as the EC2 instance type supports Amazon EBS encryption.
- You can create and attach an EBS volume at instance creation time through the specification of block device mapping.
- You can restore an EBS volume from snapshots (see note).
- You can tag the volumes when creating them to support inventory tracking.

 NOTE When you restore an EBS volume from snapshots, the storage blocks of the restored volume must be *initialized* (with the dd command on a Linux system) before they are accessed. This results in a delay when access is made for the first time to a storage block, but after the first access, performance is normal. To avoid the significant increase in latency in this situation, access each block in the restored volume before making it accessible to users and applications. This process was previously known as *pre-warming* and is now called *initialization* of the volume.

Exercise 7-1 walks you through the steps for creating an EBS volume from the console. You can also create an EBS volume from the command line with the create-volume command. Following is an example that shows how to create a 500GiB General Purpose (SSD) EBS volume:

```
$ aws ec2 create-volume -size 500 -region us-east-1 -availability-zone us-
east-1a -volume-type gp2
```

You must specify the volume size, volume type, region, and the AZ when creating an EBS volume. You can specify several optional parameters, such as `encryption`, which will encrypt the EBS volume. If provisioning an io1 volume type, you should specify the IOPS.

TIP EBS volumes that you create from an encrypted snapshot are automatically encrypted.

The previous example showed how to create a brand-new volume from scratch, but you can also create an EBS volume from a snapshot that you've stored in S3. You must specify the snapshot ID if you want to restore your EBS volume from the snapshot. The following example shows how to create an EBS volume (Provisioned IOPS) from a snapshot:

```
$ aws ec2 create-volume –size 500 –region us-east-1 –availability-zone us-
east-1a –snapshot-id snap-084028835991ca12d –volume-type io1 –iops 1000
```

The volume type is io1 (Provisioned IOPS SSD), and the `iops` attribute specifies that you want this volume to support 1000 IOPS.

When you create an EBS volume from an EBS snapshot, the volume loads lazily, meaning that the EC2 instance can start accessing the volume and all its data before all the data is transferred from S3 (snapshot) to the new EBS volume.

NOTE You can view all EBS volumes in your account by opening the EBS console and then selecting Volumes in the navigation pane.

Attaching an EBS Volume to an EC2 Instance

As long as an EC2 instance is in the same AZ as an EBS volume, you can attach the volume to an instance. You can attach multiple EBS volumes to a single EC2 instance. If the volume is encrypted, the instance must support EBS encryption. Exercise 7-2 shows how to attach an EBS volume to an EC2 instance using the console. You can also attach the volume from the command line, with the `attach-volume` command:

```
$ aws ec2 attach-volume –volume-id vol-1234567890abcdef0  --instance-id
01283ef334d86420 --device /dev/sdf
```

In this command, you specify the `volume-id` attribute to represent the volume you want to attach, and the `instance-id` attribute to specify the EC2 instance to which you want to attach the volume. You attach the volume to the instance as the device, /dev/sdf.

NOTE In most cases, you can attach a volume to a running or stopped EC2 instance.

You can view the EBS volumes attached to an EC2 instance by opening the EC2 console and selecting Instances in the navigation pane. To do so from the command line, run this command:

```
$ aws ec2 describe-volumes –region us-west-2
```

After creating an EBS volume and attaching it to an EC2 instance, you can modify the volume by increasing the volume type, increasing the volume size, or changing the volume's IOPS settings. You can make these changes to a volume that's attached to an instance as well as a detached EBS volume. AWS starts charging you at the new volume's rate once you start the change in a volume's settings.

Once you attach an EBS volume to an EC2 instance, it isn't ready for use. You must first format and mount the drive, as I explain in the next section.

Making an EBS Volume Available for Use

Before an EC2 instance can start using the EBS volume you've attached to it, you must *format* the volume with a file system and *mount* the volume. This is so because initially the instance sees only a block volume with no file system on it. Once you format and mount the volume, the instance can use it the same way it does a regular hard disk drive.

Follow these steps to format and mount an EBS volume to make it available for use on a Linux system:

1. Connect to the EC2 instance to which you've attached the new EBS volume through SSH.

2. Although you name the EBS volume something like /dev/sdf, it could be attached with a different name such as /dev/xvdh or /dev/hdf, depending on the OS of the EC2 instance. Run the `lsblk` command to view the available disk devices and their mount points; you can figure out the correct device name to specify later on:

   ```
   $ lsblk
   ```

3. If this is a volume you've restored from an EBS snapshot, you may not want to create a file system for the device because it already has one (unless you want to overwrite the existing file system). If this is a new volume, which is a raw block device, you must create a file system on the device. Run the `mkfs` command to create the file system on the device. Here's the general format of the `mkfs` command to create an ext4 file system:

   ```
   $ sudo mkfs -t ext4 device_name
   ```

   In our case, the command is as follows:

   ```
   $ sudo mkfs -t ext4 /dev/xvdf
   ```

4. Create a mount point directory for the volume with the `mkdir` command:

   ```
   $ sudo mkdir /dev/xvdf   /mydata
   ```

   This command creates the directory /mydata, where you can write and read files after you mount the volume.

5. Add an entry for the new device to the /etc/fstab file, so the EBS volume is mounted automatically after a system reboot. Just add the following line at the end of the /etc/fstab file:

```
/dev/xvdf   /data    ext4   defaults 1 2
```

6. To make sure that your entry to the /etc/fstab file is correct, unmount the new device and mount all file systems listed in the /etc/fstab file (with the mount -a command):

```
$ sudo umount /mydata
$ sudo mount -a
```

7. Assign proper file permissions for the new volume mount to ensure that your applications and users can write to and read from the new EBS volume you've made available for use.

8. To find out how much disk space is available on this EBS volume, run the following Linux command:

```
$ df -hT /dev/xvda1
```

If you modify an EBS volume by increasing its size, you must extend the volume's file system so it can use the increased storage capacity.

Attaching an EBS Volume to an Instance

In the previous section, I showed how to take a raw EBS volume, format it, and mount it to an EC2 instance. If you already have an EBS volume available to you, you can simply attach it to an instance, as long as both the volume and the instance are in the same AZ.

You can attach an EBS volume from the EC2 console or from the command line with the `attach-volume` command, as shown here (you must obtain the volume ID and the instance ID first):

```
$ aws ec2 attach-volume -volume-id vol-1234567890abcdef0  --instancce-id
i-01474ef662b89480 -device /dev/sdf
```

This command attaches an EBS volume to a running or stopped instance and makes the volume available to the instance with the device name that you specify (/dev/sdf in this example).

Detaching and Deleting an EBS Volume

You can disassociate an EBS volume from an EC2 instance by detaching the volume from the instance. You can also delete an EBS volume from your account.

There are two ways to detach an EBS volume for an EC2 instance:

- **Terminate the instance**   The EBS volume is automatically detached from the instance when you terminate an instance.

- **Unmount the volume**   If the EC2 instance is running, you must unmount the volume on the instance.

From the command line, run the `detach-volume` command to detach a volume from an instance. As you can see in the following example, to detach a volume, you need to specify the `volume-id` attribute, and there's no need to specify the instance name:

```
$ aws ec2 detach-volume –volume-id vol-1234567890abcdef0
```

 NOTE You can't detach an EBS volume that's serving as the root device for an instance without first stopping the instance. You may remount the same volume to the same instance, but it may get a different mount point.

Encrypting EBS Volumes

EBS offers encryption for most EC2 instance types. Creating an encrypted EBS volume and attaching it to an EC2 instance not only protects the data that you store on the EBS volume but offers several other encryption-related benefits.

Encrypting an EBS volume will encrypt the following:

- Data you store on the volume
- Data that flows between that volume and the EC2 instance to which you've attached it
- Snapshots that you create from that volume
- EBS volumes that you create from the snapshots that you make of that volume

EBS encryption uses AWS Key Management Service (KMS) customer master keys (CMKs) to encrypt volumes and snapshots. Unless you specify a custom CMK, AWS creates and manages a unique CMK for you in each AWS region where you own AWS resources. AWS uses the industry-standard AWS-256 encryption algorithm when it encrypts your EBS volumes with a data key. It stores the data key with the encrypted data on the volume, after first encrypting the key with your CMK. All snapshots and EBS volumes that you create from those snapshots share the same data key.

You can transfer data normally between encrypted and unencrypted EBS volumes (*volume-level encryption*). The snapshot of an unencrypted volume is by definition unencrypted. However, you can encrypt a volume's data by applying encryption to a copy of a snapshot that you've made of an unencrypted EBS volume.

You can also encrypt data at the *client level* by incorporating encryption at the OS level of the EC2 instance. When you do this, you fully manage the encryption, including the storage and availability of the encryption keys. AWS doesn't manage encryption keys for you in this case, as it does in the case of volume-level encryption.

EBS Monitoring and EBS CloudWatch Events

EBS sends notifications based on CloudWatch Events. These events can be *volume events* such as creating a volume, deleting a volume, and attaching a volume. Other EBS-related events include EBS *snapshot events*, such as creating a snapshot and copying a snapshot.

You learned about Amazon Lambda in Chapter 4. You can employ Amazon Lambda functions to handle CloudWatch Events and to help automate the workflow of a data backup. A CloudWatch Events rule that matches a new event can route the event to a

Lambda function that you create that handles that event. Suppose, for example, that you've created a Lambda function that copies an EBS snapshot to a different region. You make this Lambda function available in the CloudWatch console. When EBS emits a `createSnapshot` event, CloudWatch invokes the Lambda function, which automatically copies the snapshot created in, say, the us-east-1 region to the us-east-2 region.

 NOTE Remember that once you create an EBS volume, it continues to count toward the storage limit for your account, even if you've detached that volume from the instance or have even terminated the instance to which you had attached that volume.

For all volumes except Provisioned IOPS volumes, CloudWatch provides metrics such as the number of bytes read/written, the read and write I/O per second, idle time, queue length, and other metrics, every five minutes. For Provisioned IOPS volumes, the metrics also include the throughput percentage, which shows the percentage of throughput a volume is using, compared to the throughput that you've provisioned. If the throughput percentage is low on a regular basis, it's an indication that you've overprovisioned the IOPS for the volume, so you're paying more than you need to for that volume. For volumes such as gp2, sc1, and st1, you also get burst balance metrics, which show the burst bucket credits still available to the volume.

Backing Up EBS Volumes with Snapshots

A point-in-time EBS snapshot helps you back up data you store on the volume. A snapshot makes a copy of an EBS volume. When you create a snapshot of an EBS volume, the snapshot is automatically stored for you in Amazon S3. EBS stores the snapshots at the regional level in multiple AZs in Amazon S3. Since a snapshot is linked to the region where you create it, you must start the snapshot process in the region where you need to store copies of your data. You can use EBS snapshots for backing up data or to save data before you terminate an instance. The maximum number of EBS snapshots you can take in your AWS account is 10,000, by default.

Although EBS volumes can survive a loss of a disk, because they're redundant arrays, the volumes are located in only one AZ. If the AZ in which a volume lives becomes unavailable, your applications won't be able to access the data stored in the volume. Maintaining EBS snapshots enables you to survive an AZ failure.

 NOTE Taking a snapshot is free, but storing it isn't. AWS charges you for storing the snapshots in EBS.

How EBS Snapshots Work

To minimize the time to create a snapshot every time you back up the same volume, and to save on storage costs (by avoiding data duplication), EBS snapshots are incremental in nature. Incremental snapshots capture only the changes in a volume over time. The first snapshot you take of an EBS volume is a full snapshot that captures all the data on the volume. The second snapshot captures only the changed data blocks of the volume since the full backup of the volume. Subsequent snapshots copy and store only the amount of data that has changed since the previous incremental backup.

 NOTE If a large amount of data, such as more than 10GB, has changed since the previous snapshot, EBS will create a *full snapshot* that has all the EBS volume's data, rather than storing the large amount of changed data.

You can use an EBS snapshot to create a new EBS volume that will be a replica of the backed-up EBS volume. A point-in-time snapshot means that with this snapshot, you can restore the data up to this moment to a new EBS volume.

When you start creating a new EBS volume from a snapshot, you don't need to wait for all the data to load from the snapshot. Instead, you can start using the new volume immediately. Any data that you access that isn't already on the new volume is immediately downloaded from Amazon S3, while the download continues uninterrupted in the background. You can take a new snapshot of a volume even if a previous snapshot of the volume is in the pending state. However, the volume may take a performance hit until the snapshots complete.

EBS automatically encrypts the snapshots of an encrypted volume. Any volumes that you create from an encrypted snapshot are also automatically encrypted. You can make copies of snapshots and share them across AWS accounts. You can choose to encrypt a snapshot that's unencrypted during a copy of the unencrypted snapshot.

Using Amazon Data Lifecyle Manager for EBS Snapshots

Amazon DLM enables you to define backup and retention schedules for your snapshots, instead of relying on custom scripts to manage them. You can create snapshot lifecycle policies based on tags. DLM helps you automate the creation, deletion, and retention of the snapshots that you take to back up your EBS volumes. DLM enforces a regular backup schedule to protect your data, retains the backups required by auditing and compliance requirements, and reduces your storage costs by automatically deleting old backups that you don't need.

Creating EBS Snapshots

Unlike instance store storage, data on EBS persists, and most of the time, the data is critical. A snapshot helps you take a point-in-time backup of an EBS volume; it's a backup of an EBS volume that AWS stores in S3. You can create a new EBS volume using data stored in a snapshot by specifying the snapshot's ID.

AWS stores all snapshots in Amazon S3 at the regional level, across multiple AZs. Although the snapshots are stored in S3, they're not like other S3 objects because they contain only the data that has changed since the previous snapshot was created. You can't access your snapshots from the S3 console or APIs; instead, you must access them through the EC2 console and APIs.

TIP You can modify the permissions on EBS snapshots to share the snapshots privately with specific accounts or publicly with the greater AWS community.

Creating a snapshot could take some time and depends on the size of the source EBS volume. You can create up to five snapshots concurrently. Exercise 7-3 shows how to create an EBS snapshot from the console. You can create a snapshot from the command line by executing the `create-snapshot` command:

```
$ aws ec2 create-snapshot -volume-id vol-1234567890abcdef0 -description "Test
snapshot of an EBS volume"
```

You can view snapshot information by going to the Amazon EC2 console and selecting Snapshots in the navigation pane. Or, from the command line, run the `describe-snapshots` command to view your snapshots:

```
$ aws ec2 describe-snapshots -owner-ids 01234567890
```

This command shows all the snapshots that are available to you, including the private snapshots that you own, private snapshots owned by other AWS accounts to which you have create volume permissions, and public snapshots that are available for all AWS accounts.

 NOTE As mentioned, snapshots are incremental in nature, meaning that only the first snapshot is a full backup of the EBS volume. Other snapshots you create following this contain only those blocks on the EBS volume that have changed since the time you created the first backup. This incremental backup strategy means only the first snapshot's storage will be the same as the EBS volume it's backing up. The latter snapshots would be much smaller and are based on the amount of data that changes in between snapshots.

EBS snapshots use a *lazy loading* strategy that lets you use the snapshot immediately after you create it, even before S3 has loaded all the data in the snapshot. If your applications try to access data that hasn't been loaded on the snapshot yet, the volume downloads the required chunk of data from Amazon.

 TIP Tag the EBS snapshots you take to make it easier for you to manage the snapshots. Tags, for example, make it easier to find the name of the original volume used to make the snapshot.

Sharing EBS Snapshots and Making a Snapshot Public

You can share your EBS snapshots with other AWS accounts to enable other users to create EBS volumes with those snapshots. Although you can't make an encrypted snapshot publicly available, you can publicly share your unencrypted snapshots. If you share an encrypted snapshot, remember that you must also share the custom CMK that you've used to encrypt the snapshot.

You must modify a snapshot's permissions to enable sharing. The following example shows how to execute a `modify-snapshot-attribute` command to modify a snapshot attribute to grant the `CreateVolumePermission` for a specific AWS user:

```
$ aws ec2 modify-snapshot-attribute –snapshot-id snap-1234567890abcdef0
-attribute CreateVolumePermission –operation-type add –user-ids 123456789023
```

The `modify-snapshot-attribute` command also enables you to make a snapshot public. Just replace the `-user-ids` attribute with `–group-name all`.

NOTE A snapshot can be used to create an EBS volume in the same region where you created the snapshot. However, you can ship snapshots across regions to migrate data centers or perform disaster recovery.

Deleting a Snapshot

Deleting an EBS volume doesn't delete its snapshots. You must explicitly delete any snapshots you don't need. You can delete an EBS volume if you decide that you no longer need the volume. You can do so from the EC2 console or by running the `delete-volume` command:

```
$ aws ec2 delete-volume –volume-id vol-1234567890abcdef0
```

If you think you may need to use this volume later, you can create a snapshot of the EBS volume before deleting it.

NOTE Deleting a volume doesn't affect the snapshots you've made of the volume. Similarly, removing the snapshots doesn't affect the source volume because they are independent of each other.

Earlier, I explained that snapshots are incremental in nature, with each subsequent snapshot after the first snapshot storing only the data that has changed since the previous snapshot. When you use incremental backups for a database such as Oracle, you must retain all the incremental backups to restore the database. EBS snapshots work differently, in that you need to retain only the latest snapshot to restore the EBS volume. Snapshots contain only the changed data and *reference* the data from earlier snapshots.

Let's look at a simple example to explain the unique nature of an EBS snapshot and what happens when you delete and restore a snapshot. This sequence of events shows how you can restore an EBS volume from a later snapshot, even after removing one or more earlier snapshots. In this example, I create two snapshots: Snapshot A and Snapshot B. The EBS volume for which I am creating a snapshot has 10GiB of data.

1. I create the first snapshot, Snapshot A, which is a full copy of the 10GiB EBS volume.

2. By the time I take the next snapshot (an incremental snapshot), 2GiB of data has changed. Therefore, the snapshot I create now, Snapshot B, copies and stores only the 2GiB of changed data. Snapshot B also *references* the other 8GiB of data that was copied and stored in Snapshot A in step 1.

3. I delete Snapshot A. EBS moves the 8GiB of data stored in Snapshot A to Snapshot B after the deletion of Snapshot A. As a result, Snapshot B now has all 10GiB of data (its own 2GiB, plus the 8GiB data moved from the deleted Snapshot A).

4. I restore the EBS volume for which I took the snapshots. I can restore all 10GiB stored in Snapshot B.

TIP You need to retain only the latest snapshot of an EBS volume to be able to restore the volume.

From the storage cost point of view, you still pay for storing all 10GiB of data, since the 8GiB of data from the deleted snapshot (Snapshot A) continues to be stored in Snapshot B.

Creating an AMI from a Snapshot

You can create an AMI from the snapshot of the root volume by adding metadata and registering the snapshot as an AMI. For a Linux AMI, you can do this by running the `register-image` command from the AWS CLI. Or, you can do the same thing from the EC2 console by selecting Elastic Block Store | Snapshots | Actions | Create Image | Create Image From EBS Snapshot.

TIP As you know, EBS is block storage that you provision in terms of specific-sized volumes. AWS charges you on the basis of the size of the EBS volumes that you provision, and not on the basis of your usage of those volumes. Thus, to save costs, it's quite important that you don't overprovision EBS storage. You should provision only what you currently need for your applications, since you can easily grow the storage later.

Amazon S3: Object Storage in the Cloud

Amazon *Simple Storage Service* lives up to its name. It is an easy-to-use web service interface that you use to store and retrieve data from anywhere on the Web. S3 is primarily designed for handling read workloads, and you can use it to store data such as video clips and data for big data workflows. It is a scalable, fast, inexpensive, and reliable data storage infrastructure and offers 99.999999999 percent durability and 99.99 percent availability of objects over a year. It also automatically detects and repairs any lost data, through built-in redundancy.

Here are some key facts to remember about S3:

- You store S3 objects (data and metadata) in logical containers called buckets and manage permissions on the resources through access control and authentication policies.

- You can upload and download data using standards-based REST- and SOAP-based interfaces (APIs).

- You can store an infinite amount of data in S3 buckets.
- S3 is a regional service that offers you a high parallel throughput and stores your data within a region for compliance requirements.
- AWS automatically replicates the data that you store in S3 to at least three different data centers.
- You can configure access policies to limit who is authorized to view the data that you store in S3.
- Your S3 storage costs include the cost of the storage for the data you keep in S3, plus charges for the API calls you make to move data into and out of S3.

You can use S3 APIs to perform operations such as the following:

- Create a bucket
- Read from and write to an object
- Delete an object
- List the keys contained in a bucket

 EXAM TIP The exam is likely to test your knowledge of size limits. An S3 object can have a maximum size of 5TB. The largest object that you can upload in a single PUT request is 5GB. AWS recommends that you consider using S3's Multipart Upload capability for objects larger than 100MB for speedy transmission of the data and the ability to recover from data transmission failures.

S3 Basic Entities and Key Concepts

The key entities in S3 are buckets and objects. To store data such as photos, videos, or documents in S3, your first step is to create a bucket (in any AWS region); then you can upload your objects (files that contain text, photos, and so on) to that bucket. The following sections describe buckets, objects, and other S3 concepts.

Buckets

A bucket in which you store objects is a globally unique (across all AWS accounts) entity. Although you access individual buckets and the content that you store in those buckets from the Web with an URL, your data isn't exposed to the general public because of the security features built into S3 that require the right permissions to access the objects.

Bucket Naming Rules   Bucket names must comply with DNS naming conventions. Here are the key naming rules to which you must adhere:

- A bucket name must consist of only lowercase characters, numbers, periods, and dashes. Each of a bucket's labels must start with a lowercase character or number.

- The bucket names cannot use underscores, end with a dash, have two or more consecutive periods, or have a dash next to a period.

- A bucket name cannot be formatted as an IP address.

Addressing the Objects in a Bucket   Let's look at an example. Suppose I create a bucket named samalapati1 and store an object named photos/kitten.jpg in it. I can address this object with the following unique URL:

> http://samalapati1.s3.amazonaws.com/photos/kitten.jpg

S3 offers two differently styled URLs to access buckets: a virtual-hosted-style URL and a path-style URL. When you use a *virtual-hosted-style URL*, you specify the bucket name as part of the domain name, as in this example:

> http://samalapati1.s3.amazonaws.com

When you use a *path-style URL*, there's no need to specify the bucket name as part of the domain:

> http://s3.amazonaws.com/samalapati1

Buckets and Hierarchies   A bucket is a flat container for objects. Buckets may look like directories, but they don't have a hierarchical file organization. You can, however, create a logical file system hierarchy by using key names to stand for folders. For example, here's a bucket with four objects, each with its own key name:

```
sample1.jpg
photos/2019/Jan/sample2.jpg
photos/2019/Feb/sample3.jpg
photos/2019/Mar/sample4.jpg
```

Based on the key names, this implies the following logical folder structure:

- **sample1.jpg:** this is the root of this bucket.
- **sample2.jpg object:** this is located in the photos/2019/Jan subfolder.
- **sample3.jpg object:** this is located in the photos/2019/Feb subfolder.
- **sample4.jpb object:** this is located in the photos/2019/Mar subfolder.

Buckets are useful for organizing the S3 namespace. They also identify the account to be charged for the storage and data transfer to S3. You can control access to S3 data at the bucket level and aggregate S3 usage at the bucket level.

NOTE   You can specify a region for your buckets to provide lower latency or to meet regulatory requirements.

The Delimiter and Prefix Parameters   An S3 bucket doesn't work like a Linux directory, with files stored inside a directory. Objects within a bucket are laid out flatly and alphabetically. Unlike Linux, where a directory is a file, in S3, everything is an object, and you identify each object by its key.

You can use the `delimiter` and `prefix` parameters to make S3 buckets work like a directory. The two parameters limit the results returned by a list operation. The `prefix` parameter limits the response to the keys that begin with the prefix you specify. The `delimiter` parameter helps the `list` command roll up all the keys with a common prefix into a single summary list result.

You can also use slash (/) as a delimiter. Here's an example that shows how the `delimiter` and `prefix` parameters help. This example stores data for different cities:

```
North America/Canada/Quebec/Montreal
North America/USA/Texas/Austin
```

Instead of trying to manage a flat key namespace such as this, you can use the `delimiter` and `prefix` parameters in a list operation. So to list all the states in the United States, you can set the `delimiter='/'` and the `prefix='North America/USA/'`. A list operation with a delimiter enables you to browse the data hierarchy at just one level by summarizing the keys nested at the lower levels. If, for example, an S3 object `myobject` has the prefix `myprefix`, the S3 key would be `myprefix/myobject`.

Objects

Objects are the data that you store in S3; objects consist of data and metadata. Two items help you uniquely identify an object: a *key* (the object's name) and a *version ID*. Metadata, which is a set of key-value pairs, is helpful in describing the data, with entities such as the Content-Type and the date in which the object was last modified. You can use the standard metadata as well as configure custom metadata for a bucket.

You place objects in S3 and access those objects using standard HTTP REST verbs (also called methods) such as GET, POST, PUT, PATCH, and DELETE. These five verbs correspond to the create, read, update, and delete operations, respectively. You use these verbs with their corresponding actions in S3.

Keys

A key uniquely identifies an object within a bucket. A bucket, key, and version ID uniquely identify an object in the entire Amazon S3 storage. You can uniquely identify every object in Amazon S3 with the following four entities:

- Web service endpoint
- Bucket name
- Key
- Version (optional)

Consider the URL http://mydocs.s3.amazonaws.com/2018-12-28/AmazonS3.wsdl. In this URL,

- S3.amazonaws.com is the web service endpoint.
- mydocs is the bucket name.
- 2018-12-28/AmazonS3.wsdl is the key.

Note that there's no version entity (which is optional) in this URL.

High Availability and Durability of Data

S3 provides high availability for the data you store in it, which means that the data is almost always available to you when you need it. In addition, S3 ensures data durability, which means that the data is resilient to any storage or other types of failures. S3 offers high availability by replicating your data on multiple servers. S3 Standard storage delivers a guaranteed availability of 99.99 percent. AWS guarantees this through an SLA that penalizes AWS if the availability of your data goes below 99.99 percent in any month (roughly equal to a downtime of 44 minutes). S3 offers a data durability of 99.999999999 for your data, making it very unlikely that you'll ever lose data. This is why AWS recommends that you store your EBS snapshots in S3.

The S3 Data Consistency Model

S3 offers *eventual consistency*. A *consistent read* offers reads that aren't stale, but with a potentially higher read latency and lower throughput. Eventually consistent reads offer a lower read latency and higher read throughput, but at the cost of making stale reads possible.

When you make a PUT request and it's successful, your data is safe in S3. However, S3 takes time to replicate data to all the servers that have a copy of this data, so you may see a situation where the following is true:

- Following a PUT operation, an immediate read operation of the object may return the older data, and a *listing* of the objects may not show the new object.
- After a DELETE operation, an immediate listing of the keys might still list the deleted object, and an immediate attempt to read the data might return data that you've deleted.

When you PUT a new object in an S3 bucket, the S3 service provides *read-after-write consistency* for the PUT. S3 offers eventual consistency for overwrite PUTs and DELETEs. An update to a single key is *atomic*; a read following a PUT to an existing key (update) won't return corrupt or partial data.

S3 Storage Classes

Each object in S3 is associated with one of six storage classes: STANDARD, REDUCED_REDUNDANCY, INTELLIGENT_TIERING, STANDARD_IA, ONEZONE_IA, and Glacier. Your choice of the storage class depends on your use cases. Some types of storage are ideal for storing data that you frequently access, and others are best for less frequently used data. Objects that you store in the STANDARD, RRS, STANDARD_IA, and ONEZONE_IA storage classes are available for real-time access. Glacier objects aren't accessible in real-time; you must first *restore* the objects before accessing them. Not all storage classes offer the same levels of durability.

Storage Classes for Frequently Accessed Objects

S3 offers two storage classes for frequently accessed objects stored in S3.

STANDARD Storage Class   This default storage class offers millisecond access to your data. AWS stores STANDARD S3 data durably by replicating it across a minimum of three geographically separated data centers to ensure a guaranteed SLA of eleven 9's (99.999999999 percent) durability. There's is no minimum storage duration for the S3 objects that you store in the STANDARD storage class.

REDUCED_REDUNDANCY (RRS) Storage Class   This storage class is designed for storing non-critical data (such as thumbnails and other processed data that you can easily reproduce). This class stores data at a lower level of redundancy than S3 STANDARD storage, with "only" four 9's (99.99 percent) durability for RRS data, and it stores the data in only two data centers. RRS costs less than STANDARD S3 storage because of the lower durability of its data. If you're storing mission-critical data, RRS isn't a good choice, but if you can easily reproduce the data should you lose it, it is an appropriate choice because of its cost effectiveness—and the considerably high availability (about 400 times more durability than a typical disk drive) that it offers.

 CAUTION   RRS storage has an annual expected loss of 0.01 percent of the objects you store in S3. AWS recommends that you *not use this storage class*.

Storage Classes for Frequently and Infrequently Accessed Objects

The INTELLIGENT_TIERING storage class is designed for storing long-lived data with changing or unknown access patterns. It stores objects in two access tiers: one optimized for frequent access and a lower-cost tier for data that you infrequently access. This storage class automatically moves data to the most cost-effective storage class based on the data access patterns.

S3 monitors the access pattern of objects that you store in this storage class and moves any object that hasn't been accessed in 30 days to the (cheaper) infrequent access tier. The INTELLIGENT_TIERING autotiering of data ensures that the most cost-effective storage access tier is used, even if you can't predict your future access patterns.

This storage class is suitable for objects that are larger than 128KB that you intend to retain for longer than 30 days. Smaller objects are charged at the frequent access tier rates. If you delete objects before 30 days, you are still charged for 30 days.

Storage Classes for Infrequently Used Data

You can choose from three different storage classes for data that you access infrequently. Here are the key differences among the STANDARD_IA, ONEZONE_IA, and Glacier storage classes:

STANDARD_IA Storage Class Just like the STANDARD storage class, STANDARD_IA stores data in multiple AZs. This makes STANDARD_IA resilient because it can withstand the loss of an AZ. If your data cannot be easily (or never) re-created, use STANDARD_IA storage class. It is designed for long-lived, infrequently accessed, noncritical data, such as database backup archives. Suppose, for example, that you run a web site that stores historical photos, with most images being requested only a couple of times a year. STANDARD_IA storage would be a cost-effective and highly available choice for storing this type of data. You can serve the images directly from STANDARD_IA by hosting your web site in S3. There's is no minimum storage duration for the S3 objects that you store in the STANDARD_IA storage class.

ONEZONE_IA Storage Class ONEZONE_IA stores objects in a single AZ, so it is cheaper to store data in this class than in STANDARD_IA. However, the data isn't resilient, and you can lose data when the only AZ is lost for any reason. Use this storage class for data that can be easily re-created. ONEZONE_IA requires a minimum storage duration of 30 days.

Glacier Storage Class Designed for archiving data, Glacier offers the same resiliency as the STANDARD storage class. You cannot, however, access the objects that you store in real-time. The Glacier storage class requires a minimum duration of 90 days.

Storage Class Cost and Durability

Here are some guidelines regarding cost and durability for the various storage classes.

RRS is cheaper than STANDARD S3 storage but is significantly less durable. It's the only storage class that offers less than 99.999999999 percent durability. If, however, you know you're going to retrieve the data frequently (a few times a month or more), it's cheaper to stay with STANDARD S3 storage because it costs more to retrieve data from the storage classes designed for infrequent access. If you infrequently access data, choose a storage class other than RRS, such as STANDARD_IA, ONEZONE_IA, or Glacier.

Another cost consideration is the length of time for which you store the data. Infrequently accessed data storage classes such as STANDARD_IA have a minimum storage requirement of 30 days, meaning that AWS bills you for 30 days, even if you store the data for only a day or two. Although STANDARD_IA may be cheaper than STANDARD S3, this minimum billing structure makes it more expensive than storing short-term data in STANDARD S3 storage.

Glacier is the cheapest of all the storage classes, but it's best only if you almost never retrieve the data that you store. Unlike all the other storage classes, with Glacier, you must wait three to five hours to retrieve data; other storage classes enable you to retrieve your data in milliseconds. The minimum storage duration for Glacier is 90 days.

S3 and Object Lifecycle Management

Lifecycle policy rules apply actions to a group of objects. Using lifecycle management policies for S3 objects is a best practice that reduces your S3 storage costs and optimizes performance by removing unnecessary objects from your S3 buckets. There is no additional cost for setting up lifecycle policies.

You can configure two types of lifecycle policies:

- **Transition actions** These actions define when an object is moved to a different storage class. You can configure a lifecycle transition policy to automatically migrate objects stored in one S3 storage class to another (lower cost) storage class, based on the age of the data. You may, for example, specify that a set of S3 objects be moved to the STANDARD_IA storage class 30 days after their creation. You may also specify that a set of objects be moved to long-term Glacier storage class a year after their creation date.

- **Expiration actions** You can specify when an object can expire. A lifecycle expiration policy automatically removes objects from your account based on their age. For example, you can configure a policy that specifies that incomplete multipart uploads be deleted based on the age of the upload.

 EXAM TIP If you see a question asking about how to set up a storage policy for backups and such, know that it's asking about the S3 lifecycle management policies. For example, if you need to set a tiered storage for database backups that must be stored durably, and after two weeks, archived to a lower-priced storage tier, you can configure a lifecycle management policy that automatically transitions files older than two weeks to AWS Glacier.

You can use the Amazon S3 Analytics feature to help you determine how you should transition your S3 data to the right storage class. S3 Analytics performs a storage class analysis of your storage access patterns. This helps you determine when you can transition data stored in less frequently accessed but more expensive STANDARD S3 storage to cheaper STANDARD_IA storage, which is designed for storing infrequently accessed data. The best way to benefit from storage class analysis is by filtering the storage analysis results by object groups, rather than by a single object.

S3 Multipart Uploads

When creating a new, large S3 object or copying a large object, you can use the Multipart Upload API to upload the object in parts, in any order you choose. To improve throughput, you can upload several parts in parallel. Once you upload all the parts of an object, S3 puts together all the parts to create the object. You can retransmit a part if the transmission of that part fails.

 TIP The smaller part sizes in a Multipart Upload minimize the delays when you have to restart uploads due to a network error. You can easily resume the upload on failure.

Amazon S3 recommends that you consider using a Multipart Upload when an object's size reaches 100MB instead of attempting to upload the object in a single operation. The maximum object size for a Multipart Upload is 5TB, and the maximum number of parts per upload is 10,000.

Making Requests for S3 Data

Amazon S3 is a REST service, and, therefore, you send requests to the service via the REST API or—to make your life easy—via the AWS SDK wrapper libraries that wrap the S3 REST API. Your request can be anonymous or authenticated. An authenticated request must include a signature value that AWS partly generates from your AWS access keys (access key ID and secret access key).

You send an S3 request to an S3 service endpoint, a URL that acts as an entry point to a web service. Most AWS services offer a regional endpoint. When you create a new Amazon Virtual Private Cloud (VPC) endpoint for S3, you associate a subnet with the endpoint. When you do this, it adds a route to the endpoint in the subnet's route table.

Here's an example entry point for the DynamoDB service:

https://dynamodb.us-west-2.amazonaws.com

Using Amazon Athena to Query S3 Data

Amazon Athena is an interactive query service that enables you to query data in S3 via standard SQL statements. For example, if your developers want to query data from a set of CSV files that you've stored in S3, they can use Athena instead of going to the trouble of developing a program for querying the data. Athena is a serverless offering, meaning that there's no infrastructure or anything else for you to maintain; you pay just for the queries that you execute against your S3 data.

Hosting a Static Web Site on Amazon S3

You can host static web sites in S3 that can contain client-side, but not server-side, scripting. To host a static web site, you must first configure an S3 bucket for web site hosting, and then upload your web content to that bucket. You must enable the bucket with public read access, so everyone in the world can read objects in that bucket.

 EXAM TIP   If you're asked how you can quickly make your web site highly scalable, a good answer is to choose S3 static web site hosting, because it enables you to scale up virtually infinitely, using S3 to serve a large traffic volume. A DB server that supports your web site can't easily handle the strain of a huge increase in your web traffic.

There are three steps in setting up a static web site in S3 from the S3 bucket properties settings:

1. Enable static web site hosting in the S3 bucket properties.

2. Select the Make Public option for permissions on the bucket's objects.

3. Upload an index document to the S3 bucket.

Your static web site is available to your users at AWS region–specific endpoints of the bucket you've designated for web site hosting. Once you create a bucket and configure it as a web site, URLs such as the following examples provide users access to your web site content.

In this case, the bucket is called examplebucket and it's being created in the us-west-2 region. This URL returns the default index document that you configure for your web site:

http://examplebucket.s3-website-us-west-2.amazonaws.com/

This URL returns the photo1.jpg object that you stored at the root level of the bucket:

http://examplebucket.s3-website-us-west-2.amazonaws.com/photo123.jpg

The two examples use an S3 web site endpoint, but you can use your own custom domain when configuring a bucket for web site hosting, by adding your web site configuration to the bucket. For example, you can use a custom domain such as example.com to serve content from your web site. S3, along with Route 53, supports hosting of websites at the root domain, so your users can access your site by going to either http://www.example.com or http://example.com.

 EXAM TIP   Know how domain names and bucket names work in S3 static web site hosting. Although you can name your bucket anything when using an S3 web site endpoint, when you use a custom domain such as example.com, your bucket names must match the names of the web site. So if you want to host a web site named example.com on S3, you must create a bucket named example.com. If you want the web site to handle requests for both example.com and www.example.com, you must create two buckets: example.com and www.example.com. Subdomains must have their own S3 buckets that are named the same as the subdomain.

Managing Access to Your S3 Resources

Only the resource owner (an AWS account) has permissions to access buckets, objects, and related subresources such as lifecycle and web site configuration. By default, all S3 resources are *private*, and only the object owner has permissions to access them. However, the owner can choose to share objects with others by creating a *pre-signed URL* using the owner's security credentials. Pre-signed URLs are valid for a specific duration and enable the owner to grant time-bound permissions to a user to view, modify, delete, upload, or download objects from and to the owner's bucket. For example, the AWS account owner can create an access policy to grant an IAM user in the AWS account PUT Object permissions to enable that user to upload objects to the owner's S3 bucket.

You can grant permissions to individual users and accounts, to everyone (called *anonymous access*), or to all users who authenticate successfully with AWS credentials. When would you grant anonymous access to an S3 bucket? A good use case is when you configure the S3 bucket as a static web site. In this case, you grant the GET Object permission to everyone to make the bucket's objects public.

You manage S3 access by configuring access policies. These policies enable you to grant permissions and specify who gets the permissions, the resources for which they get the permissions, and the actions you want to allow on the resources. There are two basic types of access policy options: *resource-based policies* and *user policies.* A resource-based policy is attached to an S3 bucket such as a bucket or object. Bucket policies and access control lists (ACLs) are resource-based policies. User policies are IAM access policies that you attach to users in your AWS account. You can choose a resource-based policy, a user policy, or a combination of both to grant permissions to your S3 resources.

 TIP For mobile apps that access your AWS resources stored in S3, AWS strongly recommends that you not embed or distribute AWS credentials with the app, even in an encrypted format. You should instead have the app request temporary AWS security credentials using web identify federation. Your users can use an external identify provider (idP), such as Facebook, and receive an authorization token, and then exchange the token for temporary AWS credentials that map to a restricted IAM role with just the permissions to use the resources to perform the tasks required by the mobile app. This is a flexible method that also rotates the credentials.

It's important that you clearly understand S3 resources before you learn how to grant permissions to those resources. First, let's go over how S3 assigns ownership to resources such as buckets and objects. Here are the key things to remember regarding ownership of S3 resources:

- An S3 resource owner is the AWS account that creates the resource.
- Your AWS account is the parent owner for the IAM users that you create in your AWS account.
- When an IAM user puts an object in a bucket, the parent account is the owner of the object.
- Always use the administrative user (IAM user) accounts, and not the root AWS user account, to create buckets and grant permissions on them.

When the owner of a bucket grants permissions to users in a different AWS account to upload objects, the other AWS account becomes the owner of the object, and the bucket owner does not have permissions on the object. However, the bucket owner can deny access to the objects, archive the objects, or delete the objects, regardless of who owns them. In addition, the bucket owner pays for storing the objects, not the user who uploads the objects to the bucket.

Buckets and objects are the fundamental S3 resources, but each of these has several subresources. Bucket resources include the following subresources:

- **Lifecycle**   These resources store the bucket lifecycle configuration.
- **Website**   This subresource stores the web site configuration when you configure an S3 bucket for web site hosting.
- **Versioning**   These subresources store the versioning configuration.
- **CORS (Cross-Origin Resource Sharing)**   These help you configure buckets to allow cross-origin requests.

- **Policy and ACL**   These store the bucket's access permissions.
- **Logging**   These subresources help you request S3 to save bucket access logs.

Object subresources include the following:

- **ACL**   These resources store an object's access permissions.
- **Restore**   These resources help restore archived objects such as the objects you store in the Glacier storage class.

Resource Operations

You can manage S3 buckets and objects with the help of a set of operations that S3 provides for both buckets and objects.

Operations on Buckets   S3 bucket operations include the following:

- **DELETE Bucket**   Deletes the bucket; you must delete all the objects in a bucket before you can delete the bucket
- **GET Bucket (List Objects)**   Returns some or all the objects in a bucket up to a maximum of 1000 objects
- **GET Service**   Returns a list of your S3 buckets
- **GET Bucket acl**   Returns the ACL of a bucket
- **PUT Bucket**   Creates a bucket
- **PUT Bucket policy**   Returns the policy of the specified bucket

---

 EXAM TIP   If a question asks about the meaning of an error code, such as "403 Forbidden," know that one of the reasons for this error is the denial of access to a bucket. You'd need to check the bucket's access policy to ensure that the user can access this bucket. The "403 Bad Request" error is due to some type of invalid request. A reason for the "404 Not Found" error is that the specified bucket doesn't exist.

Operations on Objects   Object operations include the following:

- **GET Object**   Returns the current version of the object by default. To use GET Object, a user must have READ access on the object.
- **DELETE Object**   Removes the null version of an object if one exists and inserts a delete marker, which becomes the current version. Otherwise, S3 doesn't remove the object. You can remove a specific version of an object, if you own the object, by specifying the versionId subresource in your request. This request will permanently delete the object version that you specify.
- **READ Object**   Retrieves the object, provided you have read access to the object.

	Permission Keyword	Corresponding S3 Operation
Table 7-2 Permission Keywords and How They Map to S3 Operations	s3:CreateBucket	PUT Bucket operation
	s3:DeleteBucket	DELETE Bucket
	s3:ListBucket	GET Bucket (List Objects)
	s3:DeleteObject	DELETE Object
	s3:GetObject	GET Object
	s4:PutObject	PUT Object, POST Object, Upload Part

- **PUT Object**   Adds an object to a bucket, provided you have write permission on the bucket to add objects to the bucket.

- **UPLOAD Part**   Uploads a part in a Multipart Upload of an object; you must initiate a Multipart Upload before uploading a part of it.

As you'll learn shortly, you specify permissions in an access policy. You do this *not* by directly specifying an operation such as DELETE bucket or PUT Object, but by using keywords that map to specific S3 operations. Table 7-2 shows some common permission keywords and how they map to the S3 operations on buckets and objects.

Access Policy Language

In the following sections, I explain both types of resource-based policies—bucket policies and ACLs—as well as user-based policies. Both bucket policies and user policies employ a JSON-based access policy language.

Before I jump into the discussion of the various types of policies, it helps to understand the basics of the key *access policy language* elements. You use the following basic elements in a bucket or user access policy:

- **Resource**   The resource element specifies the resources for which you allow or deny permissions. Buckets and objects are the two S3 resources that you'll specify in your access policies.

- **Action**   This element enables you to specify the permission (using permission keywords) on a resource. For each S3 resource, such as a bucket or an object, S3 supports specific operations that you can perform on them. So, for example, the s3:ListBucket action grants a user permission to perform the S3 GET Bucket (List Objects) operation.

- **Effect**   The effect element shows how S3 should respond to a user request to perform a specific action and can take two values: `allow` or `deny`. If you don't specify the value `allow`, by default, access is denied. However, you can explicitly specify `deny` as a value for the effect element to ensure that a user can't access the resource, regardless of being granted access through another access policy.

- **Principal**   This element specifies the user or the AWS account that gets the access permission for the resources and actions that you've specified in the access policy statement. For a bucket policy, the principal can be a user, account, service, or another entity.

- **Condition**   Though the first four elements here are mandatory, condition is an optional policy element that enables you to specify the condition(s) under which a policy will be in effect. I show examples that illustrate how to specify the condition element later in this chapter in the section "Granting Permissions to Multiple Accounts with Conditions."

EXAM TIP   Understand that an explicit deny will keep a user from accessing a resource, even though you may have granted the user access through another access policy. You may see a situation in which there are two statements in an access policy, with the first statement specifying an allow for a specific user. However, if the second statement has a deny for all users, the deny overrides the allow in the first statement, and thus the user won't have access to that bucket.

Resource-Based Policies

In a resource-based access policy, you attach the policy directly to the S3 resource you want to manage, such as an S3 bucket or object. There are two types of resource-based access policies: *bucket policies* and *access control lists* (ACLs). Remember that both buckets and objects have associated ACLs.

Bucket Policies   You can associate a bucket policy with your S3 bucket to grant IAM users and other AWS accounts permissions on the bucket and the objects inside the bucket.

NOTE   Remember that any object permissions that you grant for the objects in a bucket apply only to those objects that you, as the bucket owner, create in that bucket.

A bucket policy supplements, and often replaces, ACL-based access policies. You use a JSON file to create a bucket policy. Here's an example:

```
{
  "Version":"2012-10-17",
  "Statement":[
    {
      "Effect":"Allow",
      "Principal": {"AWS": ["arn:aws:iam::111122223333:root","arn:aws:iam::44
4455556666:root"]},
      "Action":["s3:PutObject","s3:PutObjectAcl"],
      "Resource":["arn:aws:s3:::mybucket/*"],
        }
  ]
}
```

This bucket policy grants the following permissions on a bucket named mybucket. The `Principal`, `Action`, `Effect`, and `Resource` elements of the policy specify the user(s), permissions, whether you allow or deny the access request, and the bucket, respectively:

- **Principal**   The permissions are granted to two AWS accounts.
- **Action**   Specifies two permissions: `s3:PutObject` and `s3:PutObjectAcl`
- **Effect**   The value is allow, which allows the action that you've specified on the resource you name in this policy.
- **Resource**   Specifies the bucket name (mybucket) to which you are granting the permissions.

By specifying `s3:PutObject` as the value for the `Action` element, you're permitting two users to upload objects to this bucket. However, they can't *read* other objects in this bucket. You must specify the action `s3:GetObject` to grant a user read permission on objects in a bucket.

You can create a policy that grants anonymous access by specifying the *principal* element with a wild card (*), as shown here:

```
"Principal": "*"
```

Bucket policies offer you a way to grant access to a bucket to other accounts without having to create a role for those accounts in your root account. You can use bucket policies for a variety of use cases. I show typical use cases in this section by describing the specific elements that are most helpful to understand.

Granting Permissions to Multiple Accounts with Conditions   The following example shows how to grant the `s3:PutObject` and `s3:PutObjectAcl` permissions to multiple accounts on an S3 bucket named examplebucket:

```
{
  "Version":"2012-10-17",
  "Statement":[
    {
      "Sid":"AddCannedAcl",
      "Effect":"Allow",
      "Principal": {"AWS": ["arn:aws:iam::111122223333:root","arn:aws:iam::
444455556666:root"]},
      "Action":["s3:PutObject","s3:PutObjectAcl"],
      "Resource":["arn:aws:s3:::examplebucket/*"],
      "Condition":{"StringEquals":{"s3:x-amz-acl":["public-read"]}}
    }
  ]
}
```

The condition element requires the requests to include the public-read canned ACL.

Restricting Access to Specific IP Addresses   The following example shows the Statement portion of an access policy that allows *any user* (`"Principal": "*"`) to perform *any action* (`"Action": "s3:*"`) on objects in the S3 bucket examplebucket:

```
{
  "Version": "2012-10-17",
  "Id": "S3PolicyId1",
  "Statement": [
    {
      "Sid": "IPAllow",
      "Effect": "Allow",
      "Principal": "*",
      "Action": "s3:*",
      "Resource": "arn:aws:s3:::examplebucket/*",
      "Condition": {
        "IpAddress": {"aws:SourceIp": "54.240.143.0/24"},
        "NotIpAddress": {"aws:SourceIp": "54.240.143.188/32"}
      }
    }
  ]
}
```

The example also illustrates how to specify multiple conditions in a statement. The condition block in the statement restricts the access to requests originating from a specific range of IP addresses (54.240.143.0/24) that you specified under the `IpAddress` condition. The `NotIpAddress` condition specifies that the IP address 54.240.143.188.32 is not permitted to originate the request.

The `IpAddress` and `NotIpAddress` conditions are given a key-value pair to evaluate. Both key-value pairs use the `aws:SourceIP` *AWS-wide key*. AWS-wide keys, which have a prefix of `aws:`, are a set of common keys that all AWS services that support access policies will honor. Another example of an AWS-wide key is `aws:sourceVpc`.

In addition to AWS-wide keys, you can also specify condition keys, called Amazon S3-specific keys, that apply only in a limited context, to grant S3 permissions. Amazon S3-specific keys use the prefix `s3:` instead of `aws:`. For example, the following chunk of an access policy shows how to specify a condition that restricts a user to listing only those object keys with the *finance* prefix (`"s3:prefix": "finance"`):

```
{
        "Sid":"statement1",
        "Effect":"Allow",
        "Action":[
           "s3:ListBucket"
        ],
        "Resource":[
           "arn:aws:s3:::examplebucket"
        ],
        "Condition" : {
           "StringEquals" : {
               "s3:prefix": "finance"
           }
        }
}
```

Making a Bucket Policy Require MFA You can make a bucket policy enforce MFA by specifying the `aws:MuliFactorAuthAge` key in a bucket policy, as shown in this example:

```
"Statement": [
     {
        "Sid": "",
        "Effect": "Deny",
        "Principal": "*",
        "Action": "s3:*",
        "Resource": "arn:aws:s3:::examplebucket/hrdocuments/*",
        "Condition": { "Null": { "aws:MultiFactorAuthAge": true }}
     }
   ]
```

This access policy denies any operation on the /hrdocuments folder in the example-bucket bucket unless the request is MFA authenticated.

ACL Policies Like bucket policies, S3 ACL policies are resource-based policies that enable you to control bucket and object access. ACLs are much more limited than access policies and are designed mainly for granting simple read and write permissions (similar to Linux file permissions) to other AWS accounts.

An ACL uses an Amazon S3-specific XML schema, a set of permission grants that identify the grantee and the permissions they're granted. An ACL that you attach to a bucket or object specifies two things:

- The AWS accounts (or groups) that can access the resource
- The type of access

 NOTE Bucket policies supplement, and often replace, ACL-based access policies.

Each S3 bucket and object has an associated ACL. S3 creates a default ACL for all the buckets and objects, granting the owner of the bucket or object full control over the resource.

Here's an example of an ACL policy that contains a grant that shows the bucket owner as having full control permission (`FULL_CONTROL`) over the bucket:

```
<?xml version="1.0" encoding="UTF-8"?>
<AccessControlPolicy xmlns="http://s3.amazonaws.com/doc/2006-03-01/">
<Owner>
<ID>*** Owner-Canonical-User-ID ***</ID>
<DisplayName>owner-display-name</DisplayName>
</Owner>
<AccessControlList>
<Grant>
<Grantee xmlns:xsi="http://www.w3.org/2001/XMLSchema-instance"
xsi:type="Canonical User">
<ID>*** Owner-Canonical-User-ID ***</ID>
```

```
<DisplayName>display-name</DisplayName>
</Grantee>
<Permission>FULL_CONTROL</Permission>
</Grant>
</AccessControlList>
</AccessControlPolicy>
```

NOTE You can't grant the `FULL_CONTROL` permission in an ACL when you create the ACL through the console.

Types of Grantees in an ACL You can specify two types of grantees in an ACL: an AWS account or a predefined S3 group. You can't grant access to a single user in an ACL.

You grant permission to an AWS account by specifying either the canonical user ID or the e-mail address. Regardless, the ACL will always contain the canonical user ID for the account and not its e-mail address, as S3 replaces the e-mail address that you specify with the canonical user ID for that account. The canonical user ID associated with an AWS account is a long string that you can get from the ACL of a bucket or object to which an account has access permissions.

AWS provides the following predefined groups to help you. You specify an AWS URI instead of a canonical user ID when granting access to one of these groups. Here are the AWS predefined groups:

- **Authenticated Users group** Represents all AWS accounts, meaning that when you grant permissions to this group, all authenticated AWS accounts—any AWS authenticated user in the world—can access the resource.
- **All Users group** When you grant access permission to this group, anyone in the world can access the resource via either a signed (authenticated) or an unsigned (anonymous) request. Obviously, you must be careful when specifying this group!
- **Log Delivery group** You can grant this group the write permissions on a bucket to enable the group to write S3 server access logs to the bucket.

NOTE AWS highly recommends that you *not* grant the All Users group the `WRITE`, `WRITE_ACP`, or `FULL_CONTROL` permissions.

Permissions You Can Grant in an ACL Unlike the large number of permissions that you can grant through an access policy, an ACL enables you to grant only a small set of permissions on buckets and objects. Here are the permissions that you can grant via an ACL:

- **READ** For a bucket, it enables grantees to list the bucket's objects. For an object, it permits grantees to read the object data and metadata.
- **WRITE** Grantees can create (PUT operation), overwrite, and delete a bucket's objects. Write permission isn't applicable to objects.

- **READ_ACP and WRITE_ACP**   Grantees can read from and write to the bucket or object ACLs.
- **FULL_CONTROL**   The grantee has the READ, WRITE, READ_ACP, and WRITE_ACP permissions on the bucket. When you grant this permission on an object, the grantee gets the READ, READ_ACP, and WRITE_ACP permissions on the object.

S3 provides a set of predefined grants, called *canned ACLs*, each with a predefined set of grantees and permissions. For example, the canned ACL named *public-read* grants the owner FULL_CONTROL and READ access to the All Users group.

Here are the corresponding access policy permissions for the five types of ACL permissions that you can grant on a bucket or object:

- READ corresponds to the s3.ListBucket and s3:GetObject access policy permissions.
- WRITE corresponds to the s3:PutObject and s3:DeleteObject permissions.
- READ_ACP corresponds to the s3:GetBucketAcl and s3:GetObjectAcl permissions.
- WRITE_ACP corresponds to the s3:PutBucketAcl and s3:PutObjectAcl permissions.
- FULL CONTROL corresponds to a combination of access policy permissions.

User Policies

You can also attach IAM policies to IAM users, groups, and roles in your AWS account to grant them access to S3 resources. Let's take a case where you want an EC2 instance to have permissions to access objects in an S3 bucket. The most secure way to do this would be to create an IAM role and grant it the necessary permissions to access the S3 bucket. You then assign that role to the EC2 instance.

 NOTE   You can grant anonymous permission in an IAM bucket policy, but not in an IAM user policy, because the user policy is associated with a specific user. Thus, there's no principal element in an IAM user policy.

The following is an example user policy:

```
{
    "Version": "2012-10-17",
    "Statement": [
        {
            "Sid": "TestStatement1",
            "Effect": "Allow",
            "Action": [
                "s3:PutObject",
                "s3:GetObject",
```

```
            "s3:ListBucket",
            "s3:DeleteObject",
            "s3:GetBucketLocation"
        ],
        "Resource": [
            "arn:aws:s3:::testbucket/*",
            "arn:aws:s3:::testbucket"
        ]
    },
    {
        "Sid": "TestStatement2",
        "Effect": "Allow",
        "Action": "s3:ListAllMyBuckets",
        "Resource": "*"
    }
    ]
}
```

An access policy can have multiple sets of permissions under its Statement clause. This policy has two distinct sets of permissions:

- The first (TestStatement1) grants the user permissions to read, upload, and delete objects, among other permissions.
- The second set of permissions (TestStatement2) grants the same user permission to list all the user's buckets.

An advantage to creating a group-based policy is that you don't have to name the individual buckets. When a new bucket is created in your account, anyone to whom you granted wildcarded S3 permissions will be able to access the new bucket, without you having to modify the policies.

How Amazon S3 Authorizes Requests

S3 evaluates all the access policies related to a request, including resource-based (bucket policies plus ACLs) and user policies, to determine whether to allow or deny the request. When Amazon S3 receives a request to perform an action on an S3 resource, it processes the request in the following manner by evaluating the set of relevant access policies (user, bucket, and ACL) based on the specific *context*:

- **User context** In the user context, if the request is from an IAM user, S3 evaluates the subset of access policies owned by the parent account, including any user policies associated by the parent with this user. If the parent happens to be the owner of the S3 resource (bucket or object), S3 also evaluates the relevant resource policies (bucket policies, bucket ACLs, and object ACLs). In this case, S3 doesn't evaluate the bucket context, since it evaluates the bucket policy and the bucket ACL as part of the user context. When the parent AWS account owns a bucket or object, a user or a resource policy can grant permission to the IAM user.

- **Bucket context** In the bucket context, S3 evaluates the access policies set up by the AWS account that owns the bucket. If the parent AWS account of the IAM user making the request isn't the bucket owner, the IAM user needs permissions from both the parent AWS account and the bucket owner. For bucket operations, the bucket owner must have granted permissions to the requester through a bucket policy or a bucket ACL. For object operations, S3 ensures that there isn't an explicitly set deny policy by the bucket owner on access to this bucket's objects.

- **Object context** For requests seeking to perform operations on objects, S3 checks the object owner's access policies.

 NOTE The user context isn't evaluated for requests that you make using the root credentials of your AWS account.

Let's walk through a simple object operation request by an IAM user to learn how S3 steps through the user, bucket, and object contexts to determine whether it should grant the user's request. Let's say for an object operation, the user's parent AWS account is 1111-1111-1111. The user requests a read (GET) operation on an object owned by a different AWS account, 2222-2222-222. The bucket in which this object lives is owned by yet another AWS account, 3333-3333-3333.

Because there are different AWS entities, and the parent AWS account doesn't own the bucket in question, S3 requires the user to have permission from all three accounts—the parent AWS account, the bucket owner, and the object owner. Here's how S3 checks all the relevant access policies, one by one:

- S3 first evaluates the *user context* to ensure that the parent AWS account has an access policy that grants the user permission to perform the read operation. If the user doesn't have the permission, S3 denies the request. If the user does have the permission, S3 next evaluates the bucket context, since the parent is not the owner of the object.

- In the *bucket context*, S3 checks the bucket policies in the bucket owner's account to ensure there is no explicit deny policy for this user to access the object.

- Finally, in the *object context*, S3 checks the object ACL to verify that the user has permission to read the object. If so, it authorizes the user's read request.

Protecting Your Amazon S3 Objects

You protect your S3 data with three main strategies: *encryption, versioning and MFA delete,* and *object locking.* In addition, you may also need to durably store your S3 data across multiple regions with S3 *cross-region replication.*

Encrypting S3 Data

You can use both server-side and client-side encryption to protect your S3 data.

Server-side encryption protects data at rest in the AWS data centers. With server-side encryption, you request S3 to encrypt your objects before storing the objects on disk. S3 decrypts the data when you download the encrypted objects. You can use either AWS KMS-managed keys (SSE_KMS), Amazon S3-managed keys (SSE_S3), or your own keys (SSE-C) for encrypting the data. When you use your own encryption keys, you must provide the keys and the encryption algorithm as part of your request in each API call that you or your application makes to S3. You manage your own keys (be sure to rotate the keys regularly for additional security), but S3 handles the encryption and decryption of your data.

In *client-side encryption*, you, not Amazon, perform the encryption, and you are also in charge of the encryption keys. You encrypt the data before you send it to S3. You can use an AWS KMS-managed customer master key or your own client-side master key.

Let's say, for example, that you have some unencrypted objects in an S3 bucket. You can encrypt the objects from the Amazon S3 console. To ensure that all new objects that users place in that bucket are also encrypted, you must set a bucket policy that requires encryption when users upload the objects.

Versioning and MFA Delete

Amazon S3 offers strategies to protect data from accidental deletes and overwrites through *versioning* and *MFA Delete*.

Versioning S3 Objects   While encryption protects your data from hacking and other security vulnerabilities, there are other ways you can lose your S3 data. For example, you can accidentally delete or overwrite objects. Or an application failure may wipe out the data. Version-enabling your S3 buckets lets you access earlier versions of the objects when you accidentally delete or overwrite the objects.

Versioning maintains multiple versions of an object in a bucket. It keeps a copy of each update you make to an object. Once you enable versioning, when you delete an object, S3 inserts a *delete marker*, which becomes the current version of the object. S3 doesn't remove the object, so you can easily recover the deleted older version any time. If you accidentally or otherwise overwrite an object, S3 stores the action as a new *object version*, again helping you restore the older version.

You can configure versioning from the Amazon S3 console or programmatically using the AWS SDKs. In addition to the root account that created the bucket and owns it, an authorized user can also configure versioning for a bucket.

A bucket for which you enable versioning stores multiple object versions. One of these object versions is *current*, and the others are *noncurrent* object versions (if you have multiple versions). Exercise 7-9 shows how to enable versioning for an S3 bucket.

A bucket can be in one of three states:

- Unversioned (the default state)
- Versioning-enabled
- Versioning-suspended

You may choose to turn off versioning on a bucket. However, the bucket won't return to an unversioned state.

After you enable versioning for an object, any updates or deletes of the object introduces a new version of the object into the bucket and marks it as the current version of the object. If you just "delete" an object, it adds the new version to the bucket, but it's only a *marker* (a 0-byte file) that indicates that the object doesn't exist any longer. If you then try to access the object, you'll get an HTTP 404 error (no file found). By deleting the 0-byte version, you can restore the previous version of the object, thus providing a way to retrieve an object that you deleted by mistake. To remove a version without producing the marker file for the object, you must *purge* the object by executing a *delete version* task. You can mark any of an object's versions as the current version (also called restoring) or delete or expire any versions if you don't need them any longer.

At this point, you may wonder, if a bucket has multiple versions of an object, which versions will S3 return when you make a request to read an object (GET request)? If you make a simple GET request, you always get back the current version of the object that you had requested. You can retrieve a prior version of the object by specifying the object's version ID. Figure 7-3 shows how, by specifying a `versionId` property, a GET request obtains a specific version of an object and not the current version.

Here's what you need to know from Figure 7-3:

- The GET request seeks to retrieve the object with the key photo.gif.

- The original object in a bucket before you turn on versioning has a version ID of null. If there are no other versions, this is the version that S3 returns.

- In this example, there are three versions of the object, with the IDs null, 111111, and 121212, with the object with version ID 121212 being the current (latest) version of the object. A GET request that doesn't specify an object ID retrieves the current version of the object.

- The GET request in Figure 7-3 specifies the version ID 111111, thus retrieving this version and not the original or the current version of the object.

Although versioning of S3 objects offers several benefits, a cost is attached. AWS bills you for storing each of an object's versions, which means that your S3 storage costs are

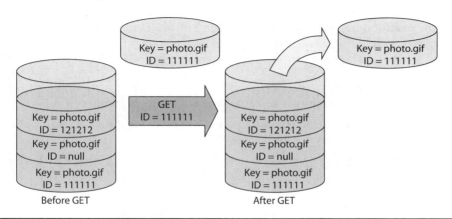

Figure 7-3   A GET request for a specific version of a versioned object

going to be higher if you have many objects with multiple versions. If it's critical for you to keep older versions in place, versioning is the way to go, but if cost is a concern, stay away from S3 versioning.

MFA Delete   For stronger protection of your S3 data, you can optionally enable Multi-Factor Authentication Delete (MFA Delete) for a bucket. MFA Delete works *together* with bucket versioning. Once you configure MFA Delete, S3 requires further authentication whenever you want to delete an object version permanently or change a bucket's versioning state.

An MFA device forces the requestor to enter an additional means of authentication in the form of an authentication code that the MFA device generates. You can use either a hardware or a virtual MFA device.

MFA Delete works together with object versioning. You can use the two together if, for example, you must retain all copies of an S3 object to satisfy a compliance requirement.

Locking Objects

Often, regulatory requirements demand that you keep critical data for a specific length of time. Amazon S3 Object Lock helps you with this by enabling you to explicitly specify an S3 object's retention period. When you specify a retention period, the object is locked by S3 and no one can delete or overwrite it.

In addition to a retention period, you can configure a *legal hold* to safeguard S3 objects. A legal hold isn't based on a time period; it prevents an object from being deleted until you remove the hold. You can use either a retention period or a legal hold, or both together, to protect objects.

To use S3 Object Lock to protect an object, you must first version-enable the S3 bucket where the object lives. Both retention period and legal hold apply to a specific object version—you specify the retention period or a legal hold, or both together, for a specific object version. The restrictions that you place apply only to this object version and new versions can still be created for that object.

How Retention Period and Legal Hold Work Together   A retention period that you specify for an object version keeps that version from being deleted for that period. S3 stores a timestamp of the object version in its metadata to indicate its retention period. When the retention period expires, you can delete or overwrite the object version, unless you've placed an additional legal hold on the object version.

Here's what you need to remember about retention periods for an object version:

- Because you specify retention periods for a specific object version, different versions of the same object can have different retention periods.

- You can explicitly set the retention period by specifying a Retain Until Date attribute for an object version.

- You can also specify the retention period for all objects in a bucket with a bucket default setting.

- An explicit retention setting for an object version overrides the bucket default settings for that object version.
- After you apply a certain retention setting of an object, you may extend it by submitting a new lock request for the object version.
- You can configure a default retention period for objects placed in an S3 bucket.

A legal hold is independent of a retention period. You can place a legal hold on an object version to keep it from being deleted or overwritten. Unlike a retention period, however, a legal hold isn't for any specific time period; it remains in effect until you explicitly remove it. You can also place a legal hold on an object version for which you've already specified a retention period. When the retention period expires, the legal hold continues to stay in effect, protecting the object from being deleted or overwritten.

Configuring Object Lock for an Object   Follow these steps to configure Object Lock for objects in S3:

1. Create a bucket with S3 Object Lock enabled.

2. Optionally, configure a retention period for the objects in the bucket.

3. Place the objects you want to lock in the new bucket.

4. Apply a retention period, a legal hold, or both to the objects.

Securing S3 Data with Cross-Region Replication

Although strategies such as versioning and MFA Delete offer protection against accidental deletions of data and such, you may also need to durably store your S3 data across multiple regions for various reasons. You can do this with S3 cross-region replication (CRR), which automatically and asynchronously copies your S3 data across buckets located in different AWS regions. Although it doesn't cost you anything to set up CRR, you are billed for transferring data across regions and for storing multiple copies of the data in those regions.

Use Cases for CRR   You can use CRR to satisfy regulatory and compliance requirements that require you to store data in multiple geographically distant AZs. By maintaining copies in various locations, you can also minimize latency in accessing key objects by maintaining copies of an object closer to your user groups.

By default, CRR replicates the replicated object's ACL along with the data. If you don't happen to own the destination bucket, you can configure CRR to change replica ownership over to the AWS accounts that own the destination buckets (this is called the *owner override* option) to maintain an object copy under a different ownership. Changing the ownership of the replicas can also safeguard key data by saving the same data under different buckets that are owned by different entities. By replicating data to a different region, you can be assured that your critical S3 data has multiple copies spread across multiple regions.

Setting Up CRR   You enable CRR at the bucket level by adding the replication configuration to your source bucket. CRR has some requirements:

- Both the source and the destination buckets must be located in different AWS regions.
- You must enable versioning for both the source and destination S3 buckets.
- If the source and destination buckets are owned by different AWS accounts (cross-account scenario), the owner of the destination bucket must grant the owner of the source bucket permissions to replicate objects through a bucket policy.

Once you meet all the requirements, you can enable CRR of data from the source bucket to the destination bucket in the other region by adding the replication configuration to the source bucket. You can replicate all or some of the objects in the source bucket to the destination bucket. For example, you can specify that S3 replicate only objects with the key name prefix *Finance/*. S3 then replicates objects such as Finance/doc1 but not objects with the key HR/doc1. Although, by default, the destination object replicas use the same S3 storage class as the source objects, you can specify a different storage class for them when configuring CRR.

Optimizing Amazon S3 Storage

Amazon S3 offers best practices for optimizing S3 performance. You can optimize performance in several areas.

You can scale read performance by creating several prefixes in a bucket to enhance performance. An application can achieve a minimum of 3500 PUT/POST/DELETE operations and 5500 GET requests per second per prefix in a bucket. You can have an unlimited number of prefixes in a bucket. A higher number of prefixes helps you increase read/write performance by parallelizing the reads and writes. So by creating 10 prefixes in an S3 bucket, you can achieve a read performance of 55,000 requests per second.

If your applications receive mostly GET requests, you can use Amazon CloudFront for enhancing performance. CloudFront reduces the number of direct requests to S3, reducing your costs for retrieving data from S3, in addition to reducing application latency. CloudFront retrieves the popular objects from S3 and caches them. It then serves requests for these objects from its cache, which reduces the number of GET requests it sends to S3.

You can improve network throughput between your OS/application layer and Amazon S3 by TCP window scaling, adjusting the TCP window sizes and setting them larger than 64KB at both the application and the kernel levels.

Finally, enabling TCP selective acknowledgment helps to improve recovery time after losing a large number of TCP packets.

Setting Up Event Notifications for an S3 Bucket

You can configure notifications to various destinations following certain S3 bucket events. When you configure the notifications, you need to specify the type of event and the destination to which the notification must be sent.

S3 can notify destinations when the following types of events occur:

- **Object creation events**   This notification is sent whenever an object is created in the bucket, with actions such as `Put`, `Post Copy`, and `CompleteMultiPartUpload`.

- **Object delete events**   You can configure the deletion of a versioned or unversioned object to trigger an event notification.

- **Restore object events**   These events send notifications when an object stored in the Glacier storage class is restored.

- **RRS object lost events**   These events send notifications when S3 finds that an object of the RRS storage class is lost. (Remember that RRS offers lower redundancy than Standard S3 storage.)

Event notifications can be sent to destinations such as an SNS topic, an SQS queue, or a Lambda function.

Archival Storage with Amazon S3 Glacier

Amazon S3 Glacier, a REST-based web service, is a storage service that's ideal for storing rarely used data, often called *cold data*. Glacier is low-cost storage for data archiving and for storing backups for long periods of time, even as long as several years. Glacier is ideal for storing data that you access rarely to infrequently. Glacier is optimized for long-term archival storage and isn't suited for data that is erased within 90 days.

Unlike the other Amazon S3 storage classes, which are all designed to provide immediate access to your data, Glacier is meant purely as storage that is not for immediate retrieval. Typically, it takes three to five hours to retrieve data from Glacier. However, by paying a much higher price for the data retrieval, you do have the option of immediately retrieving data from Glacier.

Key Glacier Concepts and Components

Vaults and *archives* are the key Glacier resources. A vault is a container for storing archives. An archive is the basic storage unit and can include data such as documents, photos, and videos that you want to store in Glacier.

 NOTE   Vaults are key entities in Glacier. You can manage vaults from the Glacier console, but for uploading data, you must use the AWS CLI or write code via the REST API (Glacier web service API) or through AWS SDKs that wrap the Glacier REST API calls, to make it easy for you to develop applications that use Glacier by taking care of tasks such as authentication and request signing.

In addition to vaults and archives, which make up the data entities of Glacier, two other concepts are important to know: *jobs* and *notifications*. Jobs perform queries on archives and retrieve the archives, among other things. The notification mechanism notifies you when jobs complete.

Vaults

Vaults are the logical containers in which you store the data you want to archive. There's no limit on the number of archives you can store within a vault.

Vault operations are region-specific. You create a vault in a specific region and request a vault list from a specific region as well. You can create up to 1000 vaults in an AWS region. You create vaults from the S3 console by following the steps in Exercise 7-10.

Glacier inventories each of your vaults every 24 hours. The inventory contains information about the archives, such as their sizes, IDs, and their creation times. Glacier also ensures that an empty vault is truly so, by checking whether any writes have occurred since it took the last inventory. You can delete a vault if there were no archives in it when Glacier computed its most recent inventory or if there were no writes since that inventory.

You refer to your vaults through unique addresses of the form:

https://*<region-specific-endpoint>*/*<account-id>*/vaults/*<vaultname>*

For example, the vault that you may create in Exercise 7-10 in the us-west-2 (Oregon) region has the following URI:

https://glacier-us-west-2.amazonaws.com/111122223333/vaults//myvault

In this URI,

- *111122223333* is your AWS account ID.
- *vaults* is the collection of vaults owned by your account.
- *myvault* is your vault's name.

Archives

An archive is data that you store in a vault. Although you can upload single files as archives, it's economical to bundle multiple files together in the form of a TAR or ZIP file before uploading it to Glacier. Once you upload an archive to Glacier, you can only delete it—you can't overwrite or edit it.

As is the case with a vault, an archive has a unique address with the following general form:

https://*<region-specific-endpoint>*/*<account-id>*/vaults/*<vaultname>*/archives/*<archive-id>*

The following is the URI for an archive that you store in the vault named myvault:

https://glacier-us-west-2.amazonaws.com/111122223333/vaults/myvault/archives/
NkbByEejwEggmBz2fHgJrg0XBoDfjP416iu87-T

You can perform three types of archive operations in Glacier: upload archives, download archives, and delete archives. You can upload archives via the AWS CLI or write code (REST APIs, or AWS SDKs) to do so. You can upload archives ranging from 1 byte to 64GB in size, which is a single operation. However, AWS recommends that you use a *multipart upload* for archives larger than 100MB. A multipart upload enables you to upload archives that are as large as 40,000GB (40TB).

You must use the AWS CLI or write code to perform any archive operation, such as uploading, downloading, or deleting archives. You can't perform archive operations from a console. The code you write may directly invoke Glacier REST APIs or the AWS SDKs, which provide a wrapper for those APIs.

Once you upload an archive, you can't update its contents (or its description). To update the archive content or its description, you must delete the archive and upload a different archive.

Jobs

You run Glacier jobs to perform queries on your archives, retrieve the archives, or retrieve a vault's contents (inventory). You use SQL queries, which Glacier Select executes, writing the query's output to Amazon S3. For example, a *select* job performs a select query on an archive, an *archive-retrieval* job retrieves an archive, and an *inventory-retrieval* job inventories a vault.

Both the retrieval of the list of archives (inventory) and the retrieval of an archive itself are actions that require you to wait. You start a job and wait to download the output once Glacier completes the job execution.

Once again, you use a unique URL of the following form to track the jobs that you initiate with Glacier:

> https://*<region-specific-endpoint>*/*<account-id>*/vaults/*<vaultname>*/jobs/*<job-id>*

Notifications

Because Glacier jobs may run for a long time, it provides notifications to let you know that your job has completed. You can configure Glacier to send the notifications to an Amazon Simple Notification Service (SNS) topic. Glacier reports the job completion in the form of a JSON document.

You can configure one notification per vault, each identified by a unique URL of the following form:

> https://*<region-specific-endpoint>*/*<account-id>*/vaults/*<vaultname>*/notification-configuraton

Because Glacier updates its inventory every 24 hours, you may not see your new archive right after you upload it to your vault.

Glacier Archive Retrieval and Data Retrieval Policies

You can specify one of three archive retrieval options when starting a job to retrieve an archive. The options differ in their access time/cost ratio:

- **Standard** Standard retrievals typically complete within a few hours—say, three to five hours. This is the *default retrieval option* if you don't specify one.

- **Expedited** An expedited retrieval makes all but very large archives (sized 250MB or larger) available within one to five minutes. You can purchase provisioned capacity to ensure that your retrieval capacity is available to you when you need it. A unit of capacity provides up to 150 MBps of throughput and ensures that at least three expedited retrievals can be made every five minutes.

- **Bulk** A bulk retrieval is the cheapest Glacier option and helps you retrieve very large amounts of data inexpensively if time isn't a big concern. Bulk retrievals complete within five to twelve hours.

You can select from the following three Glacier data retrieval policies to set limits on data retrieval and manage the data retrieval activities in your AWS account across an AWS region:

- **Free Tier Only** Your retrievals stay within your daily free tier allowance and AWS won't bill you for data retrieval. Any data revival requests that exceed the retrieval limit won't be accepted.

- **Max Retrieval Rate** You can set a data retrieval limit with a bytes-per-hour maximum. A new retrieval request that causes the peak retrieval rate of in-progress jobs to exceed the bytes-per-hour limit that you specify is rejected by Glacier. The free tier policy rate is 14MB per hour. If you set the Max retrieval rate to just 2MB per hour, you'll be wasting a lot of your daily free tier allowance. A good strategy would be to set your policy first to the Free Tier Only policy and switch it to the Max Retrieval Rate policy later, once you're more familiar with the archival retrievals.

- **No Retrieval Limit** Glacier accepts all data retrieval requests and your retrieval cost is proportional to your usage.

Data retrieval policies apply only to standard data retrievals. Your data retrieval policy settings don't have a bearing on the standard retrieval time, which is three to five hours.

S3 Glacier Vault Lock

Often, you're bound by various regulatory and compliance requirements to store key data in a way that it can't be tampered with. Glacier's *Vault Lock* feature helps you enforce compliance policies for a Glacier vault. For example, you can set up a Vault Lock policy that specifies a control such as "write once read many" (WORM). You lock up this policy in the vault, which prevents any changes to it after that.

You can use both the Vault Lock and vault access policies together. You can use the Vault Lock policy to deploy regulatory and compliance controls, which require tighter controls on data access. You can use the vault access policies for controlling noncompliance-related access.

The Lock Process

Locking a vault involves initiating the lock and then completing the lock process. You initiate the lock by attaching a vault lock policy to the vault. You do this by calling Initiate Vault Lock (POST lock-policy) with a Vault Lock policy that includes the control you want to set up. This call attaches the policy to the vault and returns a unique lock ID.

Once you create a Vault Lock policy, you have 24 hours to review and evaluate the policy with the help of the lock ID that expires after that time. After this point, you can't change the policy any longer. You call the Complete Vault Lock (POST lockId) procedure with the lock ID that was returned by the call to Initiate Vault Lock (POST lock-policy).

If a company must retain compliance data for multiple years in a form that prevents any changes in the data (immutable data), activating Vault Lock is a cost-effective and easy way to do this. No user, including the AWS root account, can change the data.

Amazon Elastic File System

Amazon Elastic File System (EFS) offers file storage for your EC2 instances in the Amazon cloud. It's a managed file storage service, which means that instead of running your own Network File System (NFS), you let Amazon handle the file storage infrastructure for you.

Although you create the file system in a specific AZ, EC2 instances running in other AZs can access the file system, thus giving you a data source that supports a large number of users.

Using Amazon EFS, you create and mount files systems on an EC2 instance and read from and write data to it as you do with any other file system. You can mount the file systems in your Amazon VPC, through the NFS versions 4.0 and 4.1 (NFSv4) protocol.

There are a few key differences between Amazon EBS and Amazon EFS. Unlike EBS volumes, in EFS, there are no unformatted blocks for you to format and use. EBS is much more flexible than EBS storage, helping you easily grow your shared storage to multiple petabytes in a single logical volume. The biggest difference between EBS and EFS is that you use EBS volumes for a single EC2 instance, whereas EFS is designed as a multiuser system, enabling multiple EC2 instances to access the same file system.

EBS is much cheaper than provisioning an EFS file system on a per-GB cost of storage basis, so if you require storage for a single EC2 system, there's no need for you to use EFS. EFS, however, is cheaper if you have a large number of users that need to access the same file system. On top of the cost savings, you won't have the overhead of setting up your own multiuser file system that's also highly available.

Setting Up an EFS-Based File System

To start using EFS files systems, you need to do the following, in order:

1. *Create mount targets.* Mount targets are endpoints in your Amazon VPC where you mount the EFS file systems on an EC2 instance running in your VPC.

2. *Create your EFS file systems.* The file systems will appear as any other file systems that an EC2 instance uses. AWS recommends that you tag the file systems with the Name tag (you can also add other tags as well) to make it easy for you to identify the file systems in the console.

3. *Mount the EFS file system.* You must mount the new EFS file system on an EC2 instance so you can access the file system.

4. *Create the necessary security groups.* You must associate both the EC2 instance and the mount targets with security groups. The security groups act as virtual firewalls to control the traffic flowing between the instance and the mount targets. The security group that you associate with a mount group controls the inbound traffic to the mount target through inbound rules that allow traffic from a specific EC2 instance.

Creating Mount Targets

Before you create an EFS file system, you must create the mount targets where you'll be mounting the file systems on EC2 instances in your VPC. The *mount target security group* controls the traffic accessing the file systems by serving as a security group. You can create the mount targets from the console, but you can also do it via the command line by executing the create-mount-target command:

```
$ aws efs create-mount-target \
--file-system-id file-system-id \
--subnet-id subnet-id \
--security-group ID -of -the-security-group-for -the-mount-target \
--region aws-region \
--profile adminuser
```

Replace the values of the parameters in italics with appropriate values for your VPC.

You can create one mount target in each AZ. If your VPC has multiple subnets in an AZ, you can create a mount target in only one of those subnets. You can create a new security group for the mount target prior to running this command if you don't want to use your default security group.

Creating an EFS File System

You can create the EFS file system from the console or the command line. Exercise 7-4 shows how to do it from the EFS Management Console.

Mounting the EFS File System

After creating an EFS file system, you must connect to an EC2 instance and mount the file system using the mount targets that you created for this file system. Exercise 7-5 shows how to do this.

AWS recommends that you use the amazon-efs-utils package that it freely makes available to help you mount the EFS file systems. This package contains the *mount helper*, a program that you can use when mounting a specific type of file system. The mount helper creates a file system type called *efs* that's compatible with the Linux mount command. It also supports mounting the EFS file system at boot time through entries you make in the /etc/fstab file. Exercise 7-5 uses the amazon-efs-utils package and shows you how to mount an EFS file system.

Creating Security Groups

When you configure EFS file systems, both the EC2 instance on which you mount the file system and the mount targets have security groups associated with them to control traffic. You can choose to create a special security group for the mount target or let EFS associate your VPC's default security group with the mount target.

You must configure the following rules for the two security groups:

- The mount target's security group must allow inbound access (on the NFS port) from all EC2 instances on which you mount the EFS file system.
- Each of the instances where you mounted the EFS file system must allow outbound access to the mount target (on the NFS port).

Using an EFS File System

Once you mount an EFS file system, there's nothing new. You work with the file system as if it were a regular local file system. By default, only the root user has rwx permissions on the root directory, but you can grant other users permissions to modify the file system.

To delete an EFS file system, you must first unmount the file system. To do this, open the Amazon EFS Management Console, select the file system you want to delete, and then, select Action | Delete File System. The command will first delete all the mount targets and then the EFS file system.

Amazon Snowball

Amazon Snowball service offers a way to bypass the Internet and directly move large chunks of data into and out of AWS. A Snowball device enables you to access AWS cloud storage (Amazon S3) locally in your own data center when connecting to the Internet to move data might not be a viable option. Snowball enables you to transport data at faster than Internet speeds, at a lower cost to boot.

A Snowball device, which is a rugged, secure (it encrypts all your data automatically) shipping container, helps you ship data through a regional carrier. Figure 7-4 shows an Amazon Snowball appliance. The device helps you transport hundreds of terabytes or petabytes of data between your data center and Amazon S3. The Snowball appliance has interfaces that you use to create data loading jobs, transfer the data to and from S3, and trace the status of your jobs until they complete.

Figure 7-4
An Amazon
Snowball
appliance

NOTE Use an alternative strategy to transfer data smaller than 10 TB. Snowball is designed for transferring very large sets of data.

Sending data via Snowball is ridiculously simple:

1. You create a job in the AWS Management Console to get a Snowball device to be shipped to you.
2. After delivery, power on the Snowball device, attach it to your network, and establish a connection with a Snowball client that you download from AWS.
3. Select the data files you want Snowball to transfer, and Snowball encrypts (encryption is mandatory) the files and transfers them to the device.
4. Once the data transfer is complete, use the provided shipping label and ship the device back to the specified AWS facility.
5. AWS imports your data into Amazon S3.

That's it. No code and no commands to run.

Snowball devices are enclosed in tamper-resistant containers, employ 256-bit encryption, and use the Trusted Platform Module (TPM) to transfer data securely. The encryption keys are safely stored in the AWS Key Management Service (KMS), and not on the device.

NOTE When downloading data from your on-premise location to S3 storage, you can choose the S3 Glacier storage type to archive the data at a low cost.

You can use storage protocols such as HDFS, S3 API, and the S3 CLI to move data into and out of a Snowball device. You can manage your Snowball data transfer jobs through the AWS Snowball Management Console or with the job management API if you want to do it programmatically.

The Snowball Edge device is like Amazon Snowball, with on-board storage and computing power. It can perform some local processing on top of transferring data between your data center and AWS.

AWS Storage Gateway

AWS Storage Gateway offers a way to connect a software or hardware appliance with S3, thus helping you integrate your on-premise environment with the AWS cloud storage infrastructure. You can run the gateway with an on-premise virtual machine (VM) appliance, use the AWS Storage Gateway hardware appliance, or set it up in AWS as an EC2 instance.

Gateway Types

AWS Storage Gateway offers three types of storage solutions: *file-based, volume-based,* and *tape-based.*

To set up AWS Storage Gateway, you must make the following choices:

- Storage solution: Choose a file, volume, or tape gateway.
- Hosting option: You can deploy the Storage Gateway on-premises as a VM appliance, or in AWS as an EC2 instance.

File Gateway

A file gateway is like a file system mount on Amazon S3. The file gateway provides a file interface to S3 by enabling you to access S3 objects as files or file share mount points and works with a virtual software appliance. The software appliance acts as the gateway and you deploy it in your data center as a VM.

Using the file gateway, you can store and retrieve objects in S3 using standard file protocols such as Network File System (NFS) and Server Message Block (SMB). You can access the S3 data from any AWS application or service.

The file gateway offers a cost-effective alternative to maintaining storage on your own premises. It integrates to your applications through standard file system protocols and provides low-latency access to the data by locally caching data. The file gateway manages all data transfers from your data center to AWS and optimizes data transfers by parallel data streaming, saving your applications from network congestion.

Volume Gateway

A volume gateway uses AWS cloud storage–backed storage volumes you mount as Internet Small Computer System Interface (ISCSI) from an application server in your data center. There are two types of volumes: cached volumes and stored volumes.

A *cached volume* lets you store your data in S3 and keep a copy of the frequently accessed portions of that data locally. This offers the twin benefits of providing your applications fast access to frequently accessed data, while reducing your local storage expenditures. This type of volume helps you grow your storage in AWS.

A *stored volume* provides fast access to all your data by letting you configure the gateway to store all your data locally in your data center. Since you won't be storing any of this data on S3, you can make snapshots of this data to S3 for disaster recovery of either your local databases or data for Amazon EC2 instances. Unlike a cached volume, which helps you grow your storage in AWS, a stored volume offers storage that has a 1:1 relationship with the volume size.

Tape Gateway

The tape gateway enables you to archive backup data to Amazon Glacier, eliminating the need for you to provision and maintain a physical tape infrastructure.

Setting Up and Activating the AWS Storage Gateway

To use the Storage Gateway, you must first create the gateway and activate it. Following this, you create file shares and start using them. You can create the gateway on-premises or in an EC2 instance. If you chose to create the gateway on-premises, you can download and deploy the gateway VM and activate the gateway. You can create the gateway on an EC2 instance using an AMI with the gateway VM image and then activate the gateway.

Creating a File Share

You can create file shares that can be accessed by NFS or SMB. You can have both NFS- and SMB-based file shares on the same file gateway. If you're using the NFS protocol, by default, everyone who can access the NFS server can also access the file share. You limit client access by IP addresses. For an SMB-based file share, authentication can be through specifying limited access to some domain users and groups, by provisioning guest access, or by using Microsoft Active Directory (AD) access.

You can encrypt the objects that a file gateway stores in S3 by using the AWS Key Management Service (KMS).

Using the File Share

To use the file share you've created, you must mount the file share on a storage drive on your client and map it to an S3 bucket. You can then test the file gateway by copying files to your mapped drive. If everything goes right, you should be able to see the files that you've uploaded in your S3 bucket after that.

Chapter Review

This is a huge chapter in many ways! AWS offers several types of storage, each designed for a set of use cases. Each of these storage types offers a different combination of cost, availability, and performance. Therefore, one of your key functions as an AWS SysOps Administrator is to match your specific use cases to the various storage types.

You use Amazon EBS volumes for persistent storage with your EC2 instances. AWS recommends that you use EBS-optimized volumes for best performance. Amazon S3 is a way to store objects in the AWS cloud. You can access these objects directly via unique URLs for each object.

Amazon S3 Glacier is meant for storing backups and other data that you must store for compliance and regulatory purposes. Unless you pay additional charges, the data you store in Glacier isn't available immediately, as is the case with EBS and S3 storage.

If you want multiple users and multiple EC2 instances to access a file system, Amazon EFS is the way to go, rather than setting up such a file system by yourself.

Amazon Snowball is quite different from all the other AWS storage services in that it enables you to transport large data sets quickly and economically to and from AWS, with the help of a storage appliance.

Finally, the Amazon Storage Gateway helps you connect your on-premise software appliance with AWS S3.

Exercises

These exercises are designed to teach you how to perform important AWS administrative tasks through the console. If you make a mistake, retrace your steps and ensure that you've correctly performed the steps. You'll know that you've correctly completed the exercise if you achieve the goal set for you in each exercise.

Exercise 7-1: Create an EBS volume from the console.

1. Open the EC2 console: https://console.aws.amazon.com/ec2/.
2. In the navigation bar, select the region where you want to create the volume.
3. In the navigation pane, select ELASTIC BLOCK STORE | Volumes.
4. Select Create Volume.
5. For Volume Type, select a volume type.
6. For Size (GiB), specify the volume size.
7. If you chose a Provisioned IOPS SSD volume, for IOPS, specify the maximum IOPS you want the volume to support.
8. For AZ, select the AZ in which you want to create the volume.
9. Select Create Volume.

Exercise 7-2: Attach an EBS volume to an EC2 instance from the console.

1. Open the EC2 console: https://console.aws.amazon.com/ec2/.
2. In the navigation pane, select ELASTIC BLOCK STORE | Volumes.
3. Select an EBS volume and then select Actions | Attach Volume.
4. For Instance, enter the name of the EC2 instance.
5. For Device, use the device name suggested by AWS or enter a different device name.
6. Select Attach.
7. Connect to the EC2 instance and mount the volume.

Exercise 7-3: Create an EBS snapshot from the EC2 console.

1. Open the EC2 console: http://console.aws.amazon.com/ec2/.
2. In the navigation pane, select Snapshots.
3. Select Create Snapshot.

4. In the Create Snapshot page, select the EBS volume that you want to back up.

5. Select Add Tags To Your Snapshot to make it easy for you to manage this snapshot.

6. Select Create Snapshot.

Exercise 7-4: Create an Amazon EFS file system.

1. Open the Amazon EFS Management Console: https://console.aws.amazon .com/efs/.

2. Select Create File System.

3. Select your default VPC from the VPC list.

4. Select all the AZs, and leave the default subnets, security groups, and automatic IP addresses alone (these are your mount targets). Click Next Step.

5. Enter a name for the file system (keep General Purpose and Bursting as the default performance and throughput modes). Click Next Step.

6. Select Create File System.

7. Make sure to note down the File System ID value, which you'll be using to mount this EFS file system

Exercise 7-5: Mount an EFS file system.

You must complete Exercise 7-4 before starting this exercise.

1. Using SSH, connect to the EC2 instance where you want to mount the EFS file system.

2. Install the amazon-efs-utils package to help mount the files:

```
$ sudo yum  install -y amazon-efs-utils
```

3. Make a directory to serve as the mount point for the EFS file system:

```
$ sudo mkdir myefs
```

4. Mount the EFS file system you created in Exercise 7-4 to the mount point myefs. The value of the *file-system-id* you must specify in this command is the File System ID that you saved in step 7 of Exercise 7-4.

5. Move to the new directory you created in step 3:

```
$ cd myefs
```

6. Make a subdirectory under the myefs directory and change ownership to your EC2 instance user (ec2-user):.

```
$ sudo mkdir test
$ sudo chown ec2-user test
```

7. Move to the subdirectory test under the myefs directory and create a test file for testing purposes:

```
$ cd test
$ touch test.txt
```

8. Run the `ls -al` command to ensure that you can see the test.txt file, with the proper permissions (`ec2-user:ec2-user`).

Exercise 7-6: Create an Amazon S3 bucket.

1. Sign in to the AWS Management Console and open the Amazon S3 console: https://console.awsamazon.com/s3.

2. Select Create Bucket.

3. Enter a bucket name that complies with the DNS naming conventions.

4. Select US West (Oregon) as the Region where the bucket will be stored.

5. Select Create.

Exercise 7-7: Upload an object to an Amazon S3 bucket.

1. Log into the Amazon S3 console as in Exercise 7-6.

2. In the Bucket Name list, select the name of the bucket where you want to upload the object.

3. Select Upload.

4. In the Upload dialog box, select Add Files.

5. Select a file to upload, and then select Open.

6. Select Upload.

Exercise 7-8: Delete an Amazon S3 object and bucket.

1. Log into the Amazon S3 console as in Exercise 7-6.

2. In the Bucket Name list, select the name of the bucket where you want to upload the object.

3. In the Bucket Name list, check the box for the object you want to delete, and then select More | Delete.

4. In the Delete Objects dialog box, select the name of the object, and then click Delete.

5. This sequence of steps is for deleting the bucket. In the bucket name list, select the bucket name, and then select Delete Bucket.

6. In the Delete Bucket dialog box, enter the name of the bucket that you want to delete, and then click Confirm.

Exercise 7-9: Enable versioning for an Amazon S3 bucket.

1. Log into the Amazon S3 console as in Exercise 7-1.

2. From the Bucket Name list, select the name of the bucket you want to enable versioning for.

3. Select Properties.

4. Select Versioning.

5. Select Enable Versioning, and then click Save.

Exercise 7-10: Create an Amazon S3 Glacier vault.

1. Log into the AWS management Console and open the Glacier console: https://console.aws.amazon.com/glacier/.

2. From the Region Selector, select a region where you want to create the vault.

3. Click Create Vault.

4. In the Vault Name field, enter a name for your new vault (**myvault**). Click Next Step.

5. Since this is only an exercise, select Do Not Enable Notifications.

6. Click Submit.

7. Verify that the new vault, myvault, is listed on the Glacier Vaults page.

Exercise 7-11: Create a lifecycle policy for an Amazon S3 bucket from the S3 console.

1. Open the Amazon S3 console: https://console.aws.amazon.com/s3/.

2. From the Bucket Name list, select the name of the bucket for which you want to create a lifecycle policy.

3. Select the Management tab, and then select Add Lifecycle Rule.

4. In the Lifecycle Rule dialog box, enter a name for your lifecycle rule. To apply this lifecycle rule to all objects in this bucket, click Next.

5. Select Current Version so that transitions are applied to the current version of the objects.

6. Select Add Transitions and specify Transition To Standard-IA After. Enter the value **30 days** as the number of days after object creation that the transition must be applied to move the object.

7. Click Next.

8. To set up the Expiration policies, select Current Version.

9. Select Expire Current Version Of Object and then enter **365 days** as the number of days after object creation that the object should be deleted.

10. Click Next.

11. For Review, verify the rule settings and click Save. You'll see your new rule in the Lifecycle page.

Questions

The following questions will help you measure your understanding of the material presented in this chapter. Read all the choices carefully because there may be more than one correct answer. Choose all the correct answers for each question.

1. When you terminate an EC2 instance that's backed by an S3-based AMI, what happens to the data on the root volume?

A. The data is automatically saved as a copy of the EBS volume.

B. The data is automatically saved as an EBS snapshot.

C. The data is automatically deleted.

D. The data is unavailable until the instance is restarted.

2. Given the following IAM policy:

```
{
"Version": "2012-10-17",
  "Statement": [
     {
       "Effect": "Allow",
       "Action": [
          "s3:Get*",  "s3:List*"
          ],
       "Resource": "*"
     },
     {
       "Effect": "Allow",
       "Action": "s3:PutObject",
       "Resource": "arn:aws:s3:::corporate_bucket/*"
     }
   ]
 }
```

What does the IAM policy allow? (Choose three)

   A. The user is allowed to read objects from all S3 buckets owned by the account.

   B. The user is allowed to write objects into the bucket named corporate_bucket.

   C. The user is allowed to change access rights for the bucket named corporate_ bucket.

   D. The user is allowed to read objects from the bucket named corporate_bucket.

3. When you're restoring an Amazon EBS volume from a snapshot, how long must you wait before the data is available to you?

   A. The data is available immediately.

   B. The length of the wait depends on the size of the EBS volume.

   C. The length of the wait depends on how much data you've stored on the volume.

   D. The length of the wait is based on the amount of storage you want to retrieve from the restored volume.

4. When you restore an EBS volume from an EBS snapshot, what happens when an application accesses data on the restored EBS volume as well as further access attempts made to the same storage blocks on the volume? (Choose two)

   A. When an access is made for the first time to a storage block, there's a delay.

   B. After the first access, performance is normal.

   C. The data is returned immediately when the data is accessed for the first time.

   D. The data is returned immediately for the first and any subsequent access attempts.

5. What's the best type of storage volume to attach to your EC2 instances, which an application running on those instances needs to edit common files in a single shared volume?

   A. A single EBS gp2 volume

   B. An Amazon Elastic File System (EFS) volume

   C. A large EBS volume

   D. An Amazon Elastic Block Store (EBS) volume with high IOPS

6. Which of the following statements are true of Amazon EBS? (Choose two)

   A. EBS automatically creates snapshots for the volumes when data changes.

   B. When you stop an instance, any EBS attached volumes are lost.

   C. Data in an EBS volume is automatically replicated within an AZ.

   D. You can encrypt all the application data that you store on an EBS volume by encrypting the volume when you create it.

7. You use S3 to store critical data for your company. Several users within your group currently have full permissions to your S3 buckets. You need to come up with a solution that doesn't adversely impact your users, but that also protects against the accidental deletion of objects. Which two options will address this issue? (Choose two)

   A. Enable versioning on your S3 buckets.

   B. Configure your S3 buckets with MFA Delete.

   C. Create a bucket policy and allow only read only permissions to all users at the bucket level.

   D. Enable object lifecycle policies and configure data older than one month to be archived in Glacier.

8. An organization's security policy requires that multiple copies of all critical data be replicated across at least a primary and a backup data center. The organization has decided to store some critical data on Amazon S3. Which option should you implement to ensure this requirement is met?

   A. Use the S3 copy API to replicate data between two S3 buckets in different regions.

   B. You don't need to implement anything since S3 data is automatically replicated between regions.

   C. Use the S3 copy API to replicate data between two S3 buckets in different facilities within an AWS region.

   D. You don't need to implement anything since S3 data is automatically replicated between multiple facilities within an AWS region.

9. Your organization must ensure that it records all the data that you upload to the Amazon S3 buckets as well as all the read activity of the S3 data by the public. How do you achieve these two goals?

   A. Turn on AWS CloudTrail logging.

   B. Turn on Amazon CloudWatch logging.

   C. Turn on server logging.

   D. Turn on Amazon Inspector.

10. How long will an Amazon EBS volume be unavailable when you take a snapshot of the volume?

    A. The length of time the EBS volume is unavailable depends on the EBS volume's size.

    B. The length of time depends on the amount of data that you've stored on the EBS volume.

    C. The length of time depends on whether you're using an Amazon EBS-optimized instance.

    D. The volume is available immediately.

11. Which of the following statements are true regarding the S3 storage classes that you can choose from? (Choose two)

    A. STANDARD_IA is the default storage class.

    B. STANDARD and STANDARD_IA are designed for long-lived and infrequently accessed data.

    C. STANDARD_IA and ONEZONE_IA are for storing infrequently accessed data that requires millisecond access.

    D. STANDARD_IA storage class is good when you have only a single copy of data that can't be re-created.

12. Who is the owner of an Amazon S3 object when the owner of an S3 bucket grants permissions to users in another AWS account to upload objects to the bucket?

    A. The other AWS account that uploaded the objects is the owner of the objects.

    B. The owner of the S3 bucket is the owner of the objects.

    C. Both the other AWS account that uploads the objects and the owner of the bucket own the objects.

    D. The root IAM account user is always the sole owner of all S3 objects.

13. You've version enabled an S3 bucket, and currently, there are three versions of an object in this bucket, with the IDs null, 1111-1111-1111, and 2222-2222-2222. When a simple GET request asks for an S3 object without specifying an object version ID, which of the three object versions does Amazon S3 return?

    A. The object version with the object ID null

    B. The original version of the object

    C. The object version with the object ID 1111-1111-1111

    D. The object version with the object ID 2222-2222-2222

14. Which of the following upload mechanisms does AWS recommend that you use when you're uploading an archive that's 1000GB in size to Amazon S3 storage?

    A. Perform the upload as a single operation.

    B. Perform a multipart upload of the archive.

    C. Use AWS Direct Connect to upload the archive.

    D. Use Amazon Snowball to move the archive to S3.

15. You've set a retention period of 30 days for a specific S3 object version. The bucket default retention period setting is 30 days. You submit a new lock request for the object version with a Retain Until Date of 120 days. When will the retention period for this object version expire?

    A. In 30 days

    B. In 60 days

    C. Immediately—because of the conflicting retention periods, the object version can't be retained for any time period

    D. 120 days

16. Which of the following EBS storage types is the best choice if your applications need a high throughput without any bottlenecks?

    A. gp2

    B. sc1

    C. io1

    D. st1

17. You're running an EC2 instance in the us-east-1a AZ. You'd like to attach an EBS volume to this instance, and you have two unattached volumes—one located in the us-east-1a AZ and the other in the us-east-1b AZ. Which of these two EBS volumes can you successfully attach to this EC2 instance?

    A. The EBS volume in us-east-1a only

    B. The EBS volume in us-east-ib only

    C. Both the EBS volumes

    D. You can't attach either of the two volumes to the instance.

18. Which of the following storage options is best suited for a scenario in which multiple EC2 instances need to attach to the storage?

    A. Amazon S3

    B. Amazon EBS

    C. Amazon EFS

    D. Amazon Glacier

19. When you encrypt an EBS volume, which of the following types of data are encrypted? (Choose all correct answers)

    A. Data-at-rest stored on the EBS volume

    B. Data that moves between EBS volume and the EC2 instance to which the volume is attached

    C. The snapshots that you create from this EBS volume

    D. The EBS volumes that you create from snapshots that you create from this volume

20. How do you update the contents of a Glacier archive?

    A. You run the upload operation to upload an archive's contents.

    B. You delete the archive and upload another archive.

    C. You keep the archive and upload another archive with different content but the same archive ID.

    D. You can't delete an archive.

21. Which of the following is the default Glacier archival retrieval option?

   A. Bulk

   B. Expedited

   C. Standard

   D. Multi-part upload

22. Which of the following AWS services provide out-of-the-box user-configurable automatic backup-as-a-service and backup rotation options? (Choose two)

   A. Amazon S3

   B. Amazon RDS

   C. Amazon EBS

   D. Amazon Redshift

23. Which of the following statements about the following S3 bucket policy is/are true?

```
{
  "Id": "IPAllowPolicy",
  "Statement": [
    {
      "Sid": "IPAllow",
      "Action": "s3:"",
      "Effect": "Allow".
      "Resource": "am:aws:s3:::mybucket/*",
      "Condition". {
        "IpAddress": {
          "aws:Sourcelp": "192.168.100.0/24"
        },
        "NotIpAddress": {
          "aws:Sourcelp": "192.168.100.188/32"
        }
      },
      "Principal": {
        "AWA": [
          "*"
        ]
      }
    }
  ]
}
```

   A. It denies the server with the IP address 192.168.100.0 full access to the mybucket bucket.

   B. It denies the server with the IP address 192.168.100.188 full access to the mybucket bucket.

   C. It grants all the servers within the 192.168.100.0/24 subnet full access to the mybucket bucket.

   D. It grants all the servers within the 192.168.100.188/32 subnet full access to the mybucket bucket.

24. When an EBS snapshot is initiated but the snapshot is still in progress, which of the following is true?

   A. You can't use the EBS volume.

   B. You can use the EBS volume in the read-only mode.

   C. You can use the EBS volume while the snapshot is in progress.

   D. You can't initiate a snapshot on an EBS volume that's in use by an instance.

25. You're running a database on an EC2 instance, with the data stored on Elastic Block Store (EBS). You are seeing occasional fluctuations in the response times of the database queries and notice that there are high wait times on the disk volume. What are the ways in which you can improve the performance of the database's storage while continuing to store data persistently? (Choose two)

   A. Move to an SSD-backed instance.

   B. Move the database to an EBS-optimized instance.

   C. Use Provisioned IOPs EBS.

   D. Use the ephemeral storage on an m2 4xiarge instance.

26. Which of the following are true of Amazon S3? (Choose two)

   A. Objects are directly accessible via a URL.

   B. S3 enables you to store objects of virtually unlimited size.

   C. S3 enables you to store virtually unlimited amounts of data that you can use to support a database.

   D. S3 offers Provisioned IOPS.

27. What is the best way to resize an instance store–backed volume?

   A. You can't resize an instance store–backed volume.

   B. Copy the data on the volume to a larger or smaller volume.

   C. Use a snapshot of the instance volume to restore data to a larger or smaller instance store–backed volume.

   D. Stop the EC2 instance first and start the resizing operation from the EC2 console.

28. You have been tasked with identifying an appropriate storage solution for a NoSQL database that requires random I/O reads of greater than 100,000 4KB IOPS. Which EC2 option will meet this requirement?

   A. EBS Provisioned IOPS

   B. SSD instance store

   C. EBS optimized instances

   D. High Storage instance configured in RAID 10

29. You need to store data long term for historical purposes. Your analysts occasionally search this data, maybe two or three times a year. Which of the following storage options is the most cost effective, as well as highly available, option?

   A. Store the data on Glacier and serve your users directly from there.

   B. Store the data in S3 and serve your users directly from there.

   C. Store the data on S3 by choosing Infrequent Access (Amazon S3-IA) and serve your users directly from S3.

   D. Store the data on EFS and run a web server on an EC2 instance to serve the data to the users.

30. You're evaluating the storage options for running a database that will have approximately 4000 transactions per second. The data stored on the database is roughly 1.6TB and will grow gradually over time. Which of the following EBS volumes would get you the optimal cost and performance ratio?

   A. One gp2 volume sized 2TB

   B. One SSD volume sized 2TB with provisioned UOPS of 4000

   C. One magnetic volume sized 2TB with a Provisioned IOPS of 4000

   D. One st1 volume sized 2TB with Provisioned IOPS of 4000

31. You want to trace all writes made to an Amazon S3 bucket as well as all the public reads of the content stored in the bucket. Which of the following steps will achieve your goals? (Choose two)

   A. Turn on CloudTrail logging.

   B. Turn on CloudWatch logging.

   C. Turn on Server Access logging.

   D. Turn on IAM logging.

32. Which of the following storage choices will ensure that key compliance can't be removed for five years, without any possibility of an erroneous or intentional access to the data?

   A. S3 with cross-region replication (CRR)

   B. S3 with Bucket Lock

   C. S3 with Versioning and Bucket Lock

   D. Glacier Vault Lock

33. Which of the following are true about Amazon EBS storage? (Choose two)

   A. When you stop an instance, all data on the EBS volume is lost.

   B. EBS automatically replicates data within an AZ.

   C. You can encrypt EBS volumes without affecting the workloads on the instance to which the volume is attached.

   D. You must always attach at least one instance store volume to an EC2 instance, in addition to the EBS volumes.

Answers

1. **C.** You cannot restart a terminated EC2 instance and the data will be deleted automatically.

2. **A, B, D. A** is correct because the first Action block in the permissions policy grants read permission (S3:Get) on all objects owned by this account in all S3 buckets. **B** is correct because the second Action block grants the user permission to write objects (S3:PutObject) to all S3 buckets (Resource": "*"). **D** is correct because the user is granted permission to read objects from the bucket corporate_bucket, not directly, but through the Resource": "*" specification, which grants the S3:Get (read permission) on all objects in all buckets in this account.

3. **A.** The data on the restored volume is immediately available. EBS uses a lazy loading algorithm. It creates the volume immediately and makes it accessible to you but loads it in a lazy fashion. When you request data that hasn't yet been restored to the volume, that data chunk is immediately restored when you first request it.

4. **A, B.** Because there's a (sometimes significant) delay when you make a request for a data chunk for the very first time, AWS recommends that you read all of the data first (this process is called *initializing*) to avoid the delays. Subsequent requests for the same data get immediate responses.

5. **B.** A single EFS file system is what you need here. Multiple EC2 instances and many users can access and share a single EFS file system, unlike an EBS volume, which you can mount only to a single EC2 instance.

6. **C, D.** EBS automatically replicates the EBS volume to multiple locations within an AZ, thus ensuring AZ level redundancy for your data. You can encrypt all data that you store on a volume by choosing the encryption option when creating the volume.

7. **A, B.** Object versioning is designed to protect data against unintentional or erroneous deletion of data by storing multiple versions of an object. MFA Delete offers strong protection against unintentional or unauthorized data deletion by requesting a one-time code from an MFA device before allowing you to delete an object.

8. **D.** You don't need to implement anything since S3 data is automatically replicated between multiple facilities within an AWS region.

9. **A, B.** CloudTrail and CloudWatch logging will show all upload as well as read activity in Amazon S3 buckets.

10. **D.** There's no delay in accessing an EBS volume after starting a snapshot on the volume. The data continues to be available immediately, as usual.

11. **C, D.** Both STANDARD_IA and ONEZONE_IA storage classes are designed for storing long-lived, infrequently accessed data that requires millisecond access. STANDARD_IA storage stores data redundantly across multiple AZs, similar to the STANDARD storage class. STANDARD_IA objects can withstand the loss of an AZ, so this storage class is a safe choice when you have only a single copy of data that you can't re-create in the case of a data loss or data unavailability.

12. **A.** The user from the other AWS account that uploaded the objects is the owner of those objects, regardless of who owns the bucket. The bucket owner doesn't have permissions on the object but can deny access to the objects, archive the objects, or delete the objects, regardless of who owns them.

13. **D.** The object version with the object ID 2222-2222-2222 is the version you'll retrieve when you don't specify an object version with your GET request. A GET request without any object version retrieves the latest version of the object.

14. **B.** AWS recommends that you perform a multipart upload for archives larger than 100MB. (You *can* upload archives ranging from 1 byte to 64GB in size in a single operation, however.)

15. **D.** The object version will be retained for 120 days since you can extend a retention period after you've applied a retention setting to an object version. An explicit retention period that you set overrides any bucket default settings for that object.

16. **A.** The EBS gp2 volume comes with 3000 IOPS as a baseline and offers the highest throughput of all the volume types listed here.

17. **A.** To ensure the lowest possible latency, EBS doesn't allow you to mount EBS volumes to an EC2 instance across AZs.

18. **C.** Amazon EFS is designed for multiple users (instances) that need to access the same file system. EFS offers an easy way to set up a file system for multiple users without your having to rig up a file system yourself that's highly available and redundant like EFS.

19. **A, B, C, D.** EBS encryption offers a comprehensive way to safeguard the data that you store on an EBS volume. When you encrypt an EBS volume, all the data that's at rest and that moves between the volume and the instance, as well as all snapshots and the EBS volumes that you create from those snapshots, are encrypted.

20. **B.** After you upload an archive, you can't update its contents or description. The only way to update an archive is to delete the archive and upload another archive.

21. **C.** Standard is the default option if a retrieval request doesn't specify a retrieval option.

22. **C, D.** Both Amazon EBS and Amazon Redshift provide out-of-the-box automatic backup and backup rotation options.

23. C. The S3 bucket policy grants all servers with an IP address that falls within the subnet 192.168.100.0/24 (`"Condition {"IpAddress {"aws:SourceIp"` `"192.168.100.0/24"`) full access to the mybucket S3 bucket (`"Resource":` `."arn.aws.s3::mybucket/""`).

24. C. You can use the snapshot for both reads and writes while the snapshot is in progress.

25. A, B. An SSD-backed instance offers persistent storage that's very fast. AWS recommends that you use an EBS-optimized instance for best performance. EBS optimization offers the best performance for EBS volumes by minimizing the network contention between EBS I/O and other traffic flowing to and from an EC2 instance.

26. A, B. You can (and must) access objects via a unique URL for each object that you store in S3. In addition, S3 enables you to store objects of virtually unlimited size.

27. A. You can't resize an instance store–backed volume.

28. A. EBS Provisioned IOPS is your choice when you want to assure yourself of a high number of IOPS, such as a large number of random reads or writes.

29. C. Storing the data on S3 enables users to directly access it via a URL, which isn't possible with any other storage solution. The S3 Infrequent Access storage tier is also low cost, compared to S3 STANDARD. The data access is slow, but it doesn't matter since your analysts request the data only a few times a year.

30. A. The 2TB gp2 volume offers the storage that the database needs and comes with a base IOPS of 6000 (3000 IOPS per TB), which more than takes care of the required IOPS of 4000, without paying a much higher cost for a provisioned SSD volume.

31. A, C. CloudTrail logs all API calls made to AWS, and since S3 access is through API calls, the writes and reads are logged. Activating Server Access logging helps track outside access to your AWS resources.

32. D. Glacier Vault offers the most robust protection for data. Until the storage period expires, no one, including the root account user, can tamper with the data once you activate Glacier Vault Lock.

33. B, C. EBS automatically replicates data in multiple data centers within an AZ. You can transparently encrypt EBS volumes while they're being used by applications.

Managing Databases in the Cloud

In this chapter, you will

- Learn about the features of relational databases
- Work with Amazon Relational Database Service
- Learn how to scale an RDS database
- Learn about Amazon DynamoDB, a highly scalable key value (and document) database
- Work with Amazon Redshift, a data warehouse for analytics
- Learn to use Amazon ElastiCache, a fully managed in-memory caching service, based on either the Memcached or Redis caching engine
- Review the AWS Database Migration Service, which helps you easily migrate your existing databases to AWS

AWS offers several types of databases, each purpose-built for a specific application use case. You can manage your databases yourself by creating the databases on Elastic Compute Cloud (EC2) servers, or you can have AWS manage them for you. The latter are called *managed database services,* and they include both relational database and non-relational databases.

Running your databases on EC2 instances and managing them yourself isn't different from how you do so in your data centers. This chapter focuses on AWS's *fully managed database service*, Amazon Relational Database Service (RDS). Amazon RDS helps you run databases such as MySQL, Oracle, PostgreSQL, and SQL Server in the AWS cloud.

Relational and Non-Relational Databases

It's common to classify databases as relational and non-relational. AWS offers both types of databases. Let's quickly review the differences between relational and non-relational databases, before plunging into the AWS database offerings. Figure 8-1 shows the wide variety of relational and non-relational databases offered by AWS.

Figure 8-1 Relational and non-relational databases offered by AWS

Relational Databases

Relational databases are the most common type of databases in use. A relational database stores data in tables that contain columns that represent various attributes and rows (fields) that store various values of the attributes. It's common for each row to have a unique identifier called a primary key. Foreign keys help link rows in multiple tables to represent relationships. Figure 8-2 shows a database model with multiple tables that are connected to each other through foreign keys.

You use Structured Query Language (SQL) to interact with relational databases to add, modify, or delete data in a relational database table. You can also select or retrieve data from a database with SQL SELECT statements. All relational databases support

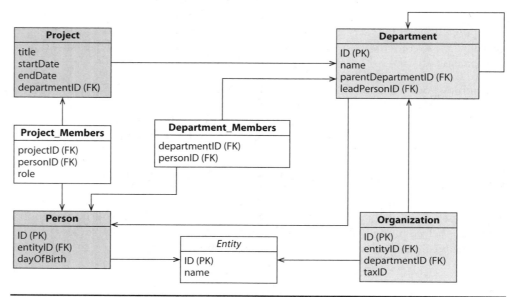

Figure 8-2 How tables are related through common keys

the standard American National Standards Institute (ANSI) SQL, and some relational database management systems (RDBMSs) support additional functionality.

Key Features of Relational Databases

Relational databases share several key features, such as normalization, data integrity, transactions, and compliance with the ACID properties (Atomicity, Consistency, Isolation, and Durability).

Normalization SQL databases commonly use a *normalization* design technique, which aims at removing, or at least minimizing, duplicate data in the database.

Data Integrity *Integrity* in the context of data means that the data is complete, accurate, and consistent. Relational databases use several data constraints to enforce data integrity. Various keys and constraints, such as the following, are how a database adheres to the business rules, thus making the data accurate and reliable:

- **Primary keys** A special column such as a Social Security number (or a combination of columns) in a table that helps uniquely identify all the table's rows.

- **Foreign keys** A column (or collection of columns) in one table that refers to the primary (unique) key in another table; foreign keys help link two tables.

- **NOT NULL constraints** By default, a table's columns can hold null values. The NOT NULL constraint forces a column not to accept null values. This means that the column must always contain a value when you're adding or updating rows.

- **Unique constraint** This ensures that all values in a column are different. You can have multiple unique keys in a table, but only one primary key.

Transactions A *transaction* is one or more SQL statements that together constitute a single, logical unit of work. A transaction provides an "all-or-nothing" proposition, in the sense that either the entire transaction completes or none of the parts of the transaction will be deemed completed.

ACID Compliance All relational database transactions are expected to be ACID compliant:

- **Atomicity** The transaction must succeed in its entirety; if a part of a transaction fails, the entire transaction fails.

- **Consistency** Data that's written to the database as part of a transaction must conform to all the business rules and restrictions, manifested through constraints and keys.

- **Isolation** A relational database handles concurrent usage of the database by multiple users by strictly isolating each transaction from the other transactions executing simultaneously in the database.

- **Durability** This ensures that all changes made to the database following the successful completion of a transaction are permanently recorded in the database and are immune to a system crash, power failure, or a similar event.

Non-Relational Databases

The failure of the relational model to scale to meet the growing demand for huge volumes of read and write operations led to the emergence of the non-relational databases. Non-relational databases are often referred to as NoSQL databases, since you can access these databases through SQL as well as other programming languages.

Non-relational databases are in general highly scalable, highly available, and resilient. These databases trade some of the ACID properties offered by relational databases for a more flexible data model that can scale easily (you can scale the database horizontally, by adding more nodes to the database cluster). Unlike relational databases, non-relational databases usually have no fixed schemas. They also don't have table joins, which are fundamental to relational databases.

Non-relational databases can run on a single server or on multiple servers; they are called *distributed databases* when they run on multiple servers. Most NoSQL databases handle large data sets and are thus distributed databases.

 NOTE A relational database normally scales up—you add bigger servers, with more and faster CPUs and more RAM. Non-relational databases scale out—you add more nodes to the database cluster to scale the database.

Unlike a relational database design, where the model is everything and the structure of the entities and the relationships among them drive the design of the database, performance is the mantra in a non-relational database. You'll still have entities and relationships, but preservation of the relationships isn't an important or a primary concern—it's performance that you're after. There are several types of NoSQL, or non-relational databases, such as key-value, document, column family, and graph databases, each of which solves a different type of problem.

Key-Value Databases

Key-value databases employ a simple data model based on sets of keys and values. The keys are the identifiers with which you look up data, and the values are the data that is associated with the keys. The simple model used by key-value databases means that there are no tables and related entities such as columns and constraints. These databases don't support using SQL to query the database.

Amazon's DynamoDB, Riak, Oracle Berkeley DB, and caching data stores such as Redis and Memcached are all key-value databases.

Document Databases

Document databases store documents—collections of data items that you store in a flexible structure. A document is simply a data structure that the database stores as strings or a binary representation of strings. Documents in this context are semistructured entities in a standard format such as JavaScript Object Notation (JSON) or Extensible Markup language (XML).

Document databases can store multiple attributes in a single document, instead of storing each attribute of an entity with a separate key, as a key-value database does. As with key-value databases, document databases use identifiers, but their values, which are stored as documents, are normally more complex than the simple keys in a key-value database.

Popular document databases include MongoDB, Apache CouchDB, and Couchbase.

Column Family Databases

Column family databases borrow some of the characteristics of relational databases by organizing data into collections of columns. However, they trade off some of the essential features of relational databases, such as the ability to join tables, for the sake of enhanced performance. The rows in a column family database can have different columns. When you're dealing with a large number of columns, you can group columns into sets of related columns called column families. It's not unheard of for a column family database to contain millions of columns.

Apache Cassandra and HBase (usually bundled with Hadoop distributions) are two well-known column family databases.

Graph Databases

A graph database is a specialized NoSQL database that uses structures (called nodes) and relationships (called vertices and edges) instead of modeling data with columns and rows. Graph databases have nothing to do with the visualization aids you normally refer to as a *graph* (or chart). They derive their name from *graph theory*, a branch of mathematics that studies objects by representing them as vertices and the relationships among them as edges.

Graph databases can represent a wide range of entities in the real world. For example, a city can be a node, and the information about the distance between the cities and the travel times between the cities can be stored in the relationships between the cities. Neo4j is a popular graph database.

Working with Amazon Relational Database Service

You can run your own custom database in AWS by deploying the database on Amazon EC2 instances and use Amazon EBS storage. However, managing those databases in the AWS cloud isn't fundamentally different from you managing them in an on-premise data center. Amazon offers several *managed database services*, including Amazon Relational Database Service (Amazon RDS), Amazon DynamoDB, Amazon Redshift, and Amazon ElastiCache.

When you opt for a managed service such as Amazon RDS, your management and administration burden is drastically reduced, with Amazon handling almost all the monitoring, backups, patching, and high availability tasks. Your database teams can focus on more valuable tasks such as optimizing the applications and enhancing them to provide more benefits to your customers. Figure 8-3 shows the difference between managing your own databases and having AWS manage them for you.

Amazon RDS web service is a fully managed database service that enables you to run industry-standard relational databases in the AWS cloud. AWS manages all the common database administration tasks for you, so you don't have to set up and manage databases on EC2 instances.

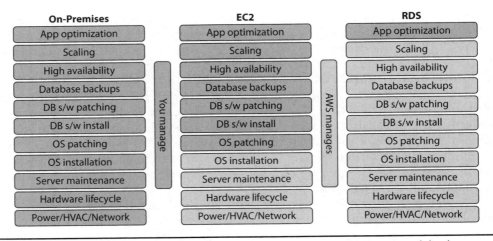

Figure 8-3 How database management changes when you move to AWS managed database services.

Amazon RDS: An Overview

Amazon RDS is a fully managed relational database service that takes over many of the routine, tedious management tasks of a relational database. Because RDS can handle all the software patching, backup and recovery, and failure detection, you can spend your time focusing on the services and applications that the database supports. You can manually create your own backup snapshots or set up RDS to automatically backup your database and maintain the database software. As with the other Amazon Web Services, there's no upfront investment—you pay only for the resources you use.

Here's a summary of the benefits offered by Amazon RDS:

- RDS can independently scale CPU, RAM, disk storage, and IOPS (I/O per second).

- RDS takes care of all mundane database administration tasks such as backups, software patching, and database recovery.

- RDS monitors the databases and automatically detects failures.

- RDS offers built-in high availability if you choose, with the standby database instance running in a different availability zone (AZ).

- RDS offers Read Replicas that enhance the scaling of database reads.

- RDS supports all major database engines, such as MySQL, MariaDB, PostgreSQL, Oracle, and Microsoft SQL Server.

- Databases can access numerous AWS features, such as AWS Identity and Access Management (IAM) and Amazon Virtual Private Cloud (VPC), to control database access and to secure data.

High Availability

For high availability, you can set up a synchronous secondary instance to take over from the primary instance when a problem occurs.

Read Replicas

You can use Read Replicas to scale read requests for MySQL, MariaDB, and PostgreSQL databases.

Security

The database engine you choose has its own security mechanisms. On top of this, you can use AWS Identity Access and Management (IAM) to create and manage users and permissions that you grant to them. You can place the databases in a virtual private cloud (VPC) to provide additional protection.

Licensing

Some of the database engines that you can choose from, such as MySQL, are open source databases. Others, such as Oracle and MySQL Server, are commercial databases that require licensing. AWS offers the "license included" model, in which the cost of the DB instance includes its license cost. It offers other DB instances under the bring your own license (BYOL) licensing model, where you purchase the license on your own and apply it to the DB instances that you run in the AWS cloud.

Access

You connect to RDS through a database endpoint that RDS exposes. You have no shell access to database instances. Also, RDS restricts access to certain system procedures and tables that require advanced privileges.

Choices in Relational Database Engines

AWS enables you to use several types of relational database engines. If you choose to use a commercial database engine, you can use your database licenses in Amazon RDS. For some types of commercial databases, such as Oracle SE (Standard Edition), AWS includes the licensing costs in the cost of the DB instance (charges are per hour of use).

Although there are differences among the various database engines, Amazon RDS offers a common management and monitoring framework, regardless of the database engine you choose. Thus, all the features are available to all database engines that you can run on Amazon RDS.

Amazon RDS supports the following relational database engines:

- **Amazon Aurora**   Aurora is a MySQL- and PostgreSQL-compatible, open source relational DB engine. Aurora provides up to five times the performance of MySQL, while providing the security, availability, and reliability of a commercial database, but at a much lower cost.

- **Oracle**   Oracle is the leading commercial database in the world. You can use your current Oracle licenses or pay for using the RDS license on an hourly basis.

- **Microsoft SQL Server**   You can deploy the Express, Web, Standard, and Enterprise editions of SQL Server.

- **MySQL**   MySQL is the most popular open source relational database.

- **PostgreSQL**   PostgreSQL is an open source object-relational database system that uses its own Procedural Language/PostgreSQL (PL/pgSQL), which is similar to Oracle's PL/SQL.

- **MariaDB**   This MySQL-compatible open source database engine is a fork of MySQL.

How to Determine the Best Database to Use

So, when do you use each type of database offered by AWS? Use a relational database when your applications demand strict ACID compliance, transaction support, and support for table joins. If your applications don't require these features, but they demand high performance and easy scalability, consider a non-relational database service such as Amazon DynamoDB.

You can consider a database based on a specific application type. The following information can help you determine which database is the best for supporting various applications:

- **Amazon RDS and Amazon Aurora**   Ideal for transactional applications such as ERP (enterprise resource planning), and CRM (customer relationship management) that involve transactions, and that store structured data.

- **Amazon DynamoDB**   This NoSQL database is suitable for Internet-scale applications like airline and hotel reservations and websites that serve content, and store both structured and unstructured data.

- **Amazon Redshift**   This is a data warehouse database that's ideal for analytical applications for reporting and querying large amounts of data.

- **Amazon ElastiCache**   Best for real-time applications that require sub-millisecond latency, such as gaming leaderboards, chat and messaging, and IoT (Internet of Things) applications.

- **Amazon Neptune**   This is a graph database that's suitable for applications that require the navigation of highly connected data like social feeds, fraud detection, and recommendations.

DB Instances

A *DB instance* is the basic building block of Amazon RDS. A DB instance is an environment in the AWS cloud in which you can run one or more databases, which act like normal databases that you run in your own data center. Each DB instance runs a DB engine, such as MySQL, PostgreSQL, or Oracle.

You can have a maximum of 40 Amazon RDS DB instances. Forty is the soft limit for DB instances per account and can include up to 10 databases that are Oracle or Microsoft SQL server DB instances under the license included model. If you're bringing your own license, you can use all 40 instances for Oracle or Microsoft SQL databases.

NOTE You can migrate an existing database to Amazon RDS. For example, you can export a MySQL database with mysqldump and import that dump file into Amazon RDS MySQL. Alternatively, you can use the AWS Database Migration Service, which can also convert a database from one database engine to another.

Amazon RDS creates a master user account for a DB instance when you create the database. The master account can create databases and select, delete, update, and insert data into the database tables.

The DB Instance Class

You can select a *DB instance class* to meet your processing and memory needs. Each DB instance class is designed for specific computing and memory capacities and performance. There are three types of instance classes:

- **Standard classes** These multipurpose DB instance classes provide a balance of compute and memory resources and are ideal for many applications. Classes include the db.m1, db.m3, db.m4, and db.m5 instance classes.

- **Memory Optimized classes** These include latest generation instances classes such as db.x1e and db.r3, 4, and 5, which are optimized for memory-intensive applications.

- **Burstable Performance classes** These classes provide a baseline performance level, with the capability to burst to full CPU usage. AWS recommends that you use these instance classes only for development and test servers, but not production servers. These include the db.t3 and db.t2 instance classes.

NOTE You can change the CPU and memory available to a DB instance by choosing a different DB instance class.

Creating a DB Instance

You can create a DB instance from the console by following the steps listed in Exercise 8-2. Figure 8-4 corresponds to step 5 of that exercise.

Figure 8-4
Creating a
MySQL DB
instance from
the Amazon RDS
console

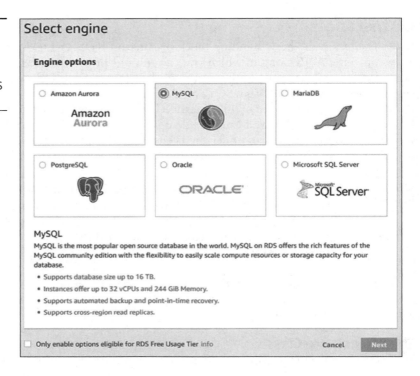

Or, from the command line, run the `create-db-instance` command to create a DB instance, as in this example, which creates a MySQL database named mydbinstance:

```
$ aws rds create-db-instance \
   --db-instance-identifier mydbinstance \
   --db-instance-class db.m1.small \
   --engine MySQL \
   --allocated-storage 20 \
   --master-username masterawsuser \
   --master-user-password masteruserpassword \
   --backup-retention-period 3
```

Connecting to the DB Instance

After you create a DB instance and the instance starts up, you'll see a Connect section in the database summary page. Here you'll see an *endpoint* for your DB instance, as shown in Figure 8-5. In my case, the endpoint for my new MySQL DB instance, named mydb, is mydb.ck31fph6zvho.us-west-2.rds.amazonaws.com.

Once you have the endpoint, you can easily connect to the MySQL database using tools such as the `mysql` command line utility. The generic format of the command line connection string using the `mysql` utility is this:

```
$ mysql -h <endpoint> -P 3306 -u <mymasteruser>
```

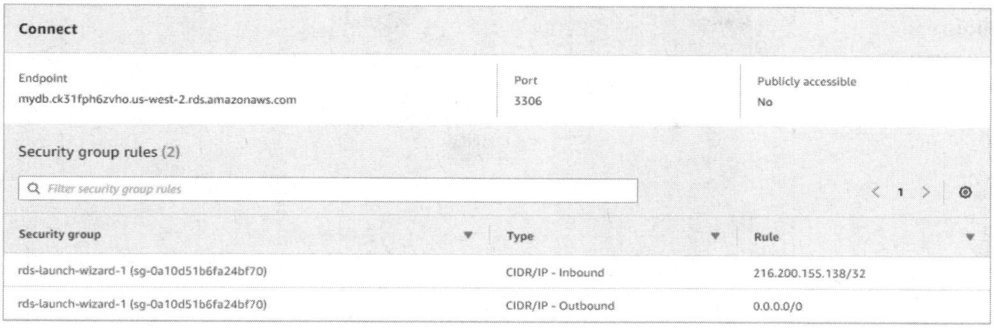
Connect
Endpoint
mydb.ck31fph6zvho.us-west-2.rds.amazonaws.com
Port
3306
Publicly accessible
No
Security group rules (2)
Filter security group rules
Security group
Type
Rule
rds-launch-wizard-1 (sg-0a10d51b6fa24bf70)
CIDR/IP - Inbound
216.200.155.138/32
rds-launch-wizard-1 (sg-0a10d51b6fa24bf70)
CIDR/IP - Outbound
0.0.0.0/0

Figure 8-5 Getting the endpoint information for a DB instance

Where `h` is the FQDN of the server on which the MySQL database instance is running, `P` is the port for the database, and `u` is the master username specified when creating the MySQL database. In my example, it looks like this:

```
$ mysql -h mydb.ck31fph6zvho.us-west-2.rds.amazonaws.com -P 3306 -u salapati -p
```

Figure 8-6 shows the output from `mysql` when you enter the server, port, and user credentials. At this point, you can start working with the MySQL database by entering SQL statements at the `mysql` prompt. Everything will work exactly as if the MySQL database were running in your on-premise data center.

Deleting a DB Instance

You can delete a DB instance anytime. You have an option to create a final snapshot of the DB instance before you delete it, so you can restore the instance later. The following example shows how to delete a DB instance from the command line with the `delete-db-instance` command:

```
aws rds delete-db-instance \
    --db-instance-identifier mydbinstance  \
    --final-db-snapshot-identifier mydbinstancefinalsnapshot
```

Figure 8-6 Connecting to a MySQL database from the `mysql` command line utility

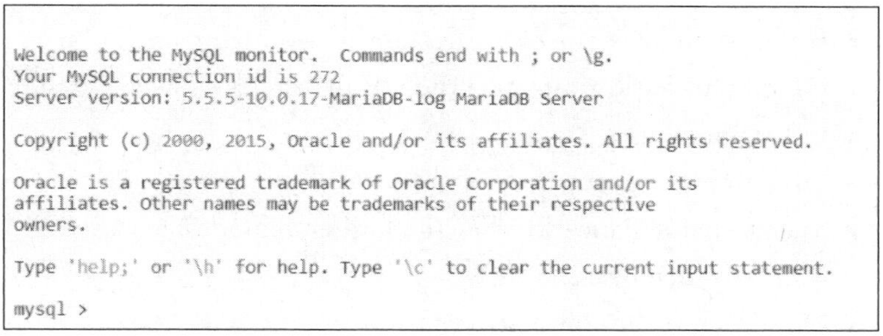
Welcome to the MySQL monitor. Commands end with ; or \g.
Your MySQL connection id is 272
Server version: 5.5.5-10.0.17-MariaDB-log MariaDB Server
Copyright (c) 2000, 2015, Oracle and/or its affiliates. All rights reserved.
Oracle is a registered trademark of Oracle Corporation and/or its
affiliates. Other names may be trademarks of their respective
owners.
Type 'help;' or '\h' for help. Type '\c' to clear the current input statement.
mysql >

Figure 8-7
Deleting an
RDS database
instance

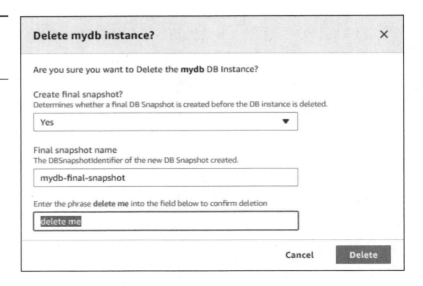

Figure 8-7 shows how to delete an RDS database instance named mydb from the console. When you click Delete, RDS starts creating a final snapshot for the database. Once the snapshot is created, it deletes the database.

NOTE When you delete an instance, all its automatic backups are deleted, and you won't be able to recover them. However, any manual snapshots you took before the database deletion *are not* deleted.

Modifying a DB Instance and Selecting When Changes Are Applied

You can change various database instance settings by modifying a DB instance. For a MySQL database instance, for example, you can modify parameters for the following settings:

- Allocated storage and storage type
- Backup retention period for automatic backups
- Backup windows
- DB engine version (upgrade the DB instance to a newer version)
- DB instance class
- DB parameter group
- System maintenance window (including upgrades)
- Multi-AZ deployment
- Option group and security group
- Subnet group to move a DB instance to a different VPC (or move an instance into a VPC, if it isn't in a VPC already)

You can modify a MySQL instance from the command line, with the `modify-db-instance` command, as shown here (for a Linux system):

```
$ aws rds modify-db-instance \
    --db-instance-identifier mydbinstance \
    --backup-retention-period 7 \
    --no-auto-minor-version-upgrade \
    --no-apply-immediately
```

To immediately apply some of the modifications to a DB instance, use the `-apply-immediately` parameter when calling the AWS CLI, or select the Apply Immediately option in the AWS Management Console. You can defer other changes until the next database maintenance window by placing them into the pending modifications queue. When you next choose to apply any of your changes, all changes in the pending modifications queue are applied as well.

Some database setting changes are applied immediately, even if you chose to defer the changes. And some modifications, such as parameter group changes, require you to reboot your DB instance before the changes can take effect. So if you choose to apply your changes immediately, be prepared for a downtime for the DB instance. It's good to be aware of when a change occurs immediately, when it's deferred, and whether the DB instance is restarted.

Following are settings for a MySQL DB instance that you can modify, when the changes will be applied, and whether the change involves downtime:

- **DB instance storage**   No downtime. If you choose Apply Immediately, the change happens right away. Otherwise, the change occurs during the next maintenance window.

- **Backup window**   This setting determines the time range during which Amazon RDS automatically backs up your database. This change is applied asynchronously, as soon as possible.

- **Database port**   This setting changes the port for accessing the database. Regardless of whether you choose to apply immediately, the change occurs immediately, with the DB instance being rebooted immediately as well.

- **DB instance identifier**   This setting changes the DB instance name. If you choose to apply immediately, the DB changes immediately; if you do not choose to apply immediately, the DB name change occurs during the next maintenance window.

Scheduling a Maintenance Window for RDS Databases

You can set up the RDS maintenance window to limit when automatically scheduled maintenance events such as instance modifications, updates to the underlying operating system, DB engine version upgrades, and software patching (only for security- and durability-related updates) can be done by AWS. If AWS schedules any maintenance event in a given week, it will do so only during the maintenance window that you configure. The maintenance events listed here require RDS to take the DB instance offline for a brief period (normally just a few minutes).

TIP   You can set up different preferred maintenance windows for your DB instances.

If you choose not to specify a preferred maintenance window during instance creation, AWS assigns a 30-minute default value for the window and selects a maintenance window for you. You can change the maintenance window after creating an instance, either from the AWS Management Console or by running the `modify-db-instance` command.

EXAM TIP   The exam usually tests you on your understanding of database maintenance windows. You should know when and how you can set one up and what AWS does if you don't configure a preferred maintenance window. When you upgrade a DB instance engine version manually from the console or from the API, by default, the upgrade is performed during your next maintenance window—unless you select the Apply Immediately option in the console or in the API, in which case the upgrade is performed right away. The same procedures apply when you modify your DB instance class or its allocated storage capacity. Remember that if you select the Apply Immediately option, all pending system requests are applied immediately as well.

You can reduce the impact of maintenance windows on critical databases by running your DB instances in a Multi-AZ deployment. If a maintenance event occurs during the maintenance window for a Multi-AZ instance, RDS performs the following actions in this sequence:

- It performs the maintenance operations on the standby first.
- It promotes the standby to primary.
- It performs the maintenance on the original primary.

The original primary becomes a standby at this point, and it's *not* promoted back as a primary after RDS performs the maintenance operations on it.

DB Instance Status

You can view the health of an instance by checking its status. Here are the common DB instance statuses:

- **Available**   The instance is healthy and available. A DB instance may be unavailable for various reasons, such as an ongoing backup, a DB instance modification you have made earlier, or a system action during a maintenance window.
- **Backing-up**   The instance is being backed up.
- **Failed**   The instance has failed, and Amazon RDS is unable to recover it. You must perform a point-in-time restore to recover the data up to the last recoverable time.

- **Incompatible parameters**   Amazon RDS cannot start the DB instance because you've specified instance parameters that aren't compatible with the instance.
- **Maintenance**   Amazon RDS is applying a maintenance update to the DB instance.

DB Instance Storage

DB instances you run in Amazon RDS use Amazon Elastic Block Store (EBS) volumes for storage. Amazon RDS automatically stripes data across multiple EBS volumes to enhance performance. Amazon RDS offers three storage types for your databases: General Purpose SSD, Provisioned IOPS, and magnetic storage.

NOTE   Amazon Aurora uses a proprietary storage system.

General Purpose SSD

General Purpose SSD (gp2) storage offers cost-effective storage for a wide variety of workloads, and it can burst up to 3000 IOPS for extended periods of time. The volume's size determines its baseline performance. A storage volume earns *I/O credits* at the baseline performance rate of 3 IOPS per GB. Since the base line I/O is 3 IOPS per GB, a 100GB volume has a 300 IOPS baseline performance.

An I/O credit represents the available bandwidth a gp2 SSD storage volume can use to burst its performance higher than its base performance level. The more the I/O credits a storage volume has, the more that storage volume can burst beyond its base performance and meet demands for higher throughput. In addition, the higher the I/O credits, the more time the storage can burst beyond its base. Performance level depends on volume size, with larger volumes having higher base performance levels and accumulating I/O credits faster. Volume size also dictates how quickly a volume accumulates I/O credits.

Burst is relevant only to storage volumes larger than 1TB; volumes smaller than 1TB can burst up to 2000 IOPS for extended periods of time. Volumes that are sized 3.34TB and larger have a baseline performance of 10,000 IOPS.

EXAM TIP   You're very likely to see questions that ask how to address high latency for an RDS database such as a MySQL database. AWS recommends the following measures when you notice a high latency for your database operations: (1) Check to ensure that your scheduled automated backups are being performed in less busy times. Backups can suspend I/O, thus leading to a higher DB latency. (2) Move to a larger EC2 instance. (3) Use Provisioned IOPS for fast, consistent performance. AWS recommends that for production workloads in a Multi-AZ environment, you use Provisioned IOPS along with DB instance classes such as m1.large, or even larger instance types, that are optimized for Provisioned IOPS, for fast and consistent performance.

When you use gp2 storage, your DB instance gets an initial I/O credit balance of 5.4 million I/O credits. This credit balance will last for 30 minutes at a burst performance of 3000 IOPS. Note that the maximum I/O credit balance for a DB instance is the same as the initial I/O credit balance of 5.4 million I/O credits. A performance burst can go to a maximum of 3000 IOPS. Since storage larger than 1000GB has a base performance that is higher than 3000 IOPS, its I/O credit balance never depletes, meaning it can burst indefinitely.

Following is how a storage volume's use of I/O credits affects its I/O credit balance:

- When a storage volume uses fewer I/O credits than what it earns (per second), the unused I/O credits are added to the unit's I/O credit balance. The maximum credit balance for a gp2 storage unit is equal to its initial credit balance, which is 5.4 million I/O credits.

- When a storage volume uses up all of its I/O credits, its maximum performance will stay at its base performance level (no burst) until the demand for I/O drops below the base level, and unused credits are added to the volume's I/O credit balance.

When you find your storage frequently limited to its base performance level due to an empty I/O credit balance, and you need a higher sustaining IOPS performance level, you have two alternatives:

- Allocate gp2 storage with a higher base performance level.
- Switch to Provisioned IOPS storage.

Provisioned IOPS

Provisioned IOPS storage is meant for supporting I/O-intensive production workloads that require fast and consistent I/O performance. This type of storage is ideal for online transaction processing (OLTP) workloads that require consistent I/O performance and consistent random access I/O throughput.

When providing IOPS, you specify the storage to be allocated and the amount of dedicated IOPS that you need. Provisioned IOPS storage helps you tune the performance of your workloads. If the workload requires low I/O latency and high, consistent throughput, for example, Provisioned IOPS storage is the best choice for you. If you see that your workload is being constrained by I/O, use Provisioned IOPS storage to increase the number of I/O requests your database can process concurrently. Increased concurrency means lower latency, as I/O requests get processed faster. Lower latency improves application response time and enhances the database throughput.

When you create a DB instance, you specify the IOPS rate and the size of the storage volume. Amazon RDS will then ensure that the IOPS rate that you've specified for that database is provided to the instance.

Table 8-1 lists the ranges of Provisioned IOP storage and the storage size range for each database engine in Amazon RDS.

Database Engine	Range of Provisioned IOPS	Range of Storage
MariaDB	1000–40,000 IOPS	100GB–16TB
SQL Server, Enterprise and Standard editions	1000–32,000 IOPS	200GB–16TB
SQL Server, Web and Express editions	1000–32,000 IOPS	100GB–16TB
MySQL	1000–40,000 IOPS	100GB–16TB
Oracle	1000–40,000 IOPS	100GB–16TB
PostgreSQL	1000–40,000 IOPS	100GB–16TB

Table 8-1   Storage Ranges for Various Database Engines

Magnetic Storage

Magnetic storage exists for backward compatibility only. AWS recommends that you use either gs2 or Provisioned IOPS SSD for your storage.

 EXAM TIP   Don't get confused between an EBS-optimized instance and Provisioned IOPS. If you are asked a question that asks which EC2 option you can choose for a NoSQL database that requires random I/O reads greater than 4KB IOPS, both EBS-optimized instances and EBS Provisioned IOPS are correct choices.

Using an EBS-Optimized Instance

You can launch specific EC2 instance types as *EBS-optimized instances*. EBS-optimized instances are designed to fully use the IOPS that you provision for an EBS volume. There's an extra, low hourly fee for using these instances. An EBS-optimized instance delivers dedicated throughput between EC2 and EBS, which minimizes the contention between EBS I/O and other traffic from an EC2 instance. You can choose a throughput option of between 500 to 10,000 Mbps, depending on the instance type that you choose.

Monitoring Storage Performance

You can view key storage performance metrics from either the Amazon RDS console (select the DB instance and click Show Monitoring) or through Amazon CloudWatch. Here are the key storage performance metrics:

- **Queue Depth**   This metric shows the number of I/O requests waiting in a queue to be served, due to the storage devices being busy with other I/O requests.
- **IOPS**   The average number of I/O operations completed per second, with read and write IOPS metrics reported separately. You can see IOPS range from zero to tens of thousands of operations per second.

- **Latency**   The time it takes for an I/O request to be completed. Read and write latencies are reported separately, and latency values are usually in milliseconds (ms).
- **Throughput**   The number of bytes per second transferred to or from the disk storage (on average). You get read and write throughput value separately in 1-minute intervals in units of megabytes per second (MBps).

System operations and database workload affect storage performance. Following are the key system activities that adversely affect database instance performance by consuming I/O capacity:

- Creation of Read Replicas
- Creation of Multi-AZ standby database instances
- Changing the storage type and scaling the storage
- Creation of automatic backups and DB snapshots

Because adding storage to a DB instance or changing the storage type for the instance can adversely affect DB instance performance, it's a good idea to schedule these types of work during off hours. The length of time it takes to complete these activities depends on the size of storage, the storage type, the database load, and the amount of IOPS that you provision.

 EXAM TIP   Your DB instance will continue to be available when you increase its storage allocation. If you decide to scale up the compute resources for of your DB instance (by choosing a larger instance, for example), the DB instance is modified, and the database will be briefly unavailable (for a few minutes). Therefore, you should schedule these types of changes during the maintenance window for your DB instance, unless you need to make those changes immediately.

Following are the main workload-related causes of adverse database instance performance:

- If your database is experiencing database contention—say, due to locking—you won't be able to use all the bandwidth you've provisioned.
- The database instance reaches its throughput limit.
- The application is not generating enough I/O operations, resulting in a queue depth that's consistently less than 1.

Setting Up High Availability
High availability is meant for protecting your database against DB instance failures and AZ disruptions, and to provide availability during system maintenance activities. It's not meant for scaling your database, since you can't use the standby server to serve read traffic.

To scale your database by servicing more read traffic, you must create a Read Replica, as I explain in this chapter in the section "Amazon RDS Read Replicas."

In Chapter 2, you learned about AWS regions and AZs. Amazon RDS enables you to place database instances in multiple locations—although, by default, an instance is created in a single AZ. An Amazon RDS instance is created and run in your default AWS region, but you can override this by specifying either the -region parameter or by setting the EC2_REGION environment variable. Unless you ask for it specially, AWS doesn't replicate data across AWS regions.

 EXAM TIP   Remember that Multi-AZ is supported for MySQL, MariaDB, Oracle, and PostgreSQL, but not for Microsoft SQL Server. For SQL Server, you must use its native mirroring capability to achieve high availability. Also, you can't configure Read Replicas with an Oracle database. You must use the proprietary Oracle tool Oracle GoldenGate to replicate transactional data between Oracle databases. You can use Oracle GoldenGate with RDS for active-active data replication, zero-downtime database migration and DB engine upgrades, disaster recovery, data protection, and in-region and cross-region data replication.

Amazon RDS uses Multi-AZ deployments to provide high availability and failover support. Amazon RDS uses different mechanisms to support failover in different databases:

- Amazon Aurora stores copies of data in a DB cluster across multiple AZs. Aurora automatically replicates a DB volume six ways across three AZs.
- SQL Server DB instances use the proprietary SQL Server mirroring (synchronous logical replication) technology instead of using AWS technology to achieve high availability.
- Oracle, PostgreSQL, MySQL, and MariaDB instances use Amazon's failover technology, which involves physical layer replication to keep the standby DB instance consistent with the primary DB instance.

High availability of a DB instance offers the following benefits:

- Provides data redundancy
- Eliminates I/O freezes
- Minimizes latency during a system backup

 NOTE   A standby replica is purely for high availability purposes. You won't be able to use the standby replica to serve as an alternative database for supporting reads. You should create a Read Replica if serving read-only traffic is your goal.

AWS recommends that you use Provisioned IOPS with Multi-AZ deployment, for a fast and predictable throughput. High availability requires a Multi-AZ deployment.

When you choose high availability, Amazon RDS sets up a standby replica in a different AZ from the one where the primary database lives. AWS replicates the primary DB instance synchronously to the standby replica in a different AZ.

Here's a summary of what it means to run a DB instance as a Multi-AZ deployment:

- You can create or modify an existing DB instance to run as a Multi-AZ deployment.
- RDS provisions a standby replica of the DB instance in a different AZ.
- The first or original DB instance is called the *primary DB instance* at this point. Only the primary instance serves database writes and reads.
- RDS automatically and synchronously replicates all the changes that you make to the DB instance to the standby, syncing the two database instances, and thus making the standby an up-to-date replica (copy) of the primary DB instance.
- If a DB instance failure or an AZ failure occurs, RDS automatically fails over to the standby and promotes it to a primary status. Failovers don't take long, usually completing within one or two minutes. AWS recommends that you use a sufficiently large instance type for best results during a failover, as a smaller instance takes longer to fail over if RDS must recover a large number of uncommitted transactions.
- The standby becomes the current primary database, and as soon as it is promoted to a primary, all database activity (both writes and reads) is resumed on this instance.
- There is no need for you to intervene manually and direct traffic to the newly promoted primary database (formerly the standby), since the DNS name record for your DB instance, called the CNAME or canonical record, remains the same. All RDS does is flip the CNAME record for your DB instance to point to the standby, which is the new primary now. RDS uses connection strings based on Route 53, and the strings are referred to as *endpoints* in RDS. An endpoint includes the DNS name and the port number of the DB instance. The switch from the primary DB instance to the standby replica doesn't impact access to the applications that the database supports. AWS recommends that you implement database connection retry at the application layer as a best practice.

 NOTE You don't interact with the standby, since it works behind the scenes. In addition, you can't use the standby to write or even read traffic, since it strictly serves as a high availability solution.

Figure 8-8 shows how a standby replica DB instance runs in a separate AZ from the one the primary DB instance runs in.

RDS creates a *DB instance event* when it automatically fails over a primary database to a standby instance. You can use the AWS RDS API `DescribeEvents` from the command line to get information about the event. `DescribeEvents` returns events concerning instances, security groups, snapshots, and DB parameter groups for the past 14 days. By default, it returns the past hour of events for any of these entities.

Figure 8-8
Standby replica
DB instance and
the primary DB
instance running
in different AZs

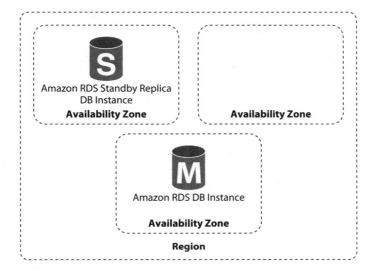

Since latency might increase in Multi-AZ deployments, especially during a DB instance failover, AWS recommends that you use Provisioned IOPS and a DB instance class optimized for Provisioned IOPS to ensure fast performance.

Using Replication and Read Replicas Together   For some databases (MySQL, MariaDB, and PostgreSQL), you can combine built-in replication with Read Replicas. That is, you can do a Multi-AZ deployment together with Read Replicas to take advantage of both types of replication. Multi-AZ deployment will provide the availability benefit and Read Replicas will provide the benefit of scaling the database reads.

NOTE   Multi-AZ deployments provide high availability and aren't designed for scaling your database. Use Read Replicas for scaling the database by serving more read traffic.

If your Read Replicas use a Multi-AZ DB instance deployment as their source, you don't need to do anything in the event of a Multi-AZ failover. All associated Read Replicas automatically resume their replication right after the failover completes by acquiring the database updates from the newly promoted primary (formerly the standby).

NOTE   If you use Amazon Aurora, Amazon RDS can also fail over to a Read Replica.

Finally, you can enable Multi-AZ configuration (for MySQL, MariaDB, and PostgreSQL) on the Read Replicas themselves. You can do this, for example, when you want to support your disaster recovery strategy or to minimize potential downtime from DB instance engine upgrades.

Setting Up a Multi-AZ Deployment   You can set up a Multi-AZ deployment either at the time you create an instance or by modifying a current DB instance. You can view the AZ of the standby replica through the console or by running the AWS CLI command `describe-db-instance`.

You can also modify a DB instance to run in a Multi-AZ deployment. Amazon RDS, in most cases, will take a snapshot of the primary DB instance and restore that snapshot to another AZ to create the standby instance. It then sets up synchronous data replication between the primary and the standby DB instances.

NOTE   If you're using the BYOL model, you need a database license for both the primary DB instance and the standby DB instance.

Remember that a DB instance using a Multi-AZ deployment has a higher write and commit latency due to the required synchronous data replication to the standby DB instance.

Failing Over to the Standby DB Instance

When there's an outage of the primary DB instance, RDS automatically fails over to the standby replica in a different AZ. The time it takes to fail over to the standby instance varies according to the size of the database and the transactions that are running at the time of failover but are typically in the 60 to 120 second range.

Failover of the primary DB instance automatically changes the DNS record of the DB instance connect string. The DNS record points to the standby DB instance, and all existing connections have to be reestablished. It's important to remember that RDS automatically handles a failover, and it doesn't require the DBA's intervention for the database operations to resume after the failover is completed.

The following conditions can set off an automatic database failover from the primary DB instance to the standby replica:

- Failure of the primary DB instance due to either a compute or storage failure
- Outage in the AZ in which the primary DB instance is running
- Patching of the primary DB instance server's operating system
- A change in the DB instance's server type

In addition to the automatic failovers, you can initiate a manual failure of a DB instance by performing a reboot with failover, as shown in this example:

```
$ aws rds reboot-db-instance \
  --db-instance-identifier mydbinstance
  --force-failover true
```

You can determine whether a Multi-AZ DB instance has failed over in multiple ways:

- Check the current state of a Multi-AZ deployment in the Amazon RDS console.
- Set up DB event subscriptions to send notifications via e-mail or Short Message Service (SMS) when a failover is initiated.
- View DB events through the Amazon RDS console or via APIs.

Key Differences Between Multi-AZ Deployments and Read Replicas

Because both a Multi-AZ deployment and Read Replicas deal with data replication and both maintain a second copy of data, there's often some confusion in understanding the essential differences between the two. For three Amazon RDS databases—MySQL, MariaDB, and PostgreSQL—Multi-AZ deployments *complement* Read Replicas. The following table shows the key differences between the two setups:

Multi-AZ Deployment	Read Replicas
Spans two AZs in the same region	Can be inside an AZ, across AZs, or across regions
Automatic failover to standby when problems occur	You can manually promote a Read Replica on a standalone DB instance
Synchronous, durable replication	Asynchronous, scalable replication
Only the database engine on the primary DB instance is active	You can access all Read Replicas for scaling reads
Automated backups are made from standby	No backups are configured by default
DB engine is upgraded on the primary instance	DB engine upgrades are independent from the source instance

You can implement *both* Multi-AZ and Read Replicas to gain multiple benefits. You can configure a database as Multi-AZ for high availability and also create a Read Replica in a single AZ for scaling your read workloads for both RDS MySQL and MariaDB (but not for PostgreSQL) databases. Finally, you can set the *Read Replica as Multi-AZ*, which enables you to use the Read Replica during a disaster recovery.

Lifecycle of a DB Instance

You have learned how to create a database and connect to it. The lifecycle of a DB instance includes other events as well, such as starting, stopping, rebooting, deleting, renaming, and modifying the instance.

Starting and Stopping an Amazon RDS DB Instance

You can start a DB instance from the AWS CLI with the `start-db-instance` command:

```
$ start-db-instance --db-instance-identifier mydbinstance
```

In this command, the `db-instance-identifier` parameter stands for the name of the DB instance.

To save money, you can stop a DB instance when the instance is not in use. To stop a DB instance, use the `stop-db-instance` command:

```
$ stop-db-instance --db-instance-identifier mydbinstance
```

When you restart the database, the instance retains its ID, DNS endpoint, its parameter and options groups (discussed in subsequent sections), and its security group.

Deleting a DB Instance

You can delete a DB instance when you don't need it any longer. Here's what you need to remember regarding the deletion of a DB instance:

- The DB instance can be in any state.
- You must specify whether RDS must take a final DB snapshot of the instance before deleting it (you can use this snapshot to restore this DB instance later, if you need to).
- All automated backups are deleted when you delete an instance.
- Earlier manual snapshots you've taken are retained.
- If the DB instance has a Read Replica, you must promote or delete the Read Replica before you can delete the DB instance.

You can delete a DB instance with the `delete-db-instance` command:

```
$ aws rds delete-db-instance \
    --db-instance-identifier mydbinstance \
    --final-db-snapshot-identifier mydbinstancefinalsnapshot
```

Rebooting an Instance

When you reboot a DB instance, it restarts the DB engine service. An instance must be in the Available state for you to reboot it. The time for rebooting the instance depends on how a specific DB engine performs crash recovery. Here's how to reboot a DB instance:

```
$ aws rds reboot-db-instance \
    --db-instance-identifier mydbinstance
```

Backing Up and Restoring an Amazon RDS DB Instance

There are two types of backups for an Amazon RDS DB instance: automatic and manual. Amazon RDS creates and saves automatic backups of all your DB instances. You perform a manual backup by taking a DB snapshot.

In both cases, Amazon RDS automatically creates a backup of the entire DB instance (not just individual databases) during the backup window of the instance, and it stores the backups according to the backup retention period that you configure. You can recover a database to any point that falls within the backup retention period. A database must be in the Active state for an automated backup to happen.

The first snapshot of a DB instance is a *full backup* of all data. Subsequent snapshots are *incremental*, with the RDS snapshots storing only the changes since the most recent backup (initial or subsequent snapshots).

You can recover a database to any point within the backup retention period. Such a recovery is called a *point-in-time recovery.* Using the RDS automated backups, you can reliably restore your database to within 5 minutes of when someone makes a mistake, such as accidentally dropping a database table. A Multi-AZ deployment or a Read Replica won't help you in this case, since the synchronization of data through replication means that the errors are replicated as well.

NOTE   You can't take a final snapshot of a DB instance that has the Failed status.

Performance Impact of a Database Backup

During a database backup, an elevated latency may occur in Multi-AZ deployments, because RDS briefly (for a few seconds) suspends storage I/O. For the MariaDB, MySQL, Oracle, and PostgreSQL databases, I/O activity isn't suspended on the primary database during a backup, because the backup is made on the standby DB instance. For SQL Server DB instances, however, I/O is briefly suspended during backups in a Multi-AZ deployment.

Backup Windows

RDS performs an automatic database backup once daily during the preferred backup window that you configure. A backup window can't overlap with the weekly mainte-nance window for a DB instance. If the backup doesn't complete within the time allowed in the backup window, it will continue until the backup successfully completes. If you don't specify a backup window, Amazon RDS assigns a default 30-minute window that it selects at random for an eight-hour block of time per region, such as 06:00–14:00 UTC for the US West (Oregon) region.

Backup Retention and Deletion

Amazon RDS retains the automated backups that it takes for the period that you specify as the backup retention period. You can use the backups to recover your database to any point of time that falls within the database retention period. In each AWS region, your DB backup storage consists of all the automated backups made for your databases and the manual DB snapshots that you've made.

NOTE Manual snapshots are never deleted. When you delete a database, only the automatic backups are deleted. You must manually remove the manual snapshots that you've made. RDS gives you an option to create a final DB snapshot before it deletes a DB instance.

By default, when you delete a DB instance, all automated backups are also deleted, so you won't be able to recover your database later with those backups. You can override this default behavior by telling RDS to retain its automated backups when you delete a DB instance. You do this by choosing the Retain Automated Backups option when deleting the instance. When you choose this option, RDS saves the automated backups for the full retention period that you've configured for automated backups.

You can configure the backup retention period for a DB instance when you create the instance. If you don't set a backup retention period, the instance uses a default backup retention period. Here are the key facts to remember about the backup retention period:

- RDS retains the backups for one day if you created the DB instance through the RDS API or the AWS CLI. For Amazon Aurora DB clusters, the default backup retention period is always one day, regardless of the way you create the cluster.
- If you've created the instance through the AWS console, the default backup retention period is seven days.
- You can change the backup retention period of a DB instance at any time.
- You can set the backup retention period to between 0 and 35 days.
- When you set the backup retention period to 0, it means you are disabling automatic backups. You may want to do this on occasion, such as when you're loading large amounts of data. Disabling automatic backup deletes all existing automated backups for that DB instance.

TIP The 35-day maximum retention period is only for automatic backups. You must manually remove manual backups, and there's no maximum retention period for them.

The following example shows how you can disable automatic backups immediately, with the `modify-db-instance` command:

```
$ aws rds modify-db-instance \
    --db-instance-identifier mydbinstance \
    --backup-retention-period 0 \
    --apply-immediately
```

You can enable automated backups by setting the `-backup-retention-period` attribute to a positive value, as in this example:

```
$ aws rds modify-db-instance \
    --db-instance-identifier mydbinstance \
    --backup-retention-period 7 \
    --apply-immediately
```

Setting the backup retention period to seven days in this example re-enables automated backups.

When you create a DB instance, you can select the backup retention period (default is 7 days, but you can go up to 35 days) and the backup time window. Figure 8-9 shows the Backup section of the Configure Advanced Settings page when you create a DB instance.

 EXAM TIP You must know when a certain RDS operation may cause a (slight) I/O delay in an RDS environment. You can expect to incur the I/O delay in two situations (and only in the case of a Single-AZ DB instance, since in a Multi-AZ deployment, the snapshots are taken from the standby): When RDS takes its automatic backups, it creates a storage volume snapshot of the DB instance to back up the entire DB instance. During the creation of this snapshot, there's a brief I/O suspension that may last between a few seconds to a few minutes, depending on the size of the database and the DB instance class. Also, when you create a Read Replica, RDS takes a snapshot of the source DB instance before it starts replicating its data. Taking the snapshot may lead to a brief I/O suspension in the source DB instance, lasting about a minute.

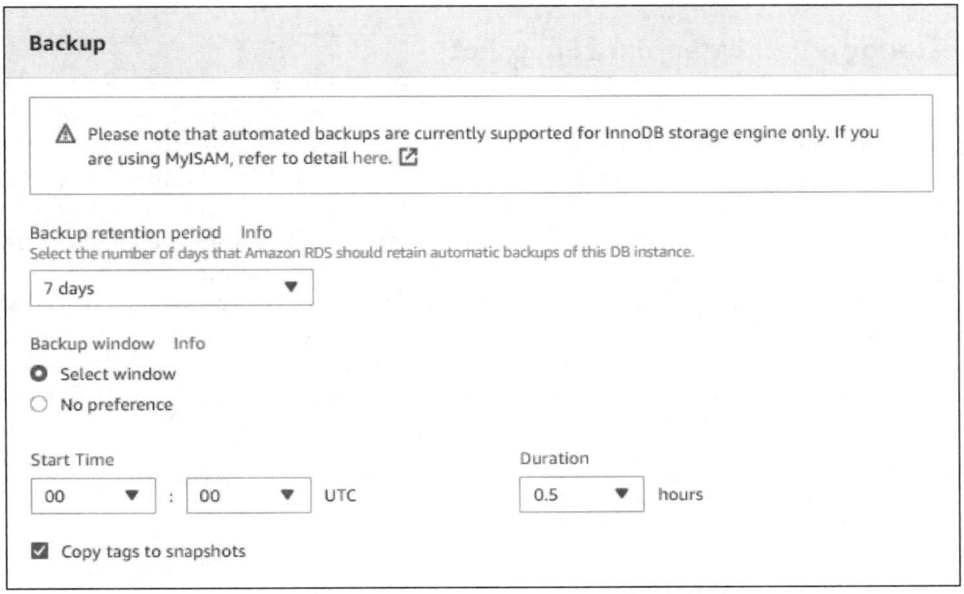

Backup

⚠ Please note that automated backups are currently supported for InnoDB storage engine only. If you are using MyISAM, refer to detail here. ☐

Backup retention period   Info
Select the number of days that Amazon RDS should retain automatic backups of this DB instance.

| 7 days ▼ |

Backup window   Info
◉ Select window
○ No preference

Start Time

| 00 ▼ | : | 00 ▼ | UTC

Duration

| 0.5 ▼ | hours

☑ Copy tags to snapshots

Figure 8-9 Configuring the backup retention period in the Backup section

Creating a Snapshot

Exercise 8-4 walks you through the steps for creating a DB snapshot of an RDS DB instance from the console. From the command line, it's very easy to take a snapshot of a DB instance with the `create-db-snapshot` command:

```
$ aws rds create-db-snapshot /
    --db-instance-identifier mydbinstance /
    --db-snapshot-identifier mydbsnapshot
```

The `db-snapshot-identifier` attribute in this command offers a way for you to name your snapshots, so you can restore from them later, if necessary.

Here are a few more bits of information about snapshots:

- Snapshots can be automatic or manual. You can copy both automated and manual DB snapshots. Once you copy an automated snapshot, you'll have a manual snapshot.

- You can configure event notifications for snapshot events, including the creation, deletion, and restoration of snapshots.

- You can view all DB snapshots by clicking Snapshots on the left side of the Amazon RDS home page.

Restoring a Database from a Snapshot

You can *restore* a DB snapshot to create a DB instance from it. It's important to understand that you aren't *recovering* an existing DB instance with a snapshot in this case—you are creating a *new* DB instance.

Once your new DB instance is available, you must associate any custom DB parameter groups that were associated with the DB instance you restored from. Amazon RDS recommends that you retain the parameter groups for all DB snapshots that you create, so you can assign the groups for the DB instances you restore from the snapshots.

As with the parameter groups, a restored DB instance will have the default security group associated with it. Once the instance is available, you can associate the custom security groups, if any, that the original instance was associated with.

You can execute the `restore-db-instance-from-db-snapshot` AWS CLI command to restore a DB instance from a DB snapshot:

```
$ aws rds restore-db-instance-from-db-snapshot \
    --db-instance-identifier mynewdbinstance \
    --db-snapshot-identifier mydbsnapshot
```

Copying an RDS Snapshot

RDS enables you to copy a snapshot from one AWS region to another. You can copy a snapshot or backup to multiple regions simultaneously.

The snapshots are incremental, including only the changed data since the last snapshot was copied. When you delete a snapshot, it doesn't affect the other snapshots. Copy operations are free; you're charged just for the data transferred from the source region and the data stored in the destination region.

Configuring a Database with DB Option Groups and Parameter Groups

RDS enables you to specify a set of database options and database parameters for an RDS DB instance via DB option groups and parameter groups.

Configuring Option Groups   Database options are additional features of a database, such as those that provide additional security for the database. An option group is a set of database options made available to an RDS DB instance. When you create a DB instance, you can associate the instance with a specific option group if you've created the group earlier. The database will inherit all the options and the option settings that you specified in the option group.

Although an option offers a feature, such as the Oracle Advanced Security option, which offers the encryption option for data, an option *setting* controls the behavior of the options. For example, the Oracle Advanced Security NATIVE_NETWORK_ENCRYPTION option has various settings to help you specify the encryption algorithm for network traffic.

Creating Option Groups and Associating Them with DB Instances   Each new DB instance comes with an empty default option group. You can't modify the default option group, but you can create new option groups that derive their settings from the default option group. You can copy or modify option groups and add options to an option group. You can then associate the option group with the DB instance to make the options available on the DB instance.

You can associate both DB instances and DB snapshots with an option group. When you restore a DB instance from a DB snapshot, the restored DB instance will have the same option group as the parent DB snapshot. Although you can associate a different option group with a restored DB instance, that option group must include all permanent and persistent options that were part of the original option group.

Modifying Option Groups and Adding Options   When you're adding options to an option group, pay attention to the special option types called *persistent* and *permanent* options:

- You can't remove a persistent option from an option group while a DB instance is associated with an option group.

- You can't remove a permanent option from an option group.

- You can't disassociate an option group that contains permanent options from the DB instance.

The following example shows how to create an option group named myoptiongroup with the Oracle RDBMS engine:

```
$ aws rds create-option-group \
--option-group-name myoptiongroup \
--engine-name oracle-ee \
--major-engine-version 12.1 \
--option-group-description "My option group"
```

And this example shows how to add the oracle OEM option to an option group, specify a custom port and a pair of security groups to use for that port, and have the changes takes place immediately:

```
$ aws rds add-option-to-option-group \
 --option-group-name testoptiongroup \
 --options OptionName=OEM,Port=5500,VpcSecurityGroupMemberships=
   "sg-test1,sg-test2" \
 --apply-immediately
```

I specify the -apply-immediately attribute, since a change to an option group must be applied immediately when the change involves an option that adds or updates a port value, which is the case here.

You can view the options and option settings for the *testoptiongroup* option group like this:

```
$ aws rds describe-option-groups --option-group-name testoptiongroup
```

For those options that are modifiable, you can modify the settings at any time. When you change an option or option setting in an option group, RDS applies that change to all the DB instances that you've associated with that option group.

Configuring DB Parameter Groups   A DB parameter group enables you to group a set of DB engine configuration parameters together and apply them to DB instances.

Creating DB Parameter Groups   When you create a DB instance and don't specify a custom DB parameter group for it, RDS creates a default parameter group for the new DB instance. The default parameter group consists of both the DB engine default configuration values and the Amazon RDS system defaults.

You aren't allowed to modify the configuration parameters within a default DB parameter group. Instead, you must create your own DB parameter group to change the default values of the configuration parameters. Some configuration parameters can't be modified by you through a custom DB parameter group.

As with option groups, when you make changes to a DB parameter group, all the DB instances associated with that parameter group will update their configuration parameter values.

Static and Dynamic Configuration Parameters   There are two broad types of database configuration parameters: *static* and *dynamic*. Any changes you make to static parameters will require you to reboot the DB instance for the changes to take effect. Changes you make to a dynamic configuration parameter are applied immediately to the running DB instance.

Selecting the Option Group and the DB Parameter Group When Creating a DB Instance   When you create a database from the RDS console, in the Configure Advanced Settings page, you'll see a section named Database Options, as shown in Figure 8-10. In this section, you can choose the DB parameter group that defines the configuration settings that you want applied to the new DB instance. You can also select an Option Group on this page.

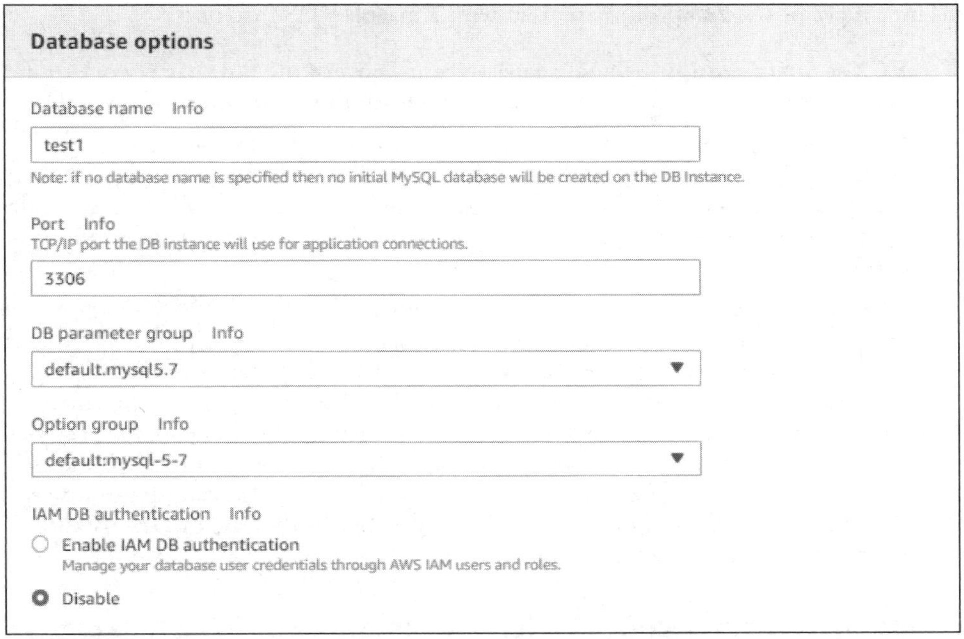

Database options

Database name   Info

test1

Note: if no database name is specified then no initial MySQL database will be created on the DB Instance.

Port   Info
TCP/IP port the DB instance will use for application connections.

3306

DB parameter group   Info

default.mysql5.7   ▼

Option group   Info

default:mysql-5-7   ▼

IAM DB authentication   Info
○ Enable IAM DB authentication
    Manage your database user credentials through AWS IAM users and roles.
● Disable

Figure 8-10   The Database Options section of the Configure Advanced Settings page

Configuring Security for Amazon RDS

Since RDS is a fully managed database service, you might be wondering how to secure the RDS databases. You use various methods to control access to your RDS DB instances as well as your other AWS-based database instances, as explained in the following sections.

Using Security Groups to Control Database Access

Security groups help you limit database access to specific IP addresses or EC2 instances. Only those connections that satisfy the rules specified by a security group are permitted to connect to the databases.

You control traffic into and out of DB instance with security groups. By default, network access is turned off for a DB instance. You can specify rules in a security group to allow access from specific IP address ranges or ports, or from an EC2 security group. You then associate the security group to a DB instance.

 NOTE   You can have a maximum of 20 security rules in each security group, a limit that you can have raised by contacting AWS Support.

Three types of security groups are used with Amazon RDS instances:

- **EC2 security groups**   These security groups govern the flow of network traffic to and from EC2 instances. (See Chapter 3 for more information.)

- **DB security groups**   These security groups are used for EC2-Classic DB instances that run outside a VPC on the EC2-Classic platform. The DB security group controls access to DB instances running outside a VPC. The security rules apply to inbound traffic only, with outbound traffic not currently allowed for the DB instances.

- **VPC security groups**   These security groups are for the EC2 VPC platform and enable access to a DB instance (and EC2 instances) running within a VPC. Each rule in the VPC security group allows a specific source (a range of IP addresses such as 203.0.113.0/24 or another security group) to access the DB instance running in a VPC associated with the VPC security group. When you specify an Amazon VPC security group as the source, incoming traffic from all instances that use the source VPC security group are permitted. VPC security groups can have both inbound and outbound traffic rules, but in the case of DB instances, there are usually no outbound rules.

Enhancing Network Security by Running Amazon RDS in an Amazon VPC

For the greatest possible network access control, you must run your DB instances in an Amazon VPC. This enables you to control your network environment by selecting your own IP address range, creating your own subnets, and configuring custom routing and access control lists (ACLs).

There's no extra cost for running your RDS DB instances in an Amazon VPC. Your databases work the same way in a VPC as they do elsewhere. Figure 8-11 shows how RDS database instances run inside an Amazon VPC.

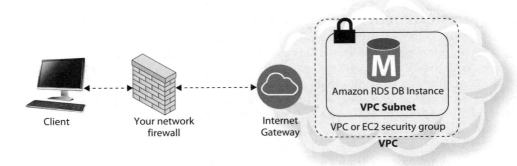

Figure 8-11   Amazon RDS VPC

Controlling Database Access with AWS IAM

You can use AWS IAM policies to control who can manage RDS DB instances. You need proper credentials so AWS can authenticate your requests, and your credentials must have permissions to access the Amazon RDS DB instances.

As you learned in Chapter 3, the best practice is not to use the AWS account root user for accessing any of your AWS resources. Instead, log in as the AWS account root user to create an IAM user in your AWS account with custom permissions that enable them to create DB instances, delete them, create DB snapshots, and so on, in Amazon RDS. You can specify IAM permissions policies that determine who can create, modify, and delete DB instances, or modify security groups. You can then associate the permissions policies to IAM identities such as users, groups, and roles.

In RDS, the primary resource is a DB instance. Resources such as DB snapshots and parameter groups are referred to as *subresources*. Each of the DB resources and subresources will have a unique Amazon Resource Name (ARN) such as the following:

A DB instance: `arn:aws:rds:region:account-id:db:db-instance-name`
A DB snapshot: `arn:aws:rds:region:account-id:snapshot:snapshot-name`

You can create an IAM policy and attach it to users in your AWS account. The following example policy enables the user to create DB instances in the AWS account and specifics that the user must use the MySQL DB engine and db.t2.micro DB instance class:

```
{
    "Version": "2012-10-17",
    "Statement": [
        {
            "Sid": "AllowCreateDBInstanceOnly",
            "Effect": "Allow",
            "Action": [
                "rds:CreateDBInstance"
            ],
            "Resource": [
                "arn:aws:rds:*:123456789012:db:test*",
                "arn:aws:rds:*:123456789012:og:default*",
                "arn:aws:rds:*:123456789012:pg:default*",
                "arn:aws:rds:*:123456789012:subgrp:default"
            ],
            "Condition": {
                "StringEquals": {
                    "rds:DatabaseEngine": "mysql",
                    "rds:DatabaseClass": "db.t2.micro"
                }
            }
        }
    ]
}
```

Amazon RDS uses AWS service-linked roles, which are unique IAM rules that are linked directly to Amazon RDS. The service-linked roles include all permissions that RDS requires to call other AWS services on your behalf.

Encrypting Database Connections, Network Traffic, and Data

You can encrypt database connections, network traffic, and the data that you store in the RDS DB instances.

Encrypting Database Connections with SSLs   You can set up Secure Sockets Layer (SSL) to encrypt connections to DB instances running MySQL, MariaDB, SQL Server, Oracle, and PostgreSQL database engines.

Encrypting Network Traffic   For an Oracle database, RDS supports native network encryption, which enables you to encrypt data as it moves to and from an Oracle DB instance.

Encrypting Data   For an Oracle database, RDS supports Oracle Transparent Data Encryption (TDE). You can use TDE if you must encrypt sensitive data in data files and backups, or if you need to comply with certain regulatory compliance requirements. TDE enables the database to encrypt data automatically before it's written to disk and decrypt data automatically when the encrypted data is read from disk.

   NOTE   Amazon RDS encryption is available for all DB engines and storage types.

You can also encrypt data-at-rest—that is, the data stored by the RDS DB instances and snapshots—by enabling the encryption option for the DB instance. Encrypted data-at-rest includes DB instance storage, automated backups, snapshots, and Read Replicas.

Once you encrypt the data, you don't need to modify the database clients to use encryption. RDS takes care of authentication access and decrypting data with a minimal performance impact.

   EXAM TIP   Encrypting a database is made possible by the AWS EBS encryption feature. When you create and attach an encrypted EBS volume to a supported instance type, all of the following types of data are encrypted: data stored on the volume (data-at-rest), including the database backups; data that moves between the volume and the instance (data-in-transit); all the snapshots that you create from the volume; and all the additional volumes that you create from the snapshot.

You use the AWS Key Management Service (KMS) to manage the keys used for encrypting and decrypting data. In addition to data, RDS encrypts all logs, backups, and snapshots of an encrypted DB instance. If the DB instance has any Read Replicas, the replicas are also encrypted using the same key as the primary instance if the replica lives in the same region, or with a different encryption key if the primary and the replica instances are in different regions.

Be aware of the limitations of Amazon RDS encryption:

- You can enable encryption only when you create a DB instance, and not after it.
- You can't modify an encryption-enabled instance to disable encryption.
- You must encrypt a Read Replica with the same key used for the source DB instance.

- You can't restore an encrypted DB instance with an unencrypted backup or snapshot.
- A source snapshot remains unencrypted during a copy from one region to another.

Finally, remember that in addition to encryption, RDS security groups, and similar security strategies, you can and must take advantage of the built-in security features of the DB engine.

 EXAM TIP You can enable encryption for an RDS DB instance only when you create it, but not afterward. Choosing the encryption option for a database encrypts the database files underlying the DB instance, as well as the automated backups, Read Replicas, and snapshots that you made to back up the database. RDS-encrypted DB instances use the industry-standard AES-256 encryption algorithm to encrypt your data on the server where your RDS DB instances run.

Monitoring Amazon RDS

You must diligently monitor all Amazon RDS databases to assure reliable performance and availability. Here are the two key things you need to do to monitor your RDS databases successfully:

- Establish your monitoring goals, determine the resources you'll monitor, and set up notifications about failures.
- Establish a baseline of RDS performance by measuring performance under different load conditions, at different times. This helps you compare the baseline against current performance data to discover performance anomalies.

You must always investigate significant variations of the metrics from their baseline values. Acceptable values for the following performance metrics depend on the baseline values of the metrics:

- **CPU, RAM, and disk space consumption**   If any of these are unexpectedly high, you must investigate further. If disk usage is higher than about 85 percent, you must look into deleting data or archiving data to free up space or change the instance size/type.
- **Network traffic**   Find out what the expected throughput is for your domain network, and investigate if throughput is consistently lower than what you expect.
- **Number of database connections**   You may want to limit database connections if you see a high number of connections associated with a decrease in performance and response time.
- **IOPS**   Investigate values for IOPS metrics that are consistently different from their baseline values.

NOTE You can set the number of database connections by configuring the User Connections parameter in the parameter group that you associate with a DB instance.

Monitoring Tools

You can use both manual and automatic tools to monitor Amazon RDS. AWS recommends that you automate monitoring tasks to the extent that you can.

Following are the key automated monitoring tools for Amazon RDS:

- **Amazon RDS event notification** Subscribe to Simple Notification Service (SNS) to be notified when any changes occur to DB instances, parameter groups, and security groups.
- **Database log files** View data and log files through the RDS console by querying the database tables, or query with RDS API actions.
- **Amazon RDS Enhanced Monitoring** View real-time metrics for the operating system.

Amazon RDS also integrates with Amazon CloudWatch to provide the following monitoring capabilities for your RDS databases:

- **Amazon CloudWatch Metrics** RDS sends DB metrics to CloudWatch every minute.
- **Amazon CloudWatch Alarms** CloudWatch can raise alarms for RDS metrics values relative to a threshold that you set. You can set up an action to be performed automatically.
- **Amazon CloudWatch Logs** Most of the DB engines enable you to access your database log files in CloudWatch Logs.

Using Amazon RDS Event Notification Amazon RDS sends notifications when an RDS event occurs through the Amazon Simple Notification Service (SNS). RDS groups the events into categories, and you can subscribe to various event categories.

Each RDS event category applies to a source types, such as DB instances, DB snapshots, DB security groups, or DB parameter groups. For example, you can subscribe to the Backup category for a DB instance, in which case, you get a notification when any backup-related event occurs for a DB instance, such as when the backup starts, completes, or fails. Similarly, by subscribing to the Configuration Change category, you'll get notifications when changes are made to a DB security group. To receive the notifications through SNS, you must do two things:

- Subscribe to the AWS events service.
- Create an SNS topic.

If you decide that you don't want to receive event notifications, you can disable the notifications from the RDS console by deselecting the Enable option for event notifications.

AWS bills for the RDS event notifications through Amazon SNS, since SNS fees apply when you use event notifications.

You can view events pertaining to RDS resources through the AWS Management Console, which stores events for 24 hours. You can use the AWS CLI command `describe-events` to view events for up to the past 14 days. This command shows all RDS instance events for the past seven days:

```
$ aws rds describe-events -duration 100080
```

Monitoring with Amazon CloudWatch   CloudWatch collects and processes RDS raw data into readable, near real-time metrics. These metrics are included for both the RDS DB instances and operating system (OS). RDS sends the metric data to CloudWatch in one-minute intervals, and CloudWatch stores the data for two weeks.

You can view the RDS metrics from the Amazon CloudWatch console or from the command line, as shown here:

```
$ aws cloudwatch list-metrics -namespace AWS/RDS
```

The AWS/RDS namespace includes metrics such as CPUUtilization, CPUCreditUsage, DatabaseConnections, ReadOPS, and FreeStorageSpace. You can filter the RDS metric data by dimensions such as DatabaseClass (for example, db.m1.small) and EngineName (for example, mysql).

You can create CloudWatch alarms to monitor RDS DB instances. Exercise 8-6 shows the steps for creating a CloudWatch alarm from the console. An alarm monitors a single topic and performs actions based on the metric values relative to their thresholds over several time periods. The actions are notifications sent to SNS topics or an Auto Scaling policy.

NOTE   CloudWatch alarms invoke actions for a state change that's maintained for a specific number of periods.

You can also configure an RDS DB instance to publish its database log files to a log group in CloudWatch Logs. CloudWatch Logs helps you analyze database log files in real time, and also help CloudWatch create alarms. CloudWatch Logs helps store your DB log files in durable storage, which you can then manage with the CloudWatch Logs Agent. You can search and filter the CloudWatch Log records.

Using RDS Enhanced Monitoring   You can use RDS Enhanced Monitoring to get IOS metrics in real time. You can view the Enhanced Monitoring metrics from the DB console or view them in the CloudWatch Logs (Enhanced Monitoring JSON output).

When you use Enhanced Monitoring, you're charged only for monitoring that exceeds the free tier offered by CloudWatch Logs. Larger monitoring intervals mean less frequent reporting of the metrics and thus lower monitoring costs. The monitoring costs apply for each DB instance for which you enable Enhanced Monitoring. Enhanced Monitoring is available for all DB instance classes, expect for the db.m1.small instance class.

Enhanced Monitoring is useful when you want to examine how different processes or threads are using the CPU. Whereas CloudWatch gets its metrics for CPU usage from the instance's hypervisor, Enhanced Monitoring uses agents running on the instances to get its metrics.

Using RDS Database Log Files   You can view and download RDS database logs from the RDS console, AWS CLI, or the Amazon RDS API. You can also publish these logs to the Amazon CloudWatch Logs service. The logs can be stored indefinitely, unless you specify a retention period (see Chapter 11). Publishing the database logs to CloudWatch Logs enables you to perform real-time analysis of the log data.

To help you understand how to use DB logs, I'll briefly describe MySQL database logs. RDS enables you to view the MYSQL error log, the slow query log, and the general log. The error log is generated by default, and you can configure a MySQL DB instance to generate the other two logs. RDS rotates all the MySQL log files.

The MySQL DB instance writes to the error log when you start up or shut down an instance, or when the instance throws any errors. You can configure the query log and general log to be written to a database table by setting the appropriate parameters in the DB parameter group. You can also configure a MySQL DB instance to publish its log files to a log group in the Amazon CloudWatch Logs service.

Enabling the error, general, and slow query logs to write to tables in the MySQL DB instance helps you easily query the logs via SQL statements. If you want to find information about a specific DB error that occurred on a specific data, directing the logs to the DB tables helps, since you can query the tables to get the information you're after. However, remember that enabling this type of logging may also degrade the DB performance if a lot of log data is written to the database tables.

Using Amazon RDS Performance Insights   You can enhance your monitoring capabilities by using Amazon RDS Performance Insights to analyze and troubleshoot database performance. Performance Insights builds on the RDS built-in monitoring features to help you view database performance in greater detail and troubleshoot performance issues. If you have multiple databases in a DB instance, Performance Insights aggregates the data for all the databases in the instance.

The Performance Insights dashboard uses the key metric DB Load, which is the average number of active sessions for a DB engine. An *active session* is a connection that's waiting for a response from the DB engine for its request. DB Load metrics are collected every second. You can filter database load by waits, SQL statements, hosts, and users.

Performance Insights combines DB Load metrics with the wait event data to show you a true picture of an active session's state. Sessions wait in the queue for a number of reasons, and a high and consistent wait state shows that there are bottlenecks or resource contentions for a specific resource. For example, if you see that the highest waits are for CPU, you may want to lower the number of DB connections (if possible), tune your SQL queries, or switch to a larger instance class. In addition to using the Performance Insights dashboard to drill down into a specific wait state, you can get information about the SQL queries, hosts, and users.

Using RDS Automated Recommendations   RDS provides automatic recommendations that provide best practice guidelines by analyzing your instance configuration, usage, and performance data. The automated recommendations cover a wide variety of areas, including outdated DB engine version, pending maintenance, disabled automatic backups, disabled Enhanced Monitoring, and disabled encryption for the instance. RDS recommends that you encrypt all your databases.

Manual Monitoring Tools   While CloudWatch alarms are automatic, you can also manually view the state of your AWS environment, in addition to reviewing the DB logs. Here's a summary of the manual monitoring strategies.

The Amazon RDS console helps you monitor items such as the following:

- Number of DB instance connections
- The amount of network traffic
- The amount of RAM, CPU, and storage being utilized for a DB instance
- The amount of reads and writes pertaining to an instance

The Amazon Trusted Advisor dashboard helps you check the following:

- RDS idle DB instances
- RDS security group access rules
- RDS backups
- RDS Multi-AZ

The CloudWatch home page shows the following:

- Current alarms and statuses
- Graphs of alarms and resources
- Status of the service health

How AWS Bills You for RDS Databases

RDS billing is based on the amount of resources that the DB instances consume, such as storage and I/O. It also depends on whether you choose On-Demand or Reserved DB instances.

Resource Usage of the DB Instances

Following are the factors that affect DB instance billing:

- **Storage (per GB per month)**   The storage capacity provisioned for the DB instance
- **Backup storage (per GB per month)**   The total storage used by all the automated backups and any active snapshots you have taken

- **DB instance hours**   Hours are based on the DB instance class of the DB instance, such as db.m4.large
- **Provisioned IOPS (per IOPS per month)**   Based on the IOPS that you have provisioned, and not the IOPS that you consumed
- **Data transfer (per GB)**   Based on the amount of data transferred in and out of the DB instances, or to and from the Internet (and other AWS regions)

On-Demand Instances

The default pricing model is an On-Demand instance, where you pay by the hour for the DB instance hours that you use. You may want to stop or delete a DB instance, if you don't want to be charged the DB instance hours. When you stop the DB instance, you will continue to be charged for provisioned storage (including Provisioned IOPS) and the amount of storage that your DB instance consumes for storing the automatic and manual backups. Thus, specifying a longer backup retention duration, or taking several DB snapshots, will end up costing you more for storage.

Reserved DB Instances

Although Amazon RDS is a fully managed service, you can optimize your costs through using Reserved DB instances. You can reserve a DB instance for a one- or three-year term at a significantly lower rate than On-Demand DB instance hours.

 NOTE   A Reserved DB instance isn't a physical instance; it's a billing discount applied to using certain On-Demand DB instances in your AWS account.

When you purchase a Reserved instance in RDS, you're guaranteed a discounted rate on a specific DB instance type for the length of the Reserved instance. The Reserved DB instances you create must match the specification of an existing Reserved instance in your AWS account. If not, RDS will apply the regular On-Demand usage rates for the DB instance.

As with the reserving of EC2 instances, which I explained in Chapter 3, you can purchase Reserved instances in three varieties: No Upfront, Partial Upfront, and All Upfront.

Factors that Affect DB Instance Usage Billing

Billing for Amazon RDS instances is based on the following DB-related resources that your DB instance consumes:

- DB instance hours consumed, based on the DB instance class (such as db.t2.small or db.m4.large)
- Total number of I/O requests that you make in a billing cycle (per 1 million I/O requests per month)
- Rate of Provisioned IOPS (per IOPS per month)

- Storage capacity that you provision for a DB instance (per GB per month)

- Backup storage associated with the automated database backups, and the database snapshots that you take (per GB per month)

- Amount of data transfer (per GB) into and out of the DB from or to the Internet and other AWS regions

Scaling RDS Databases

RDS is a managed service, so it automatically scales your relational databases to meet the growing demands of your applications that use the databases. In this context, you must understand the difference between *vertical* and *horizontal* scaling.

Vertical Scaling

You can scale databases vertically (scaling up) to meet a growing demand from your applications. Vertical scaling is ideal for applications that consist of approximately the same proportion of reads and writes.

You scale vertically by resizing your RDS MySQL, PostgreSQL, MariaDB, Oracle, or Microsoft SQL Server instances.

Considerations for Scaling Up a DB Instance   There are a few key considerations before you scale up a DB instance:

- Ensure that you have the correct licensing in place for the commercial DB instances (SQL Server and Oracle). This is especially true if you're supplying your own DB license under the BYOL model. Commercial DB engine licenses are closely tied to the CPU sockets, or cores, and, therefore, you need to take this into account when going for a larger DB instance.

- You can have instance resizing performed immediately or during the instance's maintenance window.

- When you scale your database, your storage size is unaffected by the change.

- A single-AZ database is unavailable during a scaling operation. In a Multi-AZ setup, the standby DB instance is upgraded to the new DB instance first. A failover will occur to the newly resized database, and a slight downtime is incurred during the failover.

How to Scale Vertically   It's simple to scale a database vertically. AWS RDS offers a wide selection of instance types, and you can scale a database with a simple click of a button. To change the instance type from the Amazon RDS console, select Modify from the Instance Actions menu. If you want the change to happen immediately, and not during the preferred maintenance window that you have defined, select the Apply Immediately check box at the bottom of the Modify page. You can, for example, go from a DB instance class of db.m4.xlarge (4 vCPU, 8 GB RAM) to a db.r3.4xlarge (16 vCPU, 122 GB RAM) instance class.

Horizontal Scaling with Partitioning, and Read Replicas

While vertical scaling is done through resizing DB instances, horizontal scaling (*scaling out*) is done by adding additional DB nodes. Horizontal scaling is mainly for read-heavy applications and databases. You can also scale by adding Read Replicas to a database, as explained in section "Amazon RDS Read Replicas," which follows this section.

RDS Read Replicas support load balancing of database queries or connections. Because each Read Replica has its own unique DNS endpoint, applications can implement load balancing by connecting the replica endpoints. Following are the different ways in which you can make applications aware of the RDS Read Replicas:

- For MySQL-based applications, use MySQL Connectors to configure the MySQL Read Replica as a the read-only endpoint for balancing the read workload, without making application changes.

- For a more dynamic environment where you can transparently add and remove Read Replicas behind the load balancer (without having to change database connection strings in the application), use a load balancer. The load balancer that sits between your applications and the DB instances always presents the same single DB endpoint to the application.

- You can use a transport layer 5 load balancer along with the MySQL Connector. Elastic Load Balancing (ELB) at present doesn't support the routing of traffic to RDS instances. Therefore, you may want to think of an open source load balancer such as HAProxy as a load-balancing solution.

- For a more sophisticated load balancer, use a layer 7 SQL-aware load balancer, which permits complex query forwarding rules. You can use an open source solution, such as MaxScale, ProxyScale, and MySQL Proxy for implementing this solution.

Amazon RDS Read Replicas

A Read Replica is a special type of database instance that you create from a source database. The Read Replica enables users only to read from the instance, but not write to it. The Read Replica is kept very close to the source DB instance, in terms of the database content, by asynchronously propagating changes made to the source DB instance to the Read Replica.

 NOTE A Read Replica helps you scale out your databases for read-heavy workloads. A standby DB instance, on the other hand, provides high availability for your databases.

The goal of creating Read Replicas is to reduce the load on the main DB instance by distributing some of the read requests among the Read Replicas. Thus, they enable you to scale out your DB instance for read-heavy workloads that are constrained by the performance limits of that database. You can use a Read Replica for other purposes as well. For example, you can create a snapshot of an RDS MySQL instance and use the snapshot to create an Aurora Read Replica of the MySQL database. You can then make the

Aurora Read Replica a standalone Aurora DB cluster, thus enabling you to easily migrate between the RDS MySQL and Aurora databases.

NOTE   By default, Amazon RDS creates a Read Replica with the same storage type as the source DB instance, but you can choose a different storage type.

In Amazon RDS, four DB engines—MariaDB, MySQL, Amazon Aurora, and PostgreSQL—support Read Replicas. An RDS Oracle DB engine doesn't support Read Replicas, however; you must use Oracle GoldenGate software to replicate data between Oracle databases. (There may be some differences as to how each of these DB engines implements replication, but that's not something you need to worry about when taking your AWS certification exam.)

Benefits Offered by a Read Replica   A Read Replica could help in the following scenarios:

- Helps you scale beyond the compute or I/O limits of a single DB instance, especially for databases with read-heavy workloads, by taking over excess read traffic.
- Helps you reduce the load on your production databases by running business reporting and data warehousing queries on the Read Replica.
- Offers a disaster recovery function by enabling you to promote a Read Replica to a standalone DB instance, when the source DB fails. However, the promotion isn't automatic, as in the failover of a standby DB instance, when you set up high availability through a Multi-AZ deployment of a primary and a standby DB instance.

Things to Remember About a Read Replica   Remember the following about Read Replicas:

- You can promote a Read Replica to a standalone or primary database.
- MySQL and PostgreSQL can have up to five Read Replicas, and Amazon Aurora can have up to 15 replicas.
- MySQL, PostgreSQL, and Amazon Aurora support multiregion Read Replicas.
- You can create a manual snapshot of a PostgreSQL Read Replica, but you can't enable automatic backups. You can enable automatic backups on a MySQL or MariaDB Read Replica.

TIP   Although a Read Replica is meant to serve read traffic, you can execute Data Definition Language (DDL) SQL statements against a Read Replica. For example, you may want to add an index to a Read Replica but not to the source DB instance. You can enable operations other than reads by setting the `read_only` parameter to the value `0` in the active DB parameter group for the Read Replica.

For Amazon Aurora, Amazon RDS for MySQL, and MariaDB, you can create a (second-tier) Read Replica from another (first-tier) Read Replica. This helps you offload some replication load from the master database instance to a (first-tier) Read Replica. Since the transactions are replicated first from the master DB instance to the first-tier Read Replica, and from there to the second-tier replica, the second-tier Read Replica may lag even further behind the master DB instance.

Creating a Read Replica　In a single DB instance architecture, RDS takes a DB snapshot of the source DB instance before it starts replicating data to create the Read Replica. There will be a short (about a minute) interruption of I/O in the source DB instance as a result. This, however, is true only if you're dealing with a single-AZ DB instance. In a Multi-AZ DB instance, RDS makes the snapshot from the standby DB instance, without pausing the primary DB instance. Amazon RDS synchronously replicates data from the primary DB instance to the standby DB instance in a different AZ. If there are long-running transactions in the source DB, that may delay the creation of the Read Replica.

In a Multi-AZ architecture, since RDS takes the snapshot on the secondary DB instance, there's no I/O penalty during the creation of a Read Replica.

Once it takes the snapshot of the source instance, RDS creates a read-only DB instance from the source instance. It then asynchronously replicates data from the source DB instance to the Read Replica. The Read Replica is, as its name indicates, strictly a read-only database. All databases in the source DB instance are replicated to the Read Replica.

Exercise 8-3 walks you through the steps involved in create a Read Replica from a source DB instance. From the AWS command line, you execute the `create-db-instance-read-replica` command to create a Read Replica from the source DB instance:

```
$ aws rds create-db-instance-read-replica \
    --db-instance-identifier myreadreplica \
    --source-db-instance-identifier mydbinstance
```

 NOTE　The source DB instance must be in the Available state before you can create a Read Replica instance from it.

Promoting a Read Replica to a Standalone DB Instance　You can promote a Read Replica to a standalone DB instance. RDS will reboot the Read Replica DB instance before it is available for use. You may want to promote a Read Replica to a standalone DB instance for various reasons:

- **Performing time-consuming operations**　You can perform time-consuming operations such as the creation and rebuilding of indexes on the Read Replica DB instance, and then promote it so users can use this instance.
- **Implementing failure recovery**　Earlier, I explained how you set up a standby DB instance for protection against both database and AZ failures. You can bolster your failure recovery plans by promoting a Read Replica when a source DB instance fails.

In the event of a failure, you promote the Read Replica and direct the user traffic to this promoted DB instance. You can then create a new Read Replica with the promoted DB instance acting as the source database.

- **Sharding**   Sharding involves the breaking up of a large database into smaller chunks, which are like smaller databases. You can create Read Replicas for each of the shards and promote them to standalone shards.

 NOTE   Multi-AZ Standby DB instances are replicated synchronously. A Read Replica is replicated asynchronously, meaning that the Read Replica often lags the source DB instance.

Here are a few important things to understand about Read Replicas and their promotion:

- The new DB instance that you create by promoting a Read Replica will have the backup retention period, backup window, and the parameter group of the source Read Replica.

- A promoted Read Replica is the same as any other DB instance.

- If the source DB instance has several Read Replicas, and you promote one of them to a DB instance, the other replicas will remain unaffected.

- It's a good strategy to stop transactions from being written to the source DB instance and wait for all the updates to be made to the Read Replica. This means that the source DB instance will incur a brief interruption because it won't be available for transactions.

Partitioning Data and Sharding

Another way to scale out a relational database to distribute the database load is by horizontally partitioning the data into *shards*. A shard is considered a separate instance of a database and contains a subset of the data in the database. The applications must be enhanced with the information to make them aware of the correct shard that they need to access. A shard-based architecture is also called a "shared nothing" architecture, since the shards are independent of each other.

Amazon Aurora

Amazon Aurora offers the features and capabilities of a commercial-grade relational database with the cost effectiveness of an open source database. Aurora is fully compatible with MySQL and PostgreSQL and is highly reliable and fault tolerant.

Aurora is part of RDS, so it's a managed database service. AWS promises that Aurora is more reliable and performs better than standard MySQL databases. Aurora is expected to deliver up to five times the throughput of MySQL and up to three times the throughput of PostgreSQL, without any change in your applications. All the code and applications that you use with a MySQL or PostGreSQL database work the same with Aurora.

Aurora's high performance results from its high-performance storage subsystem's database engine, which is customized to benefit from fast, distributed storage. The storage can grow automatically, up to 64TB.

Amazon Aurora offers automatic clustering, replication, and storage allocation. Database clustering and replication are typically among the most difficult tasks for database administrators.

Aurora DB Clusters

Unlike other relational databases that RDS offers, Aurora deals with clusters of database servers that are synchronized through replication, rather than individual database instances. An Aurora DB cluster consists of a set of DB instances and a cluster volume that stores the data for the instances.

There are two types of DB instances in an Aurora DB cluster:

- **Primary DB instances**   Each Aurora DB cluster has one primary DB instance. This instance manages all the reads and writes and the modifications to the cluster storage volume.
- **Aurora Replica**   An Aurora Replica supports only read operations. An Aurora DB cluster can have up to 15 replicas. You can place the replicas in multiple AZs for high availability.

 NOTE   Both primary and replica instances share the same cluster storage volume.

Aurora Replicas serve two major functions:

- A primary DB instance can fail over to an Aurora Replica when the primary instance becomes unavailable.
- A replica instance can reduce the read workload burden from the primary DB instance by handling read operations.

Aurora Endpoints

An endpoint helps you connect to DB instances in an Aurora DB cluster. An endpoint is a URL such as the following (for an Aurora MySQL DB cluster), with a host address and a port:

```
mydbcluster.cluster-123456789012.us-east-1.rds.amazonaws.com:3306
```

You can use three types of endpoints in an Aurora DB cluster: cluster endpoints, reader endpoints, and instance endpoints.

Cluster Endpoint

A cluster endpoint connects to the primary DB instance in a DB cluster. Each DB cluster has a cluster endpoint. The cluster endpoint provides failover support for both read and write connections. If the primary DB instance fails, Aurora automatically fails over to a new primary DB instance.

Reader Endpoint

A reader endpoint connects to one of the Aurora Replicas for a DB cluster. Each DB cluster has a reader endpoint. The reader endpoint provides load balancing for read connections to the database. You can't use this endpoint for write operations. The DB cluster distributes the connection requests to a reader endpoint among the available replicas. Both the cluster endpoint and reader endpoint offer support for high availability scenarios.

Instance Endpoint

An instance endpoint connects directly to a specific DB instance. The primary DB instance and all the replicas in a DB cluster have their own separate instance end-points. An instance endpoint helps you configure fine-grained load balancing of the database workload by directly controlling which specific replica instance your clients can connect to.

Aurora Storage and Reliability

The cluster volume used by Aurora instances is a single logical storage volume that con-sists of SSD drives. Aurora automatically replicates data across AZs to provide high reli-ability for your data. The data replication is independent of the number of DB instances in an Aurora DB cluster. A cluster volume automatically grows as the database needs more storage space, and can grow up to a maximum of 64TB. Aurora automatically detects storage failures in the disk volumes and repairs the disk segments, thus avoiding data loss.

Amazon DynamoDB Database

Amazon DynamoDB is a fully managed NoSQL database service. It is a highly scal-able distributed database that can handle a large number of requests by automatically spreading data and traffic over enough servers to ensure consistent and fast performance. DynamoDB is ideal for supporting web-scale applications, such as social networks, gam-ing, and IoT (Internet of Things).

 NOTE You can use AWS Data Migration Service to migrate data from a relational database to Amazon DynamoDB.

DynamoDB stores its data on SSDs and automatically replicates data across multiple AZs in an AWS region to provide built-in high availability. By default, DynamoDB is on-demand backup and restore–enabled.

Here are some of the key benefits offered by a DynamoDB database:

- It encrypts all your data by default.
- It's a schemaless database, so items in a table can belong to different schemas.
- Because it writes to servers in multiple AZs, no downtime is incurred during database changes.
- It provides in-memory caching for Internet-scale applications.
- It provides consistent performance with single-digit millisecond response times at any scale.

NOTE Check out the downloadable version of DynamoDB, which enables you to test your applications without accessing the DynamoDB web service.

Start using the DynamoDB fully managed service by going to the AWS Management Console for DynamoDB: https://console.aws.amazon.com/dynamodb/home.

Figure 8-12 shows the Amazon DynamoDB welcome page. From the console, you can create, update, and delete tables, and view, add, update, and delete items. You can also query a table, create indexes, set up and view alarms, and monitor recent alerts from the console.

NOTE Amazon DynamoDB synchronously replicates its data across three data centers in an AWS region for automatic high availability and data durability.

Figure 8-12 DynamoDB welcome page

How DynamoDB Works

DynamoDB comprises the following components:

- Core components: tables, items, and attributes
- Primary keys and secondary indexes
- DynamoDB Streams
- Read consistency
- Throughout capacity

Core Components of DynamoDB

Tables, items, and attributes are the core components of DynamoDB:

- **Tables**   A table consists of a set of data.
- **Items**   Tables contains one or more items, which are groups of attributes of the data that are uniquely identifiable from the other items stored in the table. Items are like rows and records in other databases systems. You can store an unlimited number of items in a table. The size of an item is the sum of the lengths of its attribute names and values. The maximum size of an item is 400 KB.
- **Attributes**   An attribute is a basic data element. Each item consists of several attributes. Attributes are like fields or columns in other database systems.

For example, a table named People consists of three items (rows) of data. Each item consists of the attributes `PersonID`, `LastName`, `FirstName`, and `Address`. The `Address` attribute is a nested attribute with multiple levels. Figure 8-13 shows the structure of the People table.

DynamoDB Global Tables   Suppose a customer base is spread across multiple countries—one in the United States, another in the United Kingdom, and a third in Japan. Your DynamoDB database contains a UserProfiles table that your users update when they use the applications that this database supports. You can create three identical UserProfiles tables—one for each region—but then the tables would have different data, as changes in one table won't be propagated to the other two tables.

You can write application code that replicates changes in the data to all three tables, but doing this is very time consuming and involves considerable effort by your development team. Instead, you can use DynamoDB *global tables* to do this. This fully managed replication solution helps you deploy a multiregion, multimaster database without your having to do all the work in setting it up. When creating a global table, you simply specify the regions where the table should be available to your users. DynamoDB creates identical tables in all those regions and automatically propagates all data changes to all the tables (all three in this case), so they all reflect the same data.

In addition to automatically propagating changes to all the three tables in the three regions, DynamoDB offers high availability, because if one of the three regions becomes unavailable, your users can still access the same data from other regions. Global tables help you offer low latency access to your users, regardless of their location.

Figure 8-13
A DynamoDB
table showing a
table, items, and
attributes

People

```
{
    "PersonID": 101,
    "LastName": "Smith",
    "FirstName": "Fred",
    "phone": "555-4321"
}
```

```
{
    "PersonID": 102,
    "LastName": "Jones",
    "FirstName": "Mary",
    "Address": {
        "Street": "123 Main",
        "City": "Anytown",
        "State": "OH",
        "ZIPCode": 12345
    }
}
```

```
{
    "PersonID": 103,
    "LastName": "Stephens",
    "FirstName": "Howard",
    "Address": {
        "Street": "123 Main",
        "City": "London",
        "PostalCode": "ER3 5K8"
    },
    "FavoriteColor": "Blue"
}
```

Primary Keys and Secondary Indexes   A primary key is made up of one or more attributes and has two main purposes: to uniquely identify the items in a table and partition the data, and to sort the data within each partition. An item consists of one or more attributes. Each attribute consists of a name, a data type, and a value.

It's mandatory that you specify a primary key for a table when you create the table. In our People table, PersonID is the primary key, the unique identifier that distinguishes the items in the table from one another. You can define a primary key with multiple attributes, but in our example, the primary key consists of a single attribute, PersonID.

You can use two types of primary keys in a DynamoDB table:

- **Partition key**   Also called a *simple primary key*, this consists of a single attribute: the partition key, which determines the partition on which DynamoDB stores this item. A partition is physical storage that's internal to DynamoDB. The partition key uniquely identifies an item. In our People table, for example, you can access an item by specifying the PersonID value for that item. A table cannot have duplicate partition keys.

- **Partition key and sort key**   This type of key is also called a *composite primary key*, since it consists of two attributes: the partition key and the sort key.

The partition key determines the physical location (partition) where the database stores the item. All items with the same partition key are stored physically together in the same partition and are sorted by the sort key value. More than one item can have the same partition key value, but they must have different sort key values.

 NOTE   A composite primary key gives you flexibility when querying data. For example, in a table named Music, if you provide only the value for Artist, the database retrieves all songs by that artist. If you want to retrieve only a subset of songs by an artist, you can provide a value for Artist along with a set of values for SongTitle.

In addition to primary keys, you can also create additional keys on a table, called *secondary keys* or *secondary indexes*. Unlike primary keys, which are designed mainly for uniquely identifying the items in a table, a secondary index's main purpose is to facilitate queries on a table. DynamoDB supports two types of secondary indexes:

- **Global**   This index can have a partition key and a sort key different from those on the table.
- **Local**   This index has the same partition key as the table, with a different sort key.

DynamoDB Streams

DynamoDB Streams is an optional database feature that helps you capture data modification events in DynamoDB tables. An event is represented by a stream record, and Streams writes a stream record when a new item is added to the table or when an item is deleted or updated.

A stream record consists of the table name, the timestamp for the event, and other metadata, and it is stored for 24 hours. You can configure Streams so that the stream records capture the before/after images of the items that are updated.

You can use the DynamoDB Streams feature with AWS Lambda to create code (called *triggers*) that automatically execute when a specific data modification event appears in a stream for a table.

Read Consistency

DynamoDB replicates data among multiple AZs in a region. In a distributed setup, how do you know that your application has successfully written a piece of data to a table? When your application receives a HTTP 200 response (OK) from the DynamoDB table following a write operation, that write is successful and is durable. Data will eventually be consistent across all AZs, usually within a second or less.

DynamoDB supports two types of read consistency:

- **Eventually consistent reads**   The database may return stale data sometimes. However, if you repeat your read request, the response will eventually return the most up-to-date data.
- **Strongly consistent reads**   The database always returns the most current data, incorporating all the successful write operations.

NOTE   A network outage or delay may result in a strongly consistent read not being available.

The default consistency in DynamoDB is eventually consistent reads. You can set the `ConsistentRead` parameter to true for read operations such as `GetItem` and `Query` to force DynamoDB to use strongly consistent reads.

Configuring Throughput Settings for Reads and Writes

You must specify a table's provisioned throughput capacity when you create the table. This enables DynamoDB to reserve system resources to satisfy your throughput capacity settings. You can adjust a table's throughput settings manually with the `updateTable` operation (`update-table` command).

You can also ask DynamoDB to scale a table's throughput capacity dynamically, but you must still provide the initial throughput settings when you create the table.

Read and Write Capacity Units   A *capacity unit* is the amount of data an application needs to read/write per second. To be precise, a *read capacity unit* is one strongly consistent read per second, or two eventually consistent reads per second (for an item up to 4KB in size). So if you create a table with 10 provisioned read capacity units, you can perform 10 strongly consistent reads per second (or items up to 4KB in size). A *write capacity unit* equals one write per second, for an item up to 1KB in size. A table with 10 write capacity units will allow you to perform 10 writes per second (for items up to 1KB in size).

Let's say you have an application that receives data from 80 IoT devices and writes the data to the DynamoDB table. The 80 devices write the data every 10 seconds, with each write sized at 1KB. Therefore, the number of writes per second is 80 devices/10 seconds, which is equal to 8. Based on the write size of 1KB, you must therefore provide a write capacity of 8 for this application.

When the Database Throttles Requests   If the reads and/or writes that an application performs exceed the table's throughput settings, then DynamoDB will *throttle* the requests. When a request is throttled, it fails with an HTTP 400 code (Bad Request), along with a `ProvisionedThroughputExceededException`.

You can monitor throttled read/write requests in the DynamoDB CloudWatch metrics. Obviously, if you're seeing excessive throttling, you should increase the table's throughput settings. DynamoDB may use *burst capacity* to satisfy reads and/or writes when they exceed a table's throughput settings. This will keep the requests from being throttled.

Managing Database Throughput for Reads and Writes

DynamoDB manages read and write throughput through three mechanisms: provisioned throughput, Auto Scaling, or reserved capacity.

Provisioned Throughput   You can manually define a table's throughput requirements by configuring provisioned throughput, which is the maximum capacity an application can consume from a table (or index). Once the application crosses the limit, the database can throttle the requests.

For example, let's say you want to read 200 items per second from a table. The items are 3KB in size, and you want a strongly consistent read. In this case, each read requires one provisioned read capacity unit: 3KB/4KB = 0.75, which rounds up to 1 read capacity unit.

To read 200 items per second, you must set the provisioned read capacity units to 200: 1 read capacity unit per item × 200 reads per second = 200 read capacity units.

NOTE   You configure provisioned write capacity in an analogous fashion to how you configured the read capacity in this example.

As with most other AWS services that you use, you can use CloudWatch metrics to view the amount of read and write capacity that you provision for a DynamoDB database that is being utilized.

Automatic Throughput Management with DynamoDB Auto Scaling   Often, your DynamoDB workloads are cyclical. A database that supports a social networking app, for example, is busier during the daytime hours. In other cases, an event such as the rollout of a new product or a new mobile app may lead to an unexpected spike in usage, leading to heavy demands on the database.

DynamoDB Auto Scaling uses the AWS Application Auto Scaling Service to adjust throughput capacity automatically based on actual traffic patterns. This eliminates the need for DynamoDB to throttle requests in response to sudden spikes in traffic and waste provisioned capacity when workload decreases

NOTE   DynamoDB Auto Scaling is enabled by default when you use the AWS Management Console to create a table or a global secondary index.

When you configure DynamoDB Auto Scaling, instead of manually configuring the provisioned throughput for tables, DynamoDB dynamically manages the throughput capacity for tables and global secondary indexes, subject to a range of read and write capacity units that you set.

To set up DynamoDB Auto Scaling, you must create a *scaling policy* for a table or global index and specify the following:

- Whether you want to scale read capacity, write capacity, or both

- The minimum and maximum provisioned capacity unit settings

- A target utilization rate (for example, 80 percent), which is the percentage of used provisioned throughput at a point in time

The Application Auto Scaling Service (the formal name under which DynamoDB Auto Scaling and EC2 Auto Scaling reside) strives to maintain the target utilization percentage that you set, which must fall within the range of read/write capacity units that you've configured. It uses a target tracking algorithm and adjusts the provisioned read and/or write capacity of the table or global index so that it remains at the target utilization rate that you've specified.

When you create an Application Auto Scaling policy for a DynamoDB table, DynamoDB starts publishing the table's used capacity metrics to Amazon CloudWatch. CloudWatch triggers an alarm when the table's used capacity either exceeds the target utilization rate that you've specified or falls below it for a specific length of time. The alarm leads Application Auto Scaling to issue an `UpdateTable` request to dynamically increase or decrease the table's provisioned throughput capacity so that the used capacity metric falls within the target utilization rate that you've configured.

Reserved Capacity   You can purchase reserved capacity ahead of time by paying a fee and committing to a minimum usage level over a period. Purchasing reserved capacity is significantly cheaper than buying on-demand throughput provisioning.

Backing Up, Restoring, and Recovering a DynamoDB Database

You can configure on-demand backups so that you can restore your database from them, as well as set up point-in-time recovery for the database.

On-Demand Backup and Restore

On-demand backups help you create a full backup of your tables so you can use them to restore DynamoDB tables. You can also use the backup archives for meeting regulatory compliance requirements.

On-demand backups and restores have no effect on database availability or the performance of queries that you run against the database tables. The backups that you make are consistent within seconds, and you don't have to schedule them because they're on demand. There's no charge for on-demand backups except for storing the backups.

You can restore a table from an on-demand backup from the DynamoDB console by choosing Backups | Restore, and then entering the table name and choosing Restore Table.

Using an on-demand backup, you can recover a table from AWS CLI by following these steps:

1. List the backups to get the details for the specific table backup that you want to restore the table with:

   ```
   $ aws dynamodb list-backups
   ```

2. Restore the table from the backup (in this example, the table name is MusicCollection):

   ```
   $ aws dynamodb restore-table-from-backup  \
   --target-table-name MusicCollection  \
   --backup-arn arn:aws:dynamodb:us-east-1:123456789012:table/
   MusicCollection/backup/01489173575360-b308cd7d
   ```

3. Run the `describe-table` command to describe the table you've backed up:

   ```
   $ aws dynamodb describe-table –table-name MusicCollection
   ```

Point-in-Time Recovery for a DynamoDB Database

DynamoDB point-in-time-recovery (PITR) offers an alternative (you can both configure on-demand backups and enable PITR) to on-demand backups, without the overhead of scheduling and maintaining the on-demand backups. PITR helps you protect your DynamoDB databases against accidental deletes and writes.

When you enable PITR, it provides automatic backups of your DynamoDB tables until you disable it. The retention period for the backups is fixed at 35 days and you can't modify this.

After you enable PITR, you can restore a DynamoDB database to any point in time within the following range:

```
EarliestRestorableDateTime: 5 minutes before the current time.
LatestRestorableDateTime: 35 days (fixed)
```

When you use PITR to restore a table, DynamoDB restores the table data to a new table. In addition to the table data, PITR also restores the global and local secondary indexes, provisioned read and write capacity, and the encryption settings of the table. However, you must manually set up several things, such as Auto Scaling policies, IAM policies, CloudWatch metrics and alarms, tags, TTL settings, PITR settings, and stream settings.

Using Amazon VPC Endpoints for DynamoDB

By default, all communication to and from DynamoDB uses HTTPS. You may have a privacy and security concern about sending and receiving DynamoDB via the public Internet. Although you can use a virtual private network (VPN) to route DynamoDB traffic through your own corporate network, it may not have enough bandwidth and will have availability barriers.

You can use VPC endpoints and endpoint policies to face these challenges. EC2 instances running in your VPC use their private IP addresses to access DynamoDB, without traversing the public Internet. The traffic between the AWS services and the VPC stays within the Amazon network. All requests to a DynamoDB endpoint in an AWS region (such as dynamodb.us-west-2.amazonaws.com) are routed to a private DynamoDB endpoint within the Amazon network, without the route accessing the public Internet. Figure 8-14 shows how an EC2 instance in your VPC can access DynamoDB through a VPC endpoint without traversing the public Internet.

Inserting and Querying Data

In a relational database, you use an SQL INSERT statement to add *rows* to a table; in DynamoDB, you use the PutItem API (put-item when using the aws dynamodb command) to add *items* to a table, as shown in this example:

```
$ aws dynamodb put-item \
    --table-name Thread \
    --item file://item.json
```

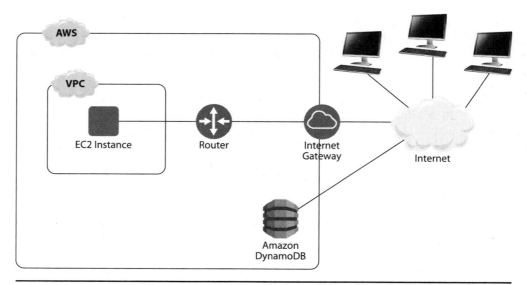

Figure 8-14 Using VPC endpoints for an Amazon DynamoDB instance to avoid using the Internet

This `aws dynamodb put-item` command creates an item if it's not in the table already. If the item exists, it replaces it.

Similarly, instead of using the `SELECT` statement to retrieve data from a table, you read data using the DynamoDB API `GetItem` (same as the `get-item` operation from the AWS CLI, `Query` to retrieve all items with the same partition key, and `Scan` to retrieve all items in a table). Here's an example that shows how to read an item using its primary key, with the DynamoDB `GetItem` action (the code uses the AWS SDK for Python [Boto 3]):

```
DynamoDB.Table.get_item():
response = table.get_item(
    Key={
        'username': 'janedoe',
        'last_name': 'Doe'
    }
)
item = response['Item']
print(item)
Expected Output:
{u'username': u'janedoe',
 u'first_name': u'Jane',
 u'last_name': u'Doe',
 u'account_type': u'standard_user',
 u'age': Decimal('25')}
```

The DynamoDB `GetItem` operation is efficient because it determines the precise storage location of the time by using the item's key value(s).

Partitioning Data

DynamoDB stores table data in partitions, which are chunks of table storage replicated across multiple AZs in an AWS region. Because DynamoDB takes care of partitioning data, you don't need to worry about managing it yourself.

When you raise the throughput settings of a table to a level at which the present number of partitions can handle it, DynamoDB adds more partitions to the table. It also adds table partitions automatically when the current partitions are filled and you need to store more data in the table.

Working with DynamoDB Data

This section covers the basics of table operations in DynamoDB, such as creating, and deleting tables.

Creating a Table

You must provide three mandatory pieces of information to create a table:

- **Table name** Tables names must be unique for an AWS account and an AWS region.
- **The primary key** The primary key consists of one (partition key) or two (partition key and sort key) attributes. Specify the attribute name, data type, and the role of each attribute, such as HASH for a partition key and RANGE for a sort key.
- **Throughput settings** Specify the initial read and write throughput settings for the table.

Here's an example:

```
$ aws dynamodb create-table \
    --table-name Music \
    --attribute-definitions \
        AttributeName=Artist,AttributeType=S \
        AttributeName=SongTitle,AttributeType=S \
    --key-schema \
        AttributeName=Artist,KeyType=HASH \
        AttributeName=SongTitle,KeyType=RANGE \
    --provisioned-throughput \
        ReadCapacityUnits=10,WriteCapacityUnits=5
```

The last two table creation attributes, ReadCapacityUnits and WriteCapacity-Units, deserve extra attention. Following are the factors that impact the setting of these attributes:

- **Size of the database items** The larger the database items that are being read or written to, the larger the amount of read and write capacity units.
- **Expected rate of reads/writes** The higher the amount of reads/writes you expect the databases to perform per second, the higher you must set the read and write capacity units.

- **Read consistency requirements** Strongly consistent read operations require more database resources compared to eventually consistent reads. If your application requires strongly consistent reads, you must configure a higher amount of read capacity units.

 NOTE By default, DynamoDB read operations are eventually consistent.

Deleting a Table

You can delete a table with the `delete-table` command:

```
$ aws dynamodb delete-table --table-name Music
```

Listing All Tables in a Database

You can list all the tables in a DynamoDB database with the `list-tables` command:

```
$ aws dynamodb list-tables
```

Describing a Table

You can view a table's details, such as its column names, with the `describe-table` command:

```
$ aws dynamodb describe-table --table-name Music
```

DynamoDB Encryption at Rest

DynamoDB offers fully managed encryption of DynamoDB data using encryption keys stored in AWS KMS.

You can choose one of the following types of customer master keys (CMKs) either when creating a table or when switching the encryption keys on a table:

- AWS owned CML: This is the default option where the key is owned by AWS, and there's no charge for it.
- AWS managed CMK: AWS stores the key in your account and manages it, and AWS KMS charges apply.

You don't need to write any code to use encrypted tables.

Amazon Redshift

Amazon Redshift is a fully managed data warehouse service in the AWS cloud that can handle petabytes of data. Redshift is a relational database, like the databases offered by Amazon RDS. Redshift helps your scale out a database by utilizing multiple nodes and server optimizations that help you process large datasets more efficiently than traditional relational databases for analytical and reporting uses.

To work with Redshift, you must launch a Redshift cluster. Exercise 8-8 shows the steps for launching a cluster.

Clusters and Nodes

A Redshift cluster is a set of nodes, with one node acting as the *leader node* and the rest as *compute nodes*. Each cluster runs a Redshift engine and contains one or more databases. You can start with a single node cluster and add nodes as your requirements change over time. You can add nodes (or remove them) to a cluster without interrupting the database service.

NOTE   You can save on cluster costs by reserving compute nodes for a one- or two-year period.

How the Leader and Compute Nodes Work Together

The leader node and the compute node work together to process client requests made to a Redshift cluster:

1. The leader node accepts client application requests and develops the execution plan for the queries. The compute nodes execute these query plans in parallel.

2. The leader node coordinates the query execution by the compute nodes and aggregates the intermediate results.

3. Finally, the leader node returns the query results to the client applications.

NOTE   AWS charges you only for the compute nodes; leader node hours aren't charged.

Selecting the Node Type

When you launch a cluster, the node type option you choose determines the CPU, RAM, storage drive type, and the storage capacity for the node. Dense storage (DS) node types are storage optimized and are meant for large data workloads. They use hard disk drive (HDD) storage. The *dense compute* (DC) node types are optimized for performance-intensive workloads and use solid state drive (SSD) storage to deliver fast I/O.

Databases

A Redshift cluster can host multiple databases. When you launch a Redshift cluster, Redshift creates a database for you. Once you connect to this initial cluster database, you can create additional databases if you want with the `create database <database name>` command. Because Redshift is a relational database, you can use standard SQL statements such as `SELECT`, `INSERT`, `UPDATE`, and `DELETE` to work with data.

Amazon Redshift Enhanced VPC Routing

Normally, Redshift routes its traffic through the Internet, including traffic to other AWS services. You can configure Enhanced VPC Routing for Redshift so that you can use the standard Amazon VPC features such as security groups, ACLs, endpoints, DNS servers, and Internet gateways together with a Redshift database.

When you configure Enhanced VPC Routing, Redshift routes all COPY and UNLOAD traffic between the Redshift cluster and your data repositories such as Amazon S3 through your VPC. There's no additional charge for using Enhanced VPC Routing.

Amazon Redshift Snapshots

A Redshift snapshot is a point-in-time backup of a Redshift cluster. There are two types of snapshots: *automatic* and *manual*. Redshift stores both types in Amazon S3.

Automated Snapshots

When you create a Redshift cluster, automatic backups are enabled by default. Redshift takes the cluster snapshots either every eight hours or after 5GB per node of data changes, whichever occurs first. You can set the retention period for automated (and manual) snapshots either when you create a cluster or later. The default retention period is one day, and you can disable the automatic snapshots by setting a retention period of zero.

 EXAM TIP If you're asked which AWS managed services have automated backup in place, remember that only AWS RDS databases and AWS Redshift clusters can be automatically backed up through snapshots. There are no automated backups for services such as EC2 and S3.

Redshift automatically deletes the automated snapshots under the following circumstances:

- When you delete a cluster
- When you disable automated snapshots for a cluster
- At the end of the snapshot's retention period

Redshift takes incremental backups that contain all the changes made in the cluster since the last automated snapshot. The automated snapshots contain everything that you need to restore a cluster. When you restore a cluster from a snapshot, the new cluster is available to you before all the data is loaded into it, and you can run your queries immediately. Redshift lazily loads the data from the snapshot as needed, when a query needs that portion of the data, while it performs loading in the background.

Redshift offers free storage for the snapshots that it stores in S3, equal to the storage capacity of your cluster. After you reach this storage limit, you're charged for storing the snapshots at the usual S3 storage rates. Remember that when you delete a Redshift cluster, you won't have access to the snapshots any longer.

 TIP You can reduce the time to create a snapshot (automatic or manual) and to restore from that snapshot by creating a *no-backup* table. To do this, include the `BACKUP NO` parameter when you create the table.

Manual Snapshots

You can take a manual snapshot of your Redshift cluster any time. Unlike automatic snapshots, you can retain these indefinitely, although you can configure a retention period for them as well. Manual snapshots can be useful if you happen to delete a cluster, since they remain even after you delete the cluster, thus enabling you to restore the cluster should you need to do so.

Copying Snapshots to Other Regions

You can configure the storage of either the automatic or manual snapshots in a different region so that you can restore your cluster in that region if your primary region becomes unavailable. You can configure Redshift to copy snapshots automatically to a different region (you can copy the snapshots only to one other region). The cluster's primary region, where the snapshot was taken, is called the *source region*, and the region where the snapshot is stored is called the *destination region*. You can also set up a retention period for the snapshots stored in the destination region. By default, automated snapshots are retained for seven days in the destination region, but for manual snapshots stored in the destination region (as is the case in the primary region), there's no default retention period.

Amazon ElastiCache

Amazon ElastiCache is a caching solution that enables you to manage distributed in-memory cache environments such as Redis and Memcached in the AWS cloud. It is a managed service. If your applications are currently using Memcached or Redis, they can use ElastiCache with minimal changes.

 NOTE You can choose to use ElastiCache with either the Memcached or the Redis engine.

Use Cases for ElastiCache

It's well known that slow web sites hurt business. Caching helps you deliver data faster to your users. An in-memory cache such as ElastiCache helps you serve your database queries or remote API calls much faster.

EXAM TIP An ElastiCache question may show up disguised in other forms. For example, if you're given a scenario where an RDS instance such as a MySQL DB instance is maxing out on its resource usage, and you are asked to choose the various ways to solve the problem, two immediate solutions should occur to you: (1) Increase the RDS DB instance size and (2) offload read-only traffic to a Read Replica, if the workload consists mostly of reads. However, a third alternative, which is to set up an ElastiCache cluster in front of the RDS DB instance, is also a valid answer, since that can relieve the heavy amount of reads in a database.

Following are a few common use cases for ElastiCache:

- **In-memory data store** The most important function of an in-memory key-value store is to provide low latency (sub-millisecond) access to data. Some database queries, especially those involving complex joins, can be quite expensive, and caching those query results will help you bypass multiple executions of the same expensive queries. Good candidates for caching are data items that are expensive and slower to acquire from a database as compared to ElastiCache. Data whose values remain static and are frequently accessed are also good candidates for caching.

- **Gaming leaderboards** Leaderboards, such as the Top 10 scorer for games, are complex to handle. *Redis sorted sets* move the complexity from the application into the Redis cluster.

- **Recommendation data (Redis hashes)** You can use ElastiCache as a real-time analytics store that can analyze fast-moving data in-memory for sub-millisecond responses. Redis hashes, for example, can maintain a list of people who liked (or disliked) a product.

ElasticCache Components

The key ElastiCache components you must understand are nodes, shards, and clusters:

- **Nodes** The smallest building block of a deployment is a node (also called a cache node). A node is a chunk of network-secured RAM that runs an instance of the ElastiCache engine (such as Redis or Memcached). An important feature of ElastiCache is that it will automatically replace a failed cache node and redirect the node's DNS name to point to the new node without you having to do anything.

- **Shards** A Redis shard is a group of one-to-six related nodes. If a shard contains more than one node (a multiple-node shard), the shard supports replication, with one read and write primary node, and one-to-five read-only replica nodes.

- **Clusters** A Redis cluster is a group of 1 or more Redis shards; each cluster has a minimum of 1 shard and a maximum of 15 shards.

Monitoring ElastiCache-Related CloudWatch Metrics

You can monitor metrics such as the memory usage, CPU utilization, number of evictions (of keys), and the cache hit ratio with metrics that ElastiCache metrics publishes to Amazon CloudWatch. If you notice alerts indicating high utilization for an ElastiCache cluster, you can resolve the issue by scaling the cluster up with a larger cache node type or scaling out the cluster by adding more cache nodes to the cluster. According to AWS, for production workloads, the R5 instance type nodes offer the best performance and RAM cost value.

The key ElastiCache-related CloudWatch metrics (AWS/ElastiCache namespace includes the Redis- and Memcached-related metrics) that you should keep an eye on are the following (some are host metrics and others are cache engine-related metrics):

- **CPUUtilization** This is a host-level metric. AWS recommends that you set a threshold of 90 percent of your available CPU, although your specific threshold should be based on the number of cores in your cache nodes, since the threshold value is calculated as a fraction of the node's total capacity. Thus, if your cache node type has two cores, the CPUUtilization threshold would be 90/2, or 45 percent. If you see your cluster exceeding the CPUUtilization threshold, and your workload consists mostly of reads, you should consider adding more Read Replicas to scale out the cluster. If the workload consists mostly of writes, AWS recommends that, based on how you've configured your cluster, you either scale up by moving to a larger cache node type or add more shards to distribute the writes across more primary nodes.

- **SwapUsage** This host-level metric is reported in megabytes and shouldn't exceed 50MB. If it does, make sure you increase the RAM available to the nodes.

- **Evictions** Evictions denote the number of keys that have been evicted due to the `maxmemory` limit. This is a cache engine metric for which AWS recommends that you set your own custom alarm thresholds based on your workload patterns. If you notice that keys are often being evicted, choose a larger node size with a larger CPU and more RAM. (The same is true if your cluster cache hit ratio is low or the cache miss ratio is high.)

- **CurrConnections** This is also a cache engine metric for which you should configure a custom threshold. A rising number of these metrics may reflect a problem in your application logic.

AWS Database Migration Service

AWS Database Migration Service (DMS) helps you easily migrate your on-premise databases to AWS. Your source database remains fully operational during the migration with minimal downtime. Once the migration is complete, the target database will remain synchronized with the source, enabling you to switch over to the database.

You can use the DMS to perform homogenous migrations, such as from Oracle to Oracle, as well as heterogeneous migrations between different database platforms, such as Microsoft SQL Server to MySQL. You can migrate from your on-premise database to

Amazon RDS or Amazon EC2. You can also migrate databases running on EC2 to RDS, or vice versa. Finally, you can migrate from one RDS database to another.

 NOTE AWS DMS offers free use for six months per instance if you're migrating to Aurora, Redshift, or DynamoDB.

Using AWS DMS, you can not only migrate a relational database to an Amazon RDS database such as Aurora, but you can also migrate those databases to Redshift or DynamoDB.

 TIP You can use AWS DMS to migrate your on-premise databases to the AWS cloud and also perform database migrations between your on-premise databases or a combination of your on-premises and cloud databases.

How AWS DMS Works

When you perform a database migration, AWS DBS connects to the source database and reads the source data. It then formats the data for consumption by the target database. Finally, it loads the data into the target database. Most of this work occurs in memory.

AWS DMS does the following for a database migration:

- **Creates a replication server**   The server is a managed Amazon EC2 instance that hosts replication.

- **Creates source and target endpoints**   Endpoints contain the connection information about the two databases.

- **Creates one or more migration tasks**   You specify settings for each replication task.

Migration Tasks

Migration tasks are how you migrate the data from the source to the target databases. You specify task settings for each replication task, such as the name of the replication instance, the source and target endpoints, and the migration type options. Migration types can be full load, full load plus replication of ongoing changes (change data capture, or CDC, replication), or just replication lag changes (CDC only). Finally, you can specify the tables to migrate and transform data, such as the schema, table, and column names during the migration.

A task can have three major phases:

1. Fully load the data.

2. Apply cached changes.

3. Replicate the new data.

During the full load of the data, AWS DMS loads data from the source database to the target database. Any changes, called *cached changes,* made to the data while the full data load is in progress are cached on the replication server. Each table may have a different change capture start time, depending on when the full load for the tables was started.

When the full load for a table is completed, AWS DBS begins the application of the cached changes to the table. Once DMS applies all the cached changes, the tables are transactionally consistent. DMS will then move on to the replication phase, applying changes as transactions.

Before migrating the data, AWS DMS creates the target schema objects such as tables, primary keys, and, in some cases, unique indexes. DMS creates only the bare minimum of objects necessary to migrate the data and doesn't create secondary indexes, primary key constraints, and so on.

AWS DMS captures both the data manipulation language (DML) and supported data definition language (DDL) changes that occur in the source database and applies the changes to the target database. It syncs the source and target databases.

If you're performing a *homogenous* migration of data (involving two databases that are identical in DB engine type), you can migrate the schema using the databases' native tools, without the data.

AWS DMS can also perform *heterogeneous* migrations, meaning the migration of data from one type of a relational database to another type of database. For example, it can migrate data from an Oracle database to a PostgreSQL database. If the migration is heterogeneous, you can use the AWS Schema Conversion Tool (SCT) to help migrate the target schema.

Amazon DMS creates the bare minimum of the database schema on the target database, including the creation of the tables and primary keys, and, in some cases, unique keys. DMS migrates the data but doesn't create the schema objects such as secondary indexes, sequences, default values, stored procedures, triggers, synonyms, views, and other schema objects that aren't related to the data migration. You must use AWS SCT to migrate these database objects.

Chapter Review

This chapter is about working with databases and focused primary on AWS's fully managed database service, the Amazon Relational Database Service (RDS), which enables you to run relational databases such as MySQL, Oracle, PostgreSQL, and SQL Server in the AWS cloud. In addition to learning how to manage Amazon RDS, you learned about managing the following non-relational databases that AWS supports: DynamoDB, Redshift, and ElastiCache.

Although you perform typical tasks, such as creating users and database objects, in the cloud similarly to how you'd perform them in your own data centers, there are several advantages to running your databases in the cloud. A managed database service such as RDS handles all your routing database administrative tasks for you, such as backups and recovery, automatic failure detection, and the patching of database software.

Features such as built-in high availability and Read Replicas that help scale your databases are key advantages to running your databases in the AWS RDS. You benefit from powerful AWS security capabilities such as AWS Identity and Access Management when you run your databases on top of the AWS cloud infrastructure.

Exercises

The exercises in this chapter show you how to use the AWS CLI and the console to perform various administrative tasks. Please create an AWS account, as explained in this chapter, before attempting the exercises. Use the Free Tier when launching AWS resources.

Exercise 8-1: Create a DB instance in Amazon RDS (using the MySQL DB engine).

1. Sign in to the AWS Management Console and the Amazon RDS console at https://console.aws.amazon.com/rds.

2. Select the region in the top-right corner of the AWS Management Console.

3. In the middle of the page, in the Create Database section, click the Oracle Create Database button.

4. In the Select Engine page, choose MySQL, and click Next.

5. In the Choose Use Case page, select the option in the middle, Production-MySQL. This comes with the default Multi-AZ deployment and Provisional IOPS storage.

6. In the Specify DB Details page, you can accept all the defaults or specify a different value for the storage size and the setting for Provisioned IOPS. Review the Estimated Monthly Costs table provided on this page. Under the Settings section, provide the DB instance name and credentials for the master user of this database. Click Next.

7. In the Configure Advanced Settings page, provide the additional information requested, such as a network, backups, and maintenance windows. Then click Create Database.

8. You'll see a message, "Your DB instance is being created." Click View DB Instance Details on this page.

Exercise 8-2: Create a MySQL DB instance.

1. Sign in to the AWS Management Console and the Amazon RDS console at https://console.aws.amazon.com/rds.

2. Choose the region in which you want to create the DB instance in the top-right corner of the AWS Management Console.

3. Choose Instances from the navigation pane.

4. Select Launch DB Instance.

5. In the Select Engine page (see Figure 8-4, earlier in the chapter), click the MySQL icon.

6. On the Specify DB Details page, specify the DB instance information:

- **License Model**   For MySQL, choose the default model.

- **DB Engine Versions**   Select the latest available version.

- **DB Instance Class**   Choose db.m1.small (1.7GB memory, 1 ECU, 64-bit platform, and a moderate amount of I/O capacity, not Provisioned IOPS).

- **Multi-AZ Deployment**   Specify Yes, so you can have a standby replica DB instance created in a separate AZ for high availability purposes.

- **Allocated Storage**   Select the amount of storage to allocate to this DB instance (up to a maximum of 16TB).

- **Storage Type**   Specify the storage types, such as Provisioned IOPS, for example.

- **DB Instance Identifier**   Type in a unique name for the DB instance.

- **Master Username**   Specify a master username to log on to the MySQL DB instance for the first time.

- **Master Password and Confirm Password**   Specify a password for the master user and confirm it.

Exercise 8-3: Create a Read Replica from a source MySQL DB instance.

1. Sign in to the AWS Management Console and open the Amazon RDS console at https://console.aws.amazon.com/rds.

2. Select Instances in the navigation pane.

3. Select the instance you want to use as the source for the Read Replica.

4. In the Instance Actions drop-down, select Create Read Replica.

5. In the Create Read Replica DB Instance page, select the options for the Read Replica DB instance. The Read Replica DB instance will have the source instance DB's security and parameter groups. You can configure different networking, security, storage type, DB instance class, monitoring, logging, and maintenance options for the Read Replica DB instance. Specify a unique name for this DB instance in the DB Instance Identifier box, under the Settings section.

6. Click Create Read Replica.

Exercise 8-4: Create a DB snapshot for an Amazon RDS DB instance.

1. Sign in to the AWS Management Console and open the Amazon RDS console at https://console.aws.amazon.com/rds.

2. Select Instances in the navigation pane.

3. In the Instances pane, select the instance you want to take a snapshot of.

4. Select Instance Actions and then choose Take DB Snapshot.

5. On the Take DB Snapshot page, in the Snapshot Name box, enter a name of your choice for the snapshot you'll be taking.

Exercise 8-5: Restore a DB instance from a DB snapshot.

1. Sign in to the AWS Management Console and open the Amazon RDS console at https://console.aws.amazon.com/rds.

2. Select Snapshots in the navigation pane.

3. Select the DB snapshot you want to use during the restoration of the DB instance.

4. Choose Snapshot Actions | Restore Snapshot.

5. Under DB Instance Identifier | Settings, enter the name for the restored DB instance.

6. Select Restore DB Instance.

Exercise 8-6: Set an alarm using the CloudWatch console.

1. Sign in to the AWS Management Console and open the Amazon RDS console at https://console.aws.amazon.com/cloudwatch.

2. Select Alarms and then select Create Alarms.

3. In the Create Alarm Wizard page, select RDS Metrics. Choose a metric for which you want to create an alarm, and then click Next.

4. Enter the Name, Description, and Whenever values for the metric.

5. To get e-mails when an alarm state is reached, do the following:
   - In the Whenever This Alarm field, select State Is ALARM.
   - In the Send Notification To field, select an existing SNS topic. If you select Create Topic, you can enter the names and e-mail addresses for a new e-mail subscription list.

6. Preview the alarm in the Alarm Preview area and click Create Alarm.

Exercise 8-7: Create an Amazon DynamoDB table.

1. Sign in to the AWS Management Console for DynamoDB at https://console.aws .amazon.com/dynamodb/home.

2. In the middle of the welcome page, click Create Table.

3. Enter a table name and a primary key (enter something like **customer** and **customer_id**).

4. Make sure the Use Default Settings check box is checked. Click Create.

5. In the main Customer table page, choose items from the menu.

6. Click Add Filter to add attributes to the customer table.

7. Once you complete adding the attributes, click Create Item so you can add data (rows) to the table

Exercise 8-8: Launch an Amazon Redshift cluster.

1. Sign in to AWS Management Console for Amazon Redshift at https://console.aws .amazon.com/redshift.

2. Select the region where you want to launch the cluster—for example, US West (Oregon).

3. In the Amazon Redshift dashboard, select Quick Launch Cluster.

4. In the Cluster Specifications page, enter values such as the following, and select Launch Cluster:

   - **Node type:** Specify dc2.large.
   - **Number Of Compute Nodes:** Use the default value of 2.
   - **Master User Name:** Use the default value of awsuser.
   - **Master User Password and Confirm Password:** Enter a password for the master user account.
   - **Database Port:** Accept the default value of 5439.
   - **Available IAM Roles:** Choose myRedshiftRole.

5. When you see the confirmation page, click Close.

6. In the Cluster page, select the cluster you've created and review its status. The Cluster Status should show Available and the Database Health should show Healthy. Then connect to the database.

Questions

The following questions will help you measure your understanding of the material presented in this chapter. Read all the choices carefully because there may be more than one correct answer. Choose all the correct answers for each question.

1. Which of the following help you to you improve your database storage performance by reducing the wait time for the database's storage volume, without affecting the persistence of the data? (Choose two)

   A. Use Amazon EBS-Optimized EC2 instance type.

   B. Switch to an Amazon S3–based storage for the database.

   C. Use an EC2 instance with an Instance Store volume.

   D. Use a Provisioned IOPS Amazon EBS volume.

2. Which of the following AWS services come with an out-of-the-box automatic backup as a service (BaaS) and backup rotation options? (Choose two)

   A. Amazon RDS

   B. Amazon Redshift

   C. Amazon DynamoDB

   D. AWS CloudFormation

3. When you configure Amazon RDS Multi-AZ deployment, which of the following is true?

   A. Amazon RDS synchronously replicates data from the primary DB instance to the standby DB instance in a different AZ.

   B. Amazon RDS asynchronously replicates data from the primary DB instance to the standby DB instance in a different AZ.

   C. Amazon RDS synchronously replicates data from the primary DB instance to the standby DB instance in a different AWS region.

   D. Amazon RDS asynchronously replicates data from the primary DB instance to the standby DB instance in a different AWS region.

4. Which of the following are true regarding Amazon RDS database backups? (Choose all that apply)

   A. All automated backups are deleted when you delete a DB instance.

   B. All manual snapshots are deleted when you delete a DB instance.

   C. You can change the engine type when performing an Amazon RDS DB instance restore operation.

   D. Manual snapshots persist until you delete them manually.

5. Which of the following can you encrypt by enabling the encryption option for an Amazon RDS DB instance? (Choose three)

   A. The file system that supports the RDS instance

   B. Automated backups of the DB instance

   C. Read Replicas of the DB instance

   D. Snapshots

6. Which of the following are true about DB security groups and VPC security groups? (Choose two)

   A. A DB security group controls access to DB instances in a VPC.

   B. A DB security group controls access to DB instances outside a VPC.

   C. A VPC security group controls access to DB instances in a VPC.

   D. A VPC security group controls access to DB instances outside a VPC.

7. Which of the following actions will help you protect your databases in the AWS cloud? (Choose three)

   A. Grant permissions on database objects to the database users.

   B. Limit network access by configuring security groups and network access control lists (ACLs).

   C. Configure AWS Identity and Access Management (IAM) permissions for the administrators.

   D. Remove all database user accounts from the databases.

8. Which of the following are true regarding an Amazon RDS Read Replica? (Choose three)

   A. It's possible to place Read Replicas in a different AWS region from that of the primary DB instance to be closer to the users and improve its performance.

   B. Read Replicas help you vertically scale a database.

   C. Read Replicas help you horizontally scale a database.

   D. Read Replicas can enhance the availability of a database.

9. What are the implications of the eventually consistent reads feature in DynamoDB? (Choose two)

   A. When you read data from a table, it can never include stale data.

   B. When you read data from a table, the response may include some stale data.

   C. The database will always return the most up-to-date data.

   D. If you repeat your read request after the initial request, the database response should return the latest data.

10. How does Amazon ElastiCache enhance application performance?

   A. It creates multiple DB instances so that they can split the work among themselves.

   B. It offers a single managed service that can run both relational and NoSQL databases.

   C. It catches rarely accessed data to reduce latency.

   D. It caches frequently accessed data.

11. Which of the following AWS cloud services enable you to store data? (Choose three)

   A. Amazon ElastiCache

   B. Amazon DynamoDB

   C. Amazon RDS

   D. Amazon Simple Queue Service (Amazon SQS)

12. When you deploy databases in a Multi-AZ setup, a planned or unplanned outage of the primary DB instance results in a switch to the secondary DB instance. Which DNS record does the automatic failover update to point to the standby DB instance?

   A. SOA

   B. CNAME

   C. MX

   D. The A Record

13. Can you force the failover of a MySQL DB instance Multi-AZ deployment?

   A. Only between some AZs

   B. Never

   C. Yes, if you run the databases in your Amazon VPC

   D. Yes

14. When you run a DB instance in a Multi-AZ primary/standby configuration in two different AZs, can you use the standby DB instance for distributing the read requests made to the database?

   A. No

   B. Yes

   C. Only for specific database engines supported by RDS

   D. Yes, provided you make the standby a read-only database

15. Can you configure an RDS standby DB instance and a primary DB instance to run in the same AZ?

    A. Yes, always

    B. No, never

    C. Yes, but only if you configure this when you create a DB instance—not by modifying the DB instance later

    D. Yes, but only for some DB engine types

16. What is the range of the backup retention period for an RDS DB instance?

    A. 1–7 days

    B. 1–28 days

    C. 1–35 days

    D. 1–365 days

17. If you accidentally delete a large amount of critical business data, which of the following will enable you to restore the deleted data very quickly?

    A. A Multi-AZ deployment of the database

    B. RDS Read Replicas

    C. RDS snapshots

    D. RDS Auto Restore feature

18. Which of the following metrics helps you know when to re-create a Read Replica when the Read Replica becomes out of sync due to replication errors?

    A. ReadReplicaLag

    B. ReplicaLag

    C. ReadTimeLag

    D. ReadThreshold

19. What happens in a DynamoDB database when an application performs more reads and writes than the configured provisioned capacity?

    A. The requests that exceed the provisioned capacity are performed but will return a 400 HTTP error code.

    B. The requests that exceed the provisioned capacity will fail with a 500 HTTP error code.

    C. The requests that exceed the provisioned capacity will be throttled, with an HTTP 400 error code.

    D. The requests that exceed the provisioned capacity will be throttled, with an HTTP 500 error code.

20. When you receive an alert that your primary RDS DB instance has gone down in a Multi-AZ RDS DB instance setup, what must you do to ensure a fast failover?

    A. Update the Domain Name System (DNS) to point to the secondary instance's new IP address.

    B. Log into the servers and update the connection strings of the applications so they communicate with the secondary DB instance.

    C. Create a new secondary DB instance from the latest snapshot of the primary DB instance.

    D. Do nothing; AWS will automatically update the database endpoint, so that it now points to the secondary DB instance. The connection string always points to the database endpoint.

21. Which of the following AWS databases offers a non-relational database?

    A. Amazon DynamoDB

    B. Amazon Redshift

    C. Amazon RDS

    D. Amazon S3

22. Which of the following methods is the quickest way to install the Microsoft SQL Server Enterprise Edition DB instance on Amazon RDS?

    A. Install the SQL Server command line tools on your laptop and use the AWS CLI to provision the new RDS instance.

    B. Amazon RDS doesn't support the SQL Server Enterprise Edition.

    C. Use the License Included Option in the RDS console to install the SQL Server Enterprise Edition.

    D. Launch an RDS DB instance and select the Enterprise Edition under the bring your own license (BYOL) model.

23. Which of the following database storage types would be best for an application that gets occasional bursts of activity throughout the day?

    A. Magnetic storage

    B. General Purpose SSD (gp2) storage

    C. Provisioned IOPS (SSD)

    D. S3 storage

24. Which of the following AWS services or databases will help a high-volume web application to scale up to handle a large number (hundreds of thousands) of concurrent users?

    A. Amazon Aurora

    B. Amazon Redshift

    C. Amazon DynamoDB

    D. Amazon ElastiCache

25. Which of the following can help an RDS MySQL database instance handle thousands of new application users? (Choose three)

  A. Upgrade storage from magnetic volumes to General Purpose SSD volumes.

  B. Use Read Replicas to distribute the read requests.

  C. Vertically scale the DB instance by switching the instance to a larger instance class.

  D. Move the database users to Amazon ElastiCache.

Answers

  1. A, D. You can improve performance by using Amazon EBS-Optimized instances and by choosing Provisioned IOPS storage.

  2. A, B. Amazon RDS and Amazon Redshift offer the ability to back up the database automatically (through automatic snapshots), and an option to store the backups in Amazon S3.

  3. A. RDS automatically creates the standby DB instance in a different AZ from that of the primary DB instance. RDS synchronously replicates the primary DB instance to the standby replica to provide data redundancy, to minimize latency hits during a system backup, and to eliminate I/O freezes.

  4. A, C, D. When you delete a DB instance, all automated backups are deleted, but manual snapshots that you've taken will persist until you manually delete them. You can change the engine when restoring an RDS DB instance.

  5. B, C, D. By enabling the encryption option for an RDS DB instance, you can encrypt automated database backups, Read Replicas of the instance, and the database instance snapshots.

  6. B, C. A DB security group controls access to EC2-Classic DB instances that are not in a VPC. A VPC security group controls access to DB instances and EC2 instances inside a VPC.

  7. A, B, C. You can enhance database security by controlling permissions on the database objects, configuring security groups and ACLs, and by configuring IAM permissions for the administrators.

  8. A, C, D. You can place the Read Replicas of a DB instance in a different AWS region from that of the primary DB instance to be closer to your users and to enhance performance. Read Replicas help you horizontally scale a database by adding more replicas to enhance read performance. Read Replicas can enhance database availability by enabling users to read from them.

  9. B, D. The eventually consistent reads feature means that when you read data, the response from the database may include stale data. However, if you repeat your read request after some time, the response includes the latest version of the data.

  10. D. Amazon ElastiCache caches frequently accessed requests. By offloading the read traffic from the databases, it reduces latencies induced by a read-heavy workload.

11. **A, B, C.** Amazon ElastiCache, Amazon DynamoDB, and Amazon RDS are all AWS database storage services.

12. **B.** When automatic failover occurs, your application can remain unaware of what's happening behind the scenes. The CNAME (canonical name) record for your DB instance is modified so it points to the newly promoted standby (which becomes the primary DB instance now).

13. **D.** By performing a reboot with failover, you can always force a failover between two AZs. When you force the failover manually, Amazon RDS makes the current standby instance the primary DB instance. It also updates the DNS record (the CNAME record) for the instance so it now points to the new primary DB instance. You must therefore reestablish all existing connections to the DB instance. You perform a reboot with failover when you want to test the impact of a DB instance failure or to restore database operations to the original AZ following a failover.

14. **A.** When you run a high availability database configuration with primary and standby database instances, you are protected against a DB instance or AZ issue that makes the primary DB instance unavailable. This is *not* a solution for scaling your database, since the standby DB instance can't serve read requests. If you want to distribute the read traffic being served by the database, you can do so by creating Read Replicas.

15. **B.** You can never configure both a primary and standby DB instance to run in the same AZ. RDS automatically provisions a standby DB instance in an AZ that's different from the region of the primary DB instance.

16. **C.** Amazon RDS saves all automated backups of a DB instance for the backup retention period that you configure. You can recover the DB instance to any point within the backup retention period. You can specify a backup retention period of 1–35 days.

17. **C.** RDS snapshots enable you to recover DB instances. If you're running a single AZ DB instance, recovery results in a slight suspension of I/O (a few seconds to a few minutes). If you're running a Multi-AZ DB instance, there won't be an I/O suspension, because RDS takes the snapshot on the standby DB instance.

18. **B.** The ReplicaLag metric reveals the time a Read Replica instance lags behind the source DB instance.

19. **C.** When the read and write requests of an application exceed the provisioned throughput for a DynamoDB table, the database might throttle new requests. The requests will fail with a HTTP 400 code message of "Bad Request." You'll also receive an exception called the `ProvisionedThroughputExceededException`.

20. **D.** You don't need to do anything, since AWS will automatically update the DB endpoint to point to the secondary instance, which now becomes the primary instance.

21. A. Amazon DynamoDB is a non-relational (NoSQL) database service.

22. D. Only the BYOL model offers the Microsoft SQL Server Enterprise Edition in RDS.

23. B. General Purpose SSD storage is best for databases that handle occasional bursts of activity.

24. C. DynamoDB is a NoSQL database that can easily scale to hundreds of thousands of concurrent requests.

25. A, **B**, **C.** General Purpose SSD volumes, Read Replicas, and larger instance classes are all good ways to handle an increasing RDS database workload.

Application Integration and Ensuring High Availability

In this chapter, you will

- Learn about Amazon Simple Queue Service
- Work with Amazon Simple Notification Service
- Learn about fault tolerance and high availability in the AWS cloud
- Learn about failure detection and disaster recovery in the AWS cloud

This chapter is about two important AWS features: application integration technologies that help distributed systems function efficiently by decoupling application tiers, and AWS support of high availability and disaster recovery with various strategies at the network, server, database, application, and other levels.

Amazon Simple Queue Service

Amazon Simple Queue Service (SQS) is a fully managed *message queueing service* that helps you decouple and scale microservices, distributed systems, and, more recently, serverless applications. A *queue*—a temporary storage location for messages that are in transit between an application's components—stores messages redundantly across several SQS servers. You use SQS to move data between the various components of a distributed application. You can send, store, and receive messages between software components without ever losing any messages, or requiring other services to be available.

An SQS queue can be used to buffer important business process event notifications. Applications that need to be made aware of these process-related events can process the messages from the queue. You can make your distributed applications more reliable by integrating SQS with various AWS infrastructure services. You can decouple application components so that they run independently of one another, with failure in one component not affecting other components, thus enhancing the overall fault tolerance of the system.

About Decoupling

You know that using HA-related strategies, such as multiple AZ-based services and configuring HA for databases and Elastic Compute Cloud (EC2) instances, helps you configure HA for your services. But there are things you can do at the application level, instead of just at the service or infrastructure level, to enhance HA for your systems running in the AWS cloud.

You can *decouple* (separate the multiple components) your applications through services such as Amazon SQS and Amazon Simple Notification Service (SNS) to provide HA, scalability, and fault tolerance for those applications. Without decoupling, an application's components remain dependent on one another, thus making the application fragile and prone to failures. By enabling the queueing of messages among an application's components and coordinating and managing the delivery of those messages to endpoints and clients, SQS and SNS help decouple your applications, so the application's components run independently. By decoupling application components and enabling them to send messages to one another, you ensure that a failure in one of the components doesn't affect the entire application. Both SQS and SNS fall under the *application integration* category of AWS services.

Unlike traditional message brokers, SQS is a managed *queue and topic service* that doesn't require you to configure and manage message brokers. You can control who can send and receive messages to and from an SQS queue. SQS stores messages safely by placing the messages on multiple servers to provide HA, and it provides highly concurrent access to those messages.

To work with SQS queues through API requests, you must construct a region-specific endpoint, such as https://sqs.us-east-2.amazonaws.com/123456789012/MyQueue. You can then use the endpoint to make GET and POST requests to perform actions on the endpoint. An *action*, for example, can be something such as `DeleteMessage`. Here's an example that shows how you can delete a specific message from a queue named MyQueue:

```
https://sqs.us-east-2.amazonaws.com/123456789012/MyQueue/
?Action=DeleteMessage
&ReceiptHandle=MbZj6wDWli%2BJvwwJaBV%2B3dcjk2YW2vA3%2BSTFFljT
M8tJJg6HRG6PYSasuWXPJB%2BCwLj1FjgXUv1uSj1gUPAWV66FU/WeR4mq2OKpEGY
WbnLmpRCJVAyeMjeU5ZBdtcQ%2BQEauMZc8ZRv37sIW2iJKq3M9MFx1YvV11A2x/K
SbkJ0=
&Expires=2020-04-18T22%3A52%3A43PST
&Version=2012-11-05
&AUTHPARAMS
```

Note that the `DeleteMessage` action shown in this example includes the most recently received ReceiptHandle for the message. It's important to include this, because if you don't, your action may succeed, but the message may not be deleted.

NOTE SQS queues in an AWS region are independent of SQS queues in other regions. Therefore, queues in different regions can't share messages.

Basic SQS Architecture

A distributed messaging system such as SQS has three main components:

- Your own distributed system components
- Your queues
- Messages in the queues

The queue plays a big role in facilitating the transmission of messages between application components that produce (or send) the messages and the components that consume (or receive) the messages by processing the messages. Here's how messaging works:

1. A producer sends a message to a queue. SQS stores the message on multiple SQL servers for redundancy purposes.

2. A consumer consumes the messages from the queue.

3. The consumer deletes the messages.

A queue isn't meant to facilitate message transmission between a single message producer and a single consumer. Multiple components of a distributed application can send messages to a queue and receive messages from the same queue. The key point here is that the application components are *decoupled* with the help of the queue, since they don't need to coordinate their actions with each other.

Producers such as a web front-end may often send messages faster than an application's components can process them. An EC2 instance may fail, for example, and thus be unable to read a message destined for application components running on the instance. Failure can happen for various reasons, including the fact that the consumer may not be connected to the network. Because the queue reliably stores the unread messages, as soon as the instance recovers, message processing is resumed. The queue buffers the messages, temporarily stores the messages, and ensures that the consumer can process the messages later. It also provides several other benefits, such as ensuring that the messages are consumed in the order they were received and that the messages are processed just once instead of repeatedly.

NOTE SQS automatically deletes messages that cross a maximum retention threshold. The default retention period for messages is 4 days, but you can set it to a value between 6 seconds and 1,209,600 seconds (14 days). So if a consumer of a queue is down for 3 days and then comes online, the consumer should be able to receive its messages from the queue. You can also delete a queue that contains messages that haven't yet been consumed by a consumer.

Standard and FIFO Queues

SQS offers two types of queues: *standard* (the default type) and *FIFO (first in, first out)*. FIFO queues offer all the standard queue capabilities, except a high throughput of messages, and they offer additional features. Both queue types support server-side encryption. The differences between the two queues are in the following areas:

- **Throughput**   How many messages per second can a queue support?
- **Message delivery**   Does the message get delivered at least once, or exactly once?
- **Message ordering**   Are the messages delivered in the order in which they're sent to a queue?

Let's consider how standard and FIFO queues differ in the areas of throughput, message delivery, and message ordering. Once you understand these differences, you can choose the queue type that best suits your use cases.

 NOTE   Standard queues support *at-least-once* message delivery and FIFO queues support *exactly-once* message processing.

Throughput

When you measure message throughput, you count all send, receive, and delete operations per second. Standard queues support almost an unlimited number of transactions per second (TPS). FIFO queues, on the other hand, can support only up to 300 messages per second and 3000 messages per second when you batch the messages. You can request an increase in the message processing limit by filing an AWS support request.

Message Delivery

An SQS message can be in three basic states:

- It is sent to a queue by a message producer.
- It is received from the queue by a message consumer.
- It is deleted from the queue.

In a standard queue, a message is delivered *at least once*. This means that sometimes multiple copies of a message are delivered. Once customers consume the messages, they delete them. FIFO queues deliver messages only once, meaning there are never duplicate messages in the queue.

SQS stores messages on multiple servers for HA. However, when using a standard queue, when one of the servers goes down, you may end up with copies of messages that were deleted on other servers, so a queue may end up sending duplicate messages. You can protect against duplicate messages by coding your applications to be *idempotent*, which means they aren't adversely affected by processing the same message more than once.

Common SQS Actions

SQS supports actions such as the following on a queue (you can embed the actions in your API calls):

- **ChangeMessageVisibility**   Changes the visibility timeout of a message to a new value. The default visibility timeout for a message is 30 seconds. The minimum is 0 seconds and the maximum is 12 hours.
- **CreateQueue**   Creates a standard or FIFO queue. Unless you specify the `FIFOQueue` attribute with the `CreateQueue` request, SQS creates a standard queue.
- **DeleteMessage**   Deletes a specific message from a queue. SQS automatically deletes all messages that are in the queue longer than the retention period that you've configured for that queue.
- **DeleteQueue**   Deletes the queue that you specify, even if it has unread messages.
- **ListQueues**   Returns a list of your queues.
- **PurgeQueue**   Deletes the messages in a queue.
- **ReceiveMessage**   Retrieves one or more messages from a queue, up to a maximum of 10 messages.
- **SendMessage**   Sends a message to a specific queue.

You can use SQS batch actions to reduce your SQS costs by sending, deleting, or changing the visibility of multiple messages (up to 10) with a single action. Here are the batch actions you can perform:

- SendMessageBatch
- DeleteMessageBatch
- ChangeMessageVisibilityBatch

NOTE   A queue without any message is an empty queue, and you may delete it. AWS may delete an inactive queue (without any notification) if none of the following actions have been performed on the queue for 30 consecutive days: `SendMessage`, `ReceiveMessage`, `DeleteMessage`, `GetQueueAttributes`, `SetQueueAttributes`, `AddPermission`, or `RemovePermission`.

Message Ordering

With a standard queue, although the queue makes a best effort to deliver messages in the order they arrived into the queue, the queue may deliver the messages in a different order. A standard queue makes an attempt to preserve the order of the messages, but it's designed to be highly scalable, so it doesn't guarantee that messages are received in the order in which they are sent. In a FIFO queue, the message order is strictly in the order the messages came into the queue—hence the name first in, first out.

Based on the message ordering criterion, standard message queues work well for applications that can handle (occasional) duplication of messages and messages that are processed out of order. Here are some examples:

- A queue that batches a large number of messages for entering data into a database table
- A queue that sends messages to multiple nodes that process a high number of credit card validation requests

If your applications and systems require strict order preservation, use the FIFO queue, because it preserves the exact order in which messages are sent and received. When you use a FIFO queue, you don't need to include sequencing information in your messages. However, you can reorder the messages through adding sequencing information to the messages. FIFO queues are ideal when preserving the order of operations is critical or when you can't have duplicate messages. Here are some examples of cases where this is true:

- A set of commands must be executed in the correct order.
- A consumer must not be able to purchase a product before creating an account.

Efficient Message Processing with SQS

AWS SQS offers several recommendations and best practices to ensure that you process messages efficiently, by handling errors, avoiding inconsistencies, and processing the messages speedily. I briefly describe these practices in the following sections.

 EXAM TIP Don't be tripped up by questions that are designed to determine whether you know the difference between SQS and SNS. SNS uses a push mechanism to send time critical messages to multiple subscribers, thus eliminating the need to periodically check (poll) for updates. SQS is a message queue service for distributed applications that exchanges messages through a polling model. SQS helps decouple message sending and receiving application components so that failure in one component doesn't affect the entire system.

Using Visibility Timeouts and Heartbeats for Fast Message Processing

You can configure *visibility timeouts* and *heartbeats* to ensure that messages are processing in a timely fashion. A visibility timeout is the period for which a message is hidden from other consumers of the queue after a consumer (application component) consumes the message by retrieving it from the queue. The consumer that receives the message must process the message and delete it from the queue within the invisibility timeout period.

The visibility timeout period (say, 40 seconds) sets the maximum time for processing and deleting a message from the queue. During the visibility timeout period, a message is invisible to other application components after an application component retrieves the message from the queue. This period provides time for the component that retrieves the message to process the message and delete it from the queue. The goal here is to keep multiple application components from processing the same message. The timeout period for a message starts when a component retrieves the message from an SQS queue. The component can process the message and delete it from the queue during the visibility period.

You must set the visibility timeout period according to your best estimate as to the maximum time it takes to process (and delete) a message. An SQS queue has a default visibility timeout of 30 seconds. You can modify the visibility timeout period setting with the `ChangeMessageVisibility` option. You can set the timeout at the queue level, or you can set a special visibility timeout for returned messages when you're receiving messages.

You can experience problems if you set the visibility timeout period too low or too high: *If you set the visibility timeout period too low,* a consumer processing the message may not have sufficient time to delete the message before the timeout expires. The message will then be visible to the consumers and will be received again by the queue. A duplicate message is received by a different consumer. If your application or system demands that there shouldn't be duplicate messages (messages must be received only once), this is a problem. *If you set the timeout period too high,* and a consumer fails to process the message successfully, the consumer is forced to wait a long time before trying to process that message again.

If you can't accurately estimate how long it takes to process messages in a queue, you can use an additional strategy to ensure speedy processing of messages. You can configure *heartbeats* for the consumer process to keep checking whether the consumer of a message is still processing a message. You configure an initial visibility timeout and extend it by a minute (or another time period) at a time, as long as the consumer is still working on the message, as indicated by the heartbeats from the consumer process.

Setting Up Polling to Reduce SQS Costs

SQS uses *polling* to determine whether messages are available for a response. During polling, SQS checks with some or all of its servers to see if they have any available messages and employs a technique that involves *sampling* a subset of its servers to check for available messages. There are two types of polling: *short polling* and *long polling*.

By default, SQS uses short polling, in which SQS queries only a subset (weighted random set) of machines, but not all its servers, to check whether there any available messages for a response. Short polling happens when the `WaitTimeSeconds` parameter of a `ReceiveMessage` request is set to `0`.

There are problems with short polling, however:

- It may result in a number of empty responses from the servers when there are no messages available for a request.

- A receive request for message may not return all your messages, since only a sample of the SQS servers is queried. Further message retrieval requests will make SQS eventually sample all its servers, and the requestor nodes get all the messages, but the application uses more CPU resources as a result of the multiple short polls of the servers.

- It may also get false responses that indicate a message isn't available, when it is.

Long polling, on the other hand, returns messages as soon as they're available in a queue. Long polling reduces your SQS costs by eliminating most empty responses by querying all the SQS servers and eliminating all false empty responses by having SQS wait until a message is available before sending a response. A response by SQS to a `ReceiveMessage` request contains at least one of the available messages, and the maximum number of messages in the response is specified in the `ReceiveMessage` action.

Handling Message Failures with Dead-Letter Queues

A *dead-letter queue* is a special queue that helps handle message failures. It receives messages not from application components, but from other SQS queues, called *source queues*. If for any reason a message wasn't processed correctly, you can set aside the failed messages in a dead-letter queue. Normally, you set up a dead-letter queue after a maximum number of processing attempts have been made. The queue helps isolate messages that couldn't be processed. Its failed message logs and the contents of the failed messages enable you to find the root causes of the message failures.

To create a dead-letter queue, you must first create a normal message queue (standard or FIFO) and then designate it as a dead-letter queue. Multiple normal queues can use the same dead-letter queue to redirect their failed messages.

You can set a *redrive policy* to specify the conditions under which SQS moves messages from the source (a standard or a FIFO queue) to a dead-letter queue. For example, you can set this policy with a `maxReceiveCount` of 3, which will move a message to the dead-letter queue if the consumer or source queue receives the same message three times without the consumer having deleted the message.

The original enqueue timestamp of a message remains the same when the message is moved to a dead-letter queue. Since the message can be deleted from the dead-letter queue based on the retention period set for it in the source queue, it's a good idea to set the retention period of the dead-letter queue to exceed that of the original source queue, so you can access those messages later for troubleshooting the message failure that led to the message being moved to the dead-letter queue.

 TIP Configuring a dead-letter queue ensures the correctness of CloudWatch Metrics and avoids false alarms due to *poison pill messages,* which are messages that a queue receives, but can't process.

It's important to understand how a dead-letter queue works with a standard and a FIFO source queue.

A standard queue is designed to handle large numbers of messages. If a message fails, the queue keeps processing the message until the expiration of the retention period. You may want to configure a policy that moves a message to a dead-letter queue after a few failures, so the queues aren't bogged down with a large number of failed messages. The best practice is to use dead-letter queues with standard queues, since standard queues don't depend on a strict ordering of messages. The only time you may not want to configure a dead-letter queue with a standard queue is when there's a dependency that forces you to retry message transmission indefinitely until it succeeds.

A FIFO queue, on the other hand, processes messages in sequence from a message group. If a failed message blocks the queue, only the messages from this message group are unavailable, but the consumer can retrieve ordered messages from other message groups.

Postponing Message Delivery with Delay Queues

You can delay the delivery of a message to a queue by configuring a *delay queue* setting. A delay queue hides a message when you add the message to the queue. By doing this, you keep the message invisible to the consumers for a set period. The default delay for a queue is 0 seconds (no delay), and the maximum duration is 15 minutes.

NOTE   The key point to remember is that for a standard queue, the delay applies only to new messages, but for FIFO queues, the delay also affects the messages that are already in the queue.

Handling Request Errors

If you're using the AWS SDK, you can use the automatic *retry and backoff* logic to handle request errors. Otherwise, configure a pause of a few milliseconds before retrying actions when you receive error messages, no messages at all, or a timeout.

Amazon Simple Notification Service

The Amazon SNS web service helps users create and send messages to clients or endpoints that subscribe to the service. If a user has deployed an application in the cloud and wants to configure a notification to be sent to her via SMS whenever the application encounters errors, she can do so with Amazon SNS. The service also enables you to send individual messages as well as fanout messages to a large number of recipients. It's a cost-efficient way to send push notifications to mobile device users and e-mail recipients, and you can also use the service to send messages to other distributed services.

SNS has three major components:

- **Topics**   These logical access points and communication channels facilitate the production and consumption of messages. You can group multiple message recipients through topics. The topics enable recipients to subscribe to identical copies of a notification. The same topic can deliver messages to various endpoint types, such as iOS, Android, and SMS endpoints. SNS formats the messages appropriately and delivers them to all the endpoint types and clients that have subscribed to that topic.

- **Publishers**   Also called *producers*, publishers communicate asynchronously with consumers by producing and sending messages to a topic. Rather than send a message to a different destination address each time, the publisher simply sends all messages to one or more topics, which act as repositories for the messages. You can configure the length of time the messages can stay in a topic, which stores the messages on disk.

- **Subscribers** Also called *consumers*, subscribers consume (receive and process) messages sent by the publishers. They consume the messages from a named topic to which the message publishers send their messages. Subscribers can be web servers, Amazon SQS queues, AWS Lambda functions, and e-mail addresses. They receive messages or notifications over a supported protocol when they subscribe to a topic.

 NOTE In Amazon SQS, there's a *one-to-one* relationship between a message and a worker. In Amazon SNS, there's a *one-to-many* relationship between a topic and its subscribers.

Keep in mind the following key points about SNS notifications:

- A message can contain a maximum of 256Kb of data and can include regular text messages, as well as XML- or JSON-formatted text.
- There's no guarantee of the message order.
- Messages can't be deleted once they're published.
- You can configure an SNS delivery policy to retry message delivery in case of a message delivery failure.

SNS supports the following protocols for sending and receiving messages and notifications:

- HTTP and HTTPS
- Email
- Amazon SQS
- Simple Message Service (SMS)
- Lambda (a Lambda function can be a subscriber)

How SNS Works

As an administrator, you can create topics and manage access to them through policies that specify which publishers can publish to that topic and which subscribers can consume those messages. Here is how you configure SNS message publishing and consumption:

1. **Create a topic.** The topic serves the communication channel for publishers and consumers to communicate with each other. Exercise 9-3 shows how to create an SNS topic.

2. **Subscribe to a topic.** You subscribe an endpoint to a topic so it can receive messages published to a topic, so that the endpoint can receive notification messages from SNS. An endpoint can be a web server, an e-mail address, a mobile app, or an Amazon SQS queue. Once you subscribe an endpoint to a queue, the endpoint starts receiving all the messages that are published to that topic. Exercise 9-4 shows how to subscribe endpoints to a topic.

3. **Publish the messages.** Publishers send messages to the topics that they've created, or to topics to which they have been authorized to publish the messages. Exercise 9-5 shows how to publish messages to a topic.

4. **Deliver the messages.** When a new message is published to a topic, SNS delivers the message to all the endpoints for which you created subscriptions in step 2.

 NOTE You can customize messages that you send to different protocols. For example, you can specify that e-mail endpoints should receive a full-length message, while SMS users get a concise version of the same message.

Interaction Between SQS and SNS

Here's what you need to do to have Amazon SNS deliver notifications to an Amazon SQS queue:

1. Subscribe to an SNS topic and specify Amazon SQS as the transport. The endpoint should be an SQS queue.

2. The SQS queue owner must subscribe the queue to the SNS topic.

3. If you are the owner of both the SNS topic that's being subscribed to and the SQS queue that will receive the notifications, you're good to go.
Or
If you are the owner of the SQS queue but not of the SNS topic, SNS requires confirmation of your subscription request.

SNS Message Durability

When a publisher publishes messages to a topic, SNS stores multiple copies of the message on disk, in different availability zones (AZs). Thus, even if there's a failure to transmit a message from a specific AZ, SNS can get the message from another AZ, thus assuring that the messages are durable.

SNS Use Cases and Scenarios

You can use Amazon SNS for various use cases and scenarios, such as sending application alerts, text messaging, and mobile push notifications.

SNS Alerts

You can configure notifications that alert you when an event occurs in any AWS services that use SNS. SNS can send application alerts in the form of notifications. You can configure the notifications to go out to users via email or SMS.

Fanout

Th *fanout* scenario is meant for parallel, asynchronous processing of messages. A message that's sent to a topic is pushed simultaneously to multiple SNS endpoints such as HTTP endpoints and e-mail addresses. For example, when a new student enrolls in a

Figure 9-1
An SNS fanout
message

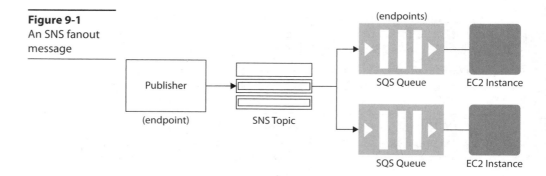

university, an SNS message is sent to a topic. SNS replicates the message and pushes it out simultaneously to all endpoints that are subscribed to this topic, such as the offices of the residence hall managers, course advisors, and the financial office of the university, to help them handle different facets of the student's enrollment.

Figure 9-1 shows the architecture of a fanout message.

Push Messages to E-mail, SMS, and Mobile Devices

You can use SNS to send mass messages, such as breaking news, to individuals and groups via e-mail and SMS. Mobile devices and mobile apps can also receive push notification messages from SNS. SNS helps you publish a message once and deliver it any number of times. With a single publish request, you can send unique messages to various Apple, Android, or Amazon devices.

AWS Fault Tolerance and High Availability

Two areas, high availability and disaster recovery (DR), should be of critical importance to you as an AWS system administrator. *High availability* ensures that your systems are available to your users and applications and that they offer their usual performance without any noticeable service interruptions, even when hardware, software, network or other failures occur. You support HA through redundant system components and by setting up automatic failover for your key services. *Disaster recovery* concerns how you prepare for and recover from a disaster, such as a natural event (flood or fire), human error, or any adverse event that disrupts your operations.

The AWS infrastructure and servers help you build reliable, fault-tolerant, and highly available systems. Providing HA and resiliency in the face of adverse events is a big motivator to move to the AWS cloud. Setting up an HA environment that matches AWS's by yourself in your on-premise environment is extremely complex and expensive. Although many HA features are already baked into the AWS infrastructure, you do need to make some HA configurations for your applications and resources.

Though any of the AWS infrastructure components, such as the compute instances, storage devices, network components, and databases, may experience failure, you can protect against failures by building resiliency for the AWS infrastructure components and all the services that you use. The most important thing to remember is that simply moving your on-premise systems to the Amazon cloud doesn't guarantee fault-tolerance and HA.

Basic infrastructure services such as EC2 and Amazon Elastic Block Storage (EBS) offer HA features such as multiple AZs, elastic IP addresses (EIPs), and EBS snapshots. To build a fault-tolerant HA system in the cloud, you must ensure that you take advantage of these and other HA-related features that AWS offers.

AWS provides resiliency and HA through its basic infrastructure services as well as its higher-level services. Most of the AWS higher-level services such as Amazon Simple Storage Service (S3), Amazon SQS, and Amazon Elastic Load Balancing (ELB) come with built-in fault tolerance and HA.

In the following sections, I explain the fault tolerance and HA capabilities of the basic AWS infrastructure services, as well that of its higher-level services. First, let's quickly review how AWS provides redundancy by placing both its services and your AWS resources in regions and AZs.

How AWS Provides Redundancy with Regions and AZs

As you know, AWS hosts its resources such as EC2 instances in multiple locations around the world. These locations consist of regions and availability zones.

Figure 9-2 shows how AWS regions and AZs are set up.

An AWS region is a geographical area that's designed to be completely isolated from other regions. At the time of this writing, there are 20 AWS regions, each of which consists of a set of data centers known as availability zones. You can place your resources such as EC2 instances and databases in multiple locations, but AWS doesn't replicate the resources across regions unless you explicitly set up the replication.

An AZ is a geographic area designed to insulate the services running in it from failures in other AZs. The AZs are situated distant from each other, with each zone in a different flood zone, and each using power from different electric grids to minimize the possibility of a simultaneous multiple AZ failure. However, the AZs are all connected with high-bandwidth, high-speed, wide area networks (WANs). An AZ may experience outages. Therefore, it's important to run your application stacks in multiple AZs to ensure HA. You must therefore understand the concept of zone dependencies.

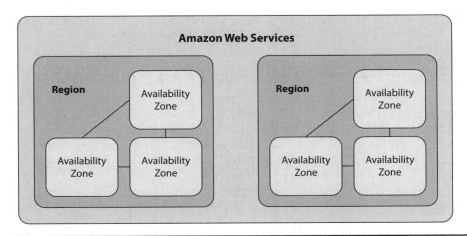

Figure 9-2   AWS regions and availability zones

NOTE Although you can deploy your web applications in multiple regions for HA, in most cases it's enough to design your applications to range over multiple AZs.

Multiple Levels of Redundancy

AWS offers globally redundant, regionally redundant, and AZ-level redundant services. A resource can be global, regional, or tied to a single AZ:

- AWS offers several globally redundant services such as Route 53 (DNS), CloudFront (content delivery network, or CDN), and Identity and Access Management (IAM), which means that these services are immune to failures of even an entire AWS region.

- Regionally redundant services are run across multiple AZs. Services such as Amazon S3, Amazon Elastic File System (EFS), DynamoDB, and ELB are some of these services that are immune to individual AZ failures.

- Services such as Amazon EBS are redundant within a data center at the AZ level.

The Cost of Higher Redundancy

It's important to be aware of the cost implications of deploying HA applications and services in the AWS cloud. In general, higher redundancy costs more than lesser or no redundancy. For example, Amazon EFS, which offers regional-level redundancy, costs more than Amazon EBS, which offers only AZ-level redundancy.

You can, however, take advantage of several AWS redundancy-related services that are either free or inexpensive to provide HA for your applications.

NOTE Not all AWS services are redundant by nature. If you're running a single EC2 instance or a database instance on a single server with no replication of the data, you could run into availability problems resulting from a server or software problem. Thus, you should design your applications for HA by leveraging AWS's redundancy features for various services.

Configuring HA for EC2 with Fully Preconfigured AMIs

By now, you know that you can spin up a virtually unlimited number of EC2 instances on demand by requesting AWS to increase the soft limit of 20. This helps you set up virtual machines quickly during disaster recovery. AWS strongly recommends that you identify fully preconfigured (with the OS and the applications that you need) Amazon Machine Images (AMIs) ahead of time so you can quickly launch instances based on those AMIs during disaster recovery.

You can copy both EBS-backed and instance store–backed AMIs within or across AWS regions. AWS doesn't charge you for copying an AMI, but you do pay for storage and for data transfer. After you copy an AMI, you must manually apply user-defined tags, launch permissions, and add S3 bucket permissions to the new AMI, since these aren't copied over. You must also modify the Auto Scaling policies in the region to which you copy the AMI, so that they use the new AMI ID.

Launching EC2 Instances in Multiple AZs

When launching EC2 instances, you can choose the AZ in which you want to locate the instance. By placing your EC2 instances in multiple AZs, you can ensure that when an instance fails, other instances in a different AZ handle the user requests. In AWS, because AZ isolates systems running in it from failures that occur in other AZs, you can launch your EC2 instances in a different AZ to protect your applications from the failure of a single AZ. You can also use EIP addresses to remap the IP address of an instance in a different AZ when an instance fails in one AZ.

Using *reserved instances* in a different AZ not only lets you provision instances at a lower price, but in the context of fault tolerance, it maximizes your chances of getting the computing capacity that you require in a disaster recovery scenario.

Using EC2 Auto Recovery to Enhance Availability

The EC2 *Auto Recovery* feature helps you increase instance availability by automatically recovering failed EC2 instances. You avoid having to move the failed instance to a new instance, because EC2 Auto Recovery can automatically recover the failed instance to new hardware, if necessary.

To enable EC2 Auto Recovery, set up an AWS CloudWatch alarm for it. Exercise 9-6 shows you how to do this. The recovered instance reboots during the recovery and retains its instance ID, EIP address(es) and configuration, as well as all its metadata.

In Exercise 9-6, you configure two key things that enable EC2 Automatic Recovery: a CloudWatch alarm (internally named as `StatusCheckField_System`), and an SNS topic. When the system status check indicates a failure, the CloudWatch alarm is triggered and the recovery action is initiated, and you'll receive a notification from the topic. Any data in the memory of the failed instance is lost, and when recovery is completed, you'll receive another notification via the same SNS topic. The recovered instance will have been rebooted, and your notification may also have additional instructions for you.

Once you set up a CloudWatch alarm for an EC2 instance, the alarm monitors the instance and automatically recovers the instance. A recovery can also be set off when AWS schedules or stops an instance or retires it due to degradation of the hardware on which the VM instance is running. The system status checks performed by CloudWatch can show failures due to various reasons, such as the loss of power or network connectivity or software or hardware issues on the physical host.

 NOTE   Remember that automatic recovery is supported only on some EC2 instance types, with the additional restriction that the instances must use EBS volumes (and not instance store volumes).

Using Auto Scaling for HA in EC2

The EC2 *Auto Scaling* service automatically launches instances based on policies, schedules, and health checks that you configure. You can specify both a minimum and a maximum number of instances for an Auto Scaling group, and AWS ensures that the specified instances are always up and running. Once you set a minimum number of running instances for your application, the EC2 Auto Scaling detects when an instance or the application itself is unhealthy and replaces the instance automatically to maintain the application availability.

Auto Scaling also enhances application availability by automatically ramping up the number of EC2 instances when your application traffic increases, and it distributes the traffic among the instances. Although you can use Auto Scaling for ensuring HA, it's more appropriate to discuss it as a tool for scaling your system (I discuss it in detail in Chapter 11).

Configuring HA for Databases

Maintaining HA for your databases is critical, since your applications can't function without data! AWS offers HA solutions for RDS databases as well as other database services such as DynamoDB.

Setting Up HA for RDS Databases with Multi-AZ

You can set up HA and failover support for an RDS database, such as Oracle or MySQL, by deploying the databases in a *Multi-AZ* deployment architecture. In a Multi-AZ deployment, RDS automatically sets up a standby replica in an AZ different from the AZ in which the primary database is running. The replica provides a redundant copy of the database and offers other benefits such as lowering latency spikes during a backup of the primary database and enhancing availability during scheduled database maintenance.

A Multi-AZ deployment protects your RDS databases against instance failures as well as disruptions in the AZ where the primary database runs. Figure 9-3 shows the architecture of a Multi-AZ RDS deployment. This figure shows three AZs in one region, with the primary and the standby replicas (also called secondary AZs) running in two different AZs. As Chapter 8 explained, setting up HA with a standby replica isn't meant for scaling the databases: you use Read Replicas to support your read-only traffic.

 NOTE You can set up a Multi-AZ deployment when creating a DB instance, or you can set it up later by modifying the instance and adding the Multi-AZ option.

Here's how RDS automatically switches to a standby replica when the primary database becomes unavailable due either to a planned or an unplanned event:

- RDS handles failovers without any intervention by you.
- The failover time is usually from 60 to 120 seconds.

Figure 9-3
Multiple-zone
RDS database
deployment in
two AZs

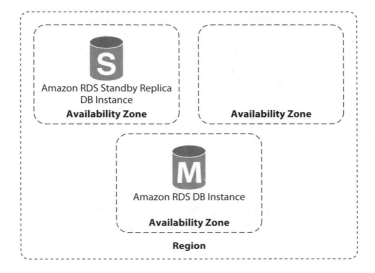

- During the failover, AWS automatically changes the DNS record of the DB instance to point to the standby DB instance, which now becomes the primary database instance.

- You must reestablish existing database connections, so they go to the new primary database.

Any of the following events result in a DB failover to the standby replica:

- A failure of the primary database or outage of the AZ of the primary database

- A change in the DB instance server type or the OS patching of the DB instance server

- A manual initiation of a failover with the `Reboot with failover` command

HA for DynamoDB

DynamoDB uses *DynamoDB Streams*, time-ordered sequences of information pertaining to table changes made to a DynamoDB table that DynamoDB stores for 24 hours in a log. Applications can access the logs to view the before-and-after change data. All modifications that you make to the table are captured by DynamoDB once you enable Streams for a table.

DynamoDB Streams has many applications, such as enabling an application to send notifications to all members of a group when one of its members uploads new data or pictures. For HA purposes, you can use DynamoDB Streams to replicate data between AWS regions when changes occur in a DynamoDB table located in a specific region. Changes made to a DynamoDB database running in one region are automatically written to a table in a different region, thus providing you with a synced-up replica of the original table.

DynamoDB offers *on-demand backup and restore* features that don't affect application availability. It uses an innovative distributed backup capability that helps you do complete backups in seconds, regardless of the size of the table. These backups are consistent within seconds over thousands of table partitions, and you don't need to set up complex backup schedules or suffer outages and application slowdowns during the backups.

DynamoDB's *point-in-time recovery* capability safeguards you from accidental or erroneous deletes and updates to a table, without your having to schedule and create an on-demand backup. DynamoDB maintains a table's incremental backups. Using the point-in-time recovery (PITR) feature, you can restore the table to a point in time within the past 35 days.

Setting Up a Fault-Tolerant and HA Network

You can configure HA and resiliency for your AWS network components, such as your Amazon VPC, with the help of various features such as NAT gateways and EIP addresses, and by configuring health checks and failover through Route 53, AWS's DNS service.

HA for NAT Gateways

You learned about network address translation gateways (NAT gateways) in Chapter 6. A NAT gateway enables instances in a private subnet to connect to the Internet or other AWS services while preventing the Internet from initiating connections to the instance.

You can locate a NAT gateway in a specific AZ and implement it with redundancy in that zone. If you run services in multiple AZs and configure just a single NAT gateway, all those resources will use that one NAT gateway.

Should the AZ in which that gateway is located become unavailable, all your resources lose their ability to access the Internet. To ensure HA, create an AZ-independent architecture by creating multiple NAT gateways, each located in a different AZ. Following this, configure routing so that resources use the NAT gateway located in the same AZ as the resources.

Using EIP Addresses

EIP addresses are associated with your AWS account, and not with any specific EC2 instance. You can programmatically map EIP addresses, which are public IP addresses, between EC2 instances running within a region.

Attaching multiple EIP addresses to an instance helps you set up a low-budget HA solution. As a simple solution, you can manually attach an EIP address to a replacement EC2 instance. You can use EC2 Auto Scaling (see Chapter 10) for an automated failover of the instances.

EIP addresses help you handle server or AZ failures by letting you quickly remap these IP addresses to a different EC2 instance that's already running, or one that you've just started up.

Using ELB for HA

Although you configure load balancing for distributing your workloads across multiple resources such as EC2 instances, load balancing also enhances availability and fault tolerance of your applications. ELB automatically distributes your traffic across multiple targets, such as EC2 instances, containers, and IP addresses, in a single AZ or multiple AZs.

Load balancing your systems increases application availability. You can set up ELB to balance traffic across EC2 instances that run in multiple AZs in an AWS region. AWS transparently replaces the failed instances behind the load balancer, while other instances service your application traffic. When you enable an AZ for a load balancer, it sets up a load balancer node in that AZ. You can then register *targets* in that AZ, such as EC2 instances, so that the load balancer can accept traffic for those targets.

TIP AWS recommends that you enable multiple AZs for your load balancer. If you're using the Application Load Balancer, enabling multiple AZs is *mandatory*.

Setting Up Redundancy for AWS Direct Connect Connections

As I explained in Chapter 6, *AWS Direct Connect* links your internal network to an AWS Direct Connect location through an Ethernet cable, helping you create virtual interfaces that connect directly to AWS services such as Amazon S3 or to your Amazon VPC, bypassing the public Internet and the Internet service providers. An AWS Direct Connect location offers access to AWS in the region to which you associate the location. If that location should become unavailable, your Direct Connect connection won't work. For HA, you can implement multiple Direct Connect connections that are dynamically routable (through the Border Gateway Protocol).

As you will recall from Chapter 6, you must work with an AWS Direct Connect partner to set up Direct Connect connectivity to your data center or on-premise network. To achieve the highest level of availability for a Direct Connect connection, AWS recommends that you employ multiple Direct Connect provider networks to configure multiple physical connections (different routers in different physical locations) to your network. Although this type of configuration does use multiple physical connections to provide resiliency, the connections appear as a single logical connection.

You may also choose to go a different route, so to speak, regarding HA for your Direct Connect connectivity, by using Direct Connect with a *backup VPN connection*. If you set up two Direct Connect connections, with two customer gateways on your end, one of the gateways uses Direct Connect. The other connection uses the second customer gateway for a VPN connection with BGP-based dynamic routing. This configuration constitutes an active-active Direct Connect connection setup.

NOTE By default, AWS Direct Connect prefers routing traffic over an AWS Direct Connect connection to sending the traffic over a VPN connection. You can, however, configure that only one particular set of static routes will be used for the customer gateway that uses the VPN connection.

HA for VPN Connectivity

A *VPN connection* (discussed in Chapter 6) enables you to connect to your Amazon VPC remotely. A virtual private gateway has two VPN endpoints, one of which it uses for static routing and the other for dynamic routing. Your router acts as the customer gateway.

To avoid a single point of failure, set up multiple customer gateways. In other words, set up multiple routers and configure dynamic routing to facilitate automatic failover between AWS and your customer VPN endpoints, for an active-active VPN connection.

> **NOTE** Your VPN network connectivity can be affected by Internet service disruptions, even if you use multiple ISPs. Direct Connect enables you to control the network path of your Internet traffic since it uses private network connectivity to connect to AWS.

Using Route 53 DNS for HA with Health Checks and Failover

As you learned in Chapter 5, Route 53 plays a crucial role in high availability. Route 53 is a highly available DNS service, and one of its three key functions is to perform health checks of your deployed AWS resources. It sends automatic requests to resources such as web servers to ensure their availability and functionality. You can set up notifications so that when a resource is unavailable, Route 53 (automatically) routes Internet traffic to the healthy resources, such as a web server, when the first web server is unhealthy.

> **NOTE** I review Route 53's HA capabilities in this chapter. There may be some overlap with the contents of Chapter 5, but that's OK, because this book is geared toward helping you pass the AWS certification exam—so, a little bit of repetition can only help you!

The two key elements to using Route 53 to provide HA for your resources are the configuration of health checks and the configuration of DNS failover.

Route 53 Health Checks

You can configure Route 53 to perform automatic health checks to monitor both the availability and the performance of web servers, web applications, and other resources. There are three types of Route 53 health checks: those that monitor the health of a resource (say, a web server), those that monitor the status of other health checks, and those that monitor the status of a CloudWatch alarm.

> **NOTE** You can receive notifications when the status of a health check changes by configuring a CloudWatch alarm for that health check.

Here's a brief explanation of the three types of Route 53 health checks that you can configure:

- **Health checks that monitor resource health** These health checks may verify that a resource that you specify with an endpoint, either by IP address or by its domain name, is available, or they may simulate user requests by performing actions such as requesting a web page from an URL.

- **Health checks that monitor the status of other health checks** These health checks, also called *calculated health checks*, help you verify that a minimum number of instances of a specific resource are healthy. For example, a health check may monitor several individual web server health checks and notify you when the number of healthy web servers falls below a number that you configure.

- **Health checks that monitor the status of a CloudWatch alarm** These health checks monitor the status of CloudWatch metrics for various resources, such as those that track the health of ELB hosts. Route 53 will go into an ALARM state even before a CloudWatch alarm does to provide resiliency and HA. Route 53's health check of the CloudWatch alarms changes to unhealthy based on the same data streams that CloudWatch monitors for an alarm and the criteria that you've configured in the CloudWatch alarm.

Route 53 DNS Basics

Before we plunge into configuring of Route 53 DNS failover (the configuration details are in Chapter 6; here I discuss additional features) for providing HA, it's a good idea to refresh your understanding of a few of the basic concepts of Route 53, such as *DNS records* and *routing policies*.

DNS Records You create DNS records to let Route 53 know where you want it to route traffic for a domain. You first create a *hosted zone* for your domain and then create the DNS records. A DNS record contains the name of the domain, a *record type* such as the MX record type for routing e-mail, and pertinent information for that record type (the MX record, for example, includes the hostname of the mail servers and the priority for the mail servers). The name of a DNS records in a hosted zone ends with the hosted zone's name (*www.mycompany.com* for the hosted zone *mycompany.com*).

DNS records can route traffic sent to a domain to the IP address of a host, route e-mail to a mail server, and route traffic for subdomains to the IP address of different hosts.

 NOTE In this context, it's important to understand the difference between a CNAME and an alias DNS record. A CNAME (canonical name) DNS record has the same format as a domain name. You can't create CNS records for the zone apex, which is the top node of a DNS namespace. For example, a zone apex is something like mycompany.com, and you can't create a CNAME record for mycompany.com, although you can do so for www.mycompany .com, newproduct.mycompany.com, and so on. An *alias* record enables you to route requests to AWS resources such as S3 buckets and CloudFront distributions. Aliases are somewhat similar to a CNAME record type, but you're allowed to create an alias for the zone apex.

Routing Policies   Although the DNS records that you create tell Route 53 *where* to send traffic coming into your systems, routing policies, which you also create, tell Route 53 *how* to respond to DNS queries. You can configure one of the following routing policies:

- **Simple routing policy**   Meant for a single resource such as a web server that serves content for your *mycompany.com* web site.

- **Failover routing policy**   Sets up an *active-passive failover*, which is one of the DNS failover types I discuss in a following section.

- **Latency routing policy**   Routes traffic to the region that currently offers the best response time (lowest latency). Use this when you've placed your resources in multiple AWS regions, and you want the best response time.

- **Weighted resource policy**   Routes traffic to various resources in proportions that you configure.

- **Geolocation routing policy**   Sends traffic to resources based on the *location of the users* making the DNS requests.

- **Geoproximity routing policy**   Sends traffic based on the *location of your resources*. This policy also enables you to divert traffic between resources in multiple locations.

- **Multivalue answer routing policy**   Enables Route 53 to respond to a DNS query with randomly selected health records (maximum of eight records).

Creating DNS Records and Associating Them with DNS Health Checks

DNS failover configuration may look a bit daunting in the beginning, but not to worry. In a routing configuration, your goal is to create DNS records and associate them with DNS health checks, so Route 53 can figure out how and when to fail over a service or resource.

The first step is to draw a *tree diagram* of your failover configuration. At the top of the tree diagram, place the DNS records that users specify to access your web site or application, such as *mycompany.com*. For the nodes, specify the routing policy for the DNS records that you create, such as a latency or failover routing policy. The records are then called latency or failover records, according to the routing policy that you assign for the record. I'll show an example configuration in Figure 9-4, so you can see that it's simple.

 NOTE   You can use the Traffic Flow visual editor to simplify the creation of records for complex configurations and save the configurations as traffic policies. You can then associate the traffic policies with domain or subdomain names in a hosted zone or zones. The editor also helps you roll back suboptimal configurations. I explained traffic flow in Chapter 6.

You can configure a *simple* or a *complex* configuration for the DNS failover. The configurations determined how to route the health checking requests to a resource such as a web server by specifying things such as the protocol (HTTP/TCP), the IP address/port, and a domain name and path (for HTTP/HTTPS health checks). DNS health checks work differently in the two configurations.

Health Checks in a Simple Failover Configuration A simple failover configuration is good for configuring failover for two identical types of resources, such as two web servers for the same domain. It enables you to route traffic to one web server if the other web server isn't in a healthy state.

In a simple failover configuration, there are restrictions on the placing of alias records. You must either not include any alias records in the configuration at all, or if you do include them, the records should route directly to a resource (such as an ELB load balancer) rather than to a different record.

Here's how you set up a simple health check configuration:

1. Determine the resources that you want Route 53 to monitor.

2. Create health checks for resources such as EC2 instances or web servers that you can't create an alias record for.

3. Create a group of records for the resource, such as a set of weighted DNS records. All the records must have identical Name, Type, and Routing Policy values.

4. Once you configure the health check, DNS selects a record based on the routing policy that you configured, such as latency, location, or weight-based policy. It checks the health state of the record that it chose, and if it's unhealthy, it picks a different healthy record and responds to the query with an IP address (*A records*). When evaluating which record to pick, DNS ignores the unhealthy records.

Figure 9-4 shows a simple health check configuration. Route 53 considers all resources that you don't specify in the set of DNS records as healthy. Route 53 doesn't perform health checks in response to a DNS query that it receives. Rather, it periodically checks the health of the endpoint you specified in the health check.

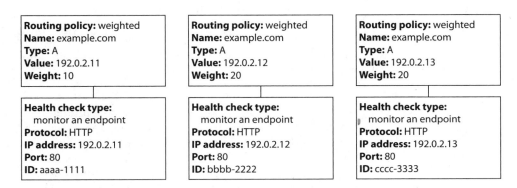

Figure 9-4 A simple Route 53 DNS health check configuration diagram

In Figure 9-4 are three A records (Record 1, Record 2, Record 3) for which a health check is configured. As you will recall, Route 53 chooses records based on the routing policy and other values that you've configured for that record. When it first selects Record 1, it does so one-fifth of the time: $10 / (10 + 20 + 20)$. Let's say the second record (weight = 20) becomes unhealthy. Route 53 now responds to requests using Record A roughly a third of the time $(10 / (10 + 20))$.

Health Checks in a Complex Failover Configuration   You configure complex health checks the same way you configure simple health checks. The big difference, however, is that your tree diagram will include both alias records (latency alias and failover alias, for example) and non-alias records. This way, you can fine-tune how Route 53 responds to requests. Here's the difference between how Route 53 determines the health of non-alias and alias records for which you've associated a health check:

- For non-alias records, Route 53 checks the current status of the health check.
- For alias records, it checks the health status of the resource such as an ELB load balancer that the alias record references.

NOTE   Although you *can* configure health checks for alias records, AWS recommends that you do so only for non-alias records.

Configuring Route 53 DNS Failover

In addition to routing DNS requests to healthy resources, Route 53 performs another, even more important function by enabling you to configure failover configurations. Here's what you need to remember when configuring a failover configuration:

- There are two types of failover configurations: *active-active* and *active-passive*.
- You can use any routing policy other than the Failover routing policy when configuring an *active-active* failover.
- You must use the Failover routing policy when configuring an *active-passive* failover.

Active-Active Failover   You use active-active failover when you want all resources to be available most of the time. When a record becomes unhealthy, Route 53 stops sending DNS requests to that resource.

Active-Passive Failover   In an active-passive failover configuration, there are two types of DNS records: *primary* and *secondary*. You use an active-passive failover configuration when you want a (primary) resource or a set of resources to be available most of the time. If all the primary resources are unhealthy, Route 53 routes requests to healthy secondary resources in response to DNS queries.

To configure an active-passive failover, you *must* specify the Failover routing policy for all the records. You can configure a single primary and secondary resource or multiple primary and secondary resources. Although you can configure an active-passive failover with weighted records as well, if some of the records have zero weights, Route 53 responds to DNS requests by using only the records with nonzero weights. It routes DNS requests to records with zero weights only when all records with nonzero weights are unhealthy.

EBS and S3: Configuring Fault Tolerance and HA for Data

As you know, protecting data is essential for ensuring a highly available system. All AWS's data-related services, such as Amazon EBS and Amazon S3, offer HA features, such as snapshots and replication.

Amazon EBS

EBS offers persistent storage volumes that are much more durable than instance storage. Furthermore, EBS automatically replicates your EBS volumes within a single AZ.

You can enhance EBS availability by taking regular point-in-time *snapshots* of the EBS volumes so that you can store the data in Amazon S3. Amazon S3 automatically replicates these snapshots to multiple AZs to provide resiliency. Although the EBS volumes are tied to a specific AZ, their snapshots are tied to the *region* and not to any AZ. Therefore, following an AZ failure, you can use the snapshots to re-create the EBS volumes in a different AZ in the same region. This strategy helps in multiple scenarios, such as server-level failures, disk failures, and AZ failures.

As I showed in Chapter 7, EBS snapshots are incremental. Make sure you protect your most recent snapshots. They are all you'll need to restore the EBS volumes in a different AZ when failure strikes.

Amazon S3

Use Amazon S3's *cross-region replication* feature to enable asynchronous automatic copying of S3 objects across multiple AWS regions. This helps make your S3 data redundant and thus enhances HA for your S3 data.

You enable cross-region replication at the *bucket level*. Cross-region replication serves several purposes, such as satisfying compliance requirements that stipulate that you store copies of data in geographical areas that are far from each other, and making it easier to process the same sets of data in multiple AWS regions. You can also use this feature to maintain copies of an S3 object under different owners, since you can specify that the destination bucket owner is also the owner of the object replicas.

From the availability perspective, cross-region replication of S3 data helps minimize latency in retrieving the objects from S3 by storing object copies in regions that are geographically close to your users.

A key requirement of S3 is extremely high availability. You can ensure this by updating the IP addresses of S3 endpoints in DNS as necessary. Short-lived clients will automatically reflect these changes, and for long-lived clients, developers must programmatically enable the applications to take the changes into consideration.

Architecting an HA System in the AWS Cloud

In the previous sections, I've explained the key fault tolerance and HA features of AWS. But how do you go about setting up HA in practice? It's hard to set up a fully fault-tolerant and highly available system from the outset. A better strategy is to understand what level of availability that you are required to provide (according

Figure 9-5
A simple deployment of all the web stack's components on a single server

to your SLAs), and then gradually enhance your systems over time to work up to the required level of availability.

In the following sections, I explain how to build a highly available system with a basic web application stack that consists of a web server, an application server, and a database that becomes more available, as well as scalable, as you gradually add HA features to the system.

Starting Out

Let's assume that your SLA calls for a 99.5 percent uptime. The simplest possible setup for your web stack would be to run all the stack's components—the web server, the app server, and the database—on a single server, as shown in Figure 9-5.

This deployment provides a total availability of just 80 percent ($0.90 \times 0.90 \times 0.99 = 0.8019$). Splitting a system into multiple *tiers*, such as the web server tier, app server tier, and database tier, helps provide availability and scalability. The total availability of a system is the product of the availability for each of its components, as I show in the following sections.

Introducing Redundancy

To enhance system availability, you must add redundancy to your system components. Let's do this by adding another web server to our web tier. This brings up the web tier availability from 90 percent for a single web server to 99 percent with the two web servers. The web tier availability is computed as follows:

$$1 - (1 - 0.9)^2 = 0.99$$

Total availability of the system goes from 80 percent to a little over 88 percent ($0.99 \times 0.90 \times 0.99 = 0.8821$). Although adding the extra web server to the web tier increases overall availability by 8 percent, you still don't get your desired availability level of 99.5 percent.

Adding more web servers obviously won't do the trick, so let's add redundancy to the application tier and the database tier as well, as shown in Figure 9-6.

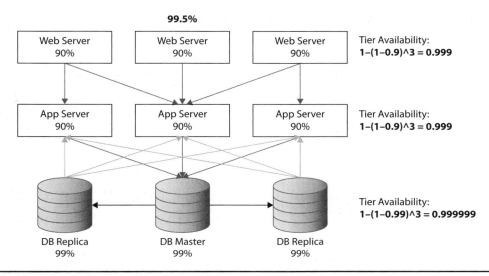

Figure 9-6 Adding redundancy to all the web stack tiers

By configuring all three tiers of my web stack with redundancy, I meet my SLA of 99.5 percent, since I now have a 99.8 percent availability for my web stack

- Web server availability: $1 - (1 - 0.9)^3 = 0.999$
- App server availability: $1 - (1 - 0.9)^3 = 0.999$
- DB tier availability: $1 - (1 - 0.99)^3 = 0.999999$
- Total availability: $0.999 \times 0.999 \times 0.999999 = 0.9980$ (99.8%)

Remember that I'm setting up my stack in a single data center. Although all three of my web stack components are redundant now, my data center isn't! What happens if my data center experiences a major failure due to a power outage, a natural disaster, or a major Internet connectivity issue? My web stack redundancy won't help me, since the multiple web servers, app servers, and DB servers all live in the same data center.

Adding Redundancy at the Data Center Level

I can make my multinode, multiple stack web stacks truly highly available by adding a redundancy component to the data center, by deploying the stack's components across multiple data centers. A highly redundant set of multiple data centers should be immune to natural disasters and have low latency connectivity among the multiple data centers. I can do this by ensuring that the data centers are close to one another, but not so close that a single disaster will bring down all of the data centers or make them all unavailable.

I can set this up in a non-AWS environment, of course, but it's going to be a very challenging process and not cost efficient, to boot. The better alternative is to take advantage of AWS's AZs by deploying my web stack to the AWS cloud. I get the benefits of HA at a low cost, and with virtually none of the headaches of setting up all the things required for HA, because everything is already there!

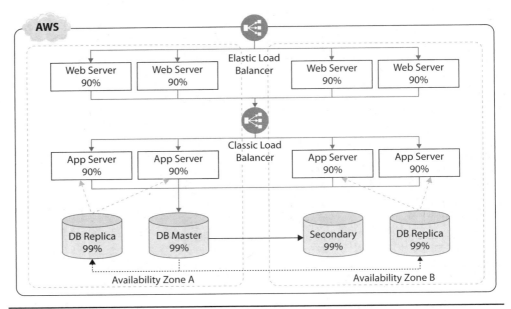

Figure 9-7 A highly available web stack deployed across two AWS AZs

Figure 9-7 shows how I can set up my web stack in two AWS AZs to provide an availability level of 99.8 percent, thus satisfying my SLA of 99.5 percent. Even if one of the two AZs experiences a major outage, I'm still good, since the web stack's tiers in the other AZ can service my users without any interruption.

By deploying my web stack across multiple AWS AZs, I assure that my web architecture is highly available at all times, since it now includes data center redundancy in addition to the redundancy at the three web stack tier levels. Not only that, but my web stack is now easily scalable as well, since I can employ strategies such as EC2 Auto Scaling to dynamically add nodes or remove them to match changes in my application workloads.

AWS Disaster Recovery

When you run your systems and applications in the AWS cloud, you want to enable fast disaster recovery (DR) of your critical systems without having to maintain a second physical site. AWS supports a variety of DR architectures to help you. These architectures range from *pilot light environments* that help in minor data center failures, to *hot standby environments* that enable you to failover large systems, to *multisite deployments* for the highest level of DR that involve running two fully fledged systems—one in the AWS cloud and the other in your onsite infrastructure. A multisite deployment provides recovery with the least amount of downtime.

With DR architectures in place, you can quickly launch services and resources pursuant to a disaster to ensure that your business runs without interruptions. AWS provides several DR services to enable you to recover your IT infrastructure and data confidently and rapidly, so that you can quickly resume normal operations when disaster strikes. You can use some or all of these DR processes to minimize the impact of a disaster on your data, systems, and business operations.

Traditional DR Strategies

When you run your operations in your own on-premise physical environment, you must duplicate your physical infrastructure to ensure that you can quickly switch to it in the event of a disaster. AWS offers you ways to spin up additional infrastructure during a DR event quickly, without your having to maintain an expensive alternative DR site. A traditional DR strategy requires organizations to maintain the DR facilities, test their DR processes regularly, secure the DR facilities, and ensure that their network infrastructure functions correctly when they turn on the DR sites following a disaster event.

AWS DR features offer several advantages over such traditional DR strategies. You can choose from a simple backup-and-recovery solution to a fault-tolerant multisite solution, based on your *recovery point objective* (RPO) and *recovery time objective* (RTO). A key advantage of AWS in the DR area is that you'll need a significant ramp-up of your infrastructure only temporarily, in the event of a disaster.

Because AWS charges you only for what you use, it's an ideal environment for setting up your DR solution. You pay for the additional resources you bring alive during a disaster as usual, based on *usage*. On the other hand, if you were to maintain a separate DR system, you'd need to pay for the infrastructure all year around, every year, even if you never use the system.

In the following sections, I explain how you can leverage AWS processes and services both to cut your DR spending and to ensure business continuity in the face of a DR event.

Recovery Time Objective and Recovery Point Objective

Many disaster recovery strategies are available to you in the AWS cloud. You base your choice of the DR strategies and the related recovery processes on your organization's RTO and RPO:

- **Recovery time objective (RTO)**   The *time* it takes for you to restore business processes to the agreed-upon levels, following a disaster. The agreements are usually codified in an SLA or an operational level agreement (OLA). For example, if your SLA stipulates an RTO of four hours, and disaster strikes at 4 P.M., your DR processes should be able to restore business processes fully by 8 P.M.

- **Recovery point objective (RPO)**   The amount of *acceptable data loss* in a specific time interval. For example, if disaster strikes at 4 P.M., and your RPO is two hours, then following the implementation of your DR processes, you should recover all the data that was in your systems before 2 P.M. So the data loss is limited to the data between 2 P.M. and 4 P.M.

Every organization has a different set of an RTO and an RPO. You plan your DR strategies based on the RPO, which determines the acceptable data loss, and the RTO, which determines the length of time for which your applications are unavailable, according to your SLAs.

Let's say you have an RTO and an RPO, both of four hours. This means that you have some leeway in terms of both the time it takes for you to become fully operations, as well as an acceptable data loss that can range over four hours. In this scenario, you might be able to get by with something like a standby database or a recovery through database backups. RDS automatically backs up your databases, but only once a day. Therefore, if your RPO is less than 24 hours, which is often the case, you must take more frequent backups to satisfy your RPO. If your RPO is 13 hours, you can take a backup every 12 hours. If, on the other hand, you have zero RTO and zero RPO, you'll need a very highly available setup, and your DR strategy should reflect that by setting up a multisite DR environment, so that your business operations can immediately switch over to the DR site following a disaster event.

AWS Services and Features that Support DR

You can adopt various DR strategies to avoid disruptions resulting from a disaster. However, before you learn about those strategies, it's important that you understand AWS services and features you can use or adopt to support your DR planning. Some of these DR supporting services and features enable you to maintain backups on which to migrate data on durable storage. Other features help you easily spin up additional computing capacity to support the DR infrastructure.

 TIP   You may want to set up your DR sites in the AWS cloud in a different region from where you deploy your production or primary systems.

The AWS DR-relevant areas you should focus on are storage, databases, computing, and the network.

Storage
The following storage-related features help you formulate an effective DR strategy:

- **Elastic Block Storage**   You can create snapshots of the EBS volumes that you use and store them durably in Amazon S3. EBS volumes are independent of the instances to which you attach them, and AWS replicates them across multiple servers to protect against data loss.

- **Simple Storage Service**   S3 stores data in multiple storage drives that live in different data centers within an AWS region. They provide a 99.999999999 percent durability. S3 data protection features such as versioning and bucket policies offer additional support for data retention and archiving.

- **Amazon Glacier**   Glacier provides low-cost storage for data archives and backups, which are critical during disaster recovery.

- **AWS Storage Gateway**   The Storage Gateway connects a software appliance that you place on your premises with AWS storage, and provides a fast, direct transfer of data into your AWS-based systems.

- **AWS Import/Export**   You can export and import critical datasets out of and into AWS by using portable storage devices that bypass the Internet. You use Amazon's fast internal networks to transfer data rather than move the data via the Internet. This is not only cost effective, but also much faster. During a disaster recovery, you can use AWS Import/Export to move data that you've transferred from S3 buckets and Glacier storage into EBS snapshots.

Databases

All AWS's managed database services and other databases contain features that help when you are recovering your systems from a disaster:

- **DynamoDB**   To prepare for DR, you can copy DynamoDB data to other AWS regions. During the DR, you can scale up the database easily with a single click from the console or with a single API call.

- **Redshift**   To prepare for DR, you can make snapshots of Redshift data and store them in S3 in the same region, or copy the snapshots to a different region. When recovering from DR, it's easy to restore the database in the same or a different region.

NOTE   You may periodically take manual snapshots of an RDS database as part of a disaster recovery drill. If you create the DB snapshot on a single-AZ instance, there's an I/O suspension (a few seconds to a few minutes), the length depending on the size and class of the DB instances. In a Multi-AZ deployment, there's no I/O suspension and thus no downtime, since RDS takes the backup on the standby and not the primary DB instance.

Network   One of the major problems in traditional DR that relies on an alternative DR site is networking. You must not only maintain the network infrastructure, such as routers, firewalls, switches, and load balancers, but you must also ensure that adequate Internet capacity exists and that all the network services are configured to work correctly, all in a very short time.

AWS offers several networking services and features to help you during DR:

- **Elastic Load Balancing**   By using ELB, you can preallocate the load balancer by configuring it with its DNS name, simplifying your DR.

- **DNS Route 53 Service**   Route 53 offers a global load balancing capability, such as DNS endpoint checks and failover between endpoints, all of which help during DR.

- **Amazon VPC**   Many enterprise applications run inside an organization's internal network. During DR, you can use your Amazon VPC to extend your internal network topology to the AWS cloud to get the applications working quickly.

NOTE In addition to the services I listed here, you can use AWS's deployment automation services such as CloudFormation, Elastic Beanstalk, and OpsWorks during the recovery phase of DR. These services help you quickly create and deploy the resources and services from stored configurations to support your RTO and RPO.

AWS Disaster Recovery Scenarios

Let's review a set of proven DR scenarios with AWS and learn how they differ from traditional DR strategies. You can use one or more of these during a DR exercise. Here are four common DR scenarios or strategies:

- Restore from backups
- Quick recovery with pilot light
- Warm standby
- Multisite DR strategy

Each of these scenarios has a DR preparation and a recovery component, with a specific set of tasks you must accomplish in each phase. Regardless of which of the four common DR strategies you choose, following a disaster recovery, there's a set of "fallback" procedures that you must perform after the restoration of your primary site. These tasks include stopping changes to the DR site, restoring backups to the primary site, and pointing your users again to the primary site.

TIP Frequent testing of your DR solutions is key to a successful DR strategy. It's cost-effective in AWS to spin up duplicate environments and test your "game-day" DR scenarios.

Restoring Backups

Restoring a backup is a minimal DR strategy. Under this scenario, you make backups of your critical data and use the backups to restore your systems during DR. In a traditional DR strategy, you back up your critical data to tape and store it offsite. Restoring from tapes takes a long time. With AWS, you store your critical backups in S3, and you can access the data via the network from anywhere in the world, making the recovery much faster than recovery with tape backups. You can store snapshots of EBS volumes, RDS datasets, and Redshift databases in S3.

NOTE You can store the backup files for RDS databases, Redshift databases, and EBS volumes in S3. You may also directly copy the files for these services into Amazon S3.

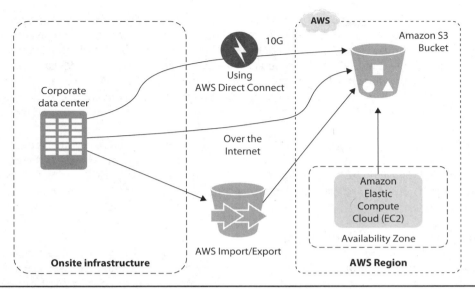

Figure 9-8 Data backup options for Amazon S3, including onsite and AWS

Remember that you can use Amazon S3 to safely store data from your onsite infrastructure or from the AWS cloud. Figure 9-8 shows the data backup options for S3, from your own onsite infrastructure or from AWS.

Restoring Backups: Preparation Phase Glacier backups are very fast to restore and recover, just like the backups that you store in Amazon S3. You can also ship data directly to AWS through a storage drive such as AWS Import/Export, making it easy to restore very large data sets.

Glacier has three types of data retrieval, and the speed of retrieval differs among these the three types:

- **Expedited** Quickly access your data during occasional urgent requests for a subset of archives. For all but the largest archives (250MB+), data accessed using expedited retrievals are typically made available within 1 to 5 minutes.

- **Standard** Access any of your archives typically within 3 to 5 hours. This is the default for retrieval requests for which you do not specify a retrieval option.

- **Bulk** Use Glacier's lowest-cost retrieval option to retrieve large amounts, even petabytes, of data inexpensively. Bulk retrievals typically complete within 5 to 12 hours.

You can copy on-premise data volumes to S3 for backups using AWS Storage Gateway. *Storage-cached volumes* work like the AWS Storage Gateway by enabling you to snapshot local data volumes to S3. You can restore these volumes to S3 or to a DR site running a storage cache gateway. Your EC2 instances can be restored with these backups as well.

NOTE EBS produces notifications based on CloudWatch Events for various types of snapshot-related events. You can use this functionality to automate some of your DR plans. For example, you can create a CloudWatch Events rule that uses AWS Lambda as a target. The rule triggers an AWS Lambda function whenever a new snapshot is made for a DB instance or an EBS volume. The Lambda function can copy the snapshot to another region to support DR.

Restoring Backups: Recovery Phase If you plan on using backup-and-recovery as a DR strategy, select a good backup tool or technique, and ensure that you retain the backup for an adequate period. Secure the backups with encryption and access policies. Finally, ensure that you can use the backups for a recovery by performing regular recovery drills.

Quick Recovery with Pilot Light

The *pilot light* strategy or scenario is similar to a backup-and-recovery DR strategy. In fact, in several cases, you take backups and restore from them under this scenario. You configure and maintain your most critical system components in AWS, apart from your production systems. During a DR, you use this core system as your base for provisioning a full-fledged alternative production system. Though you still must perform some installation and configuration, recovering your applications is much faster than it would be if you had to set up everything from scratch.

The pilot light strategy is faster than a backup-and-restore strategy because the core system is already up and running with the latest data. Core components that could be part of a pilot light system can be database servers, for example. You keep a secondary database server running and ready to go, in a different AZ than the one in which your production database is running. When a disaster event occurs, you can quickly deploy a set of EC2 instances from preconfigured AMIs around the already running pilot light system (a database in this example).

You can do several things to set up an effective pilot light strategy:

- For small systems, you can store the installation packages and configuration details in AWS as EBS snapshots to help quickly set up an application server. During DR, you use a restore of the backups to set up the system.
- For traditional web applications, the recommended approach is to use ELB to send traffic to multiple instances and use DNS to point to the EC2 instance or load balancer by using a CNAME.
- Preallocate EIP addresses and elastic network interfaces (ENIs), both of which you can associate with your instances.

Pilot Light: Preparation Phase To prepare for the pilot light scenario, you must regularly replicate or mirror data to the pilot light system (consisting of a separate set of EC2 instances). You also keep preconfigured AMIs on hand that contain the latest OS and application systems, ready for a quick install. As with the backup-and-restore strategy, regular recovery drills are key to a successful recovery after a disaster.

Pilot Light: Recovery Phase   During a recovery, your key data is already in a database that's up and running. You can resize the databases to hold production data volumes, mostly through a horizontal scaling of your systems, by adding capacity—in this case, by adding more EC2 instances. Alternatively, you can grow your systems vertically by choosing a larger EC2 instance type.

Using the preconfigured AMIs, you start your application EMI instances around the pilot light environment. You must also change the DNS to point to the new set of EC2 servers that you've started up. After the recovery is complete, set up mirroring of the data so you can recover again, following the next disaster. Since the pilot light databases are rudimentary in nature, you can add redundancy by doing things such as turning on Multi-AZ for your Amazon RDS databases.

The Warm Standby Strategy

The *warm standby* strategy goes beyond the pilot light strategy by maintaining a stripped-down version of your production system running in the AWS cloud. This is also called an *active-passive* DR confirmation. You'll have several services already running, which reduces the recovery time. So, if you have an application whose RPO is zero and the RTO is 15 minutes, the warm standby strategy is a good choice.

A warm standby requires that you set up and maintain a much larger alternative system than a simple pilot light system, so it's more expensive to implement. However, the system is much smaller than a production system and runs on the smallest possible EC2 instances to lower your DR costs.

The key element of a warm standby is *functionality*, not *scale*. The system performs all the functions of your critical production systems, but on a smaller scale. You use these setups for other work while they are in the standby mode, such as testing your new application code. When disaster strikes, you upgrade the servers to handle production workloads by adding more servers and resizing the instances to larger instance types.

Warm Standby: Preparation Phase   Set up and start running a smaller version of your application infrastructure. During the preparation phase, as with the previous two DR strategies, you set up the instances where you replicate your data with preconfigured AMIs.

Warm Standby: Recovery Phase   During the recovery phase, you scale up the small standby system either horizontally or vertically, to match the production system that's no longer usable. Change your DNS records to point all traffic to the new system, which is now your primary system, instead of being a standby. Amazon Route 53 health checks can automatically divert your traffic to the new system. Ensure that you add resiliency to the system to handle future disasters.

A Multisite DR Strategy

A multisite strategy maintains more than one full-fledged site—one in the AWS cloud and the other in your onsite infrastructure. This is also called an *active-active* DR configuration.

Depending on your RPO, you can employ a *synchronous* or an *asynchronous* data replication technique:

- **Synchronous replication**   Data is simultaneously (atomically) updated in multiple locations. For example, Amazon RDS employs synchronous replication to send data to a second AZ, ensuring that no data is lost when the primary AZ is unavailable. If you have a zero RPO and RTO, this is the ideal strategy to adopt.

- **Asynchronous replication**   The active system, whichever it happens to be, replicates data asynchronously in multiple locations, based on network performance and other factors. The two systems may not be in sync at times, because replication isn't completed to the second system.

 NOTE   Backing up data to multiple AWS regions enables you to restore services even when a large-scale, comprehensive disaster strikes your systems.

Your use case determines whether you choose synchronous or asynchronous replication. If you're using the second database as a reporting database, for example, it's fine to configure asynchronous data replication. On the other hand, if you're using both systems to support a web site with shopping carts, you must choose synchronous replication so that data is completely synchronized between the two systems.

 NOTE   Although I described database replication specifically, replication isn't limited to data. You can also set up replication for other resources, such as your network file systems.

In the active-active DR strategy, you'll have two systems, both active at the same time, splitting the production workload. You can set up DNS weighting in Route 53 to route some of your traffic to your onsite system and the rest to your system running on the AWS infrastructure. When there's a disaster onsite, you modify the DNS weighting to route all traffic to the other active system running in the AWS cloud. You can use EC2 Auto Scaling to automate the scaling of your AWS-based system, so it can now handle all the workload. After the disaster event is over, you can again use Auto Scaling to scale back to the previous level of instances.

You can cut your costs for an active-active system by adopting AWS cost optimization strategies, such as purchasing EC2 Reserved Instances for those AWS servers that always run on AWS. Once the DR is complete, and you switch your onsite systems backup, you release the additional resources that you've provisioned on AWS during the DR, so you won't have to continue to pay for them beyond the duration of the DR.

Multisite DR Strategy: Preparation Phase   You must ensure that both active systems are functioning properly, with each system a duplicate of the other. Configure a DNS service such as Route 53 to distribute portions of your web traffic between the two active systems and set up health checks so your request traffic can fail over to the alternative site when one of the systems is affected by a disaster.

Multisite DR Strategy: Recovery Phase   Unlike in the previous three scenarios, you don't have to perform any manual steps during the recovery phase in an active-active strategy. You can perform the DNS failover manually, but you can also choose to set up DNS failover to automate the DNS weighting that routes traffic to the two sites. Additionally, you can set up AWS Auto Scaling to increase the number of EC2 instances to handle the full workload that was earlier shared between the two active systems.

Chapter Review

This chapter provided an introduction to several key AWS services such as Amazon SQS and Amazon SNS that help distributed applications work together in the AWS cloud. The key benefit of using these two services is the ability to decouple a distributed application's components to enable the applications to provide high performance when dealing with many users and a heavy workload.

You must endeavor to take advantage of as many resiliency and automatic failure detection features as you can. AWS offers many of these as part of EC2, RDS, DynamoDB, VPC, and various other AWS services.

The chapter explained the key DR-related concepts RTO and RPO and showed how to set up a DR environment for various scenarios, including taking simple backups, a pilot light strategy, a warm standby setup, and the most comprehensive setup, a multisite active-active DR environment.

The most important aspects of disaster recovery are preparation and scheduled DR drills that prove to you that your DR strategies will work when they're needed.

Exercises

The exercises are designed to teach you how to perform important AWS security-related administrative tasks through the console. If you make a mistake, retrace your steps and ensure that you've correctly performed the steps. You'll know that you've correctly completed the exercise if you achieve the goal set for you in each exercise, such as creating an Amazon SQS queue.

Exercise 9-1: Create an Amazon SQS FIFO queue.

1. Log into the Amazon SQS console at https://console.aws.amazon.com/sqs/home?region=us-west-2.

2. On the Create New Queue page, under Queue Name, enter the new queue's name (for example, **MyQueue**).

3. Select FIFO (the default is Standard).

4. Select Configure Queue to begin configuring the new queue. Configure FIFO queue parameters such as the following:
   - Default Visibility Timeout
   - Message Retention Period
   - Maximum Message Size
   - Delivery Delay
   - Use Redrive Policy (under Dead Letter Queue Settings)
5. Once you finish the queue configuration, click Create Queue. Your new queue should appear shortly in the queue list.

Exercise 9-2: Send a simple message to an Amazon SQS queue.

1. Log into the Amazon SQS console: https://console.aws.amazon.com/sqs/home?region=us-west-2.
2. Select the queue that you created in Exercise 9-1 from the queue list.
3. In Queue Actions, select Send V Message.
4. In the Send A Message Queue To MyQueue.fifo dialog box, under Message Body, enter the text of the message you want to send: **My first message!**
5. In the same dialog, at the bottom, enter the following values:
   - For Message Group ID, enter **MyMessageGroupID1234567890**
   - For Message Duplication ID, enter **MyMessageDuplicationID1234567890**
6. Click Send Message.
7. You'll see a confirmation from SQS stating that your message has been sent and is ready to be received. It may take up to about 60 seconds for the Messages Available column to populate.
8. Click Close.

Exercise 9-3: Create an Amazon SNS topic.

1. Log into the AWS Management Console and open the Amazon SNS console: https://console.aws.amazon.com/sns/v2/home.
2. Select Create Topic.
3. In the Create Topic dialog box, type a topic name: **MyTopic**.

4. Click Create Topic.

5. In the Topic Details page, select MyTopic and then select the topic ARN.

6. Copy the new topic's ARN, which should be similar to this: Arn:aws:sns:us-west-2:111122223333:MyTopic.

Exercise 9-4: Subscribe to an Amazon SNS topic.

1. Log in to the AWS Management Console and open the Amazon SNS console: https://console.aws.amazon.com/sns/v2/home.

2. Click Create Subscription.

3. In the Create Subscription dialog box, go the Topic ARN field and enter the topic ARN that you created at the end of Exercise 9-3: **Arn:aws:sns:us-west-2:111122223333:MyTopic**.

4. From the Protocol drop-down, select Email.

5. In the Endpoint field, enter your e-mail address.

6. Click Create Subscription.

7. Retrieve the e-mail message from AWS Notifications in your e-mail application. Click the link to confirm your subscription. Your web browser will show a confirmation from Amazon SNS.

Exercise 9-5: Publish to an Amazon SNS topic.

1. Log in to the AWS Management Console and open the Amazon SNS console: https://console.aws.amazon.com/sns/v2/home.

2. Click Publish To Topic.

3. In the Publish A Message page, enter the following values:

- For Topic ARN, enter the topic ARN that you created at the end of Exercise 9-3: **Arn:aws:sns:us-west-2:111122223333:MyTopic**.

- For Subject, enter **Test message**.

- For Message, enter **"This is my first SNS message"**.

4. AWS SNS confirms your choices. Go to your e-mail application to open and read the message sent by AWS Notifications.

Exercise 9-6: Configure a CloudWatch alarm to recover an EC2 instance (with EC2 Recovery).

1. Log into the Amazon EC2 console at https://console.aws.amazon.com/ec2/.

2. Select Instances in the navigation pane, and then select the instance you want to set up the alarm for.

3. Select Actions | CloudWatch Monitoring | Add/Edit Alarms, and then click Create Alarm.

4. Click Create Topic.

5. In the Send A Notification field, enter a topic name.

6. In the With These Recipients field, enter your e-mail address.

7. Select Take The Action, and then select Recover.

8. Select your constraints, and then click Create Alarm.

Questions

The following questions will help you measure your understanding of the material presented in this chapter. Read all the choices carefully because there may be more than one correct answer. Choose all the correct answers for each question.

1. Your application processes messages in an Amazon SQS queue. You often notice that some messages are being processed more than once. Your application has a strict requirement that a message be processed only once. How do you deal with this situation?

   A. Decrease the visibility timeout for the queue.

   B. Advise your developers to make their application code idempotent.

   C. Raise the value of the message heartbeat.

   D. Increase the visibility timeout for the queue.

2. When setting up Amazon SNS, which of the following would be your first step?

   A. Create a subscriber.

   B. Create a subscription to a topic.

   C. Create a topic.

   D. Configure fanout.

3. When using Amazon SQS, which of the following would be true regarding polling of the SQS servers for available messages in an SQS queue?

   A. Short polling reduces SQS costs by minimizing empty responses and by eliminating false empty responses.

   B. Long polling reduces SQS costs by eliminating most empty responses and by eliminating false empty responses.

   C. Short polling reduces SQS costs by completely eliminating a majority of the empty responses.

   D. Long polling increases SQS costs by failing to eliminate most of the empty responses.

4. Which of the following protocols does AWS SNS support when you are sending notifications through SNS? (Choose all correct answers)

   A. Email, Email-JSON

   B. Amazon SQS

   C. HTTP, HTTPS

   D. SMS

5. Your application has a recovery point of objective (RPO) of zero and a recovery time objective (RTO) of zero. Which of the following disaster recovery strategies will ensure that you can satisfy both your RPO and RTO?

   A. Configure a hot standby.

   B. Store backups in S3 so that you can perform a fast restore.

   C. Use the pilot light strategy.

   D. Set up a multisite active-active disaster recovery strategy.

6. Which of the following events will result in an RDS failover when you've set up Multi-AZ deployment for high availability of your RDS databases? (Choose three)

   A. A manual failover of the primary database

   B. Software patching of the DB instance server's operating system

   C. An availability zone outage

   D. Failure of the standby replica

7. Which of the following statements are true regarding AWS regions and availability zones? (Choose two)

   A. AWS charges you for data transfers across regions.

   B. AWS charges you for data transfers across AZs.

   C. AWS doesn't automatically replicate your resources across multiple regions.

   D. AZs in an AWS region are completely isolated from each other.

8. Which of the following are valid Amazon Route 53 health checks that you can configure? (Choose three)

   A. Health checks that monitor the availability of free space on an EC2 server's file system

   B. Health checks that monitor resource health

   C. Health checks that monitor the status of other health checks

   D. Health checks that monitor the status of a CloudWatch alarm

9. A Route 53 health check alarm does which of the following? (Choose two)

   A. It waits for a CloudWatch alarm notification before it goes into the Alarm state.

   B. It doesn't wait for a CloudWatch alarm notification before it goes into the Alarm state.

   C. It bases the status of its health checks on the same data stream that CloudWatch monitors for the alarm.

   D. It uses its own health check criteria to monitor various resources by monitoring an endpoint you specify with either an IP address or a domain name.

10. You've configured a simple Route 53 health check for a set of four web server resources. You use the weighted routing policy for the records. Which of the following statements would be true when Route 53 is making its health checks? (Choose two)

    A. If you omit a health check from one of the records in the group of records you configure, Route 53 treats those records as healthy.

    B. If you omit a health check from one of the records in the group of records you configure, Route 53 treats those records as unhealthy.

    C. If Route 53 selects an unhealthy record the first time, it omits the weight of that record from its calculations when it chooses another (healthy) record.

    D. If Route 53 selects an unhealthy record the first time, it includes the weight of that record from its calculations when it chooses another (healthy) record.

11. You'd like to configure a setup that will act as a backup for your AWS Direct Connect connection because you don't have multiple redundant Direct Connect connections to connect your data center to AWS. Which of the following strategies would provide you that backup in the absence of a redundant Direct Connect connection?

    A. Use multiple routers in your data centers to provide redundancy for Direct Connect connections.

    B. Set up a direct Internet connectivity to AWS via an AWS partner location.

    C. Use multiple AWS VPCs to provide the redundancy.

    D. Configure a VPN between the data center and your VPC in the Amazon cloud.

12. When using Route 53 to configure a failover configuration, which of the following are true? (Choose two)

    A. You can configure an active-active failover with any routing policy.

    B. You can configure an active-active failover with any routing policy except the Failover routing policy.

    C. You must use the Failover routing policy when configuring an active-passive failover.

    D. You can use any routing policy to configure an active-passive failover.

13. Which of the following strategies helps you provide enhanced availability for objects that you stored in an S3 bucket?

    A. Create a destination bucket in a different region and enable cross-region replication on the source bucket so it can be replicated to the destination bucket in the other region.

    B. Enable versioning and heartbeats on the S3 bucket.

    C. Use S3 snapshots to store the bucket data in S3.

    D. S3 automatically replicates the S3 object data from one region to another.

14. You have set up redundant Direct Connect connectivity to your data center with two customer gateways and two Direct Connect physical connections from two different AWS partner locations. How does your Internet traffic fail over to a second Direct Connect connection when the first Direct Connection experiences a failure?

    A. You must change the Direct Connect configuration so that the traffic will use the second Direct Connect connection.

    B. The traffic fails over automatically to the second Direct Connect connection.

    C. You must use BGP for traffic to go to the second Direct Connect connection.

    D. It depends on whether you have set up a VPN backup for the Direct Connect connections.

15. If your recovery point objective (RPO) is 1 hour and a disaster occurs at 12:00 P.M. (noon), which of the following is/are true?

    A. The system should be able to recover all data that was in the system before 11 A.M.

    B. There is no data loss.

    C. The DR process should restore the business processes to the acceptable service level by 1 P.M.

    D. There's no disruption in the business processes.

16. Which of the following are true about Amazon EBS volumes? (Choose three)

    A. You can create point-in-time snapshots of the EBS volumes and use them as a starting point for new EBS volumes.

    B. EBS stores your EBS snapshots in Amazon S3.

    C. You can attach an EBS snapshot to a running EC2 instance.

    D. EBS snapshots are automatically replicated across multiple servers in an availability zone.

17. When the primary DB instance fails, what would happen to an RDS (Relational Database Service) database for which you've configured Multi-AZ deployment?

    A. The IP of the primary DB instance is switched to the standby DB instance.

    B. The RDS DB instance reboots.

    C. A new DB instance is created in the standby AZ.

    D. The canonical name record (CNAME) is changed from primary to standby.

18. How can AWS OpsWorks help during disaster recovery? (Choose three)

   A. OpsWorks provides automatic host replacement, so it can replace instances automatically in the event of a failure.

   B. You can use OpsWorks in the preparation phase to template your environment.

   C. You can combine OpsWorks and CloudFormation during the recovery phase.

   D. OpsWorks does not provide full control of software on EC2 instances, and you cannot integrate Chef recipes with AWS resources such as S3 and Amazon RDS.

19. OpsWorks ensures that you can re-create a stack automatically during an availability zone failure by moving the stack to a different AZ. Your web site is hosted on ten EC2 instances in five regions, with two instances per region. How would you configure your site to maintain site availability with minimum downtime if one of the five regions were to lose network connectivity for an extended period of time?

   A. Place an Elastic Load Balancer in front of the EC2 instances and set an appropriate health check on each ELB.

   B. Establish VPN connections between the instances in each region. Rely on BGP to failover in the case of a region-wide connectivity outage.

   C. Create a Route 53 latency-based routing record set that resolves to an Elastic Load Balancer in each region. Set an appropriate health check on each ELB.

   D. Create a Route 53 latency-based routing record set that resolves to Elastic Load Balancers in each region and ensure that the Evaluate Target Health flag is set to true.

20. Which of the following DR strategies offers the minimum level of DR readiness or capability?

   A. A multisite DR setup between your local data center and the AWS cloud

   B. A warm standby strategy

   C. The pilot light strategy

   D. A backup-and-restore strategy

21. You have an RPO of zero and an RTO of 1 hour. Which of the following DR strategies would be appropriate to satisfy your RTO and your RPO?

   A. A multisite DR setup between your local data center and the AWS cloud

   B. A warm standby strategy

   C. The pilot light strategy

   D. A backup-and-restore strategy

22. How do you check the status of the network traffic flow of your VPN connection to your VPC when you encounter a situation where you don't see any network traffic flow on the AWS side of the VPN connection?

    A. Check the VPN traffic flow in the AWS Management Console.

    B. Check the logs of the router on your side.

    C. Enable route propagation in your VPC's main routing table.

    D. Remove the network traffic block in your VPC.

23. Which of the following steps will help provide redundancy to your hardware VPN?

    A. Deploy the Cloud Hub solution.

    B. Enable automatic redundancy by taking advantage of the two tunnels that a hardware VPN provides.

    C. Deploy a software VPN solution to two AZs.

    D. Use two customer gateways and configure them to use the two tunnels provided by the hardware VPN.

24. How do you ensure that traffic routes over a redundant AWS Direct Connection that you've configured?

    A. Set up traffic to route over the redundant link when the first connection fails.

    B. Request your telecom provider to configure the failover for you.

    C. Traffic fails over automatically to the redundant AWS Direct Connection.

    D. You must create a second Amazon VPC and configure the redundant routing in the VPC's main routing table.

25. Which of the following are valid Amazon Route 53 failover types? (Choose three)

    A. Active-active

    B. Passive-active

    C. Latency based

    D. Weighted round robin

Answers

    1. D. Increase the visibility timeout for the queue. Visibility timeout makes the message being processed by an application component invisible (hides it) to the other application components, During the invisibility timeout period, the application component that originally picked up the message is supposed to complete the processing of the message and then delete it.

    2. C. The first step in setting up Amazon SNS notifications is to set up (create) a topic. Following this, you subscribe to the topic and publish to it, in that order.

3. B. Long polling reduces SQS costs by eliminating most empty responses and by eliminating false empty responses.

4. A, B, C, D. All the answer choices are correct because Amazon SNS supports all these protocols.

5. D. A multisite HA solution involves running your systems in AWS and in your onsite infrastructure; this is called an *active-active HA configuration.* Since your mandated RPO and RTO are both zero, you can't afford any delay in your application processing. Following a failure in your production system running in the AWS, your system must be able to switch immediately to an alternative, full-fledged DR site, so it can handle all your current production workload. This is possible only with a multisite, active-active DR configuration.

6. A, B, C. When you manually fail over a primary database, you'll switch to the standby database instance. Patching the DB instance makes the server that hosts the DB instance temporarily unavailable, making a failover to the standby DB necessary. An availability zone failure makes the primary DB instance unavailable, which forces a failover to the standby DB instance.

7. A, C. AWS bills you for all data transfers across the AWS regions. AWS doesn't automatically replicate your resources across multiple regions; you must explicitly do this to provide HA to certain AWS resources.

8. B, C, D. Health checks monitor resource health and send alerts when they detect that a resoruce such as a web server is unable to respond properly to requests. In addition to monitoring the health of resources, DNS health checks also monitor the status of other health checks and the status of CloudWatch alarms.

9. B, C. A Route 53 health check doesn't wait for a CloudWatch alarm notification before it goes into the ALARM state. Route 53 health checks are based on the same data stream monitored by CloudWatch for the alarm.

10. A, C. If you omit a health check for a record, Route 53 deems the record healthy since it has no way to check its health. Route 53 ignores the unhealthy records from its weight calculations when considering which record it must route a request to.

11. D. You can set up a VPN connection as a backup or alternative to a Direct Connect connection by configuring two customer gateways on your end. You can use the Direct Connect connection as the primary or main Direct Connect connection and use the backup VPN connection to serve your development (against production) workloads. When the Direct Connect connectivity connection goes down, you can use the backup VPN connection. Remember that AWS prefers to use the Direct Connect connectivity rather than the connectivity that you've set up with a backup VPN connection.

12. B, C. You can't use the Failover routing policy when configuring an active-active routing policy. You configure an active-passive failover only with the Failover routing policy.

13. **A.** Use cross-region replication to copy data from the original S3 bucket (source bucket) to the destination bucket that you create in a different region. This creates a synced replica of your S3 objects that serves many purposes, including lowering the latency and thus enhancing the availability of your applications.

14. **B.** The Internet traffic fails over automatically to the second Direct Connect connection; there's no need for you to anything for the failover to happen.

15. **A.** The RPO denotes the acceptable amount of data loss measured in time. In this example, your RPO is 1 hour and the disaster occurs at noon. Therefore, your DR recovery processes should enable your system to recover all the data that was in your system before 11 A.M.

16. **A, B, C.** You can create point-in-time snapshots of an EBS volume. EBS stores all your EBS snapshots in Amazon S3. After you create an EBS volume from a snapshot, you can attach the volume to a running EC2 instance. EBS stores your EBS volumes redundantly by replicating them across multiple servers in an availability zone, but it does not store snapshots.

17. **D.** When you set up a Multi-AZ failover deployment for an Amazon RDS database, in the event of a planned or unplanned outage of the primary DB instance, RDS automatically fails over to the standby DB instance in a different availability zone. The time for the failover to complete depends on the level of database activity and other conditions at the time of the primary DB failure. The failover mechanism automatically changes the DNS record (CNAME or canonical record) of the primary DB instance to point to the standby DB instance. You won't need to reestablish existing connections to the standby DB instance.

18. **A, B, C.** OpsWorks can automatically replace a failed host in the event of an instance failure. You can use OpsWorks in the disaster recovery preparation phase to template your environment. You can combine the OpsWorks template with CloudFormation during the recovery phase. You can quickly provision a new stack for the stored configuration to support your RTO.

19. **C.** Create a Route 53 latency-based routing record set that resolves to an Elastic Load Balancer in each region and configure health check on each ELB.

20. **D.** A backup-and-restore strategy is the minimum type of DR that you can perform with AWS. You can store the backups in Amazon S3 for fast retrieval and for easy access from anywhere in the world though a simple URL.

21. **B.** A warm standby already has a replicated system ready to be converted to the primary setup and therefore should be ready within a very short time to take over from the failed primary system. The warm standby is a fully functional, scaled-down version of the primary system, so all you need to do is to enlarge the instance sizes and other things to handle the full production workload.

22. **C.** After you attach a virtual private gateway to your VPC, you must enable route propagation in your VPC's main routing table. The routes that pertain to your VPN connection will automatically appear as propagated routes in the main routing table.

23. **D.** Deploy two customer gateways to make your hardware VPN redundant. Configure the two gateways to use the two tunnels provided by the hardware VPN. In the outer configuration, configure the two customer gateways with the two endpoints for the hardware VPN's virtual private gateway.

24. **C.** Traffic fails over automatically to the second Direct Connect connection.

25. **A, C, D.** Active-active, latency-based, and weighted round robin failover are among the failover types that Route 53 supports.

Monitoring, Logging, Events, and Managing Billing

In this chapter, you will

- Learn how to monitor AWS with Amazon CloudWatch
- Learn about storing the history of your AWS API calls with Amazon CloudTrail
- Get a detailed view of all your AWS resource configurations with AWS Config
- Learn how to manage costs with AWS Trusted Advisor
- Learn how to enhance your security and adhere to compliance regulations with Amazon Inspector
- Learn how to monitor and manage AWS billing

Monitoring the health and performance of your AWS resources and the applications that you run on them is critical. Amazon CloudWatch collects metrics that help you manage and optimize your workloads. While CloudWatch provides an insight into performance, you also need logs for troubleshooting, security audits, and other purposes. CloudWatch Logs and CloudWatch Events are two services that help you centrally log activity in your account.

AWS CloudTrail tracks all API calls made to AWS services. AWS Config tracks the configuration of your resources and helps you stay on top of any configuration changes made to those resources.

Billing and managing costs is a critical area. In this chapter, I show you how to use the AWS Billing and Cost Management service to optimize your AWS spending, create budgets for your AWS spending, and generate reports and set alarms when costs cross thresholds that you configure. AWS Trusted Advisor offers best practice recommendations in several areas, and I focus on its cost management recommendations in this chapter.

EXAM TIP It's easy to get confused as to the purposes served by AWS Config, AWS Trust Advisor, and other services. For example, an exam question might ask how you can ensure that SSH is always disabled on all your production servers. AWS Config would be the appropriate tool to ensure that a security check is in place, since you can configure AWS Config rules to check the security groups. If the question asks how to ensure that all your AMIs are kept updated with the latest patches, then AWS Systems Manager (discussed in Chapter 5) is the right answer.

Monitoring AWS with Amazon CloudWatch

You use several AWS services to support the applications that you run in the cloud, and monitoring all those services and applications is a huge task. You can, of course, set up your own home-grown monitoring solution with various tools such as Nagios and Zabbix. However, AWS has you well covered with its comprehensive cloud monitoring solution, Amazon CloudWatch.

CloudWatch provides data and insights to help you monitor your applications, respond to performance changes, optimize resource utilization, and gain a unified view of operational health of your systems in the AWS cloud. CloudWatch collects operational data in the form of metrics, events, and logs, providing you with a unified view of AWS resources, services, and applications that run both AWS and your on-premise servers.

To reduce latency in your applications, most AWS services offer a *regional endpoint* (a URL that serves as the entry point to that web service) to enable you to make requests. So, for example, if you are running an Elastic Compute Cloud (EC2) instance in the us-east-2a region, to get EC2 detailed monitoring metrics using the command line interface (CLI), you should use the following CloudWatch regional endpoint: monitoring. us-east-2a.amazonaws.com.

You can review and analyze CloudWatch metrics and set alarms based on how your resources, such as EC2 instances and Amazon Elastic Block Storage (EBS) volumes, are performing. Monitoring provides the real-time tracking and recording of how resources are being utilized. Alarms are notifications that are sent out based on thresholds that you configure for the metrics. CloudWatch helps you set alarms, take automated actions, optimize your applications, and ensure that they run efficiently.

CloudWatch is a metric repository. AWS services such as EC2 and Simple Storage Service (S3) deposit metrics into this repository, and you use the metrics to compute statistics and view them in the CloudWatch console. CloudWatch monitors both your AWS services and the applications that you run with the help of those services.

NOTE CloudWatch metrics are separate between AWS regions. They aren't aggregated across regions.

You can view metrics for the AWS services in the CloudWatch home page, and you can also create custom dashboards to display metrics that are of interest to you. You can create CloudWatch alarms that not only send notifications about specific metrics but can also respond to certain conditions by automatically making changes to your resource configuration based on the metric thresholds that you configure. For example, if the CPU usage metrics show that there's a heavy number of read and/or write operations, EC2 Auto Scaling can launch additional instances to handle the higher workload.

CloudWatch works closely with several Amazon services to do its work. Amazon SNS sends messages when alarm thresholds are breached. CloudWatch alarms work with EC2 Auto Scaling to scale your EC2 instances according to the current demand for computing resources. AWS CloudTrail monitors the calls made to the CloudWatch API, and CloudTrail logging ensures that it writes all CloudWatch log files to an Amazon S3 bucket.

 NOTE If your organization's compliance requirements mandate that you record all writes to an S3 bucket and the times that content was read publicly, you must activate CloudTrail logging, and enable S3 server access logging. Server access logging provides details of all requests made to a bucket and helps with security and access audits. It also provides insights into your customers and helps you understand your S3 bills.

CloudWatch Terminology and Concepts

CloudWatch uses several key concepts and terms that are important for you to know.

Namespaces

CloudWatch separates metrics from different applications by storing each application's metrics in a separate namespace, which is a logical metrics container. A namespace has a naming convention of AWS/*namespace*—for example, the AWS/EC2 namespace for EC2 metrics.

 NOTE Most AWS services such as EC2, CloudFront, DynamoDB, and Elastic Load Balancing (ELB) publish metrics to CloudWatch, so they all have a namespace. The only exception is the CloudTrail service, which doesn't publish metrics to CloudWatch.

Metrics

Metrics are a fundamental concept. A metric is a set of data points that shows the value of a monitored variable over time. CPU usage is one such metric; it tracks how the CPU usage of an EC2 instance varies over time. Metrics such as CPU usage are AWS metrics, but you can also store custom metrics by adding data points.

Metrics help you track your system resource and application performance. Most AWS services such as EC2 provide free metrics. You can use the metrics for searching, for graphing, and for configuring alarms. You can also enable *detailed monitoring* for some of those resources and publish custom metrics of your own. Metrics are saved for 16 months, providing you long-term access to historical data. CloudWatch metrics can't be deleted, and they expire after 15 months if no new data is published to them during that period.

CloudWatch groups metrics by namespace and dimension combinations (I explain dimensions in the following section) within a namespace. So you can view metrics for EC2 instances grouped by instance or by Auto Scaling group. You can view the metrics available to you by namespace/dimension from the CloudWatch console, as shown in Exercise 10-4. You can do this from the command line by running the `aws cloudwatch list-metrics` command and specifying the namespace for the metrics:

```
$ aws cloudwatch list-metrics –namespace AWS/EC2
```

You can list a metric for all your EC2 resources by adding the metric name to the command:

```
$ aws cloudwatch list-metrics –namespace AWS/EC2 –metric-name CPUUtilization
```

Almost all AWS services, including CloudFront, Direct Connect, DynamoDB, EC2 instances, EC2 Auto Scaling, Elastic Beanstalk, Amazon Elastic File System (EFS), ELB, Elastic MapReduce (EMR), Key Management Service (KMS), Lambda, Redshift, S3, and Amazon Virtual Private Cloud (VPC), can send metrics to CloudWatch.

Dimensions

A *dimension* is a name/value pair that helps uniquely identify a metric. A metric can have up to 10 dimensions that you define. You use dimensions to create categories for metrics, and they help you filter CloudWatch results. For example, you can specify the InstanceId dimension when searching for metrics for a specific EC2 instance. All AWS services attach dimensions to each of their metrics.

 TIP For several metrics such as metrics in the AWS/EC2 namespace, CloudWatch can aggregate data across dimensions, but it doesn't do so for the custom metrics that you define.

You can combine dimensions. Even if the metrics have the same metric name, Cloud-Watch treats each unique combination of dimensions as a separate metric. Following is an example that shows four distinct metrics, all named ServerStats; the four metrics share the same metric name but are distinct since each of them is a unique combination of two dimensions: Server and Domain:

```
Dimensions: Server=Prod, Domain=Frankfurt, Unit: Count, Timestamp:
2018-10-31T12:30:00Z, Value: 105
Dimensions: Server=Beta, Domain=Frankfurt, Unit: Count, Timestamp:
2018-10-31T12:31:00Z, Value: 115
Dimensions: Server=Prod, Domain=Rio, Unit: Count, Timestamp:
2018-10-31T12:32:00Z, Value: 95
Dimensions: Server=Beta, Domain=Rio, Unit: Count, Timestamp:
2018-10-31T12:33:00Z, Value: 97
```

You can retrieve statistics for combinations of dimensions that you've published, such as `Server=Prod, Domain=Frankfurt`, for example. Since you've combined the dimensions when publishing the metric, you can't retrieve statistics by specifying just one of the two dimensions, such as `Server=Prod` or `Domain=Frankfurt`.

To view all the available metrics for a specific dimension such as InstanceId from the command line, do this:

```
$ aws cloudwatch list-metrics -namespace AWS/EC2 -dimensions
Name=InstanceId,Value=i-1234567890sbcdef0
```

Timestamps

Each metric data point is associated with a timestamp, which can be up to two weeks in the past and two hours into the future. If a metric doesn't already have a timestamp, CloudWatch creates one based on when it receives the metric data point. By default, all times are UTC, and the timestamps include the data plus hours, minutes, and seconds, as in 2018-12-26T24:48:48Z.

 NOTE Custom metrics that use a non-UTC timestamp can make an alarm display the "Insufficient Data" state or delay the alarm.

Statistics

Statistics are aggregations of metric data over a specific period. CloudWatch aggregates metric data over the following entities:

- The namespace
- The metric name
- The metric dimensions
- The data point unit of measure (to be defined later)
- The time period that you specify

 NOTE Statistics aren't returned if no dimensions are specified.

The available statistics are Minimum, Maximum, Sum, Average, Samplecount (number of data points used for the aggregation), and pNN.NN (the value of a percentile that you've specified; I define percentiles later in this section). In addition to standard aggregate measures such as minimum and maximum, you can add precalculated statistics, which are aggregated by CloudWatch.

 TIP If you notice CloudWatch metrics are coming in a time zone format different from what you need, you can change the time zone (say, from UTC to Local Timezone) in the CloudWatch console by clicking on the Custom option for a metric.

There are three statistics-related concepts you need to know:

- **Units** All statistics have a unit of measure, such as bytes, seconds, count, and percent. For your custom metrics, you can specify a unit; if you don't, CloudWatch uses None as the unit.

- **Period** A period is the length of time for which CloudWatch aggregates a set of metric data. A period is defined in seconds, and you can specify 1, 5, 10, 30, or a multiple of 60 seconds, such as 360 to specify a period of 6 minutes. When you retrieve statistics, you can specify a period as well as the start and end times. You can specify not only the period over which CloudWatch compares a metric to its threshold value (to send an alarm), but also the number of evaluation periods before CloudWatch sends the alarm. For example, by specifying three evaluation periods, you make CloudWatch compare a window of three data points and send an alarm if the oldest data point exceeds the threshold (and the others also exceed the threshold or are missing). In this case, CloudWatch doesn't send a notification to you until it finds three failures.

- **Aggregation** CloudWatch aggregates statistics based on the period you specify. Only detailed monitoring provides aggregated statistics. When you need to collect multiple statistics in a short period, such as a minute (say, by using a metric that measures a web page's request latency), it's overwhelming to publish data for each occurrence of the metric. You can insert a pre-aggregated dataset called a *statistic set* to provide CloudWatch with aggregates such as the Minimum, Maximum, Sum, and SampleCount for a set of data points.

 NOTE You can watch more detailed metric data by zooming on a specific period in the console. You do this by clicking the period you want to zoom.

Percentiles

Percentiles help you better understand the distribution of metric data by showing where a value stands relative to the rest of the dataset. For example, the 95th percentile means that 95 percent of the data in a dataset is below this value, and 5 percent of the data has a value that's higher than this value. You track system and application performance with percentiles, just as you do with other statistics such as Average, Minimum, Maximum, and Sum.

Averages and the Minimum and Maximum values for a metric often hide anomalies. A low maximum CPU usage metric may hide the fact that most of the time the usage may be very high, impacting user experience. If, on the other hand, you use a 95 percentile measure for evaluating CPU utilization, you can find the instances with a very high current workload.

Alarms

CloudWatch alarms monitor a single metric over a period of time and perform one or more actions when the value of the metric crosses a threshold. The action can be a notification to a Simple Notification Service (SNS) topic or it can be sent to an EC2 Auto Scaling policy.

Remember that an alarm-directed action isn't performed when a metric crosses a threshold just once. An alarm is designed as a response to a sustained change in state, meaning that the change in state must be maintained for a specific number of periods.

Basic CloudWatch monitoring for EC2 provides instance metrics every five minutes, and detailed monitoring does so every one minute. When setting an alarm on a basic monitoring metric, select a period of at least 60 seconds (one minute), and for detailed monitoring metrics, select a period of at least 300 seconds (five minutes).

Here are some important facts about basic versus detailed monitoring:

- Some AWS services, such as EC2, enable you to set up detailed monitoring with an extra charge. Basic monitoring (five-minute frequency), however, is available at no additional charge. The same is true of other services such as EBS and the Amazon Relational Database Service (RDS).

- Some services, such as SNS, push their metrics (such as NumberOfNotificationsFailed) to CloudWatch only every five minutes, and thus you can't configure detailed monitoring for those services. The same is true of the Amazon EMR service, which updates its metrics every five minutes, and you can't configure a shorter period.

- Other services, such as AWS ELB, have detailed monitoring enabled by default, without an extra charge. ELB reports metrics only when the load balancer is handling active requests. It sends its metrics to CloudWatch in 60-second intervals. CloudWatch monitors metrics such as the number of healthy hosts, number of requests, and average latency in 60-second intervals as a standard metric for ELB.

- For the EC2 Auto Scaling service, basic monitoring is enabled by default when you create a launch template or when you use the AWS Management Console to create a launch configuration. However, detailed monitoring is enabled by default when you create a launch configuration via the AWS CLI or an SDK.

- Detailed monitoring is enabled by default for both Route 53 and RDS. Route 53 sends metrics every minute to CloudWatch, and RDS sends metrics every minute for each active DB instance.

Metric Retention

CloudWatch retains older metrics based in the period that you specify for the statistics. Here's how metric data retention works:

- Metrics with a period of less than 60 seconds are available for five hours.
- Metrics with a period of one minute are available for 15 days.
- Metrics with a period of five minutes are available for 63 days.
- Metrics with a period of one hour are available for 455 days (15 months).

Interestingly, CloudWatch aggregates data points published with shorter periods for long-term storage. Thus, data collected using a period of one minute may be available for 15 days with a one-minute detail (resolution); after the 15 days are up, the data is still

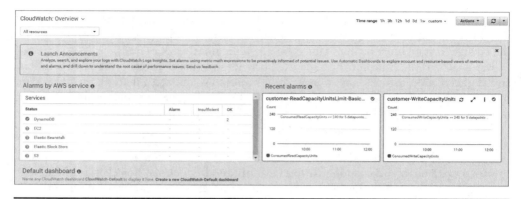

Figure 10-1   The CloudWatch Overview home page

available to you, but you can now retrieve it only at a coarser or aggregated resolution of five minutes.

CloudWatch Dashboards

You now have a basic idea of the key concepts of CloudWatch, but it helps to go to the CloudWatch Dashboard to see how everything works in practice. Figure 10-1 shows the CloudWatch Overview home page.

A CloudWatch Dashboard is a home page that you can customize to help you monitor all your AWS resources such as EC2 instances and DynamoDB databases. By creating your own dashboards, you can create customized views of the metrics and alarms for various AWS resources. You can create dashboards through the CloudWatch console, the AWS CLI, or with the PutDashboard API. Exercise 10-2 shows how to create a dashboard from the console.

The CloudWatch Overview page shows a list of the AWS services you are using, along with the state of alarms for these services. Underneath the list of services is a custom dashboard that you can create, called CloudWatch Default Dashboard, that captures key metrics pertaining to custom services or applications and shows them on the home page.

The Cross Service Dashboard, shown in Figure 10-2, displays key metrics for your AWS services and enables you to drill down to a specific service to view more metrics for that service. If you have six or more AWS services, instead of the Cross Service Dashboard on the home page, you'll see a link to that dashboard. To help you focus on key services, you can keep a service from appearing on the Cross Service dashboard by simply removing it. Any alarms that you've configured for the removed service will continue to show up in the Alarm view on the top of the Overview home page.

AWS Service Health Dashboard and AWS Personal Heath Dashboard

The AWS Service Health Dashboard, available at http://status.aws.amazon.com, shows the general status of all AWS services. Figure 10-3 shows part of the AWS Service Health Dashboard.

Figure 10-2 The Cross Service Dashboard in the CloudWatch Overview page

Figure 10-3 The AWS Service Health Dashboard

The AWS Personal Health Dashboard, which you reach from the AWS Service Health Dashboard, shows you the performance and availability of the AWS services that you are using, so you'll be aware of any issues AWS is experiencing, such as an availability zone (AZ) outage that may impact you, so you don't run around troubleshooting issues, unaware of the root cause for the issue.

The Personal Health Dashboard offers proactive notifications about the AWS services so you can plan your scheduled activities. For example, if AWS is performing a hardware maintenance activity that affects your EC2 instances, you'll receive an alert so you can proactively address any potential issues. The alerts that you receive include remediation details so that you can avoid any impact on your applications and other services. For example, if an AWS hardware failure impacts your EBS volumes, you'll get a recommendation to restore your volumes, with links to the steps that you need to perform to restore the volume from an EBS snapshot.

The Personal Health Dashboard integrates with CloudWatch Events, which helps you build rules and select targets such as AWS Lambda functions to configure automatic remediation actions.

Working with CloudWatch Alarms

A CloudWatch alarm automatically initiates actions in response to a condition or conditions that you configure. Following are the key points that you need to understand regarding the configuration of CloudWatch alarms:

- You can set up an alarm to watch a single metric or a mathematical expression encompassing multiple metrics.

- An alarm performs actions based on the threshold that you configure for a metric or expression over a set number of periods. Actions can be a notification to an SNS topic, an EC2 action, or an EC2 Auto Scaling action.

- Most important to remember is that an alarm invokes changes only for a state change that's maintained for a specific number of periods. The value of a metric or mathematical expression is, of course, relevant, but only if that value/ expression is sustained for the number of periods that you specify.

- For an SNS notification action, after the first notification, no further actions are invoked. For an EC2 Auto Scaling action, however, the alarm invokes the EC2 action during all subsequent periods when the alarm remains in that state.

- You can view an alarm's history going back to two weeks.

 NOTE Alarms invoke actions only for sustained changes in state.

Alarm States

CloudWatch alarms can be in one of three states:

- **OK**   The metric (or expression) is within the range of the threshold that you've defined.

- **ALARM**   The metric is currently outside the threshold range.

- **INSUFFICIENT_DATA**   The alarm has just started, the metric is unavailable, or there's insufficient data for the metric to determine its alarm state.

Let me explain how the three states work, with the help of a couple of scenarios.

Scenario 1: You've configured a CloudWatch alarm for an EBS-backed instance. You set up the alarm for five periods, each 5 minutes long. You stop the EC2 instance for some reason for a period of 15 minutes. Since you only stopped the instance for 15 minutes between 9 A.M. and 9:15 A.M., it doesn't exceed the threshold of 25 minutes (five periods, each 5 minutes long), and thus, the status of the alarm remains OK. The alarm status will change only if there's no instance activity for a period of 25 minutes.

Scenario 2: You've set up alarms for the EBS volumes that you've attached to an EC2 instance. You then stop the instance and detach the EBS instances. What will be the state of the CloudWatch alarm? Since the instance is stopped and the EBS volumes are detached, the alarm won't receive enough data to evaluate the health of the volumes, and hence, the alarm's state will be INSUFFICIENT_DATA.

 TIP   If you'd like to receive notifications when an RDS instance is in the unknown or unavailable state, set up a CloudWatch alarm that notifies you when the alarm state is INSUFFICIENT_DATA.

Scenario 3: You can test an alarm by temporarily setting the alarm's state to any of the three possible states for an alarm (explained in the following section). If the state you set is different from its previous value, CloudWatch invokes the action that is configured for the new state. So, if the alarm state is configured to send an SNS message when it's triggered, you can send an SNS message by temporarily changing the alarm state to ALARM. Here's an example:

```
$ aws cloudwatch set-alarm-state –alarm-name "testalarm" –state-value ALARM –
state-reason "testing"
```

How CloudWatch Evaluates Alarms

You control how CloudWatch responds to an alarm when you create the alarm. Cloud-Watch evaluations result in determination of an alarm's state (OK, ALARM, or INSUF-FICIENT_DATA). The following three entities are the three key configuration attributes that determine how CloudWatch evaluates an alarm:

- **Period**   In seconds, the time for which CloudWatch evaluates the metric to create a data point for the alarm

- **Evaluation Period**   The number of most recent periods (data points) that CloudWatch must consider before setting the state of the alarm
- **Datapoints To Alarm**   The number of data points within an evaluation period that violate the threshold that you've configured for the alarm

In brief, then, an alarm is triggered when a metric crosses a threshold and gets in a certain range, the threshold/range violation is reported several times consecutively, and the metric's value continues to stay at that value/range for multiple consecutive periods.

It helps to view a figure to explain how CloudWatch evaluates the three settings to determine the alarm state. Figure 10-4 shows the process.

In Figure 10-4, I set the alarm threshold to three units. Recall that a *unit* is a unit of measure, such as Bytes, Seconds, Count, and Percent. In this example, the unit is Count. Let's say you configure the alarm to go into the ALARM state when both the Evaluation Period and the Datapoints To Alarm are also set to three. This means that CloudWatch places the alarm in the ALARM state when all the three data points exceed their threshold value (three units) during the three most recent consecutive periods. When the alarm is in the ALARM state for these three periods consecutively, CloudWatch invokes an action to do something to fix the problem that's causing the alarm state to move to ALARM. It doesn't invoke an action if a data point goes above the threshold in just one or two periods.

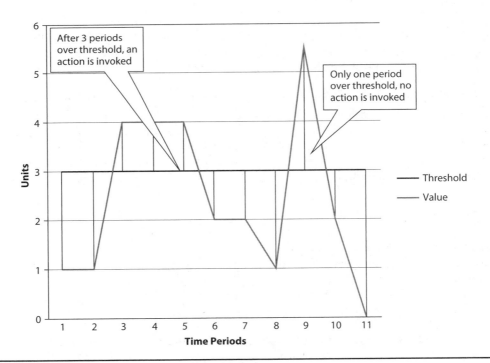

Figure 10-4   How CloudWatch evaluates an alarm's state

TIP Setting a long evaluation period could have adverse consequences. CloudWatch tends to reevaluate the last set of data points for a while after the metric has stopped reporting to CloudWatch. This may lead to a change in the alarm state and execution of the same action again. Setting a shorter period mitigates this problem.

In the example here, the Evaluation Period and the Datapoints To Alarm are both set to three. However, you can also specify an alarm by specifying a lower Datapoints To Alarm value than that of the Evaluation Period. For example, if you specify a period of 5 minutes, and configure the Evaluation Period as 8 out of 10 data points, then the evaluation interval will be 50 minutes. This is called an "M out of N" alarm, where M represents the number of Datapoints To Alarm, and N is the Evaluation Period.

NOTE There is a limit on how long all the Evaluation Periods for an alarm can last. The number of Evaluation Periods for an alarm times the length of each individual Evaluation Period must be less than 24 hours.

How CloudWatch Handles Missing Data

CloudWatch may at times miss metric data due to various reasons, such as when an EC2 instance crashes. Some metrics may report themselves sporadically as well due to the nature of the metric. You can configure how CloudWatch handles missing data so it doesn't issue false alarms.

A data point that is sent to CloudWatch as a metric can be one of the following types:

- **Not breaching**   Its value is considered as falling within the threshold that you've configured.
- **Breaching**   It falls outside the threshold.
- **Missing**   There's no data.

To handle the various missing data points, you configure a CloudWatch alarm to do one of the following when it encounters missing data:

- **missing**   Treat the missing data as missing, which means that the missing data isn't considered when determining an alarm's state.
- **notBreaching**   Treat the missing data as being within the threshold parameters.
- **breaching**   A missing data point is considered as breaching the threshold.
- **ignore**   Don't do anything and maintain the current alarm state.

The default procedure is for CloudWatch to consider all missing data as missing. How you specify missing data into one of the four missing data types depends on the metric. Some metrics such as CPUUtilization are critical, and it's best to classify those types of metrics as breaching rather than letting them be considered as merely missing.

Types of CloudWatch Alarms

Since CloudWatch uses Amazon SNS to send e-mail notifications, before you can set up CloudWatch alarms, you must first set up an Amazon SNS topic and subscribe to that topic. Chapter 9 shows how to do this. Once you set up the SNS topic, during the alarm creation process, you can add the SNS topic to send e-mail notifications when the alarm changes its state.

When you create an alarm, you choose a metric that the alarm watches and a threshold for that metric. The alarm will go to the ALARM state when that metric strays beyond the threshold for a specific number of evaluation periods. You can configure alarms based on a single CloudWatch metric or on a mathematical expression.

Following is a summary of the types of CloudWatch alarms you can configure:

- **CPU usage alarms**   These alarms change from an OK to an ALARM state when the average CPU usage of an EC2 instances crosses a threshold for, say, three consecutive periods. You'll receive an e-mail notification about the change in the alarm state.

- **Alarms that stop/terminate/reboot/recover EC2 instances**   These alarms help you terminate or stop instances that you no longer need—for example, a set of instances that perform a periodic batch job.

- **Load balancer latency alarms**   These alarms monitor latency exceeding 100 ms for a Classic Load Balancer. Exercise 10-7 shows how to set this type of alarm.

- **AWS billing alarms**   These alarms estimate charges for individual AWS services that you use, as well as the total of all your AWS charges. Exercise 10-3 shows how to set up a billing alarm to monitor your estimated AWS charges.

- **Storage throughput alarms**   These alarms send an e-mail when Amazon EBS exceeds a throughput of 100MB.

Here are some other important alarm-related concepts:

- You can set up to 5000 alarms per region per AWS account.

- When setting an alarm on a high-resolution metric, you can set a *regular* (a period that's a multiple of 60 seconds) or a *high-resolution* (a period of 10 or 30 seconds) alarm.

- You can set alarms on mathematical expressions that can include as many as 10 metrics, as long as all the metrics are from the same period.

- You can include multiple actions within a single alarm. For example, the same alarm can cause SNS to send a notification e-mail and update an Auto Scaling policy.

You can publish custom metrics to CloudWatch and view graphs of those metrics with the AWS Management Console.

A metric can have two types of resolution: *Standard resolution data* has a 1-minute granularity. *High-resolution metrics* have data at a granularity of 1 second. AWS service metrics are by default standard resolution metrics. You can define your custom metrics as standard or high resolution. So in a scenario when there's a requirement that you publish metrics from various devices into CloudWatch at an interval of 1 second, you can use high-resolution metrics to satisfy the requirements. CloudWatch stores the high-resolution metrics at a resolution of 1 second, but you can retrieve and read the metrics with a period of 1, 5, 10, 30, or any multiple of 60 seconds.

 TIP High-resolution metrics often lead to higher AWS charges.

When you set a CloudWatch alarm on a high-resolution metric, you can specify a *high-resolution alarm* with a period of 10 or 30 seconds. There are more charges for the high-resolution alarms compared to setting a regular alarm that has a period of any multiple of 60 seconds.

Publishing Custom Metrics

CloudWatch enables you to publish your own custom metrics. CloudWatch comes with a large number of standard metrics such as CPU utilization for EC2 instances and disk latency for EBS volumes. However, you'll need to create custom metrics in some cases, since CloudWatch doesn't have metrics for everything you want to monitor. For example, AWS can't access the internals of your EC2 instances and, therefore, you must configure custom metrics such as a metric that measures an instance's memory (RAM) utilization and pushes the metrics to CloudWatch. (If you need detailed memory usage reporting, such as threads and process information, you'll need a third-party monitoring application.)

As you've learned, metrics are a series of data points, and you can publish data as single data points or as an aggregated set of data points (statistics set). CloudWatch enables you to publish your custom metrics with the `put-metric-data` CLI command.

 NOTE CloudWatch doesn't differentiate among the sources of a metric that it receives. Therefore, it treats metrics that you publish from several sources with the same namespace and metric dimensions as *a single metric*. For example, if you're running multiple web servers, the application can publish identical request latency metrics from the different web servers. CloudWatch treats the metrics from the multiple web servers as a single metric, enabling you to aggregate the statistics (minimum, maximum, average, and sum) for all requests across the entire application. Similarly, you can use a third-party tool to capture memory usage details from multiple EC2 instances running in different regions and send them to CloudWatch. If you configure CloudWatch to use the same namespace and metric in all the regions, it will receive and aggregate the data based on the namespace and metric.

Aggregating the metric data reduces the number of calls to the `put-metric-data` API, for which AWS will charge you. In a scenario where you have many data points per minute, instead of calling `put-metric-data` multiple times for events that occur in quick succession, you can aggregate the data into a statistic (such as Min, Max, Average, or Sum) so you can publish it with a single call to `put-metric-data`.

Let's say you want to publish a metric such as request latency for one of your applications. You can publish data points that reflect the request latency for the application. You can name your namespace, such as MyAppStats, and name the metric as well, such as RequestLatency. You can publish the data points for the metric you have configured to CloudWatch by running the `aws cloudwatch put-metric-data` command from AWS CLI:

```
$ aws cloudwatch put-metric-data --metric-name RequestLatency --namespace MyAppStats \
--timestamp 2019-02-14T12:30:00Z --statistic-values Sum=577,Minimum=65,Maximum=18
9,SampleCount=5 –unit Milliseconds
```

NOTE A `put-metric-data` request can't be larger than 40KB for HTTP POST requests.

The `put-metric-data` command publishes metric data points to CloudWatch. You must specify the metric name and the namespace. If the metric that you specify doesn't already exist, CloudWatch creates the metric, and it may take up to 15 minutes for the new metric to appear in CloudWatch.

You specify the statistic-values attribute to publish aggregated data points as a set of statics with the four defined keys: Sum, Minimum, Maximum, and SampleCount.

You can retrieve statistics based on the metrics you've published with the `aws cloudwatch get-metric-statistics` command:

```
$ aws cloudwatch get-metric-statistics --namespace MyAppStats --metric-name
RequestLatency --statistics Average \
--start-time 2019-02-14T00:00:00Z --end-time 2019-02-15T00:00:00Z --period 60
```

Instead of specifying the metric values on the command line with the `put-metric-data` command, you can store the latency metrics inside a JSON-formatted file and supply the file as an input to the command.

In a scenario where you want an Auto Scaling group's instances to insert custom metrics into CloudWatch, create an Identity and Access Management (IAM) role with the PutMetricData permission and modify the Auto Scaling group's launch configuration (explained in Chapter 11) to launch the instances with that role.

Let's say you've deployed multiple EC2 instances and DynamoDB tables in multiple regions. To monitor your applications globally, you can graph metrics such as the average CPU utilization across all the EC2 instances and the number of requests throttled by all your DynamoDB tables. An easy way to do this is by using the `put-metric-data` command to pull the metrics that you need from all the regions, aggregate the data offline, and use it for creating graphs through the CloudWatch console. This shows the patterns of CPU utilization and DynamoDB request throttling.

If you expect some periods not to generate any metric data, you can do one of two things: publish a value of zero (0) for that period, or publish no value. If you've configured an alarm to notify you when an application doesn't publish any metrics for five minutes, you want the application to publish zeros for the periods when it has no data to report.

All metrics that CloudWatch generates are, by default, standard resolution (granularity of 1 minute). You can create a metric with a standard or high resolution (granularity of 1 second). You need to remember, however, that since AWS charges you for every `PutMetricData` call for a custom metric, high-resolution metrics can cost you a lot more than standard metrics.

How CloudWatch Monitoring Works for EC2 Instances

Before you start monitoring our EC2 instances, you should know what exactly you want to monitor and how you want to monitor. Your plan should include your monitoring goals, the frequency of monitoring, the monitoring tools, and your notification strategies when things go wrong. The next step after formulating your monitoring plan is to establish a baseline for normal performance for the instances. The baseline should include CPU, network, and disk performance.

Remember that EC2 instances have no metrics for memory utilization, including disk swap utilization and page file utilization (tracking memory utilization, disk swap utilization, and page file utilization require you to install an agent). Following this, you store historical monitoring data for the EC2 instances. Now you'll have a way of comparing normal performance to current performance. For example, if you see that current disk I/O performance falls outside the baseline figures, choose a different instance with more memory to enhance the performance.

 NOTE   You can monitor every AWS service using CloudWatch, which processes the raw data sent by the services into readable near-real-time metrics and stores them for a period of 15 months, to help you perform historical analyses of your application or service performance.

The following sections are a bit comprehensive, in the sense that they review not only CloudWatch monitoring, but also other ways to monitor your EC2 instances. I summarize various ways that you can monitor your EC2 instances in these sections.

Automated Monitoring of EC2 Instances

Several automated tools help you monitor EC2 instances.

EC2 Status Checks   EC2 status checks are performed by EC2 on running instances to identify hardware and software issues. EC2 performs system checks every minute, and the checks either pass or fail. If all checks pass, the instance status is OK. If one or more checks fail, the instance status is recorded as impaired. You can create alarms that trigger based on the status check results. You can also create CloudWatch alarms that automatically recover impaired instances.

There are two types of EC2 status checks: system status checks and instance status checks.

System Status Checks   System status checks focus on the hosts on which your instances run and uncover instance problems that may require AWS to fix them. You can either wait for AWS to fix the issues or resolve them yourself by stopping and starting the instances, in which case usually the instance (VM) moves to a different host computer, providing it's backed by an EBS volume.

System status checks can fail due to the following types of problems:

- Loss of power
- Loss of network connectivity
- Host software issues
- Host hardware issues

A good way to fix a system status check failure is to stop and start the EC2 instance (provided it's using an EBS-backed AMI) to try and change the physical server on which the instance (VM) is running. If the instance is using an instance store–backed AMI, terminate the instance and launch a replacement instance. You can also configure a *recovery alarm* to handle these failures. Finally, you can just wait for Amazon EC2 to resolve the issue (such as network connectivity failure) that caused the system status check to fail.

Instance Status Checks   Instance status checks focus on the software and network configuration of the EC2 instance. In most cases, when an instance check fails, you fix the problem yourself rather than wait for AWS to do so. You do this by rebooting the instance or changing the instance configuration.

Instance status checks can fail due to the following reasons:

- Failed system checks
- Wrong network or other configuration
- Running out of memory
- Corrupted file systems
- Incompatible OS kernel

You can view the status checks for an instance by running the `describe-instance-status` AWS CLI command. By default, this command shows the status checks for only running instances, but you can specify that it show the status of all instances. The command can show the status checks, scheduled EC2 events, and instance state. The following example shows the status of a specific instance:

```
$ aws ec2 describe-instance-status --instance-id i-1234567890abcdef0
```

You can add the `-filters` option to get the status of all instances with an instance status of impaired or OK.

CloudWatch Alarms   As explained earlier in this chapter, following a sustained state change, a CloudWatch alarm can invoke an action through a notification sent to an SNS topic or to an EC2 Auto Scaling policy.

CloudWatch Events and CloudWatch Logs   Events from AWS services, including EC2, are delivered to the CloudWatch Events service in near real-time. You can configure automatic actions by setting up rules in CloudWatch Events to match events to rules.

You can install a CloudWatch Logs agent on a web server and send all web server logs to the CloudWatch Logs service. The CloudWatch Logs service can monitor logs from EC2 instances and notify you when the number of occurrences of an error exceeds a threshold that you set up. For example, you can set up a notification when a "404" status code in an Apache web server access log occurs more than 10 times within one minute.

EC2 Monitoring Scripts   AWS offers a set of CloudWatch Monitoring Scripts for EC2 Linux-based instances. You can run these customizable scripts for reporting memory, swap, and disk space utilization metrics for the instances. The mon-put-instance-data.pl script collects system metrics such as memory, swap, and disk space utilization data for an instance and sends them to CloudWatch. The mon-get-instance-stats.pl script retrieves the most recent utilization statistics for the instance from CloudWatch, as shown in this example:

```
$ ./mon-get-instance-stats.pl --recent-hours=4
Instance metric statistics for the last 12 hours.

CPU Utilization
    Average: 1.06%, Minimum: 0.00%, Maximum: 15.22%

Memory Utilization
    Average: 6.84%, Minimum: 6.82%, Maximum: 6.89%

Swap Utilization
    Average: N/A, Minimum: N/A, Maximum: N/A

Disk Space Utilization on /dev/xvda1 mounted as /
    Average: 9.69%, Minimum: 9.69%, Maximum: 9.69%
```

The scripts report the metrics that they collect as custom metrics, so you pay the standard CloudWatch usage charges for custom metrics when you use the scripts. For some Linux versions, you must install additional modules (such as Perl modules) before running the scripts.

 NOTE   To monitor memory and disk metrics for Windows-based EC2 instances, send the metrics to CloudWatch Logs.

To run the scripts, you must first download the scripts from an AWS link, then install the scripts on a server, and ensure that the scripts have permissions to perform CloudWatch operations. You can grant the permissions in one of two ways: associate an IAM role (instance profile) with the instance or specify your AWS credentials in a credentials file.

Manual Monitoring of EC2 Instances

The various status checks, CloudWatch alarms, and monitoring scripts may not be enough to trap all issues. You must therefore make it a habit to use the EC2 and CloudWatch console dashboards to view the statuses of all your EC2 instances. The EC2 dashboard shows service health and scheduled events, status checks, alarm statuses, and instance and volume metric details. The CloudWatch Dashboard shows the current alarms and statuses, service health checks, and graphs of alarms and resources. In addition, you can graph EC2 monitoring data to troubleshoot an issue.

Basic and Detailed Monitoring

There are two types of monitoring, called *basic* and *detailed*. Basic monitoring sends data every five minutes, and detailed monitoring can make data available in one-minute periods, for an additional cost. Basic monitoring is standard for many services, including EC2, and you must explicitly enable detailed monitoring.

NOTE By default, EC2 sends data to CloudWatch every five minutes, but you can enable detailed monitoring for your instances, which sends the data every minute.

You can enable detailed monitoring for an instance when you launch it, while the instance is running, or when the instance is stopped. Exercise 10-1 shows how to enable detailed monitoring for an instance from the console. You can enable detailed monitoring for an instance when launching the instance from the command line, by adding the –monitoring flag:

```
$ aws ec2 run-instances –image-id ami-08084880 –monitoring Enabled=true…
```

When you enable detailed monitoring for a set of EC2 instances, you can also get aggregated data across groups of similar instances.

Once you launch an EC2 instance, you can open the EC2 console and, from the Monitoring tab, view the monitoring graphs for that instance, such as the Average Disk Writes and the Summary Disk Write operations graphs. You can view these graph metrics data from the CloudWatch console as well.

AWS provides several *CloudWatch Monitoring Scripts* for EC2 Linux-based instances that help produce and consume CloudWatch custom metrics. These are sample Perl scripts that include fully functional examples that report memory, swap, and disk usage metrics for the instances. The scripts make remote calls to CloudWatch to report the data that they collect as custom metrics. AWS bills you CloudWatch standard usage charges for custom metrics when you use the scripts.

The following example shows a script that collects aggregated metrics for an Auto Scaling group and sends them to CloudWatch:

```
$ ./mon-put-instance-data.pl –mem-util –mem-used –mem-avail –auto-scaling-only
```

Common CloudWatch EC2 Metrics

Common CloudWatch EC2 metrics include the following:

- **CPUUtilization**   The percentage of EC2 computing units in use on an EC2 instance
- **DiskReadOps**   The number of completed read operations from all instance store volumes available to an instance

- **DiskWriteOps** The number of completed write operations from all instance store volumes available to an instance
- **DiskReadBytes** The number of bytes read from all instance store volumes available to an instance
- **DiskWriteBytes** The number of bytes written to all instance store volumes available to an instance
- **NetworkIn** The number of bytes received on all the network interfaces attached to an instance
- **NetworkOut** The number of bytes sent via all the network interfaces attached to an instance

 EXAM TIP It's important to remember that, although I've listed several disk-related metrics such as `DiskWriteOps`, in the absence of any instance store volumes, the value for all disk-related metrics is either 0 or the metric is not reported. If a question asks about disk metrics for an EBS-backed EC2 instance, the metrics always show a 0 value unless you've attached additional instance store volumes to the instance. In other words, if the EC2 instance has only a single EBS volume, there are no values reported for these metrics.

Common CloudWatch RDS Metrics

All CloudWatch metrics are grouped first by namespace and then by a combination of dimensions within the namespace. For EC2, for example, you can view metrics from the CloudWatch console grouped by instance or by Auto Scaling group. Similarly, for RDS metrics, you use the namespace AWS/RDS.

You can view the available RDS metrics from the AWS CLI thus:

```
$ aws cloudwatch list-metrics  --namespace RDS
```

Here are some of the important RDS-related CloudWatch metrics that are available in the AWS/RDS namespace:

- **CPUUtilization** The percent of CPU utilization by the instance
- **DiskQueueDepth** The number of read and write requests that are waiting to access the disk
- **FreeableMemory** Available RAM, in bytes
- **FreeStorageSpace** Available disk storage space, in bytes
- **ReadLatency** The average amount of time taken per disk I/O operation
- **ReadThroughput** The average number of bytes read from disk per second
- **ReplicaLag** The amount of time (in seconds) by which a Read Replica DB lags behind the source DB instance

Common CloudWatch EBS Metrics

All EBS volume types send metrics every five minutes to CloudWatch, while the Provisioned IOPS SSD (io1) volumes send metrics every minute. There are two basic types of EBS metrics: volume *usage*-related metrics and volume *status*-related checks.

Common EBS volume usage–related metrics include `VolumeReadBytes`, `VolumeWriteOps`, `VolumeTotalReadTime`, `VolumeThroughputPercentage`, and `BurstBalance`. The various volume metrics capture the number of I/O operations or the total number of seconds spent by all operations in a specific period. Volume I/O performance metrics may be lower during certain actions that a volume may be undergoing, such as the creation of a snapshot during busy periods or when accessing data on a volume for the first time.

The `BurstBalance` metric is shown for EBS volumes to which burst balance applies, such as the gp2, st1, and sc1 volumes, but not to Provisioned IOPS SSD (io1) volumes. This metric shows the percentage of I/O credits (gp2) or the throughput credits (st1 and sc1) that remain in the burst bucket.

 NOTE The only dimension for EBS CloudWatch metrics is the volume ID, meaning that all statistics are filtered by volume ID.

In addition to EBS-related CloudWatch metrics, there are built-in EBS volume status checks that help you track the *consistency* of data on the EBS volumes. These volume health checks help you isolate impaired volumes and manage a potentially inconsistent volume.

EBS volume status checks run every five minutes. If all the status checks pass, the volume has the status OK. If one or more checks fail, then the volume is labeled as impaired. A status of insufficient-data means that the status checks may still be ongoing on a volume.

By default, if EBS detects potential data inconsistency on a volume, it disables I/O to that volume to prevent data corruption. This results in a failure of the subsequent volume status checks, resulting in labeling the volume as impaired. This means that the volume is unavailable for any I/O, unless you manually resolve the impaired status by enabling I/O to the volume.

You can override the default behavior by configuring a volume to enable I/O automatically to the volume that EBS has deemed potentially inconsistent, with the `AutoEnableIO` volume attribute. When you do this, the volume's status checks will pass, keeping EBS from labeling the volume as impaired.

EBS volume statuses have two components: I/O-enabled status and I/O-performance status. The I/O-enabled status applies to all EBS volumes, and the I/O-performance status applies only to Provisioned IOPS (io1) volumes.

I/O-enabled statuses can be one of the following:

- **Awaiting Action:Enable I/O**   This means that EBS considers the volume as potentially inconsistent. EBS has disabled the volume until you manually enable it. Once you do this, the status changes to I/O Enabled.

- **I/O Enabled**   I/O operations were explicitly enabled for the volume.

- **I/O Auto-Enabled**   You've configured automatic I/O operations on the volume, regardless of potential data inconsistency.

I/O-performance statuses are relevant only for Provisioned IOPS (io1) volumes:

- **Normal**   Performance is as expected.

- **Degraded**   Performance is below expectations.

- **Severely Degraded**   Performance is well below expectations.

- **Stalled**   Performance is severely impacted.

EBS considers both I/O-enabled statuses and I/O-performance statuses to determine a volume's final status at any time. Here are the four EBS volume statuses:

- **OK**   I/O-enabled status is enabled (either I/O Enabled or I/O Auto-Enabled). For io1 volumes, performance is normal.

- **warning**   I/O-enabled status is enabled. For an io1 volume, performance can be in the Degraded or Severely Degraded status.

- **impaired**   I/O-enabled status is Enabled or Disabled. If I/O is enabled (I/O Enabled or I/O Auto Enabled) the status is Enabled. If the volume has been taken offline or AWS is waiting for you to manually enable I/O, it has the I/O enabled status Disabled. The impaired status is also shown for an io1 volume that's in the Stalled status.

- **insufficient-data**   The volume check is ongoing.

CloudWatch Metrics for Amazon ElastiCache

You can access the metrics generated by ElastiCache through CloudWatch. ElastiCache offers host-level metrics such as CPU usage and metrics that pertain to the cache engine such as cache gets and cache misses. The metrics are generated for each cache node in 60-second intervals. ElastiCache metrics use the AWS/ElastiCache namespace and offer metrics for a single dimension, the `CacheNodeId`, which stands for the identifier for a node in the cache cluster.

Use the `describe-cache-clusters` command to view ElastiCache metrics. It's a good idea to configure CloudWatch alarms for key ElastiCache metrics. Host-level metrics include `CPUUtilization`, `FreeableMemory`, and `SwapUsage`. Metrics for Redis include the following:

- **ActiveDefragHits**   Value reallocations performed by the active defragmentation process per minute.

- **CacheHits**   Number of successful read-only key lookups in the main dictionary.

- **CacheMisses**   Number of unsuccessful read-only key lookups in the main dictionary.
- **CurrConnectons**   Number of current connections, excluding the connections from read replicas.
- **Eviction**   Number of keys evicted due to hitting the `maxmemory` limit. You must add more nodes or choose a larger node type if you see a high number of evictions. AWS recommends setting an alarm threshold for this metric.
- **Reclaimed**   Total number of key expiration events.
- **ReplicationLag**   How far behind a Read Replica is in applying changes from the primary node (in seconds).
- **EngineCPUUtilization**   Provides visibility into the Redis process CPU utilization.

CloudWatch Amazon RDS-Related Metrics

Amazon RDS sends metrics to CloudWatch every minute from all active database instances. Key RDS metrics include `ReadLatency`, `ReadThroughput`, `WriteLatency`, and `WriteThroughput`. You can filter RDS metric data by using instance, cluster, database class, engine, and region.

CloudWatch Metrics for the Application Load Balancer

ELB publishes data points to CloudWatch about your load balancers and targets. ELB reports data points to CloudWatch in six-second intervals. You can retrieve statistics about these data points as metrics, which enables you to verify that your system performance is up to par.

Application Load Balancer Metrics

Application load balancers send the following type of metric data points to AWS Cloud-Formation:

- **activeConnectionCount**   Total number of concurrent TCP connections active from clients to the ELB and from ELB to the targets.
- **RejectedConnectionCount**   Number of connections ELB has rejected because it reached its maximum number of connections limit.
- **HTTP_Fixed_Response_Count**   Number of successful fixed-response counts.
- **HTTP_Redirect_Count**   Number of successful redirect actions.
- **HTTPCode_ELB_3XX_Count**   Number of HTTP 3XX redirection codes originating from ELB.
- **HTTPCode_ELB_4XX_Count**   Number of HTTP 4XX client error codes originating from ELB. The client errors are due to incomplete or malformed requests.

- **HTTPCode_ELB_5XX_Count**   Number of HTTP 5XX server error codes originating from ELB.

- **UnhealthyHostCount**   Number of unhealthy targets.

- **HTTPCode_Target_2XX_Count, HTTPCode_Target_3XX_Count, HTTPCode_Target_4XX_Count, HTTPCode_Target_5XX_Count**   Number of HTTP response codes generated by the targets.

 NOTE   A HTTP-related _2XX status code represents success. A _3XX status code represents redirection. A _4XX status code represents client error, and a _5XX represents server error.

You can filter the Application Load Balancer metrics with the following dimensions:

- By availability zone
- By load balancer
- By target group

Statistics for Application Load Balancer Metrics

As you learned earlier, statistics are aggregations of metrics over a specific time period. CloudWatch provides statistics for the metric data points published by ELB. You can request ELB statistics from CloudWatch, and CloudWatch sends you a data stream along with the metric name and dimension. You'll recall that dimensions are name-value pairs that uniquely identify the metrics, enabling you to view statistics, for example, for a set of EC2 instances behind a load balancer.

Following are the key things you should remember about the ELB statistics:

- **Minimum and Maximum statistics**   Show the overall minimum and maximum statistics over all the load balancer nodes.

- **Sum**   Represents the aggregate value across all load balancer nodes.

- **SampleCount**   Represents the number of samples measured. This is not a very useful statistic, because it doesn't represent the number of hosts involved. For a statistic such as `HealthyHostCount`, the sample count is based on the number of samples reported by each load balancer and not the number of healthy hosts.

- **Percentile**   Shows how a value stacks up against the rest of the values in a data set and helps you capture abnormal behavior. The maximum and the average statistics don't usually capture the true behavior of your application. By setting the 99th percentile for a CloudWatch alarm or a trigger that Auto Scales the EC2 instances, you can ensure that, at most, 1 percent of requests have a latency that's longer than, say, 3 ms.

NOTE Statistics are metric data aggregations over a specific time.

Graphing a CloudWatch Metric and Sharing the Graph

You can use the CloudWatch console to create a graph of a metric. You can choose a detailed view such as one minute, which is helpful for troubleshooting, or a less detailed view such as one hour, when you're tracing a metric over several days and would like to see if there are any broad trends in the metric.

To view certain types of data better, you can set *custom bounds* for the Y axis on the graph—for example, you can set the bounds on a CPUUtilization graph to 100 percent, so that you can easily see if the CPU usage is low or high. Sometimes a graph may contain metrics with different units or that may differ widely in their range of values. You can switch between two different Y axes in the graph in these cases.

When you're creating a graph for a metric, you can get an URL for the graph by choosing Actions | Share during the graph creation process. You can then copy the URL and either save it for yourself or send it to others, such as your managers, so they can view the metric's graph.

Using CloudWatch Agents to Collect Additional Metrics and Logs

In addition to using the standard metrics gathered by CloudWatch, you can install the unified CloudWatch agent to collect additional custom metrics as well as additional logs from both EC2 instances and your on-premise servers. The metrics and logs include the following:

- Additional system-level metrics from EC2 instances
- System-level metrics from on-premise servers
- Logs from EC2 instances and on-premise servers
- Custom metrics from apps or services using the StatsD and collectd protocols.

TIP You can use AWS Data Pipeline to move logs, such as a web server's logs, to S3 every day and then run a weekly Amazon Elastic MapReduce (EMR) job over the logs to get insights into your web traffic.

The default namespace for the metrics gathered by the agent is CWAgent. You can view the metrics like any other metrics in CloudWatch. The metrics collected by the agent on Linux instances, for example, include `cpu_time_active`, `cpu_time_idle`, `disk_used_percent`, `diskio_reads`, `mem_available_percent`, `net_packets_sent`, and `swap_used_percent`. Metrics such as these provide a good understanding of how the instance is performing and whether any CPU, memory, disk, or network contention exists.

CloudWatch Authentication and Access Control

Anyone who uses CloudWatch must has credentials with permission to access AWS resources, such as those that enable you to retrieve metric data for EC2 resources. Dashboard access in the CloudWatch console requires the following permissions:

- cloudwatch:GetDashboard
- cloudwatch:ListDashboards
- cloudwatch:PutDashboard
- cloudwatch:DeleteDashboards

In addition, other permissions are required to work with the CloudWatch console, such as `cloudwatch:ListMetrics`, `cloudwatch:PutMetricData`, and `cloudwatch:PutMetricAlarm`.

CloudWatch Resources and Operations

Because CloudWatch itself doesn't have any resources, there's nothing to grant users access to, and, therefore, there are no CloudWatch Amazon Resource Names (ARNs) that you need to specify in a CloudWatch-related IAM policy. The permissions that you grant with IAM encompass all your resources that you monitor with CloudWatch.

When writing a policy to control access to a CloudWatch action, you use an * (asterisk) as the resource:

```
{
  "Version": "2012-10-17",
  "Statement": [{
     "Effect": "Allow",
     "Action": ["cloudwatch:GetMetricStatistics", "cloudwatch:ListMetrics"],
     "Resource": "*",
     "Condition": {
        "Bool": {
           "aws:SecureTransport": "true"
           }
        }
     }
  ]
}
```

AWS-Managed (Predefined) Policies for CloudWatch

AWS provides several standalone managed IAM policies that grant necessary permission for various use cases. Here are the AWS-managed polices that are specific to CloudWatch:

- **CloudWatchFullAccess**   Grants full access to CloudWatch.
- **CloudWatchReadOnlyAccess**   Grants read-only access.
- **CloudWatchActionsEC2Access**   Grants read-only access to CloudWatch alarms and metrics, and EC2 metadata. Also grants access to API actions for EC2 instances (Stop, Terminate, and Reboot).

Customer-Managed Policies

You can also create custom IAM policies to enable your users access to CloudWatch actions and resources. Here's an example that enables read-only access to a user to Cloud-Watch and its metrics and to CloudWatch Logs data:

```
{
  "Version": "2012-10-17",
  "Statement": [
    {
      "Action": [
        "autoscaling:Describe*",
        "cloudwatch:Describe*",
        "cloudwatch:Get*",
        "cloudwatch:List*",
        "logs:Get*",
        "logs:Describe*",
      ],
      "Effect": "Allow",
      "Resource": "*"
    }
  ]
}
```

CloudWatch Events

The CloudWatch Events service automates your AWS services by automatically responding to *system events*. Streams of events that describe changes in AWS resources such as EC2 instances, AWS Lambda functions, Amazon Kinesis streams, ECS tasks, SNS topics, SQS queues, and built-in targets are delivered to CloudWatch Events in near real-time. You can configure an automated action when an event matches a rule that you've put in place, thus enabling you to respond to operational changes in near real-time. Cloud-Watch Events also enable you to schedule actions that are triggered at certain times via a *cron* or *rate* expression that you configure in a *schedule expression* for the rules.

Types of CloudWatch Events

CloudWatch Events can use almost all the AWS services as targets. Here are some example events:

- **Amazon EC2 state change events**   These events capture EC2 state changes (running, terminated, stopped, and so on).

- **Amazon EC2 Auto Scaling events**   These events occur when an Auto Scaling group scales up or down.

- **Amazon EC2 spot instance interruption events**   CloudWatch Events detects the events that EC2 emits when it interrupts your Spot instances.

- **Amazon EBS events**   EBS generates notifications based on CloudWatch Events for volume-related events, snapshot events, and encryption state changes. Using CloudWatch Events, you can, for example, create rules that trigger actions in response to changes in the snapshot state. You can also trigger AWS Lambda functions that copy a newly created snapshot to another region for use in a disaster recovery exercise.

- **AWS CodeDeploy events** These events are emitted by CodeDeploy when there's a change in the status of a deployment.

Some AWS services don't emit any events, but you can still use CloudWatch Events with those services. As you know by now, AWS CloudTrail captures all events such as AWS API calls. You can configure CloudWatch Rules to trigger on the information in the CloudTrail logs. Only read/write events, but not read-only operations such as List, Get, or Describe, are supported.

Key Concepts of the CloudWatch Events Service

Events, targets, and rules are the key concepts of the CloudWatch Events service:

- **Events** An AWS service generates an event to indicate a change in its state, such as an EC2 instance that emits an event when the instance state changes from pending to running, or from running to terminating. You can also generate a custom application-level event. Finally, a schedule event is one that is generated periodically.

- **Targets** A target is something that processes an event, such as an EC2 instance, an AWS Lambda function, an AWS Batch job, an SNS topic, or an SQS queue.

- **Rules** A rule maps an event to a target (or multiple targets) for processing. As with CloudWatch rules, you have a set of managed rules, and you can create custom rules of your own. A rule can trigger on an event or it can trigger on a regular schedule that you configure. For example, a rule can trigger on an event emitted by an AWS service such as EC2. Exercise 10-10 shows how to create a CloudWatch Events rule that triggers an event generated by an EC2 instance.

 NOTE The log data captured by the agents and sent to CloudWatch Logs is encrypted, both during transit and while on disk.

Example CloudWatch Events

A CloudWatch Event is represented as a JSON object. Amazon EBS, for example, sends event notifications based on CloudWatch events when the encryption or snapshot status of an EBS volume changes. EBS also supports several *volume events*.

Here's a listing that shows the JSON object emitted by EBS following a successful `createVolume` event:

```
{
    "version": "0",
    "id": "01234567-0123-0123-0123-012345678901",
    "detail-type": "EBS Volume Notification",
    "source": "aws.ec2",
```

```
    "account": "012345678901",
    "time": "yyyy-mm-ddThh:mm:ssZ",
    "region": "us-east-1",
    "resources": [
        "arn:aws:ec2:us-east-1:012345678901:volume/vol-01234567"
    ],
    "detail": {
        "result": "available",
        "cause": "",
        "event": "createVolume",
        "request-id": "01234567-0123-0123-0123-0123456789ab"
    }
}
```

Here's a brief description of the fields in an event:

- **version**   Set to zero in all events.
- **id**   A unique value for every event.
- **detail-type**   Together with the `source` field, the `detail_type` field identifies the fields and their values that show up in the `detail` field.
- **source**   Identifies the AWS services that emitted the event. In this example, the source is EC2.
- **account**   A 12-digit number that identifies the AWS account.
- **time**   The event timestamp specified by the AWS service that emitted the event.
- **region**   The AWS region from which this event was generated.
- **resources**   A JSON array that shows the ARN of the resources involved in the event.
- **detail**   A JSON object with multiple fields such as the result, cause, the event, and the `request_id`.

All events have the same top-level fields, but the contents of the `detail` top-level field vary based on the AWS service that generates the event, and the event itself. The `source` and `detail-type` fields identify the fields and values shown in the `detail` field. Rules use *event patterns* to select events and send them to the correct targets.

An event pattern has a structure that's like that of an event. Here's an example:

```
{
    "source": [ "aws.ec2" ],
    "detail-type": [ "EC2 Instance State-change Notification" ],
    "detail": {
        "state": [ "running" ]
    }
}
```

For an event pattern to match an event, the event must contain *all* the fields listed in the event pattern.

In our example here, the fields under the `detail` section are pertinent to the EBS volume creation event. The `event` name is `createVolume`, and the `result` field shows the status (`available`) of the action that triggered this event.

Following is another example that shows an EC2 instance event following an instance state change:

```
{
    "id":"7bf73129-1428-4cd3-a780-95db273d1602",
    "detail-type":"EC2 Instance State-change Notification",
    "source":"aws.ec2",
    "account":"123456789012",
    "time":"2018-11-11T21:29:54Z",
    "region":"us-east-1",
    "resources":[
        "arn:aws:ec2:us-east-1:123456789012:instance/i-abcd1111"
    ],
    "detail":{
        "instance-id":"i-abcd1111",
        "state":"pending"
    }
}
```

In this example, the instance is in the pending state, and the state can take one of the various possible EC2 instance states, such as running, shutting down, stopping, stopped, and terminated.

Schedule Expressions for Rules

You can configure CloudWatch Events rules according to a regular schedule. For example, you can use rules to create a snapshot of an EBS volume on a schedule.

You can use a cron or rate expression to create rules that trigger on a schedule. The finest resolution with a cron expression is a minute. So there may be a few seconds delay when a schedule rule is triggered before the target service executes the target resource. Let's say you want to create a snapshot of an EBS volume, for example. You can configure a fixed rate to create the snapshot every few minutes. Alternatively, you can configure a cron expression to specify that the snapshot be taken at a specific time of day.

A *cron expression* looks like a regular Linux crontab entry. Here's an example of a cron expression that creates a rule that's triggered every day at 12:00 P.M. UTC.

```
$ aws events put-rule –schedule-expression "cron(0 12 * * ? *)" –name MyRule1
```

A *rate expression* starts when you create the rule and runs in the schedule that you define for it. Rate expressions consist of just two things: a *value* and *unit*, which is the unit of time. Here's an example that shows how to use a rate expression to create a rule:

```
$ aws events put-rule –schedule-expression "rate(5 minutes)" –name MyRule2
```

Event Patterns

An event pattern is a JSON object that helps rules select events and route them to their targets. You can write event patterns to match events and use the `test-event-pattern` CLI command to ensure that the pattern matches the event.

Event pattern matching requires that the event contains all the fields listed in the event pattern (the field names must appear with the same nesting structure as well), and the matching should be exact, character by character. The following two event patterns (`resources` and `detail`) match the event I described earlier. The first event pattern matches because one of the instance values mentioned here matches the event, and the second pattern also matches the event contains the "pending" state:

```
{
    "resources":[
        "arn:aws:ec2:us-east-1:123456789012:instance/i-12345678"
        "arn:aws:ec2:us-east-1:123456789012:instance/i-abcd1111"
    ]
}

{
    "detail": {
        "state": ["pending" ]
    }
}
```

CloudWatch Metrics for CloudWatch Events

The CloudWatch Events service sends metrics to CloudWatch every minute. Cloud-Watch Events metrics have a single dimension called `RuleName`. The AWS/Events namespace includes the following metrics:

- **DeadLetterInvocations**   Number of times a rules target wasn't invoked in response to an event
- **Invocations**   Number of times a target was invoked in response to an event
- **FailedInvocations**   Number of times invocations failed for good; it doesn't include retried invocations
- **TriggeredRules**   Number of triggered rules that matched an event
- **MatchedEvents**   Number of events that matched a rule
- **ThrottledRules**   Number of triggered rules that are being throttled

CloudWatch Logs

CloudWatch Logs is a log service that helps you monitor, store, access, and log files from various services such as Amazon EC2, Route 53, ELB, AWS CloudTrail, VPC, AWS Lambda, and other services. You must configure the logs for these services to be sent to and stored in CloudWatch Logs because they don't go there automatically.

You can use CloudWatch Logs to monitor both systems and applications. Cloud-Watch Logs can, for example, notify you when a specific type of error appears in the application logs and crosses a threshold that you specify. You can also create Cloud-Watch alarms to receive notifications when certain API actions show up in CloudTrail logs. CloudWatch Logs also logs information about all the DNS queries received by Route 53. The log information includes the domain and subdomain that was requested, the DNS record type, the data and time of the request, and the DNS response code (for example, NoError or SerFail). You enable Route 53 logging by configuring query logging in Route 53, so that the service can send its logs to CloudWatch Logs.

CloudWatch Logs enable you to retain log data long-term. CloudWatch Logs stores logs indefinitely, but you can configure a retention period between one day and 10 years. You can store both rotated and nonrotated log data from all your hosts to CloudWatch Logs.

CloudWatch Logs can collect logs from your EC2 instances as well as from all your on-premise servers.

Services that Work Together with CloudWatch Logs

CloudWatch Logs works closely with AWS CloudTrail. You can log all CloudWatch Logs API calls in CloudTrail, and CloudTrail delivers the log files to an S3 bucket. Some services such as VPC flow logs can be published directly to S3 buckets. You can choose to export log data from log groups to an S3 bucket for custom processing. It may take up to 12 hours before the log data is available for exporting to S3 buckets.

In addition to CloudTrail, CloudWatch Logs works with IAM, Amazon Kinesis Data Streams, and AWS Lambda.

You can create *subscriptions* to access log events in real time from CloudWatch Logs and direct the logs to other AWS services such as an Amazon Kinesis stream or AWS Lambda for processing the logs or loading them into other systems.

CloudWatch Logs Insights helps you search analyze log data stored in CloudWatch Logs. The service contains a query language with commands that help you query the data in CloudWatch Logs. It can automatically discover files in the logs sent by various AWS services.

CloudWatch Logs Concepts

Here are the key terms and concepts that CloudWatch Logs uses:

- **Log events**   A log event record shows activity by a monitored application or AWS resource. Each log event record contains a timestamp and a raw event message.

- **Log streams**   A log stream is a sequence of log events from the same source, such as an application instance or a resource.

- **Log groups**   A log group is a group of log streams with the same retention, access control, and monitoring configuration. A log stream can belong only to one log group.

- **Metric filters**   Metric filters help you extract metric data points from events and transform them to data points on CloudWatch metric. You assign metric filters to log groups. A metric filter consists of a filter pattern, the metric name, the metric namespace, and the metric value (the value published to the metric). Filters help you define the patterns to search for in log data as it's transmitted to CloudWatch Logs. Using these filters, CloudWatch Logs transforms the log data published to it into CloudWatch metrics that you can either graph or set alarms for.

- **Retention settings**   You configure retention settings to specify how long logs should be stored in CloudWatch Logs. Retention settings are assigned to log groups, and not to log streams.

Unified CloudWatch Agent

AWS provides a new unified CloudWatch agent to collect operating system logs from EC2 instances and your on-premise servers. Although an older CloudWatch Logs agent is still available, AWS recommends using the newer unified agent because it offers several advantages over the older agent:

- It offers better performance.
- It can collect both logs and advanced metrics with a single agent.
- It can collect logs from Windows servers.
- It can collect systems metrics other than CloudWatch metrics.
- It can collect custom metrics from your apps or services via the StatsD and CollectD protocols. Remember that CollectD isn't supported on Windows servers.

NOTE AWS bills the metrics collected by the CloudWatch agent as custom metrics.

If, for example, you are required to have CloudWatch respond to alerts generated by web server logs, here's what you'd need to do:

1. Install the CloudWatch Logs agent on the EC2 instance where the web server is running.
2. Direct all the web server's operating system logs to CloudWatch Logs.
3. Configure alarms according to thresholds, such as the number of 404 error messages in the logs within a specific period.

Setting Up CloudWatch Logs

You can set up CloudWatch Logs using two different techniques. The first one involves installing the unified CloudWatch agent, and the second is through AWS CloudFormation, which I explain in detail in Chapter 11.

Collecting Logs and Metrics with the Unified CloudWatch Agent When you use the unified CloudWatch agent, you must download the agent binaries and install them. Here are the steps that you must perform to install the agent on an EC2 instance and start the agent so that it can start collecting the logs and metrics:

1. Create the IAM roles and users that enable CloudWatch to collect metrics from the server on which you install the agent.
2. Attach an IAM role to the EC2 instance.
3. Using either the AWS Systems Manager Run command or an Amazon S3 download link, download the agent binary package.
4. Start the agent, either from the command line or with the Systems Manager Run command.

Using CloudFormation to Set Up CloudWatch Logs In Chapter 11, you'll learn how to create application stacks with AWS CloudFormation so that you can manage a group of AWS resources together as a single entity. You'll learn how to use templates to describe the AWS resources you want CloudFormation to provision for you. You can configure CloudWatch Logs in those templates, as shown here in a template snippet. This template snippet creates a log group as well as a metric filter that counts the number of times a 404 error occurs in the logs. The logs are retained for 30 days.

```
"WebServerLogGroup": {
    "Type": "AWS::Logs::LogGroup",
    "Properties": {
        "RetentionInDays": 30
    }
},

"404MetricFilter": {
    "Type": "AWS::Logs::MetricFilter",
    "Properties": {
        "LogGroupName": {
            "Ref": "WebServerLogGroup"
        },
        "FilterPattern": "[ip, identity, user_id, timestamp, request, status_
code = 404, size, ...]",
        "MetricTransformations": [
            {
                "MetricValue": "1",
                "MetricNamespace": "test/404s",
                "MetricName": "test404Count"
            }
        ]
    }
}
```

Searching and Filtering Log Data

CloudWatch Logs can collect humongous amounts of log data, so searching through this mass of logs isn't easy. You can create one or more metric filters to help you search through the logs that a CloudWatch Logs agent sends to CloudWatch. The metric filters help you define the terms and patterns in log data. CloudWatch Logs relies on your filters to turn the voluminous log data into meaningful CloudWatch metrics that you can set alarms on or create graphs on.

Structure of a Metric Filter

A metric filter consists of the following elements:

- **Metric name** The name of the metric, such as `FailedCount`, which counts the number of failures that appear in the log file.

- **Metric namespace** The CloudWatch namespace for the metric.

- **Metric value** Specifies the numerical value for the CloudWatch metric, such as "1," each time a failure (such as an ERROR message) shows up in the log file, or the actual number of an entity such as the number of bytes transferred.

- **Default value**   What CloudWatch should report if there are no matching logs for this filter. By setting the default value to 0, you make CloudWatch Logs always report the data.

Filter and Pattern Syntax

A metric filter helps you search your logs for a matching term, phrase, or values. For example, a metric filter that tracks the number of times the term "ERROR" occurs in a log counts the total number of occurrences during a period and sends it as a metric. So you can use case-sensitive terms, or a set of terms to filter logs. You can exclude a term as well, by placing a minus (–) in front of the term to search.

A filter pattern helps match the terms with an expression. The filter pattern matches all log events. You can specify the OR pattern (with the ? term, such as ?ERROR) to match terms in text-based filters.

Metric filters are useful in matching JSON terms. A metric filter for a JSON log event has the following format:

```
{ SELECTOR EQUALITY_OPERATOR String }
```

In this metric filter, the SELECTOR specifies the JSON property to check (for example, $.eventid). The EQUALITY_OPERATOR can be either = or !=. The string at the end of the filter is used to match text.

Here are a couple of filters that show how you can use them to match events in a log:

```
{ $.sourceIPAddress != 123.123.* }
{ $.eventType = "UpdateTrail" }
```

CloudWatch Logs Metrics

CloudWatch Logs, like several AWS services, sends metrics every minute to Amazon CloudWatch. The metrics are associated with the AWS/Logs namespace and include the following:

- **IncomingBytes**   The volume of log events, in bytes, that were uploaded to CloudWatch Logs.
- **IncomingLogEvents**   The number of log events uploaded to CloudWatch Logs.
- **ForwardedBytes**   The volume of log events forwarded to a subscription destination.
- **ForwardedLogEvents**   The number of log events forwarded to a subscription destination.
- **DeliveryErrors**   The number of log events that encountered an error when forwarding data to a subscription destination.
- **DeliveryThrottling**   The number of log events for which CloudWatch Logs was throttled when forwarding data to a destination. You can use the LogGroupName, DestinationType, and FilterName dimensions with the CloudWatch Logs metrics.

You can list (retrieve) log events from a specified log stream with the GetLogEvents API. By default, the operation returns as many log events as can fit in a response of 1MB in size, up to a maximum of 10,000 log events.

AWS CloudTrail

AWS CloudTrail helps you monitor your AWS deployment by storing a history of the AWS API calls for your account, whether they are made from the AWS Management Console, AWS SDKs, the command line, or other AWS services. CloudTrail records all API calls made in your account and delivers the log files to an S3 bucket, and it enables governance, compliance, and the operational and risk auditing of your AWS account.

You can find out the identity of the user, role, or service that made the AWS API calls, the source IP address where the calls were made from, the resource that was affected or modified, and the time when the API calls were made. CloudTrail captures API calls made by various AWS services on behalf of users. These services include CloudFormation, Auto Scaling, Elastic Beanstalk, and AWS OpsWorks.

CloudTrail is enabled when you create your AWS account and captures all activity in your AWS account in CloudTrail events. You can view, download, and analyze and respond to this account activity across your infrastructure, by going to Event History in the CloudTrail console. You can search through the past 90 days of activity in your account in the Event History.

 NOTE   CloudTrail delivers events to the CloudTrail console, S3 buckets, and optionally to CloudWatch Logs.

In addition to viewing events from the CloudTrail console (Event History), you can create a CloudTrail trail to archive and later analyze changes to your AWS resources. A *trail* refers to a configuration that determines how events are delivered to an Amazon S3 bucket of your choice. You can also analyze the events in a trail with the CloudWatch Logs and CloudWatch Events services.

You can use the CloudTrail log file integrity validation feature to determine whether a log file was modified or deleted after CloudTrail delivered the file. You can validate the files via the AWS CLI. It's impossible to modify, delete, or forge a CloudTrail log file without being discovered. The ability to validate log files is critical in security and forensic investigations.

Types of CloudTrail Trails

There are two types of trails for an account: a *common trail* and a *regional trail*. The common trail applies to all regions and is the default behavior when you create a trail from the console. A regional trail applies to a single region, and is the default option when you create a trail with the AWS CLI or the CloudTrail API.

NOTE In addition to the common and the regional trails, you can also create an organization trail if you've created an organization in AWS Organizations.

CloudTrail normally delivers the event log files within 15 minutes of account activity, stores the CloudTrail event log files in Amazon S3, and applies S3 server-side encryption (SSE) to the log files. You can choose to encrypt with an AWS KMS key. CloudTrail also publishes log files roughly every 5 minutes that contain the API calls from all AWS services that support CloudTrail.

Creating a Trail

By creating a trail, you enable the delivery of events as log files to an Amazon S3 bucket. Creating the trail ensures that an event record extends past 90 days. The trail also helps you monitor and alarm on specific events by sending the log events to CloudWatch Logs. You can create up to five trails for each AWS region. You can stop logging by turning logging off or by deleting the trail.

When creating and configuring a trail from the console or the AWS CLI, follow these basic steps:

1. Create an S3 bucket where the log files will be delivered.

2. Create the trail.

3. Create an SNS topic that receives notifications when log files are delivered. You can get the updates sent to an Amazon SQS queue, so you can handle the notifications programmatically. Notifications are optional.

4. Configure CloudWatch Logs to receive logs from CloudTrail so you can monitor and alarm on specific log events.

Exercise 10-8 shows how to create a trail from the console. You can do the same from the AWS CLI with the `create-trail` command:

```
$ aws cloudtrail create-trail --name my-trail –s3-bucket my-bucket1 –is-
multi-region-trail
```

This command creates a trail that delivers logs from all regions to the *my-bucket1* S3 bucket.

To start logging for this trail, run the `start-logging` command next:

```
$ aws cloudtrail start-logging –name my-trail
```

You can view the status of the logging with the `get-trail-status` command:

```
$ aws cloudtrail get-trail-status –name my-trail
```

Logging Management and Data Events

You can specify whether CloudTrail logs management events, data events, or both. A management event (management plane) offers details about management operations performed on your AWS resources. An event such as a user login, although it's a non-API event, is considered a management event. Data events, also known as data plane operations, capture details about operations performed on or within AWS resources.

Types of Objects to be Logged

By default, data event logging is disabled, and you must enable it by specifying the resources or resource types when creating a trail or by updating an existing trail. Data events are high-volume activities and include events such as S3 object-level API activity (GetObject, PutObject, DeleteObject) and AWS Lambda function execution activity. When logging S3 activity, you can specify that data events for all objects in a S3 bucket be logged or just specific objects in a bucket.

By default, CloudTrail logs only management events. The first copy of management events in a region is delivered free of charge. AWS charges $2.00 per 100,000 management events if you request additional copies. You may need to pay additional charges for logging data events. Data events are charged at $0.10 per 1,000,000 events. You can choose to log both data and management events to the same trail log or configure different trails for data and management events, and write them to different S3 buckets. Typical S3 charges are less than $3.00 per month for the S3 bucket.

Types of Events to be Logged

When you configure both data and management event logging, you can choose to log the following types of events:

- **Read-only events** Include API operations such as the EC2 DescribeSecurityGroups API operation that returns information but doesn't modify configuration.

- **Write-only events** Includes EC2 TerminateInstances API operations that modify resources.

- **All** A trail logs both read-only and write-only events.

- **None** The trail logs neither read-only nor write-only management events.

Monitoring CloudTrail Log Files with CloudWatch Logs

You can configure a CloudTrail trail to send data and management events from Cloud-Trail to CloudWatch Logs. If, for example, you configure a trail to log data events only, the trail delivers just the data events to your CloudWatch Logs log group.

Here are the high-level steps to configure monitoring of CloudTrail log files with CloudWatch Logs:

1. Configure a trail to send *log events* to CloudWatch Logs.

2. Define CloudWatch Logs *metric filters* to evaluate the log events.

3. Assign CloudWatch *metrics* to the metric filters.

4. Create CloudWatch *alarms* and configure them to send notifications when the alarms are triggered.

5. Configure CloudWatch to perform actions automatically in response to an alarm.

To create an alarm, you must first create a metric filter and then configure the alarm based on that metric filter. You can create metric filters and alarms with an AWS Cloud-Formation template as well. To create a CloudWatch alarm manually for an Amazon EC2 instance change, follow the steps shown in Exercise 10-9. The alarm that you create in this exercise is triggered whenever any API calls are made that terminate, create, start, stop, or reboot an EC2 instance. Similarly, you can set up alarms for events such as S3 bucket activity, security group and network ACL configuration changes, VPC changes, as well as console sign-in and authorization failures.

AWS Config

AWS Config provides a detailed view of all your AWS resources, including the resource configuration, the resource interrelationships, and how the configurations and the relationships have changed over time. You can do the following with AWS Config:

- Get a snapshot of the current resource configuration.
- Get the historical configuration of resources.
- Receive notifications when resources are created, deleted, or modified.
- View the relationships among AWS resources.

AWS Config helps you manage resource configurations, detect misconfigurations, and satisfy auditing and security compliance requirements. It also helps prevent unintended adverse effects on a resource due to configuration changes in a related resource.

AWS Config also aids in analyzing your potential security weaknesses by showing the IAM policies assigned to an IAM user, group, or role, and it helps you determine that a user or group had a specific set of permissions at a specific time when you're tracing the source of a change. You can use AWS Config to view security group configuration for your EC2 instances, such as the port rules that were open at a specific time. This information helps you figure out if a security group was blocking the incoming TCP traffic to a certain port.

You can use AWS Config logs along with CloudTrail logs (these record the API requests that were made to AWS resources in your account) to find details about configuration changes, such as who made them, when they made them, and exactly how they made them.

Key Concepts: Resources and Rules

AWS resources and AWS Config rules are the two basic concepts that determine how AWS Config helps you track your resources and their configuration changes across time.

Resources and Their Configuration

You've been working with various AWS resources such as EC2 instances, VPC, and EBS throughout this book, so by now you know what AWS resources are. AWS Config discovers your AWS resources and maps the relationships among those resources, such as a relationship that shows that a specific EBS volume is attached to a specific EC2 instance.

In the following sections, I discuss the resource-related concepts and entities that AWS Config uses.

Configuration Items A *configuration item* is a point-in-time view of a resource's attributes. AWS Config creates a configuration item when it detects a change in the resource type that it's recording at that time. When you initially turn on AWS Config, it discovers all the supported AWS resources and generates a configuration item for each resource. After this, it generates a configuration item for a resource whenever its configuration changes and keeps the historical records of the configuration items.

Configuration History A *configuration history* is a set of configuration items for a resource over a period. It helps you track changes to a resource's configuration.

Configuration Recorder The *configuration recorder* stores the configuration items for supported resources. When you turn on AWS Config, the service automatically creates and starts a configuration recorder to track the configuration changes for all your AWS resources or specific resource types that you configure.

Configuration Snapshot A *configuration snapshot* is a set of configuration items that provides a complete picture of all your resources and their configuration. You can use this snapshot periodically to validate resource configuration in your account, remove those that shouldn't exist, or correct misconfigured resources. You can navigate the configuration snapshots from the AWS Config console.

AWS Config Rules

An AWS Config rule helps you specify the ideal configuration settings for a resource or even for your entire account. AWS Config flags a resource as noncompliant when it violates a rule and notifies you through an Amazon SNS notification. AWS offers several predefined rules (AWS Config managed rules), and you can also create your own rules. Figure 10-5 shows a set of AWS Config managed rules. The figure shows 6 out of a total of 21 AWS managed rules currently available to you.

When you create and activate a rule, AWS Config performs an initial evaluation by comparing the resources to the conditions of the new rule. Following this, it runs an evaluation based on how you configure the conditions when you create the rule. You can

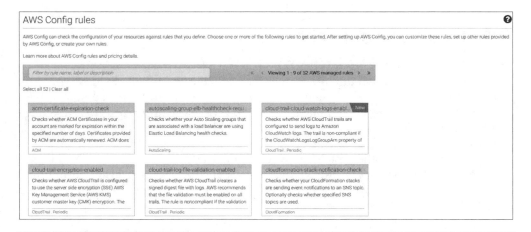

Figure 10-5 AWS Config managed rules

configure AWS Config to perform a resource evaluation when a configuration change occurs or periodically, such as every 24 hours.

You can view the compliance state of your resources by going to the AWS Management Console and selecting Rules | Rule Details. If any resources are noncompliant, you will see them here. To view compliance from the command line, run the `describe-compliance` command to show the compliance state for an AWS resource of a specific type—in this case, an EC2 instance:

```
$ aws configservice describe-compliance-by-resource --resource-type AWS::EC2::Instance
{
    "ComplianceByResources": [
        {
            "ResourceType": "AWS::EC2::Instance",
            "ResourceId": "i-nnnnnnnn",
            "Compliance": {
                "ComplianceContributorCount": {
                    "CappedCount": 1,
                    "CapExceeded": false
                },
                "ComplianceType": "NON_COMPLIANT"
            }
        },
        {
            "ResourceType": "AWS::EC2::Instance",
            "ResourceId": "i-nnnnnnnn",
            "Compliance": {
                "ComplianceType": "COMPLIANT"
            }
        },
...
```

Amazon GuardDuty   You can use Amazon GuardDuty, a threat detections service, to track malicious activity and unauthorized actions in your AWS account. GuardDuty uses machine learning, anomaly detection, and threat intelligence to identify potential threats. It analyzes events across various dta sources such as CloudTrail, VPC Flow Logs, and DNS Logs. GuardDuty can be integrated with CloudWatch Events to make GuardDuty's alerts actionable. GuardDuty's findings can also trigger AWS lambda for automatic prevention or remediation of threats.

Optimizing Resources Usage and Managing Billing and Costs

Although AWS can potentially offer a cheaper cost option in the cloud to run your systems, this isn't guaranteed by any means. A lot depends on how well you manage your AWS infrastructure, how diligently you look for and eliminate unused resources, and how eagerly you seek out ways to cut your costs—for example, by reserving EC2 instances and using the Spot pricing option to purchase your instances, rather than buying them at the much more expensive On-Demand prices.

In the next few sections, I discuss several tools and services that help you optimize your resource usage, cut your AWS spending, and manage your AWS billing. Here's a brief explanation of the tools and services:

- **AWS Trusted Advisor**   This tool helps you find unused or underused resources so that you can eliminate them to cut costs.

- **Amazon Inspector** This tool helps you enhance your security and adhere to compliance regulations.

- **AWS Billing and Cost Management** Use this AWS service to pay your bills, monitor usage, and, most importantly, budget your costs. Billing and Cost Management offers features such as the following to help you plan your AWS costs and receive alerts when costs exceed thresholds that you set and simplify your accounting:

  - **Cost Explorer** This tool helps you view your AWS costs as a graph so that you can filter the costs data according to various criteria such as EC2 instance type, region, usage type, and so on.

  - **Budgets** Budgets help you track your AWS usage and costs.

  - **Alerts and notifications** These help you avoid unexpected charges (perhaps you left servers running when they should have been stopped or terminated, or you weren't aware that AWS charges you for using certain AWS services that you chose to use).

  - **Cost allocation tags** Tags help you organize your AWS resources, and cost allocation tags help you track your AWS spending at a detailed level.

  - **AWS cost and usage reports** You can send AWS billing reports to Amazon S3 and receive reports that break down costs by various criteria, such as time period, product, or tags that you define.

AWS Trusted Advisor

The AWS Trusted Advisor is an online tool that proactively checks and analyzes your AWS environment and compares it to AWS best practices. It then offers AWS best practice recommendations in five categories: cost optimization, performance, security, fault tolerance, and service limits. Cost optimization, performance, security, and reliability are the pillars of the AWS Well-Architected Framework, and thus, Trusted Advisor evaluates how your usage of the AWS services stacks up against this framework.

For example, in the cost optimization area, the Trusted Advisor checks your EBS volume configurations and warns you when it sees a volume that's underused. Since EBS charges start accumulating right after you create the volume, if a volume has very low write activity or is unattached for a period of time, the volume is underutilized, costing you needless charges.

Trusted Advisor shows how you can cut your AWS costs by eliminating unused resources or reserving your EC2 instances instead of purchasing them on demand. Following is a summary of the cost optimization recommendations offered by the tool.

- **EC2 Reserved Instances optimization** Trusted Advisor checks your EC2 usage history and calculates the optimal number of Partial Upfront Reserved Instances. Reserved Instances require a low one-time fee to receive a substantial discount on the hourly instance charges.

- **Low utilization EC2 instances** Because all running instances incur hourly usage charges, the advisor alerts you if any of the running instances have a CPU utilization of 10 percent or lower and network I/O of 5MB or lower on four or more days during the last two weeks.

- **Unassociated Elastic IP addresses**   Trusted Advisor checks for Elastic IP (EIP) addresses that aren't associated with any EC2 instance. When this is true, the IP addresses incur a nominal charge.

- **Idle load balancers**   The advisor lets you know if any load balancers that you've configured have no backed instances associated with them, or if the network traffic is very small—both of which indicate that the load balancer isn't being used efficiently.

- **Underutilized EBS volumes**   You'll receive warnings when an EBS volume appears underused or unused because it's unattached or has very low write activity for a period of time.

- **Route 53 latency resource record sets**   The advisor checks your Route 53 latency records to ensure that you've properly configured the latency resource record sets. If you've created just one latency record set for your domain, all queries are directed to one region, so you'll be paying for the latency-based routing feature but not getting anything for it. You must create the record sets for the domain name in different regions to benefit from this feature.

- **EC2 Reserved Instance lease expiration**   The advisor checks for Reserved Instances whose leases are going to expire in the next 30 days or have expired in the last 30 days. Since Reserved Instances don't automatically review, you'll be charged the On-Demand rates when the leases expire.

- **Underutilized Redshift clusters**   If a Redshift cluster hasn't received any connection requests for a long period, or it's using very low CPU, you can cut your costs by downsizing the cluster or shutting the cluster down after taking a final snapshot.

- **RDS idle DB instances**   The advisor checks for RDS DB instances that appear to be idle, with no connections for a prolonged period of time, so you can delete the instances to reduce costs.

- **Service Limits check**   Most AWS services have default limits, and the limits are usually region-specific. You can't change the limits for many services. AWS Trusted Advisor offers a Service Limits check that shows your current usage and the limits for some aspects of some AWS services. If you want to ensure that you don't exceed the service limits for a certain service, use the AWS Trusted Advisor to check the service limits.

Amazon Inspector

Amazon Inspector is an automated security assessment service that helps you enhance your security and adhere to compliance regulations. Inspector tests both the network security of your instances as well as your applications.

Inspector assesses your applications for known security vulnerabilities, risk exposure, and deviations from common security best practices. After it completes a security assessment, it provides a list of its findings, ordered by severity level. AWS continuously updates its knowledge base security best practices and rules, and Inspector makes it easy for you to enforce those best practices in your AWS environment. Remember that under the shared security model, you, the customer, are responsible for the security of all applications, processes, and tools that run on AWS services.

 TIP Inspector identifies your security vulnerabilities, but it doesn't fix them. If your organization has mandated that all your EC2 instances be patched with the most up-to-date security patches, AWS System Manager Patch Manager is an ideal tool for fulfilling this mandate.

Following are the important terms and concepts of Inspector:

- **Amazon Inspector agent** Install this on the EC2 instances that are part of the assessment target to capture configuration data as well the behavior of the instance, including the network, file system, and process activity.

- **Assessment target** This is the set of AWS resources that Inspector assesses—currently, it can be only EC2 instances.

- **Assessment run** The process of discovering security issues by comparing Inspector's security rules packages with the assessment target's configuration and behavior. Inspector can use a combination of rules packages, such as those that assess network reachability, and others that perform host assessments. There are four main host assessment packages:
  - Common Vulnerabilities and Exposures (CVE)
  - Center for Internet Security (CIS) benchmarks
  - Security best practices for Amazon Inspector
  - Runtime behavior analysis

- **Assessment template** Use this to specify things such as the rules packages and tags for the assessment findings, and to control the duration of the assessment run.

AWS Billing and Cost Management

The AWS Billing and Cost Management service makes it easy for you to pay your bills, monitor your AWS costs and service usage, and budget your AWS spending.

Monitoring Usage and Costs

There are several ways in which you can monitor your AWS usage via Billing and Cost Management: you can read the cost and usage graphs in the dashboard through the Cost Explorer, create budgets, use cost allocation tags, use the AWS Price List API, and use strategies to avoid unexpected billing charge surprises.

To start exploring the service, log into the AWS Management Console and open the Billing and Cost Management Console at https://console.aws.amazon.com/billing. You'll see the console open to the dashboard, as shown in Figure 10-6.

Billing & Cost Management Dashboard

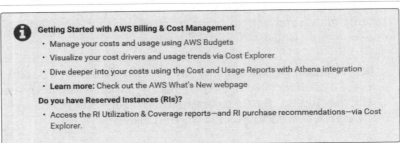

> ⓘ **Getting Started with AWS Billing & Cost Management**
> - Manage your costs and usage using AWS Budgets
> - Visualize your cost drivers and usage trends via Cost Explorer
> - Dive deeper into your costs using the Cost and Usage Reports with Athena integration
> - **Learn more:** Check out the AWS What's New webpage
>
> **Do you have Reserved Instances (RIs)?**
> - Access the RI Utilization & Coverage reports—and RI purchase recommendations—via Cost Explorer.

Figure 10-6 The AWS Billing and Cost Management Console

As Figure 10-6 shows, you can access the Cost Explorer, AWS Budgets, and Cost and Usage Reports by clicking the links in the dashboard. In addition to these links, the dashboard shows graphs for Spend Summary, Month-to-Data Spend-by-Service, and Month-to-Date Services by Spend. Figure 10-7 shows the Spend Summary, and Figure 10-8 shows the Month-to-Date Spend by Service.

In Figure 10-8, which shows your Month-to-Date Spend by Service, click Bill Details on the top right-hand side to get details about the AWS service charges broken down by service, such as CloudWatch, EC2, KMS, RDS, and S3.

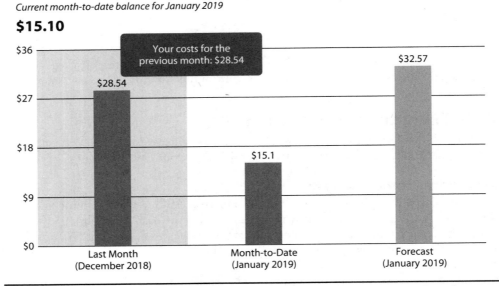

Figure 10-7 The Spend Summary graph in the AWS Billing and Cost Management Console

Figure 10-8
The Month-to-Date Spend by Service graph in the AWS Billing and Cost Management Console

Monitoring Costs with the Cost Explorer   The Cost Explorer provides analytics and visualization that help you view and manage your AWS costs and usage of the AWS resources in your AWS accounts. You can do the following with the Cost Explorer:

- Use the preconfigured views to view cost distribution by service, accounts, or daily spending over the past three months.
- Explore and analyze your historical spending. You can dive deeper into your cost and usage data to identify trends, the leading cost drivers, and any unexpected costs.
- Download the data associated with reports or benchmark your favorite reports.
- Monitor your Reserved Instance (RI) usage, so you can efficiently use those instances to lower your EC2 spending.

When you first enable the Cost Explorer, it may take up to 24 hours for the spending data in your account to be populated. Once that is done, you are ready to use the Cost Explorer and view usage reports.

In general, to cut your AWS costs, you can adopt strategies such as the following:

- Right-size your services to handle your needs at the lowest possible cost.
- Use Reserved Instances.

- Use the Spot market.

- Monitor and track service usage.

- If you see any RDS DB instances with consistently 0 connections, terminate the instances after taking a final snapshot.

- Detach unused or underused EBS volumes, and after taking a snapshot, delete them.

- Use the Cost Explorer to optimize costs and maximize savings.

Controlling Costs with AWS Budgets AWS Budgets lets you create custom budgets that alert you when your AWS costs or usage exceed or are expected to exceed the thresholds you set for your costs. By default, you have no budgets, so you must create a budget to use the Budgets feature. You can create three types of budgets:

- **Cost budget** Monitors your costs. When they hit a dollar amount that you specify, it alerts you.

- **Usage budget** Monitors your usage of a usage type or usage type group and alerts you when the usage hits a threshold that you specify.

- **Reservation budget** Monitors the RU Utilization or RI Coverage associated with your EC2 instance reservations. The budgets support EC2, RDS, Redshift, ElastiCache, and Elasticsearch reservations models. You can set expiring budgets, which stop renewing on the last day of the expiration month, and recurring budgets that renew on the first of every monthly billing period.

Using Cost Allocation Tags to Manage Costs A tag is a label that consists of a key and a value. Tags help organize your AWS resources. You can use tags for all AWS resources, such as your EC2 instances. Cost allocation tags help you organize your resource costs to manage your AWS costs. When you use tags, the cost allocation reports that you generate group your usage and costs by your active tags, such as the owner, stack, cost center, or application. If you run multiple development and production EC2 instances, you can separate the cost of the development instances from that of the production instances by using the cost allocation tags and AWS billing reports.

The cost allocation report shows your AWS costs for every billing period by product category and linked account owner. It's similar to the detailed billing report that you can generate but includes additional columns for the tag keys that you activate.

There are two types of AWS cost allocation tags: AWS-generated tags and user-defined tags. Before a tag can appear in the Cost Explorer or in a cost allocation report, you must activate it. You can't delete tags, but you can deactivate them.

Using Alerts and Notifications to Manage Costs You can monitor your costs by setting up CloudWatch billing alarms that notify you when your spending on AWS services exceeds an amount that you specify. An alarm is triggered when your account billing crosses the threshold that you specify.

To configure a billing alarm, you must first enable billing alerts. When you enable monitoring of estimated charges for your account, AWS calculates the estimated charges and sends them several times every day to CloudWatch as metrics. AWS stores all billing metrics in the US East (N. Virginia) region. The billing metrics include the estimated charges for both individual service usage as well as the overall total AWS charges. Exercise 10-11 shows how to enable billing alerts (you do this just once). After you enable billing alerts, you can create a billing alarm by subscribing to an Amazon SNS notification. Exercise 10-3 shows how to configure a billing alarm. In addition to a billing alarm, you can also subscribe to a price update notification, so you get a heads-up when AWS prices change.

 NOTE AWS provides automatic AWS Free Tier usage alerts using AWS Budgets.

AWS Cost and Usage Reports

AWS Cost and Usage Reports give you access to detailed cost and usage data, to help you understand your AWS spending and the usage amounts that led to those costs. To create a Cost and Usage Report, first click Reports on the AWS Billing Costs And Billing page (the Billing console). Click the Create Report button to create a report. Remember that you can generate three other types of reports:

- A cost and usage report through the Cost Explorer
- A Reserved Instances (RI) utilization report using the Cost Explorer
- A CSV-formatted AWS Usage Report for selected AWS services

You can configure a cost and usage report to integrate with Amazon Athena, which enables you to run standard SQL queries to analyze your billing data. You store your AWS cost and usage reports in Amazon S3 and use Athena to analyze the cost and usage data by running standard SQL statements.

AWS recommends that you create a new Amazon S3 bucket as well as a new AWS cost and usage report for use with Athena. After you do this, you can use the Athena AWS CloudFormation template to set up AWS Glue crawler, an AWS Glue database, and an AWS Lambda event.

Consolidated Billing for Organizations

The *consolidated billing* feature in AWS Organizations helps you consolidate billing and payment for multiple AWS accounts. Every organization in AWS Organizations has a master account, or *payer account*, and member accounts, or *linked accounts*. Each month, AWS charges the payer account for all the linked accounts in a single consolidated bill. The master account pays the charges for all the member accounts. There's no additional charge for using consolidated billing.

Consolidated billing provides the following benefits:

- You get a single bill for all accounts.
- You can track charges easily across accounts and download the combined cost and usage data. You can track the combined costs of all the linked accounts in your organization.
- You can combine usage across accounts to benefit from AWS's pricing tiers (volume pricing tiers) for services such as EC2 and S3 that reward higher usage with lower prices, and discounted prices for purchasing instances in advance (called *reservations* or Reserved Instances). By combining usage of services such as EC2 and S3 from multiple accounts, you can reach the lower price tiers faster. For example, if one of the AWS accounts purchases a Reserved Instance of a certain size, all the accounts in the organization can benefit from Reserved Instance pricing, provided they run the instances in the same region and use the same instance type and size. You can also apply any unused instance reservations from one member account to another.

You can set up consolidated billing by going to the AWS Billing and Cost Management Console, choosing Consolidated Billing | Getting Started, and following the directions.

Chapter Review

This chapter reviewed the key AWS monitoring services, such as AWS CloudWatch. CloudWatch is integrated with all AWS services, so you can use this service as a centralized monitoring mechanism and portal for most monitoring activities.

CloudTrail tracks and records all API activity that occurs in your account and serves as a useful auditing mechanism. AWS Config tracks your resource configuration and helps you figure out when a change occurred and who made the change. It also makes it easy for you to fix misconfigurations that adversely affect your systems, and it provides an auditing and compliance service.

Finally, this chapter explained two services and tools that help you optimize your AWS resource usage and lower your spending on AWS services. AWS Billing and Cost Management, accessible through the AWS Management Console, offers you ways to view your AWS spending according to various criteria, and it also generates reports. You can use tools such as the Cost Explorer, AWS Budgets, Cost Allocation tags, and Alerts and Notifications to stay on top of your AWS costs. AWS Trusted Advisor helps you find unused or underused resources, so that you can lower your bills by eliminating those resources from your account.

Exercises

These exercises are designed to teach you how to perform important AWS administrative tasks through the console. If you make a mistake, retrace your steps and ensure that you're correctly performing the steps. You'll know that you've correctly completed the exercise if you achieve the goal set for you in each exercise.

Exercise 10-1: Enable detailed CloudWatch monitoring for an EC2 instance.

1. Open the Amazon EC3 console: https://console.aws.amazon.com.ec2/.
2. In the navigation pane, select Instances.
3. Select the instance for which you want to enable detailed monitoring, and then select Actions | CloudWatch Monitoring | Enable Detailed Monitoring.
4. In the Enable Detailed Monitoring dialog box, select Yes, Enable.
5. Click Close.

Exercise 10-2: Create a CloudWatch dashboard.

1. Open the CloudWatch console: https://console.aws.amazon.com/cloudwatch/.
2. Select Dashboards | Create Dashboard.
3. In the Create New Dashboard dialog box, enter a name for your dashboard and click Create Dashboard.
4. In the Add To This Dashboard dialog box, add a graph to your dashboard by selecting Line | Configure. (You can also choose to add a number displaying a metric by choosing Number | Configure or add a text block by choosing Text | Configure.)
5. Click Save Dashboard.

Exercise 10-3: Create a CloudWatch billing alarm to monitor your estimated charges.

You must first enable billing alerts before you can create a billing alarm. This exercise walks you through both procedures.

1. Open the Billing and Cost Management Console: https://console.aws.amazon .com/billing/home?#.
2. In the navigation pane, select Preferences.
3. Select Receive Billing Alerts.
4. Click Save Preferences.
5. Open the CloudWatch console: https://console.aws.amazon.com/cloudwatch/.
6. In the navigation pane, select Alarms | Create Alarm.
7. Choose Select Metric | Billing | Total Estimated Charge.

8. Select the check box for Estimated Charges and click Select Metric.

9. For the Whenever My Total AWS Charges For The Month Exceed attribute, specify a monetary amount such as $500 (to trigger the alarm).

10. For Send A Notification To, select an existing notification list to specify a new one.

11. Click Create Alarm.

Exercise 10-4: View available CloudWatch EC2 metrics (by namespace/dimension) from the console.

1. Open the CloudWatch console: https://console.aws.amazon.com/cloudwatch/.

2. In the navigation pane, select Metrics.

3. Select EC2 as the metric namespace.

4. For the EC2 metric namespace, select the Per-Instance Metrics metric dimension.

5. In the All Metrics tab, select the check box in the heading row of the table to select all the EC2 metrics (you can filter the metrics).

Exercise 10-5: Create a graph for a CloudWatch metric.

1. Open the CloudWatch console: https://console.aws.amazon.com/cloudwatch/.

2. In the navigation pane, select Metrics.

3. In the All Metrics tab, enter a metric name (such as **CPUUtilization**) or resource name. Press ENTER.

4. Select one of the search results to view the metrics.

5. Select the check box next to each metric that you want to graph.

6. Select Graph Options | Add Horizontal Annotation. Enter the following:
   - Label: Enter a label for the annotation.
   - Value: Enter the metric value where the horizontal annotation appears.
   - Fill: Specify whether to use fill shading with this annotation (choose Above or Below for the corresponding area to be filled).
   - Axis: Specify whether the numbers in Value refer to the metric associated with the left Y axis or the right Y axis (if the graph includes multiple metrics).

7. Select Actions | Share to get a URL for the graph.

8. Select Actions | Add To Dashboard To add the graph to a dashboard.

Exercise 10-6: Enable detailed CloudWatch monitoring for an EC2 instance.

1. Open the EC2 console: https://console.aws.amazon.com/ec2/.

2. In the navigation pane, select Instances.

3. Select the instance and then select Actions | CloudWatch Monitoring | Enable Detailed Monitoring.

4. In the Enable Detailed Monitoring dialog box, select Yes, Enable.

5. Click Close.

Exercise 10-7: Set up a CloudWatch Load Balancer latency alarm using the AWS console.

1. Open the CloudWatch console: https://console.aws.amazon.com/cloudwatch/.

2. In the navigation pane, select Alarms | Create Alarm.

3. Under CloudWatch Metrics By Category, select ELB Metrics.

4. Select the row that contains the Classic Load Balancer and the Latency metric.

5. For the statistic attribute, select Average.

6. For the period, select 1 Minute.

7. Click Next.

8. Under Alarm Threshold, enter a name for the alarm and a description of the alarm.

9. Under Whenever, enter > for the Is attribute. Enter **3** as the value for the For attribute.

10. In Additional Settings, select Ignore for the Treat Missing Data As attribute.

11. Under Actions, select State Is ALARM for the Whenever This Alarm attribute. Select an existing SNS topic or create one for the Send Notification To attribute.

12. Click Create Alarm.

Exercise 10-8: Create a CloudTrail trail from the CloudTrail console.

1. Sign in to the AWS Management Console and open the CloudTrail console: https://console.aws.amazon.com/cloudtrail/.

2. In the Welcome to CloudTrail page, click Create trail.

3. In the Create Trail page, enter a name for the new trail in the Trail name box.

4. For the Apply Trail To All Regions attribute, select Yes (the default and recommended value).

5. In the Management Events section, select All (the default value) for Read/Write Events.

6. In the Data Events section choose the S3 tab, and then select Add S3 Bucket. Type the name of the S3 bucket (and an optional prefix) to which you want to log the data events.

7. For Storage Location | Create A New S3 Bucket, select Yes.

8. Enter a name for the S3 bucket you want to designate for storing the event log files.

9. Click Create.

10. You can see your new trail in the Trails page. CloudTrail publishes log files of all AWS API calls made in your account, starting in about 15 minutes. You can view the log files in the S3 bucket that you've specified.

Exercise 10-9: Create a CloudWatch alarm that is triggered by a CloudTrail event that makes changes to an EC2 instance.

You must first create a CloudWatch Logs log group for CloudTrail log events. You must also create a metric filter in CloudWatch Logs and then create the CloudWatch alarm based on the metric filter.

1. Open the CloudWatch console: https://console.aws.amazon.com/cloudwatch/.

2. In the navigation pane, select Logs.

3. Select the check box next to the log group that you've created for CloudTrail Logs events.

4. Select Create Metric Filter.

5. In the Define Logs Metric Filter screen, select Filter Pattern. Enter the following filter pattern (on one line):

   { ($.eventName = RunInstances) || ($.eventName = RebootInstances) || ($.eventName = StartInstances) || ($.eventName = StopInstances) || ($.eventName = TerminateInstances) }

6. Select Assign Metric.

7. Enter the following values:

   Filter Name: EC2InstanceChanges

   Metric Namespace: CloudTrailMetrics

   Metric Name: EC2InstanceEventCount

8. Select Show Advanced Metric Settings.

9. For Metric Value, enter the value **1**.

10. Select Create Filter.

11. In the Filters For *Log_Group_Name* page, select Create Alarm.

12. In the Create Alarm page, set the alarm threshold and define the actions to be taken when this alarm changes state (send notifications, Auto Scaling action, and so on).

13. Click Create Alarm.

Exercise 10-10: Create a CloudWatch event that triggers an event emitted by an EC2 instance.

1. Open the CloudWatch console: https://console.aws.amazon.com/cloudwatch/.

2. In the navigation pane, select Events | Create Rule.

3. Enter the following for Event Source attributes:

- Select Event Pattern: Build event pattern to match events by service
- Service Name: EC2
- Event Type: Select the specific event that should trigger the rule. Select Any… to have the event trigger on any type of the event that you've selected.

4. Select Add Target. For Targets, select EC2 as the service to act when an event is detected.

5. Select Use Existing Role to provide CloudWatch Events with the required permissions to send events to the target.

6. Click Configure Details. For the Rule Definition attribute, enter a name and disruption for the rule.

7. Click Create Rule.

Exercise 10-11: Enable billing alerts.

1. Open the Billing and Cost Management Console: https://console.aws.amazon .com/billing/home?#.

2. In the Billing pane, select Preferences.

3. Select Receive Billing Alerts.

4. Click Save Preferences.

Exercise 10-12: Create a billing alarm.

You must complete Exercise 10-11 (shows how to enable billing alerts) before you create a billing alarm.

1. Open the CloudWatch console: https://console.aws.amazon.com/cloudwatch/.
2. Change the Region to US East (N. Virginia), since that's where the billing metric data is stored.
3. In the navigation pane, select Alarms | Create Alarms.
4. Select Metric | Billing | Total Estimated Charge.
5. Select the check box next to EstimatedCharges, and then click Select Metric.
6. For the attribute Whenever My Total AWS Charges For The Month Exceed, specify the amount of AWS charges that must be exceeded to trigger this alarm.
7. For the Send A Notification To attribute, select a notification or create one.
8. Click Create Alarm.

Questions

The following questions will help you measure your understanding of the material presented in this chapter. Read all the choices carefully because there might be more than one correct answer. Choose all the correct answers for each question.

1. When you create custom CloudWatch metrics, which of the following are true? (Choose three)
    A. When you add a unique name/value pair (dimension) to a metric, you create a new variation of that metric.
    B. AWS can aggregate across dimensions for your custom metrics.
    C. AWS cannot aggregate across dimensions for your custom metrics.
    D. CloudWatch views each unique combination of dimensions as a separate metric.

2. For which of the following must you create a custom CloudWatch metric so you can monitor it?
    A. EC2 CPU utilization metrics
    B. EC2 Network I/O metrics
    C. EC2 Disk I/O metrics
    D. EC2 Memory utilization metrics

3. You have set up individual AWS accounts for each project. You've been asked to make sure your AWS infrastructure costs do not exceed the budget set per project per month. Which of the following approaches will help you ensure that you don't exceed your monthly budget?

  A. Consolidate your accounts so you have a single bill for all accounts and projects.

  B. Set up Auto Scaling with CloudWatch alarms using SNS to notify you when you are running too many instances in each account.

  C. Set up CloudWatch billing alerts for all AWS resources used by each project, with a notification occurring when the amount for each resource tagged to a project matches the budget allocated to the project.

  D. Set up CloudWatch billing alerts for all AWS resources used by each account, with e-mail notifications when it hits 50, 80, and 90 percent of its budgeted monthly spending.

4. A statistic set in Amazon CloudWatch is a way to do what?

  A. Specify the period length for CloudWatch to aggregate metric statistics.

  B. Specify the metrics for CloudWatch to collect metrics.

  C. Specify the unit of measure for a statistic.

  D. Specify a pre-aggregated dataset for a set of data points.

5. Which of the following services provide detailed monitoring without billing you for extra charges? (Choose two)

  A. Amazon Route 53

  B. AWS Auto Scaling

  C. Amazon RDS

  D. Amazon SNS

6. When using CloudWatch to monitor your AWS resources and applications, which of the following are true? (Choose three)

  A. Basic monitoring provides metrics for EC2 instances every one minute.

  B. Basic monitoring provides metrics for EC2 instances every five minutes.

  C. Detailed monitoring provides metrics for EC2 instances every one minute.

  D. Detailed monitoring provides metrics for EC2 instances every five minutes.

  E. When setting an alarm on a high-resolution metric, you can specify an alarm with a period of 10 or 30 seconds.

7. Which of the following are valid CloudWatch actions? (Choose three)

  A. An Amazon EC2 action

  B. An Amazon EC2 Auto Scaling action

  C. A notification to an Amazon SNS topic

  D. An Amazon DynamoDB action to stop the database

8. A CloudWatch alarm in the INSUFFICIENT_DATA state indicates which of the following?

   A. The alarm has just started.

   B. The alarm has just ended.

   C. The metric or expression is outside the threshold that you've defined for the metric.

   D. The metric is already in the ALARM state.

9. When configuring a CloudWatch alarm, you set the following values for determining the state of the alarm:

   - Period = 10 minutes
   - Evaluation Period = 6
   - Datapoints To Alarm = 6

   How long is the evaluation interval for this alarm?

   A. 10 minutes

   B. 30 minutes

   C. 60 minutes

   D. 120 minutes

10. What is the default behavior for missing data in a CloudWatch alarm?

    A. missing

    B. notBreaching

    C. breaching

    D. ignore

11. When you use CloudTrail logging, how do event logging and the billing for logging the events work? (Choose two)

    A. CloudTrail charges for both management and data events.

    B. Management events (the first copy) for each region are delivered free of charge, and there's a charge for data events.

    C. You can log events relating to activity in Amazon S3 buckets or AWS Lambda function execution activity.

    D. You can log events relating to activity occurring only in Amazon S3 buckets.

12. To which type of CloudTrail logging event do the Amazon EC2 `RunInstances` and `TerminateInstances` API operations belong?

    A. Read-Only

    B. Write-Only

    C. All

    D. None

13. Which of the following AWS services or tools can help you determine whether an EC2 security group is blocking the incoming TCP traffic to a specific port?

   A. AWS CloudFormation

   B. AWS CloudTrail

   C. AWS Inspector

   D. AWS Config

14. AWS Config evaluates your AWS resources with the AWS Config rules. Which of the following situations trigger an AWS Config evaluation of a resource to see if it violates the rule? (Choose three)

   A. When you create and activate a rule, AWS Config performs an initial evaluation of the resources to check if the resource satisfies the configuration rule.

   B. AWS Config triggers evaluations of a resource when there's a change in the configuration item's configuration.

   C. AWS Config runs periodic evaluations for a resource based on a frequency that you specify.

   D. You can use AWS Config to perform manual evaluations.

15. Which of the following is/are true regarding CloudWatch metrics and alarms?

   A. High-resolution metrics can be retrieved with a period that's a multiple of 60 seconds.

   B. You can set a high-resolution alarm with a period of 10 seconds or 30 seconds on a high-resolution metric.

   C. You can set a high-resolution alarm only with a period that's a multiple of 60 seconds on a high-resolution metric.

   D. Metrics produced by AWS services are high resolution by default.

16. When using CloudWatch, which of the following are true regarding EC2 instance status checks? (Choose all correct answers)

   A. A status check monitors CPU utilization, network, traffic, and disk activity.

   B. Status checks are performed every minute, and if all checks pass, the status of the instance is OK. If one or more of the checks fail, the overall instance status is deemed impaired.

   C. You can't disable or delete the status checks.

   D. You can create alarms that trigger based on the result of the status checks.

17. Which of the following statements are true regarding basic and detailed monitoring in AWS CloudWatch? (Choose two)

   A. Aggregate statistics are available for instances that use basic monitoring.

   B. CloudWatch doesn't aggregate data across regions.

   C. When you don't specify a dimension, CloudWatch returns statistics for all dimensions.

   D. When you don't specify a dimension, CloudWatch returns no statistics.

18. How long will a set of CloudWatch data collected using a period of one-minute detail be available to you? (Choose two)

  A. Initially for 15 days with a one-minute detail (resolution).

  B. After the 15 days are over, the data is still available, but with a coarser resolution of five minutes.

  C. After the 15 days are over, you must pay extra charges to view the data at the one-minute detail.

  D. After the 15 days are over, the data is deleted.

19. Which of the following AWS services or tools helps you answer the following question: What did my AWS resources look like six months ago?

  A. AWS Config

  B. AWS CloudTrail

  C. AWS CloudFormation

  D. AWS Inspector

20. Which of the following AWS services or tools helps you answer the following question: Who made the API calls to modify this EC2 instance, from which IP, and at what time?

  A. AWS Config

  B. AWS CloudTrail

  C. AWS CloudFormation

  D. AWS Inspector

21. Which of the following EBS checks helps you identify potential data consistency issues for an EBS volume?

  A. VolumeThroughputPercentage

  B. BurstBalance

  C. Volume usage–related checks

  D. EBS volume status checks

22. What does the EBS-related `AutoEnableIO` volume attribute do?

  A. It enables I/O to an impaired EBS volume.

  B. It enables I/O to a corrupted EBS volume.

  C. It enables I/O to an EBS volume for which EBS has disabled I/O, because it has detected potential data inconsistency on that volume.

  D. It enables I/O to a volume with the status of INSUFFICIENT-DATA.

23. Which of the following statements are correct when you're working with AWS CloudWatch Logs? (Choose two)

  A. Log retention settings are assigned to log groups.

  B. Log retention settings are assigned to log streams.

C. Metric filters are assigned to log groups.

D. Metric filters are assigned to log streams.

24. When you use the AWS-provided CloudWatch monitoring scripts for an EC2 Linux–based instance, which of the following statements are true about the metrics, and how does AWS bill you for the metrics? (Choose two)

A. The scripts report the data that they collect as standard metrics.

B. The scripts report the data that they collect as custom metrics.

C. AWS bills you CloudWatch standard usage charges for standard metrics when you use the scripts.

D. AWS bills you CloudWatch standard usage charges for custom metrics when you use the scripts.

25. Which of the following billing reports can you generate from the Billing page in the AWS Management Console? (Choose three)

A. A tag-based billing report

B. A Cost and Usage Report through the Cost Explorer

C. A Reserved Instances (RI) Utilization Report using the Cost Explorer

D. A CSV-formatted AWS Usage Report for select AWS services

Answers

1. **A, C, D. A** is true because when you assign a new dimension to a metric, such as an InstanceId dimension, you create a variation of that metric. **C** is correct because AWS can only aggregate across dimensions for metrics produced by certain AWS services, and not for your custom metrics. **D** is correct because even if the metrics have the same name, CloudWatch treats each unique combination of metrics as a different metric.

2. **D.** You must create a CloudWatch custom metric to monitor memory usage.

3. **C.** Set up CloudWatch billing alerts for all the AWS resources used by each project, with a notification occurring when the amount for each resource tagged to a project matches the budget allocated to the project.

4. **D.** You use a statistic set to insert a pre-aggregated dataset for large datasets. A statistic set provides CloudWatch the Min, Max, Sum, and SampleCount for a number of data points, and facilitates the publishing of metric data when you need to collect data several times in a minute.

5. **A, C.** CloudWatch provides detailed monitoring for Route 53 by default. Route 53 sends metrics to CloudWatch at one-minute intervals. Amazon RDS also sends its metrics to CloudWatch every minute, and detailed monitoring is enabled by default.

6. **B, C, E.** Basic monitoring provides metrics for instances every five minutes, and detailed monitoring provides metrics for instances every one minute. When setting an alarm on a high-resolution metric, you can specify an alarm (a high-resolution alarm) with a period of 10 or 30 seconds, or you can set a regular alarm with a period that's any multiple of 60 seconds.

7. **A, B, C.** A CloudWatch action can be an EC2 action, an EC2 Auto Scaling action, or an action that sends a notification to an Amazon SNS topic.

8. **A.** An alarm can be in the INSUFFICIENT_DATA state if the alarm has just started, the metric is unavailable, or there isn't sufficient data for the metric to determine the alarm state.

9. **C.** The evaluation interval is derived by multiplying the number of data points by the length of the period. In this case, the data points to alarm is 6 and the period is 10 minutes, so the evaluation interval is 60 minutes.

10. **A.** By default, missing data is considered missing.

11. **B, C.** The first copy of the management events for each region is delivered free of charge, and you're charged for all data events. You can have CloudTrail deliver trail events either to an S3 bucket or to an AWS Lambda function.

12. **B.** API activities pertaining to operations such as the Amazon EC2 `RunInstances` and `TerminateInstances` API operations modify (or might modify) your AWS resources, and hence fall under the Write-Only category of events. Read-Only events include API operations that read your resources but don't make changes. For example, read-only events include the Amazon EC2 DescribeSecurityGroups and DescribeSubnets API operations.

13. **D.** AWS Config enables you to view the configuration of your EC2 security groups, including the port rules that were open at a specific time.

14. **A, B, C.** AWS Config compares your resources to the conditions of the rule when you first activate the rule. After the initial evaluation, AWS Config triggers evaluations of a resource when there's a change in the configuration item's configuration. AWS Config runs periodic evaluations for a resource based on a frequency that you specify.

15. **B.** If you set an alarm on high-resolution metrics, you can specify a high-resolution alarm with a period of 10 seconds or 30 seconds. You can also set a regular alarm with a period that's any multiple of 60 seconds.

16. **A, B, C, D.** All four choices are correct.

17. **B, C.** CloudWatch doesn't aggregate data across regions, so metrics are separate between AWS regions. If you don't specify a dimension for a namespace, CloudWatch returns statistics for all dimensions in a namespace, such as the AWS/EC2 namespace.

18. A, B. CloudWatch stores the data points published with shorter periods for 15 days. CloudWatch aggregates data points published with shorter periods for long-term storage. Thus, data collected using a period of one minute may be available for 15 days with a one-minute detail (resolution), but after the 15 days are up, the data is still available to you, but you can retrieve it only at a coarser or aggregated resolution of five minutes.

19. A. AWS Config records point-in-time configuration details for all your AWS resources as configuration items.

20. B. AWS CloudTrail logs all API calls made to all AWS services and tracks which users made the calls, from which IP addresses, and on what day and time.

21. D. EBS volume status checks help you track and manage data inconsistencies on an EBS volume. These checks provide information that helps you ascertain whether a volume is impaired and about how to deal with a potentially inconsistent volume.

22. C. If data consistency isn't a big concern for you, and you want a volume to be available right away, you can override EBS default behavior when it encounters data inconsistency, by configuring the volume to enable I/O automatically with the `AutoEnableIO` attribute. This enables I/O to an EBS volume for which EBS has disabled I/O because it has detected potential data inconsistency on that volume.

23. A, C. Both metric filters and retention settings are assigned to log groups. All filters and retention settings that you apply to a log group are applied to log streams that belong to that log group.

24. B, D. The AWS-provided scripts make remote calls to CloudWatch to report the data that they collect as custom metrics. AWS bills you CloudWatch standard usage charges for custom metrics when you use the scripts.

25. B, C, D. You can generate a Cost and Usage Report and an RI Utilization Report, both via the Cost Explorer; you can also generate a CSV-formatted AWS Usage Report for select AWS services.

Provisioning Infrastructure, Deploying Applications, and Creating Scalable Infrastructures

In this chapter, you will

- Learn about AWS deployment and provisioning services
- Learn how AWS CloudFormation helps you provision your AWS infrastructure
- Learn how AWS OpsWorks helps you create instances and install necessary packages
- Learn how AWS CodeDeploy helps you manage your application deployments by working with your application code files and deployment scripts
- Learn how to use AWS Auto Scaling to scale your infrastructure

AWS offers several options for you to provision your infrastructure and deploy your applications. These options serve a variety of use cases, and offer scalability, performance, security, ease of deployment, and tools to migrate your applications over to the AWS cloud.

You can provision your AWS infrastructure by putting together services such as Elastic Compute Cloud (EC2), Simple Storage Service (S3), Amazon Elastic Block Storage (EBS), and Amazon Relational Database Service (RDS), and setting up an infrastructure with the help of third-party configuration management and deployment tools such as Chef, Puppet, Ansible, and Salt. However, AWS deployment services make it easy for you to automate your deployments, and they offer a flexible and easy way to set up complex infrastructures very quickly.

AWS Deployment and Provisioning Services

Each AWS deployment and provisioning service approaches application deployment differently and supports various strategies to update your applications. You can choose the deployment services that best suit your needs. In practice, you'll find that using a combination of deployment services is often best when managing several applications throughout their lifecycles.

Here's a list of the key AWS deployment and provisioning services:

- **AWS CloudFormation** This tool helps you provision and manage your cloud infrastructure. CloudFormation offers system administrators and network architects the ability to provision stacks of AWS resources based on templates that you create. Templates help you apply version control to your infrastructure and consistently replicate the infrastructure.

- **AWS OpsWorks** This tool helps developers and administrators deploy and manage applications in the AWS infrastructure. OpsWorks is ideal for complex applications, and AWS recommends that you use it whenever you think of using a configuration management tool such as Chef.

- **AWS CodeDeploy** This service manages your application deployments by working with your application code files and deployment scripts. It automates application deployments to either EC2 instances in the cloud or your on-premise instances. You can use CodeDeploy to deploy code to an infrastructure that you provision with CloudFormation or with the help of a third-party integration tool.

- **Amazon EC2 Container Service (ECS)** This service helps you manage Docker containers on a cluster of EC2 instances. ECS is a good choice if you use Docker for your deployments, or if you'd like to utilize your EC2 instance fully. (I discussed ECS in Chapter 4.)

- **AWS Elastic Beanstalk** This tool helps developers deploy their applications to AWS. Developers deploy code and don't need to bother with the underlying infrastructure. Elastic Beanstalk uses both Auto Scaling and Elastic Load Balancing (ELB) to support varying workloads and enables you to scale up your environment easily. (I discuss Elastic Beanstalk in Chapter 3.)

- **AWS CodeCommit** This AWS source control service hosts private Git repositories. You can store code and binaries in CodeCommit and integrate CodeCommit with other Git-based source control tools.

- **AWS CodePipeline** This continuous delivery and release automation service helps you check in, build, and deploy your application code into staging, testing, and production systems. AWS recommends that you use CodeCommit together with CodePipeline to make your development and release cycles more efficient.

Integration with Other AWS Services

AWS deployment and provisioning services all work well with other AWS services. For example, you can use tools such as ELB in Elastic Beanstalk, CloudFormation, and OpsWorks to help make your applications robust and resilient. Similarly, you can use AWS OpsWorks to create custom recipes to configure an application so it can access other AWS services.

Key Services Offered by AWS Deployment Services

The various AWS deployment services offer several features to help you configure and deploy applications and monitor and scale AWS services. Some deployment services offer several of these features, so there's some overlap among the services. However, each deployment service is designed to service specific needs; in this chapter, I point out the key purposes and use cases for each of the key deployment services, including AWS CloudFormation, AWS OpsWorks, and AWS CodeDeploy.

The overarching benefit of using AWS deployment services is to enable the automation of provisioning and configuring your infrastructure as well as the applications you run. Following the provisioning, these services also enable you to monitor the health of both the infrastructure and the applications. They can automatically replace failed infrastructure components and scale your infrastructure to match the needs of your applications.

I discuss the key features offered by AWS deployment services in general in the following sections.

Automating Infrastructure Provisioning

You can, of course, set up the individual pieces of your infrastructure yourself by provisioning components such as EC2 instances and S3 buckets. Deployment services can do the same thing, but they do it in a highly efficient and far less error-prone manner by enabling the automation of infrastructure provisioning.

A CloudFormation template enables you to treat *infrastructure as code*, by listing all the infrastructure components that you want to provision along with their configuration. Treating infrastructure as code also hands you a systematic, less error-prone, automatic, and repeatable means of deploying your resources. In addition to provisioning the resources, deployment services enable you to customize the AWS resources that you specify in a stack configuration, such as a CloudFormation template.

Facilitating Custom Variables

Deployment services help you customize custom configuration variables such as database connection strings and security credentials. Using variables instead of hard-coded values helps make your environment much more secure and helps you decouple your application's configuration from its code.

A good example of a custom variable is when you specify a parameter for database credentials in a CloudFormation template to enable a web server to connect to an RDS database. CloudFormation adds this parameter to the user data script of the EC2 instance on which the web server is running, making it easy for an application that you install on this EC2 instance to connect to the RDS database without having to provide separate credentials.

Custom variables enable you to separate your development, test, and nonproduction environments, which makes it easier for you to deploy different application tiers independently and helps make your applications more portable. They also enable you to scale the different tiers in a different manner.

Integrating with Instance Profiles

AWS uses *instance profiles* to embed the required Identity and Access Management (IAM) roles to perform various operations when you're working with AWS resources. An instance profile contains an IAM role that you can associate with an instance at instance launch time. Roles make secure API requests to the AWS services, without your having to manage the security credentials.

NOTE   An instance can have only a single IAM role, but you can create multiple profiles with the same IAM role.

AWS deployment services integrate with instance profiles and simplify credentials management on your part. You won't need to provide API keys as part of an application's configuration (by hard-coding the credentials) since the IAM role doesn't require you to do so. Roles help you securely handle temporary credentials for applications that run on various instances. For example, you can create an instance profile and assign write permissions on an Amazon S3 bucket to the associated IAM role. When you launch an instance, the instance profile helps specify an IAM role that should be associated with the instance. The deployment services will pass the role to EC2 instances so that the applications that run on those instances can utilize the temporary credentials provided by the role to access the Amazon S3 bucket and write to it.

Monitoring Resource and Application Health

AWS deployment services are well integrated with AWS monitoring services and provide overviews of your application's health. The CloudWatch console provides a system-wide view of all your AWS resources and their health. You can set up CloudWatch metrics to send alerts when EC2 instance status checks fail or to take a specific action (such as adding more EC2 instances) when a threshold, such as the level of CPU utilization, is crossed.

Deploying and Configuring Applications

Deployment services help you automate the deployment of your applications. All you need to do is to place your application code in a source repository and the deployment service can pick it up and provision the necessary resources to run the application.

Once an application is running, it may require changes in the underlying resources over time, whether they are for upgrading the applications, for replacing failed instances, or for automatically raising the number of instances to meet the workload demands. Deployment services can manage all these events, including the automatic scaling of resources.

The services help you customize and manage the configuration of your applications. They can perform tasks such as replacing custom configuration files for a web application (for example, httpd.conf) or updating packages.

Scaling Application Fleets

You can set various metrics for CPU, disk I/O, memory usage, and network I/O in CloudWatch that can trigger Auto Scaling to add or remove EC2 instances and other resources automatically based on the application workloads. Auto Scaling is integrated not only with CloudWatch, but also with Elastic Beanstalk, CloudFormation, and OpsWorks, to scale your resources automatically based on the workload or a specific time you set. Amazon Elastic Container Service (ECS) uses service Auto Scaling, which uses ECS, CloudWatch alarms, and Auto Scaling APIs to scale containers automatically.

Tagging Application Components

As you learned in Chapter 2, a tag consists of a key and value that you define. You can define tags for applications, projects, cost centers, and business division, all of which can help you easily identify to which unit a resource belongs. A cost allocation report summarizes your costs based on tags, helping you identify your spending for specific applications or projects.

If you specify tags during deployment with any of the AWS deployment tools, the tools propagate the tags to the infrastructure resources such as EC2 instances and RDS databases.

Monitoring Application Deployments

Deployment services offer easy visibility into the resources you run in the AWS cloud. The CloudWatch console provides a system-wide view of all your resources and their health. By configuring alarms for metric threshold violation, you can have CloudWatch send an e-mail alert when instances fail status checks or trigger an automatic scaling event when the CPU usage crosses a threshold that you configure.

Logging Applications

Logging helps you learn how your application is performing and also provides valuable debug information. All the AWS deployment services help you easily access the application logs through the AWS Management Console, CLI, and APIs, without forcing you to log into the EC2 instances to view the logs.

Deployment services are also integrated with CloudWatch Logs (see Chapter 10) to help you monitor the system and application log files. CloudWatch Logs help you monitor EC2 instance logs in real-time and archive log events in Amazon S3 for historical analysis.

Strategies for Updating Your Application Code

Often, you'll need to upgrade your application code. Upgrades can be potentially disruptive to your operations if they're not properly planned and managed. AWS deployment services help you speed up your application updates and keep the process easily manageable.

You can use several strategies for updating your application stacks, depending on which deployment service you use. The most comprehensive strategy is one where you perform an in-place upgrade. Let's start with the simplest update strategy, called *prebaking AMIs*.

Speeding Up an Application Rollout with Prebaked AMIs

In earlier chapters, you learned about Amazon Machine Images (AMI) in the context of launching EC2 instances. You must choose an AMI that you'll use for your application when you launch an EC2 instance. An AMI helps launch an instance by including the instance configuration details such as the block device mapping for the EBS volumes and the snapshot that should be used to create the EBS volume. The root volume can also consist of the base OS, as well as an application server and other application components. You can choose to install an application during an instance reboot, a process called *bootstrapping* an instance.

If your application is complex, the bootstrapping can be slow. The same is true if you've many applications to install at boot time. A better strategy would be to create your own AMIs by *prebaking* them. Prebaking an AMI speeds up an application rollout by incorporating most of the application artifacts within the base AMI. You can customize the application for various environments by specifying things such as instance tags, instance metadata, and Auto Scaling groups during the deployment. You do this through user data.

NOTE When you plan to use the same AMI in multiple regions, you must copy the AMI to all those regions, since an AMI has a regional scope.

Let's see how using prebaked AMIs eases your update process when managing a Ruby application that requires the Nginx web server (the front end), Elasticsearch Service, Logstash, Kibana (for processing logs), and MongoDB (for processing documents).

Your prebaked set of AMIs for this Ruby application will install most of the application. You can install the remaining portion of the application during the bootstrapping process and customize the installation by grouping configuration sets by instance tags, Auto Scaling tags, and so on. For example, you can tag your Nginx instances as Nginx-v-1.6.2. During the update, your deployment processes can check the instance tag for the Nginx instances to confirm that it's the latest version of Nginx.

TIP You can easily update a prebaked AMI by swapping the current AMIs with the latest versions in the deployment services you're using and updating the tags.

AWS deployment services such as CloudFormation and OpsWorks are ideal if you choose to use prebaked AMIs. You can also use third-party tools for prebaking AMIs, such as packer.io and aminator (built by Netflix), or you can use a configuration management tool such as Chef, Puppet, Salt, or Ansible.

How to Update the Application Stack

All the deployment services offer two basic methods for updating an application stack: *in-place* and *disposable* (aka replacement) upgrades:

- **In-place**   You update the applications that are running on the live EC2 instances.
- **Disposable (or replacement)**   You roll out a new application stack by provisioning a set of new EC2 instances, configuring the application traffic to go to the new set of instances, and terminating the instances in the old stack.

In-Place Upgrade   An in-place upgrade is ideal when you need to deploy an application quickly; it's also an ideal strategy when you have to perform frequent application updates. The in-place upgrade is meant for stateless applications, but even if your application is stateful, you can use the in-place upgrade strategy by implementing a *rolling deployment*. In-place upgrades can potentially lower your costs, because you reuse your AWS resources, such as the EC2 instances where the applications run. AWS CodeDeploy, AWS OpsWorks, and AWS Elastic Beanstalk are the deployment services that help with in-place upgrades.

AWS CodeDeploy helps you perform in-place application upgrades by automating application deployments. CodeDeploy primarily focuses on software updates and not on application deployment. It not only helps you upgrade applications faster by introducing code enhancements with no downtime, but it avoids the potential errors you incur when you use a manual deployment strategy. You push the application updates to deployment groups (sets of tagged EC2 instances), Auto Scaling groups, or both. You can handle the application deployment either individually (instances, database, storage) or via a build system such as GitHub, Jenkins, or Travis CI.

AWS OpsWorks helps you perform both application updates and application deployment. You can use either the built-in layers or deploy custom layers and recipes to launch the upgraded application stack.

AWS Elastic Beanstalk offers multiple options to deploy applications. Here's what you need to know regarding the various options:

- **All at Once**   This is the default deployment option.
- **Rolling**   Elastic Beanstalk splits your EC2 instances into batches and deploys the new version of the application to a batch at a time, with the other batches continuing to run the older application version. If a rolling update fails, it requires an additional rolling update to undo the changes.
- **Rolling with additional batch**   This rolling deployment with an additional branch deployment makes your environment launch a new batch of instances before it takes any instances out of service, to maintain full capacity during the deployment.
- **Immutable**   An immutable update launches a full set of instances that run the new application version in a separate Auto Scaling group (ASG), in parallel with the instances that are running the previous application version. An immutable environment update is an alternative to a rolling update and offers safety by

preventing issues due to partially completed (rolling) deployments. If the update fails, the rollback process just terminates the separate ASG, leaving the original set of instances untouched. Such in-place deployments keep you from having to provision a new stack—you can continue to use the same stack. However, they have the disadvantage that should you need to roll back the application, you must redeploy the older application version, which could be risky and could potentially disrupt your service.

Disposable Upgrade   Disposable, or replacement, upgrades are a good choice if your application has unknown dependencies that could potentially cause problems with a live upgrade of the running applications. This upgrade strategy is straightforward: you simply provision a new stack and direct your traffic to go to this new stack and stop the old stack. You don't have to bother yourself with the upgrading of the current instances and the possibility of unexpected bugs or other issues in the new application code.

A replacement upgrade avoids the problems of an incompletely rolled-out deployment. The two versions of the application, old and new, will run in separate ASGs. You also configure different ELBs for the two stacks and use a routing policy such as a weighted routing policy to gradually roll your traffic over from the old to the new stack.

You can clone your current environment with deployment services such as Elastic Beanstalk, CloudFormation, and OpsWorks. You can also use these deployment services along with Auto Scaling to perform the update process.

There are two basic ways to perform a disposable upgrade: use an Auto Scaling policy or use an update policy.

You can configure an Auto Scaling policy to specify the instances that should be added (scale out) or removed (scale in). You can use the scaling policy together with the update strategy to make the application update rollout a part of the scaling event. You can, for example, specify the OldestLaunchConfiguration attribute to terminate all instances that use the older configuration. You can configure an Auto Scaling launch configuration to use a new AMI that contains the new application code. The ASG can then use this new launch configuration to roll out the new application. You can also configure Auto Scaling policies in conjunction with your load balancer to remove the instances running the current application, and roll out the instances with the new application code.

You can alternatively configure a rolling deployment with services such as AWS CloudFormation and AWS Beanstalk. Update policies contain features that enhance application availability during an upgrade. You can use the update policies to control how the instances in an ASG are modified or replaced. You can configure update policies to enhance application availability during application updates. For example, you can do the following:

- Specify that a certain number of instances should be upgraded together.
- Specify the number of instances to be upgraded in batches.
- Specify the time to wait in between batches.
- Cancel or roll back updates if you notice errors in the new application code.

Migrating Traffic from Current to New Application Versions

A popular way to migrate traffic from your current application stack to a newer version of the stack is the *blue-green strategy*. A blue-green deployment applies to replacement upgrades. Under this strategy, you run identical stacks of your application in two different environments and migrate traffic from the current app stack to the new application version, based on your deployment needs. You can configure traffic to be switched from the old to the new stack immediately or after you complete fully vetting the new stack.

In this deployment model, the current application stack is considered *blue*, and the new version is *green*. You create the green version of the application by cloning the current (blue) version. Blue-green deployments offer several benefits when compared to an in-place deployment strategy:

- A blue-green deployment method offers zero downtime.
- Newer instances that are used in the green deployment come with update server configurations, which are more robust than the older server configurations.
- It enables you to test your new application versions fully and switch over to them when you're ready.
- As long as you terminate the instances in the old stack, you can easily switch back to the older application version quickly, should you need to do so.

Elastic Beanstalk, CloudFormation, and OpsWorks help you easily clone your current application stack to set up a green version of the application. Figure 11-1 shows a blue-green deployment.

The blue-green deployment method works differently for updating applications with session state and applications that are stateless.

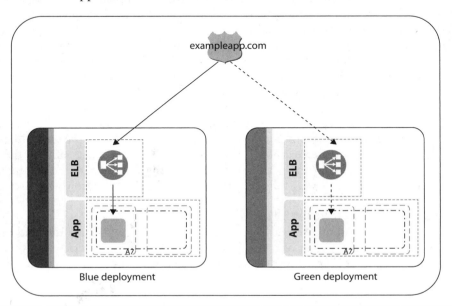

Figure 11-1 A blue-green deployment

Sessionless Applications   It's simple to update sessionless web applications. You upload the new (green) application version and submit a request to a deployment service such as Elastic Beanstalk, CloudFormation, or OpsWorks to deploy the new version. Moving to the new environment requires that you change the ELB URLs in the DNS records. You must also swap the ELB endpoints for CloudFormation or OpsWorks service, if you're using Route 53 as your DNS service. The Swap Environment URL feature in Elastic Beanstalk makes it easy to cut over to the new application version.

Stateful Applications   Applications with session states are more difficult to upgrade in a blue-green deployment strategy. To avoid end users losing data or experiencing downtime, it's a good idea to store their sessions outside the deployment service. AWS recommends that if you're using Amazon RDS or Amazon ElastiCache, you should seriously consider doing this.

TIP   You can configure a short TTL (time-to-live) for your cache on the client side to ensure that clients connect to the green deployment faster.

Amazon Route 53's Weighted Round Robin (WRR) feature is helpful when you're performing a blue-green deployment. The feature ensures that traffic moves to the new site gradually, rather than all at once, minimizing the impact on your users if you run into code bugs. You can use WRR, for example, to configure 20 percent of the traffic to go the new green deployment. As you get more confident with the new application, you can ramp up the percentage of traffic routed to the green deployment.

Blue-Green Deployments with Elastic Beanstalk

Elastic Beanstalk performs in-place updates to update an application version, which means that the application may briefly be unavailable. Perform a blue-green deployment to achieve a zero downtime capability.

You deploy the new version to a separate environment and simply swap the CNAMEs of the two environments to redirect your user traffic immediately to the new version. When you perform the blue-green deployment, swap the old environment's URL with that of the new environment to deploy the new version with no downtime.

Swapping the environment URL modifies Route 53's DNS configuration, which takes a few minutes, but the application will continue to run during this time. The CNAME records of the old and new environments are swapped, which redirects the traffic from the old version to flow to the new version. The opposite will also be true: traffic to the new instance will flow to the old environment. You must wait to terminate the old environment until the DNS changes are fully propagated and all old DNS records expire.

Using a Hybrid Deployment Model

You can choose from among several AWS deployment services. You can mix and match the services to get the most out of them. Some of the deployment services help you simplify the provisioning of the infrastructure, while others help you easily automate aspects of a deployment.

Following are some example scenarios of a hybrid deployment approach:

- Use CodeDeploy to deploy/manage multiple applications and provision infrastructure with EC2 and CloudFormation.

- Use CloudFormation to deploy an Elastic Beanstalk application.

- Use CloudFormation to deploy similar application stacks on OpsWorks and manage the infrastructure with CloudFormation.

- Use CloudFormation to deploy multiple application stacks and manage them with Elastic Beanstalk and OpsWorks.

Using AWS CloudFormation

I've shown how to configure key AWS services throughout this book. In a real-life scenario, to set up your system, you must deploy a fully configured environment with many AWS services, all of which must work well together as one cohesive system. Provisioning and configuring a full-fledged AWS infrastructure can be tedious and is prone to errors. AWS CloudFormation helps you create and provision your AWS infrastructure in a predictable fashion and enables you to repeatedly provision consistent sets of services.

 NOTE AWS CloudFormation is a free service, with you paying the standard charges of course, for the AWS resources that you create through CloudFormation.

CloudFormation lets you easily manage a set of related AWS resources as a single unit, or *stack*. You can create a *template* to describe the AWS resources that you want to provision, such as EC2 instances and DynamoDB databases.

Templates, Stacks, and Change Sets

CloudFormation uses a *template* both to provision and configure resources. CloudFormation simplifies your infrastructure management, since you use the CloudFormation template to describe all the resources and properties that you'd like to configure.

CloudFormation creates that set of resources as a *stack*. Creating a stack of resources has several advantages: you can easily modify, delete, and consistently replicate all the resources in a stack by using the template file that was the basis for the stack. You don't need to worry about the order in which to provision your AWS resources or the dependencies among the services, because CloudFormation manages all that for you.

After you deploy an environment with CloudFormation, you can modify and update it in a controlled and predictable manner with *change sets*, applying familiar version control strategies to your AWS infrastructure, just as you do with your application code. You can use CloudFormation and a source control system such as Git to deploy your infrastructure.

Templates

A CloudFormation template is a blueprint that helps you tell CloudFormation which resources it should provision and configure. A template is a JSON- or a YAML-formatted text file. You can specify multiple resources and their properties in a single template file. A template defines all the resources that you want to include in your stack, the set of related AWS resources.

I provide both a JSON and a YAML template as examples here, and going forward, I'll stick to the JSON-formatted templates when showing examples. Both the templates that I show here provision an EC2 instance and specify properties for the instance, such as the AMI ID to be used to launch the instance, the instance type, the key pair, and an EBS volume that should be attached to the instance. First, here's the template in a JSON file format:

```
{
  "AWSTemplateFormatVersion" : "2010-09-09",
  "Description" : "A sample template",
  "Resources" : {
    "MyEC2Instance" : {
      "Type" : "AWS::EC2::Instance",
      "Properties" : {
        "ImageId" : "ami-0ff8a91507f77f867",
        "InstanceType" : "t2.micro",
        "KeyName" : "testkey",
        "BlockDeviceMappings" : [
          {
            "DeviceName" : "/dev/sdm",
            "Ebs" : {
              "VolumeType" : "io1",
              "Iops" : "200",
              "DeleteOnTermination" : "false",
              "VolumeSize" : "20"
            }
          }
        ]
      }
    }
  }
}
```

Next, here's the same template as a YAML-formatted text file:

```
AWSTemplateFormatVersion: "2010-09-09"
Description: A sample template
Resources:
  MyEC2Instance:
    Type: "AWS::EC2::Instance"
    Properties:
      ImageId: "ami-0ff8a91507f77f867"
      InstanceType: t2.micro
      KeyName: testkey
      BlockDeviceMappings:
        -
          DeviceName: /dev/sdm
          Ebs:
            VolumeType: io1
            Iops: 200
            DeleteOnTermination: false
            VolumeSize: 20
```

The template shown here tells CloudFormation to launch an EC2 instance of a specific instance type from a specific AMI. An important thing to remember when creating a template is that you can also specify values such as the `InstanceType` parameter (in this example, its value is `t2.micro`) for an EC2 instance when you create the stack. This helps you use the same template for various purposes.

Templates are everything in CloudFormation. Therefore, it helps to look through a template, such as the JSON-formatted template fragment that I show here, to understand a template's structure:

```
{
  "AWSTemplateFormatVersion" : "version date",

  "Description" : "JSON string",

  "Metadata" : {
    template metadata
  },

  "Parameters" : {
    set of parameters
  },

  "Mappings" : {
    set of mappings
  },

  "Conditions" : {
    set of conditions
  },

  "Transform" : {
    set of transforms
  },

  "Resources" : {
    set of resources
  },

  "Outputs" : {
    set of outputs
  }
}
```

As you can see, there are several sections in the template, including Description, Parameters, Resources, and Outputs. Of these, only the Resources section is required; the other sections are optional. Let's quickly go over what the various sections help you do when you create a template to provision a stack or update an existing stack. (I use a JSON template fragment to show the examples for each section.)

Format Version Section This section shows the CloudFormation template version and describes the template's capabilities. Currently, the version is 2010-09-09 and is the only valid value for this section. Here's an example:

```
"AWSTemplateFormatVersion" : "2010-09-09"
```

If you don't specify a value for this section (remember that all sections except the Resources section are optional), CloudFormation assumes the latest template format version.

Description Section   This section describes the template by enabling you to include your comments about the template. Here's an example:

```
"Description" : "Here are the template details."
```

Metadata Section   This section enables you to include JSON or YAML objects that provide more information about the template, such as the template implementation details for specific resources such as instances and databases. Here's an example of a valid Metadata section declaration:

```
"Metadata" : {
  "Instances" : {"Description" : "Information about the instances"},
  "Databases" : {"Description" : "Information about the databases"}
}
```

 NOTE   You can't update the Metadata section by itself when you update a stack. You can do so only when you include changes that will add, modify, or delete the stack's resources.

CloudFormation can sometimes retrieve configuration settings that you define in the Metadata section. For example, you can use a CloudFormation-specific metadata key such as `AWS::CloudFormation::Init` to define this information and ask for a script named cfn-init that helps configure and install applications on EC2 instances.

Parameters Section   This section enables you to dynamically pass parameter values to the template at runtime, when you create or update a stack. Both the Resources and Outputs sections can access these parameters. Parameters help you customize the template each time you create or update a stack. Typical parameters are the EC2 instance type, key pairs, database ports, and so on. The following template snippet shows how you can specify `InstanceTypeParameter` to tell CloudFormation the EC2 instance type to provision for your stack:

```
"Parameters" : {
  "InstanceTypeParameter" : {
    "Type" : "String",
    "Default" : "t2.micro",
    "AllowedValues" : ["t2.micro", "m1.small", "m1.large"],
    "Description" : "Enter t2.micro, m1.small, or m1.large. Default is t2.micro."
  }
}
```

The default value of the `InstanceTypeParameter` is `t2.micro`. You should specify a different type if you don't want this instance type.

You can reference a parameter that you specify under the Parameters section from the Resources and Outputs section, through the `Ref` intrinsic function, as shown in this example:

```
"Ec2Instance" : {
  "Type" : "AWS::EC2::Instance",
  "Properties" : {
    "InstanceType" : { "Ref" : "InstanceTypeParameter" },
    "ImageId" : "ami-0ff8a91507f77f867"
  }
}
```

In this example, the `InstanceType` property of the EC2 instance under the Resource section references the value of the parameter `InstanceTypeParameter` that I've specified in the Parameters section.

NOTE There are several parameter types. The AWS-specific parameter type helps you find invalid parameter values. When you specify an AWS-specific parameter type, you must specify AWS values that currently exist in your AWS account. For example, if you specify the AWS-specific parameter type `AWS::EC2::VPC::Id`, the VPC ID that you enter must be from the AWS account and the region in which you're creating the stack. Other examples of AWS-specific parameter types are `AWS:EC2::AvailabilityZone::Name` (must enter an AZ such as us-west-2a) and `AWS::EC2::Image::id`, which requires you to enter a specific EC2 image ID such as ami-0ff4b824066h489.

Mappings Section   Use this section to specify *conditional parameter values* through key-value pairs. For example, a mapping can specify a region name as the key and the values will hold the values that you want to specify for each region. The Mappings section thus helps you run a CloudFormation script in more than one region. You can use the intrinsic function `Fn::findInMap` to retrieve the values in a map.

When you use the Mappings section, you must specify one or more keys, with each key mapping to a name-value pair that contains string values. The following example shows how to specify a mapping named `RegionAndInstanceTypeToAMIID` to map two environments, each running in a different AWS region, to a specific AMI. The keys here are the two region names, us-east-1 and us-west-2, and the name-value pair is the AMIID in each region, one for the test environment and the other for a production environment.

```
"Mappings" : {
    "RegionAndInstanceTypeToAMIID" : {
      "us-east-1": {
        "test": "ami-8ff710e2",
        "prod": "ami-f5f41398"
      },
      "us-west-2" : {
        "test" : "ami-eff1028f",
        "prod" : "ami-d0f506b0"
      },
```

```
    ...other regions and AMI IDs...

   }
 },

 "Resources" : {

  ...other resources...
```

Conditions Section   This section enables you to create a resource subject to conditions. For example, you can create a resource only for a production environment by specifying the appropriate condition.

A good scenario when you might want to use the Conditions section is when you use the same template in different environments, such as test and production. You can write a template with a Parameters section that uses the EnvType parameter with the values prod and test, and include the Conditions section to create a resource only in a specific environment, such as development or production.

You might use all of the following sections in your template to specify conditions:

- **Parameters**   Defines the input parameters that the condition must evaluate.
- **Conditions**   Uses intrinsic condition functions to define your conditions, to indicate whether CloudFormation should create the resources you associate with the condition. You use intrinsic functions such as Fn::And, Fn::If, Fn::Equals, and Fn::Or to define conditions. CloudFormation evaluates the conditions when you create or update a stack.
- **Resources**   Associates the conditions with the resources that'll be created subject to the conditions that you specify.
- **Outputs**   Associates the conditions with the outputs that'll be created subject to the conditions that you specify.

Here's an example template snippet that shows how to configure the Conditions section:

```
"Parameters" : {
    "EnvType" : {
      "Description" : "Environment type.",
      "Default" : "test",
      "Type" : "String",
      "AllowedValues" : ["prod", "test"],
      "ConstraintDescription" : "must specify prod or test."
    }
  },

  "Conditions" : {
    "CreateProdResources" : {"Fn::Equals" : [{"Ref" : "EnvType"}, "prod"]}
  },

  "Resources" : {
    "EC2Instance" : {
      "Type" : "AWS::EC2::Instance",
```

```
      "Properties" : {
        "ImageId" : { "Fn::FindInMap" : [ "RegionMap", { "Ref" :
"AWS::Region" }, "AMI" ] }
      }
    },
  "MountPoint" : {
      "Type" : "AWS::EC2::VolumeAttachment",
      "Condition" : "CreateProdResources",
      "Properties" : {
        "InstanceId" : { "Ref" : "EC2Instance" },
        "VolumeId"   : { "Ref" : "NewVolume" },
        "Device" : "/dev/sdh"
      }
    },

    "NewVolume" : {
      "Type" : "AWS::EC2::Volume",
      "Condition" : "CreateProdResources",
      "Properties" : {
        "Size" : "100",
        "AvailabilityZone" : { "Fn::GetAtt" : [ "EC2Instance",
"AvailabilityZone" ] }
      }
    }
  },
...
```

In this example, I specify an `EnvType` input parameter with two values: `test` and `prod`. For both environments, CloudFormation creates an EC2 instance, but for a production environment, it also attaches an EBS volume to the instance. As you see, the Conditions section can be very useful when reusing templates in different environments.

Transform Section   In this section, you can specify custom macros that CloudFormation can use to process a template. In addition to your own macros, CloudFormation supports the AWS::Serverless and AWS::Include macros.

The AWS::Serverless macro is meant for use with serverless (AWS Lambda) applications and enables you to specify the version of the AWS Serverless Application Model to use. Here's an example that shows how to specify two macros, one a custom macro named TestMacro, and the other, the AWS::Serverless macro.

```
AWSTemplateFormatVersion: 2010-09-09
Transform: [TestMacro, AWS::Serverless]
Resources:
    WaitCondition:
      Type: AWS::CloudFormation::WaitCondition
    MyBucket:
      Type: 'AWS::S3::Bucket'
      Properties:
        BucketName: MyBucket
        Tags: [{"key":"value"}]
        CorsConfiguration:[]
    MyEc2Instance:
      Type: 'AWS::EC2::Instance'
      Properties:
        ImageID: "ami-123"
```

Resources Section   This is the key mandatory section of a template; here you specify the stack's resources and properties. For example, you can specify an EC2 instance or an S3 bucket in this section. The two key fields of the Resources section are resource Type and resource Properties. In the following example, the value of the Type field is `AWS::EC2::Instance`, meaning that you want to create an EC2 instance. The Properties field has the value `ImageId`, which enables you to specify the AMI ID for your instance:

```
"Resources" : {
  "MyEC2Instance" : {
    "Type" : "AWS::EC2::Instance",
    "Properties" : {
      "ImageId" : "ami-0ff8a91507f77f867"
    }
  }
}
```

You can add several attributes to a resource to control the resource's behavior and relationships. I explain the key resource attributes in the following sections.

The `CreationPolicy` Attribute   When you associate the `CreationPolicy` attribute with a resource such as an EC2 instance, it prevents the status from reaching the *create complete* status until CloudFormation either receives a specific number of signals from the `cfn-signal helper script` (or with the SignalResource API) or the timeout period is exceeded.

Specify the `CreationPolicy` attribute when you want CloudFormation to wait for specific configuration actions to complete before it proceeds with the rest of the stack creation work. The `cfn-signal` script signals CloudFormation whether an instance has been successfully created or updated, and any software packages that you wanted installed on that instance have been successfully installed and are ready. You can use the `cfn-signal` script with a `CreationPolicy` or an ASG with a `WaitOnResourceSignals` update policy. When CloudFormation creates or updates the resource, it suspends work on the rest of the stack until the resource receives the required number of signals or the timeout period is exceeded.

The `DeletionPolicy` Attribute   When you delete a stack, CloudFormation deletes all resources by default. You can specify the `DeletionPolicy` attribute to tell CloudFormation to preserve or, in some cases, back up a resource when it's deleting a stack. You can also configure the attribute for stack update operations that cause a resource to be deleted from the stack. Here's an example that uses the Retain detention policy to ensure that when it deletes this stack, CloudFormation leaves the S3 bucket alone:

```
{
  "AWSTemplateFormatVersion" : "2010-09-09",
  "Resources" : {
    "myS3Bucket" : {
      "Type" : "AWS::S3::Bucket",
      "DeletionPolicy" : "Retain"
    }
  }
}
```

If, for example, you want to clean up your environment by deleting a stack but would like to retain important data stored in an RDS DB instance that's part of the stack, you can set the `DeletionPolicy` attribute for the RDS DB instance and create a snapshot of the database.

The `DependsOn` Attribute   By specifying the `DependsOn` attribute, you can specify that a resource be created after another resource is created first. Here's an example (in YAML format) that shows part of a template which specifies that when CloudFormation creates this stack, it should first create the RDS database named myDB, before creating the EC2 instance:

```
AWSTemplateFormatVersion: '2010-09-09'
Mappings:
  RegionMap:
    us-east-1:
      AMI: ami-0ff8a91507f77f867
    ...
Resources:
  Ec2Instance:
    Type: AWS::EC2::Instance
    Properties:
      ImageId:
        Fn::FindInMap:
        - RegionMap
        - Ref: AWS::Region
        - AMI
    DependsOn: myDB
  myDB:
    Type: AWS::RDS::DBInstance
    Properties:
      AllocatedStorage: '5'
      DBInstanceClass: db.m1.small
      Engine: MySQL
      EngineVersion: '5.5'
      MasterUsername: MyName
      MasterUserPassword: MyPassword
```

Outputs Section   This section specifies the values that are shown when you view a stack's properties—say when you execute the `aws cloudformation describe-stacks` command or view properties in the AWS CloudFormation console. You may, for example, want to specify an S3 bucket name in the Outputs section to make it easier for you to find the bucket. Here's an example that shows how to specify the Outputs section:

```
"Outputs" : {
    "DomainName" : {
      "Description" : "Fully qualified domain name",
      "Value" : { "Ref" : "MyDNSRecord" }
    }
```

You can also use the output values that you declare in the Outputs section to import the values into other stacks (this is called creating a *cross-stack reference*).

Using AWS-Provided Sample Templates (and Snippets) vs. Creating Your Own

AWS offers several template snippets and sample templates by AWS service, as well as complete application framework templates that help you provision application frameworks such as LAMP and Ruby on Rails. The template samples and snippets are for provisioning AWS services such as EC2 Load Balancing, Redshift, Route 53, Amazon S3, and Amazon VPC. For example, the Load-Based Auto Scaling Template helps you create an ASG with scaling policies based on CPU usage. The Route 53 Weighted Records Template creates Route 53 weighted CNAME records for you. A template's parameters (optional) enable you pass in values to a template to customize your resources.

You can create your own template in one of three ways:

- Write one in a text editor.
- Design the template in the AWS CloudFormation Designer tool. This tool helps you create and modify templates and is especially helpful to those that aren't comfortable with the JSON or YAML formats.
- Use an AWS-provided sample template, modifying it where necessary.

It's a good idea to go through the AWS CloudFormation Sample Template Library first before trying to create your own templates. From the Library web page, you can not only view the templates in the AWS CloudFormation Designer (the link to the Designer is provided on this page), but it also helps you launch the stacks described in the templates with a Launch Stack button. Here, for example, is how a sample AWS Route 53 Weighted Records Template looks (you can see this by clicking the template's View link):

```
{
  "AWSTemplateFormatVersion" : "2010-09-09",

  "Description" : "AWS CloudFormation Sample Template Route53_RoundRobin: Sample
template showing how to use weighted round robin (WRR) DNS entries via Amazon
Route 53. This contrived sample uses weighted CNAME records to illustrate that
the weighting influences the return records. It assumes that you already have a
Hosted Zone registered with Amazon Route 53. **WARNING** This template creates
one or more AWS resources. You will be billed for the AWS resources used if you
create a stack from this template.",

  "Parameters" : {
    "HostedZone" : {
      "Type" : "String",
      "Description" : "The DNS name of an existing Amazon Route 53 hosted zone",
      "AllowedPattern" : "(?!-)[a-zA-Z0-9-.]{1,63}(?<!-)",
      "ConstraintDescription" : "must be a valid DNS zone name."
    }
  },

  "Resources" : {
    "MyDNSRecord" : {
      "Type" : "AWS::Route53::RecordSetGroup",
      "Properties" : {
        "HostedZoneName" : { "Fn::Join" : [ "", [{"Ref" : "HostedZone"}, "." ]]},
        "Comment" : "Contrived example to redirect to aws.amazon.com 75% of the
```

```
time and www.amazon.com 25% of the time.",
      "RecordSets" : [{
        "SetIdentifier" : { "Fn::Join" : [ " ", [{"Ref" : "AWS::StackName"},
"AWS" ]]},
        "Name" : { "Fn::Join" : [ "", [{"Ref" : "AWS::StackName"}, ".", {"Ref"
: "AWS::Region"}, ".", {"Ref" : "HostedZone"}, "."]]},
        "Type" : "CNAME",
        "TTL" : "900",
        "ResourceRecords" : ["aws.amazon.com"],
        "Weight" : "3"
      },{
        "SetIdentifier" : { "Fn::Join" : [ " ", [{"Ref" : "AWS::StackName"},
"Amazon" ]]},
        "Name" : { "Fn::Join" : [ "", [{"Ref" : "AWS::StackName"}, ".", {"Ref"
: "AWS::Region"}, ".", {"Ref" : "HostedZone"}, "."]]},
        "Type" : "CNAME",
        "TTL" : "900",
        "ResourceRecords" : ["www.amazon.com"],
        "Weight" : "1"
      }]
    }
  }
 },

 "Outputs" : {
   "DomainName" : {
     "Description" : "Fully qualified domain name",
     "Value" : { "Ref" : "MyDNSRecord" }
   }
  }
 }
}
```

You can store the templates that you create locally or in an S3 bucket by saving the file with a file extension such as .json, .yaml, or .txt. When creating the stack, you can specify the location of your template file. If you stored the template in S3, you provide an Amazon S3 URL for the file. If you specify a local location for the file, CloudFormation uploads the file to an S3 bucket that it creates in the region in which you upload the template file. If the CloudFormation-created S3 bucket already exists, it just adds the template to that bucket.

Stacks

As I mentioned earlier, a stack is a set of AWS resources that's created as a single unit, and it enables you to update and delete those resources as a single unit. To create a set of related AWS resources such as a load balancer, a database, and a set of EC2 instances, you first create a template and then submit that template so that CloudFormation can create all those resources in one move.

 TIP A template that you store in a S3 bucket must be in the same region as that of the stack that you want to create with that template.

When you create or update a stack with CloudFormation, the service makes service calls to the pertinent AWS services to provision the resources that you specify in the template. For example, it makes a service call to the appropriate Amazon EC2 API to specify the instance type as t1.micro. You must have the required permissions for the actions that CloudFormation needs to perform.

If CloudFormation fails to create a stack, it rolls back all your changes and deletes any resources it may have created before the stack creation process hits an error. Thus, a stack is an *all or nothing* concept—CloudFormation will never create only a portion of the resources that you've specified in a stack. So, for example, if your stack includes EC2 instances, ELB, RDS, and Auto Scaling, and during the stack creation CloudFormation creates everything else but fails to create the RDS database instance, it rolls back all the changes and terminates all the services that it has created (EC2 instances and ELB in this case).

 NOTE Exercise 11-6 shows how to create a WordPress stack for an example template from the AWS CloudFormation Sample Template Library. The sample template creates a WordPress blog with one EC2 instance, a MySQL database, and an EC2 security group to control the firewall settings for the EC2 instance.

Change Sets

Updating a stack by submitting a modified template can result in unexpected consequences. You can generate a *change set* to find out how a planned change will affect a stack's resources. The change set provides a preview of the impact of the planned changes to a stack. If, for example, you rename an RDS database, CloudFormation deletes the current database and creates a new one. You may lose the data in the current database as a result. By generating a change set before you update a stack, you can avoid such events.

Although using a change set is a wise way to go about updating a stack, you can also directly update a stack. When you use a change set to update a stack, CloudFormation shows you a preview of the impact of the planned changes. It changes a stack's components only if you execute the change set.

You start a change set in motion for a currently provisioned and running stack by providing CloudFormation with a modified template (that is, a modification of the original template that you used to create this stack)—say, by adding a new resource to the stack, by providing new input parameters, or both. CloudFormation will then generate the change set by looking at the differences between the running stack and the changes that you submit.

Creating a Change Set   When you create a change set, you can provide your changes in the form of a modified template, by supplying new input parameter values, or by doing both. Exercise 11-7 shows how to create a change set from the console. In the console, select Change Sets in the Stack Detail pane to view the stack's change sets.

Executing a Change Set   After creating a change set, you can view both a summary of your changes as well as a detailed list of changes (in JSON format) from the console, or via the AWS CLI. After selecting your change set in the CloudFormation console and viewing the proposed changes, choose Execute to execute the changes. This makes CloudFormation start updating the stack. You can run the `aws cloudformation describe-stacks` command to view the progress of the stack update. By cancelling a stack update while the stack is still in the UPDATE_IN_PROGRESS state, you can roll the stack back to its original configuration.

Directly Updating a Stack   If you're certain that you don't need to preview the changes that you intend to perform, you can directly update a stack by submitting an updated template and/or the changes to the input parameters. CloudFormation *immediately* deploys the changes (deltas) to update your stack. You can do this from the console or with the `aws cloudformation update-stack` command from the command line.

AWS Best Practice Recommendations for CloudFormation

AWS offers several best practice recommendations to help you get the most out of Cloud-Formation. I summarize the key best practices in three key areas: planning and organizing, template creation, and stack management.

Planning and Organizing CloudFormation Stacks

The following strategies help you plan and organize your CloudFormation stacks.

Avoid using a single stack for everything.   Try not to use a single stack for all the resources that you want to provision. A single stack makes it more difficult to modify your stacks and leads to conflicts among the various functional groups. Group resources with similar lifecycles and the same owners into separate stacks. You can do this via a layered stack, where each layer can have multiple stacks with the requirement that those stacks should have the same owner and a similar lifecycle. You can also organize your stacks based on services by mapping each service to a separate stack.

Export shared resources.   Instead of hard-coding resource values that are in another stack or using input parameters to pass resource names and IDs, export the resources from a stack to other stacks via cross-stack references. The other stacks can import the stacks with the implicit function `Fn::ImportValue`.

Use service roles.   You can separate user permissions from those of the CloudFormation service, through a service role. A service role is an IAM role that lets CloudFormation make calls for you. Let CloudFormation use the service role's policy instead of using the user's policy to make calls to create, modify, or delete resources on your behalf. When you do this, CloudFormation uses the role's credentials. You can limit the actions that CloudFormation can perform through the service role, instead of letting it have all the privileges that you have. For example, you may have admin privileges, but you can configure the service role so that CloudFormation can perform only certain actions, such as only EC2-related actions.

Reuse your templates.   Reusing your templates helps you replace configurations in different environments such as development, test, and production environments. By using the Parameters, Mappings, and Conditions sections, you can customize your stacks and make them reusable. You can reuse common template patterns by using nested stacks within a single stack. A nested stack creates other stacks. For example, you can create a template just for configuring your EC2 instance, by specifying configurations such as the instance type and the EBS volumes you want to attach to those instances. Instead of explicitly configuring EC2 instances in your stacks, you can then use the main CloudFormation template to reference the dedicated EC2 instance template from any other stack. When you do things this way, you need to update only your EC2 instance stack templates, without having to update the entire stack configuration.

Creating a Template

Use the following strategies when creating your templates.

Don't embed credentials in templates. To secure your systems, use input parameters whenever you need to specify credentials, rather than embedding them directly within a template.

Use AWS-specific parameter types. As explained earlier, use AWS-specific parameter types such as `AWS::EC2::KeyPair::KeyName` to use existing values for instance types, VPC IDs, key pairs, and similar entities. Let CloudFormation use those existing values in your account instead of specifying them explicitly in your stack templates.

Use parameter constraints. By specifying constraints on the allowed values for stack inputs such as database user credentials, you enable CloudFormation to trap invalid values when you use a template to create a stack.

Use `AWS::CloudFormation::Init` to deploy applications. AWS CloudFormation provides the *cfn-init* helper script and the `AWS::CloudFormation::Init` resource to help you install and configure applications on EC2 instances. Using these tools, you can avoid scripting the steps for creating and configuring the applications. You avoid the usual procedural steps and instead can follow a declarative approach to creating your application stacks by using this strategy.

Ensure that your instances use the updated helper scripts. Since CloudFormation updates its helper scripts regularly, include the following command in the UserData property of your template:

```
yum install -y aws-cfn-bootstrap
```

Validate your templates. Before you create or update a stack with a template, validate the template. The CloudFormation console validates templates after you specify any input parameters, and you can validate from the command line with the `aws cloudformation validate-template` command.

Specify a wait condition (`AWS::CloudFormation::WaitCondition`). Do this for situations such as when you need to coordinate the stack resource creation with external actions, or to track the status of a configuration process. AWS recommends, however, that for EC2 and Auto Scaling resources, you use a `CreationPolicy` attribute instead of a wait condition. Add this attribute to the resources and use the `cfn-signal` helper script to notify CloudFormation when an instance creation process finishes successfully. Don't directly modify a stack's resources; use CloudFormation to update a stack's resources so that you can avoid problems when you try to update or delete the stack.

Managing a Stack

The following principles help you efficiently manage a CloudFormation stack.

Create change sets. Change sets enable you to see the impact of the changes to a stack before you implement those changes. As mentioned earlier in this chapter, CloudFormation may re-create an RDS database instance when all you want to do is to change the instance name! Create a change set every time you are planning stack changes.

Use stack policies. Probably the most important thing you can do when managing a CloudFormation stack is to create a stack policy that specifies the updates that CloudFormation can perform on critical resources. A stack policy is a JSON document that can prevent unintentional updates to key resources. This isn't mandatory, technically speaking, but from an operating perspective, not setting up the stack policy would amount to malpractice.

Log all CloudFormation calls. As you'll recall, AWS CloudTrail logs all CloudFormation API calls. By enabling the logging of all CloudFormation calls to CloudTrail and storing them in Amazon S3, you build yourself a powerful and effective audit mechanism for CloudFormation activity.

Use code reviews and revision control. By adopting code review and revision control, you can track the changes made to a template over time, and thus track all changes made to your resources. This also helps you easily reverse the changes to a template version.

Using AWS OpsWorks

Configuration management (CM) tools such as Puppet, Chef, Ansible, and Salt have become popular in many organizations. AWS OpsWorks is a CM service for the cloud based on Puppet or Chef. AWS offers the following OpsWorks services:

- **AWS OpsWorks for Puppet Enterprise** Manages Puppet Enterprise software and lets you create an AWS-managed Puppet master server that manages all the nodes in your infrastructure.

- **AWS OpsWorks for Chef Automate** Automates the management of the Chef Server and the Chef Automate Server software.

- **AWS OpsWorks Stacks** The original OpsWorks service that helps you create and manage stacks of instances and helps you deploy and monitor applications on those stacks.

To work with AWS OpsWorks, you must understand its key components:

- Stacks
- Layers
- Instances
- Apps
- Cookbooks and recipes

Earlier in this chapter, I explained the concept of a CloudFormation stack, which is a set of related instances such as application servers, database servers, and load balancers that are provisioned together as a single unit, or stack. AWS OpsWorks uses a similar stack to help you create the instances and install the necessary packages. A stack is a set of instances and related resources that serve a common purpose and that you manage together as a single, cohesive unit. In addition to serving as a provisioning tool, OpsWorks stacks also help you distribute the applications to the app servers and monitors the stack's performance.

Stacks

The stack is the fundamental OpsWorks Stacks component. A stack denotes a set of AWS resources such as EC2 instances and RDS database instances that are meant to be deployed and managed as a single unit. Stacks help you define common configuration settings such as the operating system for a set of EC2 instances.

A simple stack for serving a web application, for example, might consist of an application server instance, a load balancer instance, and a database instance. Typically, you create a separate stack for each environment, such as a development stack, a staging stack, and a production stack, so that you can manage them separately. Once you create a stack, you're free to clone and update the stack. You can create multiple stacks from the same CloudFormation template by using CloudFormation *parameters*.

A stack consists of *layers*, which I explain shortly. Thus, when you create an instance and add it to a layer through OpsWorks Stacks, the instance will have both its basic configuration settings as well as the settings that you've specified in the layer.

To manage instances, OpsWorks Stacks installs an agent on each instance. The agent helps run recipes in response to various lifecycle events. With the *autohealing* feature, if the OpsWorks Stacks agent can't communicate with service, it restarts the instance.

There are three instance types, depending on how you start and stop them:

- You can start *24/7 instances* manually and they'll run until you stop them.
- You can use *time-based instances* and run them on a specific daily/weekly schedule.
- You can use *load-based instances*, and OpsWorks stacks automatically start and stop them.

Exercise 11-9 shows how to create a demo Linux stack from the OpsWorks console. You can also create a stack from the AWS CLI by running the following command from the AWS CLI, as shown in this example:

```
$ aws opsworks --region us-west-1 create-app --stack-id 8c428b08-a1a1-46ce-a5f8-
feddc43771b8 --name SimpleJSP --type java --app-source file://appsource.json
```

Layers

A stack is made of layers, sets of EC2 instances that do a similar thing, such as those that serve applications or run database instances. Earlier, I mentioned a simple stack for serving a web application that consists of several application server instances, an ELB layer, and an RDS layer. You can also create an ECS cluster layer. Each of these is a layer in the web application stack. You can similarly have an ECS cluster layer and other layers to represent other services. A *service layer* is common to all stacks and consists of the RDS, ELB, and ECS services.

Layers enable you to customize a set of instances by installing a set of packages—for example, on all instances in a layer—and they help you deploy applications on the set of instances.

Following is what you need to remember about layers:

- Each layer must have a minimum of one instance.
- Each instance in a stack must belong to at least one layer.
- You can't directly configure an instance that belongs to a layer (except for a few things such as the hostname and the SSH key).
- You can't directly configure the instances you want to add to a layer. You must first create a layer, and then configure it, and then add the instances to that layer.
- You can stop and start the instances manually or let OpsWorks Stacks automatically scale the instances for you.

Exercise 11-10 shows how to create a layer in a stack. All stacks permit time-based automatic scaling, while a Linux stack also allows load-based scaling.

EC2 instances optionally can be members of multiple layers. Use cases for assigning the same instance to multiple layers include a situation in which you want to run both your load balancer and the database on a single instance. OpsWorks will run its recipes for each of the instance's layers. Another scenario is where you create an administrative layer to your web application stack and add one of the several application servers to the layer. You can create recipes for the administrative layer to configure this instance for administration-related tasks. You can also configure a recipe for running the application server on this instance by sourcing the recipes from the application server layer.

Instances

An instance, as you know, is a single computing resource, such as an EC2 instance. The instance defines just the basic configuration of the service, such as its operating system. The layer to which the instance belongs defines the additional configuration settings such as the instance's EIP addresses.

Remember the following about instances:

- An EC2 instance can be a member of multiple layers.
- You can't add a running instance to a layer.
- If an instance belongs to multiple layers, add the instance to all those layers before stacking the instance.
- You can register instances created outside OpsWorks Stacks with a Linux stack.

Apps

An app is the code that you want to run on an application server. You specify the application server instances when you want to deploy your code within the app. The app is a container for your application and contains metadata such as the application's name and other information, such as the repository URL that it needs to deploy the application to the instances.

OpsWorks Stacks deploys the application from a S3 bucket where you store it. (You can store the app in other places as well, such as GitHub or a publicly accessible HTTP bundle.) Deployed recipes dictate the deployment process, and the recipes are determined by the instance's layer.

The main purpose of a deployment with OpsWorks is to deploy application code and other artifacts to the application server instances. Deploying refers to the deployment of the application's code and all related files as a single unit to the application's server instances. When you run the app, OpsWorks Stacks can trigger deploy events to run the deploy recipes for each of the stack's layers on the stack's servers. The layer to which the instance belongs determines each instance's deploy recipes.

If you're starting up the instance, once the recipes are set up, OpsWorks Stacks runs the instance's deploy recipes automatically. If you add or modify an app, you must deploy it yourself to any online servers.

Cookbooks, Recipes, and Lifecycle Events

OpsWorks Stacks uses Chef cookbooks to install and configure packages and to deploy applications. OpsWorks supports various versions of Chef, ranging from version 0.89 through 12 for Linux stacks and version 12.2 for Windows stacks.

You can run the recipes manually with the `Execute Recipes stack` command or by using the agent CLI. You can also run them manually by assigning the recipes to the relevant layer in the OpsWorks Stacks lifecycle events. Each layer has a set of five lifecycle events, and there's an appropriate set of recipes for each of these five events. Here are the five OpsWorks Stacks lifecycle events:

- **Setup** This event occurs after an instance completes booting.
- **Configure** This event occurs when an instance enters or leaves the online state, when you associate/disassociate an EIP address with an instance, or when you attach/detach an ELB to a stack's layer.
- **Deploy** This event occurs when your run a `Deploy` command to deploy an application to a set of instances. The command can also update the configuration of other instances so that they can handle an app that was deployed on a set of servers.
- **Undeploy** This event occurs when you delete an application or run the `Undeploy` command to remove an app from one or more instances. The instances will then run the Chef recipes to remove all app versions and perform a cleanup.
- **Shutdown** OpsWorks Stacks runs recipes to shutdown services.

Resource Management

Resource management enables you to use your account's resources such as EIP addresses, EC2 instances, and EBS volumes in an OpsWorks Stacks stack. You can register these resources with a stack and attach, move, or detach a resource to and from the stack's instances.

AWS CodeDeploy

AWS CodeDeploy is an AWS deployment service that automates application deployments to compute services such as EC2, on-premise servers, Lambda, and ECS. CodeDeploy makes it easier to release new features and avoid downtime during the deployments. If you need to update your applications frequently, CodeDeploy is something you need to investigate, because it eliminates the complexity and error potential of messy manual deployments.

You can use the CodeDeploy service to deploy a variety of application artifacts, such as code, Lambda functions, web configuration files, scripts, executables, and packages.

CodeDeploy offers the following key benefits:

- Automated software deployments on multiple compute services.
- Centralized control over your deployments, including detailed reports about your application revisions. You can also configure push notifications to get live deployment updates.
- Maximize application uptime and easy rollback to the previous release if there are errors.
- Platform- and language-agnostic and integrates with your software release processes and continuous delivery (CD) toolchains such as AWS CodePipeline, GitHub, and Jenkins.

Key CodeDeploy Concepts and Terminology

In addition to the application that you want to deploy and the platform on which you want to deploy it, there are several key CodeDeploy components relating to the deployment process, such as deployment configuration, deployment group, deployment type, IAM instance profile, revision, and service role. I explain these concepts here.

Deployment Configuration　The deployment configuration lays out rules for a successful deployment, such as the minimum number of healthy instances in the deployment, if you're deploying to EC2 instances or an on-premise platform.

Deployment Group　This is a set of individually tagged instances, such as EC2 instances, in an EC2 Auto Scaling group. It can include the group as well.

The members of a deployment group differ between a blue-green versus an in-place deployment. In a blue-green deployment, you need two environments, and you gradually switch over traffic from the blue to the green environment. (This is true only for EC2 and on-premise instances; for ECS, the replacement is all at once.)

In a blue-green deployment, CodeDeploy creates the instances in the green (replacement) environment during deployment. You can either manually specify the instances for the replacement environment or specify an EC2 ASG as a template that CodeDeploy can use for the replacement environment, with identical number of instances as well as an identical configuration.

Deployment Type   The deployment type determines how you choose to make the new application version available to your users. The type can be an in-place deployment or a blue/green deployment.

IAM Instance Profile and Service Role   The IAM instance profile is an IAM role that you attach to the EC2 instances. The role has permissions to access the locations where you've stored the application artifacts, such as an S3 bucket or a GitHub repository. The service role is also an IAM role, and you use it to grant permissions to AWS services such as EC2 ASGs and ELBs to access and perform actions on your AWS resources such as EC2 instances. The service role also helps publish status reports to SNS topics so that push notifications are sent when deployment or instances occur as part of the deployment effort.

Revisions   Revisions (aka application revision) are files that contain information about the deployment. For an EC2 or on-premise deployment, the revision is an archive that contains the source code, executables, and scripts in an application specification file named AppSpec file. The AppSpec file contains the steps you want CodeDeploy to execute. For Lambda deployments, the revision is a YAML/JSON file that contains details of the Lambda function. The EC2/on-premise revisions are stored in S3 buckets or GitHub repositories, while Lambda revisions are stored in S3 buckets only.

A *target revision* is the most up-to-date application revision in the repository that you want to deploy to a deployment group. CodeDeploy always pulls the target revision for automatic deployments.

Outline of the CodeDeploy Deployment Process
Following is an outline of how CodeDeploy deployments work:

1. You bundle the deployment code and other artifacts along with the AppSpec file into an archive (the revision) and upload it to an S3 bucket or to a GitHub repository.

2. Let CodeDeploy know two things: the location to which you've uploaded the application revision, and the deployment group to which you want CodeDeploy to deploy the contents of the revision.

3. CodeDeploy agents on your instances (you must install these beforehand) poll CodeDeploy to find where to pull the revision from (S3 bucket/GitHub repository).

4. The CodeDeploy agent on each instance pulls the target revision and deploys the contents on the instance by following the deployment steps you've specified in the AppSpec file.

Using AWS Auto Scaling

Some applications experience daily or seasonal variations in their traffic patterns. For example, a marketing campaign for a consumer product could result in spikes in the number of visits to a web site. AWS Auto Scaling monitors your application performance automatically to adjust capacity and maintain a steady, predictable performance at a lowest cost.

You don't pay extra for using Auto Scaling—except, of course, for the AWS resources that you run. Auto Scaling features are enabled by CloudWatch metrics and alarms, so you do pay the service fees for the CloudWatch resources.

Auto Scaling was first available for EC2 instances. EC2 Auto Scaling dynamically scales your EC2 instances. AWS Auto Scaling is more comprehensive and helps you scale resources other than EC2 instances, such as DynamoDB tables and indexes, and Amazon Aurora Replicas. Currently, you can auto scale the following AWS resources:

- Amazon EC2 Auto Scaling groups (ASGs)
- Amazon EC2 Spot Fleet requests
- Amazon ECS
- Amazon DynamoDB
- Amazon Aurora

AWS Auto Scaling offers recommendations that enable you to make scaling decisions that enhance performance, lower costs, or balance between the two. If you want more guidance for defining your application scaling plans, or if you want to scale resources other than EC2 instances, such as DynamoDB tables and ECS tasks, you should use AWS Auto Scaling. Or use it if you just need to scale EC2 ASGs or want to manage the health of your EC2 fleet.

You can set up Auto Scaling for all your scalable resources from the AWS Auto Scaling console. Once you set up a scaling plan, you can view the scaling information for the resource by going to the AWS Auto Scaling console and selecting Scaling plan | *scaling_plan_name* | Scaling plan details. You can scale just a few resources or an entire application.

Amazon EC2 Auto Scaling

EC2 Auto Scaling is a fully managed service that seeks to optimize your EC2 fleet utilization. It automatically launches or terminates EC2 instances to ensure that you have the right number of instances available to handle your application workloads. EC2 Auto Scaling provides the following benefits:

- It helps maintain application availability through fleet management of your instances by detecting and replacing unhealthy instances.
- It scales your EC2 capacity up or down automatically according to the conditions that you specify (scaling plan). You set a condition to add instances in increments to the ASG when instance utilization is high and a condition to remove instances in increments from the ASG when CPU utilization falls.

- By reducing the need for you to provision a fixed number of instances manually in advance, it reduces your costs.
- If your workloads are predictable, you can schedule scaling activities through EC2 Auto Scaling.

To use AWS Auto Scaling, you must create your applications via CloudFormation or Elastic Beanstalk. You can also configure CloudWatch alarms to trigger scaling activities and ELB to distribute traffic to instances in an ASG.

How Auto Scaling Works

You must configure and manage scaling through a *scaling plan*. The scaling plans, which can be dynamic or predictive, scale the application's resources based on the app's workload, by increasing and lowering the amount of resources that are allocated to the application. When selecting a scaling plan, you can choose to optimize performance, cost, or both. You can also create custom scaling policies.

A scaling plan is how you specify resource scaling. You create one scaling plan for each application resource, such as an EC2 ASG, a set of tags, or a CloudFormation stack. There are two types of scaling strategies, *dynamic* and *predictive*, and you can combine both in your scaling plan. Both dynamic and predictive scaling seeks to maintain the resource utilization at the target value that you specify in the scaling plan.

Dynamic Scaling

Under a dynamic scaling strategy, you create a target tracking policy for the resources that you want to scale. The scaling plan adds or removes the quantities of a resource to maintain resource utilization at the target value that you specified.

Dynamic scaling helps you provision an application with more capacity than what was forecasted. As its name indicates, dynamic scaling adjusts capacity directly in response to how your applications are utilizing resources. Figure 11-2 shows how dynamic scaling smoothes resource allocation by tracking resource utilization.

Figure 11-2
Dynamic scaling

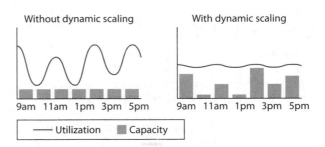

Predictive Scaling

Predictive scaling employs machine learning algorithms to analyze workload metrics to forecast future workload requirements. Currently, predictive scaling is available only for EC2 ASGs. It uses load forecasting to determine how it scales the EC2 instances. Briefly, here's how it works:

- Using *load forecasting*, Auto Scaling analyzes up to a 14-day history of a load metric to predict the demand for the next 2 days.

- Auto Scaling *schedules its scaling actions* to reflect the load forecast. At the scheduled time, it updates the resource's minimum capacity with the value specified by the scheduled scaling action. For example, if the forecast predicts a traffic spike to a web site during primetime when its ads are running, the scaling plan creates scheduling scaling actions to ensure that the ASG can handle this traffic spike.

- There's a *minimum and a maximum capacity limit,* and the values specified by the scheduled scaling actions fall in between these limits. You have the option of specifying whether an application can provision resources beyond the maximum capacity that you configured, if the load forecasting indicates a capacity that's more than the maximum.

Amazon EC2 Auto Scaling

EC2 Auto Scaling enables you to maintain the right number of running EC2 instances to handle your application workloads. To set up EC2 Auto Scaling, you create a set of EC2 instances in an ASG. You can configure both the minimum and maximum number of instances that should run in each ASG. Based on the scaling policies that you configure, Amazon EC2 Auto Scaling launches or terminates instances as workload grows and falls for your applications.

EC2 Auto Scaling performs the following three functions to help you automate your fleet of EC2 instances:

- Monitors the health of running instances through periodic heath checks

- Replaces impaired instances automatically without your intervention

- Automatically balances instance capacity across availability zones as evenly as possible

You can use Auto Scaling for various scenarios in addition to ramping capacity up or down in accordance with your workloads. For example, you can use it to ensure that a bastion host is running in every AZ, which is a security best practice. A bastion host is a special-purpose server that runs in a public subnet. It minimizes your security exposure by enabling you to log into it via SSH (or RDP), and then use that session to manage other hosts that live in your private subnets. You can configure the bastion host in an ASG and also configure the group's instances to run in multiple AZs, with a minimum and maximum size of 1. You thus will always have a single bastion host running in multiple AZs.

EC2 Auto Scaling Components

There are three key EC2 Auto Scaling components: auto scaling groups, launch configuration templates, and scaling options.

Auto Scaling Groups

An ASG is a logical collection of similar EC2 instances; grouping instances makes it easier for you to manage instance scaling. When the group starts, it launches enough instances to handle the desired capacity. It performs periodic instance health checks and replaces any unhealthy instances. Based on your scaling policy, EC2 Auto Scaling adjusts the desired capacity of the group by launching and terminating instances automatically. You can manually scale the instances as well to maintain a fixed number of instances.

After you create an ASG, the group starts out by launching the minimum (or the desired number, if you've configured it) number of instances. EC2 Auto Scaling performs periodic health checks on all running instances within an ASG, terminates unhealthy instances, and launches new ones, to maintain either the minimum or the desired number of instances. If you stop or terminate an instance, EC2 Auto Scaling considers the instance as unhealthy and replaces it.

Let's say you create an ASG with the following configuration:

- Minimum number of instances = 4
- Desired number of instances = 8
- Maximum number of instances = 16

The ASG starts with eight instances in this case, since that's your desired capacity. If you didn't specify the desired capacity, the ASG launches with four instances, which is the minimum number of instances. This ASG will scale out as needed up to a maximum of sixteen instances. Desired capacity indicates the number of instances that are started up when you launch the ASG. Since your desired capacity in this case is eight, EC2 Auto Scaling launches and keeps eight instances running until a scale-out or scale-in event occurs. If a scale-in event occurs, the number of instances will be reduced until it hits the minimum capacity you've configured. If a scale-out event occurs, the number of instances keeps going up until it hits the maximum capacity.

 TIP   If you know that your application is going to get extra traffic following a marketing e-mail or a product launch, you can scale up your desired capacity ahead of time. Launching new instances proactively also helps you when have configured ELB, by registering those instances with ELB.

Since an ASG is a regional entity, it can span AZs, but not AWS regions. You can launch different types of EC2 instances in the same EC2 ASG. You can have as many instances in an ASG as your EC2 quota permits. If you terminate an ASG with running instances, the ASG as well as the instances are terminated.

EC2 Auto Scaling automatically balances instances across AZs if you configure multiple zones in the ASG settings. It always launches instances so that the instances are balanced as evenly as possible among the AZs.

Launch Configurations and Launch Templates

You can create an ASG when launching EC2 instances via three methods:

- Use a launch configuration.
- Use a launch template.
- Use the Launch Wizard.

A launch configuration is a configuration template that an ASG uses to launch instances, and it specifies information such as the AMI ID, the instance type, a key pair, security group(s), and a block device mapping. You can't modify a launch configuration after you create it. To change the launch configuration, you must create a new launch configuration and update your ASG with the new launch configuration. New instances are launched with the new configuration parameters, but running instances will run with their old configuration. If you decide to change the EC2 instance type for the instances that are currently running in an ASG, you must copy the current launch configuration to a *new* launch configuration and then modify the instance type.

A launch template contains the same configuration information as a launch configuration, but in addition, it enables you to maintain multiple versions of the template. With a launch template, you can provision capacity across multiple EC2 instance types and use both On-Demand and Spot instances to maximize performance and minimize cost. AWS recommends that you use launch templates rather than a launch configuration, so that you can take advantage of the latest EC2 features such as T2 Unlimited instances.

 TIP You can create a launch configuration from the AWS CLI with the `aws autoscaling create-launch-configuration` command. When you create a launch configuration for an ASG from the command line or with an API, by default, detailed monitoring (metric data is sent every minute to CloudWatch) of the EC2 instances in the group is enabled. In contrast, only basic monitoring is enabled when you create a launch configuration from the AWS Management Console.

Exercise 11-1 shows how to create an ASG with the Launch Wizard. You can view a specific ASG by running the `describe-auto-scaling-groups` command:

```
$ aws autoscaling describe-auto-scaling-groups –auto-scaling-group-names my_asg1
```

Scaling Options (Scaling Policies)

Use scaling options to dynamically increase or decrease the number of EC2 instances that you make available to an application. Although you normally think of scaling as increasing or decreasing the number of instances to match the application workloads, it can also be used to maintain a set number of servers throughout an application's lifetime.

 NOTE Auto Scaling of EC2 instances relies on CloudWatch metrics.

There are several ways to scale an ASG:

- **Run a fixed number of instances**   You can run the same number of instances by having EC2 Auto Scaling perform periodic health checks within an ASG and terminating unhealthy instances and starting new instances. The ASG starts by launching the minimum number of instances that you specify (or the desired capacity, if you configure it) and maintains the number of running instances at the same level even if one or more instances become unhealthy.

- **Manual scaling**   In this most basic scaling technique, you specify a maximum, minimum, or the desired capacity for an ASG. You can change the size of an ASG any time, as well as update the desired capacity of the ASG, as shown here:

```
$ aws autoscaling set-desired-capacity --auto-scaling-group-name my-asg
--desired-capacity 2
```

- **Scheduled scaling**   You can specify when the number of instances must increase or decrease based on a predetermined schedule. Scheduled scaling is helpful when you're planning scaling for predictable traffic patterns of a web application, for example. If you know that web traffic is highest on Friday from 5 P.M. to midnight, you can use scheduled Auto Scaling to scale the number of web servers up by 5 P.M. and scale the number down after midnight. As with manual scaling, you must adjust the desired capacity of the ASG to increase or decrease the number of running instances.

  You can configure a schedule for scaling just once or on a recurring schedule using a Unix cron syntax format (UTC time), as shown in the following example, which creates a scheduled action that runs at 00:30 hours on the first of January, June, and December every year:

```
$ aws autoscaling put-scheduled-update-group-action --scheduled-action-
name scaleup-schedule-year --auto-scaling-group-name my-asg --recurrence
"30 0 1 1,6,12 *" --desired-capacity 6
```

To configure an ASG to scale according to a schedule, you must create a scheduled scaling action, which tells EC2 Auto Scaling to perform the scaling action at the specified time(s). In the scheduled scaling action, you specify the new minimum, maximum, and desired sizes for the scaling action. Auto Scaling updates the group with the desired sizes specified by the scaling action. You can't schedule an action at a time when there's already another scaling activity occurring—Auto Scaling will throw an error if you try this. A schedule action is executed within seconds of the schedule you set up, but it could be delayed for up to two minutes from the action's scheduled start time.

- **Demand-based scaling (or dynamic scaling)**   This scaling method, also called *scaling by policy,* enables you to handle unknown future demand conditions. The ASG adjusts the desired capacity of the group and launches or terminates the instances as needed. You can, for example, create a scaling policy that increases the number of EC2 instances when the average CPU utilization stays beyond 85 percent for 30 minutes. EC2 Auto Scaling launches or terminates instances as required to keep the average CPU utilization at 85 percent. Similarly, you can specify that whenever the CPU utilization remains below 10 percent, Auto Scaling should remove an instance. You configure CloudWatch to send a notification to Auto Scaling when the CPU utilization falls below 10 percent, and then configure the Auto Scaling policy to remove the instance.

 TIP You may encounter a scenario where you configure EC2 Auto Scaling to scale up an ASG based on the average CPU usage of the group, for example. You set the target CPU usage at 85 percent, but you notice that even after scaling out, the instance pool is unable to keep up with a traffic burst. The most likely reason why you may encounter such a situation is that even though more instances are launched, they aren't ready quickly enough to handle the high amount of incoming traffic. A good strategy in cases like this is to lower the target value for the CPU utilization metric—say, to 70 percent. This enables the ASG to launch instances in time to handle a spike in usage.

You can attach multiple scaling policies to the same ASG. When you do this, you could run into a situation where more than one policy instructs the ASG to increase or lower the number of instances. EC2 Auto Scaling will implement the instructions of the policy that impacts the group most. If two policies both recommend an increase in the number of instances, it'll choose the policy that recommends increasing the larger number of EC2 instances. In other words, it chooses the policy that has the greatest impact on the group.

EC2 Auto Scaling launches instances in the AZ with the fewest instances from the ASG during a *scale-out* operation, where it ramps up capacity (a *scale-in* operation removes instances from an ASG to lower capacity). You can tell EC2 Auto Scaling which instances it should terminate first during a scale-in operation by using a *termination policy*. You can configure *instance protection* to keep EC2 Auto Scaling from terminating specific instances.

Scaling Policy Types

Auto Scaling enables you use various types of scaling policies:

- **Target tracking scaling** You can change the group's capacity based in a target value for a specific metric such as CPUUtilization. You select a scaling metric and set its target value. EC2 Auto Scaling creates CloudWatch alarms that trigger the scaling policy based on the metric and the target value. You can configure alarms to monitor any metrics that EC2 sends to CloudWatch, or you can create and monitor custom metrics. The scaling policy adds or removes instances to keep the metric at, or close to, its target value. For example, suppose you select a load metric such as request count, or CPU utilization, and set your target value. EC2 Auto Scaling adjusts the number of instances in your ASG as needed, so the metric's value stays close to its target value.

- **Step scaling**   You change capacity based on a set of step adjustments based on the size of the alarm breach.
- **Simple scaling**   You change a group's capacity based on a single scaling adjustment.

NOTE   AWS recommends that you use step scaling policies, unless you base scaling on a utilization metric, in which case it recommends that you use target tracking scaling policies.

A *scaling cooldown period* ensures that a group doesn't launch or terminate instances before the previous scaling activity has completed. Auto Scaling supports cool-down periods with only the simple scaling policy.

EC2 Auto Scaling Notifications

You can configure Auto Scaling to send you SNS notifications when an ASG scales up or down. By configuring an ASG to use the autoscaling:EC2_INSTANCE_TERMINATE notification type, you can get e-mail notifications when an ASG terminates an instance.

The Auto Scaling Lifecycle

The lifecycle of an instance in an ASG starts when the ASG launches the instance, and it ends when the instance is terminated either by the ASG or by you. Understanding scale-out and scale-in events and the InService state helps you know when EC2 Auto Scaling adds or removes instances from an ASG, as the following sections explain.

Scale Out   A scale-out event makes the ASG launch one or more EC2 instances and attach them to the group. There are three scale-out events that lead an ASG to launch instances and add them to the group:

- You manually increase the ASG's size by raising the minimum or the desired capacity.
- A dynamic scaling policy adds instances to the ASG based on an increase in demand.
- A scheduled scaling action adds instances to an ASG at a specific time.

Instances in the InService State   Instances stay in the InService state until one of the following occurs:

- A scale-in event, where EC2 Auto Scaling terminates an instance to reduce the size of the ASG.
- You place the instance in the Standby state.
- You remove an instance from the ASG.
- The instance is removed from an ASG, terminated, and replaced, because it failed the required number of health checks.

Scale In   When a scale-in event occurs, an ASG detaches one or more instances from the group. Any of the following events leads an ASG to remove instances from the group and terminate them:

- You decrease the size of the ASG.
- A scaling policy that you've created decreases the size of the ASG based on a decrease in demand.
- A schooled scaling action decreases the size of the ASG at a specific time.

Lifecycle Hooks   A *lifecycle hook* helps you perform actions before an instance is added to your fleet or gets terminated. This is especially important if you're using barebones AMIs—that is, AMIs to which you haven't added your software configuration. Launch hooks perform software configuration on an instance to get it ready before EC2 Auto Scaling connects the instance to your load balancer. A *terminate hook* helps collect important data from an instance (and probably copy it somewhere, such as to an S3 bucket) before the instance is removed from service.

Attaching EC2 Instances to an ASG

You can attach a running instance to an ASG that you launch. The instances must satisfy the following requirements:

- The AMI that you used to launch the instance must exist.
- An instance can be part of only one ASG.
- The instance must be running in one of the AZs in which you've defined in your ASG.
- If the ASG has an attached load balancer, both the load balancer and the instances must be in the same VPC.
- When you attach an EC2 instance to an ASG with an attached load balancer, the instance is registered with the load balancer. If the ASG has an attached target group, the instance registers with the target group.

Exercise 11-3 shows how to attach an instance to an existing ASG using the AWS Management Console. You can also do so from the command line with the `attach-instances` command:

```
$ aws autoscaling attach-instances –instance-ids i-b5f08b8d –auto-scaling-
group-name my-asg
```

Setting Up a Scaled, Load Balanced Application

You can have a load balancer distribute incoming user traffic across the EC2 instances in an ASG by attaching a load balancer to the ASG. This ensures that the ELB service distributes your application traffic evenly across a dynamically changing set of EC2 instances.

All incoming traffic in a load-balanced setup contacts the load balancer instead of the EC2 instances. To set this up, you must first create the load balancer and then attach it to your ASG. When you attach the load balancer, it registers all the instances in the group and distributes traffic across them. Exercise 11-11 shows to attach a load balancer to an ASG.

By default, an ASG doesn't consider instances unhealthy when they fail a load balancer's health checks. However, the default health checks for a group are only EC2 status checks. If you want the group to evaluate instance health on additional tests provided by a load balancer, you must explicitly configure the ASG to use ELB health checks. When you do this, the ASG will classify an instance as unhealthy if it fails either the default EC2 status checks or the load balancer health checks. Exercise 11-5 shows how to add ELB health checks using the console. If you don't configure an ELB health check for an ASG, you may encounter situations when, even though some of the instances that you launched via an ASG are marked unhealthy, due to an ELB health check, they aren't automatically terminated or replaced.

EC2 Auto Scaling can terminate instances because of a scaling event or because of a health check. If you enable *connection draining*, EC2 Auto Scaling waits for all ongoing requests to complete or the maximum timeout expires, whichever comes first, before it terminates an instance resulting from either of the two.

When an EC2 instance fails a health check, EC2 Auto Scaling terminates the instance and replaces it with a new instance. If you're using ELB, EC2 Auto Scaling detaches the unhealthy instance from the load balancer before provisioning a new instance and attaching it to the load balancer. You don't need to perform any manual actions during this process. The turnaround time for EC2 Auto Scaling to replace an unhealthy server is a few minutes, and most replacements complete within five minutes. The length of time it takes to replace an instance depends on a number of factors, including the time it takes to boot-up the AMI of the instance.

How EC2 Auto Scaling Handles Unhealthy Instances

As mentioned, EC2 Auto Scaling receives a default EC2 status check, and by default, it also receives system status checks. It can also receive notifications from additional load balancer health checks, but only *if you configure them*. In addition, you can add *custom health checks*. If you configure ELB health checks and create custom health checks, EC2 Auto Scaling considers all three health checks—the default EC2 status checks, ELB health checks, and the custom health checks.

When Auto Scaling receives notification that an instance is unhealthy, it automatically terminates the instance and replaces it. You can specify that the group should mark the instance's health when ELB reports that those instances are in an OutOfService status. When an instance passes its initial Auto Scaling health checks, it enters the InService state. By default, Auto Scaling uses EC2 status checks, and when these checks show the instance status in a state other than running or with a status of impaired, the instance is deemed unhealthy and is replaced.

You can configure the health checks status emitted by any of your custom health checks to go to EC2 Auto Scaling for considering the health status of an instance. Your health checks can set the status of a poorly performing instance as Unhealthy, which makes Auto Scaling mark that instance as Unhealthy when it performs its instance health checks.

If you are using ELB, when it notices unhealthy instances, it will stop routing requests to the instance. If you aren't using ELB, you can integrate with Route 53 to send users to other servers in an ASG when an instance becomes unhealthy. Or you can use a reverse proxy or a service discovery solution if you're running microservices.

Scaling Processes, and How to Suspend and Resume Them

EC2 Auto Scaling supports the following scaling processes:

- **Launch** Adds a new instance to the ASG.
- **Terminate** Removes an instance from the group.
- **Healthcheck** Checks the instance's health. If EC2 or ELB tells EC2 Auto Scaling that an instance is unhealthy, it marks the instance as unhealthy.
- **AZRebalance** Balances the number of instances in an ASG across the AZs in a region, so that the instances are spread evenly across the AZs. Should an AZ become unavailable, the scaling process first launches new instances in other AZs before terminating the unavailable instances.
- **AlarmNotification** Accepts notifications from CloudWatch alarms set up for the ASG.
- **ScheduledActions** Performs the scheduled actions you configure.
- **AddToLoadBalancer** Adds EC2 instances to an attached load balancer or target group when they're launched.

Let's say you want to perform some changes to your web applications, and you bring the web servers down as part of your work. You don't want your changes to invoke the Auto Scaling processes. You can suspend and resume individual scaling processes from the AWS Management Console. If you don't want Auto Scaling to launch instances for a while, you can suspend the Launch scaling process, which keeps Auto Scaling from executing scale-out policies. A suspension of the Terminate process prevents Auto Scaling from executing a scale-in policy during the suspension. Let's say you suspend the Alarm-Notification process. AWS receives the alarms from CloudWatch but won't execute the Auto Scaling policy that would normally be triggered by such an alarm.

You can also suspend and resume individual processes or all processes from the AWS CLI by executing the `aws autoscaling suspend-processes` and the `aws autoscaling resume-processes` commands, respectively.

Auto Scaling itself can suspend processes for ASGs that repeatedly fail to launch instances over a period of 24 hours, without successfully launching any instances. This is called an *administrative suspension*, and you can manually resume these processes.

Chapter Review

Provisioning compute and other resources and deploying applications on those resources takes the bulk of your time and efforts as an AWS SysOps administrator.

This chapter reviewed several key AWS provision and deployment tools. AS Cloud-Formation helps you provision your environments based on templates that you create. Templates help you achieve consistency, minimize errors, and make your provisioning processes easily reproduceable in multiple environments.

AWS OpsWorks is based on the popular configuration management tool Chef and offers a way to use cookbooks and recipes to deploy and manage your applications.

AWS CodeDeploy can take the application artifacts and the application deployment configuration file from AWS S3 or GitHub and deploy the application on EC2 instances as well as your on-premise servers.

Scaling a growing environment is critical, and AWS's Auto Scaling feature helps you automatically scale your AWS resources such as EC2 instances, DynamoDB tables, and Aurora replicas, to ensure that your applications are continuously provisioned with the appropriate amount of resources

Exercises

The exercises are designed to teach you how to perform important AWS administrative tasks through the console. If you make a mistake, retrace your steps and ensure that you're correctly performing the steps. You'll know that you've correctly completed the exercise if you achieve the goal set for you in each exercise.

Exercise 11-1: Create an ASG with the Amazon EC2 Launch Wizard.

You start with the EC2 console and will be switched to the EC2 Launch Wizard.

1. Open the AWS Auto Scaling console: https://console.aws.amazon.com/ awsautoscaling.

2. In the dashboard, select Launch Instance.

3. Select an AMI, and on the next page, select an instance type, and then click Next: Configure Instance Details.

4. For Number Of Instances, select the number of EC2 instances you want to launch. Then select Launch Into Auto Scaling Group.

5. On the confirmation page, select Create Launch Configuration.

6. You'll now be switched to Step 3 of the Launch Configuration Wizard. Enter a name for your launch configuration, and then click Next: Add Storage.

7. Click Next: Configure Security Group.

8. Create a new security group or select an existing security group. Click Review.

9. Select Create Launch Configuration.

10. In the Configure Auto Scaling group Details page, enter a name for the group and specify a VPC, and then click Next: Configure Scaling Policies.

11. On the Configure Scaling Policies page, select one of the two options: Keep This Group At Its Initial Size, or Use Scaling Policies To Adjust The Capacity Of This Group. The first option requires you to adjust the size of the group manually, and the second option automatically adjusts the group's size.

12. In the Review page, you can add tags, notifications, and edit some other configuration elements. Then click Create Auto Scaling Group.

Exercise 11-2: Add a scaling policy to an ASG via the EC2 console.

1. Open the Amazon EC2 console: https://console.awsamazon.com/ec2/.

2. In the navigation plane, under Auto Scaling, select Auto Scaling Groups.

3. Select the ASG that you created in Exercise 11-1.

4. In the Scaling Policies tab, select Add Policy. For a target tracing scaling policy, follow the remaining steps.

5. Enter a name for the policy for the Name attribute.

6. Select a Metric Type and specify a Target Value for that metric.

7. Select an instance warm-up value for the Instances Need attribute.

8. Click Create.

Exercise 11-3: Attach an instance to an existing ASG from the AWS Management Console.

1. Open the Amazon EC2 console: https://console.awsamazon.com/ec2/.

2. In the navigation plane, select Instances.

3. Select the instance.

4. Select Actions | Instance Settings | Attach To Auto Scaling Group.

5. In the Attach To Auto Scaling Group page, select an existing Auto Scaling group. Select the instance and then click Attach.

Exercise 11-4: Create an AWS Auto Scaling plan for an EC2 ASG.

1. Open the AWS Auto Scaling console: https://console.aws.amazon.com/awsautoscaling/.

2. On the welcome page, select Get Started.

3. Select Choose EC2 Auto Scaling Groups.

4. Select an ASG from the list and then click Next.

5. To specify a scaling strategy, in the Configure A Scaling Plan page, enter a name for your scaling plan for the attribute Scaling Plan Details, Name.

6. Select the Balance Availability And Cost choice as the default strategy (it specifies a target utilization of 50 percent for the most commonly used scaling metric for the ASG resource that you're scaling).

7. In the Review And Create page, review the scaling plan and click Create Scaling Plan.

Exercise 11-5: Add Elastic Load Balancer health checks to an ASG.

You must first attach a load balancer to the ASG by completing Exercise 11-11.

1. Open the Amazon EC2 console: https://console.awsamazon.com/ec2/.

2. In the navigation plane, select Auto Scaling Groups under Auto Scaling.

3. Select the Auto Scaling group.

4. In the Details tab, select Edit.

5. For the Health Check Type attribute, select ELB.

6. For the Health Check Grace Period attribute, enter a value of **600**.

Exercise 11-6: Create a WordPress stack from the AWS CloudFormation console.

1. Open the AWS CloudFormation console: https://console.aws.amazon.com/cloudformation.

2. Click Create New Stack.

3. In the Template section, select Specify An Amazon S3 Template URL. Enter the following URL for the AWS sample WordPress template: **https://s3-us-west-2.amazonaws.com/cloudformation-templates-us-west-2/WordPress-Single_Instance.template**

4. Click Next.

5. In the Specify Details section, enter a name for the new stack in the name field—say, **MyFirstStack**.

6. In the KeyName field, enter the name of the EC2 key pair, making sure that the key pair is in the same region where you're creating the stack.

7. Click Next.

8. In this example, you won't create any tags, so click Next again.

9. Review the stack information and click Create.

10. To view the events for the stack, select MyFirstStack in the list shown in the console. In the Stack Details pane, click the Events tab.

11. Your stack takes a few minutes to be created, and when you see that the MyFirstStack has a status of CREATE_COMPLETE, you can start using it. In this example, the WordPress stack creates a WordPress web site. Perform the next two steps to complete the WordPress installation. The first step runs the installation script for your WordPress web site. The next step helps you complete the WordPress installation.

12. In the Outputs tab, click the link in the Value column, in the WebsiteURL row.

13. Follow the instructions in the web page for the WordPress installation to complete the WordPress installation.

Exercise 11-7: Create a CloudFormation change set from the CloudWatch console.

1. Open the AWS CloudFormation console: https://console.aws.amazon.com/cloudformation.

2. Select the running stack (say, MyFirstStack that you created in Exercise 11-6) from the list of stacks.

3. Select Actions | Create Change Set.

4. Select Use Current Template.

5. In the Specify Details page, Specify Details section, enter a name for your change set. Change one or more parameters in the Parameters section.

6. In the Options page, click Next.

7. Review the changes and click Create Change Set.

Exercise 11-8: Create a cookbook for use with AWS OpsWorks Stacks.

1. On your laptop or server, create a directory named my_cookbook_demo.

2. Create a file named metadata.rb in the my_cookbook_demo directory, with the following line to specify the cookbook's name:

name "my_cookbook_demo"

3. In the same directory, create a directory named recipes where you'll store the recipes you create for the cookbook named my_cookbook_demo.

4. Create a file named default.rb in the recipes directory. Add the following one-line recipe to the default.rb file:

Chef::Log info("******** My First Recipe!! ********")

5. Using the `tar` command, create a file named my_cookbook_demo.tar.gz:

```
$ tar -czvf my_cookbook_demo.tar.gz my_coookbook_demo/
```

6. Create an S3 bucket (you can also use an existing bucket).

7. Upload the my_cookbook_demo.tar.gz file to the S3 bucket.

Exercise 11-9: Create a demo Linux stack from the AWS OpsWorks console.

1. Sign in to the AWS OpsWorks console: https://console.aws.amazon.com/opsworks.

2. Select Add Your First Stack (or Add Your First AWS OpsWorks Stacks Stack).

3. In the Add Stack page, select Chef 12 stack.

4. For Stack Name, enter **MyLinuxDemostack**.

5. For Region, select US West (Oregon).

6. For VPC, select No VPC for now.

7. For Default Operating System, select Linux And Ubuntu 18.04 LTS.

8. For Use Custom Chef Cookbooks, choose Yes.

9. For Repository Type, select Http Archive.

10. For Repository URL, enter **https://s.amazonaws.com/opsworks-demo-assets/ opsworks-linux-demo-cookbooks-nodejs.tar.gz**. Leave everything else, such as Availability Zone, at the default values. The User Name and Password attributes can be left blank as well.

11. Select Advanced.

12. For IAM role, select New IAM Role.

13. For Default IAM Instance Profile, select New IAM Instance Profile.

14. For API Endpoint Region, select us-west-2.

15. Leave attributes such as Default Root Device Type and Use OpsWorks Security Groups at their default settings.

16. Select Add Stack. You should then see the MyLinuxDemostack page in the console.

Exercise 11-10: Create a layer for an AWS OpsWorks Stack from the AWS OpsWorks console.

You must complete Exercise 11-9 before completing this exercise.

1. When you create a new stack, such as the MyLinuxDemoStack in Exercise 11-9, you'll see an Add Your First Layer link on the first page that's displayed after the stack creation is completed. Click the link.

2. In the Add Layer page, select the layer you want to create.

3. Configure the layer, and then click Add Layer to add the new layer to your stack.

4. Add instances to the layer and start the instances.

Exercise 11-11: Add a load balancer to an ASG using the console.

1. Open the Amazon EC2 console: https://console.awsamazon.com/ec2/.

2. In the navigation plane, select Auto Scaling Groups under Auto Scaling.

3. Select the group to which you want to add the load balancer.

4. In the Details tab, select Edit.

5. For Target Groups, select your target EC2 scaling group.

6. Click Save.

Questions

The following questions will help you measure your understanding of the material presented in this chapter. Read all the choices carefully because there might be more than one correct answer. Choose all the correct answers for each question.

1. You have an Auto Scaling group (ASG) associated with an Elastic Load Balancer (ELB). You have noticed that instances launched via the ASG are being marked unhealthy due to an ELB health check, but these unhealthy instances aren't being terminated. What do you need to do to ensure that trial instances marked unhealthy by the ELB will be terminated and replaced?

   A. Change the thresholds set on the ASG health check.

   B. Add an ELB health check to your ASG.

   C. Increase the value for the health check interval set on the ELB.

   D. Change the health check set on the ELB to use TCP rather than HTTP checks.

2. You've attached two Auto Scaling policies to an Auto Scaling group, one based on the CPUUtilization metric, and the other based on the triggering of an alarm for a custom metric by an SQS queue. The ASG gets two instructions: one from the CPU utilization policy to launch two instances, and the other from the policy for the SQS queue to launch four instances. How many instances will this ASG launch?

   A. Two

   B. Four

   C. Six

   D. Eight

3. Which of the following sections in a CloudFormation template is a required section?

   A. Resources

   B. Parameters

   C. Conditions

   D. Outputs

4. Which of the following deployment methods does AWS OpsWorks support? (Choose three)

   A. Rolling

   B. Blue-green

   C. AWS OpsWorks layer update

   D. Immutable

5. If you're scaling based on a utilization metric that increases or decreases proportional to the number of EC2 instances in an EC2 Auto Scaling group, which type of scaling policies does AWS recommend that you use?

   A. Step scaling

   B. Target tracking scaling

   C. Auto Scaling

   D. Simple scaling

6. Which of the following are valid methods of updating an AWS CloudFormation stack? (Choose two)

   A. Direct update

   B. Blue-green update

   C. Change set

   D. Indirect update

7. You have decided to change the instance type for instances running in your application tier that's using Auto Scaling. In which area should you modify the instance type definition?

   A. Auto Scaling launch configuration

   B. Auto Scaling group

   C. Auto Scaling policy

   D. Auto Scaling tags

8. You're using EC2 Auto Scaling for your fleet of EC2 instances. The average CPU utilization stays above 90 percent for 15 minutes. Which of the following scaling strategies or policies can automatically increase the number of EC2 instances to handle the high CPU utilization rate?

   A. Dynamic scaling

   B. Scaling based on a schedule

   C. Manual scaling

   D. Automatic scaling

9. Which of the following AWS services offers your developers a way to easily provision their environment to the AWS cloud and then deploy and run applications, all without writing code to deploy this infrastructure?

   A. AWS CloudFormation

   B. AWS Elastic Beanstalk

   C. AWS OpsWorks

   D. AWS Auto Configure

10. When configuring EC2 Auto Scaling, you've attached an Elastic Load Balancer to your Auto Scaling group. Which of the following would be true regarding health checks and instance termination?

   A. If you enable connection draining, EC2 Auto Scaling waits for all ongoing requests to complete and the maximum timeout expires before it terminates an instance due to either of the two reasons.

   B. If you enable connection draining, EC2 Auto Scaling waits for all ongoing requests to complete or the maximum timeout expires, whichever comes first, before it terminates an instance due to either of the two reasons.

   C. If you disable connection draining, EC2 Auto Scaling waits for all ongoing requests to complete and the maximum timeout expires before it terminates an instance due to either of the two reasons.

   D. If you disable connection draining, EC2 Auto Scaling waits for all ongoing requests to complete or the maximum timeout expires, whichever comes first, before it terminates an instance due to either of the two reasons.

11. You have been asked to automate many routine systems administration backup and recovery activities. Your current plan is to leverage AWS-managed solutions as much as possible and automate the rest with the AWS CLI and scripts. Which task would be best accomplished with a script?

   A. Creating daily EBS snapshots with a monthly rotation of snapshots

   B. Creating daily EBS snapshots with a monthly rotation of snapshots

   C. Automatically detect and stop unused or underutilized EC2 instances

   D. Automatically add Auto Scaled EC2 instances to an Amazon Elastic Load Balancer

12. Which of the following are ways to update an AWS CloudFormation stack without having to delete and create a new stack? (Choose two)

   A. Run a script that updates the stack's resources.

   B. Create and run a change set.

   C. Use Auto Scaling to automatically adjust the resources that you've specified in the stack.

   D. Update the stack by submitting your resource configuration changes.

13. When you create a change set in AWS CloudFormation, you can do which of the following?

    A. Specify only a modified template.

    B. Specify only new parameter values.

    C. Specify new parameter values, a modified template, or both.

    D. The stack must not be running.

14. You have started a new job and are reviewing your company's infrastructure on AWS. You notice one web application with an Elastic Load Balancer (ELB) in front of web instances in an Auto Scaling group. When you check the metrics for the ELB in CloudWatch, you see four healthy instances in availability zone (AZ) A and zero in AZ B. There are zero unhealthy instances. What do you need to fix to balance the instances across AZs?

    A. Set the ELB to be attached only to another AZ.

    B. Make sure Auto Scaling is configured to launch in both AZs.

    C. Make sure your AMI is available in both AZs.

    D. Make sure the maximum size of the Auto Scaling group is greater than 4.

15. You have been asked to manage your AWS infrastructure in a manner similar to the way you might manage application code. You want to be able to deploy exact copies of different versions of your infrastructure, stage changes into different environments, revert to previous versions, and identify what versions are running at any given time. Which approach addresses this requirement?

    A. Use cost allocation reports and AWS OpsWorks to deploy and manage your infrastructure.

    B. Use AWS CloudWatch metrics and alerts along with resource tagging to deploy and manage your infrastructure.

    C. Use AWS Beanstalk and a version control system like GitHub to deploy and manage your infrastructure.

    D. Use AWS CloudFormation and a version control system like GitHub to deploy and manage your infrastructure.

16. Which of the following statements are true regarding the EC2 Auto Scaling feature? (Choose all correct answers)

    A. Auto Scaling attempts to distribute instances evenly among the availability zones.

    B. Once you create a launch configuration, you can't change it.

    C. An Auto Scaling group can't span multiple regions.

    D. When you change the launch configuration of an Auto Scaling group, new instances are launched with the new configuration, but existing instances are unaffected.

17. What does bootstrapping an application mean?

   A. Installing an application during an instance reboot

   B. Automatically restarting failed applications

   C. Installing an application on multiple instances for quick pilot light–type failover

   D. Building a completely home-grown application to replace a third-party tool

18. Which of the following AWS services or features help you configure the number of instances to be updated concurrently during a replacement application upgrade? (Choose two)

   A. AWS OpsWorks

   B. AWS CodeDeploy

   C. AWS Elastic Beanstalk

   D. AWS CloudFormation

19. Which of the following AWS CloudFormation template sections can reference a parameter that you specify in the Parameters section of a CloudFormation template? (Choose two)

   A. Resources

   B. Outputs

   C. Transform

   D. Metadata

20. When using AWS CloudFormation, which of the following helps prevent unintended changes to protected resources?

   A. Using AWS-specific parameter types

   B. Using IAM roles for CloudFormation

   C. Using change sets

   D. Using stack policies

21. You are creating an Auto Scaling group whose EC2 instances need to insert a custom metric into CloudWatch. Which method would be the best way to authenticate your CloudWatch PUT request?

   A. Create an IAM role with the PutMetricData permission and modify the Auto Scaling launch configuration to launch instances in that role.

   B. Create an IAM user with the PutMetricData permission and modify the Auto Scaling launch configuration to inject the user credentials into the instance User Data.

   C. Modify the appropriate Cloud Watch metric policies to allow the PutMetricData permission to instances from the Auto Scaling group.

   D. Create an IAM user with the PutMetricData permission, put the credentials in a private repository, and have applications on the server pull the credentials as needed.

Answers

1. **B.** Add an ELB health check to the Auto Scaling group.

2. **B.** Four instances will be launched. When multiple policies are associated with an ASG, EC2 Auto Scaling chooses the policy that has the greatest impact on the ASG. In this case, the CPU utilization policy calls for the biggest change by asking for four instances, so that instruction or recommendation is what EC2 Auto Scaling implements. This applies even when the policies use different criteria for scaling out—if one policy mandates that EC2 should launch four instances and the other policy says to increase capacity by 33 percent, EC2 Auto Scaling gives precedence to whichever policy impacts the group the most.

3. **A.** Resources is the only required section in a CloudFormation template.

4. **A, B, D.** OpsWorks supports the rolling, blue-green, and immutable deployment types.

5. **B.** If you're using scaling based on utilization metrics, AWS recommends that you use target tracking scaling policies.

6. **A, C.** Direct update is one of the two methods of updating an AWS CloudFormation stack. Creating a change set is another way to update a stack, which gives you a chance to preview the changes before you execute them.

7. **A.** Modify the instance type definition in the Auto Scaling launch configuration. When the launch configuration for the Auto Scaling group is changed, any new instances launched use the new configuration parameters, but the existing instances are not affected.

8. **A.** A dynamic scaling policy can manage scaling to respond to changing conditions, when you don't know when those conditions will change. Using a dynamic scaling policy, you can define parameters such as the levels of CPU utilization that control the scaling process.

9. **B.** Elastic Beanstalk makes it easy for developers to deploy and manage applications in the cloud. Developers simply upload their application code, and Elastic Beanstalk takes care of all aspects of application deployment, such as provisioning the servers. It also maintains the application's performance by monitoring its health. You can also use Elastic Load Balancer to load balance the applications and Auto Scaling to dynamically ramp up or down the number of EC2 instances in accordance to the application's workload.

10. **B.** If you enable connection draining, EC2 Auto Scaling waits for all ongoing requests to complete or the maximum timeout expires, whichever comes first, before it terminates an instance due to either of the two reasons.

11. **C.** Automatically detecting and stopping unused or underutilized EC2 instances would be best accomplished with a script.

12. **B, D.** Creating a change set is one way to modify a stack, and updating a stack by submitting the new configuration is another way to modify your stack. The advantage to using a change set is that you can see the impact of your modifications before you execute the change.

13. **C.** When creating a change set, you can specify new parameter values, specify a modified template, or specify both. CloudFormation generates the change set by comparing the stack with the changes that you've submitted.

14. **B.** Make sure that you've configured Auto Scaling to launch instances in both availability zones.

15. **D.** AWS CloudFormation enables you to treat infrastructure as code and enables you to modify a template so you can create entire applications stacks in multiple environments.

16. **A, B, C, D.** All choices are correct.

17. **A.** Bootstrapping an application means that you install an application at instance boot time. You do this by adding the OS, the application server, and other application components to a prebaked AMI.

18. **C, D.** Both AWS Elastic Beanstalk and AWS CloudFormation help you configure rolling application deployments. You can configure update policies to determine how instances in an Auto Scaling group are updated or replaced. You can configure the number of instances to be upgraded together, apply updates to specific instances, and also specify the time to wait between batched updates.

19. **A, B.** Both the Resources and Outputs sections of a template can reference the parameters that you specify in the Parameters section of the same template.

20. **D.** A stack policy specifies the updates that CloudFormation can perform on critical resources. The stack policy is a JSON document that can prevent unintentional updates to key resources. They help you protect your key resources from unintentional updates that may result in service interruptions. It's a best practice to specify a stack policy when you create a stack with critical resources or when you need to replace the resources.

21. **B.** The best way to authenticate your CloudWatch PUT request is to create an IAM user with the PutMetricData permission and modify the Auto Scaling launch configuration to inject the user credentials into the instance User Data.

Objective Map

Exam SOA-C01

Official Exam Objective	All-in-One Coverage	Chapter No.
1.0 Monitoring and Reporting		
1.1 Create and maintain metrics and alarms utilizing AWS monitoring services	Monitoring AWS with Amazon CloudWatch	10
1.2 Recognize and differentiate performance and availability metrics	Monitoring AWS with Amazon CloudWatch	10
1.3 Perform the steps necessary to remediate based on performance and availability metrics	AWS Fault Tolerance and High Availability	9
	AWS Disaster Recovery	9
	Amazon ElastiCache	8
2.0 High Availability		
2.1 Implement scalability and elasticity based on use case	Auto Scaling to Scale Your Infrastructure	11
	Scaling RDS Databases	8
2.2 Recognize and differentiate highly available and resilient environments on AWS	AWS Fault Tolerance and High Availability	9
3.0 Deployment and Provisioning		
3.1 Identify and execute steps required to provision cloud resources	Amazon Elastic Compute Cloud (Amazon EC2)	4
	Amazon Elastic Container Service (ECS)	5
	AWS Batch	5
	Amazon Lightsail	5
	AWS Deployment and Provisioning Services	11
	AWS Lambda	5
	AWS Elastic Beanstalk	5
3.2 Identify and remediate deployment issues	AWS Deployment and Provisioning Services	11

Official Exam Objective	All-in-One Coverage	Chapter No.
4.0 Storage and Data Management		
4.1 Create and manage data retention	Relational Databases	8
	Working with Amazon Relational Database Service (RDS)	8
	Amazon DynamoDB Database	8
	Amazon Redshift	8
	Amazon ElastiCache	8
	An Overview of AWS Storage Options	7
	Amazon Elastic Block Storage (EBS)	7
	Amazon S3: Object Storage in the Cloud	7
	Archival Storage with Amazon S3 Glacier	7
	Amazon Elastic File System	7
	AWS Storage Gateway	7
	Amazon Snowball	7
4.2 Identify and implement data protection, encryption, and capacity planning needs	Scaling RDS Databases	8
5.0 Security and Compliance		
5.1 Implement and manage security policies on AWS	AWS Account Security Features	3
	AWS Component Security	3
	Securing the Network	3
	Securing the Storage Services	3
	Securing Your Databases	3
	Application Services Security	3
	AWS Monitoring Tools and Services that Help with Security	3
5.2 Implement access controls when using AWS	AWS Identity and Access Management (IAM)	3
5.3 Differentiate between the roles and responsibility within the shared responsibility model	The AWS Shared Responsibility Security Model	3
6.0 Networking		
6.1 Apply AWS networking features	Basic Networking Features	6
	Amazon Virtual Private Cloud (VPC)	6
	Amazon Route 53	6
	Amazon CloudFront: Amazon's Content Delivery Network (CDN)	6
6.2 Implement connectivity services of AWS	Amazon Virtual Private Cloud (VPC)	6
	AWS Direct Connect	6
	Elastic Load Balancing	6
6.3 Gather and interpret relevant information for network troubleshooting	Troubleshooting AWS Network Connectivity Problems	6

Official Exam Objective	All-in-One Coverage	Chapter No.
7.0 Automation and Optimization		
7.1 Use AWS services and features to manage and assess resource utilization	Scaling RDS Databases Elastic Load Balancing	8 6
7.2 Employ cost-optimization strategies for efficient resource utilization	Optimizing Resource Usage and Managing Billing and Costs	10
7.3 Automate manual or repeatable process to minimize management overhead	Using AWS CloudFormation to Provision AWS Infrastructure AWS OpsWorks Stacks Using AWS Auto Scaling to Scale Your Infrastructure AWS Elastic Beanstalk	11 11 11 5

About the Online Content

This book comes complete with TotalTester Online customizable practice exam software with 250 practice exam questions.

System Requirements

The current and previous major versions of the following desktop browsers are recommended and supported: Chrome, Microsoft Edge, Firefox, and Safari. These browsers update frequently, and sometimes an update may cause compatibility issues with the TotalTester Online or other content hosted on the Training Hub. If you run into a problem using one of these browsers, please try using another until the problem is resolved.

Your Total Seminars Training Hub Account

To get access to the online content you will need to create an account on the Total Seminars Training Hub. Registration is free, and you will be able to track all your online content using your account. You may also opt in if you wish to receive marketing information from McGraw-Hill Education or Total Seminars, but this is not required for you to gain access to the online content.

Privacy Notice

McGraw-Hill Education values your privacy. Please be sure to read the Privacy Notice available during registration to see how the information you have provided will be used. You may view our Corporate Customer Privacy Policy by visiting the McGraw-Hill Education Privacy Center. Visit the **mheducation.com** site and click **Privacy** at the bottom of the page.

Single User License Terms and Conditions

Online access to the digital content included with this book is governed by the McGraw-Hill Education License Agreement outlined next. By using this digital content you agree to the terms of that license.

Access To register and activate your Total Seminars Training Hub account, simply follow these easy steps.

1. Go to **hub.totalsem.com/mheclaim**.

2. To register and create a new Training Hub account, enter your e-mail address, name, and password. No further personal information (such as credit card number) is required to create an account.

NOTE If you already have a Total Seminars Training Hub account, select **Log in** and enter your e-mail and password. Otherwise, follow the remaining steps.

3. Enter your Product Key: `5htf-kgp6-0777`

4. Click to accept the user license terms.

5. Click **Register and Claim** to create your account. You will be taken to the Training Hub and have access to the content for this book.

Duration of License Access to your online content through the Total Seminars Training Hub will expire one year from the date the publisher declares the book out of print.

Your purchase of this McGraw-Hill Education product, including its access code, through a retail store is subject to the refund policy of that store.

The Content is a copyrighted work of McGraw-Hill Education, and McGraw-Hill Education reserves all rights in and to the Content. The Work is © 2019 by McGraw-Hill Education, LLC.

Restrictions on Transfer The user is receiving only a limited right to use the Content for the user's own internal and personal use, dependent on purchase and continued ownership of this book. The user may not reproduce, forward, modify, create derivative works based upon, transmit, distribute, disseminate, sell, publish, or sublicense the Content or in any way commingle the Content with other third-party content without McGraw-Hill Education's consent.

Limited Warranty The McGraw-Hill Education Content is provided on an "as is" basis. Neither McGraw-Hill Education nor its licensors make any guarantees or warranties of any kind, either express or implied, including, but not limited to, implied warranties of merchantability or fitness for a particular purpose or use as to any McGraw-Hill Education Content or the information therein or any warranties as to the accuracy, completeness, correctness, or results to be obtained from, accessing or using the McGraw-Hill Education Content, or any material referenced in such Content or any information entered into licensee's product by users or other persons and/or any material available on or that can be accessed through the licensee's product (including via any hyperlink or otherwise) or as to non-infringement of third-party rights. Any warranties of any kind, whether express or implied, are disclaimed. Any material or data obtained through use of the McGraw-Hill Education Content is at your own discretion and risk and user understands that it will be solely responsible for any resulting damage to its computer system or loss of data.

Neither McGraw-Hill Education nor its licensors shall be liable to any subscriber or to any user or anyone else for any inaccuracy, delay, interruption in service, error or omission, regardless of cause, or for any damage resulting therefrom.

In no event will McGraw-Hill Education or its licensors be liable for any indirect, special or consequential damages, including but not limited to, lost time, lost money, lost profits or good will, whether in contract, tort, strict liability or otherwise, and whether or not such damages are foreseen or unforeseen with respect to any use of the McGraw-Hill Education Content.

TotalTester Online

TotalTester Online provides you with a simulation of the AWS Certified SysOps Administrator Associate (SOA-C01) exam. Exams can be taken in Practice Mode or Exam Mode. Practice Mode provides an assistance window with hints, references to the book, explanations of the correct and incorrect answers, and the option to check your answer as you take the test. Exam Mode provides a simulation of the actual exam. The number of questions, the types of questions, and the time allowed are intended to be an accurate representation of the exam environment. The option to customize your quiz allows you to create custom exams from selected domains or chapters, and you can further customize the number of questions and time allowed.

To take a test, follow the instructions provided in the previous section to register and activate your Total Seminars Training Hub account. When you register you will be taken to the Total Seminars Training Hub. From the Training Hub Home page, select **AWS SysOps Administrator Assoc (SOA-C01) TotalTester** from the Study drop-down menu at the top of the page, or from the list of Your Topics on the Home page. You can then select the option to customize your quiz and begin testing yourself in Practice Mode or Exam Mode. All exams provide an overall grade and a grade broken down by domain.

Technical Support

For questions regarding the TotalTester or operation of the Training Hub, visit **www .totalsem.com** or e-mail **support@totalsem.com**.

For questions regarding book content, e-mail **hep_customer-service@mheducation .com**. For customers outside the United States, e-mail **international_cs@mheducation .com**.

access control list (ACL)   A document that lists who can access a Simple Storage Service (S3) bucket or object and perform which actions (read or write). Each bucket and object has an ACL associated with it. ACLs are one of the resource-based access policy options in S3 that are used to manage access to S3 buckets and objects. ACLs also can be used to grant basic read/write permissions to other AWS accounts.

access key   Combination of an access key ID and a secret access key. You use the access key to sign API requests to AWS services.

access key ID   A unique identifier that's part of the access key. You use an access key ID and the secret access key to sign programmatic AWS requests in an encrypted manner.

account   Refers to an AWS account, and includes the owner's e-mail and password; the control of the resources created under this account; and payment for the resources related to activity under this account. The AWS account has full privileges to perform all actions on the AWS account resources. A user is an entity that you associate within an AWS account.

ACL   *See* access control list.

alarm   Monitors a metric over a time period and triggers either a Simple Notification Service (SNS) topic or an Elastic Compute Cloud (EC2) Auto Scaling policy when the metric crosses a threshold value over a specific number of periods.

allow   Allow and deny are the two outcomes when AWS evaluates an Identity and Access Management (IAM) policy. Based on all permissions that apply to the user, AWS evaluates the user's request and returns either allow or deny.

Amazon Aurora   A managed MySQL-compatible database engine. This fully managed relational database engine is compatible with MySQL and PostgreSQL. With some workloads, Aurora can deliver up to five times the throughput of MySQL and up to three times the throughput of PostgreSQL.

Amazon CloudFront   A content delivery service that improves the performance and availability of web sites and applications. Amazon CloudFront is a fast content delivery network (CDN) service that securely delivers data, videos, applications, and APIs to customers globally with low latency and high transfer speeds. It is integrated with AWS by physical locations that are directly connected to the AWS global infrastructure as well as other AWS services.

Amazon CloudWatch   A service that enables you to monitor and manage metrics and configure alarm actions based on the metrics. CloudWatch provides the data and actionable insights to monitor your applications, understand and respond to system-wide performance changes, optimize resource utilization, and collect data in the form of logs, metrics, and events. It provides a unified view of AWS resources, applications, and services that run on AWS and on-premise servers.

Amazon CloudWatch Events   A service that enables you to deliver a stream of system events that describe AWS resource changes to Lambda functions, Kinesis Data Streams, SNS topics, and built-in targets.

Amazon CloudWatch Logs   A service for monitoring your systems and applications using system, application, and custom log files. You can send your log files to CloudWatch Logs and monitor them in near real-time.

Amazon DynamoDB   A managed NoSQL database service that's easily scalable. DynamoDB is a key-value and document NoSQL database that delivers single-digit millisecond performance. It's a fully managed, multiregion, multimaster database with built-in security, backup and restore, and in-memory caching.

Amazon DynamoDB Streams   A service that captures and stores a sequence of item-level modifications to DynamoDB tables. Applications can view the before and after versions of the data items in near real-time.

Amazon EBS-backed AMI   An Amazon Machine Image (AMI) whose instances use an Amazon Elastic Block Storage (EBS) volume as their root device. Instances launched with an instance store–backed AMI use the instance store as their root device. It includes the launch permissions that control which AWS accounts can use the AMI to launch instances. It also includes a block device mapping that specifies the volumes to attach to the instance when it's launched.

Amazon EC2 Auto Scaling   A service that launches or terminates EC2 instances automatically based on policies, schedules, and health checks that you configure.

Amazon ElastiCache   A service that helps you deploy, operate, and scale an in-memory cache in the cloud, based either on the Memcached or Redis engine.

Amazon Elastic Block Storage (EBS)   A service that provides block storage volumes that you use with EC2 instances. It is automatically replicated within its availability zone to protect you from component failure, offering high availability and durability.

Amazon Elastic Compute Cloud (EC2)   A web service that helps you to launch and manage Linux, UNIX, and Windows server instances in Amazon's data centers.

Amazon Elastic Container Registry (ECR)   A managed Docker container registry that helps you store, manage, and deploy Docket container images.

Amazon Elastic Container Service (ECS) A container management service that helps you run and manage Docker containers on a cluster of EC2 instances.

Amazon Elastic File System (EFS) A shared file storage service for EC2 instances that provides a simple, scalable, elastic file system for Linux-based workloads for use with AWS Cloud services and on-premise resources.

Amazon Glacier A cloud storage service for storing data archives and backups that is secure, durable, and extremely low cost. Glacier delivers 99.999999999 percent durability and provides query-in-place functionality, which enables you to run powerful analytics directly on your archive data at rest.

Amazon Inspector An automated security assessment service that helps improve the security and compliance of applications that you run on AWS.

Amazon Lightsail An easy way to launch and manage a virtual private server with AWS. It provides compute, storage, and networking capacity and capabilities to deploy and manage web sites and web applications in the cloud, including a virtual machine, SSD-based storage, data transfer, DNS management, and a static IP.

Amazon Machine Image (AMI) A machine image that serves as a template for a server's root drive. It consists of the operating system and can include application software, application layers such as database servers, and web servers. AMIs are stored in Amazon EBS or Amazon S3 (instance store–backed AMIs).

Amazon Redshift A managed petabyte-scale data warehouse service that's fast and scalable.

Amazon Relational Database Service (RDS) A service that helps set up a relational database in the AWS cloud. RDS makes it easy to set up, operate, and scale a relational database in the cloud with automated hardware provisioning, database setup, patching, and backups. It is available on several database instance types from PostgreSQL, MySQL, MariaDB, Oracle, and SQL Server including Amazon Aurora.

Amazon Resource Name (ARN) The standard way to refer to an AWS resource, such as arn:aws:iam::123456789012:user/group_abc/subgroup_xyz/Sam.

Amazon Route 53 A service that helps you create a new DNS service or migrate your current DNS service to the cloud.

Amazon S3 *See* Amazon Simple Storage Service.

Amazon Simple Notification Service (SNS) A service that enables applications, users, and devices to send and receive notifications from the AWS cloud.

Amazon Simple Queue Service (SQS) A hosted queue for storing messages as they're transmitted among servers.

Amazon Simple Storage Service (S3)   An AWS data store that you can use to store and retrieve data at anytime from anywhere on the Web.

Amazon Virtual Private Cloud (VPC)   A service for provisioning a logically separate section of the AWS cloud, where you can launch AWS resources in your own virtual network. You choose your own IP address range, create your own subnets, and configure your own route tables and network gateways.

Amazon VPC   *See* Amazon Virtual Private Cloud.

Amazon Web Services (AWS)   An infrastructure web services platform in the cloud.

AMI   *See* Amazon Machine Image.

application   1. For Elastic Beanstalk, an application is a set of components such as environment, versions, and environment configurations. The application is analogous to a folder. 2. For AWS CodeDeploy, an application is a name that refers to the app that's to be deployed. CodeDeploy deploys the revision, deployment configuration, and deploy group based on the application name.

application Auto Scaling   A web service that enables you to configure automatic scaling of not only EC2 resources, but also the ECS service (containers), Elastic MapReduce (EMR) clusters, and DynamoDB tables.

application revision   1. In AWS CodeDeploy, an application version is an archive file that contains the source code and deployment scripts along with an application specification file. A revision is stored in an Amazon S3 bucket or in a GitHub repository. 2. AWS Elastic Beanstalk also uses the concept of an application revision, which represents a consistent set of deployable application code. The version refers to an Amazon S3 object (a Java Web Application Archive, or WAR file) that contains the application code.

application specification file   AWS CodeDeploy uses an application specification file to map the source files in the application revision to the destination on the instance where it deploys the application. The file specifies custom permission for the deployed files and also specifies the scripts that must be run in the instance at each stage of the deployment.

authentication   The process of proving the identity of an entity to a system.

Auto Scaling group (ASG)   A set of similar EC2 instances with identical configuration that AWS treats as a logical group for the purposes of instance scaling and instance management.

availability zone (AZ)   A distinct location within an AWS region that is insulated from failures in other zones and offers fast, inexpensive network connectivity to the other zones in the same region.

AWS Auto Scaling   A service that enables you to discover scalable AWS resources in your application and configure dynamic scaling.

AWS Billing and Cost Management   An AWS cloud computing model in which you pay for services on demand.

AWS CloudFormation   A service that enables you to create a set of AWS resources together as a single unit, through templates.

AWS CloudHSM   A web service that uses a dedicated hardware security module (HSM) appliance to help you meet your corporate and regulatory compliance requirements (mainly through data encryption).

AWS CloudSearch   A managed service that enables you to set up and manage a scalable search solution for a web site or an application.

AWS CloudTrail   A service that records all AWS API calls made in your account and delivers the log files to you. The information includes the identity of the person or service that made the API call, the source IP address, the request parameters in the API request, and the response parameters returned by the AWS service.

AWS CodeCommit   A source control service that helps you secure private Git repositories.

AWS CodeDeploy   A service that automates code deployments both to EC2 instances and to your on-premise instances.

AWS CodePipeline   A continuous delivery (CD) service that helps you automate your release pipelines for fast and reliable application and infrastructure updates by automating the build, test, and deploy phases of your release process every time there is a code change, based on the release model you define.

AWS Command Line Interface (CLI)   A tool that helps you manage AWS services from the command line and automate the services through scripts.

AWS Config   A service that provides an AWS resource inventory, configuration history, and configuration change notifications that help you secure your AWS environment and comply with regulations.

AWS Direct Connect   A service that simplifies the setup of a dedicated, private network connection from your on-premise data center, office, or a colocation environment to AWS.

AWS Directory Service   A service used for connecting your AWS cloud resources to an on-premise Microsoft Active Directory or used to set up a standalone directory in the AWS cloud.

AWS Elastic Beanstalk   A service that helps you deploy and manage your applications in the AWS cloud without having to deal with the infrastructure that runs the applications.

AWS Glue   A managed extract, transform, and load (ETL) service that helps you catalog data and load it for analytics in a serverless environment.

AWS Identity and Access Management (IAM)   A service that enables you to manage users and their permissions within AWS.

AWS Import/Export   A service that helps you transfer large amounts of data between AWS and a portable storage device.

AWS Key Management Service (KMS)   A service that helps create and manage encryption keys that you use to encrypt your data.

AWS Lambda   A serverless service that helps you run application or backend service code without your having to provision and manage any servers.

AWS managed key   One of the two types of customer master keys (CMKs) in the AWS Key Management Service (KMS).

AWS managed policy   An IAM managed policy that AWS supplies and manages.

AWS OpsWorks   A configuration management (CM) service that enables you to use Chef cookbooks and recipes to configure and manage groups of instances and applications.

AWS SDK for .NET   A software development kit that provides Java, C++, Go, .NET, Python, Ruby, and JavaScript APIs for many AWS services, including Amazon S3, Amazon EC2, and Amazon DynamoDB.

AWS Snowball   A data transport solution that uses secure devices to transfer large amounts of data to and from the AWS cloud.

AWS Storage Gateway   A web service that connects a local on-premise software appliance with the AWS cloud storage infrastructure.

AWS Trusted Advisor   A web service that checks your AWS environment and recommends measures to lower costs, enhance system availability, improve performance, and tighten security.

basic monitoring   Several AWS services offer basic monitoring, which is the monitoring of metrics derived at a five-minute frequency.

block device   A storage device that supports reading and writing data in fixed-size blocks or sectors.

block device mapping   A mapping structure for an AMI and instance that specifies the block devices that are attached to that instance.

blue-green deployment   A deployment method in which you replace the instances in the original environment with a different set of instances. The first environment is called the original, and the second, the replacement environment. AWS CodeDeploy uses the blue-green deployment model.

breach   An EC2 Auto Scaling concept. A breach occurs when a threshold that you set is crossed. If the breach continues for a significant length of time (as determined by the breach duration parameter that you set), a scaling activity (where the size of an ASG is raised or lowered) can be initiated.

bucket An Amazon S3 container for storing objects. If you store an object such as photos/kitten./jpg in a bucket named sam.alapati, the users that you authorize can access this object from the URL http://samalapati.s3.amazonaws.com/photos/kitten.jpg.

bundling In the context of creating an AMI, the creation of an instance store–backed AMI.

cache cluster A logical cache distributed across several cache nodes (Amazon ElastiCache).

cache node A chunk of network-attached RAM. Cache nodes run instances of the Memcached service (Amazon ElastiCache).

cache parameter group A set of cache engine parameter values that you can apply to a cache cluster.

canned access policy A standard access control policy that you can apply to an AWS S3 bucket or object. The policy has options such as private, public-read, public-read-write, and authenticated-read.

CDN *See* content delivery network.

CIDR (Classless Inter-Domain Routing) block An Internet protocol address allocation and route aggregation method.

CMK *See* customer master key.

CNAME (canonical name) A type of resource record in the Domain Name System (DNS) that specifies that the domain name is an alias for another canonical domain name. A CNAME entry lets you alias one fully qualified domain name (FQDN) to another.

consolidated billing A feature of the AWS Organizations services that helps you consolidate AWS costs incurred by multiple AWS accounts.

container A Linux container that you create from a Docker image. Containers package your application's code, configurations, and dependencies into a single object. They share the operating system installed on the server and run as resource-isolated processes to ensure quick, reliable, and consistent deployments, regardless of environment.

container instance An EC2 instance that runs the Elastic Container Service (ECS) agent and that's registered with a cluster. ECS tasks are placed on running container instances.

container registry A service that stores, manages, and deploys Docker images.

content delivery network (CDN) A web service that speeds up the delivery of static and dynamic web content to users through a worldwide network of data centers. User requests are routed to the data center that offers the lowest latency (delay) at that time. If the content isn't already in this location, the CDN retrieves it from an origin such as a web server or an Amazon S3 bucket. Amazon CloudFront is AWS's CDN service.

continuous delivery   A software development practice under which new code is automatically built, tested, and prepared for a production release.

continuous integration   A development practice in which developers regularly merge their code changes into a central repository, after which they run automated builds and tests.

cooldown period   The length of time during which EC2 Auto Scaling doesn't allow the desired size of an Auto Scaling group (ASG) to be changed by an Amazon CloudWatch alarm.

credentials   Also called access credentials or security credentials; in AWS, credentials are usually the access key ID and the secret access key.

cross-region replication (CRR)   A solution that maintains identical copies of DynamoDB tables in different AWS regions in near real-time.

customer gateway   A router or software application on the customer side of a VPN tunnel that's managed by Amazon VPC. You attach the internal interfaces of the gateway to devices in your on-premise network. The external interfaces are attached to the virtual private gateway across the VPN tunnel.

customer managed policy   An IAM managed policy that you create and manage in your own account.

customer master key (CMK)   The fundamental resource managed by AWS KMS that can be a set of customer managed keys or AWS managed keys. You can use a CMK to encrypt and decrypt up to 4KB (4096 bytes) of data. CMKs are created in AWS KMS and never leave AWS KMS unencrypted. There are three types of CMKs in AWS accounts: customer managed CMKs, AWS managed CMKs, and AWS owned CMKs.

database engine   The database software running on the DB instance.

DB instance   A database environment running in the AWS cloud. Each instance can contain multiple databases that you create.

DB parameter group   A set of database engine parameter values that apply to a DB instance or instances.

DB snapshot   A point-in-time backup of a DB instance that you initiate. Amazon RDS DB snapshots and automated backups are stored in S3. Automated DB snapshots are deleted when the DB instance is deleted and only manually created DB snapshots are retained after the DB instance is deleted.

dedicated host   A physical server that is fully dedicated to an AWS user for running EC2 instances.

dedicated instance   An instance that's physically isolated at the host level and that's launched within a VPC.

delete marker   An object with a key and version ID, but no content. When you delete an Amazon S3 object in a bucket for which you've enabled versioning, S3 inserts delete markers into the versioned bucket.

deployment configuration   In AWS CodeDeploy, refers to the set of deployment rules and success and failure conditions.

deployment group   In AWS CodeDeploy, refers to a set of individually tagged instances, EC2 instances in an ASG, or both.

detailed monitoring   Monitoring of AWS metrics derived at a frequency of one minute.

dimension   A name-value pair that contains additional information to identify a metric.

distribution   The link between a domain name and an origin server, such as an S3 bucket or web server. CloudFront assigns the link and uses it to identify objects that you store in the origin server.

Docker image   A file system template with multiple layers that acts as the basis for a Docker container. A Docker image can consist of an operating system or applications.

Domain Name System (DNS)   A service that routes Internet traffic to web sites by translating domain names such as www.example.com into numeric IP addresses such as 192.0.1.1 that services can use to connect to each other.

DynamoDB stream   An ordered flow of information about changes to data items in a DynamoDB table.

elastic IP (EIP) address   A fixed (static) IP address that you can assign to an EC2 instance, or that you can assign to your VPC and then attach to an EC2 instance. The IP address is called "elastic" because, unlike a traditional static IP address, you can easily attach, detach, allocate, and free it as you need. An EIP address is associated with an account and not to an instance. You can mask an instance or availability zone failure by quickly remapping your public IP addresses to another instance.

Elastic Load Balancing (ELB)   An AWS service that enhances application availability by distributing application traffic among multiple EC2 instances.

elastic network interface (ENI)   An additional network interface that you can attach to an EC2 instance. It includes a primary IP address, a private IP address, one or more secondary private IP addresses, an optional EIP address, a MAC address, membership in specified security groups, a source/destination check flag, and a description.

Elasticsearch Service   An AWS service that helps you deploy and manage the open source Elasticsearch search and analytics engine in the AWS cloud. It offers open source Elasticsearch APIs, managed Kibana, and integrations with Logstash and other AWS services, enabling you to ingest data securely from any source and search, analyze, and visualize it in real time.

endpoint   A URL that identifies a host and a port as the entry point for a web service. Most AWS services provide endpoints for an AWS region to enable fast connectivity.

environment   1. In Elastic Beanstalk, an environment is the running instance of an application. 2. In CodeDeploy, an environment is the set of instances in a deployment group in a blue-green deployment. When you begin the deployment, the instances in the deployment group constitute the original environment, and at the end of the deployment, they constitute the replacement environment.

ephemeral store   *See* instance store.

eventually consistent read   A read process that returns data from a single region and may not show the most up-to-date information. If you repeat the read request after awhile, however, the response eventually returns the latest data.

eviction   The deletion of an object from an edge location before its expiration time by CloudFront. CloudFront may evict objects that aren't frequently requested to make room for popular objects.

expiration   The time at which CloudFront stops responding to user requests for an object in its cache.

explicit launch permission   An AMI launch permission that you grant to an AWS account.

expression   In CloudWatch, how you control how search hits are sorted. An expression can use numeric fields, a rank expression, relevance scores, and standard numeric operators and functions.

facet   An index field in CloudSearch that represents a category that you use to refine and filter search results.

federated identity management (FIM)   Enables users to sign in to different networks or services using the same group or personal credentials. In AWS, federated users are external identities that are granted secure access to an AWS account's resources without your having to create IAM users. The external identities can be from a corporate identity store such as LDAP or Active Directory, or from a third party such as a login with Facebook, Amazon, or Google.

global secondary index   An index with a partition key and a sort key that can be different from those on the table. The index is called "global" because the queries that you make with the index can range over all of a table's data, across all the table's partitions.

hardware virtual machine (HVM) virtualization   Enables a guest virtual machine to function as if it's running on a native hardware platform. It uses a paravirtual (PV) network and storage drivers for enhanced performance.

hardware virtual private network (VPN)   A hardware-based IPsec VPN over the Internet. You can create a hardware VPN connection between your on-premise data center and your AWS VPC to leverage the AWS cloud as an extension of your corporate data center.

health check   A system call that checks the health status of an EC2 instance that's part of an EC2 ASG.

hosted zone   A collection of resource record sets hosted by Route 53 and managed together under a single domain name, like a traditional DNS zone file.

IAM   *See* AWS Identity and Access Management.

IAM user   *See* user.

identity provider (IdP)   An IAM entity that holds the metadata concerning external identity providers.

in-place deployment   A deployment method used by CodeDeploy, wherein the applications on all instances in the deployment group are stopped and the new application version is installed. Following this, the new application version is started and validated.

inline policy   An IAM policy that you embed in an IAM user, group, or role.

instance   A copy of an AMI running as a virtual machine. It enables you to choose the CPU, memory, storage, and networking capacity that you need to run your applications.

instance family   A general instance type grouping based on storage or CPU capacity.

instance profile   A container that passes IAM role information to an EC2 instance when you launch the instance.

instance store   Disk storage that is physically attached to the host computer on which an EC2 instance (VM) runs, and thus, lasts only during the life of the instance. When you terminate an instance, you lose the data in the instance store.

instance store–backed AMI   A type of AMI whose instances use an instance store volume as their root device.

instance type   Defines the RAM, CPU, storage capacity, and usage cost for an instance. You can have memory-intensive and CPU-intense instance types, for example.

Internet gateway   Connects a network to the Internet. You route traffic from your VPC that's destined for outside IP addresses to the Internet gateway.

key pair   A pair of security credentials, one a private key and the other a public key, that you use to connect to an EC2 instance. CloudFront uses key pairs to create signed URLs for private content.

launch configuration   A template that an ASG uses to launch new EC2 instances (EC2 Auto Scaling). The launch configuration consists of information such as the AMI ID, the instance type, key pairs, and security groups.

launch permission   An EC2 AMI attribute that specifies which users can launch the AMI.

lifecycle hook   Enables EC2 Auto Scaling to pause after it launches or terminates an instance, to enable you to perform actions when the instance is not in the running state.

load balancer   A DNS name that all your web requests use as their destination. The load balancer distributes traffic among multiple web servers running in various AZs in a region. A load balancer can span multiple AZs but can't span regions. It automatically distributes incoming application traffic across multiple targets, such as Amazon EC2 instances, containers, IP addresses, and Lambda functions. AWS offers three types of load balancers: Application Load Balancer, Network Load Balancer, and Classic Load Balancer.

main route table   The default route table for any new VPC subnet. You can associate a subnet with a different route table and also specify a different route table as the main route table.

managed policy   A standalone IAM policy that you can associate with a user, group, or role in your AWS account. There are two types of managed policies: AWS managed policies and customer managed policies that you create and manage.

mapping   An optional CloudFormation template parameter that enables you to add conditional parameter values to the template.

Multi-AZ deployment   A setup with a primary DB instance whose data is synchronously replicated to a standby replica in a different AZ.

Multipart Upload API   An Amazon S3 feature that enables you to upload a large S3 object in chunks.

NAT   *See* network address translation.

NAT gateway   A NAT device that AWS manages. The device performs network address translation in a private subnet to secure inbound Internet traffic. The gateway uses NAT and port address translation.

NAT instance   A NAT device that you configure that performs network address translation in a public subnet to secure inbound Internet traffic.

network access translation (NAT)   A way to map one or more IP addresses to another IP address. NAT is used to restrict communications from the Internet to private instances, while permitting outgoing network traffic to the Internet.

network ACL   An optional layer of network security that acts as a firewall to control network traffic flowing into and out of a subnet. You can associate a subnet only with one network ACL at a time.

object   The fundamental entity type that Amazon S3 stores. An object consists of object data and metadata.

On-Demand instance   An EC2 pricing option that charges you by the hour or per second depending on which instances you run.

organization   An AWS entity that you create to consolidate and manage multiple AWS accounts that you own. Each organization has a master account and one or more member accounts.

origin server   The Amazon S3 bucket or custom origin that contains the original version of the content that you deliver through CloudFront.

original environment   The set of instances in a deployment group at the beginning of a CodeDeploy blue-green deployment.

paravirtual (PV) virtualization   Enables guest VMs to run on host systems that don't have special support extensions for full hardware and CPU virtualization.

permission   A statement inside an IAM policy that grants allow or deny permission to an AWS resource in your account.

policy   1. In IAM, a policy is a document that specifies the permission for a user, group, or role. The permissions in the policy determine what the user, group, or role can do in AWS, by granting the entity permission to perform specific actions for specific AWS resources such as EC2 instances and S3 buckets. 2. In EC2 Auto Scaling, a policy is an object that contains the information necessary to launch or terminate instances for an ASG.

pre-signed URL   A web address that uses query string authentication.

private content   A term used when CloudFront serves content with an S3 bucket as the origin. Private content is a method that controls access to the S3 content by requiring users to use signed URLs that restrict access based on the current date and time and/or the IP address of the requestor.

private subnet   A subnet in a VPC whose instances can't be reached from the Internet.

Provisioned IOPS   An EBS storage option that delivers fast, predicable, and consistent I/O performance.

public AMI   An AMI that all AWS accounts have permission to launch.

public subnet   A subnet whose instances can be reached from the Internet.

query string authentication   A feature that enables URL-based access to objects inside an S3 bucket. The method enables you to place authentication information in the HTTP request query string instead of in the Authorization header.

queue   A sequence of messages stored temporarily, waiting to be transmitted to a subscriber of the queue.

Read Replica   A live copy of an RDS DB instance. All updates to the source DB instance are replicated to the Read Replica DB instance.

region   A set of AWS resources in the same geographical area. A region consists of at least two AZs.

replacement environment   The set of instances in a deployment group after a CodeDeploy blue-green deployment.

reservation   A set of EC2 instances that are part of the same launch request. (This is not the same as a Reserved instance.)

Reserved instance   An EC2 instance pricing option that enables you to purchase On-Demand instances at a discount. You pay for the entire term of a Reserved instance, regardless of your usage.

root credentials   Also called AWS root user credentials; the credentials associated with the AWS account owner.

root device volume   Also called a root device; a volume that contains the image used to boot the EC2 instance. When you launch an instance from an AMI backed by an instance store, the instance store volume is created from template stored in S3. If you launch the instance from an EBS-backed AMI, the EBS volume is created from an EBS snapshot.

route table   Contains a set of routing rules that control traffic that leaves any subnet that you associate with the route table. You can associate multiple subnets with the same route table.

scale in   The removal of instances from an ASG.

scale out   The addition of instances to an ASG.

scaling policy   A specification of how Auto Scaling should scale an ASG in response to changing demand conditions.

search domain   A CloudSearch term that groups together your searchable data and the search instances that handle the search requests.

secret access key   A key that you use together with an access key ID to sign programmatic AWS requests. You can generate the secret access key and the access key ID for your AWS account, IAM users, and for temporary sessions.

security group   A set of allowed inbound connections for an EC2 instance. A VPC security group includes support for outbound connections as well. A security group is a list of protocols, ports, and IP address ranges that acts as a virtual stateful firewall that controls the traffic for one or more instances.

server-side encryption (SSE)   Encryption of S3 data at the server level. S3 supports three SSE modes: SSE-S3, where S3 manages the encryption keys; SSE-C, where the customer manages the keys; and SS3-KMS, where the AWS Key Management Service (KMS) manages the keys.

service role   An IAM role that grants permission to an AWS service so it can work with AWS resources.

shared AMI   An AMI that a developer builds and makes available to others.

single-AZ DB instance   A non-Multi-AZ DB instance that you deploy in one AZ, without a standby DB instance running in another AZ.

snapshot   A backup of an EBS volume that is stored in S3 that you can use to safeguard your data or to create another EBS volume.

software VPN   A software appliance–based VPN connection over the Internet.

source/destination checking Verifies that an instance is indeed the origin of the traffic that it sends out and is the ultimate destination of the traffic that it receives. This feature is enabled by default, and you must disable it for gateway instances such as a NAT instance in your VPC.

Spot Fleet Automates the management of Spot instances. You simply tell Spot Fleet how much capacity you need, and Spot Fleet does the rest.

Spot instance An EC2 instance type that enables you to bid on its price. It can be interrupted by EC2 with two minutes of notification when EC2 needs the capacity back.

Spot price The price for a Spot instance at a given time. If your maximum bid price is more than the Spot price, EC2 launches your Spot instances.

stack 1. In CloudFormation, a stack is a set of resources that you create and delete as an unit. 2. In OpsWorks, a stack is a set of instances that you manage together, because all the instances in a stack serve the same application.

statistic An aggregate function for CloudWatch metrics gathered during a sampling period. The five aggregate functions are Maximum, Minimum, Sum, Average, and SampleCount.

sticky session An ELB term that refers to the binding of a user session to an application instance. All requests sent by that user are routed to the same application instance, instead of spreading the requests among the instances based on load, which is the default behavior of ELB.

subnet A segment of a VPC's address range to which you can attach your EC2 instances running in that VPC. Subnets are useful in grouping instances according to operational and security requirements.

supported AMI An AMI for which the owner charges for the additional software or services that customers use with their own AMIs.

tag Metadata you define and assign to your AWS resources to help you easily manage the resources. A tag enables you to categorize your AWS resources in different ways—for example, by purpose, owner, or environment.

target revision An AWS CodeDeploy term that refers to the latest version of the application revision that you've uploaded to the code repository. This is the app version that's currently targeted for deployment.

task An instantiation of a task definition that is currently running on a container instance (ECS).

task definition An ECS term that refers to the blueprint for a task and that contains the container definition, volume information, and so on.

temporary security credentials The authentication data provided by AWS Security Token Service (STS) when you call an STS API action; it includes an access key ID, a secret access key, a session token, and an expiration time.

throttling   The restriction or slowing down of a process based on the limits that you configure.

time series data   Data provided as part of a CloudWatch metric that represents a time-ordered set of data points.

topic   An SNS term that represents a communication channel to send messages and subscribe to notifications. A topic serves as an access point for message publishers and subscribers.

trust policy   An IAM policy that's part of an IAM role and specifies which principals can use the roles.

tunnel   An encrypted and secure transmission mechanism for transmitting private network traffic that uses the Internet to connect to nodes in a private network.

user   A person or an application in an AWS account that needs to make API calls to AWS services. IAM users can be privileged administrators who need console access to manage AWS resources, end users who need access to content in AWS, or systems that need privileges to programmatically access your data in AWS.

versioning   An object in an S3 bucket has a key and a version ID. Versioning is a way to keep multiple versions of an object in an S3 bucket. You use versioning to retrieve a specific version of an object or to restore it. Versioning helps you recover from erroneous use actions and application failures.

Virtual Private Cloud (VPC)   A network that contains infrastructure, platform, and application series that share common security and interconnections.

virtual private gateway   The AWS side of a VPN connection. The internal interfaces of the gateway connect to your VPC via a VPN attachment, and the external interfaces connect to the VPN connection, which leads to the customer gateway.

virtual private network (VPN) connection   An IPsec connection between your VPC and another network, such as your corporate data center.

visibility timeout   The length of time for which a message is invisible to other application components after an application component first retrieves the message from an SQS queue. To avoid multiple application components from processing the same message, the component that first received the message is expected to process and delete the message from the queue within the visibility timeout period.

VPC endpoint   A VPC feature that enables you to create private connections between your VPC and an AWS service without requiring Internet access, through a NAT instance, a VPN connection, or AWS Direct Connect.

INDEX

E

J